DISASTER LAW AND POLICY

ASPEN SELECT SERIES

DISASTER LAW AND POLICY

Third Edition

Daniel A. Farber
University of California, Berkeley

James Ming Chen
Michigan State University

Robert R.M. Verchick
Loyola University New Orleans
Tulane University

Lisa Grow Sun
Brigham Young University

 Wolters Kluwer

To contact Customer Service, e-mail customer.service@wolterskluwer.com, call 1-800-234-1660, fax 1-800-901-9075, or mail correspondence to:

Wolters Kluwer
Attn: Order Department
PO Box 990
Frederick, MD 21705

Printed in the United States of America.

1 2 3 4 5 6 7 8 9 0

ISBN 978-1-4548-6925-2

About Wolters Kluwer Law & Business

Wolters Kluwer Law & Business is a leading global provider of intelligent information and digital solutions for legal and business professionals in key specialty areas, and respected educational resources for professors and law students. Wolters Kluwer Law & Business connects legal and business professionals as well as those in the education market with timely, specialized authoritative content and information-enabled solutions to support success through productivity, accuracy and mobility.

Serving customers worldwide, Wolters Kluwer Law & Business products include those under the Aspen Publishers, CCH, Kluwer Law International, Loislaw, ftwilliam.com and MediRegs family of products.

CCH products have been a trusted resource since 1913, and are highly regarded resources for legal, securities, antitrust and trade regulation, government contracting, banking, pension, payroll, employment and labor, and healthcare reimbursement and compliance professionals.

Aspen Publishers products provide essential information to attorneys, business professionals and law students. Written by preeminent authorities, the product line offers analytical and practical information in a range of specialty practice areas from securities law and intellectual property to mergers and acquisitions and pension/benefits. Aspen's trusted legal education resources provide professors and students with high-quality, up-to-date and effective resources for successful instruction and study in all areas of the law.

Kluwer Law International products provide the global business community with reliable international legal information in English. Legal practitioners, corporate counsel and business executives around the world rely on Kluwer Law journals, looseleafs, books, and electronic products for comprehensive information in many areas of international legal practice.

Loislaw is a comprehensive online legal research product providing legal content to law firm practitioners of various specializations. Loislaw provides attorneys with the ability to quickly and efficiently find the necessary legal information they need, when and where they need it, by facilitating access to primary law as well as state-specific law, records, forms and treatises.

ftwilliam.com offers employee benefits professionals the highest quality plan documents (retirement, welfare and non-qualified) and government forms (5500/PBGC, 1099 and IRS) software at highly competitive prices.

MediRegs products provide integrated health care compliance content and software solutions for professionals in healthcare, higher education and life sciences, including professionals in accounting, law and consulting.

Wolters Kluwer Law & Business, a division of Wolters Kluwer, is headquartered in New York. Wolters Kluwer is a market-leading global information services company focused on professionals.

To my brother, Mike.
D.A.F.

To Heather Elaine, with all my love.
J.M.C.

To Laina and Egon.
R.V.

To my family: May we always be prepared.
L.G.S.

SUMMARY OF CONTENTS

CONTENTS

PREFACE

The significance of disaster law should be self-explanatory. Hurricane Katrina alone has involved many billions of dollars for compensation, insurance, and rebuilding efforts. Even as we approach the ten-year anniversary of the Katrina disaster, lawyers continue to be involved in litigating claims to these funds. The task and challenges of rebuilding New Orleans are likewise ongoing. Since Katrina, a number of other large disasters—including Hurricane Irene and Superstorm Sandy—have inflicted major damage on the United States. Smaller disasters occur on a regular basis, and the United States faces Katrina-scale disaster risk from other possible floods and earthquakes. Internationally, the threats are, if anything, graver. Law has a vital contribution to make in addressing these problems.

Apart from its practical significance, disaster law also deserves more attention because of its intellectual challenges. At first glance, disaster law seems to be nothing but a collection of legal rules of various kinds that happen to come into play when communities have suffered severe physical damage. But at a deeper level, disaster law is about assembling the best portfolio of legal rules to deal with catastrophic risks—a portfolio that includes mitigation, emergency response, compensation and insurance, and rebuilding strategies. Because of this unifying theme, we think that the topic is deserving of serious law school attention even beyond its newsworthy qualities.

The first edition of this book appeared only months after Hurricane Katrina, at a time when disaster issues were just beginning to receive sustained attention from legal scholars. The second edition—which brought on two new co-authors, Rob Verchick and Lisa Grow Sun—was published four years after Katrina and provided the opportunity to broaden the focus beyond Katrina and its aftermath. In the years since the first edition was published, courses on disaster issues have begun to spring up around the country and abroad, and a growing body of legal scholarship focused on disasters has emerged. Disaster law is increasingly establishing itself as a field in its own right, worthy of serious inquiry and investigation.

New legal developments also continue to unfold. Litigation in the aftermath of Katrina, Irene, Sandy and various other disasters has shed new light on the way legal rules and principles are being interpreted and reinterpreted in the disaster context. Important statutory and regulatory changes—including revisions of the National Response Framework and a new National Recovery Framework—have also significantly altered the legal landscape of disasters.

As a result of all of these developments, we are confident that readers will find deeper analysis, broader coverage, and richer description in this edition than the last. Unfortunately, the problem of natural disasters will always be with us. But the legal system can do more to mitigate the damage, care for and compensate victims, and rebuild sustainable communities. Our hope is that today's law students will take the lead in future efforts to accomplish these critical goals.

Dan Farber
Jim Ming Chen
Robert R.M. Verchick
Lisa Grow Sun

ACKNOWLEDGMENTS

We are grateful to many people for their help in writing this book. We are especially grateful to Steve Errick for his support as a publisher for the first two editions of this book.

Dan Farber would like to thank Leslie Stone for her deft handling of manuscript corrections and reprint permissions.

Jim Ming Chen would like to thank Marie Gordon for administrative assistance.

Rob Verchick would like to thank Erik Christensen, Rob Garda, Bonnie Haskell, and John Lovett for their valuable insights and for their help in identifying certain source materials. He is also grateful to a talented team of research assistants whose work, whether current or past, shines in this edition: Laura Ashley, Lynsey R. Johnson, Nicholas Russell, Faye Sheets, Sharon Stanley, and Sarah Thompson. He would also like to thank his students at Loyola Law and also at Tulane University's Disaster Resilience Leadership Academy for helpful feedback on the second edition. Important financial support was provided by the Loyola University New Orleans College of Law and by the Louisiana Board of Regents Endowed Chairs for Eminent Scholars Program.

Lisa Grow Sun would like to thank Karl Sun, Robert Grow, Linda Grow, RonNell Andersen Jones, and Brigham Daniels for their insightful feedback and superb advice. She also appreciates generous financial support from the J. Reuben Clark Law School, Brigham Young University; copyright permission assistance from Shawn Nevers; and the outstanding work of her research assistants from the second edition and those who helped with this edition: Sara Benzion, Josh Bishop, Sully Bryan, Christina Champenois, Victoria Chen, Brandon Curtis, Cathryn Graham, Katie James, Jessica Jardine, Christy Matelis, Garrett Messerly, Nizhone Meza, Peter Neddo, Grace Pusavat, and Chase Thomas.

In addition, we thank the following sources for their permission to reprint excerpts of their scholarship:

Action Aid International, *Tsunami Response: A Human Rights Assessment*, www.actionaid.org/docs/tsunami_human_rights.pdf (Jan. 2006). Reprinted with permission.

Anna K. Schwab & David J. Brower, *Increasing Resilience To Natural Hazards: Obstacles And Opportunities for Local Governments Under the Disaster Mitigation Act of 2000*, in Losing Ground: A Nation on Edge 281, 283-301 (John Nolon & Daniel Rodriguez eds., 2007). Reprinted with permission.

Association of State Floodplain Managers, *A Report of the 2007 Assembly of the Gilbert F. White National Flood Policy Forum* 33-36 (2007). Reprinted with permission.

B.E. Aguirre, Dialectics of Vulnerability and Resilience, 14 Geo. J. on Poverty L. & Pol'y 39, 41-45 (2007). Reprinted with permission.

Cass R. Sunstein, *Which Risks First?*, 1997 U. Chi. Legal F. 101, 103-105, 112-114 (1997). Reprinted with permission.

Charles Anderson, *Christchurch: After the Earthquake, a City Rebuilt in Whose Image?*, The Guardian (London), Jan. 27, 2014. Reprinted with permission.

Clayton P. Gilette & James E. Krier, *Risk, Court, and Agencies*, 138 U. Pa. L. Rev. 1027, 1027-1029, 1039, 1071-1073, 1076-1079 (1990). Reprinted with permission.

Dan M. Kahan, *Two Conceptions of Emotion in Risk Regulation*, 156 U. Pa. L. Rev. 741 (2008). Reprinted with permission.

David Beito & Daniel J. Smith, *Tornado Recovery, How Joplin Is Beating Tuscaloosa*, Wall St. J., April 13, 2012. Reprinted with permission.

Douglas A. Kysar, *It Might Have Been: Risk, Precaution and Opportunity Costs*, 22 J. Land Use & Envtl. L. 1 (2006). Reprinted with permission.

Elaine Enarson, *Women and Girls Last? Averting the Second Post-Katrina Disaster*, available at www.bepress.com/ev/vol2/iss4/art4i. Reprinted with permission.

Erin Ryan, *Federalism and the Tug of War Within: Seeking Checks and Balance in the Interjurisdictional Gray Area*, 66 Md. L. Rev. 503, 522-536 (2007). Reprinted with permission.

Frank Ackerman & Lisa Heinzerling, *Pricing the Priceless: Cost-Benefit Analysis of Environmental Protection*, 150 U. Pa. L. Rev. 1553 (2002). Reprinted with permission.

Hugh L. Wood, Jr., Comment, *The Insurance Fallout Following Hurricane Andrew: Whether Insurance Companies Are Legally Obligated to Pay for Building Code Upgrades despite the "Ordinance or Law" Exclusion Contained in Most Homeowners Policies,* 48 U. Miami L. Rev. 949 (1994). Reprinted with permission.

Human Rights Center, University of California, Berkeley, *After the Tsunami: Human Rights of Vulnerable Populations* (October 2005). Reprinted with permission.

Jed Horne, *Carving a Better City*, Times-Picayune (New Orleans), Nov. 13, 2005, A1. Reprinted with permission.

Marilise Turnbull, Charlotte L. Sterrett, & Amy Hilleboe, *Toward Resilience: A Guide to Disaster Risk Reduction and Climate Change Adaptation* (2013). Reprinted with permission.

Matthew D. Adler, *Policy Analysis for Natural Hazards: Some Cautionary Lessons from Environmental Policy Analysis*, 56 Duke L.J. 1 (2006). Reprinted with permission.

Metropolitan Policy Program at Brookings, *The New Orleans Index: Tracking the Recovery of New Orleans and the Metro Area* (Aug. 2009), https://gnocdc.s3.amazonaws.com/NOLAIndex/NOLAIndex.pdf. Reprinted with permission.

Mitchell Moss, Charles Schellhamer & David A. Berman, *The Stafford Act and Priorities for Reform*, 6 J. Homeland Security & Emergency Mgmt. 8-16 (2009). Reprinted with permission.

Nicholas S. Kelley & Michael T. Osterholm, Center for Infectious Disease Research and Policy (CIDRAP), *Pandemic Influenza, Electricity, and the Coal Supply Chain: Addressing Crucial Preparedness Gaps in the United States*, 7-10, 22-24, 43, 47-51 (2008), available at www.cidrapsource.com/content/do/view/marketing/mart/coalreport_landing.html. Reprinted with permission from the University Of Minnesota Board Of Regents.

Oliver A. Houck, *Rising Water: The National Flood Insurance Program and Louisiana*, 60 Tul. L. Rev. 61-164 (1985). Reprinted with permission.

Richard Campanella, Bienville's Dilemma: A Historical Geography of New Orleans 351-354 (2008). Reprinted with permission.

Robert L. Rabin & Suzanne A. Bratis, *Financial Compensation for Catastrophic Loss in The United States*, in Financial Compensation for Victims After Catastrophe (M. Faure & T. Honlief eds., Springer Verlag 2005). Reprinted with permission.

Robert R.M. Verchick, *Facing Catastrophe: Environmental Action for a Post-Katrina World* (2010). Reprinted with permission.

Sean Hecht, *Climate Change and the Transformation of Risk: Insurance Matters*, 55 UCLA L. Rev. 1559 (2008). Reprinted with permission.

Shawn Boburg, *Rebuild v. Retreat: Christie and Cuomo Offering Contrasting Plans in Wake of Sandy*, The Record (Bergen County), March 15, 2013. Reprinted with permission.

Stephen D. Sugarman, "Roles of Government in Compensating Disaster Victims," *Issues in Legal Scholarship*, (2007): Article 1, available at http://www.bepress.com/ils/iss10/art1. Reprinted with permission.

Steve P. Calandrillo, *Responsible Regulation: A Sensible Cost-Benefit, Risk versus Risk Approach to Federal Health and Safety Regulation*, 81 B.U. L. Rev. 957 (2001). Reprinted with permission.

Susan J. Popkin, Margery A. Turner & Martha Burt, *Rebuilding Affordable Housing in New Orleans: The Challenge of Creating Inclusive Communities* 2-3 (Jan. 2006). Reprinted with permission.

Susan L. Cutter, *The Geography of Social Vulnerability: Race, Class, and Catastrophe*, available at http://understandingkatrina.ssrc.org/Cutter. (Sept. 23, 2005). Reprinted with permission.

Theresa Braine, *Was 2005 the Year of Natural Disasters?*, 84:1 Bull. World Health Org. 4. Reprinted with permission.

Timothy Ingalsbee, Firefighters United for Safety, Ethics, and Ecology, *Getting Burned: A Taxpayer's Guide to Wildfire Suppression Costs* (August 2010). Reprinted with permission.

1

INTRODUCTION

A. "SUSPENDED OVER THE ABYSS"

Now I will tell how Octavia, the spider-web city, is made. There is a precipice between two steep mountains: the city is over the void, bound to the two crests with ropes and chains and catwalks. You walk on the little wooden ties, careful not to set your foot in the open spaces, or you cling to the hempen strands. Below there is nothing for hundreds and hundreds of feet: a few clouds glide past; farther down you can glimpse the chasm's bed.

This is the foundation of the city: a net which serves as passage and as support. All the rest, instead of rising up, is hung below: rope ladders, hammocks, houses made like sacks, clothes hangers, terraces like gondolas, skins of water, gas jets, spits, baskets on strings, dumb-waiters, showers, trapezes and rings for children's games, cable cars, chandeliers, pots with trailing plants.

Suspended over the abyss, the life of Octavia's inhabitants is less uncertain than in other cities. They know the net will last only so long.

—Italo Calvino, *Invisible Cities* 75 (1972)

Some modern landscapes are not that different from Calvino's fantasy city. From San Francisco to New Orleans to Miami, communities all over the country have operated for years "suspended over the abyss," awaiting the next snapped rope in the form of earthquake, hurricane, or flood. As in Octavia, the dangers in these cities are obvious and residents are aware (at least when smaller incidents focus the mind) that the place they call home is living on borrowed time. In other communities, the risks posed by natural disaster are less obvious, but often no less significant.

Politicians and civil servants have puzzled over disaster law for centuries. In 1755 an enormous earthquake rocked the city of Lisbon, followed by multiple fires and a devastating tsunami. The city was demolished. As many as 40,000 city residents are believed to have been killed; another 10,000 may have lost their lives in Spain and Morocco.

Often called "the first modern disaster," the event roused many from a complacency that had allowed them to grow too comfortable with the aristocracy and vague notions of fate. During the response and recovery phase, citizens demanded more of government and began seeing themselves as agents of change in their environment. In response, Portugal's prime minister immersed himself in the practical details of reconstruction and launched one of the first scientific inquiries into the mechanics of earthquakes. Zoning rules were imposed, as were Europe's first building codes for seismic events.

In April 1927, the great Mississippi River overflowed its banks from Illinois to the Gulf of Mexico. For six weeks more than 20,000 square miles lay submerged beneath as much as thirty feet of water. An estimated 500,000 to 1,000,000 people lost their homes and nearly 1,000 lost their lives. The consequences would lead Secretary of Commerce Herbert Hoover to take on a massive flood relief effort, establishing a national role for the region's redevelopment and setting the stage for his election to the U.S. presidency. A year after the disaster, the federal government took charge of all flood control projects on the lower Mississippi, and in 1936 it took over projects on *all* federal waterways.

On August 29, 2005, Hurricane Katrina changed the game again. The costliest disaster in American history, the storm's surge plowed across the Gulf coast from central Florida to Texas. New Orleans was the area hardest hit. The surge broke through the federal levee system in more than fifty places, swamping nearly 80 percent of the city. At least 1,836 people lost their lives in the hurricane and subsequent flood (828 in New Orleans), making it one of the deadliest catastrophes in American history. Experts estimate the storm was responsible for more than $81.2 billion in damage.

Hurricane Katrina is often described as a natural event, but the damage in New Orleans was mainly the result of a massive engineering failure. By all expert accounts, Katrina's surge was *within* the federal levee system's intended design specifications. Two professional independent reviews—and one by the U.S. Army Corps of Engineers, itself—attributed much of the flooding to mistakes in levee design and construction stretching back over decades and under the supervision and control of the federal government.[1] The storm and its aftermath

---

[1] R.B. Seed et al., Investigation of the Performance of the New Orleans Flood Protection Systems in Hurricane Katrina on August 29, 2005 xix (July 31, 2006) (attributing the flood, in part, to "the poor performance of the flood protection system, due to localized engineering failures, questionable judgments, errors, etc. involved in the detailed design, construction, operation and maintenance of the system"),

caused Americans to question many aspects of hazard protection as well as many aspects of government in general—from environmental protection to race relations, from engineering design to the responsibilities of national government. Many policy makers now wonder what the Katrina disaster might say about the importance of coastal ecosystems, the effects of sea level rise, and the social effects of environmental catastrophe.

It would be one thing if natural hazards threatened only a handful of places. But that is not the case. Disasters come in many varieties and strike in many places, from earthquakes in northern California to wildfires in Montana, from massive floods in the Great Plains to hurricanes on the mid-Atlantic coast.

Every year in the United States, events like these cause hundreds of deaths and cost billions of dollars in disaster aid, disruption of commerce, and destruction of homes and critical infrastructure. Although the number of lives lost to natural hazards has generally declined, the economic cost of major disaster response and recovery continues to rise. Every ten years, property damage from natural hazards in the United States doubles or triples in cost. Only Japan suffers more economic damage from natural hazards.

There are many reasons for this trend. Perhaps the most obvious is that the population is growing and expanding into areas that are more prone to natural hazards, such as open coasts, forested areas, or scenic hillsides. Global warming also plays a role, resulting in drier, more fire-prone forests, rising sea levels, and, according to many experts, more powerful storms. As these trends continue, such events will only get worse.

B. DEFINING DISASTER

Disasters can, of course, be understood in many different ways. In this book we focus on disasters triggered mainly by natural forces such as hurricanes, earthquakes, or wildfires. This is similar to the approach taken by many federal disaster laws, which emphasize events tied to geological or meteorological systems. Such calamities are often called "natural disasters," but, strictly speaking, that is a misnomer (even though we will occasionally use the term ourselves as a shorthand). Nearly all "natural disasters" feature some human contribution, whether it be poor construction standards (as in Lisbon), the

---

www.ce.berkeley.edu/projects/neworleans/ (Aug. 20, 2009); Ivar L. van Heerden et al., The Failure of the New Orleans Levee System during Hurricane Katrina iii-ix (Dec. 18, 2006) (noting failures in worst-case storm analysis, levee design and construction, and levee maintenance), http://www.publichealth.hurricane.lsu.edu/TeamLA.htm (Aug. 20, 2009); U.S. Army Corps of Engineers, Performance Evaluation of the New Orleans and Southeast Louisiana Hurricane Protection System: Final Report of the Interagency Performance Evaluation Task Force, vol. I (June 2009), I-3 (citing poor design and construction as the reason for levee failures), ipet.wes.army.mil (Aug. 20, 2009).

channeling of a mighty river (as in the 1927 flood), or shoddy levees and urban sprawl (as in New Orleans). As mentioned earlier, human-induced climate change has also changed the game, making it harder to distinguish "Acts of God" from "Acts of Man."

For these reasons, most serious students of disasters have moved from defining a disaster as the hazardous event itself to defining a disaster in terms of the impact that the hazardous event has on people and property—an impact that is determined not only by the magnitude of the event, but also by human interaction with nature, by our choices about where and how we live. Sociologists, for example, tend to define disasters in terms of the social disruption caused by nonroutine, destructive events. *See* What Is a Disaster? New Answers to Old Questions (Ronald W. Perry & E.L. Quarantelli eds., 2005).

For our purposes, we will define disasters, as Professor Dan Farber has, in terms of the governmental and legal responses they demand. On this view, disasters require a "circle of risk management": mitigation, emergency response, compensation, and rebuilding. Rebuilding brings us full circle, as it should occur with an eye toward mitigating impacts of the next disaster. Disasters, then, are those situations or events that require use of this suite of risk management tools.

This understanding focuses on the legal framework that will best mitigate and respond to disaster risk, as well as the concomitant human suffering. In addition, the "circle of management" directs our attention to the bread-and-butter work of many lawyers and lawmakers: mitigating future risk, responding to present damages, and making people and communities whole. At the end of the day, disaster law is an applied field, and the success of various legal tools can be judged by their results in minimizing disaster costs, as a whole, and in minimizing disparate impacts on vulnerable communities.

C. ORGANIZING DISASTER LAW AND POLICY

We have organized this book to reflect the "circle of management" approach. Chapter 2, which focuses on the causes of disaster, examines the human contribution to disaster risk and the role of law in shaping the individual and collective choices that increase our exposure to natural hazards. By understanding how our laws (and choices made in the shadow of those laws) magnify disaster risk, we begin to see the shape that effective disaster mitigation might take. The chapter also grounds our later discussion in concrete examples of disasters—including both past disasters and potential future disasters that loom on the horizon—to give us a sense of what is at stake if emergency response is ineffective and mitigation efforts are not vigorously pursued.

Chapter 3 focuses on the federal power to respond to disasters. It gives readers the opportunity to use familiar legal principles, such as federalism, and traditional legal tools, such as statutory interpretation, to understand the existing framework for disaster response. The chapter explores federal constitutional powers, gives an overview of the Stafford Act, and considers the military's role in responding to disaster.

Chapter 4, which focuses on emergency response, begins with a tabletop exercise—based on an earthquake in urban area—that introduces students to many of the chapter's issues, including the difficulties of negotiating a chain of command. The chapter then considers the federal emergency response framework in action—examining the federal regulatory scheme for disaster response, with particular focus on catastrophic disasters. Moving beyond the role of the federal government, the chapter turns to the role of state and regional disaster response and, subsequently, to the contributions of private and nongovernmental actors. The chapter ends by examining proposals for reforming the law of emergency response.

Before turning in full from disaster response to issues of risk and compensation, we consider in Chapter 5 a critical problem at the intersection of the two issues: social vulnerability. Too often the poor and other marginalized groups are more acutely affected by disaster. This chapter examines why this is so, taking up issues of poverty, race, gender, sexuality, immigrant status, and age. Observing how disasters can heighten social tensions and vulnerabilities that already exist, Chapter 5 then urges readers to consider ways in which lawyers and lawmakers might address this problem.

Chapter 6 takes up the issue of risk analysis. Everyone is in favor of taking precautions, but how cautious should we be? And how do we know what risks are really out there? In this chapter, we show how policy makers evaluate risk and examine the underlying assumptions of their techniques. We then ask how societies might respond to disaster risk after a hazard has been evaluated.

Chapter 7 shifts attention to the question of compensation and risk spreading. Should disaster survivors be compensated by the tort system, government programs, or private insurance? The chapter examines the advantages and pitfalls of each of these possibilities in turn, focusing on post-disaster litigation, the National Flood Insurance Program, and the challenges of designing insurance for catastrophic risks.

Chapter 8 then deals with questions of recovery and rebuilding. The chapter considers an array of issues, from city planning to public participation to raising funds. Throughout, readers are encouraged to think about mitigation, risk spreading, social vulnerability, and the tough question of whether or not to even rebuild. To give some context, the chapter examines a few examples of past recoveries, including the resurrection of New Orleans after Katrina, and rebuilding efforts in New York and New Jersey after Superstorm Sandy.

Finally, Chapter 9 looks at disaster from an international point of view. This provides an opportunity to see how disasters affect countries that are different from the United States—poorer countries, more populous countries, or countries closer to the warm waters of the Equator. The chapter also introduces readers to the wide range of international agreements that have relevance in disaster situations, from the Hyogo Framework for Action, aimed at reducing disaster risk throughout the world, to human rights treaties dealing with racism and sexism. Disasters in poorer parts of the world can differ substantially in terms of lives lost and percentage of the economy affected, when compared with disasters in the United States. Yet Chapter 9 also makes the point that disasters, wherever they occur, have many characteristics in common. Thus all nations have an interest in helping and learning from one another.

D. WEB RESOURCES

The World Wide Web offers an array of resources relevant to disaster law and policy, with topics ranging from emergency management to hazard mitigation to meteorology and geophysics. We have compiled a short list of some of the many fine websites now available, concentrating on those that are generally accessible to nonexperts and that have a broad scope.

NATIONAL

- Disaster Law Resources (University of California–Berkeley School of Law) http://www.law.berkeley.edu/1374.htm
- Disaster Research Center (University of Delaware) http://www.udel.edu/DRC
- Federal Emergency Management Agency http://www.fema.gov
- GAO Reports and Testimonies Related to Disaster Preparedness, Response and Reconstruction (U.S. Government Accountability Office) http://www.gao.gov/docsearch/featured/dprr.html
- Natural Hazards Center (University of Colorado–Boulder) http://www.colorado.edu/hazards
- Natural Hazards Gateway (U.S. Geological Survey) http://www.usgs.gov/hazards
- Wharton Risk Management and Decision Processes Center (University of Pennsylvania) http://opim.wharton.upenn.edu/risk

INTERNATIONAL

- International Strategy for Disaster Reduction (United Nations) http://www.unisdr.org
- PreventionWeb (United Nations) http://www.preventionweb.net/english/
- International Federation of Red Cross and Red Crescent Societies https://www.ifrc.org

E. GETTING STARTED

Before turning to the remaining chapters, and with the suite of risk management tools in mind, consider a disaster from recent history: New Mexico's Cerro Grande fire. Read the short description below and reflect on the questions that follow.

On May 4, 2000, National Park Service fire personnel initiated a prescribed burn at Bandelier National Monument, a few miles from Los Alamos, New Mexico. Although the fire plan called for burning about 900 acres to create a buffer for preventing future fires, the fire quickly burned out of control. The fire was declared a wildfire on May 5 and—fueled by high winds—eventually burned some 48,000 acres of forest. Barry T. Hill, U.S. Gen. Accounting Office, Fire Management: Lessons Learned from the Cerro Grande (Los Alamos) Fire and Actions Needed to Reduce Risks 1 (2000). Ultimately, the fire destroyed or damaged more than 439 homes, countless businesses, and 7 million trees, causing an estimated $1 billion in total damages. H.R. Rep. No. 106-710, at 175 (2000) (Conf. Rep.); Hill, *supra.* More than 1,000 families suffered injury or loss to person or property, and approximately 18,000 residents of Los Alamos were forced to evacuate. H.R. Rep. No. 106-710; Hill, *supra.* The spread of the fire was blamed in large part on the fire plan, which called for initiating the burn in close proximity to Los Alamos and for setting the fire during a three-year drought and at the beginning of the southwestern wildfire season, when winds are particularly strong. Hill, *supra* at 3-5.

Causation and Mitigation. Devastating fires such as the Cerro Grande fire that ravage communities at the wildland-urban interface are increasingly common. Why do you think fire losses are increasing and how can we mitigate these types of disasters? How do you think land use decisions impact the risk of serious fire losses? How do environmental law and policy influence fire risks? In some areas, such as Tucson, Arizona, the proliferation of nonnative vegetation such as buffelgrass is transforming fire-resistant desert into highly flammable grassland. As with the Cerro Grande fire, drought—possibly linked to climate change—is also exacerbating fire risk. What legal response would best meet these challenges?

Emergency Response. Who should be responsible for responding to and fighting this type of fire? The U.S. Forest Service? Local firefighting units? Who should provide needed coordination between different jurisdictions on the ground? Who should be in charge of evacuating residents of at-risk communities? Would your answers change if the fire initially had been sparked by lightning, rather than beginning as a prescribed burn?

Compensation. Who should be liable for the damage caused by fires such as the Cerro Grande fire? The federal government, which developed the flawed plan for the controlled burn? The city council, which approved the building of homes and businesses so close to a national forest, where fire is both an inevitable and a necessary part of the landscape? Private insurers? Individual homeowners who chose not to purchase insurance? What if private insurance is not available to homeowners because of the unpredictable, but potentially high, costs of wildfires? Should some level of government create an insurance pool?

Rebuilding. Should the devastated sections of Los Alamos have been rebuilt? To what extent? Who should have a voice in deciding what rebuilding should occur? What steps should be taken in rebuilding to mitigate future fire risk? Should a comprehensive mitigation and rebuilding plan be in place before homes and businesses are rebuilt?

2

WHY THINGS GO WRONG: DISASTER CAUSATION AND MITIGATION

Floods are acts of nature; but flood losses are largely acts of man.

—Gilbert White, father of modern floodplain management

In order to analyze the adequacy of our current legal framework for addressing disasters, and to understand how we best mitigate disaster risk, it is important to first understand the sources of disasters—why things go wrong— and how those causal factors have changed over time. No disaster is completely "natural"; human exposure and vulnerability to risk is a product of cultural patterns influenced heavily by law.

In absolute terms, at least, disaster risk is on the rise.[2] For example, from 1990 to 2007, worldwide mortality risk from floods increased by 13 percent, and the economic risk posed by floods increased by 33 percent. *See* United Nations, 2009 Global Assessment Report on Disaster Risk Reduction: Risk and Poverty in a Changing Climate 5 [hereinafter U.N. 2009 Disaster Risk Report]. Half of the ten most deadly disasters since 1975 occurred between 2003 and 2008. *See id.* at 4. The vast majority of deaths from natural disasters

---

[2] Disaster costs are arguably "fairly stable as percent of GDP." United Nations, 2009 Global Assessment Report on Disaster Risk Reduction, Summary and Recommendations 8.

occur in developing countries (*see* Charles Perrow, The Next Catastrophe: Reducing Our Vulnerabilities to Natural, Industrial, and Terrorist Disasters 15 (2007)), but Hurricane Katrina—which claimed some 1,836 lives—and the 2011 Japanese earthquake and tsunami are somber reminders that even the most developed of countries are not immune.

Moreover, the economic cost of disasters has increased dramatically over the last several decades. Total worldwide annual economic damages from natural disasters have grown from approximately $50 billion a year in the 1980s to "just under $200 billion each year in the last decade." World Bank, Damages from Extreme Weather Mount as Climate Warms, Nov. 18, 2013, http://www.worldbank.org/en/news/press-release/2013/11/18/damages-extreme-weather-mount-climate-warms. Over the past 35 years, the United States alone has experienced more than 150 weather-related disasters in which overall damages "reached or exceeded $1 billion"; together, the cost of these disasters exceeded $1 trillion. *See* National Climate Data Center, Billion Dollar U.S. Weather Disasters, http://www.ncdc.noaa.gov/billions/# chron (April 20, 2014). In just the year 2013, the U.S. experienced seven "weather and climate disasters with losses exceeding $1 billion each." *Id.*

Why are both the risks and costs of disasters increasing? Several key factors appear to be driving the upward trajectory: (1) modern economic conditions, including the just-in-time economy and the interdependence and privatization of our critical infrastructure; (2) population growth and demographic shifts that increase exposure to hazards; (3) land use planning that exacerbates, rather than mitigates, disaster risk; (4) failure to maintain green and built infrastructure; and (5) climate change. The sections of this chapter will address each of these issues in turn.

All of these drivers of disaster risk are influenced and shaped by the law. In addition to risk, some of these drivers also present opportunities to mitigate that risk. For example, population shifts and aging infrastructure mean that a large percentage of existing infrastructure will need to be replaced in the next 50 years. *See* Report of the Second Assembly of the Gilbert F. White National Flood Policy Forum, Floodplain Management 2050 xi (2007) [hereinafter, Floodplain Management 2050]. Moreover, much additional housing and commercial property will be required to accommodate increased population. Experts estimate that by 2040, the United States will need 70 million more housing units, 40 million of which will be built on new residential lots. (Current housing stock is 125 million units.) *See* Arthur C. Nelson & Robert E. Lane, *The Next 100 Million*, Planning Magazine 73(1): 4 (2007). More than a billion square feet of nonresidential space will also be constructed (30 billion of new square footage and 70 billion of rebuilt footage). *See id.* at 6. The legal structure we have in place during the next few decades will determine, at least in part, whether we capitalize on (or squander) opportunities to rebuild old infrastructure and construct new infrastructure in ways that mitigate disaster risk.

A. MODERN ECONOMIC CONDITIONS

1. THE "JUST-IN-TIME" ECONOMY AND INFRASTRUCTURE INTERDEPENDENCE

Two features of our modern economy—"just-in-time" supply chains and the increasing interconnectedness of a wide array of industries and infrastructure systems—present major challenges in preparing for and responding to disasters. The evolution of just-in-time supply chains, in which businesses seek to reduce inventory and produce goods just as the economy demands them, has eliminated buffers that would minimize the effect of disaster-related supply-chain disruptions. Moreover, the increasing interconnectedness of our critical infrastructure means that a disruption in one industry can cripple a number of other interdependent industries. The risk of pandemic has focused attention on the way that these two major changes in the American business landscape can magnify the effects and costs of disaster, creating a ripple effect through the "life support" system of critical infrastructure on which we depend. Consider the following report on the likely effect of coal-supply disruptions on electricity (and concomitantly, public health) during an influenza pandemic.

NICHOLAS S. KELLEY & MICHAEL T. OSTERHOLM, CENTER FOR INFECTIOUS DISEASE RESEARCH AND POLICY (CIDRAP), PANDEMIC INFLUENZA, ELECTRICITY, AND THE COAL SUPPLY CHAIN: ADDRESSING CRUCIAL PREPAREDNESS GAPS IN THE UNITED STATES 7-10, 22-24, 43, 47-51 (2008), http://www.cidrap.umn.edu/sites/default/files/public/downloads/cidrap_coal_report.pdf (Copyright University of Minnesota Board of Regents)

The "flattening of the world" (a term coined by New York Times columnist Thomas Friedman) has changed society dramatically since 1968, the year of the last human influenza pandemic. In a flat world, Friedman says, supply chains (all the inputs for a product, from its origin to end use) depend on rapid and reliable communication, and previous demand determines projections of products needed. Stocks of products can be kept to a minimum, thereby reducing costs up and down the supply chain.

The world has never experienced a pandemic during the just-in-time global economy. Today's supply chains lack surge capacity—the ability to quickly scale up to meet demands. During an influenza pandemic, the number of illnesses and deaths worldwide will inevitably cause problems throughout supply chains. Worker absenteeism (whether from illness, fear, need to care for dependents or loved ones, or lack of ability to travel) and disruptions in international and domestic travel will affect every facet of supply chains that deliver the critical products we depend on for immediate health and safety, such as electricity and, in turn, water supplies and sewage systems, food, prescription drugs, and community safety. So interwoven are these products and services in our lives today, their availability is simply taken for granted. Most of the critical lifesaving drugs found in every hospital, for example, are produced outside the United States, particularly in China and India. A pandemic will likely seriously disrupt the international supply chain of these pharmaceutical products, from the synthesis of an active ingredient in a facility in Asia to delivery of the finished drug to a hospital pharmacy in the United States.

Even with this economic backdrop, pandemic planning has focused primarily on public health prevention strategies. But public health planning has not historically included business continuity or critical infrastructure planning. Nor has public health had a statutory authority to require planning and preparedness of the critical infrastructure....

When one considers public health preparedness, the availability of electricity generally is not considered a factor of concern for public health planners. Electricity is typically regarded as reliable and is, in most instances, available for all public health needs. Whether planning for influenza vaccination clinics, investigating outbreaks of a foodborne disease, or responding to a bioterrorism event, public health workers almost always assume that the lights will be on and power available. For disaster scenarios that would compromise electricity, such as after a hurricane, planning activities take into account the loss of power. Most pandemic planning activities, however, do not consider the potential for the loss of electricity....

But electricity truly undergirds the public health infrastructure. It is so vital today that one of us has noted: "Thomas Edison, not John Snow, is really the father of modern public health." Without electricity or the availability or use of backup power sources, safe water treatment and distribution systems, sanitary waste treatment systems, food refrigeration processes, and vaccine manufacturing plants cannot operate. In addition, traffic lights go dark, telecommuting isn't possible, public health surveillance activities are crippled, elevators stop working, and the heating and cooling of buildings cease....

A comprehensive review of government and industry reports and guidance, scientific literature, historical accounts of the 1918-19 pandemic's impact on coal, and hearings about a 2005 train derailment that disrupted coal supply yield[] troubling findings. Despite the nation's massive reliance on the coal industry for electricity generation, little has been done to secure this critical infrastructure and the people who run it during a pandemic....

Coal-fueled power plants maintain coal stocks so that power generation can continue in the event of expected and unexpected short-term disruptions in the supply chain.... Over time, coal stocks have gradually become smaller.... Coal became a commodity that power companies assumed would be reliably transported with minor disruptions. Power companies became increasingly dependent on the coal transport system, as coal became treated as a just-in-time deliverable commodity....

Industry experts are aware [that major disruptions of coal supply in pandemics could seriously disrupt electricity production in the United States], yet little has been done to remedy [this problem]—not for lack of trying, but primarily because of the costs of increasing coal stocks at power plants in current market conditions. The amount of coal kept on the ground by coal-powered plants has decreased significantly from the 1970s, when keeping 60 to 90 days was the norm. The reduction to 30 days of coal was encouraged by public utility commissions as a way to cut costs. Most public utility commissions will not allow power companies to raise electricity rates solely for the purpose of increasing their coal stocks. Similarly, most power companies will not spend the extra capital to increase coal stocks in the competitive U.S. energy industry.

Based on an understanding of the inextricable link between public health and electricity (and the supply of coal, in particular), decision-makers should consider the following recommendations to reduce the risks posed by an inevitable pandemic:

Recommendation 1: Build coal stocks. First and foremost, every effort must be made to ensure the reliability of electricity supply during a pandemic. With coal plants, the most practical way to ensure a steady supply of fuel during a pandemic is to keep larger stocks at power plants or storage facilities. When the industry prepares for peak electrical demand (the summer in the United States), coal stocks reach their highest for the year. This peak coal stock level should now be maintained as the new minimum level at every coal power plant around the nation.... [T]his level will provide a larger buffer against supply-chain disruptions expected during a pandemic....

Recommendation 2: Place coal miners and their supporting infrastructure personnel in the highest priority levels for pandemic response. The United States government should assume primary responsibility for ensuring coal miners and their support infrastructure have priority access to antiviral drugs, pandemic vaccine, and other critical products and services (e.g., critical pharmaceutical drugs, food), because they are not currently identified as a priority in the federal or state plans for supporting the critical infrastructure during a pandemic.

Recommendation 3: Plan for disruptions in the coal supply chain. There will be disruptions in the coal supply chain during a pandemic. In the absence of prior planning, these disruptions will be more severe. It is anticipated that these disruptions will be similar in impact to the disruptions of [Powder River Basin (PRB)] coal in 2005. Coal shipments are likely to be reduced by at least 15% to 25% for periods up to 60 days. This disruption could also occur more than once if, as in other pandemics, illness comes in waves. These disruptions will occur up and down the supply chain; therefore, it is critical that the whole supply chain be involved in pandemic planning. The company that supplies the tires for the dump trucks at the surface mines in the PRB, for example, might have supply or staffing shortages that prevent it from maintaining the trucks' tires, thus reducing the number in operation. Maintaining a larger inventory of critical supplies and cross-training will help these companies continue to function when supply chains are disrupted. At mines, higher absenteeism could lead to a drop in productivity, exacerbating supply disruption with lowered output. To counter this dilemma, larger mine operations might want to consolidate operations temporarily; smaller mine operations might want to consider short-term pooling of resources (staff and equipment) to maintain the higher levels of productivity....

Recommendation 4: Anticipate and develop strategies for responding to disruptions in electrical services.... Every power company currently has procedures for such crises as blackouts caused by ice storms, but the procedures typically assume that resources (people, equipment and/or parts) can be rapidly obtained from utilities in unaffected areas. This will not be the case during a pandemic, as no area will be spared. Further, procedures are not typically developed for dealing with fuel shortages, because they are rare and localized. Planners should plan on dealing with and responding to power disruptions during periods when fuel (for power generation and response vehicles) may be scarce. As these plans are developed or modified, care should be taken to ensure that people who receive power when it is scarce are providing the most critical services to the community. These plans should be integrated with community mitigation strategies, such as closings schools and malls that do not need power.

NOTES AND QUESTIONS

1. Many of the recommendations in the preceding report will require increasing inventories (of coal at power plants, tires at trucking companies, etc.) beyond what the market would normally require. Is there an inevitable trade-off between efficiency and disaster preparedness? If so, how should we balance or prioritize these concerns?

2. One barrier to utility companies investing in disaster preparedness is uncertainty about whether such costs can be recovered (by passing them on to customers) or whether they will come out of the utility's bottom line. Immediately after 9/11, the Federal Energy Regulatory Commission stated that it would "approve applications to recover prudently incurred costs necessary to further safeguard the reliability and security of our energy supply infrastructure." 96 FERC ¶61, 299, Docket PL01-6-000 (September 14, 2001). However, a 2003 survey of state public utility commissions found that, although 45 percent of commissions had received applications from utilities for recovery of security-related costs, 85 percent of commissions still lacked standards for determining the prudence of those investments. *See* Joe McGarvey

& John D. Wilhelm, National Association of Regulatory Utility Commissioners/National Regulatory Research Institute, 2003 Survey on Critical Infrastructure Security 3-4, nrri.org/pubs/multiutility/04-01pdf. Moreover, according to one industry observer, "[r]egulators...tend to hold prudence hearings after the fact to extract revenues from the utilities" rather than being more involved in evaluating the prudence of taking (or deferring) security measures at the time the decisions are made. Jack Feinstein, *Managing Reliability in Electric Power Companies*, in Seeds of Disaster, Roots of Response: How Private Action Can Reduce Public Vulnerability 164, 178 (Philip E. Auerswald et al. eds., 2006). For a less skeptical discussion of prudence standards in the context of critical-infrastructure-protection cost recovery, see Raymond Lawton et al., Model State Protocols for Critical Infrastructure Protection Cost Recovery 20-22 (2004).

3. The 2011 Japanese earthquake and tsunami created major supply line challenges for Toyota, the company that pioneered just-in-time production, as well as other companies. While Toyota's own production facilities were not damaged by the disaster, Toyota is reported to have lost $1.2 billion in revenue because of "part shortages that caused 150,000 fewer Toyota automobiles to be manufactured" in the U.S., "production stoppages" at five U.K. plants, and production reductions "of 70 percent in India and 50 percent in China." *See* United Nations, 2013 Global Assessment Report on Disaster Risk Reduction: The Business Case for Disaster Reduction 30.

4. What are the risks of interdependent critical infrastructure—both within a critical industry (such as electricity generation) and among industries that provide critical services? The CIDRAP Report highlights some important interdependencies in our critical infrastructure: electricity generation relies on coal mining and transportation, public health relies on electricity, and so forth. The Report can hardly begin, however, to describe the depth and complexity of the interconnectedness of our critical infrastructures and the challenges that interdependence poses for disaster policy.

   One of the primary challenges posed by this interconnectedness is the potential for cascading failures in the event of a disaster. Interconnectedness magnifies disaster risk: Even a relatively small-scale event could be transformed into a major disaster, as its ripple effects spread. "The efficient function of [interconnected systems that provide key services such as transportation, information, energy, and health care] reflects great technological achievements of the past century, but interconnectedness within and among systems also means that infrastructures are vulnerable to local disruptions, which could lead to widespread or catastrophic failures." National Research Council of the National Academies, Making the Nation Safer: The Role of Science and

Technology in Countering Terrorism 1 (2002). Moreover, once a cascading failure has occurred, the interdependence of various critical industries can present a Catch-22 for disaster recovery, as each industry needs other industries to be functioning in order for it, too, to resume services.

Interdependence of critical infrastructure also can conceal a system's true vulnerabilities, thereby complicating disaster planning:

> It is one thing for a single organization to figure out how to operate reliably on its own, and then to carry out the required structural and management reforms successfully. It is another for a *web of interdependent organizations* to do the same thing. In tightly coupled systems, simply identifying vulnerabilities, let alone managing them, is a daunting task. In a sense, risk migrates to the weakest part of the system, but due to overall complexity, the migration occurs without anyone's knowledge, and without a clear understanding of where the weakest links are located. Yet not identifying such vulnerabilities and risks leaves systems unprepared to function during extreme events.

T.M. La Porte, *Managing for the Unexpected: Reliability and Organizational Resilience*, in Seeds of Disaster, *supra*, 71, 73.

Even where vulnerabilities can be accurately identified, responsibility and accountability for addressing them may be diluted by the involvement of multiple, disconnected parties, and collective action problems may arise. Regulators may need to allocate costs to multiple regulated entities to reduce risks. *See* Philip E. Auerswald, *Complexity and Interdependence*, in Seeds of Disaster, *supra*, 157, 157 ("Most pervasive and difficult to manage are the interdependence that exists among firms in different infrastructures—water authorities that depend on electric power for their pumps, or hospitals that depend on transportation providers for the delivery of needed supplies. In all of these cases, accountability for assured continuing of service is limited."); *see also id.* at 162 (describing how the interdependent risk to poultry farms of the avian flu virus might discourage any particular farmer from taking precautions, because farmers who decline to take precautions save the cost of such precautions and can free-ride on the efforts of other farmers).

The interconnectedness of different key infrastructure systems that supply essential services (transportation, electricity, fuel, water, health care, etc.) presents particularly difficult challenges for disaster response and recovery. For example, in many communities, water cannot be distributed unless there is electricity to power pumps. When South Quebec, Canada suffered a massive ice storm in January 1998 that triggered multiday power outages, Montreal's water distribution was on the brink of shutting down. *See* Patrick Lagadec & Erwann O. Michel-Kerjan, *The Paris Initiative, "Anthrax and Beyond,"* in Seeds of Disaster, *supra*, 457, 459. (Many rural Americans get their water from private wells, which also require electricity to bring groundwater to the surface.) In turn, conventional power plants need a continuous influx of makeup water (which replaces water that evaporates in the power generation cycle) both for cooling and for generating steam to turn turbines, transforming heat into mechanical energy. Moreover, the functioning of the electricity grid depends on the operation of the telecommunications network, which allows operators to shift power where it is needed, to avoid overloading (and, ultimately, failure) of power lines, to troubleshoot problems, and to communicate the status of generating systems (especially those with black-start capacity, which can resume operation without an outside source of power). *See* Feinstein, *supra*, at 187-189 (detailing how telecommunications failure could result in electricity grid failure and how recovery efforts would be deadlocked, with each industry needing the other to begin operation first); Michael Kormos & Thomas Bowe, *Coordinated and Uncoordinated Crisis Responses by the Electric Industry*, in Seeds of Disaster, *supra*, at 194, 199 (describing how Y2K fears highlighted the interdependence of electricity and telecommunications).

Intra-industry interdependencies can also pose significant challenges. Most power plants, for example, cannot perform a black-start, in which operations are restored without relying on an external source of power to start the generator. Thus, most plants require some power from elsewhere in the grid in order to resume operations after a major shutdown. Plants without black-start capability can only resume operations by coordinating with the few that have such capacity (very often large, hydroelectric plants, which usually require very little power to resume operations).

5. The August 14, 2003, blackout in Canada and the Midwest and Northeastern United States illustrates the challenges posed by both intra- and inter-industry interdependence. The U.S. electric power supply flows through three regional power grids, which together create an electricity system that is "one of the great engineering achievements of the past 100 years." U.S.-Canada Power System Outage Task Force, Final Report on the August 14, 2003 Blackout in the United States and Canada: Causes and Recommendations 5 (2004), available at http://energy.gov/sites/prod/files/oeprod/ DocumentsandMedia/ BlackoutFinal-Web.pdf (April 5, 2014). The United States' power system is dependent on the interconnections within each grid, because they allow electricity producers to sell and transport power to distant end

users. *See id.* at 6. But interconnection means that an outage in one area may affect many other locations.

The 2003 power outage began near Cleveland, Ohio, when several power transmission lines shut down because trees had grown into the cables. *See id.* at 57. Local power companies had failed to properly trim trees along transmission right-of-ways and to follow other industry reliability guidelines. *See id.* at 17. The Ohio outage caused massive swings in power transmission; the power swings caused sensors in other areas to shut down additional lines, eventually cascading from Ohio to New York to Canada. *See id.* at 73. The blackout left 50 million people without power for up to four days and cost between $4 billion and $10 billion. *See id.* at 1. Amazingly, the entire electrical event lasted only nine or ten seconds. *See* Matthew L. Wald, *The Blackout: What Went Wrong; Experts Asking Why Problems Spread So Far*, N.Y. Times, August 16, 2003, at A1. A task force appointed by President George W. Bush concluded that the disaster could have been avoided if power companies had followed reliability regulations promulgated by the North American Electric Reliability Corporation (NERC), a nongovernmental entity responsible for the security and reliability of the power grid. *See* Task Force Final Report, *supra*, at 131. But NERC was a "voluntary organization, relying on reciprocity, peer pressure and the mutual self-interest of all those involved to ensure compliance with reliability requirements." *Id.* at 9. Ultimately, NERC did not have authority to enforce its standards. In 2005, Congress passed the Energy Policy Act, which authorized enforcement of reliability standards. Pub. L. No. 109-58, 119 Stat. 594. However, the power grid remains a highly interconnected infrastructure, potentially at risk for a cascading disaster capable of rapidly affecting generation, transmission, and distribution of electricity over wide geographic areas.

The 2003 Northeast blackout also illustrates the inter-industry interdependence of critical infrastructure:

> During the one-day blackout, some hospitals and television stations in New York City, Toronto, Cleveland, and Detroit were able to stay open because they had backup generators. Services in other sectors, however, could not be delivered. Elevators in office buildings were stuck between floors, trains stopped between stations, traffic signals went dark, cell phones lost reception, and, in Cleveland, water ceased to flow and sewers overflowed when the electric-powered pumps stopped functioning. If the blackout had persisted for longer than a day, the region's public health and welfare would have begun to suffer from the failures of more and more socially critical missions.

Jay Apt et al., *Electricity: Protecting Essential Services*, in Seeds of Disaster, *supra* 211, 211-212.

6. What is the solution to disaster risks imposed by interdependence of critical services? One strategy for responding to the risks generated by interconnectedness would be to try to minimize interdependence by breaking the system into smaller, more contained parts (by, for example, decentralizing power grids). Is that a good strategy to employ? Decentralizing such services and decreasing interdependence will, in many instances, decrease efficiency and short-term profits. *See* Auerswald, *supra*, at 161. But will it increase disaster security? Consider this argument, made in the context of counterterrorism efforts:

> Our research into the resilience dimension of reliability and especially the world of reliability professionals suggests that this decoupling strategy may be misguided as a means to mitigate vulnerability to terrorism. In fact, redesigns undertaken to decrease interdependence can undermine some of the very features that ensure the operational reliability of these systems in the first place.... Complex, interdependent systems convey reliability advantages to those trained professionals who seek to protect or restore them against terrorist attacks. Their complexity allows for multiple strategies of resilience and recovery.

Paul R. Schulman & Emery Roe, *Managing for Reliability in an Age of Terrorism*, in Seeds of Disaster, *supra*, at 132-133. *See also* Kormos & Bowe, *supra*, at 196 ("The electric grid's interdependencies contribute to its resilience. The large, integrated electrical system allows for more flexible response to minute-by-minute changes, such as demand spikes and sags, generator or major transmission failures, or overloads throughout the system.").

7. Others see decentralization as an important tool for increasing disaster resilience. Yet, in some industries, there may be significant legal barriers to decentralization. For example, efforts to decentralize the power grid might include use of microgrids, in which small local power generators form local grids that can both connect up with the larger grid and operate independently in emergencies. The legal status of microgrids is murky in most states. (Much turns on whether the microgrid is characterized as a "public utility.") *See* Sara C. Bronin, *Curbing Energy Sprawl with Microgrids*, 43 Conn. L. Rev. 547, 566-68 (2010). After long power outages caused by Tropical Storm Irene and an October Nor'easter in 2011, Connecticut passed the first state law authorizing a statewide microgrid pilot program. *See* Wendy Koch, *Post Sandy, U.S. Pushes Microgrids for Backup Power*, USA Today, Oct. 31, 2013, http://www.usatoday.com/story/news/nation/2013/10/31/microgrids-increase-post-sandy/3305379/.

8. If decentralization and decoupling isn't always the right answer, what other approaches can minimize disaster vulnerability? "Most people assume that the answer to improved reliability lies in better design of complex systems. If we make them more fail-safe or less tightly coupled or more physically dispersed, we will improve their reliability.... The key to increased reliability, particularly in relation to resilience, lies not primarily in the design of large technical systems but in their management. Moreover, the preoccupation with design diverts attention from managerial skills and strategies that could improve reliability." Schulman & Roe, *supra*, at 122. How applicable is this analysis to so-called "natural" disasters? Can the law encourage the education and hiring of "reliability professionals," *id.* at 123, who are trained to maximize resilience of our interconnected infrastructure?

9. Are there some disaster-related resources that are so critical that we need to cultivate local or, at least, national capacity to produce them? The 2009 H1N1 (swine) flu pandemic underscored the difficulties posed by the United States' limited domestic vaccine production capacity. At the time of the pandemic, the United States was incapable of producing sufficient vaccine to protect substantial portions of the U.S. population and was reliant on contracting with foreign firms, whose governments might void such contracts and seize supplies to meet their own countries' needs. Production challenges are particularly difficult when the vaccines cannot be stockpiled long in advance, as is the case for new strains of flu. For a summary of U.S. efforts to improve domestic vaccine capacity, see HHS, The State of the National Vaccine Plan 2013 Annual Report, available at http://www.hhs.gov/nvpo/vacc_plan/ annual-report-2013/nvpo-annual-report2013.pdf. Are there other critical commodities that the U.S. should stockpile? Widespread shortages following Superstorm Sandy highlighted the importance of access to fuel following a disaster and spurred the federal government to build a $215 million gasoline storage reserve in New England. *See* Coral Davenport, *U.S. to Store Gasoline for Crises in the Northeast*, N.Y. Times, May 2, 2014, at A24. This new regional reserve is based on the national oil reserve and will be the first of many built in various regions across the country. *Id.*

10. Maine Senator Susan Collins famously said, "Emergency management officials should not be exchanging business cards during a crisis." It seems equally true that the CEO of the electricity company should not be exchanging business cards with the CEO of the natural gas company during a crisis. Two commentators have recommended addressing what they describe as the "network factor" ("the increasing dependence of social and economic activities on the operation of networks, combined with increasing interdependencies among these networks") by developing strategic partnerships at the senior-executive level. *See*

Lagadec & Michel-Kerjan, *supra*, at 458-62. Recognizing that the difficulty in realizing this solution lies in its implementation, they draw lessons from the Paris Initiative, which culminated in a two-day conference entitled "Anthrax and Beyond," held one year after feared anthrax contamination threatened to paralyze the international postal system. *Id.* at 472. The conference brought together high-level representatives of postal operators from nearly thirty countries, as well as several outside experts, to debrief the crisis, discuss their experiences, consider new approaches to emergency management, and develop a network of contacts that they might rely on in the next crisis. *See id.* The participants were recruited and encouraged to attend by an international team of experts who visited high-level executives in postal organizations. *See id.* at 471. The primary message of the conference was that emergency management "is a challenge for the whole organization, and especially for top-level decisionmakers, not only for technical specialists, risk managers, and people in charge of public relations." *Id.* at 472. How can top-level management be encouraged to focus on disaster preparation? The commentators suggest that every large institution should have a "Rapid Reflection Force," with access to top-level management, to develop crisis strategy. *Id.* at 477.

11. Almost certainly, managing the interdependencies of critical infrastructure to mitigate and respond to disasters requires some sharing of information between affected companies, as well as two-way information sharing between affected companies and the government (which continues to own some critical infrastructure and pursues disaster mitigation to protect the public). See Chapter 4, Section C.1 for a discussion of federal efforts to coordinate infrastructure protection.

   a. Private companies are understandably reluctant to share information with each other. Potential barriers to information sharing include fear of losing competitive advantages, confidentiality agreements with customers and suppliers, worries about negligence liability for disclosed vulnerabilities, anxiety about customer reactions to vulnerabilities, and possible antitrust violations. *See* Lewis M. Branscomb & Erwann O. Michel-Kerjan, *Public-Private Collaboration on a National and International Scale*, in Seeds of Disaster, *supra*, at 395, 398. What steps can government take to encourage beneficial exchange of private information? Should Congress carve out a new, specific exemption from antitrust laws for sharing of information necessary for critical infrastructure coordination of disaster planning and response? How would Congress decide which information sharing is truly necessary for disaster coordination? What are the risks that such an exception would swallow the rule?

b. After 9/11, government entities have become more circumspect about the public sharing of information that may reveal critical infrastructure vulnerabilities because of fears that terrorists may exploit that information to identify and target the weak points in our infrastructure systems. *See* David Zocchetti, *Public Disclosure of Information by Emergency Services Agencies: A Post–September 11 Paradigm Shift*, in A Legal Guide to Homeland Security and Emergency Management for State and Local Governments 1, 4-7 (Ernest B. Abbott & Otto J. Hetzel eds., 2005) (documenting a post-9/11 shift away from public disclosure of information about critical infrastructure vulnerabilities and emergency plans, including several new state laws amending state open-records laws to limit such disclosure). Post-9/11 reluctance to share both government and private information about critical infrastructure vulnerabilities may complicate needed coordination between the private and public sectors and between various private industries, as well as limit public participation in the development of appropriate emergency plans. *Cf.* Lisa G. Sun & RonNell A. Jones, *Disaggregating Disasters*, 60 U.C.L.A. L. Rev. 884 (2013) (arguing that invocation of "war and national security rhetoric" in natural disasters threatens ordinary norms of transparency and open government in a wide variety of disaster contexts). The 2002 Homeland Security Act exempts from public disclosure under the Freedom of Information Act "critical infrastructure information" voluntarily submitted to the Department of Homeland Security (DHS) by private entities. 6 U.S.C. §133(a)(1)(A). Is that exemption justified by the need to encourage private information sharing with the DHS? If less information about critical infrastructure vulnerability is available in the public domain, will private infrastructure owners be able to create disaster plans that accurately account for the possible failure of other infrastructure systems?

c. The creation of the DHS, in response to 9/11, also has complicated information sharing between private industry and government, by splitting information-gathering responsibilities between DHS and the other federal agencies that have traditionally regulated the industry in question:

> This split happened most notably in chemicals and hazardous materials, commercial nuclear plants, and transportation. The fragmentation has contributed to a lack of clarity regarding divisions of responsibility. For example, the Department of Transportation is responsible for regulating transport, but DHS is

> responsible for transportation security; the Environmental Protection Agency is responsible for regulating chemicals, but DHS is responsible for chemical security. As a result, private sector officials have complained about confusion, contradictory direction, and duplicative information requests and poor coordination between DHS and other federal agencies. Making matters worse, while DHS has lead responsibility for some sectors, it frequently lacks sufficient or comparable technical expertise in those areas traditionally regulated by other federal agencies...Lack of deep industry-specific expertise on DHS' part will likely impede robust information sharing between DHS and the private sector.

> Daniel B. Prieto III, *Information Sharing with the Private Sector*, in Seeds of Disaster, *supra*, at 404, 411.

2. PRIVATIZATION AND SECURITY EXTERNALITIES

"In recent years, privatization of public facilities and services, particularly at drinking water utilities, has been occurring in the United States at an increasing rate." U.S. General Accounting Office, Water Infrastructure: Information on Financing, Capital, Planning, and Privatization 16 (2002). At least 85 percent of critical infrastructure in the United States is now privately owned. *See* FEMA, Critical Infrastructure 2 (June 2011), available at http://www.fema.gov/pdf/about/programs/oppa/critical_infrastructure_paper.pdf (April 8, 2014).

Private ownership of these resources has the potential to exacerbate disaster risk and costs. Private infrastructure owners often lack adequate incentives to invest in precautions that lessen the risk of disasters and in measures that allow for optimal disaster response, because the cost to the owner of failure due to disaster does not reflect the total costs experienced by the community at large. Just as with environmental pollution, private costs and social costs diverge. Because private owners do not bear the full costs of critical infrastructure failure (and cannot capture the full benefits of critical infrastructure investment), they may not take those costs (and benefits) into account when deciding whether increased investment in disaster mitigation is justified. Disaster scholars have recently begun to identify and discuss these "security externalities":

> A rational company—with no motive other than maximizing the expected present value of net revenues—would spend on infrastructure protection up to the margin where its private value of incremental risk reduction reached its private cost of further security. Yet infrastructure protection is a government challenge, not merely a business challenge, because threats to critical infrastructure have

costs, and thus risk reduction has benefits, that extend far beyond private owners of infrastructure assets.... Collateral damage can be minor (the hot-dog stand adjacent to the oil pumping station) or major (the metropolis down-wind from the nuclear power plant)....

Private arrangements would recognize and respond appropriately to some of these external risks, even in a world without government. For example, a factory that depended on a rail link or pipeline would rationally pay some or most of the security costs for that asset, even if it did not own it. A sufficiently sophisticated insurance industry would lead firms to internalize many external liability costs. Even a rudimentary tort system would stimulate A to enhance safety for B beyond its own pure self-interested level.... But transaction costs are likely to be significant, and complex negotiations may degenerate into stalemate....However inventive private arrangements might be, when externalities abound society should still expect an inadequate supply of security absent government participation.

John D. Donahue & Richard J. Zeckhauser, *Sharing the Watch*, in Seeds of Disaster, *supra*, at 429, 448; *see also* Philip E. Auerswald et al., *Where Private Efficiency Meets Public Vulnerability: The Critical Infrastructure Challenge*, in Seeds of Disaster, *supra*, at 3, 9.

Decentralized, private ownership of critical assets and infrastructure systems also presents challenges in terms of coordination and information sharing. *See supra* Section A.1, note 10.

NOTES AND QUESTIONS

1. Professor Jim Salzman has identified five types of standard policy solutions for externality-based market failures in environmental law that he calls the five P's: prescription (prescribing behavior by "command and control" regulation); penalty (imposing financial signals such as taxes and fees); persuasion (providing information so individuals and companies can self-regulate); property rights (bestowing property rights to pollute in certain quantities, which can then be traded in a market system); and payment (providing subsidies). Jim Salzman, *A Field of Green? The Past and Future Ecosystem Services*, 21.2 J. Land Use & Envtl. L. 133, 138 (Spring 2006). Which of these policy solutions, if any, might be effective in addressing security externalities? Is the selection of an appropriate remedy complicated by the difficulty in measuring the disaster risk imposed on communities by a business's failure to take particular measures that would foster disaster resilience? By the lack of a common metric for assessing and describing that risk? Are security externalities therefore more difficult to address than environmental externalities? Consider this view:

In some respects, environmental externalities may provide elements of a model for security externalities. Major business-related environmental disasters, such as large oil spills, burst tank cars of chlorine, or unexpected releases of toxic gases from chemical plants, have been quite infrequent. Predicting how often that might happen, despite efforts to prevent them, is difficult. To that degree, there is a similarity between environmental stewardship and investments to reduce infrastructure vulnerabilities to disaster.

However, while the spatial and temporal scale of impacts make accounting difficult, whatever impacts occur can generally be measured directly in terms of the firm's output—for example, the amount of sulfur dioxide emitted as air pollution. Effluents can be monitored on a minute-to-minute basis. The same does not hold for security externalities, where the consequences of lapses in security may not materialize for months or years. Even more important, environmental compliance, like worker safety, is principally under the control of the firm. Natural disasters are under no one's control, and attacks by terrorists are under the control of attackers. Furthermore, the interdependence of elements of infrastructure makes firms in one sector subject to errors or accidents occurring in another. Thus, firms can focus on recovery from such externally caused disasters, but alone they can do little about their incidence.

Auerswald, *supra*, at 160.

2. Will the analysis of security externalities be different for terrorism risks than for natural disaster risks? Consider the fact that increasing security precautions at one site ("hardening" the site) may cause terrorists to shift to other potential targets.
3. "State and local governments could encourage or require private parties to improve the reliability of important social services in a number of ways. For example, governments could modify electricity tariffs to permit load serving entities to recover costs associated with designing, installing, testing, and maintaining backup on-site power systems for individual customers who sign up for this service." Apt et al., *supra*, at 218.
4. Are there ways in which private companies might actually be better equipped to mitigate disaster risk? Or is privatization only a negative for disaster mitigation?

B. POPULATION GROWTH AND DEMOGRAPHIC TRENDS

The U.S. Census Bureau projects that U.S. population will reach 439 million by 2050, an increase of 42 percent from 2010. U.S. Census Bureau, The Next Four Decades: Population Estimates and Projections (May 2010), http://www.census.gov/prod/2010pubs/p25-1138.pdf (April 7, 2014). World population also is increasing dramatically. The United Nations estimates that world population will reach 9.6 billion by 2050. Press Release, United Nations, World Population Projected to Reach 9.6 billion by 2050 with Most Growth in Developing Regions, Especially Africa (June 13, 2013), available at http://esa.un.org/wpp/Documentation/pdf/WPP2012_Press_Release.pdf.

Population growth will, no doubt, put increasing strains on the environment and increase disaster-related costs. Already, current demographic trends mean that population and economic resources are becoming increasingly concentrated in areas that are particularly vulnerable to natural disasters. Disaster risk itself is "geographically highly concentrated." U.N. 2009 Disaster Risk Report 19. And, like moths to a flame, we seem drawn to high-risk areas, both because disaster risk is often coupled with natural advantages and because of the natural beauty, recreational opportunities, and other amenities of many hazardous locations.

Throughout history, people have settled in places where Mother Nature is both friend and foe. Early human settlements thrived in the alluvial flood plains of the Tigris, Euphrates, and Nile rivers. The settlement of America reflects similar phenomenon. As early Americans moved inland and westward from initial settlements on the eastern seaboard, they were attracted to the banks of America's great rivers—the commercial lifeblood of the nation—which promised fertile soil and easy access to resources and distant markets. Others settled elsewhere on the shores of the great oceans, establishing ports that would service both national and international markets, and fisheries to exploit the ocean's abundance. And many later pioneers would make their homes in the shadow and shelter of the majestic mountains of the West. Of course, the very natural advantages that attracted these settlers also pose great risks: Rivers might overflow their banks, low-lying port cities are vulnerable to hurricanes and other storm damage, and the violent geological forces that created the majestic mountains might shake the earth again.

Today, two important demographic trends in the United States are putting more people and property in harm's way: (1) the increasing concentration of population within cities and (2) the choice of many to live in areas that are particularly prone to natural disasters. The first demographic trend—continuing urbanization—concentrates population and economic resources, which can amplify the costs of even relatively small disasters. *See* Dennis S. Mileti, Disasters by Design 120 (1999); Perrow, *supra*, at 30. Moreover, because many of our cities were settled, long ago, in risky locations, urbanization means concentrating population in disproportionately hazardous areas that are at risk for potentially catastrophic disasters. Although cities have often been imagined historically as "places of refuge," at least one geographer contends that they are more accurately described today as "hotspots of disaster risk." Mark Pelling, *Urbanization and Disaster Risk*, available at http://www.populationenvironmentresearch.org/ papers/Pelling_ urbanization_disaster_risk.pdf. By 2040, some two-thirds of the U.S. population will likely live in ten "megapolitan" clusters; six of these have large coastal areas (Megalopolis in the Northeast, Cascadia in the Northwest, Florida, Texas Triangle, Southwest (which includes Southern California), and Sierra Pacific), one is expanding toward the coast (Piedmont), one borders the Great Lakes (Great Lakes), one occupies large swaths of desert (Southwest), several have significant earthquake risk (including the Mountain region), and another is along the Mississippi River (Twin Cities). *See* Arthur C. Nelson & Robert E. Lang, Megapolitan America xxxii, 62 (2011). After a city suffers a disaster—even a catastrophic disaster—it is much more likely to be rebuilt than relocated. "Once a city has developed, it rarely disappears, even if it experiences some disastrous flood or earthquake[,] because there are too many individuals, enterprises, and institutions with an interest in that city's economy." David Dodman et al., *Urban Development and Intensive and Extensive Risk* (2008), available at http://www.preventionweb.net/ english/hyogo/gar/background-papers. Despite its ongoing struggles, New Orleans stands, nonetheless, as a testament to the resilience of cities.

Urbanization not only concentrates population and economic resources in dangerous areas, but it also can exacerbate those dangers. For example, urban development increases the amount of impermeable surfaces in a region, increasing the quantity and speed of runoff from rain and melting snow and contributing to flood risk. *See* U.N. 2009 Disaster Risk Report 72. Urban development also destroys or degrades floodplains and wetlands that might otherwise mitigate flood damage. *See* discussion *infra*, Section D.1. The urban heat island effect—which can elevate the temperature of "paved over" urban areas more than 22 degrees Fahrenheit over surrounding rural areas, *see* http://www.epa.gov/hiri/—can increase the risk of heat waves, already one of the most deadly of natural hazards, *see* Kevin A. Borden & Susan L. Cutter, *Spatial Patterns of Natural Hazards Mortality in the United States*, Int'l J. Health Geographics 2008 7:64. Urbanization can also amplify the effects of disasters, because city dwellers are particularly beholden to fragile distribution systems and the just-in-time economy for all basic necessities, and typically do not store provisions or have access to backup sources of food, water, or other resources. *Cf.* Citizen Corps, FEMA, Citizen Preparedness Review: Community Resilience through Civil Responsibility and Self-Reliance, Issue 5, Update on Citizen Preparedness Research 12 (Fall 2007) (reporting findings that rural California residents are most likely to report being "well prepared" for a disaster, whereas Bay Area residents are least likely to report being "well prepared"). Of course, urbanization can also mitigate some kinds of disaster relief (by, for example, allowing for the possibility of vertical evacuation in tall buildings during a flood). *See* Lisa Grow Sun, *Smart Growth in Dumb Places: Sustainability, Disaster and the Future of the American City*, 2011 BYU L. Rev. 2157, 2166-68 (describing the complex relationship "between population density and disaster risk"). Suburban and exurban sprawl also presents its own risks, such as wildfire risk to communities near forested land.

The second demographic trend exacerbating disaster risk is that people are increasingly choosing to make their homes in vulnerable areas, such as the coastal regions of the United States and in areas of the South and West that have disproportionately high exposure to natural hazards. Population has risen most quickly in states such as Florida, Maryland, North Carolina, and Texas (which face substantial hurricane risks), as well as states such as California and Washington (which face both flood and seismic risks). *See* G. van der Vink et al., *Why the United States Is Becoming More Vulnerable to Natural Disasters*, Eos, Transactions, American Geophysical Union 79(3) 533, 537 (Nov. 1998). As of 2010, nearly 40 percent of the U.S. population lives in a "coastal shoreline county." Nat'l Oceanic & Atmospheric Agency, The U.S. Population Living at the Coast, http://stateofthecoast.noaa.gov/population/ welcome.html (April 8, 2014). Other environmentally vulnerable regions of the country have also been favorite relocation spots. The West has experienced a population boom, particularly in arid regions such as Arizona and Nevada, where, for example, flood risks—though substantial—are unpredictable and poorly studied, understood, and mitigated. The natural features that make development simultaneously attractive and risky have influenced not only the siting of cities themselves but also development within cities. Indeed, many urban renewal efforts and sustainability initiatives have focused on revitalizing waterfronts and other areas with high disaster risk. *See* Sun, *supra*, at 2170.

Globally, development in risky locations is often driven by poverty, as those with the fewest resources settle in marginal, makeshift housing in hazardous areas; in the United States, however, development in hazardous locations is driven, as often as not, by wealth. In most U.S. communities, oceanfront property—with its attendant beauty and recreational access—is among the most sought-after and valuable property, despite its vulnerability to hurricanes and tsunamis. Similarly, property on the steep grade of cliffs and mountains attracts those seeking sweeping views, despite its vulnerability to landslides. Homeowners also build expensive homes on the edge of majestic forests, where they are vulnerable to wildfires.

C. LAND USE DECISIONS

The concentration of population in hazardous areas may appear to be the result of private, individual decisions. In reality, however, those private decisions to live and work in hazardous locations are shaped by local land use policies, and those local land use decisions are, in turn, heavily influenced by state and federal incentives. Effective mitigation of all types of natural hazards—including floods, earthquakes, and wildfires—thus depends heavily on governmental actions and decisions.

1. FLOODS

New Orleans is today, of course, the quintessential example of an American city built to capitalize on the very natural advantages that might prove its undoing. Many other great American urban centers, however, share similar vulnerabilities to Mother Nature. Sacramento is situated at the base of the towering Sierra Nevada range and at the confluence of two major rivers—the Sacramento River and the American River—fed by the abundant rains and snowpack of the Sierras. The abundance of water feeds Sacramento's fertile agricultural land but also presents serious flooding risks to a large, urbanized population living in low-lying regions in the Central Valley. (Most of the Central Valley is near sea level, with some areas below sea level; the Sacramento–San Joaquin Delta includes more than 60 islands below sea level.) Moreover, urban population is continually encroaching on the Central Valley's floodplains.

The entire region is also protected by an aging and poorly maintained network of publicly and privately owned levees, spanning more than 1,500 miles. A major flood that overwhelms these levees could inundate some communities with more than 20 feet of water, inflict damages of more than $25 billion in the Sacramento area alone, and cause substantial loss of life. A California Challenge—Flooding in the Central Valley, A Report from an Independent Review Panel to the Department of Water Resources, State of California iii (Oct. 15, 2007) [hereinafter Flooding in the Central Valley]. Widespread levee failure also could threaten the drinking-water supply of tens of millions of Californians. (Much of Los Angeles' water supply comes from the Central Valley, via a 444-mile long aqueduct.) These factors, combined with the region's vulnerability to earthquakes that could breach critical levees, has led many to predict that Sacramento could be the next New Orleans.

Most experts agree that current land use policies must be addressed if California is to reduce its flood risks. *See id.* at iv (describing land use planning as "critical to reducing future flood risk in the Central Valley"). A 2005 California State report described the problem as follows:

> California's population growth presents a major challenge to the State's flood management system. In the Central Valley alone, much of the new development is occurring in areas that are susceptible to flooding. In some cases, land use decisions are based on poor or outdated information regarding the seriousness of the flood threat. For example, many flood maps used by public agencies and the general public are decades old and do not reflect the most accurate information regarding potential flooding. Even worse, many

maps were made by simply assuming that federal project levees provided protection from 100-year flood events. Unfortunately, recent experience has shown that this assumption is not necessarily valid.

Land use decisions at the local level that allow developments in floodplains protected by the State-federal levee system in the Central Valley greatly increase the risk of State liability for loss of life and property damage. Better coordination is needed between agencies making land use decisions and the parties, often the State, which must bear the burdens and liabilities of those decisions. The State must develop a process that guides regional development with the goal of protecting people and property at risk in floodplains, while connecting the legal liability of ill-advised land use decisions to those making the decisions to approve development in these areas.

Another challenge is that people who live and work behind levees have a false sense of protection. Many believe that the levees will protect them against any level of flooding. Even if a levee was capable of successfully holding back a 100-year flood, a target flood event used by many insurance and public agencies when providing flood protection, it doesn't mean that a larger flood, such as a 110-year or a 150-year flood event, won't flood their property. During a typical 30-year mortgage period, there is a 26 percent chance that a homeowner living behind a levee will experience a flood larger than the 100-year flood. This risk is many times greater than the risk of a major home fire during the same period.

California Department of Water Resources, Flood Warnings: Responding to California's Flood Crisis (Jan. 2005).

Based on the concerns in this report, Governor Schwarzenegger declared a state of emergency for California's floodplains and levees, which allowed exemptions from state environmental laws to permit needed repairs to proceed more quickly. Two years later, in 2007, California passed a suite of floodplain management laws designed to respond to the flood challenges described in this report. Those laws required the California Department of Water Resources (DWR) and the Central Valley Flood Protection Board to promulgate and adopt a Central Valley Flood Protection Plan (CVFPP) by July 2012. Cal. Water Code §9612(b). The CVFPP, adopted in 2012 and available at http://www.water.ca.gov/ cvfmp/docs/2012%20CVFPP_June.pdf, was required to outline a systemic approach for floodplain management in the Central Valley, including "both structural and nonstructural" mechanisms for reducing flood risk. *Id.* §9616(a). Now that the CVFPP is adopted, cities and counties in the Sacramento–San Joaquin Valley are required to develop joint city-county emergency plans, *id.* §9621, and conform their general plans and zoning ordinances to the CVFPP, Cal. Gov. Code §65302.9; *id.* §65860.1. After cities and counties make these conforming amendments, they cannot approve development agreements, *id.* §65865.5, subdivision maps, *id.* §66474.5, or permits for construction of new residences for property, *id.* §65962, within "a flood hazard zone" unless they conclude, based on substantial record evidence, that urban or urbanizing property will be protected to the 200-year flood level by existing flood management facilities or conditions imposed on the project, or that a local flood management agency has made "adequate progress on construction of a flood protection system[,]" which will provide at least 200-year protection by 2025. *Id.*; Cal. Gov. Code §65007(n) (defining "urban level of flood protection" as that necessary to withstanding flooding that "has a 1-in-200 chance of occurring in any given year"). Nonurbanized areas need be protected only to the level required by the Federal Emergency Management Agency (FEMA).

California is, of course, not the only state with serious flooding concerns. Tropical Storm Irene and Superstorm Sandy both exposed the vulnerability of much of the U.S. Eastern Seaboard to devastating floods. The flood damage inflicted by Irene and Sandy has occasioned much debate about how flood risk should best be addressed. *See, e.g.,* Michael Kimmelman, *Vetoing Business as Usual After the Storm*, N.Y. Times, Nov. 19, 2012. There is virtual consensus among floodplain managers that current floodplain management relies too much on structural solutions—such as building codes and construction of additional levees—at the expense of nonstructural solutions—such as prohibiting additional development in certain flood-prone areas, and even relocating some existing communities away from flood-prone zones. Although additional investment to maintain existing levees is necessary, flood risk cannot effectively be built away by constructing newer, bigger levees. Indeed, though levees can protect regions from some flood risk, they can also exacerbate risk downstream and in catastrophic events, when levees are overtopped. Stricter, wiser land use restrictions are widely viewed as the most critical and indispensable element of effective floodplain management moving forward. The politics of flood protection and the reality of current urban vulnerability, however, virtually guarantee that structural protections will continue to feature prominently in future flood mitigation efforts.

What principles should guide mitigation of flood risk? Consider these "Action Guidelines" issued by a national conference of floodplain managers.

ASS'N OF STATE FLOODPLAIN MANAGERS, FLOODPLAIN MANAGEMENT 2050,
A REPORT OF THE 2007 ASSEMBLY OF THE GILBERT F. WHITE
NATIONAL FLOOD POLICY FORUM

33-36 (2007)

Action Guidelines

Floodplain management professionals and other experts gathered at the Second Assembly of the Gilbert F. White National Flood Policy Forum agreed that sweeping change is urgently needed to avoid the dismal future that awaits if the present course of scattered, short-sighted water-related policies and activities continues. All the essential technical and programmatic steps described in the previous section can be condensed into six action guidelines. These guiding principles capsulize the new ways of thinking and operating that will be needed to achieve safe and sustainable relationships with our water resources....

  1. Make room for rivers, oceans, and adjacent lands.

Beginning now, AVOIDANCE of floodprone and/or ecologically sensitive areas should be axiomatic in planning new development. Although a strategy of avoidance cannot erase unwise existing development, it will minimize the cumulative damage, losses, and degradation that otherwise will be felt sorely by 2050.

We need to begin a pattern of gradual and voluntary resettlement of those portions of communities that already have been located in the highest-risk or most ecologically sensitive areas, including areas behind levees and within the downstream influence of dams. At least four lines of attack should be employed in this strategy. First, as we repair and replace infrastructure anywhere in the nation, it should be removed from the floodplain if at all possible or, at a minimum, be brought up to higher standards of safety and environmental protection. Second, states should incorporate into their hazard mitigation plans (and localities into their comprehensive and mitigation plans) strategies to make significant changes to the land uses in certain dangerous or environmentally critical areas. Third, from now on, no state, local, or federal funds (including any type of subsidy in the tax code) should be spent that could foster development or infrastructure in high-risk and/or environmentally sensitive areas or would otherwise conflict with the provisions of Executive Orders 11988 and 11990. Fourth, new and replacement levees should be set farther back from the edges of waterways, which not only will allow more storage space for flood water but also will gradually shift existing and potential development into less hazardous areas.

No adverse impact principles should be applied in all land use and development decision making. The standard of "not causing harm," coupled with the use of future conditions as the basis for hazard and resource identification (as noted below), will result in the protection of people, property, and natural resources and functions now and into the future.

We need widespread measurement of cumulative future conditions in terms of flood flows, flood levels, riverine and coastal erosion, sedimentation, barrier and shoreline migration, sea level rise, subsidence, and other attributes. Then we must establish a policy that limits human actions in watersheds and coastal zones that would alter any of these attributes. This will result in preserving floodplain functions as well as reducing future losses.

2. Reverse perverse incentives in government programs.

An independent, comprehensive review is needed of all federal programs that fund, subsidize, license, or promote development or redevelopment (including disaster relief, the tax code, housing grants, small business loans, and many others). All of these programs should be reformed to eliminate the incentives they unwittingly provide for making unwise decisions and taking inappropriate action with regard to our water resources. In their place, we must create positive incentives for appropriate action anywhere in the watershed, but especially in areas that are floodprone and/or ecologically sensitive.

Federal agencies should adhere closely to E.O. 11988 and 11990 and thereby eliminate federal projects, funding, licenses, permits, loans, grants, or other incentives that foster new or replacement development in floodplains that exposes people, property, and taxpayers to added risk and costs. Public facilities such as causeways, bridges, evacuation routes, and water treatment plants should be treated as additional "critical facilities" under the terms of the Executive Orders.

A sunset date should be established for subsidized and grandfathered flood insurance premium rates, because subsidized rates encourage development in hazardous areas. Exemptions to the flood insurance purchase requirement must be eliminated. We should be moving toward mandatory actuarially based flood insurance (or all-hazards insurance) for all homeowners that drives mitigation and also has a pooling mechanism for coping with catastrophic losses.

3. Restore and enhance the natural, beneficial functions of riverine and coastal areas.

We must make it a national priority to reclaim, over time, our lost riparian and coastal resources wherever possible, including dunes, bottomland forests, estuaries, and marshes. This will help restore natural buffers to storms and floods, supply open space and recreational opportunities for a burgeoning population, and slow the further deterioration of some ecosystems. Generous funding must be sought from all possible sources for this effort. For example, the potential for generating revenue by trading carbon credits should be considered.

Recognition and respect for the natural and beneficial functions of floodprone areas, including the coast, must be incorporated into the programs of all federal, state, and local agencies....

4. Generate a renaissance in water resources governance.

A nationwide vision and policy for water resources sustainability and flood loss reduction are essential. This would require legislation incorporating both a national floodplain management policy and a national riparian and coastal areas policy. The act should establish unequivocally both the value to the nation of these resource areas and their natural functions, as well as their inherent hazards. This policy needs to be supported with a comprehensive legislative package to be coordinated with and implemented through states, local governments, tribes, governors, and others. We need to draw on the leaders and experts of the nation to craft and agree on outcomes and metrics for the year 2050, including how we measure success and failure.

A high-level, central point of coordination and implementation is needed to ensure that water-related laws and programs at all levels are seamlessly aligned and integrated. This could be a new federal agency or other entity but it should be dedicated solely to water-related issues. The wasteful and counterproductive fragmentation and stovepiping of federal (and state) water-related programs and of Congressional oversight of them must be eliminated.

We must consider carefully the central question of whether a national policy of water resources "development" is still relevant for 2050 and beyond or whether a policy of water resources "sustainability" that balances human and ecosystem needs is a wiser approach.

The National Water Assessment, last conducted in 1976, needs to be updated. Up to date data on streamflow, reservoirs, groundwater, and withdrawals are critical to crafting nationwide policy that is both far-seeing and grounded in science.

National programs and investment decisions should be adapted quickly to account for expected trends and impacts associated with the collision of intensified human development and climate change....

5. Identify risks and resources and communicate at public and individual levels.

A thorough, nationwide examination of our water-resources-related risks is the critical first step to understanding and resolving our present and future dilemma. Britain's Foresight Flood and Coastal Defence Project has shown that a scenario-based, comprehensive assessment of risks and resources is feasible even on a very large scale. What is more, the scenarios have proven invaluable in driving home the seriousness of the situation, in fleshing out alternatives, and in communicating with policymakers. Such an assessment should be commenced for the United States at once.

All identification of flood risks and resources should be based on future conditions. In some locales, fully built-out watersheds already are anticipated in comprehensive planning, but the increases in flood risk and the resource depletion that this level of development will bring are not considered in mapping or other management activities. Decisionmaking about all aspects of water resources and water-related hazards must be based on much longer time horizons than are being applied today.

Communication, education, and outreach efforts must be intensified immediately. We need to identify the specific behaviors that must be changed to reduce vulnerability and protect resources. Then we need to work through schools, the media, watershed councils and other local groups, and use any other available means to bring about changes in those behaviors. A communications tool kit for local opinion leaders, industry representatives, homeowners, and others will be a good start.

We must capitalize on technological advances in communication to help people understand flood hazards, the exposure and vulnerability of people to those hazards, and the fragility of water resources. We need to use visual depictions of the impacts of development on flooding and also of the adverse impact of different development scenarios on all properties and on natural resources in the watershed. These should be disseminated digitally to keep pace with other web-based attractions.

Nationwide data on many factors is absolutely critical to determining what the most efficient course will be and when progress is being made. We need to find out who is at risk from flooding and why. We need an inventory of nation's floodprone structures and risk. Existing data feeds need to be monitored so we can determine the impacts of climate change as soon as possible.

Intelligible scenario-based models are needed to help communities grasp and plan for climate change and work towards sustainability of their resources. National databases should be accessible to local governments to assist their decisionmaking.

6. Assume personal and public responsibility.

Actuarially based, all-hazards insurance must become mandatory for all properties, nationwide. The coverage should include a strong loss-reduction (mitigation) component. This will foster individual understanding of risk and acceptance of personal responsibility. If an all-hazards insurance program cannot be developed, then flood insurance under the existing mechanisms should be mandatory for all properties.

Our ethic of land and water stewardship must be revived. We need to provide a framework that will foster local responsibility for dealing with flood risk, sustaining water-related resources, and making wise use of floodprone lands. Incentives need to be institutionalized to ensure that communities that are doing a good job receive benefits related to their efforts and, in contrast, those that do not manage their risks and resources wisely are not allowed to externalize the resulting losses and costs onto the federal taxpayers. These incentives could include a sliding scale for the non-federal share of the cost of disaster relief and recovery; and preference for federal grants and loans given to communities that act to mitigate risks and protect or restore resources.

NOTES AND QUESTIONS

1. The Association of State Floodplain Manager's 2010 Report sounds many of the same themes but suggests a shift in approach from "floodplain management" to "flood risk management," with particular emphasis on defining goals, quantifying results, and rigorously assessing progress. See Ass'n of State Floodplain Mangers, Managing Flood Risks and Floodplain Resources 3 (2010), http://www.asfpmfoundation .org/forum/2010_Forum_Report.pdf. Desired outcomes include ensuring that floods cause "minimal" harm to society and the "built environment," protecting and restoring the "natural functions and resources of floodplains," building "resilient and sustainable" communities that are willing to "live with floodplains," and fairly apportioning the costs of flood and environmental damage rather than externalizing costs to federal taxpayers. *Id.* at 3-4.

2. Does California's legislation go too far or not far enough in restricting land use in floodplains and protecting existing urban areas? Is 200-year protection adequate for urban areas? Does any standard that uses historical records to assess risk adequately take account of the potential for more severe storms caused by climate change? An independent report prepared for the California Department of Water Resources suggests that the level of protection for existing urban areas "should be equivalent to protection against the Standard Project Flood, which represents a flood that can be expected from the *most severe* combination of meteorologic and hydrologic conditions that are considered *reasonably characteristic* of the region." Flooding in the Central Valley, *supra*, at v. For the Central Valley, the Standard Project Flood level falls between the 200- and 500-year protection levels. *See id.* n.6.

3. Why do we continue to develop land that has substantial exposure to natural hazards? One possible explanation mentioned in the above Report is that the artificially maintained flood insurance rates of the National Flood Insurance Program, which are not actuarially based, have subsidized development in hazardous areas, by ensuring that developers can build in floodplains confident that they can obtain relatively low-cost, below-market insurance against any flood risks. Also, numerous programs administered by a variety of federal agencies— including the Department of Housing and Urban Development, the Department of Agriculture, the U.S. Army Corps of Engineers, the Tennessee Valley Authority, and the Economic Development Administration—subsidize development and have supported

development in floodplains. Although Executive Orders 11988 and 11990 (Floodplain Management and Protection of Wetlands, respectively), require federal agencies to consider and pursue practicable alternatives before building on floodplains or wetlands, and to minimize the risk of flood loss or wetland degradation if no alternative exists, critics allege that the Orders have primarily been observed in the breach. Should these Orders be revised to include a more stringent prohibition on federal support of building on floodplains or wetlands?

4. Does the availability of federal disaster aid also encourage building in floodplains? *See* Howard C. Kunreuther & Erwann O. Michel-Kerjan, At War with the Weather 122 (2009) ("Federal disaster assistance may create a type of Samaritan's dilemma: providing assistance after a disaster reduces parties' incentives to undertak[e] loss reduction measures prior to a disaster."). Reconsider this question in connection with the readings about federal disaster aid in Chapter 4.

5. Floodplains are attractive to developers for a number of reasons. Floodplains often represent the largest undeveloped, open spaces near existing urban centers; this was certainly true in the St. Louis area after the 1993 floods. Moreover, "floodprone land is relatively less expensive, so developers see that their profit margins can be widened by using that land for development, as long as the costs of future consequences (flood damage and deterioration of the resource) can be passed along to others in the community or to future generations of taxpayers." Floodplain Management 2050, *supra*, at 9. Are there ways to alter developer incentives to develop floodplains? *See, e.g.*, Justin Pidot, *Deconstructing Disaster*, 2013 B.Y.U. L. Rev. 213, 256 (suggesting that the National Flood Insurance Program be revised to "front-load [premium] payments so that developers themselves feel the squeeze").

6. Are there other obstacles to local government adoption of stricter land use controls? Dennis S. Mileti explains that lack of political will is an important obstacle:

> Few local governments are willing to reduce natural hazards by managing development. It is not so much that they oppose land-use measures (although some do), but rather that, like individuals, they tend to view natural hazards as a minor problem that can take a back seat to more pressing local concerns such as unemployment, crime, housing, and education. Also, the costs of mitigation are immediate while the benefits are uncertain, do not occur during the tenure of current elected officials, and are not visible (like roads or a new library). In addition, property rights lobbies are growing stronger. All of these factors contribute to a lack of political leadership for limiting land use in hazardous areas.

Mileti, *supra*, at 160. Mileti also contends that local governments can be stifled in their efforts to mitigate disasters through land use planning by the expense and complexity of required techniques (such as hazard-zone mapping) and by the regional nature of hazards, which necessitates a coordinated, regional response that can be difficult to achieve. *See id.* Local governments also may lack incentives to deal with regional risks, and may focus on disaster risk—if at all—only through the narrow lens of effects within their own community. Floodplain Management 2050, *supra*, at 12. Moreover, land use decisions in most jurisdictions are made on a parcel-by-parcel basis; regional and long-term planning tools tend to be underutilized and weakened by pressure from developers.

7. Is the solution to land use problems strong federal regulation? Consider this view: "We need a more centralized regulatory system. Local initiative is simply not reliable in the case of mitigation. Localities are reluctant to enforce state standards, national standards are few, and enforcement is lax. This is an area where centralized regulation—standards and enforcement—is needed; given the political influence of growth-oriented city officials and property and building interests, there is bound to be a 'failure' of the private market." Perrow, *supra*, at 37.

8. Should all development in floodplains be restricted? *See* Carolyn Kousky, et al., *Strategically Placing Green Infrastructure: Cost-Effective Land Conservation in the Floodplain*, 47 Environ. Sci. Technol. 3563, 3563 (2013) (estimating "the avoided flood damages and the costs of preventing development of floodplain parcels" in one watershed in Wisconsin's Lower Fox River Basin and finding that preventing all floodplain development was not cost-benefit justified but that "target[ed] investments in preserving 'high-benefit, low cost parcels' can yield net benefits"). If a parcel-by-parcel analysis is required to ensure the most cost effective mitigation strategy, who is best equipped to undertake that task?

9. What does it take for a local community to commit to changes in land use? Does experiencing a serious disaster inspire change? The experience of Missouri after the 1993 Mississippi River flood illustrates the intransigence of current land use policy, at least in some localities. After a particularly cold winter and an unusually wet spring, nine states in the Mississippi River watershed—North Dakota, South Dakota, Nebraska, Kansas, Minnesota, Iowa, Missouri, Wisconsin, and Illinois—suffered record flooding in the summer of 1993. Perrow, *supra*, at 18. The flooding killed approximately 50 people, caused damage in excess of $15 billion, completely inundated 75 towns, and destroyed upwards of 10,000 homes. *See id.* at 18. In response to the flooding, the federal government bought 25,000 flooded residential properties at a cost of $1 billion in a voluntary buyout program designed to return floodplains to

their natural state. *See* Sara Shipley, *Unprecedented Growth in the Flood Plain Brings Riches and Risks: Business Grows on Land under Water 10 Years Ago*, St. Louis Post-Dispatch, July 27, 2003, at A1. Some midwestern states tightened restrictions on development of flood plains, especially on land flooded in 1993. *See id.*

Missouri, however, did not. Although 4,700 Missouri households participated in the federal buyout, the resulting gains were far outpaced by new development on Missouri's floodplains. During the decade after the 1993 floods, $2.2 billion in new development—including homes, offices, shopping centers, and highways—was built in the St. Louis area on acreage that was underwater during the 1993 floods. This new development was either elevated to the 500-year-flood level or protected by 500-year flood earthen levees. Development so protected is exempt from federal flood insurance requirements. *See id.* at A1. By 2007, approximately 28,000 homes and "more than 6,000 acres of commercial and industrial space" had been "developed on land that was underwater in 1993." *See* Susan Saulny, *Development Rises on St. Louis Area Flood Plains*, N.Y. Times, May 15, 2007, http://www.nytimes.com/2007/05/15/us/15flood.html.

Missouri has no comprehensive floodplain management legislation, so development decisions are left to local officials, who are attracted to the clarion call of tax revenue and job creation. One member of the Bridgeton (Missouri) City Council summarized the race-to-the-bottom mentality of many such floodplain development decisions: "Bridgeton in the past has hugged a lot of trees, and we've lost out on a lot of development. We're going to be surrounded by businesses while we're looking at flood plain." Christopher Carey, *Cities Look to Flood Plains for Jobs, Growth, Tax Dollars*, St. Louis Post-Dispatch, July 29, 2003, at A1 (quoting Councilwoman Barbara Abram). Floodplain development in Missouri is particularly attractive to developers, because floodplains constitute most of the available, undeveloped land in the St. Louis region. Shipley, *supra*, at A1. Moreover, Missouri has enabled new development in flood zones by allowing the building of large, new levees, the costs of which have been subsidized (to the tune of up to 65 percent for new construction and 80 percent for repair) by the Army Corps of Engineers. *See id.* A spokesman for the Corps' St. Louis district explained, "We don't make a value judgment on whether that property should be protected. As long as people can show they can meet the requirements, they'll get a permit, whether we like building in the flood plain or not." *Id.* (quoting Alan Dooley). In addition to levee subsidization, the federal government continues to pay millions of dollars in disaster aid for Missouri flooding every year. For example, in 2011, FEMA approved more than $3.6 million in flood-related disaster aid to St. Louis County alone. *See* http://www.fema.gov/news-release/2011/11/03/federal/state-disaster-assistance-st-louis-county-reaches-3655119. Missouri itself has also subsidized building behind levees by providing "tax-increment financing" to spur economic development. Shipley, *supra*, at A1.

Should we be concerned about this new development in Missouri's floodplains if, indeed, all of the developed land is elevated to the 500-year flood level or protected by 500-year levees?

10. Imagine that you are on the board of a local government. How would you balance local need for jobs and for a growing tax base against the need for flood protection? How would you answer your constituents' questions and concerns? Now imagine yourself having that same conversation in the context in which it most frequently arises: when dealing with a particular property and a particular set of people with a particular plan. Public officials facing development decisions with natural hazards implications rarely make those decisions in the spotlight of the media or with focused attention from the broader public. How does that change the political calculus of floodplain development?

11. The Floodplain Management 2050 Report mentions scenario-based planning as an effective tool for helping the public (and, concomitantly, politicians) make more informed and farsighted land use decisions. In scenario-based planning, experts typically identify a discrete number of different growth scenarios, based on different land use, transportation, and environmental decisions. The long-term effects in these scenarios (on housing, traffic, economic development, pollution, and other potential axes such as disaster costs) are then modeled and presented to the public, often using computer-aided visualization techniques. Can these techniques help overcome the political logjam that otherwise impedes more disaster-resistant land use decisions? For an overview and example of scenario-based planning, see Envision Utah, http://www.envisionutah.org/ eu_about_euprocess.html; for an interesting example of scenario-based planning in the aftermath of a disaster, see Louisiana Speaks, http://www.louisianaspeaks-parishplans.org/PlanningProcess_Louisiana Speaks.cfm.

12. If it is politically infeasible to limit all or most floodplain development, should localities at least limit building of critical infrastructure (such as hospitals, water and sewage treatment plants, and emergency operations centers) and vulnerable facilities (such as nursing homes) in floodplains? For an assessment of the wisdom and difficulties of zoning critical facilities out of floodplains, see Ass'n of State Floodplain Managers, Critical Facilities and Flood Risk (2011), http://www.ncpc.gov /floodseminar/handouts/ASFPM_Critical_Facilities_and_Flood_Risk.pdf.

13. If changes to zoning laws prove difficult to adopt and implement, can information-based solutions, which educate the public and trust them to make wiser land use decisions, be effective? California was the first

state to establish a comprehensive natural hazards disclosure requirement in conjunction with the transfer of real estate, requiring disclosure of natural hazards not only when they are within the "actual knowledge" of the seller, but also when a designated local authority has either a list of affected properties or a map of relevant hazards and has posted a notice to that effect. *See* Cal. Civil Code§1103 (requiring seller disclosure if transferred property is in a statutorily defined "special flood hazard area"—FEMA zone "A" or "V"; an "area of potential flooding"—i.e., a dam inundation zone; a "very high fire hazard severity zone"; an "earthquake fault zone"; a "seismic hazard zone"; or a "wildland area that may contain substantial forest fire risks and hazards").

Legislators hoped this law would slow the development of land in hazard zones by decreasing property values in those areas. *See* George Lefcoe, *Property Condition Disclosure Forms: How the Real Estate Industry Eased the Transition from Caveat Emptor to "Seller Tell All,"* 39 Real Prop. Prob. & Tr. J. 193, 242 (2004). Flood zone disclosure has been somewhat successful in lowering property values, as average home prices in California's flood zones dropped 4.3 percent within five years of implementing the law. *See* Austin Troy & Jeff Romm, *Assessing the Price Effects of Flood Hazard Disclosure under the California Natural Hazard Disclosure Law (AB 1195)*, 47 J. Envtl. Planning & Mgmt. 137 (Jan. 2004). This data suggests that some home buyers are choosing not to buy properties after learning that the properties are in flood zones. But fire zone disclosure has had little overall effect, and property values have only declined where the property is in close proximity to a recent fire. *See* Austin Troy & Jeff Romm, *Living on the Edge: Economic, Institutional and Management Perspectives on Wildfire Hazard in the Urban Interface,* in 6 Advances in the Economics of Environmental Resources 101 (Austin Troy & Roger G. Kennedy eds., 2007). Based on the limited data available, determining whether the disclosure law is effectively reducing development in hazard zones is very difficult. *See* Carolyn Kousky et al., *In Harm's Way: Homeowner Behavior and Wildland Fire Policy*, in Wildfire Policy: Law and Economics Perspectives (Karen M. Bradshaw & Dean Lueck eds., 2012) (noting that while there is evidence that "disclosure of risk information alters consumer behavior in many different settings," such as food safety labeling, nutrition labeling, and tobacco warnings, "[t]he literature on land development patterns and risk information is much less substantial").

California's natural hazard disclosure law also has significant shortcomings. Among them are the costs incurred by sellers who must pay for a professional hazard report; the risk of lulling buyers into assuming that disclosure reports cover every conceivable disaster or are as effective as on-site studies; inaccurate hazard maps and information;

and inability to predict when and where disasters will actually occur. *See* Lefcoe, *supra*, at 242. Furthermore, buyers' assessments of risk are often neither objective nor accurate, and they may ignore evidence of low-probability high-risk events. *See id.* at 246; *see also* Daniel Kahneman & Amos Tversky, *Prospect Theory: An Analysis of Decision under Risk*, in Choices, Values, and Frames 17, 22-25 (Daniel Kahneman & Amos Tversky eds., 2000). Reconsider the effectiveness of disclosure and education-dependent solutions when you read Chapter 6, *infra.*

Other states have enacted a variety of hazard disclosure laws. *See, e.g.,* Haw. Rev. Stat. §508D-15 (2006) (requiring disclosure when a property is in a FEMA special flood hazard area, an airport noise exposure area, a military "air installation compatibility use zone," or within an area designated a tsunami inundation zone by the Department of Defense, if the county has provided required hazard zone maps to the public); N.Y. Real Prop. Law §14-462 (McKinney 2006) (requiring a "property condition disclosure statement" for residential property that includes whether the property is in a "designated flood plain" or "designated wetland," if the seller has actual knowledge of the designation); Or. Rev. Stat. §105.464 (2007) (requiring sellers of previously occupied homes with actual knowledge of hazards to disclose whether the property is "in a designated flood zone," "a designated slide or other geologic hazard zone," or has "been classified as forestland-urban interface").

In addition to disclosure by landowners, the California Department of Water Resources is now legally obligated to send yearly notices to landowners whose property is determined to be in a "levee flood protection zone." That notice informs landowners of the residual risk in areas protected by levees (including the risk of catastrophic failure), recommends purchase of flood insurance, and refers landowners to more detailed sources of information. Cal. Water Code §9121. "Improving flood risk awareness will help insure that Californians make careful choices when deciding whether to live in Central Valley flood plains, and if so, whether to prepare for flooding and/or maintain flood insurance." California Department of Water Resources, 2007 California Flood Legislation Summary, 4. Do you think such targeted public information campaigns will have an impact on buyer decisions or local decisions about land use or disaster mitigation? Why or why not?

14. What role could or should tort liability play in altering land use patterns? Should local governments be liable for approving subdivisions or other development in floodplains if flooding later occurs? *Cf.,* Maxine Burkett, *Duty and Breach in an Era of Uncertainty*, 20 Geo. Mason L. Rev. 775 (2013) (exploring the potential contours of a local government duty to plan for and adapt to climate change, particularly

sea level rise). Should developers who build in risky locations be on the hook for flood losses incurred by later purchasers?

15. Floodplain Management 2050 suggests that optimal flood plain management would include "planned retreat" from high-hazard and environmentally sensitive areas and "massive buyouts" of "entire parcels of land that are better used as natural open space," or planted with damage-resistant crops. Floodplain Management 2050, *supra*, at 13. Environmental planning expert Dr. Robert Twiss has said that once an area has been developed for housing, it is nearly impossible to reclaim the area for flood control. How viable a solution is relocation of existing developments? *See, e.g.*, Cornelia Dean, *Some Experts Say It's Time to Evacuate the Coast (for Good)*, N.Y. Times, Oct. 4, 2005 (describing the debate over rebuilding Alabama's Dauphin Island after Katrina and one suggestion that Congress establish a commission, like the base-closing commission, to identify coastal areas that should be denied both federal rebuilding subsidies and access to federal flood insurance).

16. What legal steps can communities take to reclaim their coastal lands? As hurricanes eat away at public beaches, can states reclaim some of their remaining coastal lands from private landowners? The Texas Open Beaches Act, enacted in 1959 and amended in 1991, provides in part:

> PROHIBITION. (a) It is an offense against the public policy of this state for any person to create, erect, or construct any obstruction, barrier, or restraint that will interfere with the free and unrestricted right of the public, individually and collectively, lawfully and legally to enter or to leave any public beach or to use any public beach or any larger area abutting on or contiguous to a public beach if the public has acquired a right of use or easement to or over the area by prescription, dedication, or has retained a right by virtue of continuous right in the public....
>
> (c) For purposes of this section, "public beach" shall mean any beach bordering on the Gulf of Mexico that extends inland from the line of mean low tide to the natural line of vegetation bordering on the seaward shore of the Gulf of Mexico, or such larger contiguous area to which the public has acquired a right of use or easement to or over by prescription, dedication, or estoppel, or has retained a right by virtue of continuous right in the public since time immemorial as recognized by law or custom. This definition does not include a beach that is not accessible by a public road or public ferry as provided in Section 61.021 of this code.

Tex. Nat. Res. Code§61.103.

As originally interpreted by the Texas courts, the Act made any established public beach easement a dynamic, "rolling easement"—a public right to use the "public beach," defined not in fixed terms, but by reference to the strip of land between the current line of mean low tide and the current natural line of vegetation—lines that would creep inward as the coast itself eroded. *See, e.g.*, Feinman v. State, 717 S.W.2d 106, 110-111 (Tex. App. 1986) (holding that the "public's easement moves with the changing tide" and applying the Act to property that, while previously outside the easement, came within the easement because of coastal erosion caused by Hurricane Alicia), disapproved of by Severance v. Patterson, 370 S.W.3d 705 (Tex. 2012) Under this approach, Hurricane Rita and Ike's dramatic erosion of the Texas coast meant that many oceanfront homes that were outside the public easement before the storms were drawn within the public beach easement and thus became obstructions preventing the "free and unrestricted" right of public use. Many beachfront homes destroyed by Rita and Ike therefore arguably could not be rebuilt, and even those spared by Ike's fury might be subject to removal orders if they were seaward of the post-Ike vegetation line. The Texas Supreme Court rejected this interpretation of the Act, holding that "public easements may gradually change size and shape as the respective Gulf-front properties they burden imperceptibly change, but they do not 'roll' onto previously unencumbered private beachfront parcels . . . when avulsive events [such as hurricanes] cause dramatic changes in the coastline." Severance v. Patterson, 370 S.W.3d at 708. If the Texas Supreme Court had, instead, recognized a "rolling easement," would the landowner have been entitled to compensation for a taking? Would the state be taking the homeowner's property or would the hurricanes? For an examination of the ways that climate change may affect the evolution of property rights, see Dan Farber, Property Rights and Climate Change, available at http://papers.ssrn.com/sol3/papers.cfm?abstract _id=2418756. The takings question is considered more fully below in Section C.4.

Other states have taken different approaches to limit coastal development, but most restrictions do not apply to existing developments. Florida regulates development of hazard areas by establishing "coastal construction control lines . . . along the sand beaches of the state fronting on the Atlantic Ocean, the Gulf of Mexico, or the Straits of Florida." Fla. Stat. Ann. §161.053(1)(a) (2008). These control lines are positioned where the property is "subject to severe fluctuations based on a 100-year storm surge, storm waves, or other predictable weather conditions." *Id.* New construction within control lines is very restricted, and sellers of property located seaward of control lines must disclose that the property is subject to strict regulations. *See id.* §161.57. New York also has a law governing "coastal erosion hazard areas." N.Y. Envtl. Conserv. Law §§34-0101 to 34-0113 (McKinney 1997). This law requires the State Department of Environmental Conservation to designate coastal erosion hazard areas that are then subject to stringent development regulations and permitting requirements.

2. EARTHQUAKES

In 2001, FEMA determined that a major earthquake along the San Andreas Fault was one of the three most likely catastrophes to hit the United States. (The other two catastrophes FEMA identified have already come to pass: a terrorist attack on New York City and a major hurricane striking New Orleans.) *See* Jia-Rui Chong & Hector Becerra, *Katrina's Aftermath: California Earthquake Could Be the Next Katrina*, L.A. Times, Sept. 8, 2005, at A2. In 2008, experts estimated that there was a greater than 99 percent chance that a 6.7-magnitude earthquake would strike one of California's many major faults in the next 30 years. David Perlman, *Sure Bet: Big Quake in Next 30 Years*, S.F. Chron., April 15, 2008, at A1. One study estimated that a repeat of San Francisco's infamous 1906 earthquake today would kill between 800 and 1,500 people, seriously injure between 4,000 and 6,000 people (depending on the time of day), leave 400,000 people homeless, and cause direct economic losses of more than $93 billion. Charles A. Kircher et al., *When the Big One Strikes Again: Estimated Losses due to a Repeat of the 1906 San Francisco Earthquake*, 22 Earthquake Spectra S297 (April 2006). Different assumptions about shaking in such an earthquake result in even more horrifying statistics: between 1,800 and 3,400 people dead; between 8,000 and 12,500 seriously injured; 600,000 people homeless; and $120 billion in direct economic losses. *See id.* The number of estimated fatalities is actually quite comparable to the estimated 1906 death toll. Although building codes have made buildings much safer, San Francisco and the Greater Bay Area are now home to many more people: the population of San Francisco has more than doubled and that of the Bay Area has increased tenfold. *See id.* That population has also expanded to the west, putting many more people in closer proximity to the San Andreas Fault. *See id.*

Moreover, the rubble of the 1906 earthquake may have, quite literally, laid the groundwork for future seismic destruction. As Raymond J. Burby explains,

> San Francisco recovered rapidly from the 1906 catastrophe chiefly because the downtown business district was well insured.... However, like London after its fire in 1666, San Francisco declined to alter its basic pattern of streets and land use patterns as it rebuilt. In particular, it ignored Daniel H. Burnham's "City Beautiful" plan for the redesign of the city that had been presented to civic leaders just before the fire: "Few cities ever found themselves demolished, with a ready-made plan for a new and grander city already drawn up, awaiting implementation, and with money pouring in to help realize the plan. San Francisco chose to ignore its Burnham Plan, and decided instead to build at a rate and manner which not only made the city less beautiful than was possible, but more dangerous. The rubble of the 1906 disaster was pushed into the Bay; buildings were built on it. Those buildings will be among the most vulnerable when the next earthquake comes" (Thomas and Witts, 1971, p.274). This

statement was prophetic: the city's Marina district, built on 1906 rubble, sustained heavy damage in the 1989 Loma Prieta earthquake.

Raymond J. Burby, Cooperating with Nature 34 (1998).

The U.S. Geological Survey continues to report that, in the San Francisco Bay Area, "[t]he highest [liquefaction] hazard areas...are concentrated in regions of man-made landfill, especially fill that was placed many decades ago in areas that were once submerged bay floor. Such areas along the Bay margins are found in San Francisco, Oakland and Alameda Island, as well as other places around San Francisco Bay." http://earthquake.usgs.gov/regional/nca/qmap. (Liquefaction occurs when earthquake shaking of water-saturated, sandy soil causes that soil to liquefy and lose its strength; in essence, liquefaction results in earthquake-induced quicksand.) The Oakland approach to the San Francisco–Oakland Bay Bridge—which collapsed during the 1989 Loma Prieta earthquake, killing 42 people—was built on soft bay mud that shook much more strongly than other ground in the vicinity. See id.

In response to the 1971 San Fernando earthquake, the California Legislature passed the Alquist-Priolo Earthquake Fault Zoning Act. Cal. Pub. Res. Code §§2621-2630. The Act and its implementing regulations prohibit subdivisions and most "structures for human occupancy" across or within fifty feet of active faults. See id. §2621.5; Cal. Code Regs., tit. 14, §3603(a). The Act requires the state geologist to create Earthquake Fault Zone Maps depicting Earthquake Fault Zones and distribute them to all affected localities and state agencies. See id. §2622. Any project within an Earthquake Fault Zone, with a few limited exceptions, is then subject to regulation by the Alquist-Priolo Act and local agencies. See id. §2621.5. For example, any project proposal within an Earthquake Fault Zone must have an accompanying geologic investigation and report outlining the potential for surface fault displacement. Policies and Criteria of the State Mining and Geology Board with Reference to the Alquist-Priolo Earthquake Fault Zoning Act, http://www.conservation.ca.gov/smgb/Misc/Documents/Regulations%20and% 20Statutes/AP%20Regulations.pdf. The Act also authorizes local governments to implement stricter zoning standards, Cal. Pub. Res. Code §2624, and many localities choose to do so.

NOTES AND QUESTIONS

1. Avoiding building within close proximity to known active faults seems like a prudent zoning approach. Can zoning otherwise be useful in mitigating potential earthquake damage? Should development on landfill or in liquefaction zones be restricted? Earthquake damage is often unpredictable and does not always occur along or near identified faults. The 1994 Northridge earthquake, for instance, occurred along a

previously unknown fault and caused billions of dollars of damage to unsuspecting homeowners.

2. Should homeowners in earthquake-prone areas be required to purchase earthquake insurance? "Hurricane Katrina…has had a dual effect on homeowners in the Bay Area.… Some Californians called their insurance agents and signed up for quake coverage. But for many others, watching billions of dollars in federal aid pour into the Gulf Coast merely bolstered the sense that the government would come to the rescue after a big earthquake." Scott Lindlaw, *Homeowners Willing to Gamble*, Houston Chron., March 20, 2006. Reconsider the question in connection with Chapter 7.

3. FIRE

Like floods, wildfires have a dual nature: they are both a potentially devastating and lethal natural force and an important ecological process. Since 2000, many western states have suffered their worst fire losses on record. Review the description of the 2000 New Mexico Cerro Grande fire in Chapter 1.

The Cerro Grande fire demonstrates the increasing difficulties for wildfire management posed by the growing wildland-urban interface (WUI), the area where urban development and wildlands meet. The proximity of communities to wildlands puts those communities at risk for catastrophic fires and limits options for wildland fire management by increasing the riskiness of prescribed burns and by pressuring the Forest Service to suppress all fires on wildlands that threaten urban development, even when good forest management practices dictate allowing the fire to burn to reduce the risk of more catastrophic fires. One recent Office of Inspector General report found that 87 percent of federal wildfire suppression was undertaken for the purpose of protecting private property in the WUI. U.S. Dep't of Agric., Office of Inspector Gen. W. Region, Audit Report: Forest Service Large Fire Suppression Costs, Report. No. 08601-44-SF, at ii (Nov. 2006).

For wildfires, the costs of holding disaster at bay may be as significant as the costs of disaster-inflicted damage. A recent study found that only 14 percent of the forested wildland interface was currently developed in the United States, and that if even 50 percent of the remaining 86 percent of the wildland interface were developed, annual federal firefighting costs to protect private property would increase from the current range of $630 million to $1.2 billion per year to an estimated $2.3 to 4.3 billion per year. *See* Patricia Gude et al., *Potential for Future Development on Fire-Prone Lands*, J. Forestry, 106(4) 198, 202 (June 2008). Despite these costs, the potential for wildland interface development is immense.

Do local governments have sufficient incentives to regulate zoning in the WUI? Do homeowners have sufficient incentives to take recommended precautions for fire-proofing their homes and land? Consider this analysis of rising wildfire suppression costs.

TIMOTHY INGALSBEE, FIREFIGHTERS UNITED FOR SAFETY, ETHICS, & ECOLOGY,
GETTING BURNED: A TAXPAYER'S GUIDE TO WILDFIRE SUPPRESSION COSTS
3-4 (August 2010)
http://fusee.org/content_pages/docs/FUSEE%20suppression%20costs%20
paper%20FINALOPT.pdf?lbisphpreq=1

Wildfire suppression costs are soaring to over one billion tax dollars per year. This is causing a fiscal crisis in the Forest Service which has exceeded its suppression budget almost every year for the last 20 years.   The agency now spends nearly half of its total appropriated budget on firefighting, and has been forced to transfer billions of dollars away from several non-fire land management programs to pay for suppression. Recent legislative changes to suppression funding (e.g. the FLAME fund) may provide better accounting for suppression costs, but do not impose firm budgetary limits on suppression spending, nor absolutely prevent continued transfers of funds from other management programs to pay for firefighting.

Part of the reason suppression costs are rising is because wildfire activity is increasing, especially the frequency of large-scale wildfires. Large fires account for less than 2% of all wildfires but consume 94% of total suppression costs. Despite huge increases in money, resources, and personnel being devoted to fire suppression, the number of burned acres continues to increase. While currently 6-8 million acres defines a "bad" fire season, experts predict an average 10-12 million acres will burn annually in the near future primarily under the impact of global warming.

Suppression costs are increasing due to several reasons that can be categorized according to socioenvironmental, institutional, and operational factors. The most popularly cited reasons for rising suppression costs are the socioenviromental factors of excess fuels accumulations caused in part from past fire suppression, expansion of housing development in the wildland/urban interface (WUI), and climate change from global warming fueled primarily by human-caused fossil fuel burning. Of these three, climate change is the dominant factor affecting increased wildfire activity and fire size due to its effect on weather and vegetation and length of wildfire season.

Next to total fire size, the presence of private property or human structures in the vicinity of wildfires is the other factor most affecting the rise in suppression costs. Fire managers speculate that up to half of total suppression expenditures are related to private property protection in the WUI. Over 44 million homes in the U.S. are currently located in fire-prone WUI areas, but the Forest Service predicts a 40% increase in new homes in the WUI by 2030 which some studies estimate could raise annual suppression costs from $2 to 4 billion.

Among the institutional drivers of rising suppression costs are the budgetary structure for the Forest Service that authorized deficit spending for suppression operations. This has nurtured an "open checkbook" attitude among managers to order whatever resources or actions they desire regardless of cost, and this inhibits efforts to contain costs. Worse, some critics argue that the budget system with authorized deficit spending has set up a system of "perverse incentives" for agencies to rely on reactive fire suppression actions rather than proactive fuels reduction or ecosystem restoration projects since these must be funded by fixed budgets, and impose more legal requirements (e.g. environmental analysis and public involvement) in comparison to firefighting actions which have almost no budgetary limits, legal constraints, or public oversight due to their "emergency" status.

Another institutional driver of rising suppression costs is the growing use of private contractors to provide firefighting crews, aircraft, vehicles, supplies and services. Private contractors typically account for over half of total expenditures on large wildfire suppression incidents, with some suppression resources costing several thousands of dollars per hour to use. The privatization of firefighting has been driven largely by political and ideological interests seeking to shrink the size of the federal workforce, and has been sustained by the promise that private businesses would provide cheaper, better, more efficient service. However, private contractors not only cost more than public agency crews, but there have been concerns about the inferior work performance of some contractors whose lack of productivity (e.g. fireline construction) also raises suppression costs.

Another institutional factor is the inequity structured into cost-share agreements between the federal and state governments. The federal government usually pays the bulk of suppression expenses on multi-jurisdictional wildfires, even if the major reason a wildfire is being suppressed is to protect private or state lands. Local, country, and state governments receive all of the benefits of new development in the WUI (e.g., increased property taxes, building permits revenue, etc.), but do not pay their full share of wildfire protection costs. The result is that taxpayers across the country are essentially "subsidizing" private development in an expanding WUI by providing free/low-cost fire protection to private property owners. More equity in cost-share agreements would not necessarily reduce suppression costs, but might provide more incentives to local governments to restrict or regulate WUI development in ways that reduce the risk of wildfire damage and therefore reduce the pressure for aggressive suppression on adjacent public lands.

Operational factors are the least-discussed reasons for rising suppression costs, but the human factors influencing the objectives, strategies and tactics managers employ to respond to wildfires have huge cost implications. First, the agency is sensitive to external cultural expectations by the public and political demands by politicians to aggressively fight all wildfires. Expensive suppression resources or actions are sometimes ordered to satisfy agencies' public relations needs even though conditions on the ground make them unnecessary, inefficient, or ineffective. There is far more pressure placed on managers to prevent wildfire damage than to reduce suppression costs, consequently, there is a general lack of accountability for suppression spending, and numerous reports and recommendations for containing suppression costs have largely been ignored.

Along with external pressures to fight fires, and a lack of accountability for reducing suppression costs, there is a lack of incentives for managers to implement alternatives to aggressive suppression, especially wildland fire use. Managers fear public reaction, personal liability, or professional demerits on their careers if any accidents (e.g. firefighter fatalities, destroyed homes, scorched private lands) were to occur from a wildfire they were managing for resource benefits. These so-called "risk-adverse" managers are actually comfortable with imposing risk on firefighters by exposing them to the inherent health hazards and safety risks of firefighting, and externalizing risk to ecosystems due to the biological effects of fire suppression/exclusion and the potential increased severity of future wildfires. Consequently, many wildfires are unnecessarily or over-aggressively suppressed when they could have been managed at lower risk to firefighters and lower cost to taxpayers.

Of all the factors accounting for rising suppression costs, operational factors have the most potential to immediately reduce suppression costs. Managing wildfires—as opposed to simply "fighting" them—with alternative strategies and tactics that maximize the social and ecological benefits of burning while minimizing their potential adverse effects is far more economically and ecologically rational. A more strategic and selective approach to fire suppression would focus it on frontcountry communities which absolutely cannot tolerate fire, and then implement fire use tactics in backcountry wildlands which generally require more fire. This approach would not necessarily reduce overall taxpayer expenditures since managing wildfires that burn larger and longer will still cost money. But, instead of these being pure "costs" whose only benefit is the avoidance of adverse outcomes, fire management operations that use fire would become more like investments in beneficial community protection, fuels reduction, and ecosystem restoration that enhances long-term community sustainability and land stewardship.

NOTES AND QUESTIONS

1. How and by whom should wildfire suppression costs be funded? Should states or the federal government bear primary responsibility? Should the "blank check" approach to federal funding be reformed? The Departments of Interior and Agriculture have traditionally funded catastrophic firefighting costs that exceed agency estimates by borrowing from other agency programs, including those that fund fire prevention and mitigation programs. In 2009, Congress created the

"federal land assistance, management, and enhancement" fund (FLAME) for fighting unpredicted catastrophic wildfires (separate from amounts annually appropriated for predicted firefighting workload). 43 U.S.C. §1748a. Some critics worry that creating this separate fund for catastrophic fires—rather than requiring the Forest Service or Interior Department to find the money in their existing budgets—will remove any remaining disincentives to fighting all fires near the WUI. Others believe that wildfire suppression costs are still underfunded and have criticized Congress's failure to fully fund FLAME. The Wildfire Disaster Funding Act, supported by President Obama, would allow the Forest Service and DOI to tap into a special disaster account to fund catastrophic wildfire suppression costs, just as FEMA can for other natural disaster costs. *See* Coral Davenport, *Obama to Propose Shift in Wildfire Funding*, N.Y. Times, Feb. 22, 2014; Wildfire Disaster Funding Act of 2013, S. 1875, 113th Cong.

2. Like the excerpt above, an Office of the Inspector General Audit also criticizes cost-sharing agreements that leave the federal government with the bulk of the financial responsibility for suppressing fires that threaten homes in the WUI. That report found that "most WUI acreage is owned by private, State, or Tribal entities" and that "[f]ederal taxpayers bear the wildfire cost implications of development decisions made by local governments about where and how structures will be built in the WUI." U.S. Dep't of Agric. Audit Report No. 08601-44-SF, at 8 (Nov. 2006). Forest Service officials blame the inequity of existing protection agreements in part on states' unwillingness to renegotiate such agreements.

3. The same audit also found that federal responsibility for fighting wildfires likewise suppressed private homeowners' incentives to mitigate their own risk, explaining that "people moving into the WUI give little thought to the threat posed by wildfires, expecting to be provided with urban type emergency services if and when a wildfire occurs" and doing "little to protect themselves." *Id*. at 9. Some states have tried to respond to this problem by increasing public awareness of wildfire risk. Colorado, for example, has an online mapping tool that allows residents to assess their own wildfire risk. *See* Colorado Wildfire Risk Assessment Portal, http://www.coloradowildfirerisk.com/.

4. Most western states—which are experiencing the greatest growth at the wildland interface—have some legislation addressing construction in the WUI, though the content of the legislation varies widely. One recent study of wildfire mitigation laws in the west found that two states (California and Oregon) are so-called "common standards" states, in which "enforceable statewide wildfire mitigation standards" apply to "all property owners in the WUI." Three states (Arizona, Colorado, and New Mexico) are "local option" states, which "have no binding

statewide WUI mitigation regulations" but "empower local governments to decide whether" to require wildfire mitigation. Two more states (Utah and Nevada) employ a "hybrid" approach that "contain[s] elements" of each of the two prior approaches. Lloyd Burton, Wildfire Mitigation Law in the Mountain States of the American West: A Comparative Assessment (2012) 2-3, http://www.ucdenver.edu/academics/colleges/SPA/Research/EAWG/Research/wildfires/Documents/WhtPprIntrstStdy15jul13.pdf. The study suggests that "political culture" plays an important role in shaping state wildfire policy:

> The local option states place more emphasis on the values of personal autonomy, direct participation in rule making, and individualized, localized approaches to threat mitigation. These states then put correspondingly less emphasis on the value of mutual obligation to assure each other's safety and environmental well-being. By contrast, common standard states place a higher premium on the mutual obligation value than they do on the values of personal autonomy, localized control, and direct participation in WUI mitigation rule making.

Id., at 3-4. What other factors might influence the differing approaches of western states? Should local communities (or the state) take a harder line on WUI development by forbidding some residential development or creating special districts when subdivisions are approved to pass on the costs of fire suppression to those who build in high-risk areas?

5. In 2006, Professor Robert Keiter wrote that "[t]he law of fire is in its infancy," and consists of an "uncoordinated and fragmented welter of organic statutory provisions, environmental protection mandates, annual budget riders, site-specific legislation, judicial decisions, policy documents, management plans, and diverse state statutory prohibitions." Robert B. Keiter, *The Law of Fire: Reshaping Public Land Policy in an Era of Ecology and Litigation*, 36 Envt'l Law 301, 378, 303-304 (2006). The only significant federal statute directed at fire policy in 2006 was the 2003 Healthy Forests Restoration Act (HFRA), which focused primarily on reducing fuel loading that resulted from prior reliance on a policy of total fire suppression. Pub. L. No. 108-148, 117 Stat. 1887 (2003) (codified at 16 U.S.C. §§6501-6591 (2003)). At least one critic has charged that HFRA's focus on reducing fuel loading has encouraged more homeowners to build in the WUI, by "conveying a sense of security and federal approval" for WUI development and ignoring underlying land use issues. *See* Jamison Colburn, *The Fire Next Time: Land Use Planning in the Wildland/Urban Interface*, 28 J. Land Resources & Envtl. L. 223, 242-243 (2008). In 2009, Congress charged

the secretaries of Interior and Agriculture to develop a "cohesive wildfire management strategy," 43 U.S.C. §1748b(a), which was published in April 2014. *See* Dept's of Agriculture and Interior, The National Strategy (April 2014), http://www.doi.gov/news/upload /20140328_CSPhaseIIINationalStrategy_SurnameCopy_execSec_FINAL_ v3.pdf

6. The definition of the WUI is fluid and debatable. How close to public forest (or other forest) should construction be to be considered WUI development? By some definitions, 38 percent of all homes are located in the WUI (and more than 60 percent of new home construction in the 1990s took place there). *See* Lauren Wishnie, Student Article, *Fire and Federalism: A Forest Fire Is Always an Emergency*, 17 N.Y.U. Envtl. L.J. 1006, 1012-1013 (2008). Is a definition that includes nearly 40 percent of existing homes a legally useful category?

7. Like floodplain mapping, accurate mapping of fire zones is expensive, technologically complex, and potentially subject to local political pressures. Gude et al., *supra*, at 204. Should the federal government map wildfire hazards, as it does with special flood hazard areas? The Forest Service and Department of Interior are already engaged in some fire mapping through the joint LANDFIRE project (Landscape Fire and Resource Management Planning Tools Project).

8. Should firefighting policy encourage individual homeowners to shoulder some of the responsibility for protecting their homes by allowing them to decline evacuation and stay to defend their homes? The Australian-pioneered Leave Early or Stay and Defend approach, which encourages homeowners either to evacuate early or to make an educated choice to stay and defend their homes, was gaining some currency in Southern California, until the Black Saturday brush fires in Victoria, Australia, on February 7, 2009, claimed nearly 200 lives, including some homeowners who were actively defending their homes. *See* Catherine Saillant, *Australian Fires Give State Pause*, L.A. Times, Mar. 6, 2009.

9. Scientists have suggested that climate change may have contributed to the devastating Black Saturday brush fires that claimed so many lives and destroyed two Australian towns, incinerating at least 750 homes. *See* Meraiah Foley, *Death Toll in Australian Fire Climbs to 131*, N.Y. Times, Feb. 8, 2009, at A8. While acknowledging that it is impossible to definitively ascribe any individual fire to climate change, Australia's Commonwealth Scientific and Industrial Research Organization (CSIRO) has attributed "[t]he extreme fire weather conditions" that fueled the fire "to the very high temperatures following a 50 year warming trend, and very dry conditions following 12 years of below-average rainfall." CSIRO, Q & A: Victorian Bushfires, http://www.csiro.au/resources/ Victorian-Bushfires-QA.html#9. As the main excerpt suggests, scientists believe that severe wildfires will increase in frequency because of

climate change. *See, e.g.,* Yongqiang Liu, et al., *Wildland Fire Emissions, Carbon and Climate: Wildfire Climate Interactions,* 317 Forest Ecology & Mgmt 80, 90 (2014) (reporting estimate that wildfires in the western U.S. will increase by more than 100 percent by 2050).

10. One in five homes in the WUI is a second home. Gude, *supra,* at 200. Does this affect the equities of asking federal taxpayers to bear a substantial burden for fire suppression? Should the income of the homeowner or the value of the home matter?

11. When it comes to protecting homes from wildfire, the layout of communities is sometimes as important as their location:

> There are...a number of very poorly planned subdivisions [in the Malibu–Santa Monica mountains] which were divided in the late 1920s and 30s with lot sizes of less than an acre and many more typically 5,000 to 10,000 sq. ft. in size. These subdivisions were primarily designed for weekend cabin type[s] of use. However, today the expensive homes built on these parcels are occupied on a year-round basis. There are approximately 6,000 of these ill-conceived small parcels in the Santa Monica Mountains. These subdivisions have very narrow winding roads which cannot accommodate fire equipment and are for the most part very heavily wooded with both natural and exotic plant species. These types of subdivisions are disasters just waiting to happen.

> Proper site design on a large parcel can reduce fire danger to some extent. [H]owever, in these small lot subdivisions it is impossible in many cases to significantly reduce the fire hazards given the very steep site topography, lack of adequate water supply, proximity to other structures and limited access for fire equipment.

> Jack Ainsworth & Troy Alan Doss, Cal. Coastal Comm'n, Presentation to the Post-Fire Hazard Assessment Planning and Mitigation Workshop at the University of California, Santa Barbara: Natural History of Fire & Flood (Aug. 18, 1995). Firefighting can also be complicated in areas with very large lot sizes, because firefighters must defend large areas to protect a few homes.

4. TAKINGS DOCTRINE AS A LIMIT ON LAND USE DECISIONS

In the United States, property rights have a great deal of political weight. They also have some degree of constitutional protection. Blocking development of land can sometimes be an unconstitutional taking of property. The Takings Clause of the Fifth Amendment provides that private property shall not "be taken for public use, without just compensation." The seminal decision was Pennsylvania Coal v. Mahon, 260 U.S. 393 (1922). This case involved a

Pennsylvania statute making it unlawful for coal companies to cause the collapse or subsidence of any overlaying structure, such as a residence. In the case before the Court, the coal company contended that the effect would be to make mining completely infeasible, wiping out the value of the mining rights that they had purchased from the owner of the surface rights. In an opinion by Justice Holmes, the Court held that this was a taking of property because the statute had "very nearly the same effect for constitutional purposes as appropriating or destroying it." *Id.* at 414. Since then, courts have struggled to determine when a regulation "goes too far" and becomes a taking. The most important modern case, Penn Central Transportation Co. v. New York, 438 U.S. 104 (1978), attempted to provide a synthesis of the law. According to *Penn Central*, except where a regulation physically invades property (as by providing public access), the test is whether the regulation unreasonably "interfered with distinct investment-backed expectations." *Id.* at 123. In the following case, however, the Court attempted to provide more of a bright-line test.

LUCAS V. SOUTH CAROLINA COASTAL COUNCIL

Supreme Court of the United States, 1992, 505 U.S. 1003, 112 S. Ct. 2886, 120 L. Ed. 2d 798

Justice SCALIA delivered the opinion of the Court.

In 1986, petitioner David H. Lucas paid $975,000 for two residential lots on the Isle of Palms in Charleston County, South Carolina, on which he intended to build single-family homes. In 1988, however, the South Carolina Legislature enacted the Beachfront Management Act, which had the direct effect of barring petitioner from erecting any permanent habitable structures on his two parcels. A state trial court found that this prohibition rendered Lucas's parcels "valueless." This case requires us to decide whether the Act's dramatic effect on the economic value of Lucas's lots accomplished a taking of private property under the Fifth and Fourteenth Amendments requiring the payment of "just compensation."...

[O]ur decision in *Mahon* [an early takings decision by Justice Holmes] offered little insight into when, and under what circumstances, a given regulation would be seen as going "too far" for purposes of the Fifth Amendment. In 70-odd years of succeeding "regulatory takings" jurisprudence, we have generally eschewed any "'set formula'" for determining how far is too far, preferring to "engag[e] in...essentially ad hoc, factual inquiries." We have, however, described at least two discrete categories of regulatory action as compensable without case-specific inquiry into the public interest advanced in support of the restraint. The first encompasses regulations that compel the property owner to suffer a physical "invasion" of his property....

The second situation in which we have found categorical treatment appropriate is where regulation denies all economically beneficial or productive use of land. As we have said on numerous occasions, the Fifth Amendment is violated when land-use regulation "does not substantially advance legitimate state interests *or denies an owner economically viable use of his land.*"[3]

We have never set forth the justification for this rule. Perhaps it is simply, as Justice Brennan suggested, that total deprivation of beneficial use is, from the landowner's point of view, the equivalent of a physical appropriation.... Surely, at least, in the extraordinary circumstance when *no* productive or economically beneficial use of land is permitted, it is less realistic to indulge our usual assumption that the legislature is simply "adjusting the benefits and burdens of economic life," [*Penn Central*], in a manner that secures an "average reciprocity of advantage" to everyone concerned. And the *functional* basis for permitting the government, by regulation, to affect property values without compensation—that "Government hardly could go on if to some extent values incident to property could not be diminished without paying for every such change in the general law"—does not apply to the relatively rare situations where the government has deprived a landowner of all economically beneficial uses.

On the other side of the balance, affirmatively supporting a compensation requirement is the fact that regulations that leave the owner of land without economically beneficial or productive options for its use—typically, as here, by requiring land to be left substantially in its natural state—carry with

---

[3] Regrettably, the rhetorical force of our "deprivation of all economically feasible use" rule is greater than its precision, since the rule does not make clear the "property interest" against which the loss of value is to be measured. When, for example, a regulation requires a developer to leave 90% of a rural tract in its natural state, it is unclear whether we would analyze the situation as one in which the owner has been deprived of all economically beneficial use of the burdened portion of the tract, or as one in which the owner has suffered a mere diminution in value of the tract as a whole. (For an extreme—and, we think, unsupportable—view of the relevant calculus, see Penn Central Transportation Co. v. New York City, 42 N.Y.2d 324, 333-334, 397 N.Y.S.2d 914, 920, 366 N.E.2d 1271, 1276-1277 (1977), *aff'd*, 438 U.S. 104, 98 S. Ct. 2646, 57 L. Ed. 2d 631 (1978), where the state court examined the diminution in a particular parcel's value produced by a municipal ordinance in light of total value of the taking claimant's other holdings in the vicinity.) Unsurprisingly, this uncertainty regarding the composition of the denominator in our "deprivation" fraction has produced inconsistent pronouncements by the Court. The answer to this difficult question may lie in how the owner's reasonable expectations have been shaped by the State's law of property—i.e., whether and to what degree the State's law has accorded legal recognition and protection to the particular interest in land with respect to which the takings claimant alleges a diminution in (or elimination of) value. In any event, we avoid this difficulty in the present case, since the "interest in land" that Lucas has pleaded (a fee simple interest) is an estate with a rich tradition of protection at common law, and since the South Carolina Court of Common Pleas found that the Beachfront Management Act left each of Lucas's beachfront lots without economic value.

them a heightened risk that private property is being pressed into some form of public service under the guise of mitigating serious public harm. *See, e.g.,* Annicelli v. South Kingstown, 463 A.2d 133, 140-141 (R.I. 1983) (prohibition on construction adjacent to beach justified on twin grounds of safety and "conservation of open space"); Morris County Land Improvement Co. v. Parsippany–Troy Hills Township, 40 N.J. 539, 552-553, 193 A.2d 232, 240 (1963) (prohibition on filling marshlands imposed in order to preserve region as water detention basin and create wildlife refuge). As Justice Brennan explained: "From the government's point of view, the benefits flowing to the public from preservation of open space through regulation may be equally great as from creating a wildlife refuge through formal condemnation or increasing electricity production through a dam project that floods private property." The many statutes on the books, both state and federal, that provide for the use of eminent domain to impose servitudes on private scenic lands preventing developmental uses, or to acquire such lands altogether, suggest the practical equivalence in this setting of negative regulation and appropriation.

We think, in short, that there are good reasons for our frequently expressed belief that when the owner of real property has been called upon to sacrifice *all* economically beneficial uses in the name of the common good, that is, to leave his property economically idle, he has suffered a taking....
It is correct that many of our prior opinions have suggested that "harmful or noxious uses" of property may be proscribed by government regulation without the requirement of compensation. For a number of reasons, however, we think the South Carolina Supreme Court was too quick to conclude that that principle decides the present case. The "harmful or noxious uses" principle was the Court's early attempt to describe in theoretical terms why government may, consistent with the Takings Clause, affect property values by regulation without incurring an obligation to compensate—a reality we nowadays acknowledge explicitly with respect to the full scope of the State's police power....

The transition from our early focus on control of "noxious" uses to our contemporary understanding of the broad realm within which government may regulate without compensation was an easy one, since the distinction between "harm-preventing" and "benefit-conferring" regulation is often in the eye of the beholder. It is quite possible, for example, to describe in *either* fashion the ecological, economic, and aesthetic concerns that inspired the South Carolina legislature in the present case. One could say that imposing a servitude on Lucas's land is necessary in order to prevent his use of it from "harming" South Carolina's ecological resources; or, instead, in order to achieve the "benefits" of an ecological preserve. Whether one or the other of the competing characterizations will come to one's lips in a particular case depends primarily upon one's evaluation of the worth of competing uses of real estate....

Where the State seeks to sustain regulation that deprives land of all economically beneficial use, we think it may resist compensation only if the logically antecedent inquiry into the nature of the owner's estate shows that the proscribed use interests were not part of his title to begin with.[4] This accords, we think, with our "takings" jurisprudence, which has traditionally been guided by the understandings of our citizens regarding the content of, and the State's power over, the "bundle of rights" that they acquire when they obtain title to property. It seems to us that the property owner necessarily expects the uses of his property to be restricted, from time to time, by various measures newly enacted by the State in legitimate exercise of its police powers; "[a]s long recognized, some values are enjoyed under an implied limitation and must yield to the police power." [*Mahon.*] And in the case of personal property, by reason of the State's traditionally high degree of control over commercial dealings, he ought to be aware of the possibility that new regulation might even render his property economically worthless (at least if the property's only economically productive use is sale or manufacture for sale). In the case of land, however, we think the notion pressed by the Council that title is somehow held subject to the "implied limitation" that the State may subsequently eliminate all economically valuable use is inconsistent with the historical compact recorded in the Takings Clause that has become part of our constitutional culture....

Where "permanent physical occupation" of land is concerned, we have refused to allow the government to decree it anew (without compensation), no matter how weighty the asserted "public interests" involved, though we assuredly would permit the government to assert a permanent easement that was a preexisting limitation upon the landowner's title. We believe similar treatment must be accorded confiscatory regulations, i.e., regulations that prohibit all economically beneficial use of land: any limitation so severe cannot be newly legislated or decreed (without compensation), but must inhere in the title itself, in the restrictions that background principles of the State's law of property and nuisance already place upon land ownership. A law or decree with such an effect must, in other words, do no more than duplicate the result that could have been achieved in the courts—by adjacent landowners (or other

---

[4] Drawing on our First Amendment jurisprudence, Justice Stevens would "loo[k] to the *generality* of a regulation of property" to determine whether compensation is owing. The Beachfront Management Act is general, in his view, because it "regulates the use of the coastline of the entire state." There may be some validity to the principle Justice Stevens proposes, but it does not properly apply to the present case. The equivalent of a law of general application that inhibits the practice of religion without being aimed at religion, is a law that destroys the value of land without being aimed at land. Perhaps such a law—the generally applicable criminal prohibition on the manufacturing of alcoholic beverages challenged in *Mugler* [v. *Kansas*, 123 U.S. 623, 8 S. Ct. 273, 31 L. Ed. 205] (1887), comes to mind—cannot constitute a compensable taking. But a regulation *specifically directed to land use* no more acquires immunity by plundering landowners generally than does a law specifically directed at religious practice acquire immunity by prohibiting all religions. Justice Stevens' approach renders the Takings Clause little more than a particularized restatement of the Equal Protection Clause.

uniquely affected persons) under the State's law of private nuisance, or by the State under its complementary power to abate nuisances that affect the public generally, or otherwise.[5]

The "total taking" inquiry we require today will ordinarily entail (as the application of state nuisance law ordinarily entails) analysis of, among other things, the degree of harm to public lands and resources, or adjacent private property, posed by the claimant's proposed activities, *see, e.g.,* Restatement (Second) of Torts §§826, 827, the social value of the claimant's activities and their suitability to the locality in question, *see, e.g., id.,* §§828(a) and (b), 831, and the relative ease with which the alleged harm can be avoided through measures taken by the claimant and the government (or adjacent private landowners) alike, *see, e.g., id.,* §§827(e), 828(c), 830. The fact that a particular use has long been engaged in by similarly situated owners ordinarily imports a lack of any common-law prohibition (though changed circumstances or new knowledge may make what was previously permissible no longer so, *see id.,* §827, Comment g.) So also does the fact that other landowners, similarly situated, are permitted to continue the use denied to the claimant.
It seems unlikely that common-law principles would have prevented the erection of any habitable or productive improvements on petitioner's land; they rarely support prohibition of the "essential use" of land. The question, however, is one of state law to be dealt with on remand. We emphasize that to win its case South Carolina must do more than proffer the legislature's declaration that the uses Lucas desires are inconsistent with the public interest, or the conclusory assertion that they violate a common-law maxim such as *sic utere tuo ut alienum non laedas.* As we have said, a "State, by *ipse dixit,* may not transform private property into public property without compensation...."
Instead, as it would be required to do if it sought to restrain Lucas in a common-law action for public nuisance, South Carolina must identify background principles of nuisance and property law that prohibit the uses he now intends in the circumstances in which the property is Only on this showing can the State fairly claim that, in proscribing all such beneficial uses, the Beachfront Management Act is taking nothing.[6]

---

[5] The principal "otherwise" that we have in mind is litigation absolving the State (or private parties) of liability for the destruction of "real and personal property, in cases of actual necessity, to prevent the spreading of a fire" or to forestall other grave threats to the lives and property of others. Bowditch v. Boston, 101 U.S. 16, 18-19 (1880); see United States v. Pacific Railroad, 120 U.S. 227, 238-239 (1887).

[6] ...We stress that an affirmative decree eliminating all economically beneficial uses may be defended only if an objectively reasonable application of relevant precedents would exclude those beneficial uses in the circumstances in which the land is presently found.

Justice KENNEDY, concurring in the judgment.

In my view, reasonable expectations must be understood in light of the whole of our legal tradition. The common law of nuisance is too narrow a confine for the exercise of regulatory power in a complex and interdependent society. The State should not be prevented from enacting new regulatory initiatives in response to changing conditions, and courts must consider all reasonable expectations whatever their source. The Takings Clause does not require a static body of state property law; it protects private expectations to ensure private investment. I agree with the Court that nuisance prevention accords with the most common expectations of property owners who face regulation, but I do not believe this can be the sole source of state authority to impose severe restrictions. Coastal property may present such unique concerns for a fragile land system that the State can go further in regulating its development and use than the common law of nuisance might otherwise permit.

The Supreme Court of South Carolina erred, in my view, by reciting the general purposes for which the state regulations were enacted without a determination that they were in accord with the owner's reasonable expectations and therefore sufficient to support a severe restriction on specific parcels of property. The promotion of tourism, for instance, ought not to suffice to deprive specific property of all value without a corresponding duty to compensate. Furthermore, the means as well as the ends of regulation must accord with the owner's reasonable expectations. Here, the State did not act until after the property had been zoned for individual lot development and most other parcels had been improved, throwing the whole burden of the regulation on the remaining lots. This too must be measured in the balance.

Justice BLACKMUN, dissenting.

[T]he Court justifies its new rule that the legislature may not deprive a property owner of the only economically valuable use of his land, even if the legislature finds it to be a harmful use, because such action is not part of the "long recognized" "understandings of our citizens." These "understandings" permit such regulation only if the use is a nuisance under the common law. Any other course is "inconsistent with the historical compact recorded in the Takings Clause." It is not clear from the Court's opinion where our "historical compact" or "citizens' understanding" comes from, but it does not appear to be history.

The principle that the State should compensate individuals for property taken for public use was not widely established in America at the time of the Revolution....

Even into the 19th century, state governments often felt free to take property for roads and other public projects without paying compensation to the owners. As one court declared in 1802, citizens "were bound to contribute as much of [land], as by the laws of the country, were deemed necessary for the public convenience."...

...In short, I find no clear and accepted "historical compact" or "understanding of our citizens" justifying the Court's new taking doctrine. Instead, the Court seems to treat history as a grab-bag of principles, to be adopted where they support the Court's theory, and ignored where they do not. If the Court decided that the early common law provides the background principles for interpreting the Taking Clause, then regulation, as opposed to physical confiscation, would not be compensable. If the Court decided that the law of a later period provides the background principles, then regulation might be compensable, but the Court would have to confront the fact that legislatures regularly determined which uses were prohibited, independent of the common law, and independent of whether the uses were lawful when the owner purchased. What makes the Court's analysis unworkable is its attempt to package the law of two incompatible eras and peddle it as historical fact.

Justice STEVENS, dissenting.

In considering Lucas' claim, the generality of the Beachfront Management Act is significant. The Act does not target particular landowners, but rather regulates the use of the coastline of the entire State. Indeed, South Carolina's Act is best understood as part of a national effort to protect the coastline, one initiated by the Federal Coastal Zone Management Act of 1972....Moreover, the Act did not single out owners of undeveloped land. The Act also prohibited owners of developed land from rebuilding if their structures were destroyed, and what is equally significant, from repairing erosion control devices, such as seawalls. In addition, in some situations, owners of developed land were required to "renouris[h] the beach...on a yearly basis with an amount...of sand...not...less than one and one-half times the yearly volume of sand lost due to erosion." In short, the South Carolina Act imposed substantial burdens on owners of developed and undeveloped land alike. This generality indicates that the Act is not an effort to expropriate owners of undeveloped land.

Admittedly, the economic impact of this regulation is dramatic and petitioner's investment-backed expectations are substantial. Yet, if anything, the costs to and expectations of the owners of developed land are even greater: I doubt, however, that the cost to owners of developed land of renourishing the beach and allowing their seawalls to deteriorate effects a taking. The costs imposed on the owners of undeveloped land, such as petitioner, differ from these costs only in degree, not in kind.

NOTES AND QUESTIONS

1. After Hurricane Hugo, so many structures were damaged in the area that the state relented on its ban on rebuilding existing houses. After further negotiations, South Carolina eventually bought the *Lucas* lots for over $1.5 million. The area has been flooded many times since the Supreme Court's ruling, leaving inhabitants to "scramble for protection via beach bulldozing" and even "walls of gigantic two- and three-ton sandbags," which the government "disallowed . . . as armor in disguise." Carol M. Rose, *The Story of* Lucas: *Environmental Land Use Regulation Between Developers and the Deep Blue Sea*, in Richard J. Lazarus & Oliver A. Houck, Environmental Law Stories 268-269 (2005).

2. One noteworthy aspect of *Lucas* is Justice Scalia's use of a narrowly construed "nuisance exception," at least in total takings cases. This is in sharp contrast to the call by some for an expansive new land ethic focusing on ecological interdependency. Justice Scalia's use of nuisance law has attracted attention from commentators, who have suggested that nuisance law has been far more fluid and adaptable than Scalia suggests. *See, e.g.*, Christine A. Klein, *The New Nuisance: An Antidote to Wetland Loss, Sprawl, and Global Warming*, 48 B.C. L. Rev. 1155, 1155, 1233 (2007) (arguing that *Lucas*, with its explicit recognition that "changed circumstances or new knowledge may make what was previously permissible no longer so," has spurred the development of a new nuisance doctrine with renewed emphasis on balancing public and private interests); *see also* Richard J. Lazarus, *The Measure of a Justice: Justice Scalia and the Faltering of the Property Rights Movement within the Supreme Court*, 57 Hastings L.J. 759, 823-824 (2006) (contending that the *Lucas* rule that Justice Scalia "hoped to serve as a per se takings rule proves, in its practical operation, to work more often as a per se no takings rule").

3. What type of restrictions on land development might survive scrutiny under *Lucas?* Applying *Lucas*'s nuisance exception, "a number of state and federal courts have held that governmental efforts to protect wetlands do not constitute regulatory takings because wetland destruction constitutes a nuisance." Klein, *supra*, at 1202; *see also* Edward A. Thomas & Sam Riley Medlock, *Mitigating Misery: Land Use and Protection of Property Rights Before the Next Big Flood*, 9 Vt. Envtl. L. 155, 171 (2008) (arguing that the trend is to sustain government "hazard-based" land use regulations, particularly floodplain regulations, against takings challenges). Is it easier to see how *Lucas*'s nuisance exception might be invoked to justify floodplain or wetlands regulation than to justify earthquake zoning?

4. Justice Scalia also acknowledges in a footnote an exception absolving public and private actors from liability for destruction of property in

order to forestall a spreading fire or other "grave threat[]" to public safety. As far back as the seventeenth century, John Locke argued that power to destroy an individual's house (without compensation) in order to stop a spreading fire lay within a democratic leader's executive "prerogative" to act decisively in defense of the public when necessity demands. *See* John Locke, Second Treatise on Civil Government § 159 (1689, 1998). This notion, sometimes called the "Lockean Prerogative," has long fueled debates about when, if ever, traditional democratic values may be suspended or limited during a "state of emergency." Robert R.M. Verchick, *Disaster Justice: The Geography of Human Capability*, 23 Duke Envt'l L. & Pol'y For. 23, 50-51 (2012). How broadly should this exception be interpreted today? Could a state, for instance, escape liability for destruction of private property to forestall a grave, but *gradually increasing* threat like sea-level rise?

5. What if a regulation *temporarily* denies a landowner all economically viable use of her land? In Tahoe-Sierra Preservation Council, Inc. v. Tahoe Regional Planning Agency, 535 U.S. 302 (2002), the Supreme Court held that two moratoria on private development of land in the Lake Tahoe Basin, which together prohibited development for 32 months while the Tahoe Regional Planning Agency developed a comprehensive land-use plan for the basin, did not constitute a categorical taking under *Lucas*. The Court left open the possibility that a temporary moratorium could constitute a taking under the *Penn Central* framework. *See id*. at 321. The Court explained that while even a temporary physical occupation of land by the government constitutes a categorical taking, *see id*. at 322, the "longstanding distinction between acquisitions of property for public use, on the one hand, and regulations prohibiting private uses, on the other, makes it inappropriate to treat cases involving physical takings as controlling precedents for the evaluation of a claim that there has been a 'regulatory taking,' and vice versa," *id*. at 323.

6. In 2013, the Supreme Court decided another takings case with potentially important implications for land use planning designed to mitigate hazard risk. Prior case law, particularly Nollan v. California Coastal Comm'n, 483 U.S. 825 (1987) and Dolan v. City of Tigard, 512 U.S. 374 (1994), established that when government conditions approval of a land-use permit on a property exaction, there must be a "'nexus' and 'rough proportionality' between the government's demand and the effects of the proposed land use." Koontz v. St. Johns River Water Management District, 133 S.Ct. 2586, 2591 (2013). In *Koontz*, the Court extended the nexus and rough proportionality requirements of *Nollan* and *Dolan* to permit denials and to monetary exactions, such as the exaction at issue in *Koontz* that would have required the landowner to expend money to mitigate offsite wetlands. *Id*. at 2595-97. The Court

acknowledged that "[i]nsisting that landowners internalize the negative externalities of their conduct is a hallmark of responsible land-use policy, and we have long sustained such regulations against constitutional attack," *id.* at 2595, so long as any exactions meet the *Nollan/Dolan* test. Many questions remain (including whether the holding applies to permit fees imposed by legislation) and the long-term effects on hazard mitigation are unclear. *Cf.* Ann E. Carlson & Daniel Pollak, *Takings on the Ground: How the Supreme Court's Takings Jurisprudence Affects Local Land Use Decisions*, 35 U.C. Davis L. Rev. 103, 116 (2001) (documenting the somewhat surprising finding that *Nollan/Dolan* actually resulted in localities imposing higher impact fees).

7. What happens when a town wants to build protective sand dunes on private oceanfront property, but the owners refuse permission? When the borough of Harvey Cedars, New Jersey, launched a beach replenishment program in 2009, it offered homeowners $300 for the strip of beachfront property the Corps needed for the construction of protective sand dunes. Most homeowners accepted the offer, but Harvey and Phyllis Karan refused to sign, explaining that the dunes would block the ocean views from their $1.9 million home. Borough officials were thus forced to take the strips through eminent domain and offer "just compensation," but the parties could not agree on the amount. In 2011, a trial court set the amount at $375,000, refusing to offset the award by any "general benefit"—protection from storm surge—that the Karans might one day receive. That benefit, as it turns out, was not theoretical. When Superstorm Sandy struck the coast in 2013, the dunes held, and the Karans' home, along with the homes of their neighbors, escaped significant damage. Later, the Supreme Court of New Jersey overturned the $375,000 award, explaining that the sum must be offset by the protective benefit of the dunes. The Karans settled with the borough for $1. Almost immediately afterward, New Jersey's governor, Chris Christie, signed an executive order to acquire more than 1,000 easements to facilitate the building of sand dunes in communities hard hit by Superstorm Sandy. *See* MaryAnn Spoto, *Harvey Cedars Couple Receives $1 Settlement for Dune Blocking Ocean View*, Star-Ledger (Newark), Sept. 25, 2013, http://www.nj.com/ocean/ index.ssf/ 2013/09/harvey_cedars_sand_dune_dispute_settled.html.

D. GREEN AND BUILT INFRASTRUCTURE

1. GREEN INFRASTRUCTURE

As Professor Rob Verchick has written, although we usually think of our infrastructure (such as roads, bridges, and dams) as gray, most of our infrastructure is, in fact, green. Robert R.M. Verchick, Facing Catastrophe: Environmental Action for a Post-Katrina World (2010). And much of that natural, green infrastructure can provide some protective buffering effect against natural disasters. Mangrove forests may play a role in coastal defense, as may coral reefs, both of which can help dissipate wave intensity and storm surge under certain conditions. Wetlands can likewise dissipate storm surge and absorb flood waters. Vegetative cover and forests help prevent landslides and avalanches. Indeed, nearly two decades ago, in 1997, researchers estimated the global value of the ecosystem's role in "disturbance regulation"—including storm protection, flood control, and drought recovery—at $1.8 trillion a year. Robert Costanza et al., *The Value of the World's Ecosystem Services and Natural Capital*, Nature, vol. 387 (May 15, 1997) 253, 259.

a. Wetlands and Other Coastal Infrastructure

The role of natural infrastructure in mitigating the effects of natural disasters garnered national attention in the aftermath of Katrina, as Gulf Coast residents wondered to what extent homes and lives would have been spared but for the loss of so much of the region's wetlands:

ROBERT R.M. VERCHICK, FACING CATASTROPHE: ENVIRONMENTAL ACTION FOR A POST-KATRINA WORLD

(2010) (internal citations and footnotes omitted)

Louisiana's coastal plain contains one of the largest expanses of coastal wetlands in the contiguous United States. In fact, a quarter of *all* coastal wetlands in the Lower 48 are in Louisiana....Louisiana's coastal plain hosts an extraordinary diversity of coastal habitats, ranging from natural levees and beach ridges to large swaths of forested swamps, to freshwater, intermediate, brackish, and saline marshes. These features, which nourish wildlife, filter water, and dampen storm surges, help make the coastal plain, to quote from the Army Corps of Engineers, one of "the most productive and important natural assets" in the country.

While most people do not realize it, one of the most important services provided by coastal marshes involves storm protection. Imagine blasting water through a garden hose at full force onto a cement driveway. The water splashes and surges, fanning out in many directions. Now imagine spraying water from the same hose onto a thick, dense lawn. The difference between the cement and the lawn is the difference between a storm path composed of open water and denuded coast and one composed of lush forests and marsh. Louisiana's coastal wetlands act as vast sponges, absorbing billions of gallons of rainfall and shielding people and property from storms. The effect is impressive, even for city dwellers who have never seen a marsh: by some estimates, every two miles of wetlands south of New Orleans reduces tropical storm surges there by half a foot. For this reason, local environmentalists sometimes refer to the coast as a "horizontal levee." Coastal wetlands also help shield an internationally significant commercial-industrial complex from the destructive forces of storm-driven waves and tides....

Unbelievably, this titan among wetlands, this biotic and commercial treasure, is disappearing before our very eyes. Since Percy Viosca's enlightened plea for wetlands protection, Louisiana has lost more than *1.2 million acres* of its "trembling prairie." Today, the Army Corps of Engineers believes Louisiana is losing about 6,600 acres of coastal wetlands per year. Why is this happening? The effect is partly due to natural subsidence. The soft soils of the coastal plain naturally shift and sink over time. But this phenomenon, at best, explains only a small fraction of the loss. The real culprits are human-made: Louisiana's vast network of levees, navigational channels, and oil-and-gas infrastructure. The levee system accelerates coastal land loss by reducing the natural flow of a river's freshwater and sediment to wetland areas where lost land would then naturally be replenished. Instead, that valuable water and sediment is funneled down the Mississippi and shot into the Gulf, toward the outer continental shelf, where the formation of barrier islands is impossible.

Louisiana's coastal plain is crisscrossed with a vast matrix of navigational canals, including ten major navigational channels and literally thousands of smaller access canals serving navigation, allowing oil-rig access, and cradling oil and gas pipelines. Recall that up close, those swamps seemed lusty and vital. But from a helicopter or plane, the view is more depressing—like green shag carpet being eaten by a Pac Man. Those channels mean death to nearby marshlands. They cut the land off from the natural flow of water and starve them of nutrients. Often the banks of these channels (which are seldom maintained) crumble and fall away, expanding waterways by many yards over time. The major navigational channels pose their own special threat to flood control by sometimes acting as "hurricane highways," allowing storms to sweep inland, past marshland, like liquid bulldozers.

In the 1980s, local groups made up of environmentalists, shrimpers, scientists, and business people began pushing for plans to save the coast. One result was the federal Coastal Wetlands Planning, Protection and Restoration Act of 1990 (the "Breaux Act"), which created a federal and state task force to implement wetlands restoration projects with annual funds of around $40 million. In 1998, state and federal agencies, with the participation of a diverse group of local churches, scientists, environmentalists, and fishermen, developed a book length plan called "Coast 2050: Toward a Sustainable Coastal Louisiana," which offered a host of ecosystem restoration strategies. The underlying principles of the Coast 2050 Plan were to restore or mimic the natural processes that built and maintained coastal Louisiana. The complete plan, to be implemented over the next 50 years, carried a price tag of $14 billion, nearly twice as much as the Everglades restoration project. Though expensive, Coast 2050 actually seemed a bargain, considering the costs of doing nothing threatened to exceed $100 billion in lost jobs, lost infrastructure, lost fishing, and increased hurricane damage. But Coast 2050 was never funded. In 2004, hamstrung by climbing deficits, the Bush Administration suggested the Corps lower its sights and focus on only a few projects totaling between $1 to 2 billion. In the end, the Corps did not even receive that amount. The President's 2005 Energy Bill provided only $540 million for Louisiana's coastal restoration over four years.

Hurricanes Katrina and Rita changed all this—first by tearing its own chunks of wetlands out of the Louisiana coast, making coastal erosion an even more serious problem, and second by highlighting for the public the essential role that wetlands play in storm protection. I mentioned that the Army Corps estimates that Louisiana loses 6,600 acres, which is around 25 square miles, of its coast every year under "normal" circumstances. Over night, hurricanes Katrina and Rita destroyed *four times* that amount of wetlands, transforming 217 square miles of productive swamp and marsh into open water. Some of the most heavily damaged marshland was located south and east of Lake Borgne, wetlands that once offered protection to St. Bernard Parish, a white working-class community, and to New Orleans' own Lower Ninth Ward. In 2008 Hurricanes Ike and Gustav again raked through this fragile coast, threatening coastal protection and commerce....Talking to a local reporter, Dave Cvitanovich, an oyster grower, says "By far, coastal erosion is our biggest problem now." "I'm out on the water every day and, God, it's accelerating. There's no slowdown. It's like watching an ice cube melt on your table."

The good news is that public awareness of the problem is at an all-time high. Even school children will tell you that we are losing a football field's worth of land every half hour and that those football fields are one of the first shields against bad storms. For the first time, the federal government is getting serious about plans to restore the coast, understanding that it will take billions not millions of dollars. There is still a very long way to go, and many pitfalls along the way....But the storms of 2005 sent a clear message: in addition to *goods*, the Louisiana coast provides *services* too, most significantly storm protection. We can't afford to kill the goose that lays *that* golden egg.

NOTES AND QUESTIONS

1. Can restoration of Louisiana's coastal wetlands play an important role in protecting New Orleans from future floods? Even some who acknowledge that restoring the wetlands is a "worthy goal" worry that

there is "almost no scientific evidence that suggests that we will be able to put the wetlands back on the scale and nature needed to reduce storm impacts." *See* Soil Science Society of America, Wetlands Restoration Not a Panacea for Louisiana Coast (Sept. 30, 2008), ScienceDaily, available at http://www.sciencedaily.com/releases /2008/09/ 080924190637.htm (quoting Robert Young, Director of the Program for the Study of Developed Shorelines at Western Carolina University, summarizing the findings of a white-paper coauthored by 26 coastal scientists and engineers); *but see* Y. Peter Sheng, et al., *The Reduction of Storm Surge by Vegetative Canopies*, 39 Geophysical Research Letters (2012) (modeling the effect of vegetative canopies on storm surge and finding a protective effect under some circumstances).

2. As with wetlands, there are limited empirical data about the protective effect of other green infrastructure and the wisdom of relying heavily (or exclusively) on that infrastructure for disaster protection. Nevertheless, initial reports after the devastating 2004 Indian Ocean tsunami suggested that mangrove forests provided substantial protection from the tsunami:

> The scale of the 26 December 2004 Indian Ocean tsunami was almost unprecedented. In areas with the maximum tsunami intensity, little could have prevented catastrophic coastal destruction. Further away, however, areas with coastal tree vegetation were markedly less damaged than areas without. Mangrove forests are the one most important coastal tree vegetation in the area and are one of the world's most threatened tropical ecosystems.
>
> Measurements of wave forces and modeling of fluid dynamics suggest that tree vegetation may shield coastlines from tsunami damage by reducing wave amplitude and energy....
>
> Our results suggest that mangroves and *Casuarina* plantations attenuated tsunami-induced waves and protected shorelines against damage.... Conserving or replanting coastal mangroves and greenbelts should buffer communities from future tsunami events.

Finn Danielsen et al., *The Asian Tsunami: A Protective Role for Coastal Vegetation*, 310 Science 643 (2005). Other scientists have contested this conclusion and warn against relying on coastal vegetation to protect against tsunamis. *See, e.g.*, Papri Sri Raman, *Mangroves "Do Not Protect against Tsunamis,"* SciDevNet (Jan. 14, 2009), http://www.scidev.net /en/news/ mangroves-do-not-protect-against-tsunamis-.html (discussing researchers' conclusion that "there is no compelling evidence that coastal forests—such as mangroves—can act as 'bioshields' to adequately protect against tsunamis or cyclone storm surges").

3. Like coastal wetlands, riparian wetlands along rivers, lakes, and streams, may play an important role in flood protection. Studies estimate that the destruction of forest riparian wetlands along the Mississippi River has reduced flood storage capacity along the Mississippi's banks from approximately 60 days of river discharge to a mere 12 days. 2005 World Resources Institute Millennium Ecosystem Assessment Report, Ecosystems and Human Well-Being: Wetlands and Water 47. This loss of wetland storage capacity may have exacerbated the 1993 Mississippi floods. *See id.*

4. The federal government can control development of wetlands under Section 404 of the Clean Water Act (CWA). There has been considerable controversy over the scope of this jurisdiction. In United States v. Riverside Bayview Homes, Inc., 474 U.S. 121 (1985), the Court held that federal jurisdiction extended to wetlands that are adjacent to navigable waters or their tributaries. In Solid Waste Agency v. U.S. Army Corps of Engineers, 531 U.S. 159 (2001), the Court held that the statute did not apply to "isolated" wetlands that are not linked to navigable waters; the Court intimated that regulating those wetlands might exceed Congress's power under the Constitution. More recently, a plurality held in Rapanos v. United States, 547 U.S. 715, 742 (2006), that the government's power to regulate wetlands is confined to those wetlands that are both adjacent to, and a have a "continuous surface connection" with, "relatively permanent waters" of the United States. However, Justice Kennedy, concurring in the judgment, believed the federal jurisdiction over wetlands is limited instead to wetlands with a "significant nexus" (either physical or ecological) to navigable waters of the United States. *Id.* at 779 (Kennedy, J., concurring in judgment). Because the dissenters argued for complete deference to the Army Corps of Engineers, *id.* at 807 (Stevens, J., dissenting), Justice Kennedy's test has held sway with most lower courts. In March of 2014, EPA issued a proposed rule to clarify the CWA's definition of U.S. waters. *See* EPA, Proposed Rule, http://www2.epa.gov/sites/production/ files/2014-03/documents/wus_proposed_rule_20140325 _prepublication.pdf.

b. Forest as Green Infrastructure

Forests are also an important component of green infrastructure that can help to prevent both avalanches and mudslides. "[F]orests in potential avalanche release areas can reduce the risk of avalanches because trees break up snow cover, prevent wind-blown snow drifts, keep snow under shade and therefore colder and firmer, and their fallen boles and boughs tend to anchor snow and prevent it from moving." ProAct, The Role of Environmental

Management and Eco-Engineering in Disaster Risk Reduction and Climate Change Adaptation 9 (2008). The economic value of the avalanche-suppression effect of forests in the Swiss Alps has been estimated at approximately $100/hectare/year in open areas and as much as $170,000/hectare/year in areas surrounding significant economic assets. *Id.* at 9-10. Switzerland therefore provides federal monetary incentives for management of such protective forests. *See id.* at 28. Moreover, studies in Pakistan and Japan have demonstrated that vegetative cover—particularly dense trees—helps prevent landslides (triggered by earthquakes or otherwise), particularly relatively small landslides, which are the most common. *See id.* at 24-28.

China is hoping that forests can provide a buffering effect against a different type of natural disaster: dust storms. During the spring of 2006, Beijing experienced record dust storms, which have been aggravated in recent years by desertification. Dust storms continue to exacerbate Beijing's already poor air quality. China has attempted to mitigate some of these storms by building the Green Wall of China—a 4,500-kilometer-long forest, which it hopes will help protect settled areas from windstorms that sweep in from the Gobi and Kubuki Deserts. *See id.* at 43. Unfortunately, in some areas, large swaths of planted trees have died of drought, which has been intensified by the choice to plant poplar trees that require lots of water. *See* Jiang Jie, *The Death of Beijing's Dust Shield*, Global Times (Sept. 23, 2013), http://www.globaltimes.cn/content/813288.shtml#.U0gxDeZdXlQ.

Congress has also recognized that forests can play an important role in reducing floods. In fact, one of the primary reasons Congress authorized the creation of national forests in the 1800s was because of the fear that ravaged forests might disappear, taking with them critical watersheds that "encourage stream flows while preventing floods." United States v. New Mexico, 438 U.S. 696, 705 (1978). Wildfires that destroy vegetation significantly increase the risk of flooding and mudflows in subsequent years. *See, e.g.*, 42 U.S.C. §4013(c)(2)(C) (codifying a new exception to the 30-day waiting period for the effective date of new NFIP flood insurance policies for property "affected by flooding on Federal land that is a result of, or is exacerbated by, post-wildfire conditions).

Interfering with natural processes that shape our green infrastructure also can have unintended consequences for disaster risk. For 50 years, the U.S. Forest Service engaged in a total fire suppression policy and allowed forests to grow unchecked by natural fires that normally remove small vegetation and dead wood. *See* Evan N. Turgeon, Federal Forests, *Biomass, and Ethanol: Energy Security Sabotaged*, 39 Envtl. L. Rep. News & Analysis 10140, 10141 (2009). Fire suppression eventually created older, denser forests containing extremely high quantities of fuel and posing a much higher risk of catastrophic fire. *See id*. When the number of forest acres burned annually nearly quadrupled in the 1990s, the U.S. General Accounting Office reported that "[s]cientists and agency officials believe that this increase in large, intense, uncontrollable, and catastrophically destructive wildfires is in large part the result of the Forest Service's decades-old policy of putting out wildfires on national forests." U.S. General Accounting Office, Report to the Subcommittee on Forests and Forest Health, Committee on Resources, House of Representatives, Western National Forests: A Cohesive Strategy Is Needed to Address Catastrophic Wildfire Threats 4 (1999). Furthermore, logging, road building, and livestock grazing have altered natural forest structure and consequently increased the risk of wildfires. *See* Rebecca K Smith, *War on Wildfire: The U.S. Forest Service's Fire Suppression Policy and Its Legal, Scientific, and Political Context*, 15 U. Balt. J. Envtl. L. 25, 38 (2007).

c. Strategies for Protecting Green Infrastructure

Why have we underinvested in green infrastructure protection and what strategies could be employed to correct this market failure? Consider this approach, from a United Nations Report:

UNITED NATIONS, 2009 GLOBAL ASSESSMENT REPORT ON DISASTER RISK REDUCTION: RISK AND POVERTY IN A CHANGING CLIMATE

162-165

The management of ecosystem services

6.4.1 Approaches to ecosystem management

Resilient ecosystems are not only important for reducing disaster risks. They are critical to providing for sustainable livelihoods, in securing a reliable flow of goods and services, and in reducing vulnerability to an increasingly unpredictable climate. Building ecosystem resilience requires actions at different scales, with a wide array of stakeholders, and an understanding that different bodies of knowledge, including scientific, technical and local and traditional, are needed to understand the effects of global environmental change on local ecosystems.

The global decline in many regulating and provisioning ecosystem services contributes to increasing hazard for poor urban and rural households as well as declining livelihood resilience. From this perspective, ecosystem management is an emerging practice that can potentially contribute both to the regulation of weather-related hazards as well as to the strengthening of livelihoods....

In the case of ecosystem restoration, the avoided costs may significantly exceed the restoration costs. For example, planting and protecting 12,000 ha of mangroves by the IFRC in Viet Nam cost approximately US$ 1 million but reduced the costs of sea dyke maintenance by US$ 7.3 million per year. At the same time, the co-benefits may also greatly exceed the opportunity costs. For example, the Millennium Ecosystem Assessment estimated that the value of healthy coastal mangroves as nurseries, pollution filters and coastal defences is US$ 1,000 to US$ 36,000 for mangrove value versus US$ 200 per hectare for shrimp farming. In Malaysia, the economic value of mangroves as coastal defences has been estimated at US$ 300,000 per kilometre, taking into account the costs of hard engineering work to achieve the same protective effect. In Switzerland, the economic value of forests in preventing avalanches is valued at US$ 100 per hectare per year in open areas but up to US$ 170,000 in areas with high-value assets.

At the same time, ecosystems often provide important co-benefits if properly managed. Some of the most fertile agricultural land on the planet depends on regular flooding to recharge the soil with nutrients. Flooding can also recharge aquifers in semi-arid areas or transport vital sediments and nutrients to sustain coastal fisheries in other areas. Periodic fire is vital to the health of some forest ecosystems. In these cases the co-benefits of protecting the ecosystem usually outweigh the opportunity costs. The best examples of ecosystem management are win-win strategies that simultaneously reduce hazard and increase livelihood viability for poor households, while providing broader global co-benefits in areas such as water and energy supply, air quality and climate regulation.

Managing the provision of ecosystem services is complicated for many reasons. While the benefits may appear obvious they are often shared by many people over the long term. Ensuring that private interests do not degrade these social benefits requires effective and long-term institutional, legal and administrative systems backed up with the resources and political support to be respected. There are many opportunities to engineer ecosystems to provide multiple ecosystem services. However, engineering ecosystems to ensure that they optimally produce services that are produced and consumed by different social groups and economic and political interests at different scales is usually a daunting governance challenge. Nevertheless, there are a number of different practices that applied appropriately or in combination can facilitate ecosystem management in a way that does reduce hazard and strengthen livelihoods.

6.4.2 Environmental governance

The broad area of environmental governance involves creating policy and regulatory frameworks and institutional structures to promote environmental sustainability. Often these frameworks specify levels of environmental protection and call for means to monitor and enforce that protection. One of the best known and most widely applied tools is the use of Environmental Impact Assessments (EIA) in project and investment planning and approval. Disaster risk considerations are now increasingly factored into EIAs....

6.4.3 Integrated planning

Integrated planning, in which both environmental and disaster risk considerations are factored into land use and development planning, is another mechanism that can facilitate the management of ecosystems. This includes integrated coastal zone management, integrated water resource management, as well as specific initiatives such as the Mangroves for the Future initiative—a multi-country, multi-agency, multi-stakeholder initiative aimed at improving coastal zone management. The success of integrated planning is closely associated with the quality of governance and in most countries success has depended, as in other areas, on innovative partnerships between national agencies, local governments and civil society.

6.4.4 Protected areas

Protected areas legislation, and other methods of natural resource management to conserve and restore ecosystems, is another relevant tool. The promotion of natural floodplains and wetlands as cost effective measures for flood hazard mitigation is becoming increasingly accepted in a number of countries as an alternative to expensive hard-engineering measures such as canalizing rivers and building flood defence walls. Protected forests regulate the water cycle, can mitigate flood and drought hazard and contribute to the sustainability of rural livelihoods both through the provision of forest products as well as eco-tourism. Coastal afforestation and the protection and restoration of mangroves can complement sea walls to protect erosion prone coastlines.

6.4.5 Environmental technology

A range of new environmental technologies and innovations is being introduced by the private sector, NGOs and public sector initiatives that offer new soft or eco-engineering approaches to the management of ecosystems and hazards and of energy, as well as to the strengthening of rural and urban livelihoods. Examples include technologies for water harvesting in drought prone areas, for managing temperature extremes in housing, fuel efficient stoves aimed to limit deforestation, decentralized microhydro and solar energy, and countless others. While the potential of technological innovation is enormous, major cultural and economic barriers often exist to their adoption by risk-averse poor rural and urban communities. As a result, while pilot projects abound, cases of mainstreaming and up-scaling are still the exception.

6.4.6 Payment for ecosystem services

Payment for ecosystem services (PES) is an environmental management tool that has been in existence since the 1990s. It involves placing a monetary value upon ecosystem services and then finding both 'buyers' and 'sellers.' The costs and benefits of the different kinds of provisioning, regulatory and cultural ecosystem services are valued and systems are designed so that users pay for the services provided. For example, a protected watershed provides water for domestic consumption and hydro-energy for a nearby city but if the watershed were deforested for logging this would provide benefits for those who sold the wood. If logged, the costs in terms of reduced availability and more expensive water and electricity would be paid for by the residents of the city. Using a PES approach, the opportunity costs of protecting the watershed would be paid for by water and electricity consumers (predominantly from peri-urban and urban areas), who receive co-benefits in terms of a secure and cheap supply of water and energy. PES could therefore potentially play a major role in supporting efforts to reduce hazard both in urban and rural areas as well as to increase rural livelihood sustainability....

However, the mainstreaming of PES is still in its infancy and many current PES programmes present serious obstacles to the inclusion of poor households, given that they were originally designed to meet conservation rather than poverty reduction goals. The policy attention in many countries is indeed now shifting to identifying reforms needed to increase the potential of PES for poverty reduction and even in their current imperfect form, PES programs have managed to deliver some important benefits to low-income households, including the penetration of new markets for sustainable timber, organic coffee and other agroforestry products. Like other forms of environmental income, PES may not be sufficient in itself to raise rural households out of poverty, but it can become an important contributor to livelihood security due to the regularity of the payments and the incentive they provide to manage sustainable ecosystems....

NOTES AND QUESTIONS

1. As the report mentions, the benefits of preserving natural infrastructure may be obvious, but they are often long-term benefits shared by a diffuse group of people. What challenges are posed when the benefits of preserving a resource are widely shared by many who do not own the resource but the costs of preserving the resource (or refraining from exploiting it) are concentrated on the owner? See the discussion of externalities in the privatization section, *supra*, and the built infrastructure section, *infra*. Which of these strategies for protecting green infrastructure might make sense in the United States?

2. To what extent do U.S. laws requiring Environmental Impact Statements mandate that agencies consider the effect of natural infrastructure loss on disaster risk? The National Environmental Policy Act (NEPA) requires that a federal agency undertaking a "major Federal action significantly affecting the quality of the human environment" provide an

Environmental Impact Statement. 42 U.S.C. §4332(c) (2009). The agency is required to determine both direct and indirect effects that are "reasonably foreseeable," Metro Edison Co. v. People Against Nuclear Energy, 460 U.S. 766, 774 (1983); "[i]ndirect effects may include growth inducing effects and other effects related to induced changes in the pattern of land use, population density or growth rate, and related effects on air and water and other natural systems, including ecosystems." 40 C.F.R. §1508.8. Do these requirements adequately focus the agency's attention on disaster mitigation? *Cf.* Katherine Hausrath, *Tough Love: Should We Analyze Federal Emergency Management Agency Disaster Planning under the National Environmental Policy Act?*, 13 Hastings W.-Nw. J. Envtl. L. & Pol'y 161 (2007), 178-182 (arguing that the National Flood Insurance Program and the National Hurricane Program should require EISs, because FEMA's planning is a major federal action significantly affecting the environment; the programs do not meet an established exception; and preparing an EIS would fulfill the purposes of NEPA by allowing the public the benefit of a full analysis before moving into hurricane- or flood-prone areas). After a disaster has already occurred, some federal actions are exempted from EIS requirements by the Stafford Act, *see, e.g.*, 42 U.S.C. §5159 (2009) (exempting from NEPA an action that restores a "facility substantially to its condition prior to the disaster or emergency"), or by regulatory procedures, *see, e.g.*, 44 C.F.R. §10.8 (2009); FEMA, Alternative Arrangements to Meet NEPA Requirements for Reconstruction of New Orleans 1, available at http://www.fema.gov /pdf/plan/ehp/noma/alt_arr_nepa.pdf (providing "alternative arrangements" for numerous post-Katrina grant applications, which truncated the NEPA process).

3. One of the problems of preserving green infrastructure is that a wide number of resource users will want to use it for other purposes (and often using it means consuming it). Compare this to other infrastructure that is generally built for a specific purpose. *See* Brigham Daniels, *Emerging Commons and Tragic Institutions*, 37 Envtl. L. 515 (2007) ("It is somewhat troubling—a paradox of preservation—that the more a commons is preserved for less consumptive uses, the more attractive it might seem to those who would use the commons for more consumptive uses: the more a commons is preserved, the more it becomes a target."). For example, if a community is successful in preventing development of floodplains in the short term, over time they may become particularly attractive for development because they constitute large, contiguous open tracts of lands, which may otherwise be in short supply. Can this tendency be countered by restrictions like those in FEMA's Hazard Mitigation Grant Program (HMGP), which require for property acquired with HMPG funds to be "dedicated and

maintained in perpetuity for a use that is compatible with open space, recreational, or wetlands management practices"? 42 U.S.C. §5170c(b)(2)(B)(i).

2. BUILT INFRASTRUCTURE

Like our green infrastructure, much of the infrastructure built to protect us against disaster—such as levees—has been neglected and poorly maintained. Some levees, including those that were supposed to protect New Orleans, were poorly designed and constructed in the first instance. Others have deteriorated over time. In addition, other infrastructure whose failure could result in disaster—such as dams—has likewise been poorly maintained.

a. Levees

The failure of the flood protection system of levees and floodwalls surrounding New Orleans has been described as a catastrophic engineering failure. The Interagency Performance Evaluation Task Force (IPET), created by the U.S. Army Corps of Engineers and staffed by distinguished government, academic, and private sector scientists and engineers, concluded that approximately half of the direct losses from Katrina flooding could have been avoided if levees and floodwalls had not breached. IPET, Performance Evaluation of the New Orleans and Southeast Louisiana Hurricane Protection System: Final Report of the Interagency Performance Evaluation Task Force, Volume 1, Executive Summary and Overview, June 1, 2008, I-5, available at ipet.wes.army.mil (June 5, 2009); *see also* R.B. Seed et al., Investigation of the Performance of the New Orleans Flood Protection Systems in Hurricane Katrina on August 29, 2005 xix-xx (Final Report), July 31, 2006, (explaining that one of the root causes of the flooding was "poor performance of the flood protection system, due to localized engineering failures, questionable judgments, errors, etc. involved in the detailed design, construction, operation and maintenance of the system"), available at http://works.bepress.com/rmoss/17.

The Army Corp of Engineers, which constructed the levees, has itself acknowledged that design and construction flaws contributed to the levees' failure. *See* John Schwartz, *Army Corps Admits Flaws in New Orleans Levees*, N.Y. Times, June 1, 2006. Consider this excerpt from the IPET Report:

IPET, PERFORMANCE EVALUATION OF THE NEW ORLEANS AND SOUTHEAST LOUISIANA HURRICANE PROTECTION SYSTEM: FINAL REPORT OF THE INTERAGENCY PERFORMANCE EVALUATION TASK FORCE, VOLUME 1, EXECUTIVE SUMMARY AND OVERVIEW

(June 1, 2008), I-2 to I-3, ipet.wes.army.mil (June 5, 2009)

The System

The system did not perform as a system. In some areas it was not completed, and in others, datum misinterpretation and subsidence reduced its intended protective elevation. The capacity for protection varied because of some structures that provided no reliable protection above their design elevations and others that had inadequate designs leaving them vulnerable at water elevations significantly below the design intent. The designs of the levee-floodwall structures along the outfall canals were particularly inadequate. A series of incremental decisions...systematically increased the inherent risk in the system without recognition or acknowledgment.

The Storm

Katrina created record surge and wave conditions along the east side of New Orleans and the coast of Mississippi. Peak water levels along the Plaquemines and St. Bernard levees and within the Inner Harbor Navigation Canal (IHNC) were significantly higher than the structures leading to massive overtopping and eventually breaching. Wave heights during Katrina were typically similar to those assumed for the design of the structures, except for Plaquemines Parish where they were higher than the design assumptions. Wave periods, however, were three times longer than the design assumptions, particularly along the east side of St. Bernard and Plaquemines Parishes. The longer period, more energetic waves created much greater potential for runup and overtopping. Conditions within Lake Pontchartrain were roughly equal to the design criteria for the shoreline structures. The Mississippi River Gulf Outlet (MRGO) channel, presumed to be a major factor in propagating storm surge into the IHNC, was demonstrated to have little impact on storm water levels for large storms.

The Performance

With the exception of four foundation design failures, all of the major breaches were caused by overtopping and subsequent erosion. Reduced protective elevations increased the amount of overtopping, erosion, and subsequent flooding, particularly in Orleans East. Ironically, the structures that ultimately breached performed as designed, providing protection until overtopping occurred and then becoming vulnerable to catastrophic breaching. The levee-floodwall designs for the 17th Street and London Avenue Outfall Canals and IHNC were inadequate for the complex and challenging environment. In four cases the structures failed catastrophically prior to water reaching design elevations. A significant number of structures that were subjected to water levels beyond their design limits performed well. Typically, in the case of floodwalls, they represented more conservative design assumptions and, for levees, use of higher quality, less erodible materials.

The Consequences

Approximately 80% of New Orleans was flooded, in many areas with depth of flooding exceeding 15 ft. The majority, approximately two-thirds overall in areas such as Orleans East Bank and St. Bernard, of the flooding and half of the economic losses can be attributed to water flowing through breaches in floodwalls and levees. There were at least 727 fatalities in the five parishes in and around New Orleans, and over 70% of the fatalities were people over age 70. The poor, elderly, and disabled, the groups least likely to be able to evacuate without assistance, were disproportionately impacted. Direct property losses exceeded $20 billion, and 78% of those losses were in residential areas. There was an additional loss of over $7 billion in public structures and utilities.... Where water depths were small, recovery has been almost complete. In areas where water depths were greater, little recovery or reinvestment has taken place.

The Army Corps of Engineers rebuilt New Orleans' levee system to provide 100-year protection to New Orleans, a level that many experts feel is wholly inadequate for an urban area. *See* Report: Post-Katrina Levees Not Strong Enough (April 24, 2009), http://www.msnbc.com/id/30391989/. Most of the country's other levees are receiving even less attention and are also in dire need of renovation, repair, or replacement. In 2013, the American Society of Civil Engineers Report Card for America's Infrastructure gave America's more than 100,000 miles of levees a "D-" ("nearly failing") grade and estimated that it will cost more than $100 billion to rehabilitate the nation's levees. *See* ASCE 2013 Report Card for America's Infrastructure [hereinafter 2013 Report Card].

A number of factors contribute to the wholly unsatisfactory state of the nation's levees. First, there is neither a comprehensive inventory of existing levees nor any systematic program for assessing the condition of the more than 85 percent of levees that are locally owned. *See* 2013 Report Card, Levees: Condition & Capacity. The Water Resources Development Act of 2007, passed by Congress in response to Hurricane Katrina, requires the U.S. Army Corps of Engineers, FEMA, and DHS to develop a joint database, inventorying all federal levees, as well as non-federal levees for which state and local governments voluntarily provide information. *See* Pub. L. No. 110-114, §9004, 121 Stat. 1041, 1290 (codified at 33 U.S.C. §3303). Information about non-federal levees is limited. Of the inventoried and rated levees, only 8 percent were "found to be in acceptable condition." 2013 Report Card, Levees: Condition & Capacity.

Second, the National Flood Insurance Program requires mandatory flood insurance for federally backed mortgages on properties located in Special Flood Hazard Areas, defined as those with a 1 percent annual chance of a flood event (also referred to as a "100-year flood"); properties protected by "100-year flood" levees are exempt from the mandatory insurance requirements. ASCE 2009 Report Card for America's Infrastructure. at 43. Thus, the "100-year flood" standard, which was not intended as a safety standard, "became the target design level for many levees because it allowed development to continue while providing relief from mandatory flood insurance purchase for homeowners living behind accredited levees." *Id.* at 43-44. This level of protection not only is arguably inadequate (and based on insufficient, old data), but also creates a false sense of security about flood risk for those who live behind the levees and are unaware of the significant (even catastrophic) residual risk they would face if the levees were overtopped or breached. Many people believe that a "100-year flood" is likely to be a rare event, when—in fact—there is a 26 percent chance that it will occur in the span of a 30-year mortgage. *Id.* at 43.

Third, most existing levees were originally designed and engineered to protect cropland from flooding; development and population has exploded in the shadow of many such levees, which now are the fragile bulwark between floods and people. In 1997 alone, more than 50 California levees failed, leading to eight fatalities, damaging or destroying 24,000 homes, and forcing the evacuation of over 100,000 people. *See* John Ritter, *Several Cities Dependent on Vulnerable Levees*, U.S.A. Today, Sept. 11, 2005. Lester Snow, Director of the California Department of Water Resources characterized California's network of levee as "an old, aging system that instead of protecting farmland is actually protecting small cities" and reported that "levees of questionable integrity [are] protecting higher value real estate." *Id.*

Although most levees that protect significant urban populations are owned by federal, state, or local governments, some are privately owned. As described *supra*, private levee owners often lack adequate incentives to maintain (or strengthen) their levees because many of the risks posed by unsafe levees are external to the owner—that is, a levee failure will likely impose costs on many community members, not just the levee owner. These security externalities result in insufficient investment in levee safety.

b. Dams

As with levees, we neglect dam design and maintenance at our peril. The 1976 Teton Dam disaster—described as "one of the most colossal and dramatic failures in our national history"—demonstrates the deadly and costly consequences of dam failure. The disaster claimed 11 lives, killed approximately 13,000 head of livestock, and caused damages estimated as high as $2 billion. Eric A. Stene, The Teton Basin Project (Bureau of Reclamation History Program 1995), available at http://www.usbr.gov/dataweb/html/teton.html (quoting Teton Dam Disaster: Hearings Before a Subcomm. of the Comm. on Government Operations, H.R., 94th Cong. 1 (1976) (statement of Congressman Leo J. Ryan, Subcomm. Chairman)). The dam breached on June 5, 1976, less than seven months after the U.S. Department of Interior's Bureau of Reclamation completed its construction and before it was ever filled to capacity. *See id.* Once the reservoir broke through, the earthen dam released 250,000 acre-feet of water within six hours, Timothy J. Randle et al., Geomorphology and River Hydraulics of the Teton River Upstream of Teton Dam, Teton River, Idaho 6 (2000), washing away the embankment and damaging 427,000 acres of farmland. Stene, *supra.* The following day, President Gerald Ford declared the five surrounding counties to be a federal disaster area. *Id.* In addition to repair costs, the federal government eventually paid out more than $300 million in claims to flood survivors. *Id.*

Whatever the cause of the dam's breach—experts cite design flaws, inadequate planning, "goal-oriented" risk assessments, and poor site selection as likely contributors, *id.*—the disaster underscores the need for vigilance in dam construction and maintenance. U.S. dams received a "D" rating from the American Society of Civil Engineers 2013 Report Card for America's Infrastructure, which estimated that the United States needs to invest more than $21 billion in dam infrastructure to rehabilitate just "high-hazard" dams. That number nevertheless falls far short of the $57 billion the Association of State Dam Safety Officials has estimated is necessary to repair all the nation's dams. 2013 Report Card, *supra.* A primary driver of this near-failing grade is the number of "high hazard potential" dams (failure of which is anticipated to cause loss of life) that are deficient and in need of repair. As of 2012, the number of high-hazard-potential dams totaled 13,991; this number has increased over the last decade, largely as a result of new development beneath dams. While not all of these dams are deficient, as is the case with levees, many aging and inadequately designed dams originally built to shelter (and provide irrigation water for) agricultural lands are now being pressed into service to protect large population centers. *See id.* Moreover, "[b]y 2020, 70% of the total dams in the [U.S.] will be over 50 years old." *Id.*

The U.S. Army Corps of Engineers maintains a national inventory of the more than 85,000 dams in the United States. However, only a small percentage of dams are regulated or owned by the federal government—69 percent are privately owned and many others are owned by state and local governments—and thus the primary onus for dam maintenance and repair falls to the states. *See id.* In 1996, Congress established the National Dam Safety Program, administered by FEMA, to provide grants and technical assistance to establish state dam safety programs. *See* Pub. L. No. 104-303, §8, 110 Stat. 3658, 3658 (codified at 33 U.S.C. 467f (2006)). Although every state except Alabama now has a formal dam safety program and state dam safety programs have achieved some modest successes, including developing emergency action plans for more high-hazard dams, most state programs are insufficiently funded and staffed. *See* 2013 Report Card.

In addition to dams and levees, other aging infrastructure originally built for agricultural purposes now threatens growing communities. On January 5, 2008, a century-old irrigation canal burst in Fernley, Nevada, flooding more than

600 homes with frigid water. When the canal was built in 1903, Fernley's population was 654; in 2008, it was approximately 20,000. See Scott Sonner, *Floods Prompt Review of Canals*, Hayward Daily Rev., April 5, 2008.

c. Buildings and Building Codes

States have the power to enact building codes setting forth minimum standards for building construction or rehabilitation. States have exercised this power in divergent ways: Some have exercised the authority themselves to enact state building codes; many have delegated the power to local governments. Even those states that have statewide building codes may allow local modification of the codes. "Twenty-two states mandate local enforcement of statewide codes and 28 states have partial or complete code adoption and enforcement between the state and local levels." DHS, Including Building Codes in the National Flood Insurance Program v (Oct. 2013). Whether it is the state or a local entity doing the regulating, most jurisdictions adopt a model building code and may tailor it, by amendment, to the particular hazards of the area. Prior to 1994, there were three primary model building codes; now those codes have been merged into the model International Building Code.

There is much debate about the need for state-led code adoption and enforcement. Proposed legislation would amend the Stafford Act to encourage states to adopt and actively enforce federally approved, statewide building codes by making states that do so eligible for more post-disaster hazard mitigation grant money. *See, e.g.*, Safe Building Code Incentive Act of 2013, H.R. 1878, 113th Cong. The Biggert-Waters Flood Insurance Reform Act of 2012 required FEMA to evaluate whether the National Flood Insurance Program should be amended "to include widely used and nationally recognized building codes" as part of the NFIP's "floodplain management criteria." FEMA's report concluded that incorporating building codes into the NFIP would "help[] reduce physical losses and other hazard losses, which would in turn positively affect the land use planning and regulatory climate." Including Building Codes, *supra*, at iv.

Building codes can help reduce risks from a wide variety of hazards. Deadly tornadoes in Joplin, Missouri, and Moore, Oklahoma, for example, have helped reignite debates over whether structures in Tornado Alley should be required to have "safe rooms" to help protect occupants during tornadoes, *see* John Schwartz, *Why No Safe Room to Run to? Cost and Plains Culture*, N.Y. Times, May 21, 2013, and whether schools, in particular, should have storm shelters, *see* Erin McClam, Oklahoma Politics Snarl Push for Tornado Shelters at Schools, NBCNews.com, April 7, 2014, http://www.nbcnews.com/news/us-news/oklahoma-politics-snarl-push-tornado-shelters-schools-n70196. In 2014, the year after Moore's most recent devastating tornado, Moore became the first U.S. city to adopt new "tornado-inspired building codes," which do not include safe rooms, but which are nonetheless "expected to increase the price of home construction by $1 per square foot." Kurt Gwartney, Moore Approves

Tornado Resistant Building Codes, Mar. 18, 2014, http://kgou.org/post/moore-approves-tornado-resistant-building-codes.

Recent earthquakes have also demonstrated the close connection between the quality and design of buildings and earthquake mortality. On May 12, 2008, a 7.9-magnitude earthquake struck China's southwestern Sichuan province, killing more than 68,000 people (nearly 18,000 were still officially listed as missing one year later). At least 5,335 of the dead were schoolchildren, who were attending class in shoddily built schools at the time the earthquake hit. *See The Sichuan Earthquake: Salt in Their Wounds*, Economist, May 16, 2009, at 48. Other structures—including hospitals and factories—that shot up during China's recent building boom also collapsed, calling into question the enforcement of earthquake building codes instituted after more than 240,000 died in the 1976 Tangshan earthquake. Chinese law now requires that hospitals and schools be built to withstand 8.0-magnitude earthquakes. *See id.* (The Sichuan earthquake may, in fact, have been caused by other built infrastructure: A growing number of scientists believe the quake was triggered by the four-year-old Zipingpu Reservoir, which housed more than 320 million tons of water less than a mile from the fault. *See* Fan Xiao, *Did the Zipingpu Dam Trigger China's 2008 Earthquake?* (Dec. 2012), available at http://probeinternational.org/library/wp-content/uploads/2012/12/Fan-Xiao12-12.pdf. On April 6, 2009, a 6.3-magnitude quake in L'Aquila, Italy, claimed nearly 300 lives, left some 50,000 homeless, and destroyed not only storied medieval churches but also modern buildings, including a University of L'Aquila dormitory and L'Aquila's new hospital, completed in 2000. *See* Silvia Aloisi, *Italy Quake Exposes Poor Building Standards*, Reuters, Apr. 7, 2009, available at http://www.alertnet.org/thenews/newsdesk/ L7932819.htm (June 7, 2009). Poor construction and nonexistent building codes contributed to the horrific death toll and destruction in Haiti's 2010 earthquake. In contrast, strict Japanese building codes helped limit quake damage in Tokyo from the 2011 Tohoku earthquake and tsunami.

Seismic building codes were widely adopted in the western United States in the 1970s and gained traction in the eastern United States in the 1990s. Much of the current controversy over the disaster resilience of U.S. buildings focuses on the extent to which older buildings should be retrofitted to meet current building standards. Certain types of older buildings are particularly vulnerable to collapse in earthquakes. For example, structures with bearing walls constructed from unreinforced masonry (bricks or blocks held together by mortar only, with no steel or other reinforcement) have performed poorly in past earthquakes. Although California banned construction of unreinforced masonry buildings (URMs) after 1933, California has approximately 25,900 existing URMs in its highest earthquake zone (Seismic Zone 4). California Seismic Safety Commission, 2006 Report to the Legislature, Status of the Unreinforced Masonry Building Law (Nov. 2006) 2, available at http://www.seismic.ca.gov/

pub.html, April 19, 2014. The cost of retrofitting these buildings was estimated in the 1980s at approximately $4 billion. *See id.* at 3.

In 1986, California passed the Unreinforced Masonry Building Law, which required local building departments in Seismic Zone 4 to (1) inventory unreinforced masonry construction buildings built before adoption of local building codes requiring earthquake resistant design, Cal. Gov. Code §§8875, 8875.2(a); (2) establish a mitigation program for those buildings, *id.* §8875.2(b); and (3) report progress to the California Seismic Commission. Although the mitigation program may include strengthening and demolishing buildings, and other measures, the only mandatory measure is notifying the building's owner of the hazard. *See id.* Overall, the law has been quite effective in encouraging retrofitting of URMs: as of 2006, 70 percent of California's URMs had been either retrofitted or demolished. 2006 Report to the Legislature, *supra*, at 9. Some California localities have been very proactive in retrofitting unreinforced masonry buildings. For instance, by 2005, all but one of Los Angeles' 8,700 URMs had been retrofitted or demolished. *See* Chong & Becerra, *supra*, at A2. Rates of retrofitting/demolition are unsurprisingly much higher in local jurisdictions that mandate retrofitting (86 percent of URMS retrofitted/demolished), as compared to those jurisdictions that require owners to assess earthquake risk but make retrofitting voluntary (24 percent) or to jurisdictions that provide notice only (13 percent). 2006 Report to the Legislature, *supra*, at 7.

Many other western states with high seismicity have been somewhat less proactive in pursuing retrofitting. (According to the U.S. Geological Survey, the ten states with the most earthquakes are: Alaska, California, Hawaii, Nevada, Washington, Idaho, Wyoming, Montana, Utah, and Oregon. See http://earthquake.usgs.gov/regional/ states/top_states.php [April 16, 2014]). For example, Utah has some 200,000 unreinforced masonry buildings, many of which are single-family homes. Lee Davidson, *Shaken to Pieces*, Deseret News, April 25, 2006. More than 80 percent of Utah's population is clustered along the Wasatch Front, "an extremely active seismic zone." FEMA, HAZUS-MH Used in Support of Utah Seismic Safety Legislation, http://www.nehrpscenario. org/wp-content/uploads/2009/03/hazus_wasatch_bp.pdf (April 19, 2014). Modeling of a 7.0-magnitude daytime earthquake along the Wasatch Front predicted more than 6,000 deaths, 80 percent of which were caused by URMs. *Id.* In response, Utah's legislature passed a 2008 joint resolution "urging" Utah's Seismic Safety Commission to inventory unreinforced masonry buildings and recommend mitigation priorities, *see* Utah H.J.R. 7 (2008 General Session). Pursuing an incremental approach, Utah has amended its building code to require seismic evaluation and potential upgrading when a building is reroofed, but it has not taken more aggressive action. FEMA, Unreinforced Masonry Buildings and Earthquakes 20 (Oct. 2009). A 2011 survey by the Utah Seismic Safety Commission also found that 60 percent of Utah's schools have at least a 1 percent chance of collapse "during the maximum earthquake considered likely."

Utah Seismic Safety Commission, Utah Students at Risk 9 (Feb. 2011). Moreover, 46 schools (more than a third of those screened) had between a 10 percent and 100 percent chance of collapse during such an earthquake; of these particularly vulnerable schools, 39 are unreinforced masonry. *See id.*

Other types of structures—including those made from "non-ductile reinforced concrete" and "soft story wood-frame buildings" also are at serious risk during earthquakes. "In terms of the relative risk factor, URM and non-ductile buildings (without seismic retrofit) are at least 20 times more 'risky' than other buildings, on average." Kircher et al., *supra*. Past earthquakes have also exposed the vulnerability of "soft-story" buildings, which have a weak, inadequately braced lower story, such as homes or apartment buildings built over garages. Of the 16,000 housing units rendered uninhabitable by the Loma Prieta earthquake, 7,700 were soft-story residential buildings. Cal. Health & Safety Code §19160(g). The 1994 Northridge earthquake destroyed 34,000 soft-story housing units, *id.*, many of them multistory residential buildings with tuck-under garages.

NOTES AND QUESTIONS

1. To what standard should older buildings, such as URMs, be retrofitted? Only to the level that protects human life and safety? Or to a level that preserves the building and limits economic loss? In making this calculation, does it matter what percentage of the city's housing or building stock is made up of vulnerable buildings? For example, one survey found that approximately 50 percent of San Francisco single-family wood residences and 70 percent of multifamily wood residences had a soft story. Kircher et al., *supra*. Another report suggests that a major earthquake could destroy 25 percent of San Francisco's building stock. Is there some danger that loss of housing in a major San Francisco earthquake would reach a "tipping point," such that the city would have great difficulty recovering? *See* Memorandum, Advisory Committee, Community Action Plan for Seismic Safety, Incentives to Encourage Seismic Retrofits: Options for San Francisco (Sept. 5, 2008), available at http://www.seattle.gov/dpd/Emergency/UnreinforcedMasonry Buildings/ReportsandMaterials/default.asp (June 10, 2009). How should historic preservation be taken into account when establishing retrofit standards? *Cf.* Michael Wines, *To Protect an Ancient City, China Moves to Raze It*, N.Y. Times, May 27, 2009 (reporting China's plans to raze the ancient Silk Road city of Kashgar, ostensibly to protect residents from earthquake risks posed by centuries-old buildings).

2. Florida's experience with Hurricane Andrew in 1992 demonstrates that even the strictest of building codes will do little good if it is not vigorously enforced. Although the South Florida Building Code had some deficiencies, it was thought to be one of the most hurricane resistant in

the country, requiring design standards that would withstand a 120–mile-per-hour wind. Nevertheless, even though Andrew's wind speeds did not significantly exceed 120 miles per hour, Florida's homes and buildings suffered massive damage. Investigations lay much of the blame on insufficient inspections (Dade County employed so few building inspectors that each was required to inspect approximately thirty-five buildings a day), concessions to builders in the enforcement of code provisions, building styles that were not well suited to hurricanes, and poor workmanship (which was not adequately regulated). Mileti, *supra*, at 128-131.

3. Should Congress pass legislation authorizing taxpayers to establish tax-preferred disaster savings accounts (akin to health savings accounts) that would allow individuals to set aside funds for disaster mitigation or recovery measures? *See* Disaster Savings Account Act of 2014, S. 1991, 113th Cong.

E. CLIMATE CHANGE

In 2005, when political satirist Bill Maher interviewed Stanford climate scientist Stephen Schneider, Maher queried: "Did we put our hurricanes on steroids?" Schneider agreed it was an apt question. What will be the effects of climate change on disaster risk and costs? Scientists have been hard at work trying to answer this question, but much uncertainty remains. The estimate of climate change's potential effect on some kinds of weather extremes—particularly the frequency of hurricanes—has actually been revised downward since earlier reports of the International Panel on Climate Change. *See* IPCC, Summary for Policymakers, in Climate Change 2013: The Physical Science Basis 7 (2013). There is mounting evidence, however, that climate change is likely to exacerbate other kinds of weather disasters—such as heat waves, wildfires, heavy precipitation events, and drought. Consider this summary from the Intergovernmental Panel on Climate Change:

IPCC, Summary for Policymakers, in Managing the Risks of Extreme Events and Disasters to Advance Climate Change Adaptation

(2010), 9-14 (internal cross references, emphasis, and footnotes omitted).

Confidence in projecting changes in the direction and magnitude of climate extremes depends on many factors, including the type of extreme, the region and season, the amount and quality of observational data, the level of understanding of the underlying processes, and the reliability of their simulation in models. Projected changes in climate extremes under different emissions scenarios generally do not strongly diverge in the coming two to three decades, but these signals are relatively small compared to natural climate variability over this time frame. Even the sign of projected changes in some climate extremes over this time frame is uncertain. For projected changes by the end of the 21st century, either model uncertainty or uncertainties associated with emissions scenarios used becomes dominant, depending on the extreme. Low-probability, high-impact changes associated with the crossing of poorly understood climate thresholds cannot be excluded, given the transient and complex nature of the climate system. Assigning 'low confidence' for projections of a specific extreme neither implies nor excludes the possibility of changes in this extreme. The following assessments of the likelihood and/or confidence of projections are generally for the end of the 21st century and relative to the climate at the end of the 20th century.

Models project substantial warming in temperature extremes by the end of the 21st century. It is virtually certain that increases in the frequency and magnitude of warm daily temperature extremes and decreases in cold extremes will occur in the 21st century at the global scale. It is very likely that the length, frequency, and/or intensity of warm spells or heat waves will increase over most land areas. . . .

It is likely that the frequency of heavy precipitation or the proportion of total rainfall from heavy falls will increase in the 21st century over many areas of the globe. This is particularly the case in the high latitudes and tropical regions, and in winter in the northern mid-latitudes. Heavy rainfalls associated with tropical cyclones are likely to increase with continued warming. There is medium confidence that, in some regions, increases in heavy precipitation will occur despite projected decreases in total precipitation in those regions. . . .

Average tropical cyclone maximum wind speed is likely to increase, although increases may not occur in all ocean basins. It is likely that the global frequency of tropical cyclones will either decrease or remain essentially unchanged.

There is medium confidence that there will be a reduction in the number of extratropical cyclones averaged over each hemisphere. While there is low confidence in the detailed geographical projections of extratropical cyclone activity, there is medium confidence in a projected poleward shift of extratropical storm tracks. There is low confidence in projections of small spatial-scale phenomena such as tornadoes and hail because competing physical processes may affect future trends and because current climate models do not simulate such phenomena.

There is medium confidence that droughts will intensify in the 21st century in some seasons and areas, due to reduced precipitation and/or increased evapotranspiration. This applies to regions including southern Europe and the Mediterranean region, central Europe, central North America, Central America and Mexico, northeast Brazil, and southern Africa. Elsewhere there is overall low confidence because of inconsistent projections of drought changes (dependent both on model and dryness index). Definitional issues, lack of observational data, and the inability of models to include all the factors that influence droughts preclude stronger confidence than medium in drought projections.

Projected precipitation and temperature changes imply possible changes in floods, although overall there is low confidence in projections of changes in fluvial floods. Confidence is low due to limited evidence and because the causes of regional changes are complex, although there are exceptions to this statement. There is medium confidence (based on physical reasoning) that projected increases in heavy rainfall would contribute to increases in local flooding in some catchments or regions.

It is very likely that mean sea level rise will contribute to upward trends in extreme coastal high water levels in the future. There is high confidence that locations currently experiencing adverse impacts such as coastal erosion and inundation will continue to do so in the future due to increasing sea levels, all other contributing factors being equal. The very likely contribution of mean sea level rise to increased extreme coastal high water levels, coupled with the likely increase in tropical cyclone maximum wind speed, is a specific issue for tropical small island states.

There is high confidence that changes in heat waves, glacial retreat, and/or permafrost degradation will affect high mountain phenomena such as slope instabilities, movements of mass, and glacial lake outburst floods. There is also high confidence that changes in heavy precipitation will affect landslides in some regions.

There is low confidence in projections of changes in large-scale patterns of natural climate variability. Confidence is low in projections of changes in monsoons (rainfall, circulation) because there is little consensus in climate models regarding the sign of future change in the monsoons. Model projections of changes in El Niño–Southern Oscillation variability and the frequency of El Niño episodes are not consistent, and so there is low confidence in projections of changes in this phenomenon.

NOTES AND QUESTIONS

1. Although it seems likely that climate change will increase variability and weather extremes, uncertainty about how climate change may affect any given locality may make planning for climate change effects difficult. *See* Burkett, *supra,* at 789 (describing the difficulty of "downscal[ing]" climate projections to "provide climate forecasting for more narrow regional scales based on global climate trends").

2. In many areas of the country, disaster mitigation efforts are increasingly framed through the lens of "resilience" and climate change adaptation. How is this framing likely to influence the kind of mitigation efforts that are undertaken? The politics of disaster mitigation decisions? The equity and fairness arguments that are made in support of national

funding for mitigation efforts and disaster relief? *Cf.* Alice Kaswan, *Domestic Climate Change Adaptation and Equity*, 42 Envtl. L. Rep. 11125 (2012) (arguing that equity should play a critical role in U.S. adaptation policy).

3. Climate change adaptation efforts aside, what measures has the United States taken to regulate greenhouse gases? The United States did not ratify the Kyoto Protocol, an international treaty requiring emission reduction of six greenhouse gases: carbon dioxide, methane, nitrous oxide, sulfur hexafluoride, hydrofluorocarbons, and perfluorocarbons, Kyoto Protocol to the United Nations Framework Convention on Climate Change, Dec. 11, 1997, 2303 U.N.T.S. 148, in part because developing countries that are also major polluters, such as China and India, were not required to meet similar reduction standards. *See* Todd M. Lopez, *A Look at Climate Change and the Evolution of the Kyoto Protocol*, 43 Nat. Resources J. 285, 298 (2003).

    In 2007, the Supreme Court moved the U.S. toward domestic regulation of greenhouse gases when it held that carbon dioxide is an "air pollutant" under the Clean Air Act. Massachusetts v. E.P.A., 549 U.S. 497, 528 (2007). Accordingly, the EPA was required to regulate carbon dioxide emissions from motor vehicles if it found that motor vehicle carbon dioxide emissions "contribute[ ] to air pollution which may reasonably be anticipated to endanger public health or welfare." *Id.* at 532. The Court instructed the EPA to determine whether greenhouse gases endanger the public. *See id.* at 533. Since that time, the EPA has made the requisite "endangerment" finding, promulgated standards for new car emissions, and is proposing standards for new power plants. For a summary of EPA's greenhouse gas regulatory programs, see EPA, Climate Change Regulatory Initiatives,http://www.epa.gov /climatechange/EPAactivities/regulatory-initiatives.html. Broader federal regulation to address greenhouse gases (such as proposed cap-and-trade legislation) has proved elusive. Many states have jumped into this void to enact their own greenhouse gas regulatory initiatives. *See, e.g.*, Ann Carlson, *The President, Climate Change, and California*, 125 Harv. L. Rev. F. 156 (2013) (detailing some of California's regulatory efforts). Some of these state efforts have encountered Dormant Commerce Clause challenges. *See id.* at 159.

3

WHO'S IN CHARGE? FEDERAL POWER TO RESPOND TO DISASTER

Disasters present important governance challenges because they rarely respect political and regulatory boundaries. A single disaster can affect multiple localities, states, and even countries. The interjurisdictional nature of disaster problems poses an important question for disaster responders: Who is in charge? In recent years, the question of the proper division of authority and responsibility for disasters has been vigorously debated and even featured prominently during the 2012 presidential election debates. This chapter and the following one consider some answers to this question, exploring the roles of various actors (federal, state, regional, local, and nongovernmental) in disaster response and highlighting questions of power, capacity, and obligation. This chapter takes up the question of federal constitutional and statutory authority to respond to disasters. Section A begins by considering what constitutional powers the federal government may employ in disaster response. Section B considers the challenges federalism poses for effective disaster response and discusses which levels of government should have responsibility for responding to disasters. Finally, Section C turns to the federal statutory scheme for disaster response, including statutes authorizing federal civilian disaster aid (primarily the Stafford Act), as well as those authorizing—and limiting—the role of the military in disaster response.

A. THE U.S. CONSTITUTION: FEDERAL AND STATE POWER TO RESPOND TO DISASTERS

1. THE CONSTITUTION AND EMERGENCIES

The Constitution makes some provision for emergency situations. Article I, section 8, clause 12 grants Congress the power to raise armies, and Article II, section 2 appoints the President Commander and Chief of those armies. Article IV, section 4 obligates the United States to protect states against invasion and, when requested, against domestic violence. Article I, section 8, clause 15 empowers Congress to call out the militia to repel invasions, quell insurrections, and enforce federal law. Moreover, some provisions of the Constitution explicitly contemplate emergency situations that warrant special rules. For example, Article I, section 10, clause 3 provides: "No State shall, without the Consent of Congress, lay any Duty of Tonnage, keep Troops, or Ships of War in time of Peace...or engage in War, *unless actually invaded, or in such imminent Danger as will not admit of delay*" (emphasis added). Article I pledges that "[t]he privilege of the Writ of Habeas Corpus shall not be suspended, *unless when in Cases of Rebellion or Invasion the public Safety may require it.*" U.S. Const. art. I, §9, cl. 2 (emphasis added). The Third Amendment promises that "[n]o Soldier shall, *in time of peace* be quartered in any house, without the consent of the Owner" but allows quartering soldiers "*in time of war*" according to "a manner to be prescribed by law" (emphases added). Finally, the Fifth Amendment's promise of "presentment or indictment of a Grand Jury" applies neither to "cases arising in the land or naval forces" nor to cases "in the Militia, *when in actual service in time of War or public danger*" (emphasis added).

For the most part, however, the Constitution does not explicitly place emergencies outside of the normal constitutional order. Indeed, the American constitutional tradition has long suspected that "emergency powers...tend to kindle emergencies." Youngstown Sheet & Tube Co. v. Sawyer, 343 U.S. 579, 650 (1952) (Jackson, J., concurring). Disasters are thus to be addressed within the ordinary constitutional scheme of government.

That ordinary constitutional scheme is a federal system of government, in which sovereignty is divided between the federal and state governments. As Justice Kennedy observed, "The Framers split the atom of sovereignty." United States Term Limits v. Thornton, 514 U.S. 779, 838 (1995) (Kennedy, J., concurring). The federal government is a government of enumerated powers: it may only exercise those powers that are granted to it by the Constitution. The Tenth Amendment explicitly confirms that "[t]he powers not delegated to the United States by the Constitution, nor prohibited by it to the States, are reserved to the States respectively, or to the people." The states, in contrast, have police power to protect the health, safety, and welfare of their citizens. States therefore have plenary authority to respond to disaster in almost any way, so long as they do not violate constitutional rights and are not legitimately preempted by Congress.

Because the federal government is one of limited powers, federal authority to respond to emergencies must be derived from one of the specific constitutional grants of authority to the federal government. Both political branches of the federal government have general powers that can be invoked in disaster preparedness, mitigation, and response, as well as specific powers that come into play only during a time of crisis. In addition to the constitutional grants of power enumerated below, Congress has the power "[t]o make all Laws which shall be necessary and proper for carrying into Execution the foregoing Powers and all other Powers vested by this Constitution." U.S. Const. art. I, §8, cl. 18.

2. CONGRESSIONAL AUTHORITY TO RESPOND TO DISASTERS

Commerce Clause Authority. Article I, section 8, clause 3 of the Constitution grants Congress the power "[t]o regulate Commerce with foreign Nations, and among the several States." Since the New Deal, Congress's power to regulate interstate commerce has been sweeping. As part of the Rehnquist Court's federalism revival, however, the Supreme Court in the 1990s recognized some limits on Congress's ability to regulate local, noneconomic activity pursuant to its Commerce Clause authority. *See* United States v. Lopez, 514 U.S. 549 (1995) (striking down the Gun Free School Zones Act, which prohibited possession of a firearm in a school zone); United States v. Morrison, 529 U.S. 598 (2000) (striking down a provision of the Violence Against Women Act that granted a civil remedy for victims of private, gender-motivated violence). When Congress is regulating neither the channels nor the instrumentalities of interstate commerce, then Congress may properly exercise its Commerce Clause authority only when "the regulated activity 'substantially affects' interstate commerce." Lopez, 514 U.S. at 559. If the regulated activity is economic in nature, then the "aggregate effect" of similar conduct may be considered when judging the substantiality of the activity's effect on interstate commerce; if the regulated activity is noneconomic, then aggregation may not be allowed. *See* Morrison, 529 U.S. at 617; *see also* Gonzales v. Raich, 545 U.S. 1, 25 (2005) (defining economic activity as the production, distribution, and consumption of commodities). Most major federal statutes that impact disaster mitigation and response (including the major federal disaster statute—the Stafford Act—and federal environmental statutes) can be justified, at least in part, as exercises of Congress's Commerce Clause authority.

Yet the extent of Congress's power to regulate commerce remains hotly contested. When, in 2012, the Supreme Court upheld the individual coverage mandate in the Affordable Care Act, it did so on the basis of Congress's power to tax, rejecting any suggestion that the mandate could be defended under the Commerce Clause. NFIB v. Sebelius, 132 S. Ct. 2566. The Court distinguished prior Commerce Clause cases as addressing Congressional power to regulate "activity," observing that "[t]he individual mandate . . . does not regulate existing commercial activity" but "instead compels individuals to *become* active in commerce by purchasing a product, on the ground that their failure to do so affects interstate commerce." *Id.* at 2587. The Court explained that "[a]llowing Congress to justify federal regulation by pointing to the effect of inaction on commerce would bring countless decisions an individual could *potentially* make within the scope of federal regulation, and—under the Government's theory—empower Congress to make those decisions for him." *Id.* The Court thus rejected a construction of the Commerce Clause that would "permit Congress to regulate individuals precisely *because* they are doing nothing." *Id.*

Spending Clause Authority. Article I, Section 8, Clause 1 of the Constitution grants Congress "Power To lay and collect Taxes, Duties, Imposts and Excises, to pay the Debts and provide for the common Defense and general Welfare of the United States." It is well established that, pursuant to this Spending Clause power, Congress can spend federal funds to promote the general welfare and does not have to point to another enumerated power to justify federal expenditures. United States v. Butler, 297 U.S. 1 (1936). Pursuant to its Spending Clause authority, then, Congress has broad power to spend in response to disasters.

When exercising its Spending Clause power, Congress can condition the receipt of federal funds on a state's agreement to comply with particular standards or undertake particular activities so long as the condition is unambiguously expressed in the statute, is sufficiently related to the federal purpose for the spending, and is not unduly coercive. See South Dakota v. Dole, 483 U.S. 203 (1987). This last requirement was given teeth for the first time in NFIB v. Sebelius, when the Court invalidated a provision of the Affordable Care Act that conditioned all of a state's existing federal Medicaid funding (which made up about 10 percent of the average state's total budget) on expansion of that state's Medicaid program to cover a larger pool of individuals. 132 S. Ct. at 2603-05. The Court held that this threatened loss of funds crossed the line "where pressure gives way to coercion." *Id.* at 2605.

Congress has frequently conditioned federal disaster spending on state adoption of emergency preparedness plans. *See, e.g.*, Pet Evacuation and Transportation Standards Act of 2006, Pub. L. No. 109-308, 120 Stat. 1725 §2 (codified at 42 U.S.C. §5196) (conditioning emergency shelter funds on states sufficiently planning for the disaster relief needs of households with pets); Disaster Mitigation Act of 2000, Pub. L. No. 106-390, 114 Stat. 1552 §322 (codified at 42 U.S.C. §5165) (conditioning hazard mitigation funds on states developing approved natural disaster mitigation plans). In addition, Congress sometimes uses its Spending Clause authority as a more politically palatable alternative to Commerce Clause authority when regulating areas of traditional state concern as, for example, when it passed the Coastal Zone Management

Act, which offers federal funding for state land use plans that protect coastal environments. *See* 16 U.S.C. §§1456, §§1455(d)-1455(2)(I) (offering financial support to coastal states implementing approved state management programs that define and protect coastal zones by, inter alia, designating appropriate land and water use, and controlling and planning for shoreline erosion).

Taxing Clause Authority. Article I, Section 8, Clause 1 of the Constitution grants Congress "Power To lay and collect Taxes, Duties, Imposts and Excises, to pay the Debts and provide for the common Defense and general Welfare of the United States." One way Congress has exercised its taxing power in the disaster context is by creating the "casualty-loss deduction" within the Internal Revenue Code, which provides a tax deduction for "losses of property [. . .] from fire, storm, shipwreck, or other casualty." 26 U.S.C. §165(c)(3). The casualty-loss deduction also has special provisions for "losses in federally declared disasters." 26 U.S.C. §165(h)(3). For example, when taxpayers are required to either demolish or relocate their residences because of a disaster receiving federal assistance under the Stafford Act, those losses qualify as casualty losses. 26 U.S.C. §165(k).

Militia Clause Authority. Congress's Article I powers include the authority "[t]o provide for calling forth the Militia to execute the Laws of the Union, suppress Insurrections and repel Invasions," Art. 1, §8, cl. 15, and the related power "[t]o provide for organizing, arming, and disciplining the Militia, and for governing such Part of them as may be employed in the Service of the United States, reserving to the States respectively, the Appointment of Officers, and the Authority of training the Militia according to the discipline prescribed by Congress," Art. 1, §18, cl. 16. Thus, if a disaster impedes execution of federal law (or either causes or results from an insurrection or invasion), Congress may claim authority to federalize state militias to respond to the crisis.

Fourteenth Amendment, Section 5 Enforcement Power. Section 5 of the Fourteenth Amendment grants Congress the power "to enforce, by appropriate legislation" the guarantees of the Fourteenth Amendment, which include equal protection and due process of law. When congressional legislation is prophylactic in nature (regulating behavior that does not itself violate the Fourteenth Amendment but that might conceal, encourage, or lead to a violation), then the legislative response must be congruent and proportional to an identified pattern of injury to constitutional rights. *See* City of Boerne v. Flores, 521 U.S. 507, 520 (1997). If the constitutional right Congress is protecting receives only rational basis scrutiny, then in applying this requirement, the Court has required strong record evidence of past rights violations by states or their political subdivisions before allowing prophylactic legislation. *See, e.g.*, Kimel v. Florida Board of Regents, 528 U.S. 62 (2000) (age discrimination). If the right (or classification) in question commands heightened scrutiny, then the

Court has usually required much less justification from Congress. *See* Nevada Dept. of Human Resources v. Hibbs, 538 U.S. 721 (2003) (gender discrimination). Section 308 of the Stafford Act prohibits government bodies from discriminating on the basis of race, color, nationality, or gender (as well as other characteristics) when distributing federal disaster aid, *see* 42 U.S.C. §5151; using its Section 5 authority, Congress presumably could go farther, prohibiting state and local race- and sex-based discrimination in the provision of all disaster services, not just those that are federally funded.

NOTES AND QUESTIONS

1. Given the interdependence of local activities and the national (or indeed global) economy, is there any disaster that would not "substantially affect" interstate commerce? Of course, the disaster is not precisely what is being regulated, is it? What if Congress decided *before* a disaster to mitigate disaster risk by regulating local land use? Would it have Commerce Clause authority, for instance, to create federal zoning laws prohibiting building within 100 feet of an earthquake fault? Is federal intervention in land use more appropriate for some types of disasters than for others? *See, e.g.,* Blake Hudson, *Reconstituting Land Use Federalism to Address Transitory and Perpetual Disasters: The Bimodal Federalism Framework*, 2011 B.Y.U. L. Rev. 1991, 1992 (2011) (arguing that "federal input" in state and local land use is "more desirable and less constitutionally suspect" for "perpetual" disasters (such as sea-level rise, nonpoint source water pollution of the Gulf, and invasive species) than for more "transitory" ones (such as localized flooding, heat waves, and fires)).

2. Does the holding of NFIB v. Sebelius—that Congress lacks Commerce Clause power to regulate inaction—mean that Congress could not require everyone who lives in a floodplain to purchase flood insurance? Could Congress mandate flood insurance for everyone who owns a home in a floodplain? For everyone who builds a new home in a floodplain? If Congress lacks Commerce Clause authority to require homeowners to purchase flood insurance, could it instead tax homeowners who fail to do so? The Eleventh Circuit majority opinion in *NFIB*, which invalidated the individual mandate, cited Congress's decision not to mandate flood insurance for every homeowner in a floodplain, even when such a mandate was arguably critical to the success of the National Flood Insurance Program, as some evidence that Congress assumed it lacked the authority to do so. 648 F.3d 1235, 1289-90 (11th Cir. 2011). Does the Spending Clause holding of *NFIB* suggest that some attempts to condition federal disaster aid might prove unduly coercive?

3. Even if the activity Congress seeks to regulate falls squarely within its Commerce Clause powers, federalism may nonetheless constrain the ways in which Congress can achieve its regulatory objectives. Printz v. United States, 521 U.S. 898 (1997), established the proposition that principles of federalism and federal separation of powers bar the federal government from "commandeering" state executive officers for the purpose of enacting or implementing federal law. "The power of the Federal Government would be augmented immeasurably if it were able to impress into service—and at no cost to itself—the police officers of the 50 States." *Id.* at 922. The *Printz* dissenters expressed concern that the inability to conscript state officers to enforce federal law could hamstring federal disaster response: "[S]ince the ultimate issue is one of power, we must consider its implications in times of national emergency. Matters such as the enlistment of air raid wardens, the administration of a military draft, the mass inoculation of children to forestall an epidemic, or perhaps the threat of an international terrorist, may require a national response before federal personnel can be made available to respond." *Id.* at 940 (Stevens, J., dissenting). The majority countered that "[n]o comparative assessment of the various interests" at stake "can overcome [the] fundamental defect" of allowing the federal commandeering of state executive officers to "offend[]" the "very principle of separate state sovereignty." *Id.* at 932. Does this principle mean that state and local officials would be free to disregard any command or instructions from Federal Emergency Management Agency (FEMA) officials or other federal disaster responders?

4. While some scholars, arguing from originalist premises, have contended that Congress's Spending Clause power should be limited to "the power to spend for the 'general' welfare and not for the special welfare of particular regions or states," which might preclude federal disaster relief to individual communities, *see* John C. Eastman, *Restoring the "General" to the General Welfare Clause*, 4 Chap. L. Rev. 63, 65, 79 (2001) (arguing, for example, that "the Fourth Congress did not even believe it had the power to provide relief to the citizens of Savannah, Georgia after a devastating fire destroyed the entire city," because that expenditure would not have been for the "general welfare"), other scholars have argued that the constitutionality of federal disaster relief was quickly established and that Congressional grants of disaster relief frequently "served as precedents invoked in contested claims for [other forms of federal] relief." Michelle Landis Dauber, The Sympathetic State (2013) 19, 61 (noting that this deference to Congress contrasted with state supreme courts' treatment of state and municipal disaster relief, which "was often struck down" under state constitutions as "impermissible 'class legislation' that transferred money from the population to private interests . . . in violation of the public purpose

doctrine"); *see also* Michele L. Landis, *Let Me Next Time Be "Tried by Fire": Disaster Relief and the Origins of the American Welfare State 1789-1874*, 92 Nw. U. L. Rev. 967, 972 (1998) (contending that the historical evidence demonstrates that "during the period from 1789 to 1875, the Constitution provided no serious impediment to the development of disaster relief into the first sustained, organized social welfare program of the federal government"). In today's interconnected world, where would one draw a meaningful line between spending that benefits particular localities and spending that furthers the general welfare?

5. Do the Militia Clauses imply that Congress must use *only* state militias (called into federal service)—not regular federal troops—when deploying military forces domestically? And may troops be deployed domestically only for those purposes enumerated in Clause 15 ("execut[ing] the Laws of the Union, suppress[ing] Insurrections and repel[ling] Invasions")? *See* Stephen I. Vladeck, *The Domestic Commander in Chief*, 29 Cardozo L. Rev. 1091, 1100 (2008) (arguing that the Militia Clauses were intended to designate state militias as the exclusive military forces that could be called upon to act domestically but concluding that the Supreme Court has read the Clauses as imposing no limits on Congress's use of federal regulars). *Contrast* Jason Mazzone, *The Security Constitution*, 53 UCLA Law Rev. 29, 63 (2005) (contending that Article IV obligates the federal government to protect states from invasion or domestic violence and that Congress can choose to fulfill that obligation either by deploying federal military personnel or by employing state militias). If the Militia Clauses were interpreted to mean that only state militias could be deployed domestically and only for the purposes specified in Clause 15, would Congress have had the power to deploy state militia troops to respond to reports of civil unrest in New Orleans in Katrina's aftermath?

6. Congress has historically exercised its "calling forth" power by delegating it to the president. In a series of acts dating back to 1792, Congress has delegated to the president the power to call forth the militia (and, beginning in 1799, federal troops) to act in times of domestic crisis in at least some of the circumstances outlined in the First Militia Clause (art. I, §8, cl. 15). *See* Stephen I. Vladeck, Note, *Emergency Power and the Militia Acts*, 114 Yale L.J. 149 (2004), 159-164. The current incarnation of this power is the Insurrection Act, 10 U.S.C. §§331-334, discussed *infra*.

7. Article IV, Section 4 of the Constitution pledges that "[t]he United States shall guarantee to every State in this Union a Republican Form of Government, and shall protect each of them against Invasion; and on Application of the Legislature, or of the Executive (when the Legislature cannot be convened) against domestic Violence." In Luther v. Borden,

48 U.S. (7 How.) 1 (1849), the Supreme Court declined to decide which of two competing factions represented the lawful government of Rhode Island, reasoning that the responsibility "rests with Congress to decide what government is the established one in a State." *Id.* at 42 ("Congress must necessarily decide what government is established in the State before it can determine whether it is republican or not."); *see also* Pacific Tel. Co. v. Oregon, 223 U.S. 118 (1912). Although *Luther* is regarded as foreclosing judicial enforcement of the Republican Guaranty Clause, *see* Baker v. Carr, 369 U.S. 186, 218-224 (1962), does this provision of the Constitution empower the political branches of the federal government to "guarantee to every State...a Republican Form of Government" and to "protect [the states] against Invasion" or "domestic Violence"? Does it obligate the federal government to do so? Reconsider this question in connection with the Insurrection Act, 10 U.S.C. §§331-334. *See infra.*

8. Who is "the Militia"? In District of Columbia v. Heller, 128 S. Ct. 2783 (2008), which held that the Second Amendment confers an individual right to keep and bear arms, the majority defined "militia" to include not only organized state militias but also the unorganized militia, historically defined as all able-bodied men within a certain age range. *See id.* at 2791, 2799. Some commentators have argued that Congress, pursuant to its Calling Forth authority, could respond to a disaster by placing state and local first responders—who are part of the unorganized state militia—under federal command, even without the consent of state officials:

> The solution [to the problems of federalism in times of emergency] is to allow the national government, when it responds to certain kinds of emergencies, to call into periods of mandatory federal service the emergency response personnel of the state in which the emergency occurs and, where necessary, emergency response personnel from other states. During emergencies, these state employees—police, firefighters, emergency medical technicians, urban search and rescue teams, and public health specialists—would serve with compensation under the command of the President, as Commander in Chief. With the power to place in federal service these state and local personnel, the federal government would be able to direct the response effort without being stymied by the vagaries of state and local bureaucracies.

Jason Mazzone, *The Commandeerer in Chief,* 83 Notre Dame L. Rev. 265, 273 (2007). *See also* Brian C. Brook, Note, *Federalizing the First Responders to Acts of Terrorism via the Militia Clauses,* 54 Duke L.J. 999, 1024 (2005). Do the Militia Clauses provide Congress an alternative path for "commandeering" state and local officials to implement federal disaster response? If so, would the federal government be required to pay those "called forth" for their services? Wouldn't individuals so "called forth" be limited to executing the laws of the United States, suppressing insurrections, and repelling invasions? *See* Mazzone, *The Commandeerer in Chief, supra*, at 277 (arguing that this emergency commandeering power would be limited to "times of invasion, insurrection, and opposition to federal law," but that "many emergencies will trigger the commandeering power because of their secondary effects: as events in New Orleans following Katrina showed, natural disasters frequently produce riots and other forms of lawlessness that satisfy the Constitution's conditions for federal deployment of state personnel"). For arguments challenging the assumption that natural disasters often spur lawlessness, see Lisa Grow Sun, *Disaster Mythology and the Law*, 96 Cornell L. Rev. 1131 (2011), discussed *infra*.

9. Are National Guard troops part of the Militia? As the Supreme Court explained in Perpich v. Department of Defense, 496 U.S. 334, 345 (1990), since 1933, Congress has required by statute that all members of state National Guard units enlist, simultaneously, in the U.S. National Guard, which consists of the Army National Guard and the Air National Guard (reserve components of the U.S. Army and Air Force, respectively). This "dual enlistment" means that "a member of the Guard who is ordered to active duty in the federal service is thereby relieved of his or her status in the State Guard for the entire period of federal service." *Id.* at 346. Thus, members of State Guard units must "[k]eep three hats in their closets—a civilian hat, a state militia hat, and an army hat—only one of which is worn at any particular time." *Id.* at 348. Accordingly, when Congress federalizes state National Guardsmen by calling them into federal service, it does so pursuant to its separate Article I power to "raise armies," *see* U.S. Const. art. 1, §8, cl. 13, not pursuant to the Militia Clauses. Based on this reasoning, the Court held that it was permissible for Congress to deploy federalized National Guard troops abroad for training purposes. Does this mean that when Congress federalizes state National Guard units they can be deployed domestically for purposes other than executing federal law, suppressing insurrections, and repelling invasions? *See* Vladeck, *The Domestic Commander in Chief, supra* at 1102.

10. Can you imagine a situation in which Congress might wish to invoke its Fourteenth Amendment, Section 5 powers in the context of disaster preparation or response? Reconsider your answer in light of the reading in Chapter 5 on social vulnerability.

11. In addition to prohibiting discrimination on the basis of race, color, nationality, or sex in the provision of federal disaster relief, Section 308 of the Stafford Act forbids discrimination on the basis of religion, age,

disability, English proficiency, or economic status. *See* 42 U.S.C. §5151. Could Congress use its Section 5 authority to impose similar standards on the provision of state disaster relief, or would such standards have to be justified by some other congressional power?

3. EXECUTIVE AUTHORITY TO RESPOND TO DISASTERS

Article II of the Constitution vests the president with the "executive power," Art II, section 1, clause 1, and provides that the "President shall be the Commander in Chief of the Army and Navy of the United States, and of the Militia of the several States, when called into the actual Service of the United States," art. II, §2, cl. 1 U.S. Const. Moreover, the president is also charged with the responsibility to "take Care that the Laws be faithfully executed." Art. II, §3.U.S. Const.

One of the great constitutional debates of our day concerns the existence and extent of presidential inherent authority to respond in times of emergency, acting either without congressional authorization or—in even more aggressive and controversial formulations—in disregard of congressionally imposed limits. For a recent overview of some of the contours of this debate, *see* David J. Barron & Martin S. Lederman, *The Commander in Chief at the Lowest Ebb—A Constitutional History*, 121 Harv. L. Rev. 941 (2008). *See also* Candidus Dougherty, *"Necessity Hath No Law": Executive Power and the Posse Comitatus Act*, 31 Campbell L. Rev. 1 (2008). Much of the contemporary debate has occurred in the context of presidential wartime powers (whether a traditional ground war or a more nebulous War on Terror), but that debate has implications for the president's inherent authority to respond to domestic crises as well. For instance, would the president have the authority, without authorization from Congress, to declare martial law in the aftermath of a catastrophic disaster? "Martial law" is an imprecise term without clear legal meaning and might take many different forms—for example, enlisting the military to enforce civilian laws, suspending the writ of habeas corpus, or trying civilians in military courts. President Lincoln employed all of these forms of martial law during the Civil War. *See* Dan Farber, Lincoln's Constitution (2003) 144-175. More recently, some of President George W. Bush's top legal advisors argued that the president had the authority to deploy the military to arrest terrorist suspects (who were U.S. citizens) on U.S. soil, in upstate New York. *See* Mark Mazzetti & David Johnston, *Bush Weighed Using Military in U.S. Arrests*, N.Y. Times, July 25, 2009, at A1. In the realm of natural disasters, the president need rarely invoke any constitutional inherent authority to act, as the Stafford Act, discussed *infra*, embodies a massive congressional delegation of power to the president to commit federal resources immediately to respond to disaster and save lives and property.

B. FEDERALISM: FRIEND OR FOE?

Hurricane Katrina took an inestimable toll in human lives, suffering, and property damage; it also took a significant toll on public confidence in the ability of government at all levels—federal, state, and local—to respond effectively to natural disasters, terrorist attacks, and other emergencies. Many have laid a significant portion of the blame for the failed Katrina response squarely at the feet of jurisdictional uncertainty caused by federalism. Indeed, in the aftermath of Katrina, one commentator calls on us to "stop federalism before it kills again!" Stephen M. Griffin, *Stop Federalism Before It Kills Again: Reflections on Hurricane Katrina*, 21 St. John's J. Legal Comment 527 (2007).

There is little doubt that federalism poses some challenges for emergency response. Disasters will often require quick, decisive action. Division of power and resources between the federal government and states and localities, however, means that disaster response will also require coordination and communication, which can be difficult to achieve in real time under disaster conditions. Failure to coordinate may mean that limited resources are wasted in duplicative efforts, while other pressing matters fall through the cracks. Additionally, the existence of shared, overlapping power in disaster planning and response may encourage each level of government to shirk its own responsibilities, assuming (or hoping) that the other level of government will take the required action. This shirking might be compounded by the possibility that federalism will cloud accountability for government failures in the event of a disaster, allowing each actor to blame the botched response on others and thereby evade the political consequences of failure. Federalism has the potential to confuse lines of accountability not only among constituents but also among decision makers, who may consequently fail to learn the lessons of past disasters.

These challenges, of course, are not unique to federalism (in the disaster context or otherwise). They occur whenever power is divided, whether horizontally or vertically. Federal agencies that have some shared responsibility and jurisdiction in disaster response may encounter many of these same dynamics. Similarly, division of responsibility among private and public actors may also create many of these challenges.

How much of the tragically inept government response to Katrina can fairly be blamed on federalism? Has federalism become a convenient scapegoat to explain away other government failings? Consider this account of federalism's role in the failed Katrina response.

ERIN RYAN, FEDERALISM AND THE TUG OF WAR WITHIN: SEEKING CHECKS AND BALANCE IN THE INTERJURISDICTIONAL GRAY AREA

66 Md. L. Rev. 503, 522-536 (2007) (internal citations and footnotes omitted)

According to eyewitness accounts and primary documents cataloging the relevant events, the response to Katrina was characterized by failures in coordinated command and communications between local, state, federal, and volunteer responders, as authorities struggled to determine what the federalism directives in applicable federal laws mandated regarding whom should be responsible for which parts of the response. Revised after the 9/11 attacks and issued in 2004, the new National Response Plan (NRP) recognizes that saving lives and protecting the health of the public are top priorities of incident management. However, the NRP also demarcates that, in emergency situations, states will be responsible for the implementation of police powers traditionally within their purview (such as local law enforcement, fire protection, and delivery of food and shelter), and the federal government will act in a supportive capacity, responding to specific requests by state authorities for assistance.

Although the Federal Emergency Management Agency's (FEMA) seeming paralysis in the face of the post-Katrina crisis may suggest incompetent leadership, it is also attributable to a federalism-related "operating system crash" under the NRP, which faltered just as software does when unable to parse unanticipated inputs. According to the NRP's federalism directive, federal authorities could not act preemptively, lest they tread in the protected realm of state sovereign authority. However, state authorities were unable to make the specific requests for assistance anticipated under the NRP. Local infrastructure was so damaged by the storm that communications were down, and state and local authorities were apparently so overwhelmed themselves that they did not know what to ask for. It may also be that state authorities were simply unprepared or incompetent to play the role anticipated of them by the NRP. But as former FEMA Director Michael Brown would later testify before Congress in defense of his agency's decisionmaking: "The role of the federal government in emergency management is generally that of coordinator and supporter...[a role] fully supported by the basic concept of federalism, recognizing that the sovereign states have primary responsibility for emergency preparedness and response in their jurisdictions." Thus, as Katrina bore down on the Gulf Coast, these departures from the NRP's script left regulatory responders struggling to decipher, in essence, which parts of the response effort were the proper purview of the state, and which the proper purview of the federal government....

Federalism concerns were not limited to managerial choices in the field but pervaded the response effort up to the highest levels. News reports indicated that "[f]or days, Bush's top advisers argued over legal niceties about who was in charge," that "[i]nterviews with officials in Washington and

Louisiana show that as the situation grew worse, they were wrangling with questions of federal/state authority," and that "the crisis in New Orleans deepened because of a virtual standoff between hesitant federal officials and besieged authorities in Louisiana." The issues that most snarled the response effort were uncertainty about the point at which the federal government should stop waiting for instructions on how to assist the state and take initiative via its superior command capacity (through the deployment of U.S. military or federalized National Guard troops), and after that, confusion about who would then be in charge.

Even as it became clear that federal assistance was necessary, uncertainty unfolded among all three levels of government as to who should be in control of the troops to be deployed. Apparently desperate for results, New Orleans Mayor Ray Nagin supported federalizing the response, while Louisiana Governor Kathleen Babineaux Blanco balked, and President George W. Bush, hesitant to offend federalism principles in this interjurisdictional no man's land, waited for clarity. In one infamous exchange four days into the crisis at a strategy session aboard Air Force One, the distraught Mayor slammed the conference table with his hand and asked the President "to cut through this and do what it takes to have a more-controlled command structure. If that means federalizing it, let's do it." Mayor Nagin recommended the Pentagon's "on-scene commander," Lieutenant General Russel Honoré, to lead the flailing relief effort on behalf of the federal government. According to another meeting participant, President Bush turned to Governor Blanco and said, "[w]ell, what do you think of that, Governor?" But Governor Blanco declined to discuss the matter except in a private meeting with the President, which apparently followed the strategy session. However, there was still no agreement over one week later, leaving idle the assistance of an estimated 100,000 National Guard troops accessible on short notice in neighboring states. News accounts suggest that Governor Blanco did ask the President for 40,000 federal troops, but did not agree to surrender oversight of the relief effort to the federal government.

Had Governor Blanco surrendered her claim to control over the relief effort, President Bush would have been able to reconcile the urgency of providing needed federal assistance with the federalism principles that he believed foreclosed such authorization in the interim. Nevertheless, contemporaneous news accounts indicate that the Justice Department's Office of Legal Counsel researched the matter and "concluded that the federal government had authority to move in even over the objection of local officials."

...[W]hat is most significant about the President's decision is why he declined to exercise the potential Stafford Act authority in the first place, given such overwhelming political pressure to do so and his demonstrated confidence asserting untested federal executive authority in other realms. One patent explanation for the President's hesitancy to explore all potential avenues of authority during the most devastating natural disaster in U.S. history is the profound influence of strict-separationist idealism. Federalizing the Louisiana

National Guard and subjecting state and city police to federal command would have blurred the very lines of regulatory authority that New Federalism so endeavors to preserve. The best alternative explanation—and one equally troubling—is that the White House relied on New Federalism rhetoric for political cover in avoiding any involvement with the unfolding mess. Either way, that New Federalism ideals could stall effective governance at such a key moment or provide reliable cover to so monumental an abdication suggests their infirmity.

In the end, reasonable people may disagree on how best to apportion blame between the amply culpable local, state, and federal authorities for the failed response, subsequently heralded as "a national disgrace." That said, it remains difficult to digest the confirmed reports that after fifteen-foot floodwaters swept through the Jackson Barracks headquarters of the Louisiana National Guard Headquarters—severing communication lines, flooding high-water trucks, and converting the entire nerve center force into 375 more New Orleans refugees in need of a water rescue—White House officials stalled in Washington, debating how the finer principles of constitutional federalism dictated the scope of federal intervention. In their defense, the debate was at least warranted by a faithful interpretation of the federalism model advanced by the sitting Supreme Court. But it raises the fair question, in light of the stakes and the results that can flow from that model—is this really the federalism we intended?...

While the President's senior advisers fiddled with federalism, New Orleans drowned. The details of the debacle are by now painfully well-known to most Americans, but they bear repeating to highlight the scope of the failed response. Over a thousand residents perished in their homes and neighborhoods, and up to thirty-four died in the makeshift mass shelters at the New Orleans Superdome and convention center, where some 39,000 evacuees were encamped without adequate food, water, power, or sanitary facilities for up to seven days. Two-thirds of the occupants were women, children, or elderly, many of them infirm, and they huddled in darkness and 100-degree temperatures amidst the unbearable stench of human waste covering the floors and the ceiling debris fallen from holes torn from the roof by the storm. Unchecked lawless behavior terrorized citizens and local law enforcement alike, both within the emergency shelters and on the flooded city streets. The near total collapse of landline, satellite, and cell phone communications hindered the ability of local law enforcement and the Louisiana National Guard to coordinate a response—even available radio channels were so jammed with traffic that they became useless.

The chaotic rescue and evacuation efforts impacted families as well, as the National Center for Missing and Exploited Children reported in mid-September 2005 that 1,831 children from Louisiana, Alabama, and Mississippi were reported as missing in the aftermath of the storm, and that, weeks later, only 360 of these cases had been resolved. At least a million evacuees took shelter in other cities and states, and by March 2006 the federal government had committed $6.9 billion in shelter and direct financial assistance to Gulf Coast residents affected by the hurricane. Countless thousands of starving and injured companion animals continued to roam the streets or languish trapped within the homes of evacuated owners for weeks following the storm, most perishing before rescue but not before ghastly suffering.

Damage to oil infrastructure was the worst ever experienced by the industry. More than nine million gallons were reported spilled, and gas prices skyrocketed to as high as $6 per gallon in the following weeks. Chemical spills, rotting remains, and flooding resulted in environmental hazards ranging from land-based toxic sludge to poisoned water supplies that will continue to threaten human health and safety into the foreseeable future. Approximately $88 billion in federal aid has already been allocated toward relief, recovery, and rebuilding efforts, and an additional $20 billion has been requested to assist a variety of federal agencies in their continuing relief efforts. These moneys have been earmarked for programs including unemployment assistance, community disaster loans to local governments, housing assistance, and public assistance projects. Separate grants have also been awarded, including a $1.6 billion special congressional appropriation to the Department of Education for public and private schools where relocated students enrolled....

Of course, much of the devastation that Gulf Coast residents suffered from the winds and rain of Katrina cannot be blamed on bad disaster management. Setting aside the degree to which anthropogenic climate change contributes to the intensity of hurricanes like Katrina, hurricanes are a force of nature that we have long learned to fear. River and wetland management choices along the Mississippi Delta exacerbated the flooding that proved the worst of New Orleans's battles, and Americans are right to ask for better long-term planning from the local, state, and federal authorities responsible for these activities. Still, it was the bungled humanitarian relief effort—the disorganized response that stranded the sick and injured, separated young children from their parents, and left the most vulnerable members of society struggling to survive amidst prolonged "Lord of the Flies" conditions—that triggered public outrage.

NOTES AND QUESTIONS

1. Is the poor Katrina response (at all levels of government) an indictment of federalism itself, the model of federalism in use, or the particular leaders who failed to negotiate federalism's potential pitfalls and cooperate for the good of New Orleans? Are there advantages to having a federalist system that are manifest during disaster response? Is it beneficial to have expertise and resources available at multiple levels of government? Are disaster survivors more likely to trust and take direction from federal or local officials? For a further explication of

some of these issues, see Erin Ryan, Federalism and the Tug of War Within (2012) (advancing a dynamic theory of balanced federalism that better integrates local and national capacity).

2. If divided power is the problem, is federal control over major—or at least catastrophic—disasters the answer? Will state personnel respond well to being commanded by federal authorities? Do federal authorities have the capacity to mount an effective response without state and local input and resources? A wholly federal response to even a catastrophic disaster would appear nearly impossible, as federal officials lack the intimate knowledge of the area and its conditions that local officials possess.

3. In addition to issues of power and capacity, the question of who is in charge of disaster response implicates notions of responsibility and obligation. Historically, states have been charged with ensuring the health and safety of their citizens. Although this obligation has not abated, is it, perhaps, increasingly shared with federal authorities?

Most of us have grown up in a world in which federal assistance in time of disaster is taken for granted. Consider the primary conclusion of the House Select Committee: "Our investigation revealed that Katrina was a national failure, an abdication of the most solemn obligation to provide for the common welfare." This conclusion implies that the nation fell short on a key constitutional commitment. But is this conclusion consistent with historic understandings of federalism? To put this in a more pointed way, when did the national government formally commit itself to having primary responsibility for the welfare of the people of the states? Of course, the Committee could not point to a constitutional amendment or a widely understood legal commitment originating from the Preamble to the Constitution.

The Committee report is quite revealing on this score. As noted above, the Committee argued that the federal government must respond "proactively" to a disaster like Katrina. Yet when discussing the military's role, the Committee made this general remark: "The Select Committee does not believe there is a simple answer to improving state and federal integration. Local control and state sovereignty are important principles rooted in the nation's birth that cannot be discarded merely to achieve more efficient joint military operations on American soil." Thus, the Committee's report points ultimately in two directions—both toward greater federal responsibility in time of national catastrophe and toward a continued essential role for state and local governments. How could it be otherwise? The Committee could not by itself surmount the conflicts inherent in American federalism.

Why was the Committee confused in this way? The answer lies in the process of constitutional change. When it criticized the national response, the Committee invoked a value system that was a product of informal twentieth century constitutional change and was not implied by anything in the text of the Constitution. This kind of criticism would not have occurred to anyone in the eighteenth or nineteenth centuries. During the twentieth century and especially during the New Deal, the constitutional order changed in a somewhat helter-skelter unplanned fashion. Certainly no constitutional amendment was approved that might have provided firm legitimacy and guidance to the federal government's new power. The formal structure of American federalism remained intact.

Stephen M. Griffin, *Stop Federalism Before It Kills Again: Reflections on Hurricane Katrina*, 21 St. John's J. Legal Comment 527, 536-538 (2007) (citations omitted).

4. Why would the federal government be obligated to respond to disasters? Because it has committed itself to do so? Because it has the capacity to respond when states and localities are overwhelmed? Because citizens expect it to fill that role? In the aftermath of Hurricane Andrew, a Category 5 hurricane that devastated southern Florida in August 1992, the Director of the Dade County (Florida) Office of Emergency Management voiced a common reaction when he asked, "Where in the hell is the cavalry?" Mary Jordan, *President Orders Military to Aid Florida*, Wash. Post, Aug 28, 1992, at A1.

5. Throughout the twentieth century, especially after the Mississippi River flood of 1927, the federal government became progressively more involved in emergencies. The "role of the Federal government in disaster response has evolved significantly throughout the past 200 years":

> In 1803, in what is widely seen as the first instance of Federal intervention in a disaster scenario, Congress approved the use of Federal resources to assist the recovery of Portsmouth, New Hampshire, following a devastating urban fire. Between 1803 and 1950, the Federal government intervened in over 100 incidents (earthquakes, fires, floods, and tornados), making Federal resources available to affected jurisdictions. These interventions were limited and were delivered in an ad hoc manner without an established Federal role or coordinated response plan. The Federal government also quickly recognized the role that private non-profit organizations can play. In 1905, Congress chartered the American Red Cross as a charitable organization to provide disaster relief support during crises....

During the Great Depression, the approach of the Federal government became more proactive. For example, Congress endowed the Bureau of Public Roads with the authority to provide continuous grants to States for the repair of disaster-damaged infrastructure and charged the Army Corps of Engineers with the task of mitigating flood-related threats. This piecemeal legislative approach was eventually replaced by the Civil Defense Act of 1950[,] the first comprehensive legislation pertaining to Federal disaster relief.

In 1952, President Truman issued Executive Order 10427, which emphasized that Federal disaster assistance was intended to supplement, not supplant, the resources of State, local, and private sector organizations. This theme was echoed two decades later [by] President Nixon...." Federal disaster assistance is intended to supplement individual, local and state resources."...

Th[e] piecemeal approach to disaster assistance was problematic and it prompted legislation that required greater cooperation between Federal agencies and authorized the President to coordinate these activities.

The 1960s and early 1970s brought massive disasters requiring major Federal response and recovery operations by the Federal Disaster Assistance Administration, established within the Department of Housing and Urban Development (HUD). Hurricane Carla struck in 1962, Hurricane Betsy in 1965, Hurricane Camille in 1969 and Hurricane Agnes in 1972. The Alaskan Earthquake hit in 1964 and the San Fernando Earthquake rocked Southern California in 1971. These events served to focus attention on the issue of natural disasters and brought about increased legislation. In 1968, the National Flood Insurance Act offered new flood protection to homeowners, and in 1974 the Disaster Relief Act firmly established the process of Presidential disaster declarations.

However, emergency and disaster activities were still fragmented. When hazards associated with nuclear power plants and the transportation of hazardous substances were added to natural disasters, more than 100 Federal agencies were involved in some aspect of disasters, hazards and emergencies. Many parallel programs and policies existed at the State and local level, compounding the complexity of Federal disaster relief efforts. The National Governor's Association...asked President Jimmy Carter to centralize Federal emergency functions.

President Carter's 1979 executive order merged many of the separate disaster-related responsibilities into a new Federal Emergency Management Agency (FEMA). Among other agencies, FEMA absorbed: the Federal Insurance Administration, the National Fire Prevention and Control Administration, the National Weather Service Community Preparedness Program, the Federal Preparedness Agency of the General Services Administration and the Federal Disaster Assistance Administration activities from HUD. Civil defense responsibilities were also transferred to the new agency from the Defense Department's Defense Civil Preparedness Agency.

The White House, The Federal Response to Hurricane Katrina: Lessons Learned 11-12, 158-159 n.11 (2006). FEMA itself was absorbed in 2002 into a new bureaucracy that united emergency response and defense against terrorism within the Department of Homeland Security. For a detailed history of the expansion of the federal role in emergency management, *see* Emergency Management: The American Experience 1900-2005 (Claire B. Rubin ed., 2007).

6. The conclusion that "informal . . . constitutional change" and recent historical practice justify an ongoing, expansive role for the federal government in disaster response was vigorously contested in the run-up to the 2012 presidential election and in the aftermath of Superstorm Sandy. In a 2011 Republican debate, Mitt Romney suggested that disaster relief should be the states' responsibility: "Every time you have an occasion to take something from the federal government and send it back to the states, that's the right direction." *CNN Live Republican Debate* (CNN television broadcast June 13, 2011) (transcript available at http://transcripts.cnn.com/TRANSCRIPTS/1106/13/se.02.html). This position proved unpopular when, just a week before the general election, Superstorm Sandy slammed the East Coast. As state politicians praised the quick federal response and a New York Times editorial declared, "A Big Storm Requires Big Government," N.Y. Times, Oct. 29, 2012, the Romney campaign attempted to clarify its candidate's position, saying that he continued to believe "states should be in charge of emergency management in responding to storms and other natural disasters in their jurisdictions" but that "[t]his includes help from the federal government and FEMA." Tom Cohen, *Disaster Relief: Obama, Romney Differ on Federal Role*, CNN (Oct. 31, 2012), http://www.cnn.com/2012/10/30/ politics/disaster-role-government/.

With the presidential race over, the disaster aid issue continued to attract attention when Congress voted on a relief package for Hurricane Sandy victims. *See* Al Shaw, et al., *How Disaster Aid Recipients Voted on Sandy Relief*, ProPublica, http://projects.propublica.org/sandyvote/#view=sandy_2_vote (last visited Mar. 5, 2014) (mapping House and

Senate votes on the Sandy relief bill alongside federal disaster relief dollars each state received in 2012-13). Republicans in both the House and Senate seemed to champion Romney's state-centered perspective, as a majority of the GOP voted against the bill, though some Republicans later explained that their disapproval stemmed from the bill's inclusion of several spending measures unrelated to disaster relief.

C. THE FEDERAL STATUTORY SCHEME

Constitutional provisions and Supreme Court case law on federalism represent only the first step in understanding the relationship between federal, state, and local authorities during disasters. Of far greater practical significance are the statutes, regulations, and guidelines that implement federal power and define the federal government's role in disasters. Much of this work is delegated to the Federal Emergency Management Agency (FEMA), now located within the Department of Homeland Security. Created by an executive order signed by President Jimmy Carter in 1979, FEMA helps Americans (in the words of its mission statement) "prepare for, prevent, respond to and recover from disasters." The agency operates from its headquarters in Washington, D.C. and from ten regional offices. Its activities are organized around five "preparedness goals"—prevention, protection, mitigation, response, and recovery—each of which is outlined in a document called a "National Planning Framework." The most notable of these documents are the National Response Framework (NRF), which we will examine more fully in Chapter 4, and the National Disaster Recovery Framework, which we will examine in Chapter 8. *See* Federal Emergency Response Agency, National Planning Frameworks, http://www.fema.gov/national-planning-frameworks (May 16, 2014). The main disaster-related duties of the federal government are laid out in the Robert T. Stafford Disaster Relief and Emergency Assistance Act, 42 U.S.C. §§5121-5208 (2009), which FEMA administers.

1. THE STAFFORD ACT: DEPLOYMENT OF FEDERAL CIVILIAN AID AND RESOURCES

a. Triggers for Federal Aid: Emergencies and Major Disasters
The basic premise of the Stafford Act, passed in 1988, is that the federal government will step in to provide disaster aid to affected states when the disaster is of sufficient magnitude and severity that it overwhelms state and local capacity to respond. Accordingly, most relief provisions of the Act are not triggered until a state governor requests, and the president issues, a disaster (or emergency) declaration. The accompanying graphic, taken from FEMA's 2008 NRF Overview Document, outlines the process for states obtaining aid under the Stafford Act.

Overview of Stafford Act Support to States

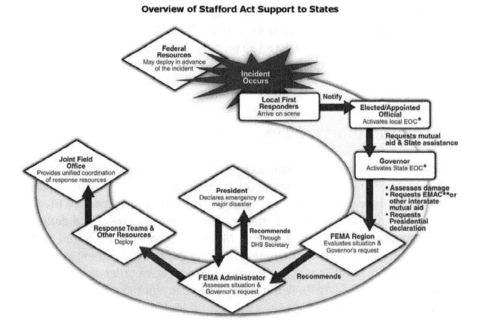

* Emergency Operations Center
** Emergency Management Assistance Compact

Moreover, the Stafford Act distinguishes between two disaster incident levels—emergencies and major disasters—and establishes parallel, though not identical, procedures for obtaining the requisite declarations. Section 401 of the Stafford Act, 42 U.S.C. §5170, governs major disaster declarations. Section 501, 42 U.S.C. §5191, governs emergency declarations.

§5122. Definitions
As used in this Act—

(1) "Emergency" means any occasion or instance for which, in the determination of the President, Federal assistance is needed to supplement State and local efforts and capabilities to save lives and to protect property and public health and safety, or to lessen or avert the threat of a catastrophe in any part of the United States.

(2) "Major Disaster" means any natural catastrophe (including any hurricane, tornado, storm, high water, winddriven water, tidal wave, tsunami, earthquake, volcanic eruption, landslide, mudslide, snowstorm, or drought), or, regardless of cause, any fire, flood, or explosion, in any part of the United States, which in the determination of the President causes damage of sufficient severity and magnitude to warrant major disaster assistance under this Act to supplement the

efforts and available resources of States, local governments, and disaster relief organizations in alleviating the damage, loss, hardship, or suffering caused thereby.

§5170. Procedure for [major disaster] declaration.
All requests for a declaration by the President that a major disaster exists shall be made by the Governor of the affected State. Such a request shall be based on a finding that the disaster is of such severity and magnitude that effective response is beyond the capabilities of the State and the affected local governments and that Federal assistance is necessary. As part of such request, and as a prerequisite to major disaster assistance under this chapter, the Governor shall take appropriate response action under State law and direct execution of the State's emergency plan. The Governor shall furnish information on the nature and amount of State and local resources which have been or will be committed to alleviating the results of the disaster, and shall certify that, for the current disaster, State and local government obligations and expenditures (of which State commitments must be a significant proportion) will comply with all applicable cost-sharing requirements of this chapter. Based on the request of a Governor under this section, the President may declare under this chapter that a major disaster or emergency exists.

§5191. Procedure for [emergency] declaration.
(a) Request and declaration
All requests for a declaration by the President that an emergency exists shall be made by the Governor of the affected State. Such a request shall be based on a finding that the situation is of such severity and magnitude that effective response is beyond the capabilities of the State and the affected local governments and that Federal assistance is necessary. As a part of such request, and as a prerequisite to emergency assistance under this chapter, the Governor shall take appropriate action under State law and direct execution of the State's emergency plan. The Governor shall furnish information describing the State and local efforts and resources which have been or will be used to alleviate the emergency, and will define the type and extent of Federal aid required. Based upon such Governor's request, the President may declare that an emergency exists.

NOTES AND QUESTIONS

1. Does the definition of "major disaster" cover a disease outbreak, such as an influenza pandemic? Does your analysis depend on whether the influenza is a naturally occurring strain or a biologically engineered

strain released in a bioterrorist attack? Historically, FEMA has taken the position that "biological disasters" do not qualify as Stafford Act "major disasters." Department of Homeland Security, *A Review of the Top Officials 3 Exercise* (Nov. 2005), available at http://www.oig.dhs.gov /assets/Mgmt/OIG_06-07_Nov05.pdf. However, the Homeland Security Council asserted in its Implementation Plan for the National Strategy for Pandemic Influenza that "the President could declare either an emergency or a major disaster with respect to an influenza pandemic." *See* Homeland Security Council, *Implementation Plan for the National Strategy for Pandemic Influenza* 212, available at http://www.flu .gov/planning-preparedness/federal/pandemic-influenza-implementation.pdf. For a discussion of statutory arguments as to whether pandemic influenza can qualify as a "major disaster," *see* Edward C. Liu, *Would an Influenza Pandemic Qualify as a Major Disaster under the Stafford Act?* (CRS Report for Congress, Order Code RL34724, Oct. 20, 2008) (concluding that the president could reasonably interpret "major disaster" to cover a flu pandemic). Congress has made several unsuccessful attempts to amend the definition of "major disaster" to explicitly include infectious disease outbreaks. *See, e.g.,* S. 2863, 111th Cong., 1st Session (2009).

2. Would the definition of "major disaster" cover a nonnatural event, such as an electronic attack on the Internet, not attributable to fire, flood, or explosion? *See* Ernest B. Abbott, *Representing Local Governments in Catastrophic Events: DHS/FEMA Response and Recovery Issues*, 37 Urb. Law. 467, 471 (2005) (suggesting it does not).

3. Do these definitional difficulties suggest that, rather than defining "major disaster" by reference to specific hazard events, the Act should instead define disaster in terms of some other referent, such as societal or community disruption? For example, the International Disaster Response Guidelines, adopted unanimously by the International Conference of the Red Cross and Red Crescent in 2007, define "disaster" as a "serious disruption of the functioning of society, which poses a significant, widespread threat to human life, health, property or the environment, whether arising from accident, nature or human activity, whether developing suddenly or as a result of long-term processes, but excluding armed conflict." The Secretariat of the United Nations International Strategy for Disaster Reduction defines disaster as "a serious disruption of the functioning of a community or a society causing widespread human, material, economic or environmental losses which exceed the ability of the affected community or society to cope using its own resources." Would one of these definitions better serve the purposes of the statute? Is the solution instead for Congress to amend the Act whenever any new threat seems to warrant inclusion as a "major disaster"?

4. In the run-up to President Obama's first inauguration, Washington, D.C., Mayor Adrian Fenty requested, and President Bush granted, an emergency declaration for Washington, D.C., for the days immediately prior to and including the inauguration. The request was prompted, in part, by Congress's allocation of only $15 million to cover D.C.'s inauguration costs, which was some $2.3 million less than the District had spent on security for President Bush's (smaller) second inauguration. *See* Dan Leaderman & John Ward, *Inauguration Declared "Emergency,"* Wash. Times, Jan. 14, 2009. Was this a proper declaration of "emergency" or an improper end run around Congress's appropriation process?

5. Should the president's decision to grant or withhold an emergency or major disaster declaration be subject to judicial review? Section 305 of the Act (42 U.S.C. §5148) provides that "[t]he Federal Government shall not be liable for any claim based upon the exercise or performance of or the failure to exercise or perform a discretionary function or duty on the part of a Federal Agency or an employee of the Federal Government in carrying out the provisions of the Act." This provision would seem to immunize the president's decision from review. *See* Kansas v. United States, 748 F. Supp. 797, 799-800 (D. Kan. 1990) (holding that the "President's decision on a request for a declaration of major disaster is not subject to [judicial] review"). More generally, Section 305's language is almost identical to the Federal Tort Claims Act's (FTCA) exception for "[a]ny claim...based upon the exercise or performance or the failure to exercise or perform a discretionary function or duty" by a federal employee. 28 U.S.C. §2680(a). The Stafford Act's immunity provision is interpreted *in pari materia* with the FTCA's frequently litigated "discretionary function" exception. *See* Freeman v. United States, 556 F.3d 326, 336-337 (5th Cir. 2009) (holding that the Stafford Act's "discretionary function" exception, as interpreted by reference to the FTCA's exception, precluded liability for the federal government's failure to provide Katrina survivors with adequate food, water, shelter, and medical assistance in accordance with provisions of the Catastrophic Index Annex of the National Response Plan); Graham v. FEMA, 149 F.3d 997, 1006 (9th Cir. 1998); McWaters v. FEMA, 436 F. Supp. 2d 802, 811-12, 814 (E.D. La. 2006) (holding that FEMA was not immune from post-Katrina claims based on the Constitution or statutory mandates that precluded agency discretion).

6. The disaster declaration process has been criticized as overly political. *See, e.g.,* Daniel C. Vock, *Disaster Declaration Denials Exasperate Governors*, Aug. 23, 2013, http://www.pewstates.org/projects/stateline/headlines/disaster-declaration-denials-exasperate-governors-85899499704. Recent empirical work suggests that political influences do have a substantial effect on both the president's decision as to

whether to declare a disaster and to subsequent decisions about the amount of aid to provide. *See, e.g.*, Thomas Husted & David Nickerson, *Political Economy of Presidential Disaster Declarations and Federal Disaster Assistance,* 42 Public Finance R. 35, 51 (2014) (finding, inter alia, that "the president is more likely to grant a governor's request to declare a major disaster when the president is facing reelection, particularly in those states with a larger number of electoral votes" and to grant a governor's request "when an incumbent governor who is facing reelection is from the same political party as the president"). Does this evidence of political influence suggest that presidential disaster declarations should be subject to judicial review? Is it enough that states may be able to sue FEMA if FEMA doesn't follow proper procedures in presenting a request to the president? *See* State of Kan. ex rel. Hayden v. U.S., 748 F. Supp. 797 (D.Kan. 1990) (allowing such a claim to proceed).

7. Rather than expanding judicial review, should there be more objective statutory or regulatory criteria to guide the declaration process? After Superstorm Sandy, Congress directed FEMA to revise its factors, codified in 44 C.F.R. 206.48, for determining whether a particular disaster warrants certain types of assistance to individuals. The revisions, which are now underway, are supposed to "provide more objective criteria" and to give more consideration to "trauma" to the affected community. Disaster Relief Appropriations Act of 2013, Pub. L. No. 113-2, 127 Stat. 47. More generally, some critics assert that, in evaluating requests for major disaster declarations, FEMA now gives too much weight to a formula—designed to determine if the damage is too high for the state and local governments to absorb on their own—that recommends the president deny the request unless the total damage exceeds some number ($1.39 in 2014) multiplied by the state's population. *See* Cheryl Corley, *States, Lawmakers Want Feds to Use New Math for FEMA Calculations*, April 9, 2014, http://www.npr.org/2014/04/09/300519019/states-lawmakers-want-feds-to-use-new-math-for-fema-calculations. Others suggest that there are far too many federal disaster declarations for relatively small disasters, thus sapping federal resources and decreasing state and local incentives to mitigate risk. *See* Steven P. Bucci et al., *After Hurricane Sandy: Time to Learn and Implement the Lessons in Preparedness, Response, and Resilience*, The Heritage Foundation, http://www.heritage.org/research/reports/2013/10/after-hurricane-sandy-time-to-learn-and-implement-the-lessons (May 27, 2014) (finding that "[t]he pace of FEMA declarations has increased with each new President" and recommending that the Stafford Act be modified "to establish clear requirements that limit the situations in which FEMA can issue declarations"). What factors should the president consider when making the declaration decisions? *See,*

e.g., Fairness in Federal Disaster Declarations Act of 2014, S. 1960, 113th Cong. (proposing to require FEMA to give specific weight to a variety of factors).

8. When can the federal government respond to a disaster or potential disaster without a request from the affected state? Section 501(b) of the Stafford Act (42 U.S.C. §5191(b)) provides that the president may exercise his authority to provide federal emergency assistance pursuant to sections 5192 and 5193 without a state request for an emergency declaration when the president "determines that an emergency exists for which the primary responsibility for response rests with the United States because the emergency involves a subject area for which, under the Constitution or laws of the United States, the United States exercises exclusive or preeminent responsibility and authority." Although the section directs the president to "consult with the Governor of any affected State, if practicable," the president can proceed without the governor's consent. Presumably, this authority enables the president to declare an emergency in the event of disasters or attacks affecting military installations and other federal properties. This authority was first invoked by President Clinton in the aftermath of the Oklahoma City bombings. *See* Jim Winthrop, *The Oklahoma City Bombing: Immediate Response Authority and Other Military Assistance to Civil Authority (MACA)*, 1997-JUL Army Law 3, 10-11. Might this provision also authorize the federal government to declare an emergency and respond without a state request to a catastrophic disaster that cripples state and local government? *See* Ryan, *supra*, at 530 (concluding that "the question is unsettled").

9. In 2013, Congress amended the Stafford Act to authorize the "Chief Executive of an affected Indian tribal government" to request a major disaster or emergency declaration directly from the president, *see* 42 U.S.C. §5170(b)(1) (major disaster), *id*. §5191(c)(1) (emergency), rather than having to submit a request through a state governor. These changes more fully recognize and respect the sovereignty of tribes and decrease coordination, communication, and hold-up difficulties. Tribes remain eligible for assistance under state disaster declarations when no tribal declaration is granted. *Id*. §5191(c)(3)

b. Federal Aid Available for Major Disasters

The president's issuance of a major disaster declaration authorizes (but does not require) the president to provide various types of federal disaster assistance to affected states, localities, and individuals. Major disaster assistance can include (1) response and recovery aid to states and localities (including General Federal Assistance, Essential Assistance, other Public Assistance (to permanently repair infrastructure), and Community Disaster Loans); (2) hazard mitigation assistance; and (3) individual assistance.

i. RESPONSE AND RECOVERY AID TO STATES AND LOCALITIES

§5170a. General Federal assistance.

In any major disaster, the President may—

(1) direct any Federal agency, with or without reimbursement, to utilize its authorities and the resources granted to it under Federal law (including personnel, equipment, supplies, facilities, and managerial, technical, and advisory services) in support of State and local assistance response and recovery efforts, including precautionary evacuations;

(2) coordinate all disaster relief assistance (including voluntary assistance) provided by Federal agencies, private organizations, and State and local governments, including precautionary evacuations and recovery;

(3) provide technical and advisory assistance to affected State and local governments for—

(A) the performance of essential community services;

(B) issuance of warnings of risks and hazards;

(C) public health and safety information, including dissemination of such information;

(D) provision of health and safety measures;

(E) management, control, and reduction of immediate threats to public health and safety; and

(F) recovery activities, including disaster impact assessments and planning;

(4) assist State and local governments in the distribution of medicine, food, and other consumable supplies, and emergency assistance; and

(5) provide accelerated Federal assistance and Federal support where necessary to save lives, prevent human suffering, or mitigate severe damage, which may be provided in the absence of a specific request and in which case the President

(A) shall, to the fullest extent practicable, promptly notify and coordinate with officials in a State in which such assistance or support is provided; and

(B) shall not, in notifying and coordinating with a State under subparagraph (A), delay or impede the rapid deployment, use, and distribution of resources to victims of a major disaster.

§5170b. Essential assistance

(a) In general—Federal agencies may on the direction of the President, provide assistance essential to meeting immediate threats to life and property resulting from a major disaster, as follows:

(1) Federal resources, generally—Utilizing, lending, or donating to State and local governments Federal equipment, supplies, facilities, personnel, and other resources, other than the extension of credit, for use or distribution by such governments in accordance with the purposes of this chapter.

(2) Medicine, food, and other consumables—Distributing or rendering through State and local governments, the American National Red Cross, the Salvation Army, the Mennonite Disaster Service, and other relief and disaster assistance organizations medicine, durable medical equipment, food, and other consumable supplies, and other services and assistance to disaster victims.

(3) Work and services to save lives and protect property— Performing on public or private lands or waters any work or services essential to saving lives and protecting and preserving property or public health and safety, including—

(A) debris removal;

(B) search and rescue, emergency medical care, emergency mass care, emergency shelter, and provision of food, water, medicine, durable medical equipment, and other essential needs, including movement of supplies or persons;

(C) clearance of roads and construction of temporary bridges necessary to the performance of emergency tasks and essential community services;

(D) provision of temporary facilities for schools and other essential community services;

(E) demolition of unsafe structures which endanger the public;

(F) warning of further risks and hazards;

(G) dissemination of public information and assistance regarding health and safety measures;

(H) provision of technical advice to State and local governments on disaster management and control;

(I) reduction of immediate threats to life, property, and public health and safety; and

(J) provision of rescue, care, shelter, and essential needs—

(i) to individuals with household pets and service animals; and

(ii) to such pets and animals.

(4) Contributions—Making contributions to State or local governments or owners or operators of private nonprofit facilities for the purpose of carrying out the provisions of this subsection.

(b) Federal share—The Federal share of assistance under this section shall be not less than 75 percent of the eligible cost of such assistance.

(c) Utilization of DOD resources

(1) General rule—During the immediate aftermath of an incident which may ultimately qualify for assistance under this subchapter [major disaster assistance] or subchapter IV-A of this chapter [emergency assistance], the Governor of the State in which such incident occurred may request the President to direct the Secretary of Defense to utilize the resources of the Department of Defense for the purpose of performing on public and private lands any emergency work which is made necessary by such incident and which is essential for the preservation of life and property. If the President determines that such work is essential for the preservation of life and property, the President shall grant such request to the extent the President determines practicable. Such emergency work may only be carried out for a period not to exceed 10 days.

. . .

(6) Definitions—For purposes of this section

(A) Department of Defense—The term "Department of Defense" has the meaning the term "department" has under section 101 of Title 10.

(B) Emergency work—The term "emergency work" includes clearance and removal of debris and wreckage and temporary restoration of essential public facilities and services.

Public Assistance Grant Program. Under the foregoing provisions, federal disaster aid can take two forms: either emergency measures can be taken by the federal government itself, or the federal government can reimburse states and localities for debris removal and other "emergency protective measures" (such as search and rescue and sheltering) taken by the state and local governments to respond to the disaster. Federal reimbursement for state and local "emergency measures" takes place pursuant to FEMA's Public Assistance Grant Program. *See* FEMA, Public Assistance Guide 3 (2007), available at http://www.fema.gov/public-assistance-policy-and-guidance/public-assistance-guide.

Another critical component of the Public Assistance Grant Program for major disasters is outlined in Section 406 of the Stafford Act, which authorizes the president to make contributions "to a State or local government for the repair, restoration, reconstruction, or replacement of a public facility damaged or destroyed by a major disaster," 42 U.S.C. §5172(a)(1)(A), and—under certain circumstances—to make similar grants to private nonprofit facilities, including facilities that provide "critical services...in the event of a major disaster," *id.* §5172(a)(3)(i), or facilities that have already sought the maximum Small Business Act disaster loan for which they are eligible, *id.* §5172(a)(3)(ii). The federal government will bear at least 75 percent of eligible costs, unless the facility has previously been damaged "on more than one occasion" in the preceding ten years by a similar event and the owner failed to "implement appropriate mitigation measures to address the hazard," *id.* §5172(b)(2), in which case the minimum federal share is 25 percent. If the owner decides not to repair or replace the facility, it can elect instead to receive a grant equal to 90 percent of the federal share of eligible costs (for public entities) or 75 percent of the federal share (for private nonprofits). *Id.* §51724(c).

Community Disaster Loans. Section 417 of the Stafford Act, 42 U.S.C. §5184, authorizes the president to make loans to local governments affected by major disasters:

> **§5184. Community Disaster Loans**
> (a) In General—The President is authorized to make loans to any local government which may suffer a substantial loss of tax and other revenues as a result of a major disaster, and has demonstrated a need for financial assistance in order to perform its government functions.
> (b) Amount—The amount of any such loan shall be based on need, shall not exceed
>   (1) 25 percent of the annual operating budget of that local government for the fiscal year in which the major disaster occurs, and shall not exceed $5,000,000; or
>   (2) if the loss of tax and other revenues of the local government as a result of the major disaster is at least 75 percent of the annual operating budget of that local government for the fiscal year in which the major disaster occurs, 50 percent of the annual operating budget of that local government for the fiscal year in which the major disaster occurs, and shall not exceed $5,000,000.

Repayment of the loan is cancelled if, for the three years subsequent to the disaster, local government revenues are insufficient to meet the operating budget of that local government. §417(c), 42 U.S.C. §5184(c).

Other Response and Recovery Aid to States and Localities. Other provisions of the Stafford Act also authorize the federal government to provide direct aid to communities affected by major disasters, by supplying food "for emergency mass feeding,"§413, 42 U.S.C. §5180 (authorizing and "direct[ing]" the president to assure an adequate food stock); emergency public transportation, §419, 42 U.S.C. §5186; temporary emergency communications systems in anticipation of a major disaster or emergency, §418, 42 U.S.C. §5185; and debris removal (or grants for debris removal) from publicly and privately owned lands, §407, 42 U.S.C. §5173.

NOTES AND QUESTIONS

1. The provisions outlined above reflect a number of changes prompted by FEMA's response to Katrina. One of the most significant additions is §5170a(5), which allows FEMA, in a declared "major disaster," to provide accelerated federal assistance and support, without a state request, when necessary to save lives, prevent suffering, and mitigate severe damage. This provision explicitly confirms authority that FEMA has long claimed but exercised only sporadically: the power to implement a proactive federal response utilizing a "push" system for deploying assets to devastated areas, rather than a traditional "pull" system:

   What is a push system? In response to most disasters, the federal government provides assistance in response to state requests. This reactive approach is often referred to as a "pull" system in that it relies on states knowing what they need and being able to request it from the federal government. States may make these requests either before disasters strike because of the near certainty that federal assistance will be necessary after such an event, e.g., with hurricanes, or afterwards, once they have conducted preliminary damage assessments and determined their response capabilities are overwhelmed.

   Unlike the bulk of the disasters requiring FEMA's response, catastrophic disasters require the federal response to be more proactive. This proactive response is referred to as a "push" system, in which federal assistance is provided and moved into the affected area prior to a disaster or without waiting for specific requests from the state or local governments....

   ...[P]re-positioning of disaster supplies and assets is not in and of itself a push of commodities. Once assets are pre-positioned to go into the field, they still need to be mobilized and deployed into the field either proactively by pushing the commodities to the state or reactively by waiting for a request from the state.

   Operational procedures for a push are not well exercised, practiced, or utilized. The majority of declared disasters are not catastrophic. Because of this, the pull system is most commonly used during disasters and training exercises and, therefore, is more familiar to disaster response personnel. In fact, the NRP-CIA [National Response Plan Catastrophic Incident Annex] has never been appropriately exercised. As a result, federal personnel have little experience or comfort with instituting a proactive response.

   Additionally, if the Homeland Security Secretary does not invoke the NRP-CIA, federal personnel have no clear instruction to switch from a reactive approach to a proactive approach. Without this clear direction, federal personnel can be uncomfortable pushing resources into the state because of the inherent risks, such as complicating the disaster response by diverting needed resources from other areas or wasting millions of dollars in a duplication of effort.

U.S. House of Representatives, A Failure of Initiative, Final Report of the Select Bipartisan Committee to Investigate the Preparation for and Response to Hurricane Katrina 136-137 (2006) [hereinafter House Katrina Report]. Is this new authority sufficient to allow a fully effective federal response to a catastrophic disaster? Should there be a separate, explicit federal power to push resources into a devastated area even without a major disaster declaration (which requires a state request), when a disaster incapacitates the state's chain of command and continuity of government? (For example, what if a major earthquake destroyed a state's historic capitol building while the governor was there and the legislature was in session?) Should there be federal power to push resources into devastated areas where lives are at stake when the governor is not incapacitated but is either incompetent or unwilling to request a federal disaster declaration?

Section 5170a was also amended to make clear that the federal government has the authority to support and coordinate precautionary evacuations. *See* 42 U.S.C. §5170(a)(1)-(2).

2. Another post-Katrina addition was section 5170b(a)(3)(J), which allows the federal government to provide assistance for rescuing, sheltering, and caring for individuals with pets and service animals (as well as the animals themselves). Many residents of New Orleans apparently refused to evacuate because doing so would have forced them to abandon their pets:

> In hurricane-ravaged New Orleans, the lack of planning added to the burden and stress of both rescuers and residents. In a city of 500,000 as many as 69 percent of the people are pet owners and, by some estimates, there are as many as 600,000 pets and animals affected by the devastation of hurricane Katrina. Private rescue organizations estimate they have saved about 5,000 animals so far and have reunited only 600 animals with their owners. Estimates indicate there are an equal percentage of pet owners nationwide.

Introduction of the Pets Evacuation and Transportation Standards (PETS) Act of 2005, 151 Cong. Rec. E1943, E1943 (Sept. 22, 2005) (statement of Rep. Tom Lantos, D-Cal.); *see also Pets Evacuation and Transportation Standards Act of 2005*, 152 Cong. Rec. H2985, H2986 (May 22, 2006) (statement of Rep. Christopher Shays, R-Conn.). According to an animal search and rescue expert, "There is a direct correlation between people risking their lives in a disaster and the presence of pets in the home." Jay Romano, *Protecting Pets in a Disaster*, N.Y. Times, Sept. 25, 2005, at 14 (quoting Joseph Buttito). In addition to expanding essential assistance to encompass the needs of households with animals, the Pet Evacuation and Transportation Standards Act of 2006 requires, as a condition of federal funding, that state and local preparedness plans address those needs. Pub. L. No. 109-38, 120 Stat. 1725 §2, codified at 42 U.S.C. §5196b(g). How hard will it be to provide shelters that accommodate pets and service animals? Given the possibility of allergies, will separate shelters be required for pet owners? The Red Cross generally has responsibility for shelters, but its policies forbid allowing pets in its shelters.

3. Other revisions to emergency response law enacted in response to Katrina include the creation of the National Emergency Child Locator Center and the National Emergency Family Registry and Locator System. *See* Post-Katrina Emergency Management Reform Act of 2006, Pub. L. No. 109-295, §§689b(b)-689c, 120 Stat. 1394, 1449 (2006), codified at 6 U.S.C. §§774-775. During a major disaster or emergency, the National Emergency Child Locator Center serves as a clearinghouse for information about displaced children: it assists law enforcement in locating children and in reuniting children with their families. *See* 6 U.S.C. §774(b)(2)(C). The Center provides a toll-free number to receive reports about displaced children, creates a Web site to provide information about children to those who might be looking for them, and deploys staff to gather necessary information. *See id.* §§774(b)(3)(A)-774(b)(3)(C). Similarly, the National Emergency Family Registry and Locator System is designed to help reunify families separated after an emergency or major disaster. *See id.* §775(b). Displaced adults register voluntarily by submitting personal information to the database, and this information is accessible to individuals named by the displaced adult as well as law enforcement officials. *See id.* §§775(c)(1)-775(c)(2).

4. Like Hurricane Katrina, Superstorm Sandy, which affected 24 states in October of 2012, spawned many amendments to the Stafford Act. Responding to concerns about bureaucratic red-tape and long delays for federal aid, many of these amendments were designed to speed and streamline the delivery of disaster assistance. For example, building on earlier pilot projects, the amendments confirm FEMA's authority to create alternative procedures for Public Assistance grants that allow aid recipients to secure funding based on fixed estimates of eligible costs instead of waiting until the work is done to be reimbursed for actual expenditures. 42 U.S.C. §5189f(e)(1)(A). The recipient bears the risk that repairs will prove more costly than the estimate, *id.*, but can also use any extra money to fund projects that reduce future risk or improve

public assistance operations or planning. *Id.* §5189f(e)(1)(D). These changes are designed to decrease the administrative costs of grants, ensure that funding reaches recipients more quickly, and incentivize efficient completion of repair work. The provisions would also allow aid applicants, with FEMA's approval, to consolidate multiple public assistance projects under one grant. *Id*. §5189f(e)(1)(C). Moreover, if the aid applicant decides not to rebuild a particular facility, it can elect to receive an "in lieu contribution" to fund an alternate project that meets certain criteria. While FEMA already had this authority to fund alternate projects, the Stafford Act required a reduction in grant amount (10 percent for state and local governments, 25 percent for eligible private non-profits) for such in lieu contributions. Public assistance grants authorized under the alternative procedures are now exempt from this reduction requirement, which was widely criticized as penalizing decisions to relocate infrastructure to less risky areas. *Id.* §5189f(e)(1)(B). Another post-Sandy change expands a pilot-project requiring FEMA to establish alternative dispute resolution procedures to resolve high-value conflicts between the federal government and state and local governments over eligible assistance. *Id*. §5189a(b)(1).

5. Federal aid for both major disasters and emergencies under the Stafford Act is funded through the Disaster Relief Fund (DRF). The DRF is a no-year account, which means the fund's balance rolls over from year-to-year, rather than expiring on a set date. Congressional appropriations to the DRF are based on a number of factors, including on "a ten-year rolling average of normal disaster costs." Bruce R. Lindsay, et al., *An Examination of Federal Disaster Relief Under the Budget Control Act* 3 (CRS Report for Congress, Order Code R42352, Nov. 18, 2013). This historical calculation excludes disasters that cost more than $500 million, as these events are considered "outliers." *Id*. at 3. Consequently, while the "average budget request for the DRF between FY2000 and FY2011 was roughly $2 billion," the DRF's "average spend-out rate" for those same years was 4.2 billion. *Id*. These shortfalls are met by supplemental appropriations, usually in response to individual large disasters, such as Superstorm Sandy. Under the Budget Control Act, supplemental appropriations—within certain limits—to fund most major disaster activities (but not emergency assistance) are exempt from offset requirements. *See id*. at 7-8. Is this the best way for Congress to fund disasters? Should all disaster relief spending be subject to budgetary offset requirements?

ii. FEDERAL HAZARD MITIGATION ASSISTANCE

Section 404 of the Stafford Act (42 U.S.C. §5170c) authorizes the president to contribute to hazard mitigation efforts in the wake of a major disaster. Pursuant to this authority, FEMA created the Hazard Mitigation Grant

Program (HMGP). After the president has made a major disaster declaration, the HMGP provides grants to states and local governments to implement long-term hazard mitigation measures within a presidentially declared disaster area. The HMGP allows communities to implement disaster mitigation measures during the immediate recovery period, when destruction occasioned by the disaster already necessitates repair or replacement of infrastructure, and when communities are most amenable to mitigation. (The Disaster Mitigation Act of 2000, Pub. L. No. 106-390, 114 Stat. 1552, amended the Stafford Act to provide for pre-disaster hazard mitigation as well, by authorizing pre-disaster mitigation grants to fund cost-effective hazard mitigation measures before disaster strikes. See 42 U.S.C. §5133.)

Although FEMA has the authority to provide HMGP grants, certain limitations apply, including applicant and project eligibility requirements and ceilings on federal contributions. Eligible applicants include state and local governments, Indian tribes or other tribal organizations, and certain nonprofit organizations. Individuals may not apply, but state or local governments may apply on their behalf. Though FEMA may administer HMGP grants, under 42 U.S.C. §5170c(c)(1), a state wishing to administer grants may submit an application for delegation of the authority to administer the program. Eligible projects include those that will reduce or eliminate losses from future disasters. Section 5170c(a) states that FEMA "may contribute up to 75 percent of the cost of hazard mitigation measures which the President has determined are cost-effective and which substantially reduce the risk of future damage, hardship, loss, or suffering in any area affected by a major disaster." FEMA's total HMGP contributions must not exceed a certain percentage of the total, estimated Stafford Act aid for the disaster. See 42 U.S.C. §5170c(a). However, states may receive increased funding if, at the time of the disaster declaration, the state has in place a federally approved hazard mitigation plan. See 42 U.S.C. §5165. Post-Sandy amendments to the Stafford Act attempt to streamline HMGP grant procedures and to advance states up to 25 percent of grant funds "before eligible costs are incurred." Id. §5170c(d),(e).

iii. FEDERAL ASSISTANCE TO INDIVIDUALS AND HOUSEHOLDS

Pursuant to §408 of the Stafford Act (42 U.S.C. §5174), the president is authorized "in consultation with the Governor of a State" to "provide financial assistance and, if necessary, direct services, to individuals and households in the State who, as a direct result of a major disaster, have necessary expenses and serious needs in cases in which the individuals and households are unable to meet such needs through other means."

Specifically, §408 authorizes "housing assistance" to respond to "disaster-related housing needs" (including financial assistance for rent, direct provision of temporary housing units where the housing stock would otherwise be inadequate, and financial assistance for the repair or replacement of "owner-occupied private residences"). 42 U.S.C. §5174(b)-(c). Post-Sandy amendments specifically authorize the president to lease and repair privately owned "multifamily rental property" to provide temporary housing in disaster areas. *Id.* §5174(c)(1)(B)(ii). Section 408 also authorizes financial assistance for "disaster-related medical, dental, child care, and funeral expenses," as well as "personal property, transportation, and other necessary expenses or serious needs resulting from the major disaster." *Id.* §5174(e)(1)-(2). The maximum amount of financial assistance an individual or household can receive under §408 was capped at $32,400 in 2014 (the cap is adjusted annually based on the Consumer Price Index).

FEMA administers §408 through its Individuals and Households Program. After a disaster incident, affected individuals may apply for aid directly to FEMA through its disaster helpline or Web site. http://www.fema.gov. Once an individual files an application, one of FEMA's ten regional offices sends an inspector to the damaged property to make a decision regarding eligibility for aid. Eligible individuals must live in a presidentially declared disaster area and have losses that are not otherwise covered by insurance. Details of the application process for individual aid are available at http://www.fema.gov/pdf/assistance/process/help_after_disaster_english.pdf. Other sections of the Stafford Act also authorize aid to individuals affected by major disasters. For example, §410, 42 U.S.C. §5177, authorizes the president "to provide to any individual unemployed as a result of a major disaster such benefit assistance as he deems appropriate." Section 412, 42 U.S.C. §5179, authorizes the president to distribute food coupons, pursuant to the 1964 Food Stamp Act, if he determines that "low-income households are unable to purchase adequate amounts of nutritious food" due to a major disaster. The president is also authorized to provide professional counseling services (or training), §416, 42 U.S.C. §5182, and to oversee legal services, §415, 42 U.S.C. §5182, for victims of major disasters. In addition to Stafford Act assistance, homeowners and business owners may be eligible for federally subsidized U.S. Small Business Association loans to cover uninsured losses. 15 U.S.C. §636.

c. Federal Aid Available for "Emergencies"

In a presidentially declared "emergency," the Stafford Act provides for more limited aid to states, localities, and individuals. Section 501, 42 U.S.C. §5192, governs "federal emergency assistance."

§5192. Federal emergency assistance

(a) Specified—In any emergency, the President may—

(1) direct any Federal agency, with or without reimbursement, to utilize its authorities and the resources granted to it under Federal law (including personnel, equipment, supplies, facilities, and managerial, technical and advisory services) in support of State and local emergency assistance efforts to save lives, protect property and

public health and safety, and lessen or avert the threat of a catastrophe, including precautionary evacuations;

(2) coordinate all disaster relief assistance (including voluntary assistance) provided by Federal agencies, private organizations, and State and local governments;

(3) provide technical and advisory assistance to affected State and local governments for—

(A) the performance of essential community services;

(B) issuance of warnings of risks or hazards;

(C) public health and safety information, including dissemination of such information;

(D) provision of health and safety measures; and

(E) management, control, and reduction of immediate threats to public health and safety;

(4) provide emergency assistance through Federal agencies;

(5) remove debris in accordance with the terms and conditions of section 5173 of this title;

(6) provide assistance in accordance with section 5174 of this title [federal assistance to individuals and households];

(7) assist State and local governments in the distribution of medicine, food, and other consumable supplies, and emergency assistance; and

(8) provide accelerated Federal assistance and Federal support where necessary to save lives, prevent human suffering, or mitigate severe damage, which may be provided in the absence of a special request and in which case the President—

(A) shall, to the fullest extent practicable, promptly notify and coordinate with a State in which such assistance or support is provided; and

(B) shall not, in notifying and coordinating with a State under subparagraph (A), delay or impeded the rapid deployment, use and distribution of critical resources to victims of an emergency.

(b) General—Whenever the Federal assistance provided under subsection (a) of this section with respect to an emergency is inadequate, the President may also provide assistance with respect to efforts to save lives, protect property and public health and safety, and lessen or avert the threat of a catastrophe, including precautionary evacuations.

(c) Guidelines—The President shall promulgate and maintain guidelines to assist Governors in requesting the declaration of an emergency in advance of a natural or man-made disaster (including for the purpose of seeking assistance with special needs and other evacuation efforts) under this section by defining the types of assistance available to affected States and the circumstances under which such requests are likely to be approved.

The federal share of emergency assistance provided must be at least 75 percent of eligible costs. *See* 42 U.S.C. §5193(a).

Much of this aid is identical to that provided for major disasters. As suggested by §5192(c), one common use of emergency declarations is to call upon federal resources in advance of an anticipated disaster to aid with tasks like sheltering and evacuation. *See* FEMA, Pre-Disaster Emergency Declaration Requests, http://www.fema.gov/media-library-data/20130726-1845-25045-8572/pre_disaster_emergency_declaration_requests_policy_fp010_4.pdf. Recall, too, that the president has 10-Day Authority under 42 U.S.C. §5170b to use DOD resources to perform "emergency work" in advance of an emergency declaration. Perhaps the most important limitation on federal assistance in an emergency (as opposed to a major disaster), however, is that the total amount of emergency assistance provided under the foregoing provisions is capped at $5 million, *see id.*§5193(b)(1), unless the president determines that "(A) continued emergency assistance is immediately required; (B) there is a continuing and immediate risk to lives, property, public health or safety; and (C) necessary assistance will not otherwise be provided on a timely basis," *id.*§5193(b)(2). Moreover, in contrast to a major disaster declaration, an emergency declaration does not trigger grants for hazard mitigation, community disaster loans, emergency public transportation, unemployment assistance, food stamps, legal services, or crisis counseling assistance and training.

2. OTHER STATUTES AUTHORIZING FEDERAL CIVILIAN DISASTER RESPONSE

A number of specific statutory schemes supplement the Stafford Act when the nation confronts certain types of disasters. *See, e.g.,* Defense Against Weapons of Mass Destruction Act, 50 U.S.C. §§2301-2368 (2008) (providing federal aid to state and local emergency agencies responding to terrorist incidents involving weapons of mass destruction). One of the most important of these statutes is the Public Health Service Act, 42 U.S.C. §201 et seq., which gives the secretary of Health and Human Services broad emergency authority to respond to public health disasters, including the power to deploy the U.S. Public Health Service Commissioned Corps and other instruments of the Department of HHS, such as the Centers for Disease Control, the Food and Drug Administration, and the National Institutes of Health. The secretary's primary authority under the Act is found in 42 U.S.C. §247d(a), which allows the secretary to declare a public health emergency and then take appropriate steps to respond:

> If the Secretary determines, after consultation with such public health officials as may be necessary, that (1) a disease or disorder presents a

public health emergency; or (2) a public health emergency, including significant outbreaks of infectious diseases or bioterrorist attacks, otherwise exists, the Secretary may take such action as may be appropriate to respond to the public health emergency, including making grants, providing awards for expenses, and entering into contracts and conducting and supporting investigations into the cause, treatment, or prevention of a disease or disorder as described in [other sections of the Act].

For a fuller discussion of the secretary's powers in a public health emergency see Public Health Emergency, Legal Authority of the Secretary, https://www.phe.gov/Preparedness/support/secauthority/Pages/default.aspx#phe. On April 26, 2009, the acting HHS secretary exercised this authority to declare a nationwide public health emergency for influenza A (H1N1), the so-called swine flu virus.

The Public Health Service Act also outlines a variety of other powers the secretary has for preparing for, and responding to, public health emergencies. These include:

Establishing international and interstate isolation and quarantine. Although the primary authority of the states over public health includes the power to isolate and quarantine individuals, the federal government regulates individuals who are entering the United States or crossing state boundaries. Under 42 U.S.C. §264, the secretary of HHS has the power "to prevent the introduction, transmission, or spread of communicable diseases from foreign countries into the States or possessions, or from one State or possession into any other State or possession." The secretary's isolation and quarantine authority is limited to those communicable diseases listed in a presidential Executive Order. *See* 42 U.S.C. §264(b); E.O. 13295 (April 2003); E.O.13375 (April 2005). The secretary may issue regulations for the apprehension and examination of "any individual reasonably believed to be infected with a communicable disease" who is moving or about to move from one state to another or who poses a probable source of infection to individuals who will be moving from one state to another. 42 U.S.C. §264(d). The secretary has broader authority to issue regulations providing for the apprehension and detention of individuals entering the United States from foreign countries in order to prevent the spread of disease, and may also inspect, disinfect, or destroy infected animals or articles that pose a danger to humans. The HHS secretary has delegated interstate and foreign quarantine authority to the director of the Centers for Disease Control (CDC). *See* 42 C.F.R. Part 70-71.

The federal government is directed to cooperate with and aid state and local authorities in the enforcement of their quarantines and health regulations, and the federal government may accept assistance from state and local authorities in enforcement of federal quarantine regulations. *See* 42 U.S.C. §243(a). Generally, federal authority does not supersede state law; however, to the extent that state measures conflict with an exercise of federal quarantine authority under 42 U.S.C. §264 (granting federal authority over international and interstate quarantines) or under §266 (granting federal authority over quarantines conducted in times of war), federal authority may supersede state provisions. *See* 42 U.S.C §264(e). Federal regulations implement the power to override state measures in order to control the interstate transmission of a communicable disease by vesting in the director of the CDC the authority to take control of state efforts (and implement such measures as he or she deems reasonably necessary to prevent the spread of the disease) when the director determines that measures taken by state health authorities are insufficient to prevent the disease's spread. *See* 42 C.F.R. §70.2. A U.S. attorney general memorandum to the secretaries of DHS, HHS, and other relevant agencies explained that "[t]he authority to implement an intrastate federal quarantine is less clear [than that for interstate quarantine], although the statutes and regulations provide some authority for HHS and CDC to take some intrastate measures." Office of the Attorney General, Memorandum to the President, Summary of Legal Authorities for Use in Response to an Outbreak of Pandemic Influenza (April 25, 2009), available at http://www.fema.gov/media-library-data/20130726-1845-25045-8572/pre_disaster_emergency_declaration_requests_policy_fp010_4.pdf.

Maintaining the Strategic National Stockpile (SNS). The Public Health Service Act directs the secretary of HHS to collaborate with the Centers for Disease Control and Prevention and to coordinate with the Department of Homeland Security in maintaining a stockpile of "drugs, vaccines and other biological products, medical devices and other supplies" needed to protect the nation during a bioterrorist attack or other public health emergency. *See* 42 U.S.C. §247d-6b(a)(1). A "stockpile" may consist of either a physical accumulation of supplies or a contractual agreement with vendors to deliver the needed supplies. *See id.*§247d-6b(e).

Credentialing of health professionals. The Public Health Service Act directs the secretary of HHS to link existing state verification systems to maintain a single, national, interoperable network for verifying the credentials and licenses of health care professionals who volunteer to provide health services during a public health emergency. 42 U.S.C. §247d-7b(a). The secretary is also directed to "encourage" states to adopt mechanisms for waiving state licensing requirements for health professionals seeking to provide medical services during a state health emergency, upon verification that the professional is licensed and in good standing in another state. *Id.* §247d-7b(i).

In addition to the authority granted to the secretary pursuant to the Public Health Service Act, federal law also provides for the waiver of a wide variety of regulatory requirements in cases of public health emergency. For instance, the Food, Drug, and Cosmetics Act permits the emergency use of an unapproved new drug, an unlicensed biological product, or a medical device that has not been approved or cleared for commercial distribution in the event of an "actual or potential emergency" involving a biological, chemical, radiological, or nuclear agent. *See* 21 U.S.C. §360bbb-3(a). In 2004 a federal district court enjoined the Department of Defense's mandatory anthrax vaccination program based on the FDA's failure to solicit additional public comments before certifying the safety and efficacy of the anthrax vaccine. *See* Doe v. Rumsfeld, 341 F. Supp. 2d 1, 16 (D.D.C. 2004). The HHS responded by issuing its first authorization for emergency use so that the Defense Department could continue anthrax vaccinations. *See* Determination and Declaration Regarding Emergency Use of Anthrax Vaccine Absorbed for Prevention of Inhalation Anthrax, 70 Fed. Reg. 5450 (Feb. 2, 2005). This waiver authority seems geared primarily toward terrorist attacks. Does it extend to a naturally occurring pandemic virus? On April 27, 2009, pursuant to this emergency authority, the FDA authorized use of a new swine flu diagnostic test, as well as widespread distribution of the antiviral drugs Relenza and Tamiflu, without compliance with label requirements. *See* FDA News Release (April 27, 2009), available at http://www.fda.gov/NewsEvents/ Newsroom/PressAnnouncements/ucm149571.htm (June 19, 2009).

The federal government also has two statutory tools for shielding health care professionals when they volunteer services during emergencies. First, the Volunteer Protection Act, 42 U.S.C. §§14501-14505, shields from liability some individuals providing volunteer services to nonprofit or governmental organizations. The institutions themselves, however, are not immunized in this way. *See id.* §14503(c). Second, the federal government may also protect health care providers by hiring them directly. *See* Public Health Security and Bioterrorism Preparedness and Response Act of 2002, Pub. L. No. 107-188, §102, 116 Stat. 594, 599-603 (amending 42 U.S.C. §300hh-11(d) to authorize the secretary of Homeland Security to appoint intermittent employees "in accordance with applicable civil service laws and regulations"); 42 U.S.C. §5149(b)(1) (enabling federal agencies, for purposes of carrying out the Stafford Act, to appoint temporary personnel without regard to federal civil service requirements); 42 U.S.C. §209(f) (authorizing the secretary of HHS to hire public health consultants without regard to civil service rules).

3. DEPLOYMENT OF FEDERAL MILITARY FORCES AND THE POSSE COMITATUS ACT

a. The Posse Comitatus Act

Federal military forces can, and often do, play an important role in disaster relief. In the aftermath of Katrina, for example, 50,116 National Guard personnel and 22,670 federal troops were deployed to aid in disaster relief. *See* House Katrina Report, *supra*, at 202 (chart). Under the Stafford Act, the Department of Defense (DOD) is a "federal agency," that the president may call upon in a declared major disaster to provide "general federal assistance" under §5170a or "essential assistance" under §5170b. *See* 42 U.S.C. §5122(8)

("'Federal agency' means any department, independent establishment, Government corporation, or other agency of the executive branch of the Federal Government, including the United States Postal Service, but shall not include the American National Red Cross."). Similarly, in a declared emergency, the DOD is one of the federal agencies the president can call upon to provide "federal emergency assistance" under §5192.

Moreover, pursuant to §5170b(c) of the Stafford Act, the DOD is singled out as the agency on whom the president may call in the "immediate aftermath of an incident which may ultimately qualify" as a major disaster or emergency but has not yet been declared as such. Upon the request of the governor of the affected state, the president may—for a period of ten days in advance of a major disaster or emergency declaration—direct the DOD "for the purpose of performing on public and private lands any emergency work which is made necessary by the incident and which is essential for the preservation of life and property." *Id.* §5170b(c)(1). For purposes of this ten-day authority, "'emergency work' includes clearance and removal of debris and wreckage and temporary restoration of essential public facilities and services." *Id.* §5170b(c)(6)(B). This provision allows the president to put the DOD to work meeting critical public needs even if communication failures or other difficulties prevent the governor from immediately transmitting all the information necessary for a major disaster or emergency declaration.

Despite these clear authorizations to use DOD resources, President Bush in the immediate aftermath of Katrina professed uncertainty about his ability to send federal troops into Louisiana. The president's reluctance to commit federal military personnel hinged, at least in part, on an old law, the Posse Comitatus Act, 18 U.S.C. §1385, and its exceptions. The Posse Comitatus Act provides that "[w]hoever, except in cases and under circumstances expressly authorized by the Constitution or Act of Congress, willfully uses any part of the Army or the Air Force as a posse comitatus or otherwise to execute the laws shall be fined under this title or imprisoned not more than two years, or both." *Id.*

"The phrase 'posse comitatus' is literally translated from Latin as the 'power of the county' and is defined at common law to refer to all those over the age of 15 upon whom a sheriff could call for assistance in preventing any type of civil disorder." United States v. Hartley, 796 F.2d 112, 114 n.3 (5th Cir. 1986); *accord* United States v. Yunis, 681 F. Supp. 891, 891 n.1 (D.D.C. 1988); *see also* H.R. Rep. No. 97-71, Part II, 97th Cong., 1st Sess. 4 (1981) (citing 1 William Blackstone, Commentaries*343-344), *reprinted in* 1981 U.S.C.C.A.N. 1781, 1786. Before states and localities had sizable police forces, the sheriff would supplement his numbers by calling for local citizens to aid him—as a posse comitatus—in pursuing and apprehending criminals. The first significant (and very controversial) use of posse comitatus to enforce federal law was the notorious 1850 Fugitive Slave Law, which required citizens to aid federal marshals in pursuing and detaining fugitive slaves. *See* Gautham Rao, *The Federal Posse Comitatus Doctrine: Slavery, Compulsion, and Statecraft in Mid-*

Nineteenth Century America, 26 Law & Hist. Rev. 1, 24 (2008). In 1854, Attorney General Caleb Cushing issued an opinion concluding that military troops (including militia and federal regulars) could be enlisted in the posse comitatus. *See id.* at 36.

The use of the federal military as a posse comitatus to enforce the laws came to full fruition during military reconstruction of the South. During the fiercely contested presidential election of 1876, President Ulysses S. Grant sent federal troops to police federal polling places in Florida, Louisiana, and South Carolina, whose electoral votes were the subject of partisan disputes over the popular vote. An electoral commission, controlled by the Republican Congress that appointed it, awarded all of the contested electoral votes to Republican candidate Rutherford B. Hayes, who prevailed by a single electoral vote over Democrat Samuel J. Tilden. *See* H.W.C. Furman, *Restrictions upon Use of the Army Imposed by the Posse Comitatus Act*, 27 Mil. L. Rev. 85, 94-95 (1960). *See generally* David E. Engdahl, *Soldiers, Riots and Revolution: The Law and History of Military Troops in Civil Disorders*, 57 Iowa L. Rev. 1 (1971). Congress then passed the Posse Comitatus Act in response to Southern objections that federal military power was being abused and civil authority subordinated to military might.

Despite its ugly roots in Reconstruction politics, the Posse Comitatus Act has often been viewed as embodying the broader notion that using military troops as a domestic police force risks both individual rights and civilian supremacy over the military. This understanding still requires policy makers and courts to delineate those situations in which the military's role in law enforcement is substantial enough to constitute a violation of the Act. Of course, the Posse Comitatus Act does not forbid all use of federal military troops to respond to natural or other disasters. The Act, by its terms, forbids deploying federal troops only when they are to be used "as a posse comitatus or otherwise to execute the laws." If "execute the laws" were read very broadly— as coincident, for instance, with the president's constitutional charge to see that the laws are faithfully executed—then the Act would forbid all but expressly authorized use of the federal military to implement or carry into effect any state or federal law, including disaster relief programs. In context, however, it is clear that "execute the laws" has the narrower meaning of enforcing laws against civilians and compelling citizens to comply with the law, such that the Act only forbids assigning civilian law enforcement functions to federal troops.

Prosecutions under the Act itself have been virtually nonexistent, *see, e.g.*, Matthew Carlton Hammond, Note, *The Posse Comitatus Act: A Principle in Need of Renewal*, 75 Wash. U. L.Q. 953, 961 (1997), so most of the judicial interpretation of the Act has occurred when an individual is prosecuted for another crime and defends on the ground that federal military involvement in his investigation or apprehension rendered the actions of law enforcement officers illegal. Consider the *Red Feather* case below, which arose out of military involvement in the federal response to the February 1973 occupation of

Wounded Knee, South Dakota, by followers of the American Indian Movement. The defendant was charged under 18 U.S.C. §231(a)(3) with interfering with law enforcement officers engaged in the lawful performance of their official duties—officers who had received federal military assistance in the form of equipment, supplies, advice, and aerial reconnaissance.

UNITED STATES V. RED FEATHER

392 F. Supp. 916, 921-924 (D.S.D. 1975), *aff'd sub nom.*
United States v. Casper, 541 F.2d 1275 (8th Cir. 1976)

Bogue, District Judge....

Upon careful examination of the legislative history of 18 U.S.C. §1385, this Court has reached several conclusions of law. First, the clause contained in 18 U.S.C. §1385 "uses any part of the Army or the Air Force as a posse comitatus or otherwise" means the direct active use of Army or Air Force personnel and does not mean the use of Army or Air Force equipment or materiel. 18 U.S.C. §1385 was intended by Congress...to eliminate the direct active use of federal troops by civil law enforcement officers. The prevention of the use of military supplies and equipment was never mentioned in the debates, nor can it reasonably be read into the words of the Act. Only the direct active use of federal [troops is] forbidden, unless expressly authorized by the Constitution or by Act of Congress. An Act of Congress, 10 U.S.C. §331, has authorized the President of the United States to order use of the militia and armed forces, but no such order was issued by the President as to the Wounded Knee occupation. The Congressional debates clearly reveal that...Congress intended to prohibit the direct active use of any unit of federal military troops of whatever size or designation to include one single soldier or large units such as a platoon or squadron, to execute the laws....[W]hen 18 U.S.C. §1385 was enacted, many Southerners resented the use of federal troops in places in which government had been reestablished, especially since such use was often directed, in their view, toward altering the outcome of elections in Southern states. For example, in the disputed Tilden-Hayes election of 1876, Rutherford B. Hayes obtained the necessary electoral votes only because the disputed votes of South Carolina, Louisiana, and Florida were all awarded to him. In each of these states the elections were accomplished by the use of federal troops, ostensibly to preserve the peace, and in each state when elections were contested, the troops supported the reconstruction candidates. Of primary concern was the prospect of United States marshals, on their own initiative, calling upon troops to form a posse or to otherwise perform direct law enforcement functions to execute the law. Thus,...the act was intended to stop army troops, whether one or many, from answering the call of any marshal or deputy marshal to perform direct law enforcement duties to aid in execution of the law....

[T]he intent of Congress in enacting this statute and by using the clause "uses any part of the Army or the Air Force as a posse comitatus or otherwise," was to prevent the direct active use of federal troops, one soldier or many, to execute the laws. Congress did not intend to prevent the use of Army or Air Force materiel or equipment in aid of execution of the laws. Moreover, through enactment of the Economy Act of 1932, 31 U.S.C. §686, Congress has provided extremely broad authorization for any executive department or independent establishment to place orders with any other willing department for materials, supplies, equipment, work, or service....

[T]his Court concludes that 18 U.S.C. §1385 may be violated only through the direct active use of troops for the purpose of executing the laws and 18 U.S.C. §1385 is not violated by the use of Army or Air Force materiel, supplies, or equipment of any type or kind in execution of the law....

[T]his holding is not only dictated by the statute and its legislative history, but from a practical economic standpoint, this holding is supported by common sense. During and after any natural disaster in this country whether due to flood, heavy snowstorms, earthquake, tornado or otherwise, there is always the possibility of looting and other acts of civil disorder. Most of this nation's smaller governmental units simply cannot maintain an inventory of emergency vehicles and other equipment adequate to meet such a crisis. If the affected municipality or county requests and receives, and law enforcement officers are using Department of Defense equipment or supplies to aid in enforcing the laws,...it would violate common sense and do violence to the intent of Congress in passing 18 U.S.C. §1385 to hold that those arrested for criminal acts must be released because law enforcement officers were using military equipment to aid in executing the law....

In order to more fully establish what evidence of military involvement would constitute unlawful conduct under 18 U.S.C. §1385 and thus be relevant to disprove the third element of the charge against the defendants under 18 U.S.C. §231(a)(3), the clause "to execute the laws" contained in 18 U.S.C. §1385 must be construed. It is the opinion of this Court that Congress intended, by use of the clause "to execute the laws," to make unlawful the direct active participation of federal military troops in law enforcement activities. Congress did not intend to make unlawful the involvement of federal troops in a passive role in civilian law enforcement activities....

Activities which constitute an active role in direct law enforcement are: arrest; seizure of evidence; search of a person; search of a building; investigation of crime; interviewing witnesses; pursuit of an escaped civilian prisoner; search of an area for a suspect and other like activities....Activities which constitute a passive role which might indirectly aid [law enforcement include] aerial photographic reconnaissance[;] military personnel under orders to report on the necessity of military intervention; preparation of emergency contingency plans to be used if military intervention is ordered; advice or recommendations given to civilian law enforcement officers by military personnel on tactics or logistics; presence of military personnel to deliver military material, equipment or supplies, to train local law enforcement officials on the proper use and care of such material or equipment, and to maintain such material or equipment....

[Therefore,] any evidence that United States marshals or agents of the Federal Bureau of Investigation used Army or Air Force Troops, one soldier or many, in an active role of direct law enforcement by performing one or more of the specific acts set forth above during the occupation of Wounded Knee, is admissible. Such [activity] is unlawful under 18 U.S.C. §1385 and therefore relevant and material to disprove the third element of the 18 U.S.C. §231(a)(3) charge against defendants, i.e., that law enforcement officers were lawfully performing their official duties....

NOTES AND QUESTIONS

1. The Department of Defense has interpreted the Posse Comitatus Act as generally prohibiting "direct" military involvement in civilian law enforcement but permitting "indirect" assistance such as the transfer of information obtained during normal military operations, as well as other actions that "do not subject civilians to the use of DoD power that is regulatory, prescriptive, or compulsory." DOD Directive 3025.21 §E3.1.g(3); *accord* United States v. Hitchcock, 286 F.3d 1064, 1069, *amended on other grounds*, 298 F.3d 1021 (9th Cir. 2002). Specifically, the DOD has interpreted the prohibition on using military personnel "as a posse comitatus or otherwise to execute the laws" as usually including, inter alia, "[i]nterdict[ing] a vehicle, vessel, aircraft"; engaging in "[a] search or seizure"; executing "[a]n arrest[,] apprehension[, or] stop and frisk"; interviewing witnesses or suspects; using, "brandishing" or "threatening" to use a weapon, except in self defense or defense of others; collecting evidence; "operating, manning, or staffing checkpoints"; or performing "security functions" or "crowd and traffic control." DOD Directive 3025.21 §E3.1.c(1).

2. Federal courts typically classify potential violations of the Act by using three tests to determine when military involvement in law enforcement transcends the presumptively permissible zone of "indirect" assistance: (1) whether civilian law enforcement officials have made "direct active use" of military personnel (as in *Red Feather*), (2) whether military involvement has "pervaded the activities" of civilian authorities, and (3) whether the military has become so entangled in civilian law enforcement as to subject citizens to the "exercise of military power that is regulatory, proscriptive, or compulsory in nature." *See* United States v. Kahn, 35 F.3d 426, 431 (9th Cir. 1994); United States v. Yunis, 924 F.2d 1086, 1094 (D.C. Cir. 1991); United States v. Hartley, 678 F.2d 961, 978 n.24 (11th Cir. 1982).

3. Would it violate the Posse Comitatus Act for federal troops to enforce an evacuation order? To provide security for distribution of food and other essential supplies? To direct traffic? To police the perimeter of a disaster scene? To operate a checkpoint allowing residents (but excluding nonresidents) from reentering a disaster area? To enforce a quarantine or isolation order? To administer compelled vaccination during a pandemic? *See* James Balcius & Bryan A. Liang, *Public Health Law & Military Medical Assets: Legal Issues in Federalizing National Guard Personnel*, 18 Annals Health L. 35, 55-57 (2009).

4. Even without the express statutory authority granted in the Stafford Act, President Bush could have deployed federal troops to provide every type of assistance outlined under the Stafford Act (search and rescue, food distribution, debris removal, etc.) without running afoul of the Posse Comitatus Act because those activities do not involve federal military participation in law enforcement. What, then, was the source of the president's reluctance to send federal troops to New Orleans? Apparently, based on widespread reports of looting and violence on New Orleans' streets, "Pentagon and military officials [believed] that no active-duty forces could have been sent into the chaos of New Orleans on Wednesday or Thursday [immediately after the hurricane made landfall] without confronting law-and-order challenges." Eric Lipton et al., *Storm and Crisis: Military Response; Political Issues Snarled Plans for Troop Aid*, N.Y. Times, Sept. 9, 2005, at A1. Thus, federal officials were reluctant to send federal troops to New Orleans because they believed the troops necessarily would have to engage in law enforcement functions in order to protect themselves and carry out their mission. They feared that federal troops would therefore be forced to violate the Posse Comitatus Act unless they could be deployed under the Insurrection Act, an exception to the Posse Comitatus Act. *See infra.*

5. Most of the reports of post-Katrina looting and violence were unsubstantiated or exaggerated and many were later retracted. Sun, *supra*, at 1134. Disaster sociologists have found that disasters often spur false or overblown reporting of looting and violence and that this reporting perpetuates a common "disaster myth" that people tend to engage in antisocial behavior in disaster's aftermath. *See id.* at 1134-35. Does this sociological evidence suggest that using federal military in a law enforcement capacity during disasters will rarely be necessary or justified?

6. Consider one author's contention that the behavior of military troops responding to Katrina underscores the necessity of the Posse Comitatus Act:

> Soon after troops began arriving in New Orleans, television news broadcasts repeatedly showed footage of General Honoré yelling at a

group of soldiers in the back of a pickup truck who were training their M-16s on haggard-looking civilian men, women, and children. The General said: "Point your weapons to the ground, this is not Iraq." The soldiers epitomized a posse comitatus and appeared to be playing out a scene from a developing country run by aberrant gangs.

Scenes like this were precisely why the PCA was passed: to enforce civilian authority over the military in order to maintain a democratic form of government. Unfortunately, Congress and the courts have created so many exceptions that the PCA has lost its teeth. The modern PCA appears to be nothing more than a legacy law.

Candidus Dougherty, *While the Government Fiddled Around, The Big Easy Drowned: How the Posse Comitatus Act Became the Government's Alibi for the Hurricane Katrina Disaster*, 29 N. Ill. U. L. Rev. 117, 146 (2008). Dougherty contends that the PCA presented no real obstacle to the government's provision of humanitarian aid and was simply a convenient scapegoat to justify the government's inadequate response. *See id.*

7. Is continued application of the Posse Comitatus Act justified by the fact that military troops are not trained to deal with the nuances of civilian law enforcement, including the difficulties of crowd control, restraints on the use of deadly force, and respect for constitutional rights?

> Modern combat is very fast-paced: decisions are made quickly in the heat and stress of a life-and-death struggle. Soldiers are highly trained to use force in the furtherance of the mission. They are trained to respond with force when facing an adversary because the adversary is likely to do the same. Being under fire changes the landscape and changes the stakes....Military personnel have different approaches to tactical situations than what is required in a law enforcement situation. The appropriate reaction to an adversarial law enforcement situation is not necessarily the use of deadly force; a more deliberative approach may be more appropriate. Conversely, military personnel involved in a combat situation need to quickly decide when deadly force should be used. Moving military personnel between these two situations may cause the soldier to misread or misunderstand a situation and use the wrong kind of force.

Michael T. Cunningham, *The Military's Involvement in Law Enforcement: The Threat Is Not What You Think*, 26 Seattle U. L. Rev. 699, 715-716 (2003). *See also* Dan Bennett, Note, *The Domestic Role of the Military in America: Why Modifying or Repealing the Posse Comitatus Act Would Be a Mistake*, 10 Lewis & Clark L. Rev. 935, 944 (2006) ("[T]here is no reason to assume that the military is often, or even ever, suited to the tasks of domestic law enforcement. As Lawrence Korb, the former Assistant Secretary of Defense puts it, the armed forces are 'trained to vaporize, not Mirandize.'").

8. Does allowing the military to assume responsibility for civilian law enforcement in the aftermath of disasters present any real risk that civilian institutions will be subordinated to military control? *See* Bennett, *supra*, at 935, 943-944 (describing the Posse Comitatus Act as a "crucial bulwark for liberty" and arguing that increased use of military in domestic law enforcement presents a "very real, if remote, danger that the military will seek to gain supremacy over the civilian institutions of government," threatens "universal trust in the military as a non-political body," and is "inherently repugnant to most Americans"). Would the risk be greater in a disaster that spanned many months or even years, such as a virulent flu pandemic? Is the notion that the military threatens civilian rule outdated?

> The change in Americans' perception of the military...warrants a change in the PCA. Present-day Americans view the military much more favorably than [they] did at the dawn of the Revolution. American troops no longer symbolize suppression; instead to some they represent "beacons of freedom" at home and abroad. The rise of American nationalism post–September 11th causes citizens to perceive soldiers as heroes, not villains, and to perceive the Army as protector of safety, not an imposer of threat. Consequently, Americans no longer mandate the artificial construct separating civilian law enforcement from military operations when the immediacy of a disaster requires otherwise.

Jessica DeBianchi, Note, *Military Law: Winds of Change—Examining the Present-Day Propriety of the Posse Comitatus Act after Hurricane Katrina*, 17 U. Fla. J.L. & Pub. Pol'y 473, 500 (2006).

9. Are Posse Comitatus Act restrictions justified by the effect on military readiness of domestic disaster deployments? *See, e.g., supra*, at 701-702. Many of the troops sent to relieve conditions in the wake of Hurricane Katrina had returned from or were en route to foreign tours of duty (particularly in Iraq and Afghanistan). Does the liberal use of military personnel and material during disasters effectively open an additional front for these troops at the very moment when American forces are stretched to their limits by active military engagements across the globe? Or is it the overseas deployment of National Guard troops that unduly drains state military (militia) resources that should be available for domestic disaster response? *See Hurricane Katrina: The Role of the Governors in Managing the Catastrophe: Hearing before the S. Comm. on Homeland Sec. and Governmental Affairs*, 109th Cong. 25 (2006) (statement of Kathleen Blanco, Gov., State of Louisiana)

(explaining that some 6,000 of Louisiana's 11,000 National Guardsmen were not available to respond to Katrina because they were deployed overseas).

10. What personnel are covered by the Posse Comitatus Act?

    a. Does the Posse Comitatus Act apply to the Navy (including the Marine Corps) even though it is not specifically named in the statute? Courts have divided over this question, but the debate is of little practical significance because the Department of Defense has applied the proscriptions of the Posse Comitatus Act to the Navy (including the Marine Corps), as well as the Army and the Air Force. *See* U.S. Dept. of Defense, Directive No. 3025.21, Defense Support of Civilian Law Enforcement Agencies encl. 3.3 (Feb. 27, 2013). Despite its application to the other military branches, the Posse Comitatus Act does not constrain the Coast Guard—which is charged by statute with certain law enforcement functions—unless the Coast Guard is operating under the DOD's command and control. 14 U.S.C. §2; 1 Center for Law & Military Operations, Domestic Operational Law (DOPLAW) Handbook for Judge Advocates 71 (2013) [hereinafter DOPLAW].

    b. Does the Posse Comitatus Act apply to National Guard troops? National Guard troops can be activated in three different legal capacities. First, a state governor can activate National Guard troops to "state active duty status." When acting in this capacity, National Guard troops are commanded by the state governor and compensated with state funds. Second, pursuant to Title 32 of the U.S. Code, a state governor may, with the permission of the secretary of the Army or Air Force, activate National Guard troops to "full-time National Guard duty" status. *See* 32 U.S.C. §§328, 502(f). Title 32 troops are under the direction of the state governor, who acts as commander in chief; however, the federal government pays them. 32 U.S.C. §§902, 905. Third, under Title 10, the president may call National Guard troops into federal "Active Duty." 10 U.S.C. §12406 authorizes the president to call the National Guard into federal service to repel an invasion, suppress a rebellion, or to aid in the execution of federal law, when those laws cannot be executed with federal regular forces alone. The president is the commander in chief of these federal active duty troops (who are considered regular federal Army or Air Force), and the troops are paid federal salaries.

        The PCA...applies to Reserve members of the Army, Navy, Air Force, and Marine Corps who are on active duty, active duty for training, or inactive duty training in a Title 10 duty status. Members of the National Guard performing operational support duties, active duty for training, or inactive duty training in a Title 32 duty status are not subject to the PCA. Only when members of the National Guard are in a Title 10 duty status (federal status) are they subject to the PCA. Members of the National Guard may also perform additional duties in a State Active Duty (SAD) status and are not subject to PCA in that capacity. Civilian employees of the Department of Defense are only subject to the prohibitions of the PCA...if they are under the direct command and control of a military officer.

DOPLAW, *supra*, at 71 (footnotes omitted).*See also* Gilbert v. United States, 165 F.3d 470, 473 (6th Cir 1999) ("The [Posse Comitatus] Act does not apply to members of the National Guard unless they have been called into 'federal service.'").

After Katrina, Louisiana Governor Blanco refused to consent to federalization of the Louisiana National Guard. In an attempted compromise, President Bush proposed a hybrid structure, in which one National Guard commander would have been authorized to command both Title 10 and Title 32 personnel, and would have been required to report both to the president and the governor. 2006 A.B.A. Hurricane Katrina Task Force Rep. 66. Governor Blanco rejected this alternative. However, following Superstorm Sandy, "temporary dual-status commanders" who could command both Title 10 and Title 32 troops were appointed for six states (Maryland, Massachusetts, New Hampshire, New Jersey, New York, and Rhode Island) in order to lead the military's disaster response operations. William Matthews, *Two Hats Are Better Than One*, National Guard Magazine, http://nationalguardmagazine.com/article/Two+Hats+Are+Better+Than +One /1341937/149143/article.html (May 27, 2014).

b. Statutory Exemptions to the Posse Comitatus Act

The prohibitions of the Posse Comitatus Act do *not* apply "in cases and under circumstances expressly authorized by the Constitution or Act of Congress." 18 U.S.C. §1385. A number of statutes expressly authorize the federal military to engage in civilian law enforcement. *See* DOPLAW, *supra*, at 82-83.

Several of the exceptions are of particular interest in disaster (or potential disaster) situations. For example, in an emergency situation in which civilian law enforcement officers lack capacity to enforce the law, the DOD, upon request by the attorney general, is permitted to deploy military forces to assist in enforcing federal restrictions on the handling of nuclear materials; such assistance may include conducting searches and seizures and arresting suspects.

18 U.S.C. §831(e). DOD may likewise provide assistance, at the request of the attorney general, in "an emergency situation involving a weapon of mass destruction,"10 U.S.C. §382(a), but participation in arrest and search and seizure are authorized—if at all—under only the most limited of emergency circumstances, *id.* §382(d). In addition, the secretary of Health and Human Services can authorize military officers stationed at seacoast posts (and Coast Guard personnel) to aid states in executing state quarantines and health laws, "respecting any vessel arriving in, or bound to, any port or district thereof." 42 U.S.C. §97.

One of the most important exceptions to the Posse Comitatus Act is the Insurrection Act, 10 U.S.C. §§331-335. When invoked, the Insurrection Act authorizes the president to invest members of federalized state militias or federal regulars with broad civil law enforcement powers. The Insurrection Act—originally enacted during the Civil War, *see* Act of July 29, 1861, ch. 25, 12 Stat. 281—is the most recent in a long series of statutes, dating back to 1792, delegating Congress's power "[t]o provide for calling forth the Militia to execute the Laws of the Union, suppress Insurrections and repel Invasions," U.S. Const. art. I, §8, cl. 15, *see* Vladeck, Note, *supra*, at 159, to implement Article IV, Section 4 of the Constitution, and (post–Civil War) to enforce the Fourteenth Amendment.

INSURRECTION ACT

10 U.S.C. §§331-334

§331. Federal aid for State governments.

Whenever there is an insurrection in any State against its government, the President may, upon the request of its legislature or of its governor if the legislature cannot be convened, call into Federal service such of the militia of the other States, in the number requested by that State, and use such of the armed forces, as he considers necessary to suppress the insurrection.

§332. Use of militia and armed forces to enforce Federal authority.

Whenever the President considers that unlawful obstructions, combinations, or assemblages, or rebellion against the authority of the United States, make it impracticable to enforce the laws of the United States in any State by the ordinary course of judicial proceedings, he may call into Federal service such of the militia of any State, and use such of the armed forces, as he considers necessary to enforce those laws or to suppress the rebellion.

§333. Interference with State and Federal law.

The President, by using the militia or the armed forces, or both, or by any other means, shall take such measures as he considers necessary to suppress, in a State, any insurrection, domestic violence, unlawful combination, or conspiracy, if it—

(1) so hinders the execution of the laws of that State, and of the United States within the State, that any part or class of its people is deprived of a right, privilege, immunity, or protection named in the Constitution and secured by law, and the constituted authorities of that State are unable, fail, or refuse to protect that right, privilege, or immunity, or to give that protection; or

(2) opposes or obstructs the execution of the laws of the United States or impedes the course of justice under those laws.

In any situation covered by clause (1), the State shall be considered to have denied the equal protection of the laws secured by the Constitution.

§334. Proclamation to disperse.

Whenever the President considers it necessary to use the militia or the armed forces under this chapter, he shall, by proclamation, immediately order the insurgents to disperse and retire peaceably to their abodes within a limited time.

NOTES AND QUESTIONS

1. What constitutes an insurrection? Consider the following jury charge, issued by the federal district court that tried members of the American Railway Union for their role in the legendary Pullman Strike of 1894:

   Insurrection is a rising against civil or political authority, the open and active opposition of a number of persons to the execution of law in a city or state. Now, the laws of the United States forbid, under penalty, any person from obstructing or retarding the passage of the mail, and make it the duty of the officers to arrest such offenders, and bring them before the court. If, therefore, it shall appear to you that any person or persons have willfully obstructed or retarded the mails, and that their attempted arrest for such offense has been opposed by such a number of persons as would constitute a general uprising in that particular locality, then the fact of an insurrection, within the meaning of the law, has been established; and he who by speech, writing, or other inducement assists in setting it on foot, or carrying it along, or gives it aid or comfort, is guilty of a violation of law. It is not necessary that there should be bloodshed; it is not necessary that its dimensions should be so portentous as to insure probable success, to constitute an insurrection. It is necessary, however, that the rising should be in opposition to the execution of the laws of the United States, and should be so formidable as for the time being to defy the authority of the

United States. When men gather to resist the civil or political power of the United States, or to oppose the execution of its laws, and are in such force that the civil authorities are inadequate to put them down, and a considerable military force is needed to accomplish that result, they become insurgents . . .

In re Charge to Grand Jury, 62 F. 828, 830 (N.D. Ill. 1894). *See generally* William Cawardine, The Pullman Strike (1973).

2. Much of the Fourteenth Amendment was aimed at imposing special disabilities on the losers of the Civil War. Sections 2, 3, and 4 of that amendment continue to serve notice that those who engage in insurrection or rebellion against the United States do so at their peril. *See, e.g.*, U.S. Const. amend. XIV §3 (disqualifying from federal office any person "who, having previously taken an oath, as a member of Congress, or as an officer of the United States, or as a member of any State legislature, or as an executive or judicial officer of any State, to support the Constitution of the United States, shall have engaged in insurrection or rebellion against the same, or given aid or comfort to the enemies thereof"). Does the stigma of the word "insurrection," as reflected in the punitive provisions of the Fourteenth Amendment and court decisions such as the Pullman Strike case, impede the contemporary use of the Insurrection Act? Is there another word without this stigma that would convey the same meaning?

3. Recall that the National Guard may be called into the service of the United States "[w]henever—(1) the United States, or any of the Commonwealths or possessions, is invaded or is in danger of invasion by a foreign nation; (2) there is a rebellion or danger of a rebellion against the authority of the Government of the United States; or (3) the President is unable with the regular forces to execute the laws of the United States." 10 U.S.C. §12406. The Insurrection Act has been used to deploy National Guard units in support of desegregation orders that met "massive resistance" during the 1950s and 1960s. Perhaps the most prominent use of this power took place in September 1957, when President Eisenhower ordered the National Guard and Air National Guard of Arkansas to remove "obstruction of justice...with respect to...enrollment and attendance at public schools in the Little Rock School District." Order No. 10,730, 22 Fed. Reg. 7628 (Sept. 24, 1957); *see also* Exec. Order No. 11,053, 27 Fed. Reg. 9681 (Sept. 30, 1962) (Mississippi public schools); Exec. Order No. 11,111, 28 Fed. Reg. 5709 (June 11, 1963) (University of Alabama); Exec. Order No. 11,118, 28 Fed. Reg. 9863 (Sept. 10, 1963) (Alabama public schools). These executive orders were preceded by presidential proclamations, issued under 10 U.S.C. §334, commanding private citizens engaged in an insurgency to disperse and retire peaceably to their homes. *See, e.g.*, Proc. No. 3204,

22 Fed. Reg. 7628 (Sept. 23, 1957) (Little Rock public schools, particularly Central Little Rock High School). Similar proclamations were issued in connection with Martin Luther King Jr.'s peace march from Selma to Montgomery, *see* Proc. No. 3645, 30 Fed. Reg. 3739 (March 23, 1965), and urban riots throughout 1967 and 1968, *see, e.g.*, Proc. No. 3795, 32 Fed. Reg. 10,905 (July 26, 1967) (Detroit).

4. The Insurrection Act enabled the first President Bush to send troops to quell civil unrest in the U.S. Virgin Islands after Hurricane Hugo in 1989. *See* Proc. No. 6023, 54 Fed. Reg. 39,151 (Sept. 20, 1989); Exec. Order No. 12,690, 54 Fed. Reg. 39, 153 (Sept. 20, 1989). Three years later, President Bush again invoked the Insurrection Act in response to the Rodney King riots in Los Angeles. *See* Proc. No. 6427, 57 Fed. Reg. 19,359 (May 1, 1992); Exec. Order No. 12,804, 57 Fed. Reg. 19,361 (May 1, 1992).

5. If President George W. Bush and his advisors believed that lawlessness in New Orleans was so prevalent that federal troops necessarily would be required to engage in some law enforcement functions, why didn't he invoke the Insurrection Act to justify his deployment of troops to New Orleans to put down looting and lawlessness? Governor Blanco did not make the requisite request under §331 (and, in fact, was anxious to retain control over National Guard troops and objected to any suggestion that these troops be federalized). Could President Bush have invoked §332 or §333? It appears that politics, as much as legal uncertainty, made President Bush reluctant to invoke the Insurrection Act. Said one senior administration official, "Can you imagine how it would have been perceived if a president of the United States of one party had pre-emptively taken from the female governor of another party the command and control of her forces, unless the security situation made it completely clear that she was unable to effectively execute her command authority and that lawlessness was the inevitable result?" Lipton et al., *supra*, at A1. If President Bush believed lawlessness was prevalent in New Orleans, couldn't he have invoked the Insurrection Act but then sent federal regular troops, rather than federalizing the National Guard? Apparently, Defense Secretary Donald Rumsfeld actively resisted the deployment of federal active-duty troops to New Orleans and relented only under direct presidential order. *See* Stephanie Grace, *Defiant Rumsfeld Left City to Suffer*, Time-Picayune, May 21, 2009.

6. If a pandemic were to overwhelm the ability of state and local civilian authorities to enforce quarantine and other public health measures such as those suggested in the Model State Emergency Health Powers Act, *see* The Center for Law and the Public's Health, The Model State Emergency Health Powers Act (2001), could the Insurrection Act be invoked to authorize military officials to enforce those measures? *See*

Jennifer Elsea & Kathleen Swendiman, *Federal and State Quarantine and Isolation Authority* 20-21 (CRS Report for Congress, Order Code RL33201, Aug. 16, 2006) (yes).

c. Nonstatutory Exceptions to the Posse Comitatus Act

In addition to exceptions "expressly authorized by...Act of Congress," the Posse Comitatus Act is suspended also "in cases and under circumstances expressly authorized *by the Constitution*." 18 U.S.C. §1385 (emphasis added). Relying on the "inherent legal right of the U.S. Government—a sovereign national entity under the Federal Constitution—to insure the preservation of public order and the carrying out of governmental operations within its territorial limits, by force if necessary," the DOD has long asserted two "constitutional exceptions" to the Posse Comitatus Act. *See* 32 C.F.R. §215.4(c)(1). First, the DOD claims authority to protect federal property and functions when local authorities cannot or will not. *See id.* §215.4(c)(1)(ii). Second, the DOD claims nonstatutory emergency response authority to respond in the immediate aftermath of disasters, when local capacity is overwhelmed, to save lives, prevent human suffering, mitigate serious property damage, and restore government functioning and public order. *See id.* §215.4(c)(1)(i). This claimed authority is neither subject to the limitations of the Posse Comitatus Act nor conferred by the Stafford Act or other federal statute.

NOTES AND QUESTIONS

1. To the extent that DOD claims emergency response authority to engage in civil law enforcement functions (without constraint by the Posse Comitatus Act) to "prevent loss of life or wanton destruction or property" in the aftermath of natural disasters, can that authority be grounded in the Constitution? Is it expressly authorized? Does your answer depend on whether the natural disaster has triggered civil unrest? If constitutional authority is found in a constitutional power granted to the president (such as inherent commander-in-chief authority) or a power granted to Congress (such as calling forth the militia), how could immediate response actions taken by low-level military officers—without presidential authorization—be justified? Are these actions justified by some extraconstitutional notion of necessity? *Cf.* Mitchell v. Harmony, 54 U.S. (13 How.) 115, 134 (1851) (reasoning that an emergency can vest a military officer with "discretionary power" to take private property for the public good if the officer had reasonable grounds to believe that the necessity was imminent).

2. Should historical practice be enough to justify a nonstatutory exception to the Posse Comitatus Act, even if it does not rise to the level of an express constitutional authorization? The immediate response authority, derived from no statute, appears to stem from the historical

practice of the armed forces. For instance, during the 1906 San Francisco earthquake and fire, the commander of the Army's Pacific Division unilaterally directed all troops under his command to help civilian law enforcement officers in their effort to stop alleged looting, fight fires, and protect federal buildings. *See* Winthrop, *supra*, at 5.

3. Does the DOD's assertion of inherent emergency authority and immediate response authority upset the balance of powers established through the Posse Comitatus Act, Stafford Act, Insurrection Act, and other statutes governing the deployment of federal troops and resources in civilian law enforcement?

d. Reforming the Posse Comitatus Act for Disaster Response?

Does the Insurrection Act strike the right balance with the Posse Comitatus Act in the context of disaster response? In the aftermath of Hurricane Katrina, President Bush asserted that "a challenge on this scale requires greater federal authority and a broader role for the armed forces—the institution of our government most capable of massive logistical operations on a moment's notice." Julian E. Barnes & Kenneth T. Walsh, *A Uniform Response?*, U.S. News & World Rep., Oct. 3, 2005, at 28. In response to President Bush's call for greater authority to use the military in disaster response, Congress passed Section 1076 of the John Warner National Defense Authorization Act of 2007, 109 P.L. 364, 120 Stat. 2083, which changed the title of the Insurrection Act to "Enforcement of the Laws to Restore Public Order" and amended §333 as follows:

> **§333. Major public emergencies; interference with State and Federal law**
>
> (a) USE OF ARMED FORCES IN MAJOR PUBLIC EMERGENCIES.—
>
> (1) The President may employ the armed forces, including the National Guard in Federal service, to—
>
> (A) restore public order and enforce the laws of the United States when, as a result of a natural disaster, epidemic, or other serious public health emergency, terrorist attack or incident, or other condition in any State or possession of the United States, the President determines that—
>
> (i) domestic violence has occurred to such an extent that the constituted authorities of the State or possession are incapable of maintaining public order; and
>
> (ii) such violence results in a condition described in paragraph (2); or
>
> (B) suppress, in a State, any insurrection, domestic violence, unlawful combination, or conspiracy if such insurrection, violation, combination, or conspiracy results in a condition described in paragraph (2).

(2) A condition described in this paragraph is a condition that—

(A) so hinders the execution of the laws of a State or possession, as applicable, and of the United States within that State or possession, that any part or class of its people is deprived of a right, privilege, immunity, or protection named in the Constitution and secured by law, and the constituted authorities of that State or possession are unable, fail, or refuse to protect that right, privilege, or immunity, or to give that protection; or

(B) opposes or obstructs the execution of the laws of the United States or impedes the course of justice under those laws.

(3) In any situation covered by paragraph (1)(B), the State shall be considered to have denied the equal protection of the laws secured by the Constitution.

(b) NOTICE TO CONGRESS.—The President shall notify Congress of the determination to exercise the authority in subsection (a)(1)(A) as soon as practicable after the determination and every 14 days thereafter during the duration of the exercise of that authority.

This provision—which was embedded in a massive appropriations bill—passed over the objection of all fifty state governors, who claimed that the amendment was an unwarranted expansion of the president's power to federalize the National Guard without the consent of the affected state governor. *See* Letter from Janet Napolitano et al., to Bill Frist, Majority Leader, et al. (Aug. 31, 2006). Senator Patrick Leahy also objected on the ground that the "constructive friction in existing law when it comes to martial law declarations" is beneficial because "[u]sing the military for law enforcement goes against one of the founding tenets of our democracy." 152 Cong. Rec. S10808-09 (daily ed. Sept. 29, 2006).

The amendment had an extremely short shelf life: it was overturned and the Insurrection Act restored to its previous form by the 2008 Defense Appropriations Bill. *See* National Defense Authorization Act for Fiscal Year 2008, 110 Pub. L. No. 181, 122 Stat. 3 §1068.

NOTES AND QUESTIONS

1. If natural disasters generally do not spark widespread antisocial behavior, *see* Sun, at 1134, *supra*, is the Insurrection Act in any form relevant to disaster response? If so, which version of the Insurrection Act do you prefer? Is there a major substantive difference between the two versions in terms of the conditions that allow the president to use military troops for civilian law enforcement? Or did the Amendments simply clarify that the requisite conditions could occur as the result of

natural disasters? *See* Michael Greenberger, *Yes, Virginia, the President Can Deploy Federal Troops to Prevent the Loss of a Major American City from a Devastating Natural Catastrophe*, 26 Miss. C. L. Rev. 107, 108 (2006) (arguing that the Warner Act's amendment of §333 "merely codifie[d] and clarifie[d] the federal power that existed prior to its enactment"). Would changing the name of the Act, alone, have been enough to make invocation of the Act's authority more politically palatable for the president? (The 2008 bill reinstated the title "Insurrection Act.") Does the repeal of the Warner Act's amendment to the Insurrection Act imply that the now reinstated Act should be read narrowly (and perhaps read not to apply in natural disaster situations at all)?

2. Some commentators have argued that, rather than amending the Insurrection Act to better account for disaster situations, Congress should create a new, distinct disaster relief exception to the Posse Comitatus Act as part of the Stafford Act:

> As the name suggests, the Insurrection Act contemplates heavy-handed military tactics in order to quell threats to the legitimacy of state and federal governments. . . . Ironically, by granting the military so much power, the Insurrection Act grants them too little, as it suggests overkill and often fits poorly into primarily disaster relief missions....Instead of relying on ill-fitted exceptions [like the Insurrection Act] and fine distinctions, necessary military activities should fall under the statutory framework of the Stafford Act....The military's primary focus remains humanitarian relief, but providing relief may necessitate the exercise of power that is regulatory, proscriptive, or compulsory in nature....[Without such authority,] the military may be reluctant to take on relief missions where it foresees a high probability of having to set up road blocks, control traffic, or restore order. Scenarios like this, which do not always fit easily into the Insurrection Act, could be met by allowing state officials the statutory option of coupling essential law enforcement with the [humanitarian] mission.

Isaac Tekie, Note, *Bringing the Troops Home to a Disaster: Law, Order, and Humanitarian Relief*, 67 Ohio St. L.J. 1227, 1261-1262 (2006). If such an exception were created, what particular law enforcement activities should the military be allowed to undertake? Providing security at emergency shelters? Directing traffic? Enforcing quarantines? Arresting looters?

3. Other commentators have suggested that, rather than creating new Posse Comitatus Act exceptions, Congress should cut back on existing exceptions:

The struggle to define the appropriate role of the military in domestic life comes at a critical juncture in our nation's development. With an increased emphasis on homeland security following the 9/11 attack, the government and the public have yielded to the military's growing involvement in domestic affairs. Such acquiescence is not surprising. Following 9/11, public confidence in the military reached record highs. But even before that, the U.S. military had consistently rated as the most trustworthy of public and private institutions—even more trustworthy than churches, universities, hospitals, the U.S. Supreme Court, and any other part of the government. In the last two decades, the military has been steadily used to aid law enforcement in a variety of domestic situations....The government's and public's reliance on the military is only magnified by concerns regarding another terrorist attack. The line between civil disorder and national security—between domestic law enforcement and military necessity—is continually blurred.

By increasing the military's presence in the domestic sphere, however, the federal government is obscuring the traditional lines between military and civilian roles. Even when sanctioned by civil leaders, the increased role of the armed forces in the domestic life endangers civil liberties and the democratic process....A fundamental tenet of our society, first reflected in the Declaration of Independence, is the desire of civilian supremacy over military power....

[Sections 331 to 334] should be combined and new language inserted that restricts the President's discretion, increases the states' role in the decision-making process, and provides the National Guard—not the standing Army—with the primary domestic security responsibilities.

Jackie Gardina, *Toward Military Rule? A Critique of Executive Discretion to Use the Military in Domestic Emergencies*, 91 Marq. L. Rev. 1027, 1029-1031, 1073 (2008).

4

EMERGENCY RESPONSE

Emergency response poses unique challenges for every level of government. Section A of this chapter sets forth a disaster scenario tabletop exercise to introduce many of the chapter's issue, including negotiating a chain of command. The prior chapter considered the federal constitutional and statutory framework for disaster response, and Section B examines that federal framework in action as implemented through the federal regulatory scheme for disaster response, focusing in particular on the evolution of FEMA, the federal regulatory framework for disaster response, and planning for catastrophic disasters (those that cause extraordinary levels of casualties or damage). Moving beyond the role of the federal government, Section C turns to state and regional disaster response and considers state disaster laws and the multijurisdictional Emergency Management Assistance Compact (EMAC). Section D explores the role of private and nongovernmental actors (including individual citizens) in disaster response. The final section of the chapter, Section E, then takes up the future of disaster response law and examines models for reform.

A. A SIMULATION EXERCISE: MAJOR EARTHQUAKE

This scenario is based, in part, on one of the 15 National Planning Scenarios (Scenario 9: Natural Disaster—Major Earthquake) developed to implement the now-rescinded HSPD-8. *See* National Planning Scenarios: Executive Summaries. For interesting visual depictions of the consequences of a large-scale earthquake along the San Andreas fault, see http://www.shakeout.org /resources/videos.html (cataloguing videos prepared for California Shakeout earthquake drills) (May 16, 2014). Read through the exercise and the questions once to familiarize yourself with the situation; then read the remaining sections of the chapter. When you've finished the reading, return to this section and prepare for the exercise.

At 9:15 a.m. on Tuesday, February 7, a 7.2-magnitude earthquake struck the major metropolitan area of Fault City. Located in the Intermountain West, the Fault City metropolitan area is home to some 3 million people (10 million people live in the six-county area). Although scientists had long predicted a moderate to catastrophic earthquake in the region, there were no specific seismic changes in the days and weeks leading up to the event that indicated that a major quake was imminent. Approximately three hours after the initial quake, at 12:03 p.m., another massive quake—registering 8.0 on the Richter Scale—shook the already devastated region. Subsurface faulting has occurred along sixty miles of the fault zone; the areas of greatest destruction are densely populated urban and suburban areas. It is now 1:10 p.m.; aftershocks (perhaps in the 7.0-8.0 range) are expected and could continue for months.

Damage reports are beginning to trickle in. No one can say for sure how reliable the reports are, as telecommunications networks are functioning sporadically, at best. Extrapolating from initial reports, the State's Head of Emergency Management estimates that there may be 1,400 fatalities, 100,000 injuries requiring medical care, and more than 18,000 people in need of hospitalization for serious and life-threatening injuries. Many of the city's largest hospitals have suffered extensive damage and cannot care for existing patients, much less the surge of injured who are flooding emergency rooms.

Hundreds of thousands of homes—and some 150,000 other buildings—have been destroyed, as a result of the shaking and concomitant liquefaction (earthquake-induced quicksand). Many of those homes shifted off their foundations. Several tall buildings in the downtown area—including one recently completed high-rise apartment building—collapsed completely, "pancaking" as floors collapsed down onto one another. As many as 20,000 people may be trapped in collapsed homes and buildings.

Additionally, most of the homes and buildings in the area that are still standing have neither electricity nor natural gas (and most homes and buildings in the area require both electricity and natural gas in order for their heating systems to work). The downtown area (including the State Capitol, which houses the State Emergency Management Department's Emergency Response Center) and the closest suburbs have gone completely dark. The State Capitol's emergency generator, which had not been tested in several years, has malfunctioned and will not start. Natural gas leaks have sparked a number of fires throughout the city, at least one of which is threatening a large hospital and several adjacent long-term care facilities. A large number of fire stations and fire trucks have been destroyed.

Many water mains have broken; wastewater treatment plants have been heavily damaged, and raw sewage is leaking into the streets in many neighborhoods. (The city's water distribution system also requires electric pumps to function.) The infrastructure damage is particularly extensive because the area's geography dictates that nearly every major natural gas and water pipeline in the city crosses over the major fault line. It is now 39 degrees outside, and weather forecasts indicate that snow or sleeting rain can be expected as evening approaches. Lows in the 20s are expected overnight.

Reports of serious environmental threats are also beginning to surface. Fuel pumps at several gas stations have ruptured, leaking thousands of gallons of gasoline onto city streets. Several large chemical facilities in the city have sustained serious damage. One unsubstantiated report indicates that there may be a small chlorine gas leak at a municipal water treatment center. (Chlorine gas was used as a weapon during World War I.)

Estimates suggest that at least 500,000 people are already planning to evacuate (including some who must evacuate to seek shelter and those who will choose to self-evacuate regardless of official evacuation advice). Both evacuations and transport of needed emergency supplies will be hampered by the state of major highways and bridges: many have buckled, making them all but impassable, and others are completely blocked by debris. Many freeway overpasses have also collapsed. The city's underground commuter system is in shambles, and many are feared trapped in underground stations and trains. An entire section of the city located along the eastern mountain range—home to 35,000 people—has been all but cut off from the surrounding area by a new 12-foot-high fault scarp. Thousands of skiers are potentially trapped in the city's many ski resorts, which are also located primarily in the eastern mountains.

Ten miles northeast of the city, Hill Side Reservoir has suffered major damage. Although the dam has not yet ruptured, experts on site are concerned that even another small aftershock could cause a catastrophic failure. The dam is relatively small in comparison to others in the area—holding back only 300 million gallons of water—but its rupture could nonetheless flood 30,000 houses, and floodwaters could reach the downtown area.

Communities some 70 miles outside of the city also felt significant shaking, but damage there is much less extensive. Most homes and buildings appear to be intact. Unfortunately, the CEO of the natural gas company—Intermountain Gas—has received numerous reports from the company's emergency call center that many homeowners in these less damaged areas are following advice (widely repeated on the radio) to turn off their natural gas. Those homes are now without heat as well. The CEO reports that once a customer's natural gas is turned off, it can only be turned back on by a power company technician; the unnecessary gas shutoffs are going to create a huge additional burden on the relatively small Intermountain Gas repair crew.

The governor has gathered his core staff, the head of the state's Emergency Management Department, and Fault City's mayor, in a makeshift emergency center at a military base on the outskirts of the city. Officials from the Army Corps of Engineers, EPA, Red Cross, and FEMA's Regional Office (also located in Fault City) are on their way. The governor is also in touch by satellite phone with the CEO of Intermountain Gas, the CEO of MountainWest

Construction (a large, regional construction company headquartered in Fault City), the president of Charity Hospital (a large nonprofit hospital with moderate damage), and the heads of several local water districts.

Assign individuals to play some of the different roles outlined above. For purposes of this exercise, assume that the state has the same emergency response law as Texas. Working together, negotiate a chain of command and establish emergency response priorities and plans.

Consider at least the following questions as you work on this tabletop exercise:

1. In your assigned role, consider what actions you should take first. What actions will you suggest to others as priorities? Who will be in charge of setting priorities? Will priorities be set by negotiation? By dictate (by the governor or someone else)?

2. How will communication be established and maintained? In making your decisions, how will you account for uncertainties about what is happening on the ground in different areas of the city? How will you improve situational awareness?

3. What steps does the governor need to take to ensure that the state gets necessary federal aid? Are there any obstacles to fulfilling those responsibilities?

4. What would an evacuation look like under these circumstances and how could it be accomplished? Where will shelters be established? How will the displaced (particularly those with special needs) be located and transported?

5. Consider how the dynamic at this makeshift emergency center changes as federal officials become involved. What will the chain of command look like? How will it be negotiated? How will it evolve over time? Beyond the assigned roles, who else needs to be involved at this early stage of response?

6. What is the role of private actors in the immediate aftermath of the disaster? How will questions of liability affect private- (and public-) actor behavior?

B. THE FEDERAL EMERGENCY REGULATORY SCHEME

In times of disaster, even the soundest legal structure is only as effective as its implementation. When Katrina struck, "the System did not perform as a system"; "the hurricane protection in New Orleans and Southeast Louisiana was a system in name only." 1 Army Corps of Engineers, Final Report of the Interagency Performance Evaluation Taskforce (IPET) 3 (June 1, 2006). As it was with infrastructure, so, too, with personnel: By most accounts, the federal and state agencies charged with coordinating the response to Hurricane Katrina performed abysmally. The federal framework had been developed in response to the terrorist attacks of September 11, 2001. The four-year cycle from September 11 to Hurricane Katrina—from the worst mass crime to the worst natural disaster in American history—severely tested the law of emergency response. Unfortunately, the federal response system, with some notable exceptions such as the Coast Guard, did not perform well.

This section begins by exploring the evolution of the Federal Emergency Management Agency (including the creation of the Department of Homeland Security). The section then turns to federal emergency response plans and evaluates how the post-9/11 scheme fared during Hurricane Katrina before considering how the current regulatory scheme, particularly the National Response Framework, deals with both "routine" and catastrophic disasters.

1. EVOLUTION OF THE FEDERAL EMERGENCY MANAGEMENT AGENCY

The Federal Emergency Management Agency (FEMA) was created as an independent agency by President Carter to forge a comprehensive, federal approach to emergency management. *See* Reorganization Plan No. 3, 43 Fed. Reg. 41,943 (June 19, 1978); Exec. Order No. 12,127, 44 Fed. Reg. 19,369 (March 31, 1979); Exec. Order No. 12,148, 44 Fed. Reg. 43,239 (July 20, 1979). The new agency assumed responsibility for emergency functions that previously had been distributed among a variety of federal agencies (including the Department of Defense, which had responsibility for civil defense, and the Department of Housing and Urban Development's Federal Disaster Assistance Administration). Even before the terrorist attacks of September 11, 2001, President Bush had begun reorganizing FEMA to focus on terrorist threats. *See* Keith Bea, *Federal Emergency Management Policy Changes after Hurricane Katrina: A Summary of Statutory Provisions* (CRS Report for Congress, Order Code RL33729, Dec. 15, 2006). After 9/11, Congress passed the Homeland Security Act of 2002, Pub. L. No. 107-296, 116 Stat. 2135 (codified at 6 U.S.C. §§101-557), which created the Department of Homeland Security (DHS). The Department's "primary mission" is described principally in terms of terrorism; the first three responsibilities of the DHS are to "prevent terrorist attacks within the United States," to "reduce the vulnerability of the United States to terrorism," and to "minimize the damage, and assist in the recovery, from terrorist attacks that do occur within the United States." 6 U.S.C. §111(b)(1). Only then does the Homeland Security Act direct DHS to "act[ ] as a focal point regarding natural and man-made crises and emergency planning." *Id.* §111(b)(1)(D).

The Homeland Security Act consolidated the functions of FEMA within DHS and made FEMA a subordinate organization within DHS, subject to the secretary of Homeland Security's broad power to reorganize the Department. The Act thus represented the most comprehensive reorganization of federal emergency authority since FEMA's creation. The Homeland Security Act assigned the secretary of Homeland Security a wide range of responsibilities for emergency preparedness and response. In addition to "helping to ensure the effectiveness of emergency response providers to terrorist attacks, major disasters, and other emergencies," the secretary must manage "the Federal Government's response to terrorist attacks and major disasters" and "coordinat[e]...Federal response resources...in the event of a terrorist attack or major disaster." *Id.*§314(a)(1), (3). The secretary is also directed to "aid[ ] the recovery from terrorist attacks and major disasters." *Id.* §314(a)(4).

The reorganized FEMA retained all of its Stafford Act "functions and authorities" and was directed to "lead[ ] and support[ ] the Nation in a comprehensive, risk-based emergency management program" for all hazards, centered around mitigation, preparedness planning, response, recovery, and coordination of emergency management to increase efficiency. *See* Pub. L. No. 107-296, §507(a)(1)-(2). In the years following the Homeland Security Act's enactment, however, the secretary of Homeland Security used his reorganizational authority to transfer some former FEMA functions to other components of the DHS. These changes culminated in a Department-wide reorganization by Secretary Michael Chertoff, announced on July 13, 2005 (before Katrina) and effective on October 1, 2005, which transferred most preparedness functions of the Directorate of Emergency Preparedness and Response (of which FEMA was a part) to a newly created Preparedness Directorate. *See* Henry B. Hogue, *Federal Emergency Management and Homeland Security Organization: Historical Developments and Legislative Options* 20-21 (CRS Report for Congress, Order Code RL33369, June 1, 2006).

In the aftermath of Hurricane Katrina, many blamed FEMA's anemic response on the agency's submersion in a sprawling bureaucracy focused primarily on terrorism, as well as the accelerating reassignment of many of FEMA's preparedness functions to other DHS divisions. In response to these and other criticisms, Congress enacted the Post-Katrina Emergency Management Reform Act of 2006. Pub. L. No. 109-295, 120 Stat. 1355 (2006) [hereinafter Post-Katrina Act]. The Act transferred back to FEMA most (but not all) of the preparedness functions that had been reassigned to the Preparedness Directorate of the DHS, 6 U.S.C. §315, and imposed qualifications for the newly created head (administrator) of FEMA, *id.* §313(c). Moreover, the Post-Katrina Act elevated FEMA's status in the Department, by establishing it as a "distinct entity" within the DHS, *id.* §316; exempting it from the secretary's reorganization authority, *id.*; giving the newly created FEMA administrator direct access to the president and Congress, *id.* §313(c); designating the FEMA administrator as the principal advisor to the president, the secretary, and the Homeland Security Council on all emergency management matters, *id.* §313(c)(4); authorizing the president to designate the administrator to serve as a member of the Cabinet during disasters, *id.* §313(c)(5)(A); and limiting the secretary's ability to reduce FEMA's authority or divert its assets, *id.* §316(c)(1).

The Post-Katrina Act affirmed that FEMA's primary mission "is to reduce the loss of life and property and protect the Nation from all hazards, including natural disasters, acts of terrorism, and other man-made disasters, by leading and supporting the Nation in a risk-based, comprehensive emergency management system of preparedness, protection, response, recovery, and mitigation." 6 U.S.C. §313(b)(1). Accordingly, the Act reiterates that the responsibilities of the FEMA administrator include:

> (8) assisting the President in carrying out the functions under the Robert T. Stafford Disaster Relief and Emergency Assistance Act...and carrying out all functions and authorities given to the Administrator under that Act;
>
> (9) carrying out the mission of the Agency to reduce the loss of life and property and protect the Nation from all hazards by leading and supporting the Nation in a risk-based, comprehensive emergency management system of—
>
> > (A) mitigation, by taking sustained actions to reduce or eliminate long-term risks to people and property from hazards and their effects;
> >
> > (B) preparedness, by planning, training, and building the emergency management profession to prepare effectively for, mitigate against, respond to, and recover from any hazard;
> >
> > (C) response, by conducting emergency operations to save lives and property through positioning emergency equipment, personnel, and supplies, through evacuating potential victims, through providing food, water, shelter, and medical care to those in need, and through restoring critical public services; and
> >
> > (D) recovery, by rebuilding communities, so individuals, businesses, and governments can function on their own, return to normal life, and protect against future hazards[.]

6 U.S.C. §314(a).

NOTES AND QUESTIONS

1. In carrying out his or her responsibilities, the FEMA administrator is instructed to "coordinate the implementation of a risk-based, all-hazards strategy that builds those common capabilities necessary to prepare for, protect against, respond to, recover from, or mitigate against natural disasters, acts of terrorism, and other man-made disasters, while also building the unique capabilities necessary to prepare for, protect against, respond to, recover from, or mitigate against the risks of specific types of incidents that pose the greatest risk to the Nation." 6 U.S.C. §314(b). Is this "all-hazards approach" the most efficient and effective way to organize emergency management authority or would we do better to establish separate agencies tasked with responding to specific types of emergencies? More specifically, how compatible are the tasks of combating terror and responding to other emergencies, especially natural disasters?

The all-hazards approach focuses on developing common capabilities and plans that can be utilized in a wide array of different disasters. And, indeed, many terrorist incidents, industrial accidents, and natural disasters share a common core of challenges: warnings, evacuation, provision of medical care, sheltering, debris removal, etc. Common planning avoids both duplication of effort and creation of multiple, potentially overlapping and conflicting response plans, so responders need only remember and practice a single set of procedures and protocols. Additionally, for some disasters, it will be impossible to tell at the outset whether the event is natural, accidental, or intentional, so having a single response framework can minimize confusion about which plan should be implemented. On the other hand, all-hazards plans will inevitably be developed with a certain set of "likely" disasters in mind, and because terrorism typically inspires more fear and garners more attention than natural disasters (see Chapter 6 for a discussion of heuristics that influence this reaction), response plans may be skewed toward terrorism. All-hazards planning dominated by terrorism scenarios may also lead to a greater emphasis on law enforcement than is optimal for natural disaster response. *See* Lisa Grow Sun, *Disaster Mythology and the Law*, 96 Cornell L. Rev. 1131, 1203-06 (2011).

2. Despite FEMA's elevated status within the DHS, there are continuing calls to return FEMA to its status as an independent agency outside of DHS. *See, e.g.*, Federal Emergency Management Advancement Act, S. 412, 111th Cong. (2009). Would removing FEMA from the DHS be beneficial? Does continued focus on FEMA's organizational structure divert attention from more important substantive questions about FEMA's mission performance?

3. As FEMA fumbled and New Orleans suffered, President Bush's chummy praise for FEMA Director Michael Brown ("Brownie, you're doing a heckuva job!") came to exemplify much of what was wrong with out-of-touch presidential and inexperienced FEMA leadership during the disaster. Brown, it appeared, had been elevated to the post despite his lack of any substantial emergency management experience. The Post-Katrina Act requires that the FEMA administrator have "a demonstrated ability in and knowledge of emergency management and homeland security" and "not less than 5 years of executive leadership and management experience in the public or private sector." 6 U.S.C. §313(c). In a Signing Statement to the law, President Bush objected to this provision on the grounds that it eliminated too many qualified individuals from the pool. Statement on Signing the Department of Homeland Security Appropriations Act, 2007, 42 Weekly Comp. Pres. Doc. 1742 (Oct. 4, 2006).

2. FEDERAL EMERGENCY RESPONSE PLANS

a. The Post-9/11 Framework and Hurricane Katrina

In addition to the other emergency management responsibilities assigned to the secretary of the DHS by the Homeland Security Act of 2002, the Act also directed the secretary to perform two specific tasks to coordinate and plan multijurisdictional response to disasters and terrorism. First, the Act directed the secretary to "build[ ] a comprehensive *national incident management system* with Federal, State, and local government personnel, agencies, and authorities, to respond to such attacks and disasters." 6 U.S.C. §314(a)(5) (emphasis added). Second, the Act required the secretary to "consolidat[e] existing Federal Government emergency response plans into a single, coordinated *national response plan*." *Id.* §314(a)(6) (emphasis added).

In 2003, President Bush issued Homeland Security Presidential Directive 5 (HSPD-5), a blueprint for the "management of domestic incidents." *See* Homeland Security Presidential Directive/HSPD-5, 39 Weekly Comp. Pres. Doc. 263 (March 7, 2003). The directive was designed to facilitate cooperation between all levels of government by "using a national approach to domestic incident management." *Id.* ¶(3). It also designated the secretary of Homeland Security as the principal federal official for domestic incident management. *See id.* ¶(4) Specifically, the directive provided:

> [T]he Secretary is responsible for coordinating Federal operations within the United States to prepare for, respond to, and recover from terrorist attacks, major disasters, and other emergencies. The Secretary shall coordinate the Federal Government's resources utilized in response to or recovery from terrorist attacks, major disasters, or other emergencies if and when any one of the following four conditions applies: (1) a Federal department or agency acting under its own authority has requested the assistance of the Secretary; (2) the resources of State and local authorities are overwhelmed and Federal assistance has been requested by the appropriate State and local authorities; (3) more than one Federal department or agency has become substantially involved in responding to the incident; or (4) the Secretary has been directed to assume responsibility for managing the domestic incident by the President.

Id. The directive also recognized the primary role of states in responding to disasters, specifying that the secretary would coordinate with the states to ensure adequate planning and that the federal government would "assist State and local authorities when their resources are overwhelmed, or when Federal interests are involved." *Id.* ¶(6). The guidance also acknowledged the role of nongovernmental entities in disaster response, and directed the secretary to coordinate with the private sector. *See id.* ¶(7).

HSPD-5 implemented the requirements of the 2002 Homeland Security Act by directing the secretary to establish two complementary components of a plan for managing "domestic incidents": a National Incident Management System (NIMS) and a National Response Plan (NRP). Together, the NIMS and the NRP (now the National Response Framework (NRF)) represented the heart of the post–September 11 framework for federal emergency response. The directive encouraged states to adopt the NIMS by conditioning federal preparedness assistance to the states (including grants, contracts, and other activities) on state adoption of NIMS. *See id.* ¶(20).

Hurricane Katrina posed the first serious test of HSPD-5 and the twin cornerstones of its approach to managing disasters, the NIMS and the NRP. The post–September 11 framework for emergency response failed many aspects of this initial challenge. Most of these failures were related to the catastrophic magnitude of the Katrina disaster—both the extraordinary number of casualties and the extraordinary amount of damage inflicted on the Gulf Coast. Additionally, the first iteration of the NRP—adopted by the federal government in December 2004—suffered from several infirmities, which became painfully obvious in the aftermath of the storm. First, it was unclear what triggered the NRP (both substantively and procedurally). The NRP was designed to deal with "Incidents of National Significance," but the NRP neither precisely defined those incidents nor specified the procedure for invoking the Plan. Perhaps more importantly, the NRP did not indicate what actions were to be taken once an Incident of National Significance was declared. *See* The White House, The Federal Response to Hurricane Katrina: Lessons Learned 13-15 (2006) [hereinafter Lessons Learned]. Consider this critique from the House Report on Hurricane Katrina:

U.S. HOUSE OF REPRESENTATIVES, A FAILURE OF INITIATIVE

Final Report of the Select Bipartisan Committee to Investigate the Preparation for and Response to Hurricane Katrina 131-132 (2006)

With the creation of the Department of Homeland Security (DHS) and the development of the National Response Plan (NRP), an additional layer of management and response authority was placed between the President and FEMA, and additional response coordinating structures were established. The Secretary of Homeland Security became the President's principal disaster advisor responsible for enabling the President to effectively utilize his authority under the Stafford Act to direct all federal agencies, particularly the Department of Defense (DOD), to respond in a coordinated and expeditious fashion. As part of these changes, critical response decision points were assigned to the Secretary of Homeland Security. Secretary [Michael] Chertoff executed these responsibilities late, ineffectively, or not at all. These secretarial authorities include:

The designation of an incident of national significance (INS);

The authority to convene the Interagency Incident Management Group (IIMG);

The designation of the principal federal official (PFO); and

The invocation of the national response plan's catastrophic incident annex (NRP-CIA).

There was plenty of advance warning by the National Weather Service, and the consequences of a category 4 hurricane striking New Orleans were well-documented. Fifty-six hours prior to landfall, Hurricane Katrina presented an extremely high probability threat that 75 percent of New Orleans would be flooded, tens of thousands of residents may be killed, hundreds of thousands trapped in flood waters up to 20 feet, hundreds of thousands of homes and other structures destroyed, a million people evacuated from their homes, and the greater New Orleans area would be rendered uninhabitable for several months or years. An August 28 report by the department's National Infrastructure Simulation and Analysis Center concluded: "Any storm rated Category 4 or greater...will likely lead to severe flooding and/or levee breaching, leaving the New Orleans metro area submerged for weeks or months."

Under these conditions it seems reasonable to expect the criteria for designating an INS would have been met, the appointment of a PFO would be necessary to coordinate an unprecedented federal response, the IIMG would be convened to provide strategic guidance and recommendations to the Secretary and the President, and the NRP-CIA would be invoked to shift the federal response posture from a reactive to proactive mode in order to save lives and accelerate assistance to overwhelmed state and local systems. According to a recent letter submitted by DHS...in response to the preliminary observations of the Comptroller General..., DHS viewed the NRP-CIA as applicable only to no-notice or short-notice events. And the Select Committee acknowledges that the State of Louisiana expressed its satisfaction with the supplies and that former FEMA Director Michael Brown directed that commodities be "jammed up" the supply chain.

While the NRP-CIA may be particularly applicable to a no-notice event, the Annex itself reflects only that a catastrophic incident may occur with little or no warning. And the pre-positioning of supplies to the satisfaction of state and local authorities, while an appropriate measure for a disaster without catastrophic consequences, was clearly not sufficient for the catastrophic consequences of Hurricane Katrina.

Instead, absent a catastrophic disaster designation from Chertoff, federal response officials in the field eventually made the difficult decisions to bypass established procedures and provide assistance without waiting for appropriate requests from the states or for clear direction from Washington. These decisions to switch from a "pull" to a "push" system were made individually, over several days, and in an uncoordinated fashion as circumstances required. The federal government stumbled into a proactive response during the first several days after Hurricane Katrina made landfall, as opposed to the Secretary making a clear and decisive choice to respond proactively at the beginning of the disaster. The White House Homeland Security Council (HSC), situated at the apex of the policy coordination framework for DHS issues, itself failed to proactively de-conflict varying damage assessments. One example included an eyewitness account of a levee breach supplied by a FEMA official at 7:00 p.m. on August 29. The White House did not consider this assessment confirmed for 11 more hours, when, after 6:00 a.m. the next morning, it received a Homeland Security Operations Center (HSOC) Situation Report confirming the breach.

The catastrophic nature of Katrina confirmed once again that the standard "reactive" nature of federal assistance, while appropriate for most disasters, does not work during disasters of this scale. When local and state governments are functionally overwhelmed or incapacitated, the federal government must be prepared to respond proactively. It will need to anticipate state and local requirements, move commodities and assets into the area on its own initiative, and shore up or even help reconstitute critical state and local emergency management and response structures.

The need for assistance is extreme during the initial period of a catastrophic hurricane, yet the ability of state and local responders to meet that need is limited. That is why it is so important for the federal government, particularly DOD resources, to respond proactively and fill that gap as quickly as possible. Because it takes several days to mobilize federal resources, critical decisions must be made as early as possible so that massive assistance can surge into the area during the first two days, not several days or weeks later. The NRP-CIA was drafted to meet this specific and well known requirement, yet Chertoff never invoked it for Katrina.

NOTES AND QUESTIONS

1. Scholars in many fields distinguish between failures of capacity and failures of performance. For example, tort law distinguishes between design defects and manufacturing defects. *Compare* Restatement (Third) of Torts: Products Liability §2(b) *with* Restatement (Second) of Torts §402A. *See generally* Frank J. Vandall & Joshua F. Vandall, *A Call for an Accurate Restatement (Third) of Torts: Design Defect*, 33 U. Mem. L. Rev. 909 (2003). Linguists distinguish between competence and performance, between the innate capacity to speak and speech as it actually occurs. *See, e.g.*, Noam Chomsky, Language and Mind 4 (enlarged ed. 1972). Was the failure of the NRP during Katrina one of design and capacity, or was it one of execution and performance? The former suggests that the proper remedy lies in legislative reform, perhaps to the point of overhauling the entire law of emergency response. The latter suggests that fault is more appropriately assigned to

individual actors: FEMA Director Michael Brown, Secretary of Homeland Security Michael Chertoff, or perhaps even President George W. Bush.

2. The Senate assigned blame at all levels, describing Katrina's relief effort as one plagued by "failures in design, implementation, and execution of the National Response Plan." United States Senate, Committee on Homeland Security and Governmental Affairs, Hurricane Katrina: A Nation Still Unprepared 27-1 (2006) [hereinafter Senate Katrina Report]. The Senate's report identified the following as some of the major failures of the Katrina response, *see generally id.* at 27-1 to 27-17:

    a. *Insufficient training and exercises.* The NRP "is a complex, ambitious, 400-plus-page high-level plan," a "very detailed, acronym-heavy document that is not easily accessible to the first-time user." Beyond an initial wave of training for headquarters staff of component agencies, DHS evidently made no further efforts to "ensur[e] that the NRP would be well implemented."

    b. *The roles of the principal federal official (PFO) and the federal coordinating officer (FCO).* The Stafford Act directs the president to appoint an FCO immediately upon declaring a major disaster or emergency. *See* 42 U.S.C. §5143. Under the Stafford Act, the FCO appraises the most urgent needs, establishes field offices, coordinates relief efforts, and takes other appropriate action to guide citizens and public officials. *See id.* The NRP, however, had created the new (nonstatutory) position of principal federal officer, "personally designated" by the secretary of Homeland Security as his or her representative as "the lead federal official." Department of Homeland Security, National Response Plan 33 (2004). However, the NRP created confusion and impeded coordination by failing to "define the role of the PFO or distinguish it from that of the FCO." Senate Katrina Report at 552. (FEMA no longer appoints PFOs for major disasters.)

    c. *Potentially overlapping agency roles.* The NRP "fail[ed] to delineate areas of potentially overlapping responsibility among federal agencies." For instance, the NRP assigned responsibility for Emergency Support Function 8, Public Health and Medical Services, to HHS, even though one of the response mechanisms, the National Disaster Medical System, answers to FEMA and DHS. Consequently, "[i]n the response to Katrina, FEMA and HHS engaged in minimal coordination on pre-positioning and deploying Disaster Medical Assistance Teams."

    d. *Contingency and catastrophic planning.* As "a high-level plan, with a core set of principles meant to apply to a wide range of possible events," the NRP "was not designed to address specific scenarios or geographic areas, or to provide operational details." The plan simply failed to "'contemplate' an event on the massive scale of Katrina."

  e. *Mistakes in declaring an Incident of National Significance.* According to the NRP, "every event that provokes a Presidential declaration under the Stafford Act automatically becomes an Incident of National Significance." President Bush's August 27, 2005, emergency declaration for portions of Louisiana automatically transformed Hurricane Katrina into an INS. Nevertheless, three days later, Secretary of Homeland Security Chertoff issued another "declaration" designating Katrina an INS. "At minimum, the Secretary's redundant declaration of an Incident of National Significance confused an already difficult situation and suggested a lack of familiarity with core concepts of the NRP within the Secretary's Office."

  f. *The appointment of Michael Brown as principal federal official.* Apart from the wisdom of appointing a principal federal official "who had no experience as an emergency manager," Secretary Chertoff's appointment of FEMA Director Michael Brown as PFO for Katrina "violated the literal requirements of the NRP." The NRP prohibits the PFO "from occupying another position or having another set of conflicting or distracting obligations at the same time."

  g. *Non-implementation of the Catastrophic Incident Annex.* "In failing to implement the National Response Plan's Catastrophic Incident Annex (NRP-CIA), Secretary Chertoff ignored a potentially powerful tool that might have alleviated difficulties in the federal response to Katrina." Though not accompanied by changes in the Stafford Act or other legislation (and therefore unable to provide new emergency response authority to federal officials), the NRP-CIA does "set a policy and tone for an urgent and proactive response that moves beyond the usual procedures in responding to an 'ordinary' disaster."

3. In addition to these many difficulties, the NRP arguably relied on planning assumptions that "skewed toward...terrorist attacks" and were therefore less well suited for "address[ing] the complications evident in the evacuation of New Orleans." Keith Bea, *Disaster Evacuation and Displacement Policy: Issues for Congress* 5 (CRS Report for Congress, Order Code RS22235, Sept. 2, 2005). For example, "[t]he Catastrophic Incident Annex of the NRP includes the assumption that large-scale evacuations, whether spontaneous or directed pursuant to authorities, may be more likely to occur after attacks than natural disasters, and that the maintenance of public health will 'aggravate attempts to implement a coordinated evacuation management strategy.'" *Id.* Nearly four years after September 11, 2001, Katrina posed the question as squarely as possible: Did the United

States fundamentally err in assigning responsibility for all emergency response, including relief and rebuilding efforts in connection with natural disasters, to an agency whose principal mission is directed toward detecting and preventing terrorist attacks? The current iteration of the Catastrophic Incident Annex has eliminated this planning assumption. *See infra.*

b. The Post-Katrina Regulatory Framework for Disaster Response

In order to address some of these failings, a second iteration of the NRP, renamed the National Response Framework (NRF), was issued in 2008; it emphasized, for example, that the NRF was always in effect and attempted to clarify the respective responsibilities of the FCO and PFO. Then in March 2011, President Obama issued Presidential Policy Directive 8: National Preparedness (PPD-8) "aimed at strengthening the security and resilience of the United States through systematic preparation for the threats that pose the greatest risk to the security of the Nation, including acts of terrorism, cyber attacks, pandemics, and catastrophic natural disasters." PPD-8. While PPD-8 does not displace HSPD-5, it embeds the NRF in a larger network of frameworks designed to meet preparedness goals. Rather than a stand-alone document, the NRF, which was revised again in 2013 to align with PPD-8, is now one in a "series of integrated national planning frameworks covering prevention, protection, mitigation, response, and recovery" that are part of the "national preparedness system." PPD-8.

As you read the following excerpt from the 2013 NRF, consider how effective the framework is likely to be in addressing both catastrophic and more routine disasters:

FEMA, NATIONAL RESPONSE FRAMEWORK

3-7 (2d. ed. May 2013) (footnotes omitted)

Evolution of the Framework

This NRF is currently the most mature of the National Planning Frameworks because it builds on 20 years of Federal response guidance. The Federal Response Plan published in 1992 focused largely on Federal roles and responsibilities. The establishment of the Department of Homeland Security (DHS) and the emphasis on the development and implementation of common incident management and response principles led to the development of the National Response Plan (NRP) in 2004. The NRP broke new ground by integrating all levels of government, the private sector, and nongovernmental organizations (NGOs) into a common incident management framework. In 2008, the NRP was superseded by the first NRF, which streamlined the guidance and integrated lessons learned from Hurricane Katrina and other incidents.

This NRF reiterates the principles and concepts of the 2008 version of the NRF and implements the new requirements and terminology of PPD-8. By fostering a holistic approach to response, this NRF emphasizes the need for the involvement of the whole community. Along with the National Planning Frameworks for other mission areas, this document now describes the all-important integration and inter-relationships among the mission areas of Prevention, Protection, Mitigation, Response, and Recovery.

. . .

Intended Audience
The NRF is intended to be used by the whole community. This all-inclusive concept focuses efforts and enables a full range of stakeholders—individuals, families, communities, the private and nonprofit sectors, faith-based organizations, and local, state, tribal, territorial, insular area, and Federal governments—to participate in national preparedness activities and to be full partners in incident response. Government resources alone cannot meet all the needs of those affected by major disasters. All elements of the community must be activated, engaged, and integrated to respond to a major or catastrophic incident. . . . Engaging the whole community is essential to the Nation's success in achieving resilience and national preparedness. . . .

Scope
The NRF describes structures for implementing nationwide response policy and operational coordination for all types of domestic incidents. This section describes the scope of the Response mission area, the guiding principles of response doctrine and their application, and how risk informs response planning.

The Response mission area focuses on ensuring that the Nation is able to respond effectively to all types of incidents that range from those that are adequately handled with local assets to those of catastrophic proportion that require marshaling the capabilities of the entire Nation. The objectives of the Response mission area define the capabilities necessary to save lives, protect property and the environment, meet basic human needs, stabilize the incident, restore basic services and community functionality, and establish a safe and secure environment moving toward the transition to recovery. [The Response mission area includes 14 core capabilities: planning, public information and warning, operational coordination, critical transportation, environmental response/health and safety, fatality management services, infrastructure systems, mass care services, mass search and rescue operations, on-scene security and protection, operational communications, public and private services and resources, public health and medical services, and situational assessment.]

The NRF describes the principles, roles and responsibilities, and coordinating structures for delivering the core capabilities required to respond to an incident and further describes how response efforts integrate with those of the other mission areas. **The NRF is always in effect, and elements can be implemented at any time.** The structures, roles, and responsibilities described in the NRF can be partially or fully implemented in the context of a threat or hazard, in anticipation of a significant event, or in response to an incident. Selective implementation of NRF structures and procedures allows for a scaled response, delivery of the specific resources and capabilities, and a level of coordination appropriate to each incident.

In this Framework, the term incident includes actual or potential emergencies and disasters resulting from all types of threats and hazards, ranging from accidents and natural disasters to cyber intrusions and terrorist attacks. The NRF's structures and procedures address incidents where Federal support to local, state, tribal, territorial, and insular area governments is coordinated under the Robert T. Stafford Disaster Relief and Emergency Assistance Act (Stafford Act), as well as incidents where Federal departments and agencies exercise other authorities and responsibilities. . . .

Guiding Principles

The priorities of response are to save lives, protect property and the environment, stabilize the incident and provide for basic human needs. The following principles establish fundamental doctrine for the Response mission area: (1) engaged partnership, (2) tiered response, (3) scalable, flexible, and adaptable operational capabilities, (4) unity of effort through unified command, and (5) readiness to act. These principles are rooted in the Federal system and the Constitution's division of responsibilities between state and Federal governments. These principles reflect the history of emergency management and the distilled wisdom of responders and leaders across the whole community.

Engaged Partnership

Effective partnership relies on engaging all elements of the whole community, as well as international partners in some cases. This also includes survivors who may require assistance and who may also be resources to support community response and recovery.

Those who lead emergency response efforts must communicate and support engagement with the whole community by developing shared goals and aligning capabilities to reduce the risk of any jurisdiction being overwhelmed in times of crisis. Layered, mutually supporting capabilities of individuals, communities, the private sector, NGOs, and governments at all levels allow for coordinated planning in times of calm and effective response in times of crisis. Engaged partnership and coalition building includes ongoing clear, consistent, effective, and culturally appropriate communication and shared situational awareness about an incident to ensure an appropriate response.

Tiered Response

Most incidents begin and end locally and are managed at the local level. These incidents typically require a unified response from local agencies, the private sector, and NGOs. Some may require additional support from neighboring jurisdictions or state governments. A smaller number of incidents require Federal support or are led by the Federal Government. National response protocols are structured to provide tiered levels of support when additional resources or capabilities are needed.

Scalable, Flexible, and Adaptable Operational Capabilities

As incidents change in size, scope, and complexity, response efforts must adapt to meet evolving requirements. The number, type, and sources of resources must be able to expand rapidly to meet the changing needs associated with a given incident and its cascading effects. As needs grow and change, response processes must remain nimble and adaptable. The structures and processes described in the NRF must be able to surge resources from the whole community. As incidents stabilize, response efforts must be flexible to support the transition from response to recovery.

Unity of Effort through Unified Command

Effective, unified command is indispensable to response activities and requires a clear understanding of the roles and responsibilities of all participating organizations. The Incident Command System (ICS), a component of NIMS [National Incident Management System], is an important element in ensuring interoperability across multi-jurisdictional or multi-agency incident management activities. Unified command, a central tenet of ICS, enables organizations with jurisdictional authority or functional responsibility for an incident to support each other through the use of mutually developed incident objectives. Each participating agency maintains its own authority, responsibility, and accountability.

Readiness to Act

Effective response requires a readiness to act that is balanced with an understanding of the risks and hazards responders face. From individuals, families, and communities to local, state, tribal, territorial, insular area, and Federal governments, national response depends on the ability to act decisively. A forward-leaning posture is imperative for incidents that may expand rapidly in size, scope, or complexity, as well as incidents that occur without warning. Decisive action is often required to save lives and protect property and the environment. Although some risk to responders may be unavoidable, all response personnel are responsible for anticipating and managing risk through proper planning, organizing, equipping, training, and exercising. Effective response relies on disciplined processes, procedures, and systems to communicate timely, accurate, and accessible information about an incident's cause, size, and current status to the public, responders, and other stakeholders.

Risk Basis

The NRF leverages the findings from the Strategic National Risk Assessment (SNRA) to build and deliver the response core capabilities. The SNRA identifies the threats and hazards that pose the greatest risk to the Nation. These findings affirm the need for an all-hazards, capability-based approach to preparedness to ensure that all types of scenarios are accounted for. The risks and threats identified by SNRA include [natural hazards; pandemics; technological and accidental hazards, such as dam failures or chemical substance spills or releases; and terrorist attacks, including cyber attacks].

In addition to these sweeping (and somewhat vague) principles, the NRF attempts to define the roles and responsibilities of local, tribal, state, and federal governments (as well as individuals, communities, NGOs (nongovernmental organizations), and the private sector). Indeed, it even outlines specific roles for particular state-level officials, including governors, state homeland security advisors, and directors of state emergency management agencies. *See id.* at 13-14.

Like its previous iterations, the 2013 NRF builds on the principles of the National Incident Management System (NIMS) to organize governmental response at all levels. NIMS is designed to provide "a consistent nationwide template to enable Federal, State, tribal, and local governments, nongovernmental organizations (NGOs), and the private sector to work together to prevent, protect against, respond to, recover from, and mitigate the effects of incidents, regardless of cause, size, location, or complexity." DHS, National Incident Management System 3 (Dec. 2008). The five major components of NIMS are preparedness (including a "continuous cycle of planning, organizing, training, equipping, exercising, evaluating, and taking corrective action"); communications and information management (developing a "standardized framework for communications and emphasiz[ing] the need for a common operating picture"); resource management ("defin[ing] standardized mechanisms and establish[ing] the resource management process to identify requirements, order and acquire, mobilize, track and report, recover and demobilize, reimburse, and inventory resources"); command and management (building on the "Incident Command System, Multiagency Coordination Systems, and Public Information"); and ongoing management and maintenance (coordinating through the National Integration Center and developing supporting technologies). *Id.* at 7-9.

NOTES AND QUESTIONS

1. Both the 2008 and 2013 versions of this document hold that the NRF is "always in effect," eliminating designations like "Incident of National Significance." While this approach may obviate questions about when the NRF, as a whole, is triggered, does it go any distance in clarifying when particular actions are to be taken under the NRF? Does the NRF provide sufficient clarity about when the DHS should assume the responsibility for coordinating federal response? More specifically, the NRF explains that the Secretary of DHS "coordinates the Federal response, as required" and "may monitor activities and activate specific response mechanisms to support other Federal departments and agencies without assuming the overall coordination of the Federal response during incidents that do not require the Secretary to coordinate the response or do not result in a Stafford Act declaration." NRF at 16.

2. The earlier 2008 NRF referred to a "bias toward action" and a "forward-leaning posture." The 2013 version retains only the latter formulation. What specific steps would the federal government take to implement this "forward-leaning posture"?

3. Like previous iterations of the framework, the current NRF proceeds on the premise that "incidents should be handled at the lowest jurisdictional level capable of handling the mission." NRF at 30. Should the potential scope of modern disasters—hurricanes bearing down on major population centers, pandemics that can spread across the globe in days or weeks—cause us to reconsider this fundamental proposition? Consider this opinion expressed by the Bush Administration:

> Disaster response in America traditionally has been handled by State and local governments, with the Federal government playing a supporting role. Limits on the Federal government's role in disaster response are deeply rooted in American tradition. State and local governments—who know the unique requirements of their citizens and geography and are best positioned to respond to incidents in their own jurisdictions—will always play a large role in disaster response. The Federal government's supporting role respects these practical points and the sovereignty of the States as well as the power of governors to direct activities and coordinate efforts within their States. While we remain faithful to basic constitutional doctrine and time tested principles, we must likewise accept that events such as Hurricane Katrina and the terrorist attacks of September 11, 2001, require us to tailor the application of these principles to the threats we confront in the 21st Century.

> Lessons Learned, *supra*, at 11. What procedural mechanisms and substantive factors should the federal government use to determine the

lowest level of government capable of responding to a particular disaster situation?

4. Obama's preparedness directive (PPD-8) and the Bush administration's now-rescinded predecessor (HSPD-8) each endorse "capability-based planning," which FEMA has defined as "[p]lanning, under uncertainty, to provide capabilities suitable for a wide range of threats and hazards while working within an economic framework that necessitates prioritization and choice." *See* Jared T. Brown, *Presidential Policy Directive 8 and the National Preparedness System: Background and Issues for Congress* 4 (CRS Report for Congress, Order Code R42073, Oct. 21, 2011). In conjunction with HSPD-8, the federal government had developed fifteen National Planning Scenarios, three of which dealt primarily with naturally occurring disasters (Scenario 9: Natural Disaster—Major Earthquake; Scenario 10: Natural Disaster—Major Hurricane; and Scenario 3: Biological Disease Outbreak—Pandemic Influenza). The others were various nightmare terrorism scenarios, ranging from the detonation of improvised nuclear devices to the release of pneumonic plague in a major metropolis. PPD-8 deemphasizes the role such scenarios in capability-based planning. Brown, *supra*, at 2-4. What are the advantages and disadvantages of focusing on specific disaster scenarios while developing response policy and plans?

5. In 2011, the Centers for Disease Control (CDC) proposed what might be considered a *sixteenth* emergency scenario: "zombie apocalypse." In a tongue-in-cheek effort to grab public attention, the CDC launched a zombie-apocalypse social media campaign, complete with zombie blog, downloadable posters, and a graphic novella. Centers for Disease Control, Zombie Preparedness, at http://www.cdc.gov/phpr/zombies.htm (last visited May 20, 2014). Evoking an all-hazards approach, CDC official Ali Khan explained, "If you are generally well equipped to deal with a zombie apocalypse you will be prepared for a hurricane, pandemic, earthquake, or terrorist attack." *Id.* FEMA later followed up with an online emergency-planning seminar focusing on the flesh-eating walking dead. Government officials stressed the importance of having an evacuation plan, a change of clothes, and emergency flashlights. Alicia A. Caldwell, *Zombie Apocalypse: "The Zombies Are Coming," Homeland Security Warns*, Huffington Post Sept. 6, 2012, http://www.huffingtonpost.com/2012/09/06/ homeland-security-warns-the-zombies-are-coming_n_1862768.html (May 20, 2014).

6. What exactly is the Incident Command System (ICS)?

> ICS was developed and refined over many years by incident commanders at the Federal, State, and local levels and was being successfully implemented throughout the country prior to being included in the NIMS. The ICS provides a means to coordinate the efforts of individual responders and agencies as they respond to and help manage an incident. The ICS organization, the structure and size of which can be tailored to the complexity and size of any given

incident, comprises five major functional areas—Command, Planning, Operations, Logistics, and Finance/Administration. This system grew out of the challenges of interagency coordination experienced when fighting wildfires in western states....Recognizing that most incidents are managed locally, the command function under ICS is set up at the lowest level of the response, and grows to encompass other agencies and jurisdictions as they arrive.

Lessons Learned, *supra*, at 13. There are several key roles defined by ICS, including an Incident Commander (who has authority and responsibility for managing all incident operations at the incident site), and the Command Staff (a Public Information Officer, Safety Officer, Liaison Officer, and other positions). NIMS at 49-53. In an incident involving multiple jurisdictions or agencies, the incident can be led by a "Unified Command" of agency officials "represent[ing] different legal authorities and functional areas of responsibility" and "us[ing] a collaborative process to establish, identify, and rank incident priorities." *Id.* at 51. For a fuller explanation of ICS, see Clifford J. Villa, *Law and Lawyers in the Incident Command System*, 36 Seattle U. L. Rev. 1855 (2013).

7. What is "unified command"? Compare "unity of command" with "unified command":

    Unity of command: The concept by which each person within an organization reports to one and only one designated person. The purpose of unity of command is to ensure unity of effort under one responsible commander for every objective.

    Unified command: An application of the Incident Command System used when there is more than one agency with incident jurisdiction or when incidents cross political jurisdictions. Agencies work together through the designated members of the Unified Command, often the senior person from agencies and/or disciplines participating in the Unified Command, to establish a common set of objectives and strategies and a single incident action plan.

    Lessons Learned, *supra*, at 13. NIMS and the NRF apparently aspire to unified command, but not unity of command. Can unity of command be achieved in a program for emergency response? Should it?

8. How well is unified command—which admittedly requires a "team effort"— likely to work in an emergency situation that involves federal, state, and local responders (and potentially responders from a number of states and localities)? Is it wishful thinking to expect that unified command can produce "unity of effort"? Reconsider, in this regard, the conflict between President Bush and Louisiana Governor Blanco over the control of National Guard troops in Katrina's aftermath. *See* Chapter 3, Section B, *supra.* In addition to difficulties in coordinating federal and state response, disputes

between different federal agencies with overlapping jurisdiction may challenge notions of "unified command." The federal BP oil spill response illustrates some of these difficulties in an analogous context. Federal response to large oil spills is governed by the National Oil and Hazardous Substance Pollution Contingency Plan (NCP), rather than the NRF, and federal spill response is coordinated by the National Response Team, which itself represents fifteen federal agencies. United States Coast Guard, BP Deepwater Horizon Oil Spill: Incident Specific Preparedness Review 1, 9 (Jan. 2011). During spill response, confusion over appropriate roles was rampant, and the Coast Guard's incident review concluded that "[t]he extensive involvement of the White House and top Administration officials resulted in what many have termed the 'political nullification' of the NRT [National Response Team] in the Deepwater Horizon incident," as "the NRT was essentially bypassed as the central policymaking body for oil spill response." *Id.* at 86.

9. The NRF and NIMS attempt to facilitate "unified command" by coordinating federal incident support to states through a Joint Field Office (JFO), which provides a common physical location for the members of the "Unified Coordination Group." The Unified Coordination Group "comprises senior officials representing Federal and state interests and, in certain circumstances, tribal governments, local jurisdictions, and the private sector," NRF at 40, and is charged with developing common objectives and strategies. State officials represented in the Unified Coordination Group include the State Coordinating Officer and other senior officials who "have significant jurisdictional responsibility and authority." *Id.* at 40-41. The role of the JFO is not to "manage on-scene operations," but rather to "support... on-scene efforts and conduct[ ] broader support operations." *Id.* at 40. On-scene operations are managed by the local incident command.

10. Another way the federal government coordinates and delivers disaster aid is through rapidly deployable "strike teams" with specific skill sets. The Post-Katrina Act directed FEMA to establish Incident Management Assistance Teams (IMATs) to support local incident command and facilitate establishment of unified command. 42 U.S.C. §5144. Designed to activate in two hours and arrive on-site within twelve hours, IMATs are staffed by full-time emergency management personnel and tasked with providing leadership in delivering federal aid, coordinating interjurisdictional response, and supplying decision makers with initial situational awareness. *See* FEMA Fact Sheet: IMAT (2010), https://www.fema.gov/pdf/media/factsheets/2010/imat_fact_sheet_10_05_10.pdf.

11. Another of FEMA's primary mechanisms for coordinating federal support is calling up one of the Emergency Support Functions (ESFs) outlined in the NRF. "The Federal ESFs bring together the capabilities of Federal departments and agencies and other national-level assets. ESFs are not based on the capabilities of a single department or agency, and the

functions for which they are responsible cannot be accomplished by any single department or agency. Instead, Federal ESFs are groups of organizations that work together to deliver core capabilities and support an effective response." NRF at 31. Each ESF covers one functional area and is headed by a coordinating agency.

12. The following table classifies Emergency Support Functions according to ESF number, function, and coordinating agency:

ESF #	Emergency Support Function	ESF Coordinator
ESF #1	Transportation	DOT
ESF #2	Communications	DHS (NCS)
ESF #3	Public Works and Engineering	DOD (USACE)
ESF #4	Firefighting	USDA (Forest Service) and DHS (FEMA/USFA)
ESF #5	Information and Planning	DHS (FEMA)
ESF #6	Mass Care, Emergency Assistance, Temporary Housing, and Human Services	DHS (FEMA)
ESF #7	Logistics	GSA and DHS (FEMA)
ESF #8	Public Health and Medical Services	HHS
ESF #9	Search and Rescue	DHS (FEMA)
ESF #10	Oil and Hazardous Materials Response	EPA
ESF #11	Agriculture and Natural Resources	USDA
ESF #12	Energy	DOE
ESF #13	Public Safety and Security	DOJ (ATF)
ESF #14	Superseded by National Disaster Recovery Framework	
ESF #15	External Affairs	DHS

NRF at 32-35.

13. Among the functions laid out in the NRF, ESF #8 (Public Health and Medical Services) figures very prominently. Because natural disasters often damage hospitals and strain infrastructure in every respect, disease looms large as a source of secondary casualties after a catastrophe. Moreover, the 2009 H1N1 pandemic heightened interest in strategies for combating public-

health risks such as pandemic flu and bioterrorism. ESF #8 provides the general "mechanism for coordinated Federal assistance...in response to a public health and medical disaster." FEMA, Emergency Support Function #8—Public Health and Medical Services Annex (2008), available at http://www.fema.gov/pdf/ emergency/nrf/nrf-esf-08.pdf. Some of the core functional areas for which ESF #8 provides assistance are assessment of public health/medical needs; health surveillance; medical care personnel; health/medical/veterinary equipment and supplies; patient evacuation; food safety and security; agricultural safety and security; potable water/wastewater and solid waste disposal; and mass fatality management, victim identification, and decontamination of remains. *Id.* at 8-1. The primary agency of ESF #8 is the Department of Health and Human Services (HHS), which leads the federal effort to provide public health and medical assistance to affected areas by giving instructions to fifteen federal agencies and the American Red Cross, and by coordinating national preparedness, response, and recovery actions. *Id.* at 8-2.

The Biological Incident Annex is another mechanism aimed at preventing the possibility of widespread disease outbreak. FEMA, Biological Incident Annex (2008), available at http://www.fema.gov/pdf/emergency /nrf/nrf_Biological IncidentAnnex.pdf. Again, HHS is the primary federal agency for public health, medical preparation, and response to a biological terrorism attack or naturally occurring outbreak. *Id.* at BIO-2. Once HHS is notified of a threat or disease outbreak that requires federal assistance, HHS will request activation of ESF #8 from FEMA. *Id.* at BIO-8. The Annex then outlines "actions, roles, and responsibilities associated with response to a human disease outbreak," as well as response actions, such as threat assessment notification procedures, laboratory testing, joint investigative/response procedures, and activities related to recovery. *Id.* at BIO-1. Some of the federal government's objectives in response to a biological terrorism event or a naturally occurring disease outbreak are to "detect the event through disease surveillance and environmental monitoring; identify and protect the population(s) at risk; determine the source of the disease; assess the public health, law enforcement, and international implications; control and contain any possible epidemic (including providing guidance to State, tribal, territorial, and local public health authorities); augment and surge public health and medical services; identify the cause and prevent the recurrence of any potential resurgence, additional outbreaks, or further spread of disease; and assess the extent of residual biological contamination and conduct response, restoration, and recovery actions as necessary." *Id.* The Annex provides for "environmental surveillance systems," which detect agents that could cause a biological incident and allow for rapid mobilization of a public health response if necessary. *Id.* at BIO-2, BIO-6. An incident may also be detected by "clinical or hospital presentation." *Id.* at BIO-4.

14. In addition to the ESFs, the National Response Framework also has "Incident Annexes," such as the Biological Incident Annex discussed in the prior note, that outline response for different types of disasters. Currently, there are separate annexes for biological incidents, catastrophic incidents, cyber incidents, food and agriculture incidents, mass evacuation incidents, nuclear/radiological incidents, and terrorism incidents. One of the most important of these annexes—and one that has received extensive attention post-Katrina—is the Catastrophic Incident Annex, discussed below.

c. The Regulatory Framework for Catastrophic Disasters

Particular attention continues to be focused on the issue of "catastrophic" disasters, defined by the 2006 Post-Katrina Act as "any natural disaster, act of terrorism, or other man-made disaster that results in extraordinary levels of casualties or damage or disruption severely affecting the population (including mass evacuations), infrastructure, environment, economy, national morale, or government functions in an area." *See* 6 U.S.C. §701(4). As you read the following excerpt from the current Catastrophic Incident Annex, think about whether, if properly invoked, it would help avoid some of the problems that plagued the Katrina response.

FEMA, NATIONAL RESPONSE FRAMEWORK, CATASTROPHIC INCIDENT ANNEX
(2008), available at http://www.fema.gov/emergency/nrf/incidentannexes.htm

Coordinating Agency: Department of Homeland Security/Federal Emergency Management Agency

Cooperating Agencies: All Federal departments and agencies (and other organizations) with assigned primary or supporting Emergency Support Function responsibilities

Introduction

Purpose

The Catastrophic Incident Annex to the National Response Framework (NRF-CIA) establishes the context and overarching strategy for implementing and coordinating an accelerated, proactive national response to a catastrophic incident.

A more detailed and operationally specific National Response Framework Catastrophic Incident Supplement (NRF-CIS) is published independently of the NRF and annexes.

Scope

A catastrophic incident, as defined by the NRF, is any natural or manmade incident, including terrorism, that results in extraordinary levels of mass casualties, damage, or disruption severely affecting the population, infrastructure, environment, economy, national morale, and/or government functions. A catastrophic incident could result in sustained nationwide impacts over a prolonged period of time; almost immediately exceeds resources normally available to State, tribal, local, and private-sector authorities in the impacted area; and significantly interrupts governmental operations and emergency services to such an extent that national security could be threatened. These factors drive the urgency for coordinated national planning to ensure accelerated Federal and/or national assistance.

Recognizing that Federal and/or national resources are required to augment overwhelmed State, tribal, and local response efforts, the NRF-CIA establishes protocols to preidentify and rapidly deploy key essential resources (e.g., medical teams, search and rescue teams, transportable shelters, medical and equipment caches, etc.) that are expected to be urgently needed/required to save lives and contain incidents.

Upon the occurrence of a catastrophic incident, or in advance if determined by the Secretary of Homeland Security, the Government will deploy Federal resources, organized into incident-specific "packages," in accordance with the NRF-CIS and in coordination with the affected State and incident command structure.

Where State, tribal, or local governments are unable to establish or maintain an effective incident command structure due to catastrophic conditions, the Federal Government, at the direction of the Secretary of Homeland Security, may establish a unified command structure, led by the Unified Coordination Group (UCG), to save lives, protect property, maintain operation of critical infrastructure/key resources (CIKR), contain the event, and protect national security. The Federal Government shall transition to its role of coordinating and supporting the State, tribal, or local government when they are capable of reestablishing their incident command.

The NRF-CIA is primarily designed to address no-notice or short-notice incidents of catastrophic magnitude, where the need for Federal assistance is obvious and immediate, where anticipatory planning and resource pre-positioning were precluded, and where the exact nature of needed resources and assets is not known. Appropriately tailored assets and responses identified in the NRF-CIS, as well as other select Federal resources and assets, may also be deployed in support of a projected catastrophic event (e.g., a major hurricane) with advance warning in support of the anticipated requests of State, tribal, and local governments.

Policies

A catastrophic incident will likely trigger a Presidential major disaster declaration and result in the Secretary of Homeland Security or a designee implementing the NRF-CIA/CIS.

All deploying Federal resources remain under the control of their respective Federal department or agency during mobilization and deployment. Some Federal departments and agencies have the authority, under their own statutes, to deploy directly to the incident scene.

Federal resources arriving at a National Logistics Staging Area (NLSA) remain there until requested by State/local incident command authorities, when they are integrated into the response effort.

Federal assets unilaterally deployed to the NLSA in accordance with the NRF-CIS do not require a State cost share. However, in accordance with the Stafford Act, State requests for use of deployed Federal assets may require cost-sharing.

For no-notice or short-notice catastrophic incidents, Federal resources identified in the execution schedule of the NRF-CIS will be mobilized and deployed, unless it can be credibly established that an action listed is not needed at the catastrophic incident venue.

If during a response, it is determined that the incident is catastrophic in nature, any remaining actions not originally initiated from the execution schedule will be initiated.

States are encouraged to conduct planning in collaboration with the Federal Government for catastrophic incidents as part of their steady-state preparedness activities.

The Federal Government, in collaboration with States, tribes, local governments, the private sector, and nongovernmental organizations (NGOs), develops proactive plans for activation and implementation of the NRF-CIA, to include situations where the need exceeds or challenges the resources and/or capabilities of State and local governments to respond and where the Federal Government may temporarily assume roles typically performed by State, tribal, and local governments.

The occurrence or threat of multiple or successive catastrophic incidents may significantly reduce the size, speed, and depth of the Federal response. If deemed necessary or prudent, the Federal Government may reduce the allocation of finite resources when multiple venues are competing for the same resources.

Situation

The initial response to a catastrophic incident starts on a local level with the local, tribal and/or State responders. However, there may be circumstances that exceed the capabilities of State, local, or tribal authorities in which they are unable to initially establish or maintain a command structure for incident response. In these instances, accelerated Federal response may be warranted, and the Department of Homeland Security (DHS)/Federal Emergency

Management Agency (FEMA) will coordinate response activities until local, tribal, and/or State authorities are capable or have re-established their incident command structure.

Continuity of Operations (COOP)/Continuity of Government (COG): Following a catastrophic event, segments of State, tribal, and local governments as well as NGOs and the private sector may be severely compromised. The Federal Government and its national partners must be prepared to fill potential gaps to ensure continuity of government and public- and private-sector operations. The incident may cause significant disruption of the impacted area's CIKR, such as energy, transportation, telecommunications, law enforcement, and public health and health care systems.

Incident Condition: Normal procedures for certain Emergency Support Functions (ESFs) may be expedited or streamlined to address the magnitude of urgent requirements of the incident. All ESFs must explore economies of scale to maximize utilization and efficiency of limited resources. In the case of a catastrophic incident, it is expected that the Federal Government or other national entities will provide expedited assistance in one or more of the following areas: [mass evacuations (ESF #5); mass care, housing, and human services (ESF #6); search and rescue (ESF #9); victim decontamination (ESF #8); environmental assessment and decontamination (ESF #10); public health and medical support (ESF #8); medical equipment and supplies (ESF #8); casualty transportation (ESF #8); public safety and security (ESF #13); public information (ESF #15); and critical infrastructure (CIKR Support Annex).]...

Planning Assumptions

A catastrophic incident will result in large numbers of casualties and/or displaced persons, possibly in the tens to hundreds of thousands. During a catastrophic incident response, priority is given to human life-saving operations.

The nature and scope of a catastrophic incident will immediately overwhelm State, tribal, and local response capabilities and require immediate Federal support.

A detailed and credible common operating picture will not be achievable for 24 to 48 hours (or longer) after the incident. As a result, response activities may have to begin without the benefit of a detailed or complete situation and critical needs assessment.

The nature and scope of the catastrophic incident will include major natural or manmade hazards including chemical, biological, radiological, nuclear, or high-yield explosive attacks, and cyber attacks.

A catastrophic incident has unique dimensions/characteristics requiring that response plans/strategies be flexible enough to effectively address emerging needs and requirements.

A catastrophic incident will occur with little or no warning. Some incidents may be well underway before detection.

Multiple incidents will occur simultaneously or sequentially in contiguous and/or noncontiguous areas. Some incidents, such as a biological WMD attack, may be dispersed over a large geographic area and lack a defined incident site.

A catastrophic incident will produce environmental impacts that severely challenge the ability and capacity of governments and communities to achieve a timely recovery.

Federal resources must be capable of mobilization and deployment before they are requested via normal NRF protocols.

Large-scale evacuations, organized or self-directed, may occur.

Existing health care systems in the impacted area are expected to be quickly overwhelmed, requiring evacuation of existing patients from these facilities to accommodate increased patient workload if the facility remains operational. Additionally, those persons with special needs, including residents of nursing homes and extended care facilities, will require special attention during evacuation.

Large numbers of people will be left temporarily or permanently homeless and may require prolonged temporary housing. Some displaced people will require specialized attention, healthcare assistance, and assistance with activities of daily living based on their special needs.

A large number of household pets and service animals will require appropriate care, sheltering, medical attention, and transportation.

A catastrophic incident will have significant international dimensions, including impacts on the health and welfare of border community populations, cross-border trade, transit, law enforcement coordination, and others....

Federal Response

In accordance with NRF provisions for a proactive Federal response to catastrophic incidents, the NRF-CIA employs an expedited approach to the provision of Federal resources to save lives and contain the incident.

Guiding principles for a proactive Federal catastrophic incident response include the following:

* The primary mission is to save lives, protect property and critical infrastructure, contain the event, and protect the national security.
* Standard procedures outlined in the NRF regarding requests for assistance may be expedited or, under extreme circumstances, temporarily suspended in the immediate aftermath of an incident of catastrophic magnitude, pursuant to existing law.
* Preidentified Federal response resources are mobilized and deployed, and, if required, begin emergency operations to commence life-safety activities.

*   Notification and full coordination with States occur, but the coordination process should not delay or impede the rapid mobilization and deployment of critical Federal resources.

*   Upon recognition that a catastrophic incident condition (e.g., involving mass casualties and/or mass evacuation) exists, the Secretary of Homeland Security immediately begins implementation of the NRF-CIA. Upon notification from the National Operations Center (NOC) that the NRF-CIA has been implemented, Federal departments and agencies immediately:

    *   Take actions to activate, mobilize, and deploy incident-specific resources in accordance with the NRF-CIS.

    *   Take actions to protect life, property, and critical infrastructure under their jurisdiction, and provide assistance within the affected area.

    *   Commence those hazard-specific activities established under the appropriate and applicable NRF Incident Annex(es), including the NRF-CIA.

    *   Commence functional activities and responsibilities established under the NRF ESF Annexes.

NRF-CIA actions that the Federal Government takes in response to a catastrophic incident include:

*   For no-notice or short-notice catastrophic events resulting in little or no time to assess the requirements of the State, tribal, and local governments, all Federal departments and agencies initiate actions to mobilize and deploy resources by scenario type as planned for in the NRF-CIS.

*   For those potential catastrophic incidents where there is time to coordinate with State, tribal, and local governments, as well as private-sector and NGO authorities, Federal departments and agencies will pre-deploy appropriately tailored elements specified in the NRF-CIS, as well as other Federal resources as required to meet the anticipated demands of the specific incident scenario.

*   For no-notice/short-notice catastrophic events when there is little or no time to assess the requirements of the State, tribal, and local governments, Federal departments and agencies initiate actions to mobilize and deploy resources by scenario type as planned for in the NRF-CIS. To that end, the Department of Defense (DOD) is prepared to provide capabilities in the following support categories: aviation, communication, defense coordinating officer/defense coordinating element, medical treatment, patient evacuation, decontamination, and logistics.

All Federal departments and agencies and organizations assigned primary or supporting ESF responsibilities immediately begin implementation of those responsibilities, as appropriate or when directed by the President.

Incident-specific resources and capabilities (e.g., medical teams, search and rescue teams, equipment, transportable shelters, preventive and therapeutic pharmaceutical caches, etc.) are activated and prepared for deployment to an NLSA near the incident site. The development of site-specific catastrophic incident response strategies (as detailed in the NRF-CIS) that include the preidentification of incident-specific critical resource requirements and corresponding deployment/employment strategies accelerate the timely provision of critical capabilities.

Regional Federal facilities are activated and prepared to receive and treat casualties from the incident area. Federal facilities are directed to reprioritize services (in some cases possibly reducing or postponing certain customary services) until life-saving activities are concluded. The development of site-specific catastrophic incident response plans that include the preidentification of projected casualty and mass care support requirements and potentially available facilities expands the response architecture and accelerates the availability of such resources.

Supplementary support agreements with NGOs and the private sector are activated. Given the projected high demand for Federal support, as well as the potential national security implications of a catastrophic incident, Federal departments and agencies may be asked to redirect efforts from their day-to-day responsibilities to support the response effort....

NOTES AND QUESTIONS

1. The NRF-CIA continues to emphasize that the Annex is primarily for "no-notice or short-notice events." Does that language make it less likely that the Annex will be invoked in events such as major predicted hurricanes, even if the hurricane has catastrophic effects? Or is it likely that Katrina sufficiently impressed on federal leaders the importance of invoking the Annex?

2. The NRF-CIA, like the NRP-CIA, establishes an alternative "push" system for catastrophic incidents, identifying the conditions under which federal emergency response may proactively deploy resources to mobilization centers close to disaster areas, in contrast to the traditional "pull" system in which federal officials await requests from state or local officials. It also prescribes expedited and streamlined protocols for performing Emergency Support Functions. How can the government know *ex ante* which events should be handled with the default "pull" system and which events qualify for the NRF-CIA's "push" treatment? Compounding the difficulty is the way in which hurricanes, earthquakes, and other natural disasters follow a right-skewed distribution characteristic of complex systems rather than the usual

Gaussian ("bell curve") distribution. *See generally* Daniel A. Farber, *Probabilities Behaving Badly: Complexity Theory and Environmental Uncertainty*, 37 U.C. Davis L. Rev. 145 (2003).

3. Recall that after Katrina, when Secretary Chertoff did not invoke the NRP-CIA to provide clear authority for pushing resources into affected areas, the "pull" system nonetheless evolved into a "push" system over a number of days because of individual decisions of FEMA personnel on the ground. A similar evolution had occurred after Hurricane Iniki in Hawaii. The House Final Report on Katrina concluded:

> [The efforts behind] the switch to a push response [illustrate] important principles of effective emergency management. First, they demonstrate the importance of having qualified and experienced professionals in charge of operations. Second, these officials need to have the authority to commit resources as they see fit without waiting to seek approval from above. And, third, federal officials need to have good working relationships with their state counterparts....

U.S. House of Representatives, A Failure of Initiative, Final Report of the Select Bipartisan Committee to Investigate the Preparation for and Response to Hurricane Katrina 138-139 (2006) [hereinafter House Katrina Report]. Does this analysis suggest that disaster planning should not be so detailed and specific that it precludes experienced emergency management personnel on the ground from making informed choices about what measures the particular situation demands?

4. The ad hoc evolution of the push system (in the absence of clear legal authority, let alone coordinated direction from a hierarchical command structure) epitomizes "emergent" behavior, as identified by complexity theory, in which uncoordinated actors following small-scale rules generate systemic effects transcending any one actor's local conduct. *See* John H. Holland, Emergence: From Chaos to Order (1998); Steven Johnson, Emergence: The Connected Lives of Ants, Brains, Cities, and Software (2001). Does the ability of on-site officials to make quick judgments, informed by firsthand observations not available to faraway supervisors, have greater potential to engender good outcomes in emergencies than coordination decisions by higher level officials?

5. To what extent can we truly plan for large-scale, unprecedented, catastrophic disasters? One scholar suggests that we should be skeptical of claims that advance planning for large disasters is too difficult and that disaster decision makers therefore need broad discretion to make ad hoc policy determinations. *See* David A. Super, *Against Flexibility*, 96 Cornell L. Rev. 1375, 1428 (2011) (arguing that while disasters "would seem to present the perfect case for postponing decisions" because "information about the . . . disaster are extremely valuable decisional inputs" that are not available in

advance, in fact "[d]isasters shrink our decisional resources while generating a host of new decisions we must make" and thus discretion can result in paralysis, delays, and poorly considered choices). Disaster sociologist Lee Clarke is less sanguine about the ability of advance planning to deal with unprecedented catastrophes and suggests that one function of planning for disasters such as large oil spills on open seas or nuclear meltdowns that affect large numbers of people is symbolic: "[S]ymbolic plans, [or] fantasy documents, are rhetorical instruments that have political utility in reducing uncertainty for organizations and experts." Lee Clarke, Mission Improbable 13 (1999). What are the benefits and risks of constructing disaster response plans that are largely rhetorical tools?

6. The definition of "catastrophic incident" in the 2006 Post-Katrina Act quoted at the beginning of this section is virtually identical to that then in use in both the NRP and the NRP-CIA. It is unclear why Congress felt it necessary to include this definition at all, although the Act does direct FEMA to make specific provision for catastrophic incidents when undertaking certain preparedness functions, including establishing adequate Surge Capacity Force to deal with catastrophic incidents, *see* Pub. L. No. 109-295, §624(a)(1), codified at 6 U.S.C. §711(a)(1), and training regional office Strike Teams to respond to catastrophic disasters, *see* Pub. L. No. 109-295, §507(f)(5), codified at 6 U.S.C. §317(f)(5). *See also* Mitchell Moss et al., *The Stafford Act and Priorities for Reform*, 6 J. Homeland Security & Emergency Mgmt. 8-9 (2009) (arguing that this definition of catastrophic incident should have been integrated into the Stafford Act, rather than simply included in new sections of law dealing with national emergency management). Rather than just providing a definition, should Congress have added a "catastrophic incident" level to the Stafford Act? *See id.* If a catastrophic incident level were added to the Act, should Congress also add new powers or procedures that would be triggered by declaration of a catastrophic event? The Stafford Act gives the president authority to deploy federal resources without further congressional action. Are catastrophic events so outside the norm that Congress cannot realistically decide in advance what additional resources ought to be committed, such that post hoc, event-specific legislation—rather than a Stafford Act amendment—is required?

7. If another catastrophic hurricane were to strike the Gulf coast today, would the new NRF function better than the NRP did during Katrina? The current NRF, like the NRP, calls specifically for proactive response to catastrophic incidents: "Prior to and during catastrophic incidents, especially those that occur with little or no notice, the Federal governments may mobilize and deploy assets in anticipation of a formal request from the state." NRF at 29. These proactive measures would be taken for "catastrophic events involving chemical, biological, radiological, nuclear, or high-yield explosive weapons of mass destruction; large-magnitude earthquakes; or other incidents

affecting heavily populated areas" and would be coordinated with state and local governments "when possible." *Id.*

8. In all disasters, but particularly catastrophic disasters, the need for quick and efficient disaster response may be in tension with other preexisting policies, particularly environmental regulations. For example, after Superstorm Sandy, a federal contractor and others burned debris in open pits. *See* Sierra Club, *Clean Air Victory*, Feb. 20, 2013, http://nyc.sierraclub .org/clean-air-victory/. Likewise, after Katrina, toxic water that had accumulated in New Orleans was pumped into Lake Pontchartrain. Julia C. Webb, *Responsible Response: Do the Emergency and Major Disaster Exceptions to Federal Environmental Laws Make Sense from a Restoration and Mitigation Perspective?*, 31 Wm. & Mary Envtl. L. & Pol'y Rev. 529, 544 (2007). Should categorical exemptions from federal environmental laws be granted for disaster response or is a more ad-hoc approach preferable? *See, e.g., id.*; Michael B. Gerrard, *Disasters First: Rethinking Environmental Law After September 11*, 9 Widener L. Symp. J. 223, 230 (2003) (cataloguing emergency exemptions in a wide variety of environmental statutes).

C. STATE, LOCAL, AND REGIONAL EMERGENCY RESPONSE

Notwithstanding the elaborate legal structures of the Stafford Act, the Homeland Security Act, PPD-8, and the National Response Framework, emergency response for both routine and catastrophic disasters remains in the first instance a state and local government responsibility. For example, although the federal response to Katrina attracted intense scrutiny in the popular press and by the federal government itself, much of the success or failure of the response to Katrina hinged on the actions—and omissions—of state and local officials such as Louisiana Governor Kathleen Blanco and New Orleans Mayor Ray Nagin. This section turns to state and regional emergency response authority. After considering some of the many challenges of state and local disaster response, we will examine a representative state emergency management statute and then the interstate Emergency Management Assistance Compact (EMAC), which won praise for its effectiveness in delivering relief during Katrina.

1. STATE AND LOCAL EMERGENCY RESPONSE

States have broad authority to respond to disasters. Indeed, "[t]he authority of state and local elected officials to act under a state's police powers is at its apex during a disaster." Ernest B. Abbott, Otto J. Hetzel & Alan D. Cohn, *State, Local, and First Responder Issues, in* American Bar Association, Hurricane Katrina Task Force Subcommittee Report 14 (Feb. 2006). State law generally vests governors and other state and local officials with "broad discretion . . . to take actions deemed necessary to reduce imminent threats to life, property, and public health and safety" and grants "extraordinary powers, upon declaration of a state of emergency, to commandeer resources, control property, order evacuations, suspend laws and administrative requirements, and take other measures necessary to respond to the emergency." *Id.* This section explores some of the disaster response challenges that state and local officials often confront and examines one state's attempt to codify state and local emergency powers.

a. Planning and Coordination

Although state power to respond to disasters is broader than federal authority, like their federal counterparts, state officials confront many difficulties in coordinating response—deciding who will take what response actions when—and likewise confront important questions about the extent to which those difficulties can be managed by legal structures put in place before a disaster occurs. Some experts have suggested that any evaluation of state disaster response capacity should be guided by four central questions focused on this disaster authority: "[H]ow did the state *express or clarify* its authority through statutes or executive orders; how was that authority *implemented* through plans, procedures, and protocols; in what manner did the state *execute* that authority during incidents; and how did the state *delegate* its authority to local units of government?" *Id.*

Many of the issues that plague the coordination of federal relief efforts with state-level efforts reappear in the coordination of statewide relief with local governments. Others, such as the Posse Comitatus Act's attempt to resolve the inherent tension between military and civilian authority, are noticeably absent in the relationship between state governments and their subdivisions. Some of the common issues involve questions of governmental structure. Additionally, questions of finance and competence are even more salient at the state level than they are in the relationship between the federal government and the states. Apart from granting money to local governments and conducting extensive training for local officials, which most states would gladly do if only they had unlimited resources, what concrete measures can states take to coordinate emergency response efforts with their constituent localities?

Just as in federal/state relationships, overlapping authority and confusion about lines of authority within a state can potentially hinder both disaster response and accountability. For example, on Friday, August 26, 2005, three days before Hurricane Katrina made landfall, Louisiana Governor Kathleen Blanco declared a state of emergency. *See id.* That declaration triggered the Governor's authority under the Louisiana Disaster Act to order the evacuation of any threatened area, but Louisiana's Hurricane Evacuation and Sheltering Plan ("Evacuation Plan") assigned each parish, rather than the state, the power to decide whether to order a voluntary or mandatory evacuation. *See id.* Under the plan, the state was to "play[] only a supporting and consulting role, aside from the implementation of the contra-flow plan," *id.* at 16, which would speed evacuation by altering traffic flow on highways so that travel in all lanes would be in the direction of the evacuation. State police implemented contra-flow on highways leading out of New Orleans on Saturday, August 27, but New Orleans Mayor Ray Nagin did not order evacuation until Sunday, August 28, shortly before Katrina made landfall on Monday morning. *See id.* After Katrina, the Louisiana legislature clarified the concurrent authority of parish presidents and the governor to order evacuation, providing that "[the governor] may order a forced evacuation order for one or more parishes or parts thereof if a forced evacuation is not issued by the parish president." Act effective June 16, 2008, No. 214, sec. 1, §730.3, 2008 La. Sess. Law Serv. (West) (codified as amended at La. Rev. Stat. §29:730.3 (2009)). Will this change help Louisiana deal with future hurricanes, or is the real problem failure to utilize existing authority?

b. Resource Allocation and Compensation

Questions of resource allocation likewise loom large for state and local officials responding to disaster. Yet failure to plan for how particular authority will be exercised during disasters can mean that state officials fail to tap available resources. For example, Louisiana law clearly granted the governor and parish presidents authority to commandeer unused school buses (and even private buses) to aid in evacuation of residents who lacked transportation, and the failure to use this authority left many New Orleanians stranded and unable to comply with evacuation orders. *See* Abbott et al., *supra,* at 16. After Hurricane Katrina, the Louisiana legislature directed the state to promulgate regulations to guide local governments in utilizing all available transportation resources. *See* Act of Feb. 23, 2006, No. 36, Sec. 1, §726, 2006 La. Sess. Law Serv. (West) (codified as amended at La. Rev. Stat. §29:726(E)(17) (2009)). The legislature emphasized that school and city buses, as well as government and other relief vehicles, should be used with special consideration for the elderly, the infirm, tourists, those without personal transportation, and those that refuse to leave. *See* Abbott et al., *supra.*

Beyond the challenge of channeling available resources where they are most needed, another important question for public officials is when private individuals will be compensated for resources government officials either seize to use in disaster response or destroy in the course of response efforts. Despite the Fifth Amendment's compensation requirement, in some circumstances, the tort law doctrine of public necessity "absolves the State . . . of liability for the destruction of 'real and personal property, in cases of actual necessity, to prevent the spreading of a fire' or to forestall other grave threats to the lives and property of others." Lucas v. South Carolina Coastal Council, 505 U.S. 1003, 1029 n.16 (1992). When should the government be able to escape liability for destruction or use of private property in disaster response? For an argument that the doctrine of public necessity should be abolished, see Susan S. Kuo,

Disaster Tradeoffs: The Doubtful Case for Public Necessity, 54 B.C. L. Rev. 127 (2013).

c. Evacuation: Logistics and Vulnerable Populations

All evacuations pose major logistical challenges, and these difficulties are magnified for densely populated cities threatened by potentially devastating, but also uncertain, disasters. On Sunday, August 28, 2005, Mayor Ray Nagin issued the first mandatory evacuation in the history of New Orleans. Aided by contraflow (the practice of converting all highway lanes outbound) more than a million people evacuated southeastern Louisiana within 24 hours. Nearly 100,000 New Orleanians, however, remained in the city. Though some residents sought refuge at "shelters of last resort"—the Louisiana Superdome, the Convention Center, and the I-10 "cloverleaf"—others rode out the storm at home. *See* Senate Katrina Report, *supra*, at 1-4 to 1-5, 16-1 to 16-14.

Why did so many New Orleanians play "hurricane roulette"? One study identified many factors that affect individual evacuation decisions, including the severity of the storm, the existence of evacuation orders, the absence of a clear evacuation destination, confidence in rescue, and experience with prior storms, among others. Daniel R. Petrolia, et al., *Why Don't Coastal Residents Choose to Evacuate for Hurricanes?* 38 Coastal Management 97, 110 (2010). Many of these factors were evident in New Orleans. Snarled traffic associated with previous evacuations evidently persuaded some residents to stay, as did the experience of surviving earlier storms (particularly Camille, a Category 5 hurricane that struck the Gulf Coast in 1969). It also appears that many residents of New Orleans refused to evacuate because they did not want to abandon their pets. See discussion *supra*, Chapter 3, Section C.1.b., note 3. The timing of evacuation orders has also been blamed for some residents' failure to evacuate. Parishes did not begin to issue orders until the morning of August 27, 2005, and this notice proved insufficient for many. Moreover, many of the initial evacuation orders were recommended rather than mandatory, contributing to residents' inaccurate perception of the storm's severity. Beyond those choosing to stay, many residents did so out of necessity. Poor residents lacked cars to leave. They did not have the estimated $1,000 needed to shelter a family of four or, alternatively, a meaningful social network outside the city upon which they could rely for temporary shelter. Many even lacked access to information about the severity of the impending storm. City, state, and federal officials failed to coordinate bus evacuations until after the storm had struck and the levees had been breached. Ultimately, the poorest residents of the city had no choice. Others were likewise impaired due to age or infirmity. Evacuating prisoners also became a problem, and many were forced to ride out the storm.

Asking why people fail to evacuate invites discussion of whether the government's policies adequately address those motivations. Should the government focus on coercion, facilitation, or some combination of the two? Does serving one goal detract from the other? A focus on coercion inspires more aggressive enforcement tactics, such as forcible removal, civil penalties, or criminal liability. Moreover, a focus on coercion reflects certain assumptions about evacuation behavior, namely, that the primary factor impeding evacuation is choice. On the other hand, a focus on facilitation shifts the focus from changing people's minds to changing people's options. Indeed, such a focus assumes that the primary impediment to evacuation is not choice, but capacity. Of course, it is hard to imagine a state government that does not endeavor to both persuade and provide for its citizens in times of crisis. Undoubtedly, any given area has both stubborn residents needing coercion and vulnerable residents needing assistance. The question then becomes, what is the appropriate balance? How effective can any evacuation order be, at any level of government, if it is not backed by (1) some measure of coercion for those who might otherwise risk staying and (2) transportation or other provisions for those who lack the means to evacuate themselves?

What measures, then, should states take to enforce mandatory evacuations? Should police attempt to impress on evacuation resisters the gravity of the situation by asking them to provide next-of-kin information or write their social security numbers on their arms for possible identification purposes? Should those who ignore evacuation orders face monetary penalties or criminal prosecution? *See, e.g.*, N.C. Stat. §166A-19.62. (imposing civil liability for the cost of rescue on a person who willfully ignores a disaster-related warning about personal safety); Utah Crim. Code §76-8-317 (making failure to obey an evacuation order a class B misdemeanor, punishable by up to six months in jail and a fine of up to $1,000). In light of the disparities among residents' ability to comply, what risks arise when the government penalizes those remaining behind? On a related note, where the state imposes criminal penalties, should law enforcement rely on the statute to assert probable cause and forcibly remove noncompliant residents? Texas law gives law enforcement the right to use reasonable force to remove such residents. Tex. Gov't Code Ann. §418.185(b). In contrast, Louisiana has taken a hands-off approach to noncompliant residents after Katrina, explicitly providing that a "person who refuses to comply with a mandatory evacuation order may remain in his home and not be forcibly removed." La. Rev. Stat. Ann. §29:730.3. However, storm riders surrender the right to be rescued or receive other lifesaving assistance. *Id.*

When residents refuse to leave their homes, should they forfeit the right to be rescued? Social science has revealed the injustice and illogic of blaming victims for their plights. Yet one study that polled both rescue workers and laypeople found that respondents overwhelmingly described those failing to evacuate as "passive (e.g., lazy, dependent), irresponsible (e.g., careless, negligent), and inflexible (e.g., stubborn, uncompromising)." Nicole M. Stephens, et al., *Why Did They "Choose" to Stay? Perspectives of Hurricane Katrina Observers and Survivors*, 20 Ass'n Psychol. Sci. 878, 880 (2009). To what extent might this perception affect policy makers' calculus about the proper balance of coercion versus facilitation?

In addition to enforcement mechanisms, what measures should states take to provide for their citizens? What steps should be taken to ensure that vulnerable populations are not left behind? How should officials decide whether and when to evacuate hospitals and care facilities, given that evacuation poses its own risks to vulnerable patients? How should officials prioritize different types of facilities (hospitals, nursing homes, schools) for evacuation (or other response measures) and should those priorities be established and codified in advance?

d. Risk Communication and Warnings

Evacuation orders and other official warnings issued before and during disasters require public officials to decide how, when, and what information to communicate to the public. Some of the many challenges of risk communication are explored more fully in Chapter 6. What factors should influence official decisions about how and when to share disaster information with the public? *See, e.g.*, Lisa G. Sun & RonNell A. Jones, *Disaggregating Disasters*, 60 U.C.L.A. L. Rev. 884 (2013) (exploring the advantages of transparency during disasters). Should officials have a tort duty to warn or a duty to share material information with the public during disasters? *Cf. id.* 898 n.74 (recounting how "[s]even members of Italy's prestigious National Commission for the Forecast and Prevention of Major Risks" were convicted of manslaughter "for allegedly giving false reassurances to the public about swarm earthquake activity a week before L'Aquila's devastating 6.3 magnitude earthquake claimed more than three hundred lives"). If precursors to major earthquakes can eventually be identified, *see* Emily E. Brodsky & Thorne Lay, *Recognizing Foreshocks from the 1 April 2014 Chile Earthquake*, 344 Science 700 (May 16, 2014) (suggesting "that observable precursors may exist before large earthquakes"), should government have a duty to monitor and warn the public when earthquake activity is likely? What level of risk would trigger an official duty to warn?

e. Public Health and Balancing Individual Rights

One area in which state disaster laws have undergone significant revision in recent years is public health authority to respond to pandemics. After the 2001 anthrax attacks in the United States, many public health experts were concerned that state health laws were antiquated and inadequate for potential modern public health emergencies, including pandemics and bioterrorism. In late 2001, legal experts at the Center for Law and the Public's Health at Georgetown and Johns Hopkins universities drafted the Model State Emergency Health Powers Act (MSEHPA). The Center for Law and the Public's Health, The Model State Emergency Health Powers Act (2001), available at http://www.publichealthlaw.net/ModelLaws/MSEHPA.php (June 22, 2009).

MSEHPA addresses planning for public health emergencies; surveillance, and reporting measures (to detect and track public health emergencies);

management of public and private property (including establishing decontamination facilities, acquiring medical supplies, and using private property for quarantine); power over persons (including power to vaccinate, test, treat, isolate, and quarantine individuals); liability of government and private medical workers during public health emergencies; and public communication. Under MSEHPA, during a "public health emergency" declared by the state governor, public health authorities can issue mandatory isolation orders (for infected individuals) and mandatory quarantine orders (for exposed individuals), violation of which constitutes a misdemeanor. *Id.* §604(a). Although individuals may refuse vaccination, testing, or treatment, those who do are subject to involuntary isolation or quarantine. *See id.* §§601-604. MSEHPA does provide some due process protections before quarantine or isolation (including a court order), although most pre-quarantine/pre-isolation procedures may be suspended where immediate action is needed to protect the public health. *See id.* §605. Other controversial provisions allow public health authorities to condition a health worker's continuing license to practice medicine on rendering of requested aid during the public health emergency, *see id.* §608, and limit state (and most private) liability to "gross negligence or willful misconduct," *see id.* §804.

In 2003, representatives from five states and numerous public health experts, organizations, and agencies, collaborated to produce the more comprehensive Turning Point Model State Public Health Act (MSPHA), which includes some provisions from the MSEHPA. The MSPHA provides for compulsory testing, treatment, and vaccination under certain circumstances, *see* MSPHA §§5-106 to 5-107, 5-109, and, like the MSEHPA, provides for temporary quarantine and isolation before a court hearing is held, if delay would jeopardize the public health, *see id.* §5-108[d]. It also sets standards for quarantine and isolation (including using the least restrictive means necessary to prevent spread of disease and requiring competent medical care for those detained). The full text of the MSPHA is available at http://www.hss.state .ak.us/dph/improving/turningpoint/ MSPHA.htm (June 22, 2009).

Overall, James Hodge, executive director of the Center for Law and the Public's Health, reports that more than half of the states have adopted some version of one of the two model laws. *See* Debra Cassens Weiss, *Will Swine Flu Merit Quarantines? If So, New Laws Give States Authority*, ABA Journal, Apr. 27, 2009, available at http://www.abajournal.com/mobile/article/will_swine_ flu_merit_quarantines_if_so_new_laws_give_states_authority/Swine%20Flu%2 0Fear%20Prompts%20Some%20Changes%20in%20Law%20Firm%20Protocol(M ay 7, 2014). For a detailed cataloguing of state isolation and quarantine laws, see http://www.ncsl.org/research/health/state-quarantine-and-isolation-statutes.aspx (May 14, 2014). Despite this widespread enactment of at least portions of these statutes, the Model Acts have "become a lightning rod for criticism from both ends of the political spectrum" regarding the balance struck between personal rights and the public good. Lawrence O. Gostin, *The Model*

State Emergency Health Powers Act: Public Health and Civil Liberties in a Time of Terrorism, 13 Health Matrix 3, 6 (2003) (*citing* Ronald Bayer & James Colgrove, Public Health vs. Civil Liberties, 297 Science 1811, 1811 (2002) (relating the critical response to the MSEHPA raised by AIDS advocates, physicians, hospitals, antivaccination advocates, privacy advocates, and civil liberties advocates). For a review of these concerns, see, for example, Sue Blevins, *The Model State Emergency Health Powers Act: An Assault on Civil Liberties in the Name of Homeland Security*, Heritage Found. Lecture 748 (2002), available athttp://www.heritage.org/research/lecture/the-model-state-emergency-health-powers-act; George J. Annas, *Bioterrorism, Public Health, and Civil Liberties*, 346 New Eng. J. Med. 1337 (2002), available at http://www.nejm.org/doi/full/10.1056/NEJM20020425 3461722. Furthermore, some critics of the Model Acts suggest the Acts add layers of administrative "red tape" in an already over-legislated and confusing arena. *See, e.g.*, Edward P. Richards &Katharine C. Rathbun, *Legislative Alternatives to the Model State Emergency Health Powers Act (MSEHPA)*,LSU Program in Law, Science, and Public Health White Paper #2 (April 21, 2003), available at http://biotech.law.lsu.edu/blaw/bt/ MSEHPA_review.htm.

   To what extent does due process constrain a state's ability to force treatment or isolate or quarantine individuals during a pandemic or other public health emergency? *See* George J. Annas, *Blinded by Bioterrorism: Public Health and Liberty in the 21st Century*, 13 Health Matrix 33, 58 (2003) (criticizing MSEHPA for allowing a person to be quarantined on the basis of a "written directive by a public health official" for fifteen days before a hearing is required and allowing group rather than individual quarantine hearings). In 1905, the Supreme Court upheld a Massachusetts statute that permitted local boards of health to require compulsory vaccination—on pain of a $5 fine—when they deemed it "necessary for the public health or safety." Jacobson v. Massachusetts, 197 U.S. 11, 12, 27 (1905). Is this holding undermined by more recent substantive due process cases establishing a right to privacy and suggesting a right to refuse medical treatment? *See, e.g.*, Cruzan v. Missouri Dep't of Health, 497 U.S. 261 (1990) (stating, in dicta, that "[t]he principle that a competent person has a constitutionally protected liberty interest in refusing unwanted medical treatment may be inferred from our prior decisions"). In any event, are compulsory measures likely to be effective, or can quarantine succeed only if most people willingly comply?

   State laws creating public health authority triggered by the governor's declaration of a "public health emergency" often overlap with more general state emergency management laws, most of which are triggered by a governor's declaration of a "disaster" or a "general emergency," in accordance with statutory definitions and procedures. Every state currently has a law authorizing the declaration of a "general emergency," a "disaster," or both. *See* James G. Hodge, Jr. & Evan D. Anderson, *Principles and Practice of Legal Triage during Public Health Emergencies*, 64 N.Y.U. Ann. Surv. Am. L. 249, 264 (2008). The declaration typically triggers extraordinary powers vested in the state's governor. Consider the Texas version of a state emergency management law.

TEXAS DISASTER ACT OF 1975

codified at Texas Gov Code Section 418

Sec. 418.004. DEFINITIONS. In this chapter:

> (1) "Disaster" means the occurrence or imminent threat of widespread or severe damage, injury, or loss of life or property resulting from any natural or man-made cause, including fire, flood, earthquake, wind, storm, wave action, oil spill or other water contamination, volcanic activity, epidemic, air contamination, blight, drought, infestation, explosion, riot, hostile military or paramilitary action, extreme heat, other public calamity requiring emergency action, or energy emergency.

...

Subchapter B. Powers and Duties of Governor

Sec. 418.011. RESPONSIBILITY OF GOVERNOR. The governor is responsible for meeting:
> (1) the dangers to the state and people presented by disasters;
and
> (2) disruptions to the state and people caused by energy emergencies.

Sec. 418.012. EXECUTIVE ORDERS. Under this chapter, the governor may issue executive orders, proclamations, and regulations and amend or rescind them. Executive orders, proclamations, and regulations have the force and effect of law.

Sec. 418.013. EMERGENCY MANAGEMENT COUNCIL. (a) The governor by executive order may establish an emergency management council to advise and assist the governor in all matters relating to disaster mitigation, preparedness, response, and recovery....

Sec. 418.014. DECLARATION OF STATE OF DISASTER. (a) The governor by executive order or proclamation may declare a state of disaster if the governor finds a disaster has occurred or that the occurrence or threat of disaster is imminent.
> (b) Except as provided by Subsection (c), the state of disaster continues until the governor:

(1) finds that:

    (A) the threat or danger has passed; or

    (B) the disaster has been dealt with to the extent that emergency conditions no longer exist; and

(2) terminates the state of disaster by executive order.

(c) A state of disaster may not continue for more than 30 days unless renewed by the governor. The legislature by law may terminate a state of disaster at any time. On termination by the legislature, the governor shall issue an executive order ending the state of disaster.

(d) An executive order or proclamation issued under this section must include:

(1) a description of the nature of the disaster;

(2) a designation of the area threatened; and

(3) a description of the conditions that have brought the state of disaster about or made possible the termination of the state of disaster.

(e) An executive order or proclamation shall be disseminated promptly by means intended to bring its contents to the attention of the general public. An order or proclamation shall be filed promptly with the division [of emergency management], the secretary of state, and the county clerk or city secretary in each area to which it applies unless the circumstances attendant on the disaster prevent or impede the filing.

Sec. 418.015. EFFECT OF DISASTER DECLARATION. (a) An executive order or proclamation declaring a state of disaster:

(1) activates the disaster recovery and rehabilitation aspects of the state emergency management plan applicable to the area subject to the declaration; and

(2) authorizes the deployment and use of any forces to which the plan applies and the use or distribution of any supplies, equipment, and materials or facilities assembled, stockpiled, or arranged to be made available under this chapter or other law relating to disasters.

(b) The preparedness and response aspects of the state emergency management plan are activated as provided by that plan.

(c) During a state of disaster and the following recovery period, the governor is the commander in chief of state agencies, boards, and commissions having emergency responsibilities. To the greatest extent possible, the governor shall delegate or assign command authority by prior arrangement embodied in appropriate executive orders or plans, but this chapter does not restrict the governor's authority to do so by orders issued at the time of the disaster.

Sec. 418.016. SUSPENSION OF CERTAIN LAWS AND RULES. (a) The governor may suspend the provisions of any regulatory statute prescribing the procedures for conduct of state business or the orders or rules of a state agency if strict compliance with the provisions, orders, or rules would in any way prevent, hinder, or delay necessary action in coping with a disaster. . . .

Sec. 418.017. USE OF PUBLIC AND PRIVATE RESOURCES. (a) The governor may use all available resources of state government and of political subdivisions that are reasonably necessary to cope with a disaster.

(b) The governor may temporarily reassign resources, personnel, or functions of state executive departments and agencies or their units for the purpose of performing or facilitating emergency services.

(c) The governor may commandeer or use any private property if the governor finds it necessary to cope with a disaster, subject to the compensation requirements of this chapter.

Sec. 418.018. MOVEMENT OF PEOPLE. (a) The governor may recommend the evacuation of all or part of the population from a stricken or threatened area in the state if the governor considers the action necessary for the preservation of life or other disaster mitigation, response, or recovery.

(b) The governor may prescribe routes, modes of transportation, and destinations in connection with an evacuation.

(c) The governor may control ingress and egress to and from a disaster area and the movement of persons and the occupancy of premises in the area.

Sec. 418.019. RESTRICTED SALE AND TRANSPORTATION OF MATERIALS. The governor may suspend or limit the sale, dispensing, or transportation of alcoholic beverages, firearms, explosives, and combustibles.
. . .

Sec. 418.020. TEMPORARY HOUSING AND EMERGENCY SHELTER. (a) The governor may enter into purchase, lease, or other arrangements with an agency of the United States for temporary housing units to be occupied by disaster victims and may make units available to any political subdivision....

(c) Under regulations prescribed by the governor, the governor may temporarily suspend or modify for a period of not more than 60 days any public health, safety, zoning, intrastate transportation, or other law or regulation if by proclamation the governor considers the suspension or modification essential to provide temporary housing or emergency shelter for disaster victims....

Sec. 418.021. FEDERAL AID FOR LOCAL GOVERNMENT. (a) On the governor's determination that a local government of the state has suffered or will suffer a substantial loss of tax and other revenue from a major disaster and has demonstrated a need for financial assistance to perform its governmental functions, the governor may apply to the federal government on behalf of the local government for a loan and may receive and disburse the proceeds of an approved loan to the local government....

Sec. 418.022. AID FOR INDIVIDUALS. (a) On the governor's determination that financial assistance is essential to meet disaster-related necessary expenses or serious needs of individuals or families adversely affected by a major disaster that cannot be otherwise adequately met from other means of assistance, the governor may accept a grant by the federal government to fund the financial assistance, subject to the terms and conditions imposed on the grant. The governor may agree with the federal government or any officer or agency of the United States pledging the state to participate in funding not more than 25 percent of the financial assistance.

(b) The governor may make financial grants to meet disaster-related necessary expenses or serious needs of individuals or families adversely affected by a major disaster that cannot otherwise adequately be met from other means of assistance. The grants may not exceed an aggregate amount in excess of that established by federal statute for an individual or family in any single major disaster declared by the president of the United States.

(c) The governor may designate in the state emergency management plan the Department of Human Services or another state agency to carry out the functions of providing financial aid to individuals or families qualified for disaster relief. The designated agency may employ temporary personnel for those functions to be paid from funds appropriated to the agency, from federal funds, or from the disaster contingency fund. The merit system does not apply to the temporary positions. The governor may allocate funds appropriated under this chapter to implement the purposes of this chapter.

Sec. 418.023. CLEARANCE OF DEBRIS. (a) Through the use of any state agency or instrumentality, the governor, acting through members of the Emergency Management Council, may clear or remove debris or wreckage from public or private land or water if it threatens public health or safety or public or private property in a state of disaster declared by the governor or major disaster declared by the president of the United States.

(b) The governor may accept funds from the federal government and use the funds to make grants to a local government for the purpose of removing debris or wreckage from public or private land or water.

(c) Debris or wreckage may not be removed from public or private property until the affected local government, corporation, organization, or individual presents to the governor or member of the Emergency Management Council an unconditional authorization for removal. Debris or wreckage may not be removed from private property until the state is indemnified against any claim arising from removal. In instances where it is not practical and further delay would create a greater risk to public health or safety, the governor, acting through the Emergency Management Council, may remove debris or wreckage from public or private property without an unconditional authorization or indemnification.

(d) If the governor provides for clearance of debris or wreckage under this chapter, state employees or other individuals acting by authority of the governor may enter on private land or water to perform tasks necessary to the removal or clearance operation. Except in cases of wilful misconduct, gross negligence, or bad faith, a state employee or agent performing his duties while complying with orders of the governor issued under this chapter is not liable for the death of or injury to a person or for damage to property....

NOTES AND QUESTIONS

1. How does the Texas definition of a "disaster" differ from the Stafford Act's definition of "major disaster"? Does having a different trigger for state and federal emergency powers create confusion or is a natural consequence of differing state and federal roles? Why might Texas have chosen its definition?
2. Does this statute give the Texas governor sufficient powers to respond to disasters? Given that the governor is charged with protecting Texas citizens from disaster-related danger, should he have the power to mandate evacuation, rather than simply recommend evacuation?
3. How should the governor determine whether (and how) to exercise his authority to recommend evacuation and restrict access to the affected area?
4. Are there adequate legislative checks on the governor's exercise of disaster-triggered powers? What role, if any, should the state legislature play in the immediate aftermath of a major disaster?

2. REGIONAL EMERGENCY RESPONSE

The structure of federal disaster relief suggests that, for most non-catastrophic events, affected communities should rely initially on state and local resources. It follows that some emergencies, even those affecting more than one state, may not warrant full federal involvement. In the antiterrorism context, the Justice Department has fostered multijurisdictional partnerships for meeting regional threats. *See generally* Department of Justice, Bureau of Justice Assistance, Mutual Aid: Multijurisdictional Partnerships for Meeting Regional Threats (September 2005). Even in circumstances meriting aggressive federal intervention, interstate cooperation can supplement federal aid. The Emergency Management Assistance Compact (EMAC), an interstate compact ratified by Congress in 1996, provides the framework for mutual cooperation.

Please read the text of EMAC, which is available at the EMAC website: http://www.emacweb.org/index.php/learnaboutemac/emac-legislation

NOTES AND QUESTIONS

1. Mutual aid as a tool for emergency management traces its origins to global instability in 1949, when President Truman responded to the Soviet Union's explosion of its first nuclear device and North Korea's invasion of South Korea by establishing the Federal Civil Defense Administration. In 1950, Congress passed the Federal Civil Defense Act, the Defense Production Act, and the Disaster Relief Act. (Only the Disaster Relief Act addressed both natural and military disasters.) In connection with these statutes, Congress also ratified the Civil Defense Compact of 1950.

   Nearly half a century later, EMAC became the first interstate compact since the Civil Defense Compact to facilitate interstate cooperation as a way to supplement federal emergency response. After Hurricane Andrew struck Florida in 1992, the Southern Governors' Association formed the Southern Regional Emergency Management Assistance Compact (SREMAC) in 1993. In 1995 the SREMAC opened membership to any state or territory that wished to join; one year later, Congress ratified the broadened agreement as EMAC.

2. All 50 states, the District of Columbia, Guam, Puerto Rico, and the U.S. Virgin Islands have passed the requisite legislation to become members of EMAC. The National Emergency Management Association has also drafted Model Intrastate Mutual Aid Legislation, based on the interstate compact, to facilitate mutual aid agreements between political subdivisions of a state. *See* http://www.emacweb.org/index.php/mutualaidresources/intrastate-mutual-aid/modellegislation (April 1, 2014).

3. Whether implemented on a regional or an intrastate basis, EMAC actively pursues a decentralized approach to emergency response. Does decentralization of response authority to states or to counties and municipalities supply a viable alternative to prevailing systems such as the Stafford Act and the NRF? Consider the performance of EMAC in the aftermath of Katrina:

U.S. House of Representatives, A Failure of Initiative

Final Report of the Select Bipartisan Committee to Investigate the Preparation for and Response to Hurricane Katrina 144-145 (2006)

Finding: Once activated, the Emergency Management Assistance Compact (EMAC) enabled an unprecedented level of mutual aid assistance to reach the disaster area in a timely and effective manner

EMAC provided invaluable interstate mutual aid in support of Hurricane Katrina by deploying more than 67,891 personnel (19,481 civilians and 48,477 National Guard) to Louisiana and Mississippi. EMAC facilitated mutual assistance from 48 states, the District of Columbia, the Virgin Islands and Puerto Rico.

In support of Hurricane Katrina, more than 2,188 resource requests (missions) were filled. Record numbers of National Guard troops, local responders, and health/medical personnel were deployed through the compact. EMAC also works in cooperation with the federal government by co-locating personnel, when requested, in the NRCC or Regional Response Coordination Center (RRCC) in order to share information on EMAC activities in the affected states, monitor the availability of needed resources being offered by assisting states, and facilitate overall emergency response and recovery activities.

Through state statute, EMAC addresses the legal issues of liability, workers compensation, reimbursement, and professional licensure—prior to a disaster or emergency when resource needs and timing are critical. State and territory members must pre-designate personnel with the authority to request and commit resources. Standard operating procedures exist for compact members and training and exercise of state personnel is required. While formalized protocols are in place, EMAC is designed to be adaptable and scaleable to meet the changing needs of each event.

Following each large scale activation of the compact, a review and evaluation of the response is conducted and standard operating procedures revised and updated to reflect lessons learned and best practices. For example, lessons learned from the 2004 Florida hurricanes led to an overhaul of some operational procedures related to mobilization and deployment of resources, an enhanced automation system to provide more accurate data and electronic tracking of resources, and a new standardized EMAC training curriculum and updated operations manual. These enhancements were either in progress or completed prior to Hurricane Katrina.

In Mississippi, EMAC assistance was considered a success. The assistance in Mississippi included help from other states' security agencies (such as their state police) as well as various states' National Guards (troops and hard assets)....Louisiana state officials also viewed EMAC assistance as very successful. One state official said there were almost 900 EMAC agreements for assistance. Although the EMAC response from surrounding states varied, state officials applauded EMAC for successfully getting law enforcement manpower assistance. According to state police officers Ralph Mitchell and Joseph Booth, Arkansas, Tennessee, New Jersey, and California all sent law enforcement officers through EMAC.

FEMA officials also noted the general success of EMAC. Because of the magnitude of the disaster, however, Louisiana was unable to handle all of the EMAC requests, requiring FEMA to become more involved in the process than normal. In particular, FCO Scott Wells noted some state offers of assistance through FEMA were rejected by Louisiana. He said these offers were rejected by SCO Smith because of concerns about the costs to the state.

NOTES AND QUESTIONS

1. Why did EMAC succeed where so many other response systems failed either partially or catastrophically? What distinguished EMAC, an interstate compact, from counterparts that covered either a smaller geographic footprint (local and state plans) or the entire United States (the NIMS and NRP)?

2. By the same token, EMAC did not perform flawlessly. Louisiana affirmatively rejected some offers of assistance from other states, evidently concerned that Louisiana would bear the eventual costs. Articles VIII and IX of EMAC, respectively, address "compensation" and "reimbursement." What is the distinction between these categories? Did EMAC offer Louisiana some alternative to refusing aid on grounds of cost? Article IX stipulates "that any aiding party state may assume in whole or in part such loss, damage, expense, or other cost, or may loan such equipment or donate such services to the receiving party state without charge or cost." It also provides "that any two or more party states may enter into supplementary agreements establishing a different allocation of costs among those states." "Compensation" under article VIII, however, may not be "reimbursable" under article IX.

3. Multijurisdictional emergency response systems, whether implemented through federal law (the Stafford Act and NRF) or through an interstate compact (such as EMAC) may be viewed as a form of insurance among participating governments. Increasing the geographic footprint of an emergency response system has the effect of deepening an insurance pool: It allows participants to spread risks across a deeper and therefore more stable source of financial resources. The simultaneous presence of federal response and EMAC can be analogized to the presence of multiple layers of insurance against risk that defies any single state's ability to manage.

4. Of course, the insurance analogy suggests a fundamental weakness of these arrangements within a country with persistent differences along two dimensions. First, states have predictably different risk profiles. For instance, states with seashores are more vulnerable to hurricanes and typhoons, whereas states near geologically active faults, such as the San Andreas and New Madrid faults, are more prone to earthquakes. Second, states also have different levels of income and wealth. Environmental and economic differences impair the management of federal response, EMAC, and other multijurisdictional emergency response systems. These schemes strongly resemble a health insurance system in which some beneficiaries are predictably poorer and sicker than others.

5. Reconsider article VII of EMAC:

> Inasmuch as it is probable that the pattern and detail of the machinery for mutual aid among two or more states may differ from that among the states

that are party hereto, this compact contains elements of a broad base common to all states, and nothing herein shall preclude any state entering into supplementary agreements with another state or affect any other agreements already in force between states.

Is this provision an adequate tool for overcoming persistent differences in the economic and risk profiles among states?

D. PRIVATE AND NONGOVERNMENTAL RESPONSE

1. PRIVATE ENTITIES

When the Mississippi River valley was inundated by massive flooding in 1927, the federal government response relied heavily on private-sector resources. Secretary of Commerce Herbert Hoover served as disaster czar, but the federal government supplied little else by way of muscle or materiel. As discussed in Chapter 2, nongovernmental actors remain crucial today, especially in restoring critical infrastructure and services after a disaster. *See* Lee M. Zeichner, *Private Sector Integration, in* American Bar Association, Hurricane Katrina Task Force Subcommittee Report 33, 34-38 (Feb. 2006). Almost all communications and energy facilities in the United States are privately controlled. *See* Jim Chen, *The Nature of the Public Utility: Infrastructure, the Market, and the Law*, 98 Nw. U. L. Rev. 1617, 1633-1640 (2004). Ensuring the continued supply of fuel and health care likewise demands more comprehensive interaction with the private sector. *Cf.* Homeland Security Council, National Strategy for Pandemic Influenza (2005); U.S. Department of Health & Human Services, HHS Pandemic Influenza Plan (2005). The Department of Homeland Security's blueprint for protecting "critical infrastructure and key resources (CI/KR)," Department of Homeland Security, Interim National Infrastructure Protection Plan 1 (2005), acknowledges the importance of the private entities that "own[ ] and operate[ ] the vast majority of the Nation's CI/KR," *id.* at 4. DHS contemplates "CI/KR Sector Coordinating Councils" that would engage private owners and operators of infrastructure with their public-sector counterparts in emergency planning and response. *See id.* at 5, 33-34.

Nonetheless, although the United States is dependent on privately owned infrastructure, the Stafford Act does not explicitly authorize FEMA to provide federal aid to some of the private entities that may play critical roles in response and recovery. The current statutory framework gives FEMA the authority to coordinate all relief efforts, including private responses, *see* 42 U.S.C. §5170a(2), and to contract with private entities to perform certain response functions or to use their equipment for those functions, *see, e.g., id.* §5150 (contracts with local private firms). However, although the Stafford Act does not preclude federal assistance to other private, for-profit companies engaged in disaster relief efforts, it does not specifically authorize such support. Indeed, legal confusion may have impaired efforts by private entities to restore communications and other critical services in areas crippled by Katrina:

> Many companies turned to the Federal Government for support because the civil unrest, coupled with the unprecedented level of damage from the storm and subsequent flooding, hindered their access to the disaster site and to necessary resources, thus impairing their ability to repair the damaged critical infrastructure on their own. When requesting support from the Federal Government, many companies were unable to receive assistance because Federal agencies indicated that they did not have the authority to provide them support under the Stafford Act, and the NRP did not guide an interpretation that would enable that support....
>
> The [Stafford] Act acknowledges the need for robust coordination; however, it does not clearly address coordination with the private sector. The Stafford Act provides assistance to "State or local Governments for the repair, restoration, reconstruction, or replacement of a public facility damaged or destroyed by a major disaster and for associated expenses incurred by the Government."[*Id.* §5172(a)(1)(A).]
>
> Although the language of the statute does not specifically preclude the private sector from receiving resources under the Act, it does not clearly grant the Federal Government authority to provide assistance to private entities, apart from nonprofit organizations. It states that the president can provide resources to "a person that owns or operates a private non-profit facility damaged or destroyed by a major disaster for the repair, restoration, reconstruction, or replacement of the facility and for associated expenses incurred by the person."[*Id.* §5172(a)(1)(B).] In addition, the law states that the president can "coordinate all disaster relief assistance (including voluntary assistance) provided by Federal agencies, private organizations, and State and local Governments."[*Id.* §5170(a)(2).] Section 5170(b)(3) of the Act also allows Federal departments and agencies to "provide assistance essential to meeting immediate threats to life and property resulting from a major disaster." . . .
>
> Absent from the Stafford Act is any direct reference to Federal assistance to "for-profit" entities, and it does not recognize that [telecommunications infrastructure providers], which own about 80 percent of the Nation's critical infrastructure, play a critical recovery role in disasters to address the threats to public health and safety, life, and property.

The president's National Security Telecommunications Advisory Committee, Legislative and Regulatory Task Force, *Federal Support to Telecommunications Infrastructure Providers in National Emergencies: Designation as "Emergency Responders (Private Sector)"* 7-9 (Jan. 31, 2006). Should the Stafford Act be amended to authorize emergency response actions by private-sector, for-profit entities and to authorize federal aid to private responders? If so, what measures can best facilitate voluntary relief efforts by the private parties who supply vital infrastructure and services? (The NRF does acknowledge that the private sector and NGOs play an "essential role" in disaster response, NRF at 6-7, and NIMS defines "emergency responder" to include "Federal, State, territorial, tribal, substate regional, and local governments, NGOs, private sector-organizations, critical infrastructure owners and operators, and all other organizations and individuals who assume an emergency management role," NIMS at 139.)

The Task Force report quoted above advocates the creation of a new legal category, "emergency responders (private sector)," that would enable private owners of infrastructure to secure governmental protection and other "nonmonetary" assistance as their employees work to restore service. Thus far, this recommendation has not been implemented. The only post-Katrina amendment to the Stafford Act to address the role of private disaster responders was contained in the Safe Ports Act, enacted October 13, 2006. *See* Pub. L. No. 109-347, §607, 120 Stat. 1941. The provision added a requirement to the Stafford Act that, absent exceptional circumstances, federal agencies shall not "deny or impede access to the disaster site to an essential service provider whose access is necessary to restore and repair an essential service" or otherwise "impede the restoration or repair" of essential services. *See* 42 U.S.C. §5189e(b). The definition of "essential service provider" specifically includes "a private, for profit entity," contributing to disaster response efforts, that provides telecommunications service, electrical power, natural gas, water and sewer services, or any other essential service, as determined by the president. *See id.* §5189(a). Thus, though the Stafford Act prohibits federal agencies from actively denying or impeding private utility companies' access to the disaster area, it does not specifically authorize federal agencies to help private infrastructure companies gain access to the site, secure safe working conditions for employees, or give other nonmonetary aid to companies working to restore essential services.

Moreover, the current statutory scheme does not recognize the disaster response role that may be played by private companies that are not necessarily "essential service providers." Large corporations can make a substantial difference in disaster relief because of their "economic resources," "logistical capacity," and "operational expertise." Susan S. Kuo & Benjamin Means, *Corporate Social Responsibility After Disaster*, 89 Wash. U. L. Rev. 973, 974 (2012). Much of the critical assistance supplied to devastated areas in the aftermath of Hurricane Katrina was provided voluntarily by various private companies. For instance, Wal-Mart donated more than $18 million to emergency relief efforts, delivered 150 Internet-ready computers to shelters to help family members find one another, dispatched over 2,450 truckloads of supplies, filled prescriptions free of charge to evacuees with emergency medical needs, and donated more than 25 vacant facilities to impacted states for relief

efforts. Wal-Mart, Fact Sheets, available at http://walmartstores.com
/FactsNews/FactSheets, June 24, 2009. Home Depot dispatched more than 800
truckloads of supplies to impacted areas and also used buses to transport 1,000
employees into the region from other areas. Steven Horwitz, *Making Hurricane
Response More Effective: Lessons from the Private Sector and the Coast Guard
During Katrina* (March 2008), available at mercatus.org/uploadedFiles/Mercatus
/Publications/PDF_20080319_MakingHurricaneReponseEffective.pdf.
Budweiser delivered truckloads of water and ice, and Ford provided vehicles for
search and rescue. Mary L.G. Theroux, *Public and Private Responses to Katrina:
What Can We Learn?* (October 2005), available at http://www.independent.org/
newsroom/article.asp?id= 1589 (June 24, 2009).

Beyond the sheer magnitude of the private relief effort was the
swiftness with which supplies reached the public. Professor Steven Horwitz
observed that "Wal-Mart and Home Depot were able to get...assistance to the
disaster areas almost immediately after the storm had passed, in comparison to
the days—in some cases weeks—that residents waited for government agencies
to provide relief." Horwitz, *supra.* Sheriff Harry Lee of Jefferson Parish (which
borders New Orleans) opined that "if the American government would have
responded like Wal-Mart has responded, we wouldn't be in this crisis." *Id.* One
particularly interesting comparison of private versus public relief efforts comes
from contrasting the disaster response of a private hospital, the Hospital
Corporation of America [HCA], with that of a government-owned hospital,
Charity, across the street. *See* Theroux, *supra.* In the immediate aftermath of
Katrina, HCA executives determined that they would need to lease 20
helicopters to safely evacuate their patients. HCA acted quickly on these plans
and was able to evacuate its critically ill patients without one mishap. Charity
Hospital, on the other hand, was completely without emergency supplies and
unable to get government help in evacuating. *See id.* Charity's patients were
finally rescued by privately leased helicopters on HCA's tab. *See* Hospital
Corporation of America, *HCA Completes Airlift Evacuation at Tulane University
Hospital and Clinic; Assists Nearby Hospitals*, available at http://phx.corporate-
ir.net/phoenix.zhtml?c= 63489&p=irol-newsArticle&ID=752385&highlight=
(June 24, 2009). Why were some private actors arguably more adept at
responding to Katrina than the government?

Many utility companies also were extremely effective at reestablishing
services for their customers. Even though all 195,000 Mississippi Power
customers were without power, nearly two-thirds of the company's
transmission and distribution system was damaged or destroyed, and its
second-largest electric generating plant was flooded, Southern Power was able
to restore power in just 12 days, thanks in large part to the aid of many other
utility companies throughout the country. *See* Transmission & Distribution,
*Southern Company CEO Shares Details of Successful Hurricane Katrina Response
with Senate Committee*, available at http://tdworld.com/hurricane-katrina-
relief/Southern-Company-response (June 24, 2009). In Louisiana, Cleco Power

was able to restore power to 80 percent of its customers in just three weeks. *See* Terry Wildman, *Cleco Faces the Beast*, available at http://tdworld.com /katrina_ reflections_supp/Cleco-Katrina-reflection (June 24, 2009).

Locally owned businesses are also essential to disaster relief and long-term recovery. *See* Kuo & Means, *supra*, at *Corporate Social Responsibility After Disaster*, 89 Wash. U. L. Rev. 977-79 (2012). Local businesses that rebuild and survive following a disaster "not only restore economic vibrancy but also replenish and strengthen the community's social capital." *Id.* at 979. For example, Johnny White's, a New Orlean's bar that "never closes," remained open throughout Hurricane Katrina and its aftermath. *Id.* at 982. This local business was "an essential part of the community's resilience" as it became a community center for those affected by the storm and a "favorite among journalists and rescue workers who needed a place they could go to forget the despair and destruction." *Id.* Although the National Recovery Framework acknowledges the importance of local businesses in disaster recovery, some argue that in order to fully capitalize on their economic and social importance, local businesses should be included in the development of short-term relief and recovery plans, not simply in long-term recovery plans. *See* Kuo & Means, *supra*, at 1010–16. Additionally, "public relief efforts should take care to avoid squelching [or crowding out] the efforts of locally owned businesses." *Id.* at 1012.

2. THE AMERICAN RED CROSS

Perhaps the most important nongovernmental organization involved in emergency response and disaster relief is the American Red Cross. When originally chartered by Congress in 1900, the American Red Cross was assigned the role of "carry[ing] on a system of national and international relief in time of peace...in mitigating the sufferings caused by pestilence, famine, fires, floods, and other great national calamities." See Kevin R. Kosar, *The Congressional Charter of the American National Red Cross: Overview, History, and Analysis* 19, Table 2 (CRS Report for Congress, Order Code RL33314, March 15, 2006) (quoting the 1900 charter). Six years later, in 1906, when an earthquake struck San Francisco and an ensuing fire engulfed the city, President Theodore Roosevelt announced that all federal aid would be channeled through the Red Cross. *See* National Academy of Public Administration, Coping with Catastrophe: Building an Emergency Management System to Meet People's Needs in Natural and Manmade Disasters 10 (1993). The American Red Cross continues to play a unique and critical role in U.S. disaster response:

> The Red Cross is an independent, non-governmental organization...that operates as a nonprofit, tax-exempt, charitable institution pursuant to a charter granted by the United States Congress. [*See* 36 U.S.C. §300101.] It has

the legal status of a "federal instrumentality" due to its charter requirements to carry out responsibilities delegated by the federal government.

[The Red Cross has the responsibility] to perform all duties incumbent upon a national society in accordance with the spirit and conditions of the Geneva Conventions to which the United States is a signatory, to provide family communications and other forms of assistance to members of the U.S. military, and to maintain a system of domestic and international disaster relief, including mandated responsibilities under the Federal Response Plan coordinated by the Federal Emergency Management Agency.

The Red Cross is not a federal agency, nor does it receive federal funding on a regular basis to carry out its services and programs. It receives financial support from voluntary public contributions and from cost recovery charges for some services. Its stated mission is to "provide relief to victims of disasters and help people prevent, prepare for, and respond to emergencies."

To meet its mandated responsibilities under the NRP, the Red Cross functions as an ESF primary organization in coordinating the use of mass care resources in a presidentially declared disaster or emergency. As the lead agency for ESF #6, dealing with Mass Care, Housing and Human Services, the Red Cross assumes the role of providing food, shelter, emergency first aid, disaster welfare information and bulk distribution of emergency relief items.

House Katrina Report, *supra*, at 42. In the current ESF #6, the Red Cross is a support agency, while DHS/FEMA is the lead. Relying on a nongovernmental entity to carry out critical components of federal disaster relief policy has both advantages and disadvantages. For example, as a well-respected charitable organization, the Red Cross has significant fund-raising capacity. On the other hand, federal and Red Cross policies may sometimes conflict. Implementation of federal policy favoring accommodation of pets in shelters may be hindered by the Red Cross's reluctance (for liability and other reasons) to accept pets at its shelters, which are often the only shelters provided when disaster strikes. In the wake of Superstorm Sandy, the Red Cross has been criticized for slow response times, denial of aid to many applicants, and mismanagement of collected funds. *See* Liz Goodwin, *A Year After Sandy, Red Cross Still Dogged by Criticism*, Yahoo News, Oct. 23, 2013, http://news.yahoo.com/a-year-later-after-sandy--red-cross-still-dogged-by-criticism-145155111.html; John Stossel, *Commentary: More Red Cross Criticism*, ABC News, Jan. 25, 2014, http://abcnews.go.com/2020/story?id=123956.

3. CITIZENS AND CITIZEN GROUPS

In addition to the Red Cross and private-sector corporations, individual citizens can play an important role in disaster response. Indeed, sociological literature commonly recognizes that the true first responders in any disaster tend to be the survivors themselves, as they extricate themselves from danger and begin to aid their family members and neighbors. People from outside the disaster area typically converge on the disaster scene, as well, many of them hoping to help. To capitalize on the post-9/11 national spirit of volunteerism and in recognition of the critical role that local citizens play in the aftermath of disasters, President Bush, in January 2001, established the Citizen Corps, which is coordinated by FEMA. According to the Citizen Corps Web site, its mission is to "harness the power of every individual through education, training, and volunteer service to make communities, safer, stronger, and better prepared to respond to threats of terrorism, crime, public health issues, and disasters of all kinds." Consider the following description of the role of the Citizen Corps in community disaster preparedness and response.

> The Citizen Corps mission is accomplished through a national network of state, local, and tribal Citizen Corps Councils. These Councils build on community strengths to implement the Citizen Corps preparedness programs and carry out a local strategy to involve government, community leaders, and citizens in all-hazards preparedness and resilience
>
> Citizens Corp Councils encourage citizens to help make our communities safer through:
> Personal responsibility: Developing a household preparedness plan and disaster supplies kits, observing home health and safety practices, implementing disaster mitigation measures, and participating in crime prevention and reporting.
> Training: Taking classes in emergency preparedness, response capabilities, first aid, CPR, fire suppression, and search and rescue procedures.
> Volunteer service: Engaging individuals in volunteer activities that support first responders, disaster relief groups, and community safety organizations. Everyone can do something to support local law enforcement, fire, emergency medical services, community public health efforts, and the four stages of emergency management: prevention, mitigation, response and recovery efforts.

See http://www.citizencorps.fema.gov/councils/.
Of particular interest to disaster response are local Community Emergency Response Teams (CERT) teams. The CERT concept was first developed by the Los Angeles City Fire Department in 1985, and has since been implemented in more than twenty-eight states. CERT teams are sponsored by

state, county, or local emergency management agencies and provide classroom and simulation training to interested citizens (on a voluntary basis) in disaster preparedness, fire suppression, medical operations, light search and rescue, disaster psychology, and team building. FEMA supports CERT teams by providing training materials for local entities. *See* http://www.fema.gov/community-emergency-response-teams/about-community-emergency-response-team (May 14, 2014).

In the aftermath of Katrina, a morbid joke that made the rounds of the emergency management community suggested that FEMA's new disaster policy was "YOYO" ("You're on your own."). Regardless of any post-Katrina improvements made to government's capacity to respond to disasters, there remains some truth in this assessment. In the immediate aftermath of disasters, local citizens are well advised to have their own disaster plans and resources at the ready. Despite public information campaigns urging people to have an emergency supply of food and water, a portable seventy-two-hour survival kit, and a written plan in case of emergency, most citizens have not complied with these recommendations. In a recent study, only 57 percent reported having any sort of specifically designated emergency supplies. *See* Fed. Emergency Mgmt. Agency, Personal Preparedness in America: Findings from the Citizen Corps National Survey 7 (2009), available at http://www.ready.gov/ personal-preparedness-survey-2009 [hereinafter *Findings*]. Of those who reported having emergency supplies, only 42 percent reported including a flashlight in their emergency kit and only 39 percent included a first aid kit. *See id.*

Indeed, even those who report that they are prepared for disasters admit to being less prepared when asked more specific questions. For example, one study found that only 55 percent of those reporting that they had an emergency kit reported that they had enough food, and only 36 percent reported having enough water. *See* Fed. Emergency Mgmt. Agency, Citizen Preparedness Review, Update on Citizen Preparedness Research 5 (2007), available at https://www.citizencorps.fema.gov/downloads/ pdf/ready/citizen_prep_review_issue_5.pdf. In a separate study, among those who reported that they "have been prepared for at least the past six months," over 33 percent did not have a household plan, "nearly 80 percent had not conducted a home evacuation drill, and nearly 70 percent did not know their community's evacuation routes." *Findings, supra*, at 18. Barriers to individual preparedness include the public's low perception of community risk and the fact that 61 percent of those surveyed "expected to rely on emergency responders in the first 72 hours following a disaster." *Id.* at 47. One report suggests that education specifically targeting the public's underestimation of community risk and unrealistic expectations of outside assistance could help motivate greater individual preparedness. *See id.* at 47-50.

NOTES AND QUESTIONS

1. How can state and local governments integrate private resources more fully into disaster planning? If efforts focus on low- to mid-level private company employees (rather than high-level management), will such efforts be effective?

2. How much are CERT teams likely to contribute to disaster response? For a listing of some ways in which CERT teams have responded to disasters, see http://www.fema.gov/community-emergency-response-teams/cert-action (May 14, 2014). Beyond creating CERT teams, how can states and communities more effectively encourage and organize disaster volunteers? Twenty-two states have State Defense Forces that can be activated during disasters. These forces are "largely made up of volunteers from local and state communities and are often composed of retired service members and reservist, along with other professionals, such as doctors, lawyers, and engineers, seeking to give back." Steven P. Bucci, et al., *After Hurricane Sandy: Time to Learn and Implement the Lessons in Preparedness, Response, and Resilience*, http://www.heritage.org/ research/reports /2013/10/after-hurricane-sandy-time-to-learn-and-implement-the-lessons.

3. How can government (or other organizations) more effectively encourage personal disaster preparedness? Is it unrealistic to expect that more citizens could comply with the hallmarks of disaster preparedness such as a written family disaster plan, a 72-hour kit, and an emergency supply of food and water? How much food and water can individuals and families reasonably be urged to store? Consider that experts recommend at least a 72-hour supply of water, which includes—at a minimum—one gallon per person per day.

E. REFORMING THE LAW OF EMERGENCY RESPONSE

The response to Katrina was so roundly denounced that proposals for reform arose almost immediately. The perceived failure of the law of emergency response prompted a long season of political introspection. Many of the proposed statutory reforms were adopted by the 2006 Post-Katrina Act and incorporated into the National Response Framework. As the notes throughout this chapter reveal, however, many questions remain about the effectiveness of individual reforms, as well as about the direction that future reform should take. This chapter concludes with two readings that suggest different possible directions for the future of disaster response law. The first reading draws on history to consider, as a possible model for reform, the federal government's concentration of authority in a single "recovery czar" in response to the Mississippi River flood of 1927. A second reading presents a vision of future response needs generated by FEMA's Strategic Foresight Initiative to spark a broader assessment of the ways in which response law might evolve.

KEVIN R. KOSAR, DISASTER RESPONSE AND APPOINTMENT OF A RECOVERY CZAR: THE EXECUTIVE BRANCH'S RESPONSE TO THE FLOOD OF 1927

(Oct. 25, 2005) (CRS Order Code RL33126)

In the wake of the destruction caused by Hurricanes Katrina and Rita, the press and policymakers have looked to the past for examples of federal responses to natural disasters that might serve as models for emulation today. A number of newspaper articles have referred to the executive branch's response to the 1927 Mississippi River flood. Some Members of Congress have expressed an interest in creating a cabinet-level "czar" to administer Hurricane Katrina and Hurricane Rita relief programs. Since the federal response to the flood of 1927 featured Secretary of Commerce Herbert Hoover as the director of the flood response and wielding immense executive powers, this episode... may be of particular interest....

[The federal response to the 1927 flood] was primarily an executive branch response. President Calvin Coolidge created a quasi-governmental commission that included members of his Cabinet and the American National Red Cross. This commission encouraged the public to donate funds to the relief effort and utilized federal resources, American National Red Cross volunteers, and the private sector to carry out the relief and recovery program. The commission also gave Secretary of Commerce Herbert Hoover near-absolute authority.

The concentration of power and the blending of the governmental and private sectors in Hoover's hands enabled the relief effort to be carried out expeditiously and creatively. President Coolidge's empowerment of Hoover alone as director of the flood response clarified to federal, state, and local officials and the public who was in charge. As will be seen, historical accounts and assessments of the federal flood response failed to locate any instances of jurisdictional confusion or power struggles between agencies.

However, this administrative structure was not without costs. There was little direct federal oversight of actual relief provision....Furthermore, the concentration of power in a single set of hands enabled Secretary Hoover to undertake inadvisable actions with nearly no constraints.

The Mississippi River Flood of 1927

...From late August 1926 through the spring of 1927, unusually heavy precipitation fell upon the Mississippi River Valley. "From January 1 to April 30, 1927, enough rain fell in various sections of [the Mississippi River basin] to cover the entire territory to a depth of 10.79 inches."...

In April 1927, the Mississippi River began bursting levees. The first was at Dorena, MO, where on April 16, 1,200 feet of levee crumbled. Five days later, massive crevasses opened in levees in Mounds Landing, MS, and then Pendleton, AR; hundreds of millions of gallons of water violently washed over the land. The flood had begun and its end was not declared until late July. People were drowned in the fields and in their homes. The rush of the water was so immense and violent that it permanently altered the topography in areas. Near the levee break at Mounds Landing, for example, the flood left a 65 acre lake that remains to this day.

In all, levees in Arkansas, Louisiana, Mississippi, and Missouri broke in 145 places. Over 26,000 square miles of land in seven states inhabited by some 930,000 persons were flooded. The damage was immense—41,487 buildings were destroyed, 162,017 homes flooded, and over $100 million [about $1.12 billion in 2005 dollars] in crops and farm animals destroyed. It is unclear how many persons were killed—accounts vary widely—but, it seems clear that at least 246 died....

Federal Disaster Response, Relief, and Reconstruction

The federal government's response to the disaster was a mixture of pre-New Deal minimalist federal governance and, to use recent parlance, "governing by network." The federal government would make no immediate appropriations to the affected area. Instead, it would utilize federal resources and coordinate networks of federal, state, private, and not-for-profit organizations to deliver relief services. The President's Cabinet would direct the relief effort in close consultation with the American National Red Cross. Thus, flood response policy was centralized, but, its execution was decentralized.

In 1927, there was no federal disaster-response agency. Instead, the federal government had a partnership with the Red Cross, a congressionally chartered quasi-governmental entity, established for a number of purposes, including the carrying out of "a system of national and international relief in time of peace, and to apply the same in mitigating the suffering caused by pestilence, famine, fire, floods, and other great national calamities, and to devise and carry out measures for preventing the same." Under the charter, the President of the United States was to appoint six members, one of whom was to serve as chairman, of the eighteen-person central committee. The other five members were to be "named by him from the Departments of State, War, Navy, Treasury, and Justice." While the law did not provide a position for the President himself, Coolidge had been asked and agreed to serve as President of the Red Cross.

On April 22, 1927, President Calvin Coolidge issued a proclamation to the nation. He declared, "The Government is giving such aid as lies within its powers....But the burden of caring for the homeless rests upon the agency designated by Government charter to provide relief in disaster—the American National Red Cross." He made no mention of emergency appropriations. Rather,

Coolidge, as President of the United States and the Red Cross, asked for the public to donate $5 million [$55.9 million in 2005 dollars] to the Red Cross. Additionally, the President created a quasi-governmental commission to assist the Red Cross in the relief effort. Coolidge appointed Herbert Hoover, Secretary of Commerce, as chairman.

Hoover was an apt choice—he had been elected to the Central Committee of the Red Cross by the incorporators and he had experience managing post–World War I relief and reconstruction efforts in Europe. Hoover was directly assisted by James L. Fieser, acting chairman of the Red Cross. The remainder of the commission, whose roles, according to President Coolidge, were to lend expert advice and expedite resource provision, included the secretaries of the Departments of the Treasury, War, and Navy, and the members of the Red Cross Central Committee.

That same day—April 22—[the "Hoover Flood Commission"] met for the first time and made three major decisions. First, it effectively turned over direction of the Red Cross's relief effort to Secretary Hoover. Second, it appointed Henry M. Baker, disaster relief director for the Red Cross, as the actual administrator of the response effort. As "dictator," Baker would do the work to execute Hoover's directions. Third, the Flood Commission agreed that each of the affected states should appoint a "dictator"; this individual would serve as the point-person for the state, and who would see to it that state resources were provided to the centrally directed response. These decisions made Hoover, to use recent nomenclature, the "czar" for federal disaster response, likely the first.

This concentration of a wide array of governmental powers in a single set of hands enabled the federal government to respond rapidly without bureaucratic impediments. If Hoover asked for a federal resource, the Hoover Flood Commission would see that it was provided. The Memphis flood response headquarters served as an "administrative pump." A hodgepodge of resources from the many partners in the relief effort flowed in, as did advice from the Hoover Flood Commission and local relief workers. The headquarters, which was divided into operational units, including purchase and supply, river transportation and rescue work, rail transportation, and so forth, served as a processor…. Out of the pump flowed streams of coordinated responses. A single, official channel of communication—"Field Operations Letters"—was established; through it, the headquarters delivered relief plan directions to local personnel and groups by telephone calls and radio communications directed to regional Red Cross offices.

Furthermore, coordinating the federal response with the Red Cross gave the relief effort the power to draw upon thousands of already-trained Red Cross volunteers in affected areas. These volunteers on the scene provided information to the [Hoover Commission's] headquarters for use in planning and coordinating the response, and utilized relationships they had with affected residents and governments to help execute the response. Federal, state, and quasi-governmental entities and private citizens and businesses were linked to form an "administrative machine."

The President, for his part, let the Hoover Flood Commission run relief administration. He issued a further plea for another $5 million in donations to the Red Cross on May 2. Hoover, though, directed the expenditure of the funds, often shipping allotments to local Red Cross chapters to expend according to their directions.

The scale of the relief effort was massive. Approximately 640,000 displaced persons were aided by the Red Cross; 307,208 stayed in over 150 Red Cross camps, many for up to four months; the remainder of evacuees stayed elsewhere, but, received food from the Red Cross. The Red Cross provided those in the camps with food, tobacco, medical care, clothing, and some entertainment. Evacuees, typically, lived in tents donated by the Department of War, and had access to simple bathing and toilet facilities. They received rudimentary medical care; some entertainment and courses in home economics were provided.

While the relief operations were of considerable breadth, federal recovery and reconstruction efforts were quite modest. The Army Corp of Engineers, after some delay, repaired the levees. Hoover encouraged affected states to incorporate state reconstruction corporations. He also strongly encouraged banks in affected areas and the captains of industries of the day to provide working capital for the banks by buying stock in them. His plan was for state reconstruction corporations to lend money to farmers, sell these loans to the Federal Intermediate Credit Corporation, and use the proceeds to make more loans. The Red Cross, meanwhile, helped citizens rebuild some of their homes, and provided them with seeds, farm implements, basic household furnishings, and other items to help them regain the ability to sustain themselves....

An Assessment of the Executive Branch's Response

The public donated and the Red Cross delivered over $21 million [$234.9 million] in aid. The federal government provided, perhaps, $10 million [$111.8 million] in resources and manpower—nearly $32 million [$346.7 million] in all. On the whole, the response and relief provided by the federal government and Red Cross appear to have been well executed. The concentration of great power in the person of Secretary Hoover enabled quick and creative responses. By April 23, 1927, U.S. Coast Guard boats were rescuing citizens trapped in trees and on rooftops, bridges, and high grounds, the U.S. Army had shipped thousands of tents, cots, and blankets to areas where Red Cross camps were being set up, and the Navy had received Hoover's request to dispatch boats and rescue crews....

The blending of governmental and private resources enabled creative responses. For example, the Red Cross Rescue Fleet was cobbled together from privately owned yachts, commercial barges, boats belonging to federal agencies such as the U.S. Army, Navy, Coast Guard, and river steamships. Railroads were employed to move...materials, manpower, and evacuees. Hoover also brought into the mix the Rockefeller Foundation, which provided public health assistance to affected counties.

Additionally, President Coolidge's employment of a Cabinet-based commission helped clarify to the public and local, state, and federal officials who was in charge of the flood response. Secretary Hoover was widely known throughout the nation, and the President made sure that everyone got the message that Hoover was in charge by utilizing the bully pulpit—he issued a presidential proclamation to the press. That same day—April 23—Hoover and Fieser made contact with governors to let them know that the federal government and Red Cross would jointly direct all activities. The scholarly and press accounts on the flood response cited above reveal no jurisdictional disputes between federal agencies or between federal and state agencies. Again, Hoover created an "administrative machine."

That said, the federal response has been faulted on at least four points. First, while the employment of governmental and private sector resources allowed for creative responses, it also opened the door to potential abuses. For example, Hoover, reportedly, empowered Baker to order the seizure of privately owned boats by relief workers. Thus, with no executive order or statute, private individuals were authorized to take the property of others. To whom individuals affected and aggrieved by civilian exercise of federal powers would protest or appeal is simply unclear.

Second, decentralized execution meant that the federal government had little oversight of the actual operations of the relief camps. Two significant incidents illustrate the limitations of this method of administration. First, critics accused the Red Cross of being slow to respond to the spread of venereal diseases among camp residents. Second, in some Red Cross camps, local officials brutalized Black evacuees and disallowed them to leave the camps.[6]... [T]he federal government had no one at these sites to provide accurate reports on the conditions or put a halt to these actions.[7]

---

[6]Under the sharecropper relationship, a farmer would work land owned by another person and turn over to the landowner the products thereof. The landowner would sell the agricultural products and give the farmer a "share" of the proceeds. Under such an arrangement, many Blacks in the South had fallen into near or outright peonage. Farmers fell into debt when landowners would charge them for various items and services—such as loans for seed—and provided small returns. Bound by debt, farmers could not leave the land. After the flood of 1927, landowners had a strong interest in seeing that their sharecroppers returned to their fields. Therefore, they often employed threats of violence and called upon state and local governments to help them force farmers to return to work.

[7]...President Coolidge empowered Hoover to issue reports on the progress of flood recovery. With an eye on a run for the presidency in 1928, this gave Hoover a strong incentive to be less than objective about inadequate results. Thus, he would often claim

Third, directions from headquarters and Hoover to field operations were very explicit as to the goals desired. In one instance, Hoover [ordered] a regional representative...to erect a camp to hold 10,000 persons and gave instructions on the proper construction and installation of the facilities, including tent platforms, latrines, pipelines, wells, and power lines. However, these same directions provided little direction as to the appropriate means. Locals were to figure it out themselves. Free to use whatever means they felt necessary to achieve these ends, local relief workers, in many instances, forced Black males, sometimes at gun point, to participate in flood response work. In short, workers carrying out ostensibly federal work were not federal workers, and did not have to follow federal administrative laws.

Finally, there is the matter of power concentration in the hands of a Cabinet-level czar. As head of the Hoover Flood Commission, head of the Red Cross flood relief effort, and the public face of flood relief—thanks to his tireless public relations efforts—Secretary Hoover held an immense amount of administrative and political power....While this empowered him to do much good work, Hoover also made glaring mistakes, and made matters worse by refusing to admit his errors and make amends. Critically, nobody, the President excepted, could force Hoover to change course. For example,

> [t]here is evidence that Hoover was aware of the mistreatment of Blacks in the camps and the shortcomings of his credit provision plan. Yet, he did little to fix these problems.
>
> In late May of 1927, the Secretary decided that the farmers of the area should plant soybeans, instead of cotton. He directed the Red Cross, which received public donations for the flood response, to buy enough soybean seed for 400,000 acres. When informed by agricultural scientists that soybeans were not an advisable crop choice for the affected areas, Hoover disregarded this counsel and contacted banks to urge them to loan monies to farmers for soybean crops.
>
> A destitute victim departing a relief camp might receive no more than "tickets that entitled him to railway fare..., and to a tent if his house was gone, tickets that gave him lumber, seeds, implements [for gardening], and a mule or cow." Many newspapers...argued that the federal government, which was running a massive surplus, should provide direct aid to flood victims in order to help them regain self-sustenance. Hoover disagreed—he thought flood victims had received enough to get back on their feet. Unfortunately, even these modest resources did not reach those in need. Red Cross officials distributed some

---

that six or fewer persons died once he was put in control of flood response. This figure is not deemed credible.

evacuees' allotments to the planters for whom they worked. Some planters charged evacuees for the goods.

In summation, President Coolidge's version of a disaster response and recovery czar enabled quick and apparently efficient utilization of governmental and private sector resources and personnel. It also, though, gave a single administrator a large quantity of power with only presidential oversight, and, in some instances, that power appears to have been used inadvisably.

NOTES AND QUESTIONS

1. The definitive book on the 1927 flood is John M. Barry, Rising Tide: The Great Mississippi Flood of 1927 and How It Changed America (1998). Kevin Kosar's CRS report draws heavily from Barry's book.

2. John Barry notes that the displacement of African Americans from flooded homes and their mistreatment in Hoover's camps pushed thousands of Blacks out of the Mississippi Delta. See Barry, supra, at 417. Coupled with the invention of the mechanical cotton picker and the boll weevil infestation, see Nicholas Lemann, The Promised Land: The Great Black Migration and How It Changed America 5-6 (1991); Jim Chen, Of Agriculture's First Disobedience and Its Fruit, 48 Vand. L. Rev. 1261, 1302-1312 (1995), the flood of 1927 sparked the eventual movement of more than 6 million African Americans from the rural South to the urban North between the Great War and the Great Society. Do disasters often have the capacity to trigger major societal movements?

3. How would the federal government appoint a "disaster czar"? He or she would surely "exercis[e] significant authority pursuant to the laws of the United States," Buckley v. Valeo, 424 U.S. 1, 126 (1976), and be subject to the Appointments Clause, U.S. Const. art II, §2, cl. 2. Unless the czar's mission can be characterized as limited in time and scope, cf. Morrison v. Olson, 487 U.S. 659, 671-673 (1988) (describing the traits of an "inferior" officer), or unless the czar is already a principal officer of the United States, the Senate must confirm his or her appointment.

4. Given the scale and scope of federal involvement in emergencies, especially its escalation since 1927, a straightforward restoration of the Mississippi River flood's "disaster czar" approach seems fanciful. The experience of 1927 nevertheless retains enough allure to prompt a congressional inquiry after Katrina. Insofar as today's federal emergency response system aspires to "unified command" across jurisdictions and to a more rational coordination of fifteen emergency support functions, in what respects does Herbert Hoover's 1927 experience remain pertinent?

5. Another proposal for disaster reform draws on the Hoover-as-disaster-czar experience to suggest creating a statutory basis for a "Presidential Officer-

in-Charge," who would have flexibility to respond to megadisasters that, the authors contend, are essentially "unplannable":

> We recommend stand-by federal legislation to enable the president to appoint an officer-in-charge, not to take over state and local responsibilities, but to do two essential things. First, to provide the authority and resources to mobilize the federal establishment (and, by virtue of being able to do this, being in a stronger position to influence major institutions on the scene to get their act together). Second, to enable the national government to adopt extraordinary measures. A major charge to the person assigned as this "presidentially designated driver" would be to report to the president and the Congress within a prescribed period of time on whether extraordinary national action is needed, and if so what it should be. In doing so, the officer-in-charge and the staff of this office would draw on the expertise of federal, state, and local officials and agencies, voluntary groups, and outside experts.
>
> Proposals that emerge out of this process would be time sensitive. At the discretion of the officer-in-charge, we suggest that these proposals be subject to special Congressional procedures like those for international trade agreements and, at the discretion of the officer-in-charge, that they could be considered en bloc under processes like those for base-closing commissions. Such authority to put forward legislative proposals for fast, special action would not infringe on the authority of the president and the Congress to reject them, nor on the powers and responsibilities that policymakers and first responders at the state and local levels must retain. What such authority would accomplish—in government jargon—is provide the officer-in-charge with the capacity to collaborate and facilitate—and in plain English, to lead.

Richard P. Nathan & Marc Luncy, *Who's in Charge? Who Should Be? The Role of the Federal Government in Megadisasters: Based on Lessons from Hurricane Katrina* (June 2, 2009), available at http://www.rockinst.org/pdf/disaster_recovery/gulfgov/gulfgov_reports/2009-06-02-Whos_in_Charge.PDF.

In July 2011, as part of FEMA's Strategic Foresight Initiative, a group of emergency management experts participated in a scenario-planning workshop that considered future emergency management needs in 2030 under five different scenarios featuring different economic, political, and social conditions. The scenarios were called "Quantum Leap," "Bet on the Wrong Horse," "Dragon vs. Tiger," "Dude, Where's My Sovereignty?," and "Treading Water." The workshop participants identified fifteen "common strategic needs that applied across all five scenario worlds" across three categories: essential capabilities, innovative models and tools, and dynamic partnerships.

As you read about the fifteen strategic needs and the workshop's vision of emergency management in 2030, consider what role the law could and should play in achieving that vision.

FEMA, CRISIS RESPONSE AND DISASTER RESILIENCE 2030
13-20 (January 2012), available at http://www.fema.gov/media-library-data/20130726-1816-25045-5167/sfi_report_13.jan.2012_final.docx.pdf

ESSENTIAL CAPABILITIES

[B]listeringly rapid change and complexity will define the emergency management environment over the next few decades. Even demographics, here in the U.S. traditionally one of the more slow-moving and predictable trends, could be subject to sudden and unpredictable lurches, in the face of climate change, pandemic outbreaks, refugee surges or some other factor not even considered today. Meanwhile, new service challenges are arising as government agencies – from Washington down to the smallest towns – wrestle with new responsibilities and extremely challenging fiscal conditions. All of this is playing out in a data-rich but often knowledge-poor environment, where nearly everyone is an information consumer, contributor, and critic.

Not surprisingly, these dynamics will drive demand for new, augmented, or otherwise different emergency management capabilities. Several of the suggested capabilities highlighted during the July 2011 SFI scenario workshop are explained below.

1. Develop emergency management capabilities to address dynamic and unprecedented shifts in local and regional population characteristics and migratory flows. Among other things, this could include building multi-lingual proficiencies and understanding risks associated with both heavily populated coastal areas and urban centers and more remote locations where new population centers are forming. This will require close dialogue with community leaders to better understand local needs, including new vulnerable populations and emergency operating challenges related to issues like aging infrastructure. And it will mean involving traditionally underrepresented populations in planning and service delivery.

Why this need? Emergency managers will be faced with complex demographics shifts as the United States' population increases, ages, and becomes more culturally and linguistically diverse. New challenges will arise from migrations within the U.S., possibly because of environmental issues and changes in regional climates. There will also be changes in the size and nature of traditionally underrepresented and elusive populations, including the extremely poor; the homeless; those volunteering to live "off the grid"; refugees from disasters; and victims of pandemics.

2. Practice omni-directional knowledge sharing. This means employing all relevant forums, networks (including sensitive and classified), and technologies so that information created and distributed by government remains relevant to the public in complex information and media environments. And it will mean

staying abreast of the rapidly evolving world of social networks and knowing how to leverage their power and influence.

Why this need? The proliferation of information from all sources (including private sector and social media) intensifies the need to make emergency management information and knowledge useful and accessible. Advanced tools to collect, analyze and disseminate information represent potentially valuable new tools for emergency managers. As information flows become more widely distributed, the connectivity of networks will be significantly more important than any single hierarchical solution. And the public's role as an information source will be vital.

3. Infuse emergency management principles and life skills across the entire educational experience to empower individuals to assume more responsibility. This means continuing to build emergency management awareness, from K through 12, with community-tailored curricula shaped by the local environment. It is about communicating the importance of partnering with individuals and community organizations to build self-reliance and individual initiative.

Why this need? Future operating environments may well be characterized by significant decline in governmental resources for emergency management. Such fiscal constraints could tempt emergency managers to pull back from community engagement, which would widen the gap that already exists. Instead, it will be important to use the fiscal environment as an opportunity to reinvent and innovate. Schools and youth programs will be critically important channels, especially in creating awareness of new and unfamiliar threats such as pandemics or cyber attacks.

4. Build a shared vision for the emergency management community of the future and a culture that embraces forward thinking to anticipate emerging challenges and develops appropriate plans and contingencies. This might include building "futures" knowledge and insights into operational and leadership training, examining and adopting global best practices, or exploring the development of an emergency management academy that has a foresight component.

Why this need? The SFI scenarios depict increasingly complex, rapidly changing worlds – even for economically troubled and less technologically vibrant scenarios. Since current operational strategies and plans may not be applicable in the future, the emergency management community will have to deliberately explore future issues as it prepares for the challenges that face our community.

5. Leverage volunteer capabilities across all emergency management phases. This need is about creatively incorporating volunteers into our operating models – and dealing with the non-trivial risks involved, particularly in supervision,

training, and liability. Technology may come to play an important role in volunteer organization and training.

Why this need? Emergency management resources, especially personnel, are apt to be stretched in future operating environments marked by tight budgets and/or more frequent national emergencies. In some cases, skill gaps may become more pronounced, and alternative staffing models will become important. How might we further incorporate volunteers into our operating models? What limitations must we understand to mitigate undue risk exposure? Further, even though it is already used to mobilize communities, how can we better use technology to inform and organize volunteers?

INNOVATIVE MODELS & TOOLS

Foresight tells us that the future will challenge us to be even more inventive in our thinking about the tools and solutions we will need to be successful. For one, we expect that the future operating environment will be characterized by more frequent emergency events, many of which will be simultaneous. In addition, these events are apt to have more far-reaching impacts, simply because the world is more complex, networked, and interdependent. Combined with aging infrastructure, potential supply chain risks, and technological advancements, our environment becomes even more difficult to navigate. Thus, we will need to employ, and in some cases develop, new and improved models and tools to successfully meet our critical missions.

SFI scenario workshop participants identified tremendous opportunities in the Innovative Models & Tools category. Related Strategic Needs that proved effective across scenario worlds are explained below.

6. Adopt new risk management tools and processes in order to manage cascading consequences of interactions among infrastructure and all hazards. Emergency managers will need advanced modeling and tools to prospectively assess and manage risks related to climate, power, transport, telecommunications, and water, among other domains. Additionally, understanding and remediating potential points of catastrophic failure will be important. And as populations shift we will have to plan more appropriately to provide services to the public.

Why this need? Current risk management tools and processes already are outdated. For example, our risk management models are typically retrospective and do not account for climate change impacts we are experiencing today. If climate change is exacerbated, we will be even further behind the curve, our mitigation efforts will prove insufficient, and our response and recovery operations will suffer. The risks of aging infrastructure due to budget pressures, political and jurisdictional conflicts, and potential failures to initiate or sustain the long-term investments required also will challenge us in the future. Aging infrastructure also represents a highly interconnected form of risk, with many secondary and tertiary risks to populations during and following emergency situations.

7. Employ alternative surge models to meet the challenging confluences of social, technological, environmental, economic, and political factors and conditions. This could include regional and sub-regional sharing of assets, infrastructure, and logistics capabilities. Considering new staffing models that include greater volunteer, private sector, non-governmental organization, and armed forces support also could help meet this need.

Why this need? Acute and possibly chronic fiscal pressure could create highly challenging deficits in emergency management resources relative to needs, and public safety and emergency management practitioners could see reduced funding at all levels. Possible offsetting factors, such as technology, could be an important force multiplier in some situations. However, all of this suggests the need for new approaches and models for marshaling resources to deal with the possibility of more frequent and more complex emergency situations.

8. Establish flexible frameworks that optimize emergency management inter-operability across all boundaries, because of increasing jurisdictional and technological complexities. These include, but are not limited to, medical professional licensures, communication and messaging, equipment training, and security standards. This could require comprehensive frameworks to remediate; engaging the public and private sectors will be important to ensure we are meeting differing communities' needs.

Why this need? The future operating environment will challenge individual emergency management entities to accomplish more with fewer of their own resources. This underlines the importance of resource-sharing arrangements across jurisdictions, especially during emergency situations. In 2011, doctors and nurses cannot cross state lines to help in emergencies unless a governor declares a state of emergency. Obstacles to many other forms of interoperability, including security, law enforcement, and technology, to include our hemispheric partners, will be magnified unless there is reform in this area.

9. Plan and coordinate around shared interests and interdependencies to exercise the entire range of emergency management capabilities. This will require effective leadership, which can come from multiple sources, aligning strategies and operations across sectors, and using tools such as models, scenarios, and simulations as learning opportunities to tease out stress points and gaps and address them.

Why this need? The future may challenge our community with chronic resource constraints at times of rising demands for emergency management services. Current regional approaches are limited. Planners need to be motivated and empowered to look beyond short-term concerns and narrow stovepipes and recognize opportunities for collaboration around shared interests.

10. Remediate hidden vulnerabilities in critical supplies—from water to energy to medical products—to offset threats to the full scope of emergency management activities. Having an understanding of supply chain vulnerabilities of all supplies, not just commodities, would benefit the emergency management community when considering future supply lines. Further, developing contingencies in anticipation of both global and local supply challenges is in our best interest.

Why this need? Future availability of important emergency supplies cannot be assured. Global and national supply chains, some of which have limited capacity to begin with, may be vulnerable to infrastructure degradation, interruptions in foreign trade, and cyber attacks, and they are undergoing radical structural changes in warehousing demand signaling and logistics. Water, especially in drought-stricken areas of the country, may not be available in sufficient amounts to fully support emergency management missions. Climate change may negatively affect access to power and energy; so may man-made problems, such as foreign conflicts and trade embargoes.

11. Influence the development of emerging technologies that advance emergency management capabilities. This will require sustained dialogue between the emergency management and technology communities. We will have to help technologists understand the technological requirements of emergency managers so that appropriate technologies can be developed. Ensuring technological interoperability with our stakeholders as technology evolves will also be a critical consideration.

Why this need? Technology will become a more important element in future emergency management mission execution, from information management to communications, to sensing, to transportation and logistics, and much more. In fact, there is a case to be made that technology will be even more important in tight budget environments. This argues not just for proactive technology adoption, but actually getting out ahead and influencing the development of products that have emergency management applications.

DYNAMIC PARTNERSHIPS

Partnerships are and will continue to be critical to the future of emergency management. For this community, partnerships are not merely standard operating procedures—they are essential. In an environment of fiscal constraints and changing government roles and responsibilities, the partnership imperative must rise to a whole new level, involving new associations, broader and deeper interactions, and immense fluidity.

It begins with individuals and communities. Working with communities to understand their needs, and where emergency managers can empower and assist, is a shift in approach, but it is necessary. Further, as we look to the future, businesses will continue to serve as a core member of the emergency management team, and they will be crucial to successful service delivery. We also will need to engage our international partners, in particular Canada and Mexico, around several shared interests, including border security, immigration, water management, and disease surveillance. And our partnership with the U.S. Armed Forces as we respond to and recover from complex disaster situations will benefit our collective efforts.

Strengthening (and, in some cases, building) these partnerships will be important to meeting longer-term strategic needs, as further explained below.

12. Empower individuals, neighborhoods, and communities to play a greater role throughout all phases of disasters. We know that regardless of the situation, the public will be involved, as first responders, as eyewitnesses, providing updates, serving as information nodes, or relaying critical information to authorities. Engagement with communities offers an opportunity to partner with individuals and organizations in life-saving and life-sustaining actions to strengthen their role in emergency management. The question is whether the emergency management community will succeed in building a constructive relationship with the public to empower them as a full partner in realizing mission success.

Why this need? There are real shifts underway in how people are processing information and how and where they will produce and consume it in the future. Additionally, there are corresponding shifts in the nature of trust, with public trust placed less in large organizations and increasingly in social networks. Along with these changes, the SFI scenarios depict a range of U.S. economic futures with spending constraints—especially over the next decade— as a repeated theme. Inevitably this will mean changes in how government services are delivered before, during, and after an emergency or disaster event. Understanding how to empower communities and individuals in new and different ways holds a critical key to enhancing our ability to achieve successful emergency management outcomes in the future; it also challenges our current public engagement approaches and expectations.

13. Proactively engage business in all emergency management phases and solicit its contribution to policy development, in light of the critical nature of private sector capabilities. We already engage the private sector in much of what we do. Moving forward, promoting further collaboration, cooperation, and appropriately close relationships between the private sector and the emergency management community will be vital. We will have to consider what legal and regulatory frameworks we will need in order to avoid conflicts of interest, since

furthering our partnership with the private sector is a necessary element of serving the public in the future.

Why this need? The private sector meets the public's needs every day. With close to 90% of the labor force and tremendous specialized capabilities, the private sector is a key partner before, during, and after disasters. This partnership will become increasingly important in the future. Working in concert with the private sector, rather than competing with it, the public sector has an opportunity to further enable private sector resources and capabilities to assist in recovery efforts and resilience-building throughout communities. Engaging the private sector in policy development is also important so that the private sector has the appropriate frameworks in place to work effectively and cooperatively with the public sector to address issues of mutual concern.

14. Intensify disaster-response collaboration and planning with Canada and Mexico, recognizing scope for both national and local actions. Sharing critical emergency management information is a start to building collaborative cross-border relationships. As we do this, engaging the State Department and other authorities to ensure we have the appropriate agreements and frameworks in place will be important in the effort to intensify these relationships.

Why this need? Emergencies and disasters do not respect national boundaries. A number of the SFI scenarios anticipated the need for significantly closer U.S. collaboration with Canada and Mexico around several shared emergency management interest areas, including immigration, border security, drought and water management, disease surveillance, trade and commerce, and critical infrastructure. The scenarios made a strong case for anticipatory action to ensure the highest levels of cooperation are in place before actual emergencies or disasters occur.

15. Foster increased collaboration to ensure appropriate use of the military to provide specialized capabilities or to augment capacity in complex, overwhelming disaster incidents. This includes building on ties that already exist with respect to existing state and National Guard relationships. Strengthening dialogue between the military and local communities to coordinate resources and to foster trust and understanding will also be important. This is not uncharted territory, per se, but a new era of closer collaboration will be necessary.

Why this need? The SFI scenario discussions covered a range of complex emergency situations including weapons of mass destruction (WMDs), cyber attacks, and the potential need for quarantining pandemic victims showing up on U.S. shores. Responding to such threats will require scale, as well as specialized skills, some of which are within the purview of U.S. armed forces. If the U.S. reduces its global military footprint, the armed forces may be more available for domestic missions, including emergency management.

NOTES AND QUESTIONS

1. Which of the many future emergency management needs identified in the report seem most critical? Are there important needs not addressed by the report? Which needs can the law most effectively address?
2. Do current laws and regulations impede addressing any of these needs? Can the federal regulatory framework respond to evolving needs within the current statutory framework or is statutory reform required?

CHAPTER 5

SOCIAL VULNERABILITY

Sometime that night the winds came back. Everything in the world had a strong rattle, sharp and short.... [Janie] saw the drifting mists gathered in the west—that cloud field of the sky—to arm themselves with thunders and march forth against the world. Louder and higher and lower and wider the sound and motion spread, mounting, sinking, darking.

It woke up old Okechobee and the monster began to roll in his bed. Began to roll and complain like a peevish world on a grumble. The folks in the quarters and the people in the big houses further around the shore heard the big lake and wondered. The people felt uncomfortable but safe because there were the seawalls to chain the senseless monster in his bed. The folks let the people do the thinking. If the castles thought themselves secure, the cabins needn't worry. Their decision was already made as always. Chink up your cracks, shiver in your wet beds and wait on the mercy of the Lord....

They huddled closer and stared at the door. They just didn't use another part of their bodies, and they didn't look at anything but the door. The time was past for asking the white folks what to look for through that door. Six eyes were questioning God.

—Zora Neale Hurston, *Their Eyes Were Watching God,* 158-59 (1937)

"The moral test of government," said Hubert H. Humphrey, "is how it treats those who are in the dawn of life, the children; those who are in the twilight of life, the aged; and those who are in the shadows of life, the sick, the needy and the handicapped." Arnold v. Arizona Dept. of Health Servs., 160 Ariz. 593, 775 P.2d 521, 537 (1989) (quoting Humphrey). Natural disaster puts government to an extreme version of this test. This chapter addresses the relationship between social vulnerability and natural disasters. It begins with a global overview. Disasters are never strictly "natural"; they invariably stem from social as well as environmental factors. *See, e.g.*, Gregory Squires & Chester Hartman, There's No Such Thing as a Natural Disaster: Race, Class, and Hurricane Katrina (2006). Even more bluntly: "Floods are 'acts of God,' but flood losses are largely acts of man." Gilbert F. White, *Human Adjustment to Floods, in* 1 Geography, Resources, and Environment: Selected Writings of Gilbert F. White 12 (Robert W. Kates & Ian Burton eds., 1986).

Hurricane Katrina inspired the first edition of this book. Although the current edition looks beyond Katrina, the societal heartbreak associated with that storm continues to loom prominently in this chapter. No previous natural disaster in the nation's history exacted a grimmer toll. More than a thousand Americans died; another million evacuated the Gulf Coast. The legendary city of New Orleans all but sank when its levees failed and the resulting storm surge drowned many of the city's feeblest, most vulnerable residents. The flood waters consumed the forlorn hope that the United States could rescue its citizens during their darkest and neediest hour.

Precisely because Katrina unfolded as a tragedy of race and class, of official incompetence and social injustice, the story of that disaster, in its often gruesome detail, continues to provide the ideal backdrop against which to examine the racial and class-based dimensions of social vulnerability during and after natural disasters. This chapter then addresses other vectors of discrimination laid bare by disaster: sex, age, disability, and immigrant status. A discussion of price-gouging laws rounds out this chapter's exploration of economic exploitation during disaster.

A. DISASTERS AS A FUNCTION OF INJUSTICE

Natural disaster supposedly does not discriminate; it putatively strikes everyone in its path, without regard to race, class, sex, age, or disability. In other words, "poverty is hierarchic, smog is democratic." Ulrich Beck, Risk Society: Toward a New Modernity 36 (1986); *accord* Scott Frickel, *Our Toxic Gumbo: Recipe for a Politics of Environmental Knowledge,* http://understandingkatrina.ssrc.org /Frickel (June 11, 2009). Closer examination of the natural and social factors in any disaster, however, belies this assumption. Disaster does not so much erase as expose social vulnerability. Though " '[n]atural disasters' such as hurricanes, earthquakes, and floods are sometimes viewed as 'great social equalizers' " that "strike unpredictably and at random, affecting black and white, rich and poor, sick and well alike," harms from disasters "are not visited randomly or equally in our society." Center for Progressive Reform, An Unnatural Disaster: The Aftermath of Hurricane Katrina 34 (2005). Around the world, social injustice contributes so heavily to the incidence and intensity of natural disasters that the quest for equality may be regarded as a valuable tool for improving disaster preparedness, response, mitigation, compensation, and rebuilding.

This section begins with a global view of the relationship between natural disasters and social injustice. Losses from catastrophic events will not be stemmed until the law honestly confronts the contribution of "civilized" society to "natural" disasters:

THERESA BRAINE, WAS 2005 THE YEAR OF NATURAL DISASTERS?

84:1 Bull. World Health Org. 4 (Jan. 2006)

The year 2005 saw the aftermath of the 26 December 2004 earthquake and tsunami waves in Asia, hurricanes in central and north America, notably Katrina,...and the 8 October earthquake in Pakistan and India. The year also saw famine after crops were destroyed by locusts in Niger. Virtually unnoticed by the outside world was tiny El Salvador where the country's highest volcano, Ilamatepec, erupted on 1 October, displacing more than 7,500 people and killing two. A few days later Hurricane Stan swept through and killed about 70 people with floods and mudslides.

From January to October 2005, an estimated 97,490 people were killed in disasters globally and 88,117 of them in natural disasters....[T]he number of natural disasters—floods, windstorms, droughts and geological disasters— recorded since 1900 have increased and the number of people affected by such disasters has also increased since 1975.

Is this as bad as it gets, or could it get worse? Why do natural disasters appear to be increasingly frequent and increasingly deadly?

Today's disasters stem from a complex mix of factors, including routine climate change, global warming influenced by human behaviour, socioeconomic factors causing poorer people to live in risky areas, and inadequate disaster preparedness and education on the part of governments as well as the general population.

Some disasters experts reject the term "natural disasters," arguing that there is almost always a man-made element....Dr Ciro Ugarte [of the Pan American Health Organization (PAHO)], explain[ed] that natural disasters would not have such a devastating effect on people's lives if they were not exposed to such risks in the first place.

Natural phenomena do not always generate human disasters. Ugarte noted that in 2005, several earthquakes that struck in South America were of a higher magnitude than the one that devastated northern Pakistan and parts of India in October, but these hit sparsely populated areas and therefore caused less damage. The same goes for several tsunamis in 2005 which were not deemed "disasters" because they didn't endanger anyone, Ugarte said.

Natural phenomena are likely to affect more people because Earth's population has increased. According to the United Nations Population Fund, this stands at about 6.5 billion people and is projected to reach 9.1 billion people in 2050.

Marko Kokic, spokesperson for WHO's Health Action in Crisis department, said that some communities are more vulnerable to the effects of natural disasters than 100 years ago because of ecological degradation. He said that, for example, when tropical storms hit the Caribbean in September 2004, there was nothing to stop storm waters gathering and wreaking devastation in Haiti because of deforestation. "We need to tackle the underlying issues, such as poverty and inequity," Kokic said, adding: "In many countries, people cut down trees because wood is the cheapest fuel."

Disasters are also a consequence of development and industrialization. In Europe, experts believe that countries such as France and Germany are more adversely affected by floods today because major rivers, such as the Rhine, have been straightened to ease commercial traffic.

Global warming as well as routine, cyclical climate changes are causing a higher number of strong hurricanes in the Caribbean, meteorologists say. Add to that the increasing number of people living in areas such as coastlines, in substandard housing and the destruction in a crisis of essential infrastructure, such as hospitals, and you have the potential for more devastating disasters than a few decades ago.

There have always been disasters. The bubonic plague wiped out more than 25 million people, or 37% of Europe's population, in the 1300s. More recently, the 1918-19 flu pandemic killed between 20 and 40 million people worldwide. One of the earliest recorded disasters, the eruption of Vesuvius in 79 AD, buried the ancient Roman city of Pompeii killing about 10,000 people. Today, two million people live within its possible range, illustrating one major difference between then and now.

About 75 disasters were reported globally in 1975....In 2000 the figure peaked at 525 and dropped to just under 400 in 2004. By far the highest number of fatalities—about 450,000—occurred in 1984. In 2004 nearly 300,000 died in disasters, but the number of people affected has soared since 1975 with about 600 million people affected by disasters of all kinds in 2002.

So complex and intertwined are the factors behind these disasters that some experts believe the most practical approach to preparedness may be to focus on reducing the risks rather than factors behind the risks.

Dave Paul Zervaas, regional coordinator for Latin America and the Caribbean at the United Nations' International Strategy for Disaster Reduction, argued that preparation should focus on making people less vulnerable to disasters. "We think it's much more important now to look at vulnerabilities, because you have factors you can control," Zervaas said. "You can work to lower vulnerability [to disasters]."

Hurricane Katrina in the United States is a good example, Zervaas said. A number of factors contributed to the damage and loss of life. The storm was huge. It struck a city whose levees had not been maintained or strengthened for years, and government agencies' response to the emergency was at first inadequate.

In Central America storms such as hurricanes Mitch and Stan have wrought damage with rain and landslides rather than wind. "The poverty issue and the social inequity situation have not become much better in most places," said Zervaas, adding that migration to cities conspires with a lack of urban planning to put people in danger.

Clearly, climate change—whether helped by human behaviour or not—is playing a role. Hurricane experts say the world is in the midst of a routine, cyclical climate change that causes the Caribbean to heat up, increasing the frequency of powerful storms. The effect of this is greater than that of global warming....

Experts agree that the poor are disproportionately hit. "In several of these countries, the poor people are looking for spaces to build their houses or their communities [and] they find spaces that are not already used," Ugarte said. "And those spaces that are not already used are usually the spaces at higher risk for natural phenomena. There's a huge relationship between this kind of damage and poverty."

For this reason financial services play a role in both prevention, and damage limitation and recovery....[T]he risks generated by climate change [include]..."blows to the world economy sufficiently severe to cripple the resilience that enables affluent countries to respond to catastrophes."... While it is important to encourage people, governments and companies to buy insurance, not everyone can afford it or see the need.

Microfinancing is another avenue, giving poor people the means to improve their economic situation so that a disaster does not hit them as hard as it would otherwise, and also by lending them money to use in recovering from it....

PAHO has expanded its programmes to focus not only on preparedness but also on mitigation. This involves reducing secondary deaths and destruction that can occur in the aftermath of a disaster, and implementing building codes that require hospitals, schools, military bases, and other vital structures to be built to withstand such disasters.

Many countries say they can't afford more preparation, but some measures are simple and can be inexpensive, such as a tsunami warning system, Ugarte said. "But from there to Banda Aceh, that is another step," Ugarte said, referring to the capital of the Indonesian province that was worst hit by the earthquake and tsunami of December 2004. "And from Banda Aceh to all the little communities on the coast, that's another issue. That last link of the chain is not in place. And that is the system that we need to build."

Disaster experts say early warning systems and education are essential to prevent and mitigate against the effects of natural disasters....[A] simple phone call saved thousands of lives when the giant tsunami waves hit India in 2004. A fisherman's son named Vijayakumar Gunasekaran, who lives in

Singapore, heard about the tsunami early on the radio and phoned relatives living on the east coast of India. Following his warning, all 3,630 residents evacuated their village there before the waves arrived.

NOTES AND QUESTIONS

1. The increase in the frequency and intensity of natural disasters depends on a complex web of interrelated factors. Climate change, environmental degradation, population growth, social and economic inequality, and governmental policy all contribute. These factors span a spectrum that can be calibrated according to the degree of putative control that governments can exert.

   a. *Climate change.* Though "environmental geographers [say] there is no such thing as a natural disaster," Neil Smith, *There's No Such Thing as a Natural Disaster,* http://understandingkatrina.ssrc.org/Smith (June 11, 2009), the factors that contribute to disasters do vary in the degree of effective control that humans can exert. Perhaps the most complex and therefore most unmanageable natural phenomenon, climate change is affected by a staggering range of factors. Since the Industrial Revolution, however, the earth's climate has begun to exhibit two disturbing trends. First, overall temperature has risen. Second, departures from "normal" conditions are becoming more frequent and more intense. Storms and temperature extremes—in both directions—are rapidly becoming the norm rather than the exception. *See generally, e.g.,* Intergovernmental Panel on Climate Change, Climate Change 2014: Working Group II, Impacts, Adaptation and Vulnerability (2014); Howard C. Kunreuther & Erwann O. Michel-Kerjan, At War with the Weather: Managing Large-Scale Risks in a New Era of Catastrophes (2009).

   Greenhouse gas emissions represent the very sort of "diffuse, cross-jurisdictional" crises that defy "haphazard local encouragement" and require cooperative solutions. Stephen M. Nickelsburg, Note, *Mere Volunteers? The Promise and Limits of Community-Based Environmental Protection,* 84 Va. L. Rev. 1371, 1409 (1998); *see also* Daniel A. Farber, *Stretching the Margins: The Geographic Nexus in Environmental Law,* 48 Stan. L. Rev. 1247, 1271 (1996). Because individual contributions to climate change are hard to quantify and even harder to control, whether through incentives or coercive regulation, governments will have great difficulty fashioning satisfactory *ex post* remedies, let alone effective *ex ante* prevention.

   b. *Localized environmental degradation.* Environmental conditions on a smaller footprint also affect the probability and impact of natural disasters. Wealth and poverty are each capable of degrading the environment and thereby contributing to disaster. Whereas poverty and desperation have driven deforestation in Haiti, the urge to move more barge traffic in western Europe has driven the straightening of the Rhine. For strikingly different reasons, both regions find themselves more vulnerable to storms, flooding, and other putatively natural phenomena.

c. *Population growth and distribution.* The mere existence of more humans increases the number of potential casualties. *See generally* Joel Cohen, How Many People Can the Earth Support? (1995); Paul Ehrlich & Anne Ehrlich, The Population Explosion (1990). These population increases are not distributed evenly. The rich and the poor alike are crowding seashores and other environmentally vulnerable areas. Poverty arguably poses a greater challenge for disaster management, since the poor often have no choice but to live in risky areas. The inability of the poor to heed evacuation orders, examined in Chapter 4, finds a distressing corollary in the continued presence of the poor in areas prone to storms, flooding, earthquakes, and other disasters.

d. *Governmental policies.* Katrina represented merely one prominent instance of legal failure. The federal government and the most directly affected states shared responsibility for failure on at least three distinct levels. First, these governments fell short of optimal *preparedness,* in the sense of educating themselves and the public on ways to minimize risk and on the division of authority in the event of disaster. Early warning systems and evacuation protocols had to be improvised, even though the probability of a strong hurricane hitting New Orleans was substantial and anticipated, and even though officials at all levels of government knew that such a strike could inflict many casualties. Second, once Katrina struck, officials did not carry out the best available plans for *response and mitigation.* For instance, Secretary of Homeland Security Michael Chertoff failed to invoke the National Response Plan's Catastrophic Incident Annex. Finally, the Gulf Coast sustained intense *secondary damage* to hospitals and other elements of public infrastructure that contribute most to mitigation and recovery. Governments should strive to minimize secondary casualties attributable more directly to these losses than to the disaster itself.

e. *Idiosyncratic barriers to perceiving problems and prescribing change.* Decision makers are heavily influenced by their personal experiences. Walter Isaacson, vice-chairman of the Louisiana Recovery Authority, was initially an advocate of aggressive, top-down urban planning as a precondition to the disbursement of Community Block Development Grants and other publicly controlled funds set aside for recovery efforts after Katrina. He reversed field when he learned that his family's neighborhood, Broadmoor, had been targeted for bulldozing and conversion into green space. Perhaps belatedly, Walter Isaacson came to appreciate that a planning official's preferred "urban footprint" may demand the bulldozing of someone else's neighborhood. *See* Jim Chen,

*Law Among the Ruins, in*Law and Recovery from Disaster: Hurricane
Katrina 1, 3 (Robin Paul Malloy ed., 2009).

To be sure, failed policies are more readily remedied than broader
social and environmental problems, such as economic inequality or
global climate change. The structure of this chapter and of this book as
a whole reflects this instinct. We have focused so far on the initial
allocation of governmental authority and the actual implementation of
emergency response measures, leaving to later chapters more diffuse
issues of compensation, risk spreading, prevention, mitigation, and
long-term environmental protection. The immediate subject of social
vulnerability and its contribution to a natural disaster illustrates the
interplay of governmental, economic, social, and environmental forces.
Precisely because there is no such thing as a strictly natural disaster,
government should focus in the first instance on matters more within its
control, hopeful that success in overcoming economic and social
injustice will lessen the suffering from disasters.

2. Consider this summary of human factors that contribute to the "mortality,
displacement, [and] economic destruction" wrought by disasters:

The first of these is pre-disaster preparedness and mitigation. From
constructing housing (or levees) to withstand natural [shocks] to pre-
positioning adequate relief supplies and preparing realistic evacuation plans,
the ability of communities and societies to plan ahead to resist disaster is
critical.

Second, the in-disaster coping capacities of affected populations: are there
resources on which they are able to fall back? In some hunger-prone regions of
the world, for example, 'famine foods'—not eaten in good times but growing
wild and freely available—can provide some meager support in periods of
scarcity. In developed ones, have communities been able to build up and
ensure access to stockpiles of canned goods, drinking water and first aid
supplies? Or has their ability to build up a margin of safety been whittled away
by poverty and marginalisation?

Third, the immediacy, quantity, efficiency and coverage of the disaster
response: each element is critical. Response may be timely but insufficient,
ignoring key communities; or, as is all too frequent in the case of major "CNN
catastrophes" which creep onto the world's television screens, the response
may eventually be large but months too late....
Finally, the longer term commitment of governments and other actors to post-
disaster recovery: long after the flood waters and the TV cameras both recede,
reconstruction and rehabilitation are critical in rebuilding shattered lives and
livelihoods. But continued commitment (and investment) at this point can

capitalise on a unique opportunity to build towards the reduction of future disasters.

Stephen Jackson, *Un/natural Disasters, Here and There*, http://understanding katrina.ssrc.org/Jackson (June 11, 2009).

3. Katrina capped a global year of misery that began with a natural disaster of even greater geographic and social scale. Roughly a quarter of a million people died in the Indian Ocean tsunami of December 26, 2004. Another million people were displaced. Though spread across three continents, the populations most directly affected by the tsunami were united in poverty and their vulnerability to one of the most destructive disasters in history:

Human Rights Center, University of California, Berkeley
After the Tsunami: Human Rights of Vulnerable Populations 1 (October 2005)

The tsunami of December 26, 2004, devastated thousands of communities along the coastline of the Indian Ocean. More than 240,000 people were killed. Tens of thousands went missing and are presumed dead, and more than a million people were displaced. Those most affected by the tsunami were the poor, including fisher folk, coastal workers with small retail or tourist businesses, workers in the tourism industry, migrants, and those who farmed close to coastal areas. The majority of those who died were women and children.

Immediately following the tsunami, international aid agencies feared that human traffickers might seize the opportunity to compel those most vulnerable (women, children, and migrant workers) into situations of forced labor....[O]ther human rights problems, including arbitrary arrests, recruitment of children into fighting forces, discrimination in aid distribution, enforced relocation, sexual and gender-based violence, loss of documentation, as well as issues of restitution, and land and property tenure soon emerged in certain tsunami-affected areas.

As we have seen in the aftermath of hurricane Katrina, which devastated coastal areas in the southern United States, natural disasters often catch national and local governments and relief agencies unprepared to deal with the massive exigencies of emergency relief and management, and can expose victims of these catastrophes to violations of human rights.

Victims of natural disasters are protected by a host of human rights treaties and agreements. Both the UN Guiding Principles on Internal Displacement and the Sphere Project's Humanitarian Charter and Minimum Standards in Disaster Response protect victims of natural disaster and guide relief efforts to ensure that those displaced receive access to adequate and essential relief—including food, shelter, and medical care. These guiding principles maintain that internally displaced persons (IDP) have the right to request and to receive protection and assistance from national authorities who, in turn, have the primary duty and responsibility to protect and assist populations within their jurisdiction.

Natural disasters can exacerbate pre-existing vulnerabilities of populations already at risk. Poverty-stricken groups living in substandard housing, on unstable ground, or in flood plains are usually the principal victims of these disasters. Often these groups have experienced ongoing discrimination because of their ethnicity, religion, class, or gender, which has left them living in fragile physical environments. Moreover, pre-existing civil war or a history of ongoing human rights abuses can complicate or interfere with aid relief and reconstruction.

In countries where corruption and bureaucratic incompetence are rife, certain individuals and groups may manipulate their political connections to receive or distribute aid at the expense of others. Still other groups may receive little or no aid because of their ethnicity, religion, gender, age, or social standing. These abuses can leave individuals and families at risk and prolong the time they have to stay in poorly built and even dangerous camps and shelters for internally displaced people.

Isolated in camps, the internally displaced often are sidelined as government officials in distant towns and cities formulate and implement resettlement and rebuilding programs, sometimes in favor of special interests. Uncoordinated relief efforts run the risk of exacerbating these problems, especially where there is weak government oversight of the activities of international agencies and aid organizations. A tension can develop between government appropriating all decision-making to itself or allowing nongovernmental organizations to carry out their missions as they see fit. Lack of a middle ground leaves survivors with no one to turn to for assistance.

NOTES AND QUESTIONS

1. Compare Hurricane Katrina with the Indian Ocean tsunami. What might American policy makers learn from an even greater tragedy that spanned the entire Indian Ocean rim? Conversely, can global efforts against staggering losses to natural disaster learn from domestic failures in one of the world's wealthiest nations? The parallels between Katrina and the tsunami are fairly obvious: catastrophic loss of life and property, disparate impact based on social and economic status, and a distressing degree of official incompetence. Some salient differences, however, do distinguish the two disasters:

   a. *Preexisting human rights violations.* Whatever else might be said of inequality, civil rights, and human dignity in the United States, none of Katrina's victims were exposed to conscription into civil wars or opportunistic human trafficking. North America, to put it mildly, knows nothing of the misery that afflicts less developed parts of the world.

b. *Corruption and lack of transparency and accountability in government.* Again, official fecklessness in America falls short of the sheer ineptitude of governments in many of the world's poorest countries. Katrina's impact on New Orleans and the Gulf Coast was the subject of extensive public discussion. The House of Representatives, the Senate, and the White House all delivered scathing reports on the failures of the response effort, complete with concrete platforms for reform. Some officials perceived as having performed poorly during Katrina, such as former FEMA chairman Michael Brown, lost power.

c. *Wealth, poverty, and inequality.* According to the World Bank's gauges of absolute poverty, the world's poorest subsist on $1 per day in purchasing power parity (relative to the value of U.S. dollars in 1985). Such extreme levels of poverty are unknown—and politically unthinkable—in the United States. By the same token, *relative* poverty exists everywhere, and by this standard the United States fares poorly, at least as compared with other industrialized countries. According to the United Nations, *see* United Nations, Human Development Indicators 270 (2005), the United States reported a Gini coefficient of 40.8, which corresponds to a higher level of economic inequality than either India (32.5) or Bangladesh (31.8), two significantly poorer countries that suffered mightily during the 2004 tsunami, *see id.* at 272.[8]

d. *War.* Nearly a century and a half after Appomattox Court House, every American combat veteran is eligible for membership in the Veterans of Foreign Wars. Many other countries, sadly, continue to experience war as a thoroughly domestic phenomenon. Most Americans have no personal experience with the conscription of children or the exploitation of civilians as human shields against organized violence.

2. In the end, Katrina and the Indian Ocean tsunami should not be compared as part of an exercise to determine which victims suffered more, but rather as part of a learning experience by which policy makers might minimize future suffering. Taking account of geographic, social, economic, and political differences represents an important step in that learning process. "If the Indian Ocean Tsunami and Hurricane Katrina can be said to have any 'lessons' for us, it is to suggest that western developed countries may have as much to learn about disaster preparedness, management and recovery from non-western developing countries in terms of community-based assistance and the integrated flexible use of technology as the latter do from the former in terms of technocratic know-how and scientific expertise."

---

[8] The Gini coefficient is a measure of economic inequality; a higher score on this gauge indicates greater disparities in income within a country. *See* Philip M. Dixon, Jacob Weiner, Thomas Mitchell-Olds & Robert Woodley, *Bootstrapping the Gini Coefficient of Inequality*, 68 Ecology 1548 (1988).

3. The Berkeley tsunami report identifies two sources of international norms that might govern disaster relief efforts. One of these is the United Nations' Guiding Principles on Internal Displacement, which will receive more consideration in Chapter 9 (international law). The other is the handbook of the Sphere Project, a collaborative effort of the Red Cross, Red Crescent, and other humanitarian organizations. A substantial portion of the Sphere Project's handbook outlines the "Humanitarian Charter" to which participating organizations aspire. The handbook's "Minimum Standards," by contrast, "are based on agencies' experience of providing humanitarian assistance":

> Though the achievement of the standards depends on a range of factors, many of which may be beyond our control, we commit ourselves to attempt consistently to achieve them and we expect to be held to account accordingly. We invite other humanitarian actors, including states themselves, to adopt these standards as accepted norms....
>
> [W]e commit ourselves to make every effort to ensure that people affected by disasters have access to at least the minimum requirements (water, sanitation, food, nutrition, shelter and health care) to satisfy their basic right to life with dignity. To this end we will continue to advocate that governments and other parties meet their obligations under international human rights law, international humanitarian law and refugee law.

The Sphere Project Handbook: Humanitarian Charter and Minimum Standards in Disaster Response 19 (2004).

4. Social vulnerability in times of disaster raises questions of human rights. How can international human rights law balance the proposition that environmental quality is "essential to...the enjoyment of human rights," Stockholm Declaration, Report of the United Nations Conference on the Human Environment, U.N. Doc. A/Conf.48/14, 11 I.L.M. 1416, 1416 (1972) (preamble), with the equally solemn pronouncement that economic development is also a "universal and inalienable right and an integral part of fundamental human rights"? Vienna Declaration and Programme of Action, U.N. Doc. A/CONF.157/24, *adopted at* Vienna, June 14-25, 1993, *reprinted in* 32 I.L.M. 1661 (1993). Environmental sustainability may hinge on a global transition from poverty to affluence and from authoritarianism to democracy rather than the suppression of economic development. *See* Jack M. Hollander, The Real Environmental Crisis: Why Poverty, Not Affluence, Is the Environment's Number One Enemy (2003). Of the world's myriad environmental problems, "persistent poverty may turn out to be the most aggravating and destructive." Patrick Low, *Trade and the Environment: What Worries the Developing Countries?*, 23 Envtl. L. 705, 706 (1993).

5. Katrina and the tsunami exposed serious flaws in several nations' capacity for preparedness, response, mitigation, and recovery in the event of natural disaster. Many of those flaws are attributable to—or at least exacerbated by—social, economic, and political inequalities expressed by the catchall phrase, "social vulnerability." To what extent is the global community willing to engage problems of social vulnerability once a single, catastrophic event has subsided? Or is the world doomed to remain inherently unequal and unjust—and correspondingly unprepared for the next tragedy that blends natural calamity with human injustice?

B. THE SCARS OF RACE, CLASS, AND INJUSTICE

Among Hurricane Katrina's first casualties was any expectation that the storm and the governmental response to it would deal equally with all victims, without regard to race or class. In a survey of Katrina evacuees living in Houston, "68 percent of respondents thought the federal government would have responded more quickly if people trapped in the floodwaters were 'wealthier and white rather than poorer and black.' " U.S. House of Representatives, A Failure of Initiative: Final Report of the Select Bipartisan Committee to Investigate the Preparation for and Response to Hurricane Katrina 19 (2006). At its worst, the storm exposed longstanding racial, social, and economic inequities. To be effective and legitimate, the legal response to disasters must address these injustices.

SUSAN L. CUTTER, THE GEOGRAPHY OF SOCIAL VULNERABILITY: RACE, CLASS, AND CATASTROPHE

http://understandingkatrina.ssrc.org/Cutter (June 11, 2009)

The revelations of inadequate response to the hurricane's aftermath are not just about failures in emergency response at the local, state, and federal levels or failures in the overall emergency management system. They are also about failures of the social support systems for America's impoverished—the largely invisible inner city poor. The former can be rectified quickly (months to years) through organizational restructuring or training; the latter requires much more time, resources, and the political will to redress social inequities and inequalities that have been sustained for more than a half century and show little signs of dissipating.

How did we arrive at such a confluence of natural and social vulnerabilities manifested as the Hurricane Katrina disaster? This complex emergency began with geography—the spatial interaction of humans and their environment over time. Officially founded in 1718 by Jean-Baptiste Le Moyne de Bienville, New Orleans was strategically located at the crossroads of three navigable water bodies, Lake Pontchartrain, the Gulf of Mexico, and the Mississippi River. Important primarily as a trading depot for French fur trappers, the city evolved into one of the most important ports in America providing a gateway to the nation's agricultural riches.

The original settlement was on the highest ground in the bayou, Vieux Carré (the French Quarter), which later became the heart and soul of the modern city. How prescient for the early settlers to build on the highest ground available. As the settlement grew in the ensuing decades, New Orleans became a major American port city and a sprawling metropolis sandwiched between and surrounded by water....

To reduce the natural risks of flooding, the physical environment surrounding New Orleans was re-engineered, spawning an era of structural river control. Levees were built to control the flow of the mighty Mississippi, but they were also built to contain flooding from Lake Pontchartrain, especially useful during hurricane season....Instead of seeing the deposition of alluvium that one expects in a deltaic coastline, the levees channeled the river and its sediment, destroying protective wetlands south and east of the city. With many areas of the city below sea level, even heavy rainfall became a problem filling the city with water just like a giant punchbowl. An elaborate pumping system was required to keep the city dry during heavy rains, let alone tropical storms. What would happen during a hurricane, a levee failure, or an intentional levee breach used to divert floodwaters away from the city as was done in 1927?

Concurrent with the physical transformation of the city, a new social geography was being created as well. The South's segregated past was best seen in the spatial and social evolution of southern cities, including New Orleans. Migration from the rural impoverished areas to the city was followed by white flight from urban areas to more suburban communities. Public housing was constructed to cope with Black population influxes during the 1950s and 1960s and in a pattern repeated throughout America, the housing was invariably located in the most undesirable areas—along major transportation corridors, on reclaimed land, or next to industrial facilities. Employment opportunities were limited for inner city residents as jobs moved outward from the central city to suburban locations, or overseas as the process of globalization reduced even further the number of low skilled jobs. The most impoverished lived in squalor-like conditions concentrated in certain neighborhoods within cities, with little or no employment, poor education, and little hope for the future for their children or grandchildren. It is against this backdrop of the social geography of cities and the differential access to resources that we can best understand the Hurricane Katrina disaster.

Socially created vulnerabilities are largely ignored in the hazards and disaster literature because they are so hard to measure and quantify. Social vulnerability is partially a product of social inequalities—those social factors and forces that create the susceptibility of various groups to harm, and in turn affect their ability to respond, and bounce back (resilience) after the disaster. But it is much more than that. Social vulnerability involves the basic provision of health care, the livability of places, overall indicators of quality of life, and accessibility to lifelines (goods, services, emergency response personnel), capital, and political representation.

Race and class are certainly factors that help explain the social vulnerability in the South, while ethnicity plays an additional role in many cities. When the middle classes (both White and Black) abandon a city, the disparities between the very rich and the very poor expand. Add to this an increasing elderly population, the homeless, transients (including tourists), and other special needs populations, and the prospects for evacuating a city during times of emergencies becomes a daunting challenge for most American cities. What is a major challenge for other cities became a virtual impossibility for New Orleans. Those that could muster the personal resources evacuated the city. With no welfare check (the hurricane struck near the end of the month), little food, and no help from the city, state, or federal officials, the poor were forced to ride out the storm in their homes or move to the shelters of last resort. This is the enduring face of Hurricane Katrina—poor, black, single mothers, young, and old—struggling just to survive; options limited by the ineffectiveness of preparedness and the inadequacy of response....

As a nation, we have very little experience with evacuating cities from natural hazards....Crisis relocation planning was the norm during the height of the Reagan administration, but many social scientists scoffed at the implausibility of the effort as a precautionary measure against a nuclear attack. Our collective experience with evacuations is based on chemical spills or toxic releases, planning for nuclear power plant accidents, and hurricanes. In most cases, but certainly not all, the evacuations have been in rural or suburban places, not a major U.S. city....The potential differences in response are critical and highlight the difficulties in emergency preparedness for major cities. The number of large urban hospitals, the dependence on public transportation, and the need for mass sheltering all complicate preparedness efforts in these dense multi-ethnic and multi-racial cities. In addition to the sheer number of people at risk, emergency managers have the additional task of identifying those residents who may be the most vulnerable—the poor, the infirm, the elderly, the homeless, women, and children. The nescient result is an ever-widening disparity in society's ability to cope with more persistent social and economic problems in urban areas, let alone a potential mass impact event of unknown origin. This is the story of Hurricane Katrina and its aftermath....

Just as there is variation in the physical landscape, the landscape of social inequity has increased the division between rich and poor in this country and has led to the increasing social vulnerability of our residents, especially to coastal hazards. Strained race relations and the seeming differential response to the disaster suggest[ ] that in planning for future catastrophes, we need to not only look at the natural environment in the development of mitigation programs, but the social environment as well. It is the interaction between nature and society that produces the vulnerability of places. While physical vulnerability is reduced through the construction of disaster-resistant buildings, changes in land use, and restoration of wetlands and floodways, a marked reduction in social vulnerability will require an improvement in the overall quality of life for the inner city poor. We should not have the equivalent of developing world conditions in a nation as wealthy as the United States. This is the tragedy of Hurricane Katrina....

Disasters will happen. To lessen their impacts in the future, we need to reduce our social vulnerability and increase disaster resilience with improvements in the social conditions and living standards in our cities. We need to build (and rebuild) damaged housing and infrastructure in harmony with nature and design cities to be resilient to environmental threats even if it means smaller, more livable places, and fewer profits for land and urban developers and a smaller tax base for the city. Disasters are income neutral and color-blind. Their impacts, however, are not.

NOTES AND QUESTIONS

1. Reconsider this statement by Susan Cutter: "Social vulnerability is partially a product of social inequalities—those social factors and forces that create the susceptibility of various groups to harm, and in turn affect their ability to respond, and bounce back (resilience) after the disaster." This pivotal passage suggests that social vulnerability consists of two distinct components: the *susceptibility* of certain groups to harm and the *resilience* of these groups. *See generally* Susan L. Cutter, Bryan. J. Boruff & W. Lynn Shirley, *Social Vulnerability to Environmental Hazards,* 84 Soc. Sci. Q. 242 (2003).

   a. *Susceptibility* is an *ex ante* quality; it is already in place when disaster strikes. Inequality in New Orleans and other parts of the South has taken hundreds of years to build. Differences in living conditions, wealth, and power rendered the poorest, often black victims of Katrina susceptible to disproportionate loss.

   b. *Resilience,* by contrast, assumes importance after the fact. Rebuilding destroyed communities demands extraordinary human and material resources. Capital available—and often taken for granted—for recovery in more affluent communities may simply not exist in poorer communities. Crucial physical and social infrastructure, often strained or undermined by disaster and its aftermath, is not as readily reestablished.

2. Consider also this definition of vulnerability:

   By vulnerability we mean the characteristics of a person or group in terms of their capacity to anticipate, cope with, resist, and recover from the impact of a natural hazard. It involves a combination of factors that determine the degree to which someone's life and livelihood is put at risk by a discrete and identifiable event in nature or in society.

Piers Blaikie, Terry Cannon, Ian Davis & Ben Wisner, At Risk: Natural Hazards, People's Vulnerability and Disasters 9 (1994). Even more succinctly: "risk = exposure × vulnerability." Robert R.M. Verchick, Facing Catastrophe: Environmental Action for a Post-Katrina World 128 (2010). Conversely, "disaster justice" consists of discharging collective responsibility to minimize social vulnerability and to optimize social resilience. Robert R.M. Verchick, *Disaster Justice: The Geography of Human Capability*, 23 Duke Envtl. L. & Pol'y 23 (2013).

B.E. AGUIRRE, DIALECTICS OF VULNERABILITY AND RESILIENCE

14 Geo. J. on Poverty L. & Pol'y 39, 41-45 (2007)

The complexity inherent in the concepts of vulnerability and resilience is in part due to the multiple systems in which they operate simultaneously...and from the interactions and inter-effects that take place among these systems. Resilience is an example of morphostasis—that is, a process directed to preserve the social system. Vulnerability is a type of morphogenesis, for it facilitates changes in the system, at times by becoming more differentiated. Vulnerability is a synonym of exhaustion, impotence, weakness, or exposure to harm. [There are] three types of vulnerabilities: a pre-existing condition in a social organization; a social product, in which vulnerability is the outcome of the differential distribution of power and privilege in society; and bio-physical risks associated with specific geographical sites. [An even more] comprehensive list of vulnerabilities...includes natural, physical, economic, social, political, technical, ideological, cultural, educational, ecological, and institutional risks, all of these subsumed in the concept of global vulnerability. It is seldom noted, however, that from an open system dialectic perspective, a state of vulnerability of social organization reveals the presence and operation of risks and may constitute a window of opportunity calling for mitigations, which may improve its resilience and its adaptive capacity in the face of crises and disasters. The absence of an awareness of vulnerability may also be associated with the presence of unknown risks. Known vulnerability illuminates the need of social organizations to change so as to minimize risks and increase their capability to adjust to their environment, and may bring about efforts at mitigation....

Resilience has been defined in many ways, including an ability to "bounce back" and continue to function; predict and prevent potential problems; improvise and recombine resources in new ways; develop a collective and shared vision of dangers and what to do about them; and constantly monitor threatening contextual conditions....[R]esilience "is also about the opportunities that disturbance opens up in terms of recombination of evolved structures and processes, renewal of the system and emergence of new trajectories." Resilience is partly a recursive function of conscious awareness, planning, and training that anticipates or responds to the presence of vulnerabilities and tries to mitigate and provide solutions to them. These are all dimensions of resilient systems. Resilient actions do not merely reflect the capacity of systems to reconstitute themselves as they existed prior to the crisis, but show a system's ability to absorb, respond, recover, and reorganize from an internally or externally induced set of demands which reveal the presence of vulnerability and bring about mitigation efforts. As indicated previously, it is a never-ending open process, for multiple sources of often unanticipated demands create changes in the known dynamics of the systems. Past experiences cannot be used as the only source of information to anticipate new risks. Imagination, creativity, and careful historical reconstructions of past disastrous events, including both cross national and international scientific assessments of major crises and disasters, are needed to attempt to anticipate and prevent new risks' effects. Inherent in the very solution meant to bring about temporary adaptation is the creation of new and frequently unanticipated vulnerabilities, resulting in the need for new efforts at mitigation and resilience. This is due in part to the incomplete nature of human knowledge, our inability to foresee the multilevel and contradictory impacts of our actions regardless of our intent, and the weight of traditions which limit creative adaptation, as well as exogenous changes in the natural and social environments....

Resilience is also the ability to take action in anticipation of demands and known vulnerabilities to forestall or minimize them, although...the effectiveness of such efforts is always open to the vagaries of limited human knowledge, entrenched interest, and inability to come up with solutions outside prevailing cultural practices. [A] study of Sydney, Australia, [has] demonstrated that the city so far has escaped major disasters mostly because of a relatively benign natural environment even as other vulnerabilities, such as environmental degradation and poverty, are largely ignored. What could happen in less benign environments is evidenced by Katrina, for it was an announced catastrophe that revealed the rigidities of political interests and narrow-minded public service. Local scientists for at least a decade earlier had outlined what would happen in the absence of adaptive change, and how to bring such change about, which involved learning to live with the Mississippi River rather than against it. A contrasting example is the "growing with the sea" strategy of the Netherlands, in which the Dutch recognized that their coastal mitigation measures were not working and adopted a system that allows for occasional extreme flooding while minimizing the damages. These cases show that often disasters are the indirect effects of political traditions, entrenched economic and social power, and the presence or lack of leadership, rather than a lack of scientific knowledge about what needs to be done. These processes of political economy often determine whether or not societies recognize their risks and associated vulnerabilities, and whether they engage in mitigation efforts that enhance their resilience and their adaptive capacity.

Resilience of social organizations is one of a number of factors that determine their adaptive capacity. Changes which enhance resilience take place neither in a linear fashion nor without conflicting objectives: policy changes are often contentious, technological changes have unintended consequences, demographic transitions can bring their own pressures through changes in resource needs, and the built environment is subject to constant maintenance needs and changes in usage. The challenge for the incorporation of resiliency is to identify what enhances the ability of social organizations to rebound effectively, taking into account the actual physical, biological, personality, social, and cultural systems that are present and the limited amount of economic and other resources that may be available to lessen vulnerability.

In an immediate sense, disasters are the outcome of the interaction between a hazard and a social organization with a portfolio of risks, vulnerabilities, and resilience. Disasters are disturbances that have the "potential to create opportunity for doing new things, for innovation and for development." They are not solely caused by vulnerabilities, but also, counter-intuitively, by previous efforts at mitigation and enhancement of resilience. Disasters are moments of rupture in the "normal" or taken-for-granted operations of social organizations. They reveal the critical balance existing among vulnerability, mitigation, resilience, and community recovery, and the extent to which the social organization has not been able to adapt effectively to its environments. Both vulnerability and resilience fluctuate over time and space, allowing for the differential impacts of hazards on the built and social systems. A dialectical approach to vulnerability and resilience to disaster necessitates a shift in our conceptualizations from discrete strategies to reduce disaster-related risks and vulnerability to more dynamic, holistic, and integrated approaches to enhance societal adaptation.

NOTES AND QUESTIONS

1. May disaster victims seek legal relief from the officials who supervised an emergency preparedness and response effort that appears not only to have been wholly inadequate? Begin with this summary of the law of post-disaster compensation, elaborated at greater length in Chapters 3 and 7:
   a. Numerous statutes immunize governments from liability for negligent disaster management. *See generally* Ken Lerner, *Governmental Negligence Liability Exposure in Disaster Management*, 23 Urb. Law. 333, 336-340 (1991). Under certain conditions, plaintiffs may sue public operators of large-scale infrastructure that fails during disaster. *Cf.* Kunz v. Utah Power & Light Co., 526 F.2d 500, 504 (9th Cir. 1975) (recognizing a common law duty arising from a utility's adoption of flood control measures).

b. For losses attributable to failed public infrastructure, governments may face inverse condemnation liability under state law. *See* Paterno v. California, 113 Cal. App. 4th 998, 6 Cal. Rptr. 3d 854 (2003). Similarly, the federal government may face takings clause liability for government-induced flood control measures that effect a permanent or even temporary occupation of private property. Arkansas Game & Fish Comm'n v. United States, 133 S. Ct. 511 (2012).

c. Within limits imposed by the Federal Tort Claims Act, 28 U.S.C. §2674, disaster victims may recover damages from the United States. In litigation arising from Hurricane Katrina, the federal government could not claim immunity under the Flood Control Act (FCA), 33 U.S.C. §702c, on claims related to the dredging of the Mississippi River Gulf Outlet, but could assert (1) immunity under the Flood Control Act against claims stemming from levee breaches caused by the dredging of the canal and (2) immunity under the discretionary-function exception to the Federal Tort Claims Act against other claims. *See In re* Katrina Canal Breaches Litig., 696 F.3d 436, 444-52 (5th Cir. 2012).*Compare* United States v. James, 478 U.S. 597 (1986) (shielding the United States from liability arising from flood control projects conducted by the Corps of Engineers) *with* Central Green Co. v. United States, 531 U.S. 425 (2001) (holding that Flood Control Act immunity depends upon "the character of the waters that cause the relevant damage rather than the relation between that damage and a [federal] flood control project").

d. Tort actions treat official defendants in their proprietary rather than their regulatory capacities—that is, as owners of property as opposed to sovereigns capable of regulating private actors, collecting taxes, and redistributing wealth. *See* Lockheed Aircraft Corp. v. United States, 460 U.S. 190, 198 (1986).

2. What of disaster response that not only fell short in absolute terms, but also arguably exposed blacks to greater harm than similarly situated whites? Some relief may lie in disparate impact claims under federal anti-discrimination laws. In 2011, the U.S. Department of Housing and Urban Development (HUD) and the State of Louisiana settled a class action suit alleging that the formula for administering post-Katrina "Road Home" housing recovery grants—which awarded grants based on the lesser of the home's pre-storm value or repair costs—violated the Fair Housing Act because it imposed a disparate impact on African Americans, whose homes, on average, were worth less before the storm. *See* HUD Press Release, July 6, 2011, http://portal.hud.gov/hudportal/HUD?src=/press/press_releases_media_advisories/2011/HUDNo.11-138.

3. An even more aggressive approach to holding government responsible for compensating disaster victims consists of framing the question as one of federal constitutional rights. Aside from the question of whether government had a duty to act, *cf.* DeShaney v. Winnebago County Dept. of

Soc. Servs., 489 U.S. 189 (1989), formidable barriers block the path to relief. A direct claim that government inaction violates disaster victims' civil rights seems remote at best.

a. Constitutional law does not recognize an equal protection claim based solely on the claim that otherwise neutral conduct has a racially disparate impact. *See* Washington v. Davis, 426 U.S. 229, 242 (1976). An equal protection violation typically hinges on "[p]roof of racially discriminatory intent or purpose." Village of Arlington Heights v. Metropolitan Housing Dev. Corp., 429 U.S. 252, 265 (1977); *accord, e.g.,* City of Cuyahoga Falls v. Buckeye Community Hope Found., 538 U.S. 188, 194 (2003). The government must have chosen a particular course "because of" and not merely "in spite of" the decision's adverse impact on "an identifiable group." Personnel Adm'r v. Feeney, 442 U.S. 256, 279 (1979); *accord* McCleskey v. Kemp, 481 U.S. 279, 298 (1987).

b. On the other hand, when even neutral legislation or governmental conduct produces a clear pattern that cannot be explained except on racial grounds, a constitutional violation may lie. *See* Gomillion v. Lightfoot, 364 U.S. 339 (1960); Yick Wo v. Hopkins, 118 U.S. 356 (1886); *cf.* Lane v. Wilson, 307 U.S. 268 (1939); Guinn v. United States, 238 U.S. 347 (1915). The appearance of "a clear pattern, unexplainable on grounds other than race," makes the "evidentiary inquiry...relatively easy." 429 U.S. at 266. Because cases presenting "a pattern [this] stark" are "rare," however, "impact alone is [seldom] determinative, and [a reviewing] Court must look to other evidence." *Id.*

c. In most cases, evidence of "invidious discriminatory purpose" demands a deeper inquiry into the "historical background" underlying official conduct. *Arlington Heights,* 429 U.S. at 267. "The specific sequence of events leading up the challenged decision also may shed some light on the decisionmaker's purposes." *Id.* Departures from "the normal procedural sequence" or from substantive decision-making criteria "also might afford evidence that improper purposes are playing a role." *Id.* Finally, "[t]he legislative or administrative history may be highly relevant, especially where there are contemporary statements by members of the decisionmaking body, minutes of its meetings, or reports." *Id.* at 268. What evidence can be found in the record of official conduct during the preparation for a hypothetical hurricane hitting New Orleans, during Katrina itself, and throughout recovery after the storm?

d. The use of legislative or administrative history gives rise to another basis for relief, albeit one rarely encountered. The Supreme Court has invalidated an otherwise facially neutral law that disenfranchised all persons convicted of crimes of moral turpitude, citing statements showing that the law's proponents intended to prevent blacks from voting. *See* Hunter v. Underwood, 471 U.S. 222 (1985). *But cf.* Palmer v. Thompson, 403 U.S. 217, 224 (1971) ("[N]o case in this Court has held that a legislative act may violate equal protection solely because of the motivations of the men who voted for it.").

e. "In many instances, to recognize the limited probative value of disproportionate impact is merely to acknowledge the 'heterogeneity' of the Nation's population." *Arlington Heights,* 429 U.S. at 266 n.15 (quoting Jefferson v. Hackney, 406 U.S. 535, 548 (1972)).

f. Notwithstanding Washington v. Davis and *Arlington Heights,* the Supreme Court is more willing in certain contexts to infer discriminatory purpose from disparate impact. *See, e.g.,* Shaw v. Reno, 509 U.S. 630 (1993) (gerrymandering); Batson v. Kentucky, 476 U.S. 79 (1986) (peremptory jury challenges); Rogers v. Lodge, 458 U.S. 613 (1982) (vote dilution); Swann v. Charlotte-Mecklenburg Bd. of Educ., 402 U.S. 1 (1971) (school desegregation). Does anything about natural disasters, the nature of social vulnerability during disaster, or the role of government warrant a comparable judicial willingness to infer purpose from effect? Or, as in the context of selective prosecution, must a claim alleging a racially uneven response to a disaster "draw on 'ordinary equal protection standards' "? United States v. Armstrong, 517 U.S. 456, 465 (1996).

4. The Eighth Amendment supplies another constitutional analogy by which policy vis-à-vis vulnerable populations during a disaster may be judged. A prison official's "deliberate indifference" to a substantial risk of serious harm to an inmate violates the prohibition on "cruel and unusual punishments." *See, e.g.,* Helling v. McKinney, 509 U.S. 25 (1993); Wilson v. Seiter, 501 U.S. 294 (1991); Estelle v. Gamble, 429 U.S. 97 (1976).

a. "Deliberate indifference" demands that an official have a state of mind more blameworthy than negligence. In considering a claim that inadequate medical care violated the Eighth Amendment, the Supreme Court has distinguished "deliberate indifference to serious medical needs of prisoners," *Estelle,* 429 U.S. at 104, from mere "negligen[ce] in diagnosing or treating a medical condition," *id.* at 106. Transcending the "ordinary lack of due care for the prisoner's interests or safety," Whitley v. Albers, 475 U.S. 312, 319 (1986), deliberate indifference ultimately requires subjective intent:

> [A] prison official cannot be found liable under the Eighth Amendment for denying an inmate humane conditions of confinement unless the official knows of and disregards an excessive risk to inmate health or safety; the official must both be aware of facts from which the inference could be drawn that a substantial risk of serious harm exists, and he must also draw the inference.

Farmer v. Brennan, 511 U.S. 825, 837 (1994).

b. Perhaps the officials in charge of preparing for and responding to Katrina can be accused of *passive* rather than deliberate indifference:

> [R]acial exclusion...today happens not so much through active bigotry as it does through the tacit exclusions created by these sorts of unstated, unconsidered social habits....[I]f your social network is, for purely historical reasons, defined by color lines that were drawn long ago in a different and undeniably widely bigoted age, then you don't have to be a bigot yourself to be perpetuating the institutional structures of racial exclusion....This was exactly Illinois Senator Barack Obama's point when he declared on the Senate floor that the poor response to Katrina was not "evidence of active malice," but merely the result of "a continuation of passive indifference." These structural exclusions matter very much for one's total life opportunities, including crucially one's economic opportunities—and thus greatly affect one's opportunities to, say, escape from deadly hurricanes.

Nils Gilman, *What Katrina Teaches about the Meaning of Racism,* http://understandingkatrina.ssrc.org/Gilman (June 11, 2009). Is "passive indifference" less blameworthy than its deliberate counterpart?

5. Disaster relief arguably provides the constitutional foundation for the contemporary American welfare state. Constitutional justifications for federal intervention on behalf of victims of fires, floods, storms, earthquakes, and wars reach back beyond the New Deal and even the Progressive Era, to the earliest days of the Republic. *See generally* Michele Landis Dauber, The Sympathetic State: Disaster Relief and the Origins of the American Welfare State (2012). From this perspective, it is not so far fetched to examine social vulnerability to disaster—and to frame the appropriate legal response to such vulnerability—in explicitly constitutional terms.

6. For yet another legal perspective on vulnerability, consider U.S. Sentencing Guidelines §3A1.1, which instructs judges to enhance the sentence of a federal criminal defendant who "intentionally selected any victim or any property as the object of the offense of conviction because of the actual or perceived race, color, religion, national origin, ethnicity, gender, disability, or sexual orientation of any person" or who "knew or should have known that a victim of the offense was a vulnerable victim."

a. The Guidelines are structured so that the presence of "race, color, religion, national origin, ethnicity, gender, disability, or sexual orientation" automatically qualifies a defendant for an enhanced sentence, independent of any inquiry into the victim's vulnerability.

b. With respect to the sentencing enhancement for a "vulnerable victim," the following three-pronged test applies:

> The enhancement may be applied where: (1) the victim was particularly susceptible or vulnerable to the criminal conduct; (2) the defendant knew or should have known of this susceptibility or vulnerability; and (3) this vulnerability or susceptibility facilitated the defendant's crime in some manner; that is, there was "a nexus between the victim's vulnerability and the crime's ultimate success."

United States v. Iannone, 184 F.3d 214, 220 (3d Cir. 1999); *accord, e.g.,* United States v. Zats, 298 F.3d 182, 186 (3d Cir. 2002). At least the first two prongs of this test can be applied by analogy to officials accused of failing to address social vulnerabilities during a natural disaster. Certain victims are "particularly susceptible or vulnerable" in times of disaster, and public officials "kn[o]w or should have known of this susceptibility or vulnerability." Because the Sentencing Guidelines are an artifact of criminal law, the analogy degrades somewhat with respect to the third prong. But some connection remains. The presence of a "nexus between the victim's vulnerability" and the social harm attributable to a natural disaster arguably should bear on the degree of official responsibility for shortcomings in remedying social vulnerabilities through preparation, response, mitigation, or recovery.

7. In assessing the moral (if not legal) culpability that should be assigned for the socially lopsided effects of natural disasters, consider the following account:

> It is society's most vulnerable who were "left behind" by government efforts to assess, to plan for, and to respond to a storm of Katrina's magnitude. And this was predictably so. A host of government decisions were made—each of which had the potential to mitigate or exacerbate the effects of a hurricane for the people of New Orleans—against a social, economic, and political backdrop that made the disproportionate impacts of certain government choices virtually inevitable. Where the choice was to forego the basic services and protections typically provided by a government, it should have been clear to decision makers precisely who would be left to fend for themselves.

> Twenty-eight percent of people in New Orleans live in poverty. Of these, 84 percent are African American. Twenty-three percent of people five years and older living in New Orleans are disabled. An estimated 15,000 to 17,000 men, women, and children in the New Orleans area are homeless. The lowest lying areas of New Orleans tend to be populated by those without economic or political resources. The city's Lower Ninth Ward, for example, which was especially hard hit and completely inundated by water, is among its poorest and lowest lying areas. Ninety-eight percent of its residents are African American.... "[I]n New Orleans, water flows away from money. Those with

resources who control where the drainage goes have always chosen to live on the high ground. So the people in the low areas were the hardest hit."

Of the households living in poverty, many have no access to a car: 21,787 of these households without a car are black; 2,606 are white. This lack of access became crucial, given an evacuation plan premised on the ability of people to get in their cars and drive out of New Orleans.

Center for Progressive Reform, An Unnatural Disaster: The Aftermath of Hurricane Katrina 34-35 (2005).

8. The Congressional Research Service has quantified the unequal social impact of Hurricane Katrina:

> Hurricane Katrina disproportionately impacted communities where the poor and minorities, mostly African Americans, resided. The three states where communities were damaged or flooded by the hurricane rank among the poorest in the nation. According to the 2000 Census, Mississippi ranked second only to the District of Columbia in its poverty rate; Louisiana was right behind it ranking third, and Alabama ranked sixth. CRS estimates that about one-fifth of the population most directly impacted by the storm was poor. That poverty rate (21%) was well above the national poverty rate of 12.4% recorded in the 2000 Census....In addition, over 30% of the most impacted population had incomes below one-and-one-half times the poverty line and over 40% had income below twice the poverty line....

> The hurricane's impact on New Orleans also took a disproportionate toll on African Americans. An estimated 310,000 black people were directly impacted by the storm, largely due to flooding in Orleans Parish. Blacks are estimated to have accounted for 44% of storm victims. In Orleans Parish, an estimated 272,000 black people were displaced by flooding or damage, accounting for 73% of the population affected by the storm in the parish. In contrast, an estimated 101,000 non-black people in Orleans Parish were displaced by flooding or damage, accounting for about 63% of the non-black population living in the parish; still a high proportion affected, but somewhat less than that experienced by blacks.
> Among blacks living in Orleans Parish who were most likely displaced by the storm, over one-third (89,000 people, or 34.0% of displaced blacks) were estimated to have been poor, based on 2000 Census data. Among non-black (predominantly white) persons living in the parish who were likely displaced by the storm, an estimated 14.6% (14,000) were poor.

Thomas Gabe, Gene Falk & Maggie McCarty, *Hurricane Katrina: Social-Demographic Characteristics of Impacted Areas* 14, 16-17 (Nov. 4, 2005) (CRS Order Code RL33141).

9. Katrina's disparate impact on poor and non-white individuals has been characterized as part of a larger pattern of "environmental injustice":

> Katrina...was an exceptionally large echo of a socioeconomic political condition known popularly as environmental injustice, the longstanding pattern whereby people of color and the poor are exposed to greater environmental risk while receiving fewer environmental amenities. Between the two, race has a statistically stronger link than class, and recent reports reveal that the association between race and environmental hazards is increasing. If we examine the background policies and decisions that ultimately led to the devastation in the wake of Katrina, we begin to see the event as part of this larger pattern.
>
> For example, planners anticipated that approximately 100,000 transit-dependent residents of New Orleans, mostly poor and black, would have no private transportation out of the city in an emergency. The federal, state and local governments made no provision for them. Instead, evacuation plans relied on private automobiles. Environmental justice activists, citing Hurricane Hugo in 1989 and the 2005 release of chlorine gas from a train crash in South Carolina, note that this is not the first time people of color have been overlooked by emergency planners and then received slower assistance afterwards.

> Eileen Gauna, *Katrina and Environmental Injustice,* http://jurist.law.pitt.edu /forumy/2005/10/katrina-and-environmental-injustice.php (Oct. 10, 2005). Other critics have argued that Katrina's indignities are "part of a pattern of environmental disasters in which low-income communities and communities of color are overlooked in the preparations before such disasters occur and receive less rapid assistance afterwards." Center for Progressive Reform, An Unnatural Disaster: The Aftermath of Hurricane Katrina 35-36 (2005). *See generally* Robert D. Bullard, Dumping in Dixie: Race, Class and Environmental Quality (3d ed. 2000); Luke W. Cole & Sheila Foster, Environmental Racism and the Rise of the Environmental Justice Movement (2000).

10. In addition to environmental injustice, racial bias manifested itself in the New Orleans housing market before and after Katrina:

> [M]any residents lacked the insurance and assets needed to recover from the storm. New Orleans had a relatively low homeownership rate—just 47 percent compared to 67 percent nationally....And much of the housing stock was old (though not necessarily in bad condition), with 45 percent of the units constructed before 1950, more than twice the national figure (21 percent). Without mortgages, many low-income longtime home-owners opted out of costly homeowners insurance or flood insurance. Moreover, FEMA had

designated many of these areas to be at "low" flood risk, so lenders did not require flood insurance.

Like most cities across the country, New Orleans already had an affordable housing crisis before Katrina. According to the 2000 Census, two-thirds (67 percent) of extremely low income households in New Orleans bore excessive housing cost burdens (by federal standards, housing costs that exceed 30 percent of income), a figure slightly higher than average for Louisiana and slightly lower than that for the nation as a whole. More than half (56 percent) of very low income households in New Orleans were paying more than half their income for housing, also comparable to national figures. Both owners and renters were equally disadvantaged, with majorities of both groups facing excessive housing cost burdens.

Only a small proportion of needy households received federal housing assistance—a public housing apartment, other federally subsidized housing, or Housing Choice Voucher (Section 8). Those that did receive assistance had lower housing costs, but many had to cope with living in some of the nation's worst public housing....

Historically, the city's public housing projects were sited in low-income neighborhoods, isolating low-income residents from the rest of the city and exacerbating both racial segregation and the concentration of black poverty. Decades of neglect and mismanagement had left these developments in severe distress. Residents of projects like Desire, Florida, and Iberville endured intolerable physical conditions, high levels of violent crime, rampant drug trafficking, and myriad other social ills. These distressed public housing communities blighted the surrounding neighborhoods and exacerbated the overall racial and economic segregation in the city.

Susan J. Popkin, Margery A. Turner & Martha Burt, *Rebuilding Affordable Housing in New Orleans: The Challenge of Creating Inclusive Communities* 2-3 (Jan. 2006) (available at http://www.urban.org/UploadedPDF/900914_ affordable _housing.pdf).

11. Destruction of housing stock poses especially pointed issues of social injustice. Of the more than $20 billion in direct property damage caused by Katrina, nearly four-fifths ($16 billion) involved residential property. *See* 1 Army Corps of Engineers, Final Report of the Interagency Performance Evaluation Taskforce (IPET) 8 (June 1, 2006). In Katrina's immediate aftermath, FEMA placed an estimated 125,000 evacuees in hotels; "an untold number" of additional evacuees "stay[ed] with friends and family or liv[ed] in cars, tents, or damaged homes." National Fair Housing Alliance, *No Home for the Holidays: Report on Housing Discrimination Against Hurricane Katrina Survivors* 4-5 (Dec. 20, 2005) (available at http://newreconstruction

.civilrights.org/LinkClick.aspx?fileticket=dhpik3cZYgc=&tabid=2555 &mid=5418).

12. Nearly half the persons displaced by Katrina were renters. *See* Olympia Duhart & Eloisa C. Rodriguez-Dod, *Legislation and Criminalization Impacting Renters Displaced by Katrina,* in Law and Recovery from Disaster, *supra,* at 141, 141-142. For three months in 2006, St. Bernard Parish banned the renting of residential property to anyone besides blood relatives. *See* St. Bernard Parish (La.) Ord. 670-09-06 (Sept. 16, 2006), *amended,* Ord. 697-12-06 (Dec. 19, 2006). *See generally* Duhart & Rodriguez-Dod, *supra,* at 143-148.

13. "The longer-term challenge" is to rebuild New Orleans "without recreating intense concentrations of minority poverty and distress":

> Instead of isolating needy families in pockets of extreme poverty, affordable housing should be provided throughout the metropolitan area so low-income households choosing to return to New Orleans have safe and secure places to live, along with access to the good jobs and schools needed to get ahead. And for those who do not return, affordable housing policies should help ensure that people left homeless by Katrina enjoy the same opportunities in their new communities, do not wind up concentrated in the poorest neighborhoods, and receive the supports they need so they do not end up even worse off than they were in New Orleans.

> To expand the stock of moderately priced rental and for-sale housing, while allowing returning residents flexibility and choice about where to live, we recommend a strategy that addresses both the supply side and the demand side of the housing market. More specifically, regulatory incentives and capital subsidies should be used to encourage and support the construction of affordable housing units throughout the metropolitan region (by both for-profit and nonprofit developers). At the same time, low-income households returning to the area should receive vouchers to supplement what they can afford to pay to rent or buy modest housing in neighborhoods of their choice....

> Whatever decisions are ultimately made about how to move forward, reconstruction should be based on what is known about how to incorporate high-quality, affordable housing into healthy mixed-income communities that offer real opportunities for low-income families....[T]he city may not be able to recover economically unless its low-wage workforce returns—both the reconstruction effort itself and the city's tourism industry depend on them. And much of what creates the unique and vibrant New Orleans culture grows directly out of its lower-income and minority communities with their many deeply rooted families.

Popkin et al., *supra,* at 8-9. *See generally* Myron Orfield, *Land Use and Housing Policies to Reduce Concentrated Poverty and Racial Segregation,* 33 Fordham Urb. L.J. 877 (2006). On the other hand, in what might be regarded as a form of creative destruction, *see generally* Joseph A. Schumpeter, Capitalism, Socialism and Democracy (1975) (1st ed. 1942), disaster enables government to remedy past segregation through integrative reconstruction. *See* Michèle Alexandre, *Navigating the Topography of Inequality Post-Disaster: A Propose for Remedying Past Geographic Segregation during Rebuilding,* in Law and Recovery from Disaster, *supra,* at 157.

14. One proactive way to assimilate lessons from disasters is to think of ways that the government and other parties involved in preparing for, responding to, and recovering from disasters can develop greater cultural competence in order to minimize the effects of social vulnerability. The "cultural competence continuum" developed in Terry L. Cross et al., Towards a Culturally Competent System of Care, Volume I: A Monograph of Effective Services for Minority Children Who Are Severely Emotionally Disturbed (1989) describes a spectrum ranging from least to greatest cultural competence: (1) destructiveness, (2) incapacity, (3) blindness, (4) precompetence, (5) competence, and finally (6) proficiency.

The following excerpt, though aimed at the narrower question of mental health services, illustrates how greater cultural competence can improve disaster assistance of all kinds.

U.S. DEPARTMENT OF HEALTH AND HUMAN SERVICES, DEVELOPING CULTURAL COMPETENCE IN DISASTER MENTAL HEALTH PROGRAMS: GUIDING PRINCIPLES AND RECOMMENDATIONS
(DHHS Pub. No. SMA 3828), 14-17 (2003)

Culture as a source of knowledge, information, and support provides continuity and a process for healing during times of tragedy. Survivors react to and recover from disaster within the context of their individual racial and ethnic backgrounds, cultural viewpoints, life experiences, and values. Culture offers a protective system that is comfortable and reassuring. It defines appropriate behavior and furnishes social support, identity, and a shared vision for recovery. For example, stories, rituals, and legends that are part of a culture's fabric help people adjust to catastrophic losses by highlighting the mastery of communal trauma and explaining the relationship of individuals to the spiritual. Despite the strengths that culture can provide, responses to disaster also fall on a continuum. Persons from disadvantaged racial and ethnic communities may be more vulnerable to problems associated with preparing for and recovering from disaster than persons of higher socioeconomic status.

Because of the strong role that culture plays in disaster response, disaster mental health services are most effective when survivors receive assistance that is in accord with their cultural beliefs and consistent with their needs. As disaster mental health service providers seek to become more culturally competent, they must recognize three important social and historical influences that can affect the success of their efforts. These three influences are the importance of community, racism and discrimination, and social and economic inequality.

The Importance of Community

Disasters affect both individuals and communities. Following a disaster, there may be individual trauma, characterized as "a blow to the psyche that breaks through one's defenses so suddenly and with such brutal force that one cannot react to it effectively." There also may be collective trauma—"a blow to the basic tissues of social life that damages the bonds attaching people together and impairs the prevailing sense of community." Cultural and socioeconomic factors contribute to both individual and community responses to the trauma caused by disaster.

The culture of the community provides the lens through which its members view and interpret the disaster....[A] disrupted and fragmented [community] will be able to provide less support than a cohesive community.

A classic example is...the devastating 1972 flood in Buffalo Creek, West Virginia. The flood led to relocation of the entire community [and] a "loss of community," in which people lost not only their sense of connection with the locale but also the support of people and institutions. Results of this community's fragmentation included fear, anger, anxiety, and depression.

Other studies have emphasized positive effects that can result from disaster experiences in communities that perform a protective role and cushion the stress of the disaster. Compared with non-disaster-related suffering, which is isolating and private, the suffering of disaster survivors can be collective and public. However, devastating disasters can have positive outcomes. They can bring a community closer or reorient its members to new priorities or values. Individuals may exhibit courage, selflessness, gratitude, and hope that they may not have shown or felt before the disaster.

Community often is extremely important for racial and ethnic minority groups, and it may dramatically affect their ability to recover from disaster. For example, a racial or ethnic minority community may provide especially strong social support functions for its members, particularly when it is surrounded by a hostile society. However, its smaller size may render it more fragile and more subject to dispersion and destruction after a disaster. Members of some racial and ethnic minority groups, such as refugees, previously have experienced destruction of their social support systems, and the destruction of a second support system may be particularly difficult.

Racism and Discrimination

Many racial and ethnic minority groups, including African Americans, American Indians, and Chinese and Japanese Americans, have experienced racism, discrimination, or persecution for many years....[R]acial discrimination persists in housing rentals and sales, hiring practices, and medical care. Racism also takes the form of demeaning comments, hate crimes, and other violence by institutions or individuals, either intentionally or unintentionally.

As a result of past or present experiences with racism and discrimination, racial and ethnic minority groups may distrust offers of outside assistance at any time, even following a disaster. They may not be accustomed to receiving support and assistance from persons outside of their own group in non-disaster circumstances. Therefore, they may be unfamiliar with the social and cultural mechanisms of receiving assistance and remain outside the network of aid....For example, following the 1994 California earthquake,...many immigrants' distrust of government posed a barrier to their use of disaster services. Likewise, some of the survivors of a hurricane in Alabama were immigrants from Asian Communist countries who did not trust any government and were not accustomed to receiving Government assistance.

Social and Economic Inequality

Poverty disproportionately affects racial and ethnic minority groups. For example, in 1999, 8 percent of whites, 11 percent of Asian Americans and Pacific Islanders, 23 percent of Hispanic Americans, 24 percent of African Americans, and 26 percent of American Indians and Alaska Natives lived in poverty. Significant socioeconomic differences also exist within racial and ethnic minority groups. For example, although some subgroups of Asian Americans have prospered, others remain at low socioeconomic levels.

Social and economic inequality also leads to reduced access to resources, including employment; financial credit; legal rights; and education, health, and mental health services. Poor neighborhoods also have high rates of homelessness, substance abuse, and crime.

Poverty makes people more susceptible than others to harm from disaster and less able to access help. Low-income individuals and families typically lose a much larger part of their material assets and suffer more lasting negative effects from disaster than do those with higher incomes. Often, disadvantaged persons live in the least desirable and most hazardous areas of a community, and their homes may be older and not as sound as those in higher income areas....

[S]ome groups cannot readily access [disaster relief] services. Negative perceptions derived from pre-disaster experiences may serve as a barrier to seeking care. Lack of familiarity with sources of community support [and] lack of transportation are common barriers for many immigrants and unwillingness to disclose their immigration status is a major barrier.

Middle-class disaster survivors are more likely than lower-income people...to know how to complete forms, communicate adequately, talk to the "right" people, or otherwise maneuver within the system. Thus, they may be more likely to receive aid than survivors with fewer means or those from different cultures. On the other hand, affluent groups...may fear a loss of control and find it humiliating to accept emergency assistance such as clothing, food, loans, and emotional support from disaster workers.

In some instances, people of lower socioeconomic status exhibit strong coping skills in disaster situations because they have seen difficult times before and have survived. In other instances, the loss of what little one had may leave an individual feeling completely hopeless.

NOTES AND QUESTIONS

1. Mental health experts have identified certain characteristics of disasters that bear heavily on the emotional distress felt by survivors and on health professionals' efforts to assist in their recovery. *See* Robert Bolin & Lois Stanford, *The Northridge Earthquake: Community-Based Approaches to Unmet Recovery Needs,* 22 Disasters 21 (1998); Department of Health & Human Services, *Assuring Cultural Competence in Health Care: Recommendations for National Standards and an Outcomes-Focused Research Agenda* 6 (2000):

   a. *Intensity of the impact.* Disasters that effect intense destruction within a brief period are more likely to cause emotional distress than slower, less destructive disasters.

   b. *Impact ratio.* When a significant proportion of a community sustains losses, there are fewer survivors available to lend material and emotional support to others.

   c. *Potential for recurrence.* The threat of recurrence, real or perceived, of the disaster or of associated hazards can increase stress in survivors.

   d. *Cultural and symbolic aspects.* Survivors may be deeply disturbed by disaster-related changes in their lives, even in their routines. Natural and human-caused disasters can have great symbolic effects.

   e. *Extent and type of loss.* Deaths of loved ones, personal injury, property damage or loss, and job loss can affect emotional recovery.

2. How did Katrina measure on these gauges? Consider the Corps of Engineers' assessment of the storm's physical and social consequences:

   The most serious direct impact of Katrina was the high number of deaths. While large numbers of people were able to evacuate, the groups least likely to be able to do so on their own, the poor, elderly, and disabled, were hardest hit....[F]looding was highly correlated to land elevation, and the areas with the lowest elevations were largely residential. This places the residential population who cannot readily evacuate at the greatest risk.

Katrina caused direct property losses (excluding Plaquemines Parish) of over $20 billion, approximately 78 percent ($16 billion) of which was attributed to residential losses. The next largest component was the 11.5 percent ($2.4 billion) attributed to commercial losses. There was an additional $6.0 to $6.7 billion in losses attributed to public infrastructure, including the hurricane protection system itself. The most significant infrastructure impact was incurred by the hurricane protection system (1.8 to 2.08 billion) followed by roadway networks and assets of the regional electrical distribution/transmission grid. Together, the damages to these categories of infrastructure totaled approximately $2.0 billion. This estimate is followed by damages to public transit assets of approximately $690 to $730 million followed by damages to rail lines, airport facilities, gas and water distribution, telecommunications assets, and assets for waterborne transportation totaling an additional $1.7 to $1.9 billion. Approximately half of the direct economic losses, excluding public and utilities infrastructure, can be associated with breaching of levees and floodwalls. The remaining losses alone, attributable to rainfall and overtopping, constitute the largest losses experienced in any disaster in the New Orleans vicinity.

Combined with the significant and far-reaching impact of Hurricane Katrina regarding initial displacement of population, workforce, and businesses, the impacts to infrastructure and affiliated public welfare and services will contribute to slowed phasing of recovery with regard to return of populace and business activities. Orleans Parish alone is estimated to have lost over 60 percent of its population and St. Bernard Parish nearly 80 percent. On the other hand, St. Charles and Tammany Parishes have increased in population since before the storm....

[T]he social organization of the community and region has been compromised by the mass exodus of the population, the structural damage, and the demands to respond and rebuild. The flooding caused a breakdown in New Orleans' social structure, a loss of cultural heritage, and dramatically altered the physical, economic, political, social, and psychological character of the area.... The immediate physical damage made large portions of the city uninhabitable, with thousands of residential, commercial, and public structures destroyed. Basic infrastructure facilities, such as power, water, sewer, and natural gas lines, were made inoperable and continued to be out of service for months after the event. Many victims not only lost their homes, but also their schools, health care, places of worship, places of trade, and jobs. The forced relocations disrupted family and friend networks. As a result, the event not only had an immediate impact on the well being of the population of those living and working in the metropolitan area, but also resulted in basic changes in the social organization of all aspects of that population.

1 Army Corps of Engineers, Final Report of the Interagency Performance Evaluation Taskforce (IPET) 8-9 (June 1, 2006). "These impacts are unprecedented in their social consequence and unparalleled in the modern era of the United States." *Id.* at 9.

C. SEX, SEXUALITY, AGE, DISABILITY, AND IMMIGRANT STATUS

Bias has many manifestations. Women, children, the elderly, persons with disabilities, and immigrants (documented and otherwise) all suffer from disaster in ways that other victims do not. *See generally* Daniel A. Farber, *Disaster Law and Inequality,* 25 Law & Ineq. 297, 302-308 (2007). Justice John Paul Stevens's frequent admonition, that there indeed "is only one...Equal Protection Clause," serves as a reminder that the aspiration to equality persists no matter what the source of injustice.[9] This section therefore examines social vulnerability by sex, sexuality, age, disability, and immigration status.

1. SEX: WOMEN AND WOMEN'S CONTRIBUTIONS TO POST-DISASTER RECOVERY

Although Katrina is most often framed as a tragedy of race and class, at least one commentator argues that it should also be regarded as a tragedy of sex.

ELAINE ENARSON, WOMEN AND GIRLS LAST? AVERTING THE SECOND POST-KATRINA DISASTER
http://understandingkatrina.ssrc.org/Enarson (June 11, 2009)

The fault lines of American society, as much as the failings of its infrastructure, are shamefully on display in the aftermath of Hurricane Katrina. Race, class, age and (dis)ability are now at the heart of the public debate about vulnerability, preparedness and emergency response, but this is also a story, as yet untold, about women and men.

It was low-income African American women, many single mothers among them, whose pleas for food and water were broadcast around the world

---

[9] Adarand Constructors, Inc. v. Pena, 515 U.S. 200, 246 (1995) (Stevens, J., dissenting); *see also* City of Richmond v. J.A. Croson Co., 488 U.S. 469, 514 n.5 (1989) (Stevens, J., concurring in part and concurring in the judgment); Karcher v. Daggett, 462 U.S. 725, 749 (1983) (Stevens, J., concurring); Craig v. Boren, 429 U.S. 190, 211 (1976) (Stevens, J., concurring). *See generally* James Fleming, *There Is Only One Equal Protection Clause: An Appreciation of Justice Stevens's Equal Protection Jurisprudence,* 74 Fordham L. Rev. 2301 (2006).

from the Superdome, women more than men who were evacuated from nursing homes, and women more than men whose escape of sorts was made with infants, children and elders in tow. Now we see on nightly TV the faces of exhausted women standing in seemingly endless lines seeking help of any kind. In the long run, as we have learned from studies of past disasters, women will be at the heart of this great city's rebirth, and the emotional center of gravity for their families on the long road to the "new normal." They will stitch the commemorative quilts, organize community festivals and hurricane anniversary events, support their schools and faith-based organizations and relief agencies, and compose and sing many of the Katrina songs to come. Though not this simple, it is often said that men rebuild buildings while women reweave the social fabric of community life.

We are transfixed now by images of needy women and strong men (a few with female partners) wearing badges, carrying weapons and riding in armored vehicles, and will soon be treated to endless photos of hardworking men hauling garbage, replacing roofs, making speeches and decisions. Behind the scenes (taking nothing away from others), women labor, too. In the dreary months ahead, after the nation's attention wanes, the burdens on women will be exceptional and exceptionally invisible. Imagine cleaning just one flooded room, helping just one toddler or teen to sleep well again, restoring the sense of security to a widowed mother's life. The basic domestic chores of "homemaking" gain new significance and are vastly more difficult in a FEMA trailer, a friend's apartment or the basement of a church—and parents will call upon daughters more than sons for help. Nothing will change in a hurry as women pack and unpack, moving from place to place across the nation with distracted partners, bewildered children, pets and whatever possessions remain or are gathered piecemeal. The demands on the women who take them in and make them at home are incalculable, and displaced families will stay longer than anyone now imagines. Women across the nation are also the lifeblood of voluntary organizations of all descriptions, now being pulled inexorably into relief work. They will continue to do this work when the funds dry up and women (and to a lesser extent men) marginalized by race and class fall between the (gaping) cracks of the relief system. Long after we think Katrina over and done with, women whose jobs and professions in teaching, health care, mental health, crisis work, and community advocacy bring them into direct contact with affected families will feel the stress of "first responders" whose work never ends.

NOTES AND QUESTIONS

1. As women go during and after disaster, so goes society at large:

    > The hallmark of such a mega-disaster as Hurricane Katrina is that it shreds the social networks and institutions, which provide a modicum of stability and coherence in people's lives. Women are particularly vulnerable when these social institutions deteriorate, particularly in their role as caregivers. Nearly forty percent of children in Mississippi had either not completed their school year or had missed a significant amount of class time. Combined with unsafe housing and neighborhoods, and unreliable systems of criminal justice and police protection, women often find themselves in a volatile home environment—the children are at home, disengaged from school; their spouse or partner is unemployed, with little economic opportunity available; their material possessions have mostly been destroyed; and they are living in extremely close quarters—often four or five family members in a 250 square foot trailer, for over a year, with no certain housing solution in sight. Many respondents spoke to us of the enormous strain on personal relationships, and it is not surprising that mental health disability is so endemic.

    Irwin Redlener, David M. Abramson & Richard Garfield, *Lessons from Katrina: What Went Wrong, What Was Learned, Who's Most Vulnerable,* 13 Cardozo J.L. & Gender 783, 786-787 (2008).

2. Disaster affects women and men differently. *Compare, e.g.,* Jane C. Ollenburger & Graham A. Tobin, *Women and Postdisaster Stress,* in The Gendered Terrain of Disaster: Through Women's Eyes 95 (Elaine Enarson & Betty Hearn Morrow eds., 1998) *and* Jane C. Ollenburger & Graham A. Tobin, *Women, Aging, and Post-Disaster Stress: Risk Factors,* 17 Intl. J. Mass Emergencies & Disasters 65 (1999) *with, e.g.,* Lawrence A. Palinkas et al., *Social, Cultural, and Psychological Impacts of the Exxon Valdez Oil Spill,* 52 Human Org. 1 (1993). The very condition of "being female is a risk factor for experiencing post-disaster psychological trauma." Farber, *supra,* 25 Law & Ineq. at 305-306. Nor have observers failed to account for differences in women's vis-à-vis men's contributions to disaster relief and recovery. *See, e.g.,* Ayse Yonder, Sengul Akcar & Prema Gopalan, Women's Participation in Disaster Relief and Recovery (2005). Enarson transcends these first-order differences. Unless women recover on terms equivalent to men after a disaster, the area's social fabric will suffer long-term secondary damage.

3. Recall how *susceptibility* and *resilience* represent distinct components of vulnerability. The disproportionate number of women trapped inside New Orleans suggests that women were more *susceptible* during the hurricane. Enarson argues that New Orleans will not be as *resilient* unless women contribute significantly to the recovery. Women play a pivotal role in combating poverty and other social ills. "Teach a man to fish, and he eats.

Teach a woman to fish, and everyone eats." Elizabeth Palmberg, *"Teach a Woman to Fish...and Everyone Eats." Why Women Are Key to Fighting Global Poverty,* Sojourners Mag., June 2005 (quoting Ritu Sharma of the Women's Edge Coalition). *See generally, e.g.,* Manisha Desai, Hope in Hard Times: Women's Empowerment and Human Development (2010) (United Nations Development Programme, Human Development Research Paper 2010/14);Elizabeth M. King & Andrew D. Mason, Engendering Development—Through Gender Equality in Rights, Resources, and Voice (2001).

Are there other groups or individuals whose postdisaster welfare heavily affects a community's resilience? How might the law recognize "keystone" actors who are most likely to make the greatest contribution to recovery? Social capital, the often fickle and fragile fabric of a community, holds the key to a population's vulnerability to disaster and its ability to bounce back. *See* Eric Klinenberg, Heat Wave: A Social Autopsy of Disaster in Chicago 19 (2002).

2. SEXUALITY

Sexuality may also give rise to social vulnerability during disaster. In *Sexuality and Natural Disaster: Challenges of LGBT Communities Facing Hurricane Katrina* (May 2010), http://papers.ssrn.com/sol3/papers.cfm?abstract_id=2513650, Bonnie Haskell documented the challenges that LGBT (lesbian, gay, bisexual, transgender) individuals and the LGBT community experienced in the wake of Hurricane Katrina:

First, LGBT persons were scapegoated when influential clergymen publicly described the storm as divine punishment for New Orleans' annual "gay pride" parade and assorted "sexual sin[s]." *See* Mark Guarino, *Fear the Almighty Wrath: Five Natural Disasters "Caused" by Gays*, Salon, Oct. 30, 2012, http://www.salon.com/2012/10/30/fear_the_almighty_wrath_five_ natural_disasters_caused_by_gays. LGBT persons have likewise drawn blame for Superstorm Sandy, Hurricane Isaac, and the Haitian earthquake of 2010. *Id.* Grandstanding like this stokes animus within some religious groups, weakening the humanitarian ethos we often associate with (and expect of) faith-based communities in times of disaster. *See Matthew* 25:40 (New International Version) ("Truly I tell you, whatever you did for one of the least of these brothers and sisters of mine, you did for me."). *Compare* Snyder v. Phelps, 131 S. Ct. 1207 (2011) (striking down a tort judgment against Fred Phelps, pastor of the Westboro Baptist Church, for leading anti-homosexual protests at the military funeral of Lance Cpl. Matthew Snyder) *with* Honoring America's Veterans and Caring for Camp Lejeune Families Act of 2012, Pub. L. No. 112-154, § 601, 126 Stat. 1165, 1195 (2012) (banning disruptions at the funerals of members or former members of the Armed Services, in response to Snyder v. Phelps).

Second, LGBT residents in some Gulf States already had less financial security than their similarly situated straight neighbors. For instance, despite evidence of discrimination against gays and lesbians in the housing and job markets, no state on the Gulf Coast prohibits such conduct. The unavailability of marriage for same-sex couples in Gulf States also brought special challenges. In the absence of lawful marital status, it was harder for an individual to consent to the medical treatment of an incapacitated same-sex partner. Lack of marital status likewise obstructs the smooth transfer of property upon the death of a same-sex partner. Members of one New Orleans couple, registered as domestic partners under city law, expressed anger and confusion when they were directed to apply for FEMA assistance as separate individuals. Haskell, *supra*, at 8-9. Paradoxically, their registered partnership prevented them from qualifying for a second FEMA trailer. *Id.* Now that same-sex marriage is legal throughout the United States, some of these hardships are avoidable.

Third, many shelters and aid stations were simply unequipped (or in some cases unwilling) to meet the privacy and security needs of transgendered persons or the medical needs of HIV-positive individuals. *See id.* at 9. Although challenges like these are not limited to Katrina or the Gulf Coast, research on the LGBT experience during disaster remains scarce—as does awareness among responders and policy makers of this community's vulnerability.

3. AGE AND DISABILITY

THOMAS GABE, GENE FALK & MAGGIE McCARTY, HURRICANE KATRINA: SOCIAL-DEMOGRAPHIC CHARACTERISTICS OF IMPACTED AREAS

(CRS Order Code RL33141), 17-19 (Nov. 4, 2005)

The Aged. The aged may have been especially affected by Katrina. Many had close ties to their communities, having resided there for years, and for some, their entire lifetimes. Some may have found it more difficult than others to evacuate. The elderly are more likely to live alone, and less likely to own a car, or be able to drive. Some may have been more isolated, living alone, or homebound due to frailty or disability.

Home Ownership Status and Community Ties. Among households headed by persons age 65 or older who were likely displaced by the storm, 70% are estimated to have owned their own home—an ownership rate higher than any other age group. Among aged homeowners likely displaced by the storm, over 70% had lived in their homes for over 20 years, and 47% over 30 years, in the year 2000. Among likely displaced aged renters, an estimated 55% had lived in their rental units for over 20 years, and 36% over 30 years, based on 2000 Census data.

Living Arrangements. An estimated 88,000 persons age 65 and older were likely displaced by Hurricane Katrina, or 12.4% of the population affected by flooding and/or storm damage. Among the aged population affected, an estimated 27,000 lived alone, in one-person households, which accounted for 41% of households with an aged member.

The hurricane likely displaced an estimated 45,000 persons age 75 and older, a population prone to frailty. Among this group, nearly 15,000 are estimated to have lived alone, in one-person households, which accounted for 45% of the households with a member age 75 or older.

Disability Status. Nearly half (48%) of all persons age 65 or older living in flooded or damage-affected areas reported having a disability, and over one-quarter (26%) reported two or more types of disability. Reported disabilities included sensory disabilities (blindness, deafness, or severe hearing impairment), and other disabilities reflecting conditions lasting more than six months that limit various activities. These activity-limiting disabilities include mental disabilities (difficulty learning, remembering, or concentrating); self-care disabilities (difficulty dressing, bathing, or getting around inside the home); and, going outside disabilities (difficulty going outside the home alone to shop or visit a doctor's office). An estimated 13% of persons age 65 and older in the flood or damage-affected areas reported a self-care disability, and 19% of those age 75 and older; one-quarter of those age 65 and older reported a disability that made it difficult to go outside, unassisted, and of those age 75 and older, one-third reported such a disability.

Poverty Status. Among aged persons likely displaced by the storm, an estimated 12,600, based on 2000 Census data, were poor, or about 14.7% of the aged displaced population, and nearly 23,600 (27.6%) had incomes below 150% of the poverty line.

Vehicle Availability. Among all households living in the flood or damage-affected areas, an estimated 19% had no vehicle available to the household. Among households with heads age 65 or older, over one-quarter (26%) were without a vehicle, and among those age 75 or older, one-third (33%). In order to evacuate from the storm, these households would have been dependent on other nonresident family members, friends, neighbors, or public or specially arranged transportation.

Children. About one-fourth of the people who lived in areas damaged or flooded by Hurricane Katrina were children (under age 18). Hurricane Katrina struck at the beginning of the school year, potentially displacing an estimated 183,000 children,...including an estimated 136,000 children who were of school age. An estimated 47,000 children under the age of 5 lived in neighborhoods that experienced flooding or damage from the hurricane.

Child Poverty Rates in Areas Acutely Affected by Hurricane Katrina. The characteristics of the children in the damaged and flooded areas reflect greater disadvantage compared with the characteristics of children in the nation as a whole. Many of the children in affected areas were poor. [Among 180,102 children in areas flooded or damaged by Hurricane Katrina, 54,646, or 30.3 percent, were poor. Among children aged 0-4, 32.8 percent, or 15,079 out of 46,025, were poor.]...The poverty rate of 30% for children in hurricane-flooded or damaged areas is almost twice the 2000 Census child poverty rate for the nation as a whole of 16.6%....

[A]bout 15,000 children of preschool age (age 0-4), or about one-third of all children in that age group, were poor. Another 40,000 school age children who lived in flooded or hurricane-damaged areas were poor. Over half (55%) of the children most likely to have been displaced by the hurricane were African American....Approximately 45% of the displaced black children were estimated to have been poor (about 45,000 children), accounting for 25% of all children displaced by the storm, and 82% of all poor displaced children.

Living Arrangements of Children in Hurricane-Affected Areas. Children in the areas damaged and flooded by Hurricane Katrina were more likely than children nationwide to live in female-headed families....Overall, 38% of children under the age of 18 in the hurricane-affected areas lived with a female head; nationally, this percentage is 20%. Children in female-headed families are more likely to be poor than children living in married couple or other families....[N]ationwide, 41% of children in female-headed families were in poverty versus an overall poverty rate of 16%. Further, a single mother often needs child care to enter the workforce or remain working. In the Hurricane Katrina-damaged and flooded areas, there were 12,000 preschool children living in families headed by a single mother. The high rate of children living with single mothers also is consistent with the hurricane having disproportionately affected African Americans, as African American children are more likely than children of other racial and ethnic groups to be raised by a single mother.

NOTES AND QUESTIONS

1. Age classifications warrant no special scrutiny as a matter of equal protection jurisprudence. *See* Massachusetts Bd. of Retirement v. Murgia, 427 U.S. 307 (1976). Limits on constitutional relief do not necessarily govern other sources of law. Should problems of age—whether applied to the elderly or to children—warrant special attention during disasters? In what ways are the aged and the young especially *susceptible?* To what extent are these groups less *resilient* than others during recovery? You may find it helpful to distinguish between the general difficulties posed by poverty

(which disproportionately affect children and the elderly) and unique problems associated with youth or old age.

2. In political, social, and physical terms, children face drastically different challenges in times of disaster than do the elderly. Even if the very young and the very old posed challenges of precisely the same difficulty, however, the law could be more responsive to one class at the apparent expense of the other. Because children cannot vote, whereas the elderly represent a politically potent constituency, children rarely secure as much legal protection as do their elders. How seriously does American society take its nominal commitment to "the upbringing and education of children"? Pierce v. Society of Sisters, 268 U.S. 510, 534-535 (1925).

3. Certain types of bias, though expressed along some vector besides age, reap their heaviest toll from the very young and the very old. Discrimination in health care is one example. *See, e.g.*, Lindsey J. Hopper, Note, *Striking a Balance: An Open Courts Analysis of the Uniform Emergency Volunteer Health Practitioners Act,* 92 Minn. L. Rev. 1924 (2008). Another is housing. *See, e.g., supra;* Duhart & Rodriguez-Dod, *supra.* What both types of bias have in common is their disparate impact on the physically vulnerable, a condition that corresponds (roughly) with youth and senescence. Laws against health care and housing discrimination target the use of race as an illicit factor in allocating these scarce, potentially life-saving resources. The primary beneficiaries, however, tend to be the youngest and oldest members of the protected groups.

4. Like classifications based on age, classifications based on disability do not trigger heightened constitutional scrutiny. *See* Heller v. Doe, 509 U.S. 312 (1993); City of Cleburne v. Cleburne Living Center, 473 U.S. 432 (1985). Nearly half of the elderly victims of Katrina had one disability; more than a quarter reported multiple disabilities. The disabled are uniquely vulnerable to disaster. *See generally* Debra Lyn Bassett, *Place, Disasters, and Disabilities,* in Law and Recovery from Disaster, *supra,* at 51, 61-69. Although accounting for persons with disabilities "when planning disaster relief in the first instance minimizes harm and reduces (re)development costs in the future," Janet E. Lord, Michael E. Waterstone & Michael Ashley Stein, *Natural Disasters and Persons with Disabilities,* in Law and Recovery from Disaster, *supra,* at 71, 72, this call for prescient preparation goes unheeded:

> Emergency situations arising from natural disasters invariably cause human suffering. It is the responsibility of domestic governments and international humanitarian assistance organizations to minimize this anguish to the greatest extent possible, especially for vulnerable populations. Almost by definition, advance planning is crucial. Yet all too often governments, humanitarian assistance agencies, and other policy makers fail to adopt a disability perspective in natural disaster humanitarian crisis situations. With distressing

frequency, the disability experience is either neglected completely or lost when cast among other vulnerable groups.

Id. Put bluntly, "poor people with chronic health conditions" in times of disaster "suffer[] disproportionately—and unnecessarily." Leah J. Tulin, Note, *Poverty and Chronic Conditions During Natural Disaster: A Glimpse at Health, Healing and Hurricane Katrina,* 14 Geo. J. on Poverty L. & Pol'y 115, 115 (2007).

5. The Americans with Disabilities Act (ADA), 42 U.S.C. §12101 et seq., and other statutory protections against discrimination on the basis of disability can be successfully invoked to require cities to account for the needs of the disabled in disaster response planning. In Brooklyn Center for Independence of the Disabled v. Bloomberg, 980 F. Supp. 2d 588 (S.D.N.Y. 2013), New York City was found to have violated the ADA by virtue of the failure of its disaster planning to account for the emergency sheltering, evacuation, transportation, and communication needs of the disabled. Los Angeles has been held accountable under the ADA on similar claims. *See* Communities Actively Living Independent & Free v. City of Los Angeles, 2011 WL 4595993 (C.D. Cal.).

4. ALIENAGE AND IMMIGRATION

Immediately after Hurricane Katrina, the Department of Homeland Security announced that it would "refrain from initiating employer sanction enforcement actions for the next 45 days for civil violations, under Section 274A of the Immigration and Nationality Act [8 U.S.C. §1324a], with regard to individuals who are currently unable to provide identity and eligibility documents as a result of the hurricane." Department of Homeland Security, *Notice Regarding I-9 Documentation Requirements for Hiring Hurricane Victims* (Sept. 6, 2005). The decision to suspend enforcement of the immigration laws triggered an uptick in Latino immigration:

> In the weeks following the storm, the construction industry quickly became a magnet for Latino immigrants who were lured by the promise of paychecks and an emergency federal decree temporarily suspending immigration-enforcement sanctions....

> The media picked up on the trend in early October 2005 and described how employers were seeking Latino immigrants to help rebuild the affected areas. Together with a cartoon in the *Los Angeles Times* that depicts an African American walking out of New Orleans holding two suitcases and a Mexican laborer walking in holding tools to repair a broken levee, articles with titles such as "Illegal Workers Eying the Gulf Coast," "Big Easy Uneasy about Migrant Wave," "La Nueva Orleans" and "A New Spice in the Gumbo" all signal the role

that immigrants, many of them Latino laborers, will play in the efforts to rebuild.

Yet Latinos responding to labor-market demand have not been all that welcome. New Orleans Mayor Ray Nagin famously asked at a forum with business leaders, "How do I make sure New Orleans is not overrun with Mexican workers?" Although he quickly distanced himself from the remark— which provoked a joint statement about unity by civil rights and Latino organizations—many in the region believe contractors favor cheap, foreign labor over local, native workers.

Katharine Donato & Shirin Hakimzadeh, *The Changing Face of the Gulf Coast: Immigration to Louisiana, Mississippi, and Alabama,* http://www.migration information.org/Feature/display.cfm?id=368 (June 11, 2009). Conflict with Latino newcomers illustrates merely one of the many legal issues surrounding immigrants, immigration, and Hurricane Katrina.

RUTH ELLEN WASEM, KATRINA-RELATED IMMIGRATION ISSUES AND LEGISLATION
(Sept. 19, 2005) (CRS Order Code RL33091)

Caught in the web of [Katrina's] tragedy and its sweeping dilemmas are a unique subset of immigration-related issues. The loss of livelihood, habitat, and life itself has very specific implications for foreign nationals who lived in the Gulf Coast region....

This report focuses on four immigration policy implications of Hurricane Katrina. It opens with a discussion of employment verification and other documentary problems arising for those who have lost their personal identification documents. It follows with an overview of the rules for noncitizen eligibility for federal benefits. Issues pertaining to how the loss of life or livelihood affects eligibility for immigration visa benefits are discussed next. The report closes with...background on relief from removal options for Katrina-affected aliens....

Personal Identification and Employment Eligibility. Many of the victims of Hurricane Katrina lack personal identification documents as a result of being evacuated from their homes, loss or damage to personal items and records, and ongoing displacement in shelters and temporary housing. As a result of the widespread damage and destruction to government facilities in the area affected by the hurricane, moreover, many victims will be unable to have personal documents re-issued in the near future. Lack of adequate personal identification documentation...has specific consequences under immigration law, especially when it comes to employment.

The Immigration and Nationality Act (INA) requires employers to verify employment eligibility and establish identity through specified documents presented by the employee—citizens and foreign nationals alike. Specifically, §274(a)(1)(B) of the INA makes it illegal for an employer to hire any person— citizen or alien—without first verifying the person's authorization to work in the United States....

Noncitizen Eligibility for Federal Assistance. Lack of sufficient documentation to confirm eligibility for federal programs and assistance is a core issue for all victims, not merely those who are noncitizens. The eligibility of noncitizens for public assistance programs, moreover, is based on a complex set of rules that are determined largely by the type of noncitizen in question and the nature of services being offered. The Personal Responsibility and Work Opportunity Reconciliation Act of 1996 [Pub. L. No. 104-193] is the key statute that spells out the eligibility rules for noncitizens seeking federal assistance....

Legal Permanent Residents. Under current law, noncitizens' eligibility for the major federal means-tested benefit programs largely depends on their immigration status and whether they arrived in the United States (or were on a program's rolls) before August 22, 1996, the enactment date of the Personal Responsibility and Work Opportunity Reconciliation Act of 1996....Several bills that would waive the categorical [eligibility] requirements for various federal programs in the case of Hurricane Katrina victims have been introduced, but most are silent on the issue of noncitizens. On September 13, however, legislation to provide the Secretary of Agriculture with additional authority and funding to provide emergency relief to victims of Hurricane Katrina (S. 1695) was introduced, and, among other provisions, this bill would treat legal immigrants in the United States who are victims of Hurricane Katrina as refugees for the purposes of food stamps.

Unauthorized Aliens. The PRWOR of 1996...also denies most federal benefits, regardless of whether they are means tested, to unauthorized aliens....The class of benefits denied is broad and covers: (1) grants, contracts, loans, and licenses; and (2) retirement, welfare, health, disability, housing, food, unemployment, postsecondary education, and similar benefits. So defined, this bar covers many programs whose enabling statutes do not individually make citizenship or immigration status a criterion for participation. Thus, programs that previously were not individually restricted—the earned income tax credit, social services block grants, and migrant health centers, for example—became unavailable to unauthorized aliens, unless they fall within the act's limited exceptions. These programmatic exceptions include: treatment under Medicaid for emergency medical conditions (other than those related to an organ transplant); short-term, in-kind emergency disaster relief; immunizations against immunizable diseases and testing for and treatment of symptoms of communicable diseases;

[certain] services or assistance (such as soup kitchens, crisis counseling and intervention, and short-term shelters)....

P.L. 104-193 also permits unauthorized aliens to receive Old Age, Survivors, and Disability Insurance benefits under Title II of the Social Security Act (SSA), if the benefits are protected by that title or by treaty or are paid under applications made before August 22, 1996. Separately, the P.L. 104-193 states that individuals who are eligible for free public education benefits under state and local law shall remain eligible to receive school lunch and school breakfast benefits. (The act itself does not address a state's obligation to grant all aliens equal access to education under the Supreme Court's decision in Plyler v. Doe, 457 U.S. 202 (1982).) P.L. 104-193 expressly bars unauthorized aliens from most state and locally funded benefits. The restrictions on these benefits parallel the restrictions on federal benefits.

Disaster Assistance. ...[N]oncitizens—regardless of their immigration status— are not barred from short-term, in-kind emergency disaster relief and services or assistance that deliver in-kind services at the community level, provide assistance without individual determinations of each recipient's needs, and are necessary for the protection of life and safety. Moreover, the [Stafford Act]...requires nondiscrimination and equitable treatment in disaster assistance:

> The President shall issue, and may alter and amend, such regulations as may be necessary for the guidance of personnel carrying out Federal assistance functions at the site of a major disaster or emergency. Such regulations shall include provisions for insuring that the distribution of supplies, the processing of applications, and other relief and assistance activities shall be accomplished in an equitable and impartial manner, without discrimination on the grounds of race, color, religion, nationality, sex, age, or economic status.

FEMA assistance provided under the Stafford Act includes (but is not limited to) grants for immediate temporary shelter, cash grants for uninsured emergency personal needs, temporary housing assistance, home repair grants, unemployment assistance due to the disaster, emergency food supplies, legal aid for low-income individuals, and crisis counseling....

Relief from Removal. At various times in the past, the Attorney General has provided, under certain conditions, discretionary relief from deportation so that aliens who have not been legally admitted to the United States or whose temporary visa has expired nonetheless may remain in this country temporarily....The Attorney General has provided blanket relief by means of the suspension of enforcement of the immigration laws against a particular group of individuals. In addition to Temporary Protected Status (TPS) which may be provided by the Secretary of DHS, the two most common discretionary procedures to provide relief from deportation have been deferred departure or deferred enforced departure (DED) and extended voluntary departure (EVD). Unlike TPS, aliens who benefit from EVD or DED do not necessarily register for the status with [U.S. Citizenship and Immigration Services], but they trigger the protection when they are identified for deportation....

NOTES AND QUESTIONS

1. Migrants rarely come from the poorest sectors of society. The truly abject have too few resources to move. Migrants typically have at least modest resources and social networks at their disposal. *See* Elizabeth Fussell, *Leaving New Orleans: Social Stratification, Networks, and Hurricane Evacuation,* http://understanding katrina.ssrc.org/Fussell (June 11, 2009); Douglas S. Massey & Kristin Espinosa, *What's Driving Mexico-US Migration? A Theoretical, Empirical and Policy Analysis,* 102 Am. J. Sociology 939 (1997); J. Edward Taylor, *Differential Migration, Networks, Information and Risk, in* Migration Theory, Human Capital and Development 147 (Oded Stark ed., 1986).

2. Section 308 of the Stafford Act, 42 U.S.C. §5151, as amended by the Post-Katrina Emergency Management Reform Act of 2006, Pub. L. No. 109-295, §689a, 120 Stat. 1335, 1449, prohibits discrimination on the basis of "English proficiency." The Post-Katrina Act also instructs the director of FEMA to "identify, in coordination with State and local governments, population groups with limited English proficiency and take into account such groups in planning for an emergency or major disaster." *Id.* §616(a)(1), *codified at* 42 U.S.C. §5196f.

D. PRICE GOUGING AFTER NATURAL DISASTERS

Natural disasters routinely create shortages. High prices are the predictable response of markets to shortages. Although price gouging affects all survivors of a disaster, policy makers often worry that it falls most heavily upon the most vulnerable survivors. In the immediate aftermath of a disaster, legislatures often restrict the ability of vendors to charge what the market will bear for food, water, medicine, and other essential supplies. This section reviews those laws, their constitutionality, and their efficacy.

ANGIE A. WELBORN & AARON M. FLYNN, PRICE INCREASES IN THE AFTERMATH OF HURRICANE KATRINA: AUTHORITY TO LIMIT PRICE GOUGING

(CRS Order Code RS22236), 1-4 (Sept. 2, 2005)

There are no federal laws that specifically address price gouging. Price gouging laws exist at the state level and are generally applicable in situations arising from a declared emergency. An increase in prices alone does not necessarily constitute price gouging, and technically, price gouging only occurs when the trigger event has been met in a particular state. If there exists evidence of collusive activity among retailers, suppliers, or manufacturers, federal antitrust laws could be applicable. The Federal Trade Commission monitors gas prices and investigates possible antitrust violations in the petroleum industry....

While there is no federal price gouging law, many states have enacted some type of prohibition or limitation on price increases during declared emergencies. All of the affected states—Louisiana, Mississippi, Alabama, and Florida—have price gouging laws that are triggered by the declaration of an emergency in the state. Generally, the laws prohibit the sale of goods and services in the designated emergency area at prices that exceed the prices ordinarily charged for comparable goods or services in the same market area at or immediately before the declaration of an emergency. However, there exists a general exemption for increased prices that are the result of additional costs incurred for procuring the goods or services in question, or "national or international market trends."

The Florida statute [Fla. Stat. §501.160] is the most detailed of the four. It establishes a prima facie case of unconscionable pricing, if:

1) The amount charged represents a gross disparity between the price of the commodity or rental or lease of any dwelling unit or self-storage facility that is the subject of the offer or transaction and the average price at which that commodity or dwelling unit or self-storage facility was rented, leased, sold, or offered for rent or sale in the usual course of business during the 30 days immediately prior to a declaration of a state of emergency, and the increase in the amount charged is not attributable to additional costs incurred in connection with the rental or sale of the commodity or rental or lease of any dwelling unit or self-storage facility, or national or international market trends; or

2) The amount charged grossly exceeds the average price at which the same or similar commodity was readily obtainable in the trade area during the 30 days immediately prior to a declaration of a state of emergency, and the increase in the amount charged is not attributable to additional costs incurred in connection with the rental or sale of the commodity or rental or lease of any dwelling unit or self-storage facility, or national or international market trends.

Commodity is broadly defined to include "any goods, services, materials, merchandise, supplies, equipment, resources, or other article of commerce," and specifically includes, "without limitation, food, water, ice, chemicals, petroleum products, and lumber necessary for consumption or use as a direct result of the emergency."...

Typically, state price gouging laws are triggered only when there has been a declaration of emergency in the state. The laws, therefore, are only applicable in areas affected by the declared emergency. Thus, in other parts of the country, not directly affected by Hurricane Katrina, state price gouging laws, where they exist, are not likely to be generally applicable to any price increases occurring subsequent to the hurricane. While price increases may not fall within the definition of price gouging, if the raising of prices by retailers, suppliers, or manufacturers is the result of collusive activity, the federal antitrust laws could be applicable.

Under special circumstances and depending on the scope of the statute in question, state price gouging laws could be triggered by the declaration of an emergency not specifically related to a natural disaster occurring in the state. For example, Georgia's price gouging statute can be triggered by the declaration of an "energy emergency," which is defined as "a condition of danger to the health, safety, welfare, or economic well-being of the citizens of this state arising out of a present or threatened shortage of usable energy resources." [Ga. Code Ann. §§10-1-393, 38-3-3.] The Governor of Georgia declared such an emergency on August 31, 2005, triggering the state's price gouging statute.

NOTES AND QUESTIONS

1. At least 15 states and Guam have statutes that specifically address price gouging during emergencies. *See* Ala. Code §8-31-3 to -6; Ark. Code Ann. §4-88-301 to -305; Cal. Bus. & Prof. Code §7123.5; Cal. Civ. Code §§1689.5-.14; Cal. Penal Code §396; Conn. Gen. Stat. §42-232; Fla. Stat. Ann. §§501.160, .201-.213; Ga. Code Ann. §10-1-393; Guam Code Ann. §32201; Ind. Code §§4-6-9.1-1 to -7; La. Rev. Stat. Ann. §29:732; Miss. Code Ann. §75-24-25; N.Y. Gen. Bus. Law §396-r; N.C. Gen. Stat. Ann. §75-37; S.C. Code 1976 §39-5-145; Tex. Bus. & Com. Code Ann. §1746(25); Va. Code Ann. §59.1-525 to -529; W. Va. Code §46A-6J-1 to -6. Ordinary trade regulation laws may also address price increases during disasters and other emergencies. For an evaluation of Florida's price-gouging statute, see Gary E. Lehman, *Price Gouging: Application of Florida's Unfair Trade Practices Act in the Aftermath of Hurricane Andrew,* 17 Nova L. Rev. 1029 (1993). For a study of California's legislation, see Sean P. Lafferty, *Consumer Protection, Emergencies— Protection against Price Gouging,* 26 Pac. L.J. 215 (1995).

2. Tennessee and Virginia regulate price gouging in vaccines during medical emergencies. *See* Tenn. Code Ann. §47-18-2801 to -2805; Va. Code Ann. §59.1-533 to -37. California penalizes an engineer who offers to practice engineering without legal authority, impersonates or uses the seal of another practitioner, or uses an expired or revoked certificate in connection with repairing structures damaged by natural disasters. *See* Cal. Bus. & Prof. Code §6788.

3. On June 28, 2005, two months before Hurricane Katrina, Louisiana very presciently amended its price-gouging statute. 2005 La. Sess. Law Serv. Act No. 149 (S.B. No. 162) reenacted La. Rev. Stat. Ann. §29:732 and added the following italicized language:

During a state of emergency as declared by the governor or as declared by the parish president, *or during a named tropical storm or hurricane in or threatening the Gulf of Mexico,* the value received for goods and services sold within the designated emergency area may not exceed the prices ordinarily charged for comparable goods and services in the same market area at, or immediately before, the time of the state of emergency. However, the value received may include reasonable expenses and a charge for any attendant business risk, in addition to the cost of the goods and services which necessarily are incurred in procuring the goods and services during the state of emergency.

4. Retail gasoline prices, already a subject of political concern, often rise after a disaster. The federal government has occasionally imposed price controls on petroleum products. *See generally* Wellborn & Flynn, *supra,* at 4-6. The Economic Stabilization Act of 1970, Pub. L. No. 91-379, 84 Stat. 796, authorized the President to control commodity prices, including crude oil and refined petroleum. President Nixon exercised this authority in 1971 before it expired in 1974. The Emergency Petroleum Allocation Act of 1973 (EPAA), Pub. L. No. 93-159, 87 Stat. 627 (codified at 15 U.S.C. §§751-760), directed the President to adopt temporary measures "to deal with shortages of crude oil, residual fuel oil, and refined petroleum products or dislocations in their national distribution system" and to "minimiz[e] the adverse impacts of such shortages or dislocations on the American people and the domestic economy." Until it expired in 1981, the EPAA authorized the President to allocate oil and to set its price. Finally, the federal government can influence oil supplies and prices by manipulating the Strategic Petroleum Reserve (SPR). *See* Energy Policy and Conservation Act of 1975, Pub. L. No. 94-163, 89 Stat. 871 (codified as amended at 42 U.S.C. §§6231-6247).

5. Price-gouging laws are rationalized as a tool for correcting a temporary market failure. The market's ordinary ability to allocate goods and services to buyers who value them most is thought to be impaired by a temporary spike in prices. Price-gouging statutes and their functional equivalents (such as state trade regulation laws and federal antitrust laws) are thought to strip sellers of a windfall attributable solely to high prices that cannot spur further output within an emergency's time frame. *See, e.g.,* United States v. Eli Lilly & Co., 1959 Trade Cas. (CCH) ¶69,536 (D.N.J. 1959); Almarin Phillips & George R. Hall, *The Salk Vaccine Case: Parallelism, Conspiracy and Other Hypotheses,* 46 Va. L. Rev. 717 (1960). Conventional economic wisdom, however, disfavors price-gouging statutes. During shortages, high prices are the most efficient market-clearing mechanism. Suppressing prices serves solely to discourage vendors of essentials from entering the market. *See, e.g.,* Richard G. Lipsey & Peter O. Steiner, Economics 83-88 (5th ed. 1978); P.D. Byrnes, W.J. Lowry & E.J. Bondurant II, *Product Shortages, Allocation and the Antitrust Laws,* 20 Antitrust Bull. 713 (1975); James I. Serota,

Monopoly Pricing in a Time of Shortage, 33 Loy. U. Chi. L.J. 791 (2002). One study concludes that federal price control legislation, such as the proposed (but never enacted) Federal Price Gouging Prevention Act,[10] would have increased the economic damage from hurricanes Katrina and Rita by $1.5 to $2.9 billion. W. David Montgomery, Robert A. Baron & Mary K. Weinkopf, *Potential Effects of Proposed Price Gouging Legislation on the Cost and Severity of Gas Supply Interruptions,* 3 J. Compet. L. & Econ. 357 (2007).

6. Notwithstanding conventional economic objections to price gouging statutes, they may play a limited role during catastrophic breakdowns of ordinary commercial conditions:

> Natural disasters...have the potential to cause mass market failures in this era of electronic consumerism. Price gouging may be fine so long as consumers can access their financial assets or credit markets to pay according to their reservation price. But where payment mechanisms have broken down and uncertainty prevents the development of alternative measures, anti-gouging laws may actually be necessary to facilitate a minimum level of commerce. Because postdisaster commercial transactions often help reduce the negative externalities that natural disasters and terrorist attacks might produce, the result of facilitating a minimal level of commerce may actually be more optimal than what a free market would yield.

> This analysis reveals, however, the efficiency limits of anti-gouging laws. Only where the payment systems supporting consumer markets have collapsed is the enforcement of such laws appropriate. Non-coordinated price hikes in areas unaffected by the actual physical impact or secondary consequences of disasters should be permitted without government interference. Because existing state anti-gouging laws do not distinguish adequately between affected and unaffected areas, legislative reform is required.

> Moreover, anti-gouging laws may make sense where markets price inefficiently. To the extent that a product is affected by an "availability" or "anchoring" heuristic, the result of a supply-or demand-shock may be an increase in price beyond the market optimum. Price increases may become "sticky." If such heuristics are widespread, it may take too much time for a market to correct naturally. Anti-gouging laws, by preventing rapid price hikes, help avoid this problem of asymmetric market correction.

> Geoffrey C. Rapp, *Gouging: Terrorist Attacks, Hurricanes, and the Legal and Economic Aspects of Post-Disaster Price Regulation,* 94 Ky. L.J. 535, 538-539

---

[10] H.R. 1252, 110th Cong., 1st Sess. (May 24, 2007). The Price Gouging Act passed the House on May 23, 2007, but never reached a Senate vote. http://www.govtrack.us/congress/bill.xpd?bill=h110-1252.

(2005-06); *cf.* David Skarbeck, *Market Failure and Natural Disasters: A Reexamination of Anti-Gouging Laws,* 37 Pub. Contract L.J. 771 (2008) (rejecting Rapp's hypotheses by defending the role of the market as a facilitator of discoveries about the elasticity of demand for commodities in shortage).

7. Curbing the urge to reap windfall profits from others' misery after disaster may be framed as a question of business ethics. *See* Susan S. Kuo & Benjamin Means, *Corporate Social Responsibility After Disaster*, 89 Wash. U. L. Rev. 973 (2012).

8. To what extent does the Constitution constrain the regulation of price gouging? The Supreme Court has addressed this question in the context of laws designed to curb windfall profits during wartime:

UNITED STATES V. COMMODITIES TRADING CORP.

Supreme Court of the United States, 339 U.S. 121, 70 S. Ct. 547, 94 L. Ed. 707 (1950)

Mr. Justice Black delivered the opinion of the Court.

Commodities Trading Corporation brought this suit in the Court of Claims to recover "just compensation" for about 760,000 pounds of whole black pepper requisitioned by the War Department in 1944....The United States contended that the [Office of Price Administration] ceiling price of 6.63 cents per pound was just compensation. Commodities denied this, claiming 22 cents per pound. It argued that Congress did not and could not constitutionally fix the ceiling price as a measure for determining what is just compensation under the Constitution....

[This case is] controlled by the clause of the Fifth Amendment providing that private property shall not be "taken for public use, without just compensation." This Court has never attempted to prescribe a rigid rule for determining what is "just compensation" under all circumstances and in all cases. Fair market value has normally been accepted as a just standard. But when market value has been too difficult to find, or when its application would result in manifest injustice to owner or public, courts have fashioned and applied other standards. Since the market value standard was developed in the context of a market largely free from government controls, prices rigidly fixed by law raise questions concerning whether a "market value" so fixed can be a measure of "just compensation."...

The word "just" in the Fifth Amendment evokes ideas of "fairness" and "equity," and these were the primary standards prescribed for ceiling prices under the Emergency Price Control Act. As assurance that prices fixed under its authority by the administrative agency would be "generally fair and equitable," Congress provided that price regulations could be subjected to judicial review. All legitimate purchases and sales had to be made at or below ceiling prices.

And most businessmen were compelled to sell because, for example, their goods were perishable or their businesses depended on continuous sales. Thus ceiling prices of commodities held for sale represented not only market value but in fact the only value that could be realized by most owners. Under these circumstances they cannot properly be ignored in deciding what is just compensation.

The extent to which ceiling prices should govern courts in such a decision is another matter. Congress did not expressly provide that prices fixed under the Price Control Act should constitute the measure of just compensation for property taken under the Fifth Amendment. And §4(d) provides that the Act shall not be construed as requiring any person to sell. But §1(a) declared the Act's purposes "to assure that defense appropriations are not dissipated by excessive prices" and to "prevent hardships...to the Federal, State, and local governments, which would result from abnormal increases in prices...." Congress thus plainly contemplated that these governments should be able to buy goods fulfilling their wartime needs at the prices fixed for other purchasers. The crucial importance of this in the congressional plan for a stabilized war economy to limit inflation and prevent profiteering is shown by the fact that during the war approximately one-half of the nation's output of goods and services went to federal, state and local governments. And should judicial awards of just compensation be uniformly greater in amount than ceiling prices, expectations of pecuniary gains from condemnations might prompt many owners to withhold essential materials until the Government requisitioned them. We think the congressional purpose and the necessities of a wartime economy require that ceiling prices be accepted as the measure of just compensation, so far as that can be done consistently with the objectives of the Fifth Amendment.

NOTES AND QUESTIONS

Commodities Trading appears to foreclose takings clause objections to price-fixing statutes adopted in response to war, disaster, or other emergency.[11] Suppose that the government, as an alternative to regulating prices, purchased supplies for distribution on some basis other than willingness and ability to pay. If the government is the primary or exclusive purchaser of a commodity, vendors may respond by raising prices. This issue arose in United States v. Cors, 337 U.S. 325 (1949), a case involving the pricing of tugboats purchased by the federal government during wartime:

---

[11] On the melding of war and disaster, and the pitfalls of such rhetoric, see Lisa Grow Sun & RonNell Anderson Jones, *Disaggregating Disasters*, 60 UCLA L. Rev. 884, 910-921 (2013).

The special value to the condemner as distinguished from others who may or may not possess the power to condemn has long been excluded as an element from market value. In time of war or other national emergency the demand of the government for an article or commodity often causes the market to be an unfair indication of value. The special needs of the government create a demand that outruns the supply. The market, sensitive to the bullish pressure, responds with a spiraling of prices.

The normal market price for the commodity becomes inflated. And so the market value of the commodity is enhanced by the special need which the government has for it....[A]t the time of the requisition there was "a rising market and a strong demand for tugs of all types" in and around the Port of New York, due in part at least to the shortage of tugs resulting from the government's requisitioning program.

It is not fair that the government be required to pay the enhanced price which its demand alone has created. That enhancement reflects elements of the value that was created by the urgency of its need for the article. It does not reflect what "a willing buyer would pay in cash to a willing seller" in a fair market. It represents what can be exacted from the government whose demands in the emergency have created a sellers' market. In this situation, as in the case of land included in a proposed project of the government, the enhanced value reflects speculation as to what the government can be compelled to pay. That is a hold-up value, not a fair market value. That is a value which the government itself created and hence in fairness should not be required to pay.

Id. at 333-334. For an analysis of *Commodities Trading* and *Cors,* see Gregory R. Kirsch, Note, *Hurricanes and Windfalls: Takings and Price Controls in Emergencies,* 79 Va. L. Rev. 1235 (1993).

NOTE: BEHAVIORAL BIAS IN DISASTER LAW AND POLICY

Legislative responses to price-gouging may reflect a deeper behavioral limit on the ability of lawmakers to formulate cogent policies in response to disaster. Scholars have speculated that price-gouging laws emerge in response to recent, salient experiences with calamity. *See* Christine Jolls, Cass R. Sunstein & Richard Thaler, *A Behavioral Approach to Law and Economics,* 50 Stan. L. Rev. 1471, 1513 (1998). Of the 16 jurisdictions with all-purpose price-gouging statutes, nine are prone to hurricanes: Alabama, Florida, Georgia, Louisiana, Mississippi, North Carolina, South Carolina, Texas, and Virginia. Guam is prone to typhoons. So is California, although earthquakes probably figure more prominently in that state's political consciousness. Of the remaining five states, Connecticut and New York are marginally susceptible to hurricanes. The presence of landlocked Arkansas, Indiana, and West Virginia counsels "[m]ore in-depth empirical research...to determine" whether behavioral considerations provide the most convincing explanation, or "whether conventional interest-group theories provide an alternative account." *Id. See generally* Justin Pidot, *Deconstructing Disaster*, 2013 BYU L. Rev. 213, 235-243 (surveying the cognitive psychology of disaster law and policy).

The behavioral shortcomings of disaster law and policy are worth further elaboration in their own right. Behavioral limitations on rational models of human conduct profoundly affect public preparedness for all forms of risk and uncertainty, and especially losses whose magnitude overwhelms prior expectations and preparations. *See, e.g.*, Joshua P. Fershee, *The Rising Tide of Climate Change: What America's Flood Cities Can Teach Us About Green Energy Policy, and Why We Should Be Worried*, 39 Envtl. L. 1109 (2009); Clayton P. Gillette & James E. Krier, *Risk, Courts, and Agencies*, 138 U. Pa. L. Rev. 1027 (1990); Dan M. Kahan, *Two Conceptions of Emotion in Risk Regulation*, 156 U. Pa. L. Rev. 741 (2008). The public mechanisms that generate disaster law and policy are themselves products of behavioral bias. Countervailing advice is easier to dispense than it is to implement:

- [D]isasters are not exceptional events. Disasters, large and small, occur all the time. They are as ubiquitous as the uncertainty that follows in their wake. ...
- [S]top focusing only on the sensational disasters. ... Disasters both large and small reveal a disturbing sameness and have great potential to teach us about our culture. ...
- [D]isasters are grounded in the powerfully political world of social relations. Disasters are not simply socially and politically disruptive; they are *political events* themselves.

Gregory Button, Disaster Culture: Knowledge and Uncertainty in the Wake of Human and Environmental Catastrophe 247 (2010).

Perhaps the most dramatic of behavioral departures from rationality is "disaster mythology," the belief that disaster plunges its victims "into a lawless, chaotic world of looting, violence, and human depravity, where they either 'flee in panic' ... or curl up in fetal position, paralyzed by fear and unable to muster the will to go on." Lisa Grow Sun, *Disaster Mythology and the Law*, 96 Cornell L. Rev. 1131, 1134 (2011). Powerful behavioral biases cement disaster mythology within the public imagination. The same behavioral cascades that inspire overblown fear of environmental and health risks in general work with especially insidious effectiveness in the context of disasters. *Cf.* Timur Kuran & Cass R. Sunstein, *Availability Cascades and Risk Regulation*, 51 Stan. L. Rev. 683, 685-86 (1999) (addressing behavioral biases in the context of pollution and food contamination). Disaster mythology is gripping because it is easily conjured.

Because actual research to debunk disaster mythology takes effort, individuals join the bandwagon of passing along each other's uninformed narratives, going so far as to profess beliefs they may not fully hold solely to gain social approval or to avoid ostracism.

Despite its powerful grip, disaster mythology remains brittle precisely because it is based on falsehood. Because "cascade-generated equilibria" such as disaster mythology "rest subtly on preference and knowledge falsification," they can be vulnerable to "even an inherently minor shock." *Id.* at 746. But disaster law operates under psychological distortions that become even more profound in the wake of catastrophe. The brooding omnipresence of behavioral bias in disaster policy concentrates policy makers' "window of opportunity for implementing mitigation measures" into a "finite and perhaps quite small" space. Sun, *Disaster Mythology*, at 1198; *see also* Henry W. Fischer III, Response to Disaster: Fact Versus Fiction and Its Perpetuation: The Sociology of Disaster 146 (3d ed. 2008) ("The *decay curve* works to reduce the likelihood of a community adopting mitigation measures. Over time, the effects of the event are no longer as salient and individuals become less concerned with the possibility of a disaster striking their community again.").

E. CONCLUSION: LAW AMONG THE RUINS

At first glance, disaster law may appear to be nothing more than a collection of rules that happen to come into play when localities suffer severe physical damage. Upon deeper examination, especially of the social dimensions of catastrophic loss, disaster law emerges as the enterprise of assembling the best portfolio of legal rules to deal with catastrophic risks.

To prevent or at least to mitigate future disasters, we must confront social vulnerability in all its forms, from racial and class-based vectors of discrimination to sex, age, disability, and immigrant status. These factors contribute to the susceptibility of specific individuals and groups to disaster. In addition to recognizing these sources of susceptibility to harm during disasters and ameliorating their impacts, government owes its weakest citizens a corresponding responsibility to maximize their resilience in a disaster's wake.

Recovery from disaster almost invariably generates a narrative of personal survival, suffering, and heroism. The time eventually comes when "the needles thick on the ground" destroyed by a storm, tsunami, or earthquake "will deaden the footfall so that we shall move among trees as soundlessly as smoke." Robert Penn Warren, All the King's Men 438 (Harvest 1996, 1st ed. 1946). "But that will be a long time from now, and soon now we shall go...into the convulsion of the world, out of history into history and the awful responsibility of Time." *Id.*

In the meanwhile, those of us charged with debating, designing, and deploying the entire battery of legal tools designed to prevent and mitigate disaster face a twofold challenge. First, law must seek to minimize social susceptibility before the next natural event becomes a social catastrophe. Second, during times of relative tranquility, the law should strive to improve resilience within vulnerable communities so that they might recover more rapidly and effectively should disaster strike. Addressing both of these dimensions of social justice in times of disaster fulfills the highest calling in public governance, that of law among the ruins.

CHAPTER 6

EVALUATING AND
RESPONDING TO RISK

This chapter is devoted to the concept of risk. Precautions and planning about disasters must be geared to the risk of a disaster. But how should we measure risk, and once we have measured it, how should we decide on the appropriate level of precautions?

The standard approach to risk analysis used by experts is based on probability theory. Here is how it works. We begin with the probability of an event—for example, the odds that a tossed coin will come up heads or tails, which is 50-50 or a probability of 0.5. Suppose that you can win $10 if the coin comes up heads, but lose $5 if it comes up tails. The question is whether to take the bet. If you repeated a bet of this type many times, on average you would expect to win $10 half the time and lose $5 half the time. So your expected return is [(.5×10) − (.5×5)] = 2.50. Thus, on average you would expect to win $2.50 each time. This is called the "expected value" of the bet. It's a fair bet statistically so long as you do not have to pay more than $2.50 to play.

Even though a bet is statistically fair, you might prefer to pass it up. People are often risk averse—that is, they prefer not to gamble. For instance, they may strongly prefer a sure thing of losing $1,000 in the form of paying an insurance premium rather than take a 1 percent chance of losing $100,000. Yet, if you do the arithmetic, you will see that in expected value terms, the two are equivalent. (1 × 1,000 = .01 × 100,000). Economists explain this by saying that the utility of an additional dollar declines as wealth rises. This seems intuitively right—a homeless person would surely care far more than Bill Gates or Warren Buffett about the loss of $20. For this reason, among others, there is social value in providing insurance against disasters.

All of this sounds simple in theory. In practice, of course, finding the correct probabilities is not as easy as it is with coin tosses. In some cases, we can find the probabilities by examining the historical record, but the record may not be extensive enough or we may have reason to think that the probabilities are shifting (for instance, due to climate change). For further discussion of the techniques used by risk analysts, you may want to consult a standard text such as Daniel M. Kammen & David M. Hassenzahl, Should We Risk It? Exploring Environmental, Health, and Technological Problem Solving (1999), or M. Granger Morgan & Max Henrion, Uncertainty: A Guide to Dealing with Uncertainty in Quantitative Risk and Policy Analysis (1990).

Partly because of risk aversion, it is important to know the probabilities associated with the full range of possible harms, not just the most likely level of harm. In other words, we should not consider merely the "typical" California earthquake or the "typical" Gulf Coast hurricane. (Using the term "typical" may actually be misleading, as we will see.)

A graph of the probability of harm as against the extent of that harm can take various shapes. When an event is caused by a large number of random factors, the resulting probability distribution is often the famous bell-shaped curve (also called the normal or Gaussian distribution). A lot of statistical analysis is based on normal distributions.

Even people who have never heard of a bell curve have an intuitive sense of its properties, with most events bunched near the average and extreme outcomes fading away quickly. If the average cat weighs 10 pounds, we can expect that most cats will be within a few pounds of the average, and we can safely disregard the possibility of a 200-pound tabby.

Complex systems, however, are often characterized by a different type of statistical distribution called a "power law." [12] If feline weight were subject to a power law, we would find that the vast majority of cats were tiny or even microscopic but that 1,000-pound housecats would cross our paths now and then. Under a power law, the possibility of freak outcomes, a one-ton Siamese, weighs heavily in the analysis, often more heavily than the far more numerous "routine" outcomes, the tiny micro-cats. Indeed, a power law probability distribution makes it somewhat misleading to even talk about "typical" outcomes. This is definitely not true of the sizes of cats, but it may well be true of magnitude of damage from hurricanes.

The difference between complexity and randomness is that random factors operate independently of each other whereas complexity involves interactive systems. In statistical terms, this difference is reflected in the difference between a normal distribution and a power law distribution. In

---

[12] For an introduction to power laws, see Manfred Schroeder, Fractals, Chaos, Power Laws: Minutes from an Infinite Paradise 103-119 (1991). For discussion of the broader category of fat-tailed distributions, including power laws, see Roger M. Cooke and Dean Nieboer, Fat-Tailed Distributions: Data, Diagnostics, and Dependence (2011) (RFF Discussion Paper DP 11-9-REV).

practical terms, the difference is that extreme events are more likely in complex systems—obviously something that's very relevant to disaster issues.

In this chapter, we will begin by looking closely at the meaning of "risk" – is it just a combination of probability and harm, or are there other dimensions? The quantitative methods used by risk analysts and economists are at odds with the intuitive reactions of people to hazards. We will probe these differences in depth and discuss the issues they raise for policy makers. At its most fundamental, the question relates to the role of expertise versus democracy in making decisions about risk.

We will then consider approaches to deciding on the proper response. Knowing the risk that an earthquake will occur does not directly tell us how much we should spend on precautions. That determination may be made in terms of standard engineering practices, cost-benefit analysis, or the precautionary principle. Complete safety is impossible, much as we might want to believe otherwise. So the question is: How safe is safe enough?

In this analysis, in order to determine the seriousness of a risk, we only need to know the odds that it will materialize and the amount of "utility" that will be lost. We will see in Section A, however, that human beings do not necessarily conform to this model, which raises the question of whether the economist approach is a more rational alternative to ordinary attitudes toward risk.

A. EVALUATING RISKS

CLAYTON P. GILETTE & JAMES E. KRIER, RISK, COURT, AND AGENCIES
138 U. Pa. L. Rev. 1027, 1027-1029, 1039, 1071-1073, 1076-1079 (1990)[13]

...What does "risk" *mean?* To anticipate our argument, suppose that the concept signifies different things to different people—more particularly, one thing to agency experts and another to the lay public....The resulting contest is, at bottom, one of competing rationalities, and its resolution is a matter of ethics and politics, not technical expertise. Nothing in the training, credentials, or legitimacy of risk assessors or bureaucrats qualifies them to settle the issue. Hence deference to agencies would grant them ground they have no right to claim. Deference would beg a central question in the control of public risk....

...[G]enerally speaking "experts appear to see riskiness as synonymous with expected annual mortality [and morbidity]."[14] So, for example, when

---

[13] Copyright © 1990, University of Pennsylvania Law Review. Reprinted by permission.

[14] Slovic, *"Perception of Risk,"* 236 Sci. 280, 283 (1983) (citation omitted); *see also* Slovic, Fischhoff & Lichtenstein, *Facts and Fears: Understanding Perceived Risk,* in

technical experts are asked to rank the risks of various activities and technologies, "their responses correlate highly with technical estimates of annual fatalities." [15] When experts write about relative risk, they implicitly or explicitly use body counts as the relevant measure. And, in a way seemingly consistent with the logic of their method, they insist that a death is a death is a death—1,000 lives lost in a single anticipated annual catastrophe, or through many accidents expected every year, or lost ten-fold but only once every decade on average, or lost in a single community or across the country, are all the same to them.

In the view of experts, then, risk is a one-dimensional phenomenon....

For the lay person, risk is *n*-dimensional, as William Lowrance suggested in an early study. He observed that a variety of considerations in addition to expected fatalities and injuries affect people's judgments about risk: involuntary exposure, delayed effects, scientific uncertainty about the hazard in question, "dreaded" versus common hazards (for example, the threat of death from invisible radiation as opposed to an auto accident), irreversible consequences, and others. Since the time of Lowrance's work, any number of studies have found "that many attributes other than death rates determine judgments of riskiness" by lay people, whose "model of what constitutes risk appears to be much richer than that held by most technical experts." Thus the public is known to be concerned about risks that have catastrophic potential, that are unfamiliar, uncontrollable, or involuntary, that threaten future generations, that would concentrate fatalities in time or space, that are distinctively threatening as opposed to widespread and shared by the general population, that are manmade as opposed to natural....,

Return, then, to the public's rich image of risk, and reflect for a moment on its many dimensions. People have a lower tolerance for involuntary than for voluntary exposure. [16] Even on its surface, the concern here is easily understood, and closely related to the dimensions of uncontrollability and uncertainty. Voluntary exposure presupposes knowledge. Knowledge coupled with freedom of action facilitates individual choice and efforts to control events bearing on the choice. To be forced to face a risk, on the other hand, or to be ignorant of it, or to sense that no one is really in command of it, leaves one's well-being in the

---

Societal Risk Assessment: How Safe Is Safe Enough? 181, 191-192 (R. Schwing & W. Albers, Jr., eds. 1980) (experts view risk as synonymous with technical fatality estimates).

[15] Slovic, Fischhoff & Lichtenstein, *Regulation of Risk: A Psychological Perspective*, in Regulatory Policy and the Social Sciences 241, 263 (R. Noll ed., 1985) [hereinafter Slovic, Fischhoff & Lichtenstein, *Regulation of Risk*]; *see also id.* at 266 (Fig. 4) (showing that experts' risk judgments are closely associated with annual fatality rates)....

[16] There is some indication that the voluntary-involuntary distinction actually serves as a proxy for other concerns, such as catastrophic potential, dread, uncontrollability, and like factors....

hands of others, or of no one. Either alternative is obviously inferior, under most circumstances, to being in charge.

Upon deeper examination, this sense of voluntariness might trivialize the true concern. Suppose my situation (say I am an unskilled worker) "forces" me to "choose" a risky occupation, in exchange for some wage premium. Is my exposure to the risk "voluntary"? Suppose, more generally, that I rightly see life as full of difficult choices. Is it sensible to say that, given my power to choose—given that any choice is "voluntary"—I should accept without complaint whatever consequences follow? The answer might be yes if the world were organized in a way consistent with ideal values and principles, but it is not. Behind the notion of voluntariness, then, there may lurk more fundamental concerns about autonomy and equality and power among individuals in the society, for it is the pre-existence of these that lets free choice be morally interesting. People perhaps are saying that some risks seem consistent with such ideals and others not, and registering the view by showing a greater acceptance of risks that they regard as "voluntary" in fundamentally important ways, as opposed to "chosen" in some narrower sense.

The foregoing account enlightens us about other popular dimensions of risk, such as the enhanced dislike of delayed (latent) effects, and of irreversible ones. Latency frustrates knowledge, and irreversibility frustrates control. They make it more difficult for us to govern our own circumstances—and also to govern our governors. How do we hold accountable officials whose mistakes or misdeeds manifest themselves only decades after a term of office? And how do we correct for what they have done, if what they have done is uncorrectable? Latency and irreversibility practically deny us the fruits of trial-and-error, perhaps the best means yet devised by which to resolve uncertainty.

What of the special dislike of manmade as opposed to natural hazards? Once again, a story grows out of what has been said thus far: Humans might treat each other with motives that Nature could never have, and this matters....First, people are responsible for artificial risks, but not for natural ones, and the government's job is to regulate what people do. Second, only manmade risks can, in any meaningful sense, threaten autonomy, an additional reason to be especially wary of them. Third, the harms we suffer because of the acts of others carry special injury; we mourn the deaths from a natural flood but resent, deeply, the ones from a broken dam. We "are concerned not simply with safety but with responsibility and guilt as well."

These same concerns arise in the case of those manmade risks we and others classify as "public": risks generated by highly centralized high technologies. This is especially so because public risks entail so much uncertainty (given their complexity), imply such considerable power, and are capable of such calamitous effects. The last consideration, in particular, implicates the public's aversion to the possibility of disastrous consequences and brings us to the cluster of factors that enter into what is termed "dread." Dread correlates significantly with some aspects of risk that we have already discussed, such as involuntariness and uncontrollability, but also with such others as inequitable distributions, threats to future generations, and catastrophic potential—each of which speaks almost for itself.

The idea of inequitable distributions, for example, reflects the view that just as a right thinking society should concern itself with the distribution of wealth, so too should it do so with the distribution of risk. For example, risks that might result in death or disease are often considered worth taking because they confer significant benefits not otherwise available. This risk burden may be regarded as equitably distributed only if it is borne by those who simultaneously enjoy the benefits. Burdens imposed on others, or diverted to future generations, generate worries about exploitation. Alternatively, risks concentrated in time and space might be regarded as inequitable or otherwise unacceptable because concentration can result in losses that are avoided by broader distributions. This suggests, then, a link between inequitable distributions and catastrophic potential. Concentrated risks can threaten whole communities, and the loss of a community is the loss of a valued thing distinct and apart from the disaggregated bodies of a community's citizens.

NOTES AND QUESTIONS

1. Cognitive psychologists have developed a descriptive theory of how people make decisions under conditions of risk and uncertainty. A dominant theme in the theory is that most people do not evaluate risky circumstances in the manner assumed by conventional decision theory. People make systematic mistakes in evaluating the likelihood of good and bad outcomes; they also assess the value of outcomes in ways that are difficult to square with economic theory. Thus, human behavior often deviates from what is considered "economically rational." These findings have implications for regulatory policies designed to control risk to life, health, and the environment. For further discussion, *see* Roger G. Noll & James E. Krier, *Some Implications of Cognitive Psychology for Risk Regulation*, 19 J. Legal Stud. 747 (1990).

2. For more discussion of how and why experts and lay persons assess environmental risks differently, *see* Howard Margolis, Dealing with Risk: Why the Public and the Experts Disagree on Environmental Issues (1996); Cass R. Sunstein, *The Laws of Fear*, 115 Harv. L. Rev. 1119 (2002); Howard Margolis, *A New Account of Expert/Lay Conflicts of Risk Intuition*, 8 Duke Envtl. L. & Pol'y F. 115 (1997). Cognitive bias can adversely affect decision making. For instance, millions of Americans substituted driving for air travel in the months after September 11, 2001 because of fear of terrorists. Yet, the chance of any given airplane being attacked was much smaller than the chance of being in a traffic accident. Consequently, this change in behavior caused an estimated 353 deaths in the final months of 2001. *See* Rerd

Gigerenzer, *Dread Risk, September 11, and Fatal Traffic Accidents*, 15 Psych. Sci. 286 (2004).

3. The analysis above suggests that a number of factors besides probabilities and estimated harms may affect public response to disaster risks: risks will get the most attention if they have catastrophic potential, are unfamiliar or uncontrollable, or result in geographically concentrated fatalities. This suggests that potentially catastrophic events may get more attention than more routine disasters, even if the routine disasters are cumulatively quite damaging. Also, natural disasters get less attention than man-made events—imagine if the New Orleans levees had been blown up by terrorists, or on the other hand, if the Twin Towers had been hit by a meteor.

4. Gillette and Krier focus on the different aspects of risk that are relevant to the public. In the next excerpt, Dan Kahan considers how emotion affects perception of risk and how this may lead different individuals to divergent perceptions. The two excerpts can be considered complementary: one focuses on risk characteristics and the other on the individual characteristics of the person assessing the risk. They have in common an interest in the distinction between expert and lay opinions about risk.

5. Kahan explores different perspectives on how ordinary people approach risk. One approach views individual behavior as irrational because people rely on conceptual shortcuts and are misled by emotion, using more primitive portions of their brains rather than high-level intellectual analysis. Some psychologists call such emotional intuitive reaction part of "System 1" in the brain, while the more deliberative thinking process is called "System 2." The alternative approach to the issue views many of the same behaviors differently. Rather than viewing individuals as suffering from defective thinking, this approach sees their actions as reflections of the meanings that cultures attach to different situations. In reading Kahan's article, consider some scenarios that might cause identical mortality, but which the public might view very differently:

> (A) Because they lived in older homes that did not have seismic retrofits, a number of people were killed in an earthquake when their houses collapsed.
>
> (B) The same number of people died because a radioactive release after an earthquake from a nuclear plant that was built close to the fault line.
>
> (C) The same radioactivity release occurred because of a terrorist attack on the nuclear plant.

Are differing reactions to these scenarios simply evidence of human susceptibility to ill-considered emotional reactions? Or do they reflect valid differences in how our culture thinks about the responsibilities of businesses, government, and individual actors? That's the focus of Kahan's article. He essentially seeks to explain the same phenomena as Gillette and Krier, but from a perspective that is more sympathetic to the way ordinary people perceive risks.

In reading Kahan's article, it may also be helpful to think in terms of risk communication. If understanding of risks is mediated by cultural attitudes, then communicating the extent of a risk may be a very delicate undertaking requiring close attention to the audience's cultural values.

DAN M. KAHAN, TWO CONCEPTIONS OF EMOTION IN RISK REGULATION
156 U. Pa. L. Rev. 741 (2008)

Recent work in cognitive and social psychology makes it clear that emotion plays a critical role in public perceptions of risk, but doesn't make clear exactly what that role is or why it matters. This Article examines two competing theories of risk perception, which generate two corresponding understandings of emotion and its significance for risk regulation. The "irrational weigher" theory asserts that laypersons' emotional apprehensions of risk are heuristic substitutes for more reflective judgments, and as such lead to systematic errors. It therefore counsels that risk regulation be assigned to politically insulated experts whose judgments are free of emotion's distorting impact. The "cultural evaluator" theory, in contrast, asserts that emotional apprehensions of risk reflect persons' expressive appraisals of putatively dangerous activities. It implies that emotional apprehensions of risk should at least sometimes be afforded normative weight in law and also generates distinctive strategies for reconciling sound risk regulation with genuinely participatory, democratic policymaking....

Recent advances in the study of risk perception seem to furnish decisive evidence of emotion's antagonism to reason. A growing body of empirical research supplies compelling proof of the critical role that emotions play in the apprehension of personal and societal dangers. This role, according to the predominant understanding, is a heuristic one. Lacking access to sound empirical information, or the time and cognitive capacity to make sense of it, ordinary people conform their perceptions of risk to the visceral reactions that putatively dangerous activities evoke. These snap judgments might serve individuals better than nothing, the conventional account suggests. But they don't serve individuals nearly as well as the type of considered, reflective assessment for which they are a substitute. A substantial body of writing in the field of risk perception documents the numerous ways in which affect-driven risk appraisals lead ordinary people, and their popularly accountable representatives, to take positions inimical to society's well-being. The remedy, according to this work, is to shield law from the distorting influence of emotion, primarily by delegating regulatory power to politically insulated experts, who can evaluate the costs and benefits of asserted hazards (nuclear power, genetically modified foods, handguns, etc.) in a deliberate and reasoned fashion.

My goal in this Article is to challenge this position. I don't mean to raise any question about the demonstrated centrality of emotions to risk perception, but only about the prevailing interpretation of it. The conclusion that emotional appraisals are irrational is integral, I'll argue, to a model of risk perception that sees the positions people take toward putatively dangerous activities as reflecting their implicit (and usually skewed) weighing of instrumental costs and benefits. I will lay emphasis instead on an account that sees risk perceptions as embodying individuals' cultural evaluations of the meanings expressed by society's decision to tolerate or abate particular risks. This model of risk perception, I'll argue, suggests that emotion functions not as a heuristic substitute for considered appraisals of information but rather as a perceptive faculty uniquely suited to discerning what stance toward risk best coheres with a person's values. Without the power this affective capacity supplies, it would be impossible for individuals to form rational cultural evaluations of risk. This account suggests that it would also be a mistake to seal off risk regulation from the influence of affect-driven risk appraisals or to assume that affect-driven appraisals cannot themselves be influenced by education and deliberation.

I will develop this argument in three steps. I will begin, in Part I, by describing three theories of risk perception, two of which treat emotion as essential to the cognition of risk. In Part II, I will canvass empirical findings that bear on these alternative understandings of how emotion contributes to risk perception. Finally, in Part III, I will examine what is at stake as a normative and prescriptive matter in the contest between these two conceptions of emotion in risk regulation.

I. Three Theories of Risk Perception, Two Conceptions of Emotion

The profound impact of emotion on risk perception cannot be seriously disputed. Distinct emotional states—from fear to dread to anger to disgust and distinct emotional phenomena—from affective orientations to symbolic associations and imagery have been found to explain perceptions of the dangerousness of all manner of activities and things—from pesticides to mobile phones, from red meat consumption to cigarette smoking.

More amenable to dispute, however, is exactly why emotions exert this influence. Obviously, emotions work in conjunction with more discrete mechanisms of cognition in some fashion. But which ones and how? To sharpen the assessment of the evidence that bears on these questions, I will now sketch out three alternative models of risk perception—the rational weigher, the irrational weigher, and the cultural evaluator theories—and their respective accounts of what (if anything) emotions contribute to the cognition of risk.

A. The Rational Weigher Theory: Emotion as Byproduct

Based on the premises of neoclassical economics, the rational weigher theory asserts that individuals, over time and in aggregate, process information about risky undertakings in a way that maximizes their expected utility. The decision whether to accept hazardous occupations in exchange for higher wages, to engage in unhealthy forms of recreation in exchange for hedonic pleasure, to accept intrusive regulation to mitigate threats to national security or the environment, all turn on a utilitarian balancing of costs and benefits.

On this theory, emotions don't make any contribution to the cognition of risk. They enter into the process, if they do at all, only as reactive byproducts of individuals' processing of information: if a risk appears high relative to benefits, individuals will likely experience a negative emotion (perhaps fear, dread, or anger), whereas if the risk appears low, they will likely experience a positive one (such as hope or relief).

B. The Irrational Weigher Theory: Emotions as Bias

The irrational weigher theory asserts that individuals lack the capacity to process information that maximizes their expected utility. Because of constraints on information, time, and computational power, ordinary individuals must resort to heuristic substitutes for considered analysis; those heuristics, moreover, invariably cause individuals' evaluations of risks to err in substantial and recurring ways. Much of contemporary social psychology and behavioral economics has been dedicated to cataloging the myriad distortions—from the "availability cascades" to "probability neglect" to "overconfidence bias" to "status quo bias" that systematically skew risk perceptions, particularly those of the lay public.

For the irrational weigher theory, the contribution that emotion makes to risk perception is, in the first instance, a heuristic one. Individuals rely on their visceral, affective reactions to compensate for the limits on their ability to engage in more considered assessments. More specifically, irrational weigher theorists have identified emotion or affect as a central component of "System 1 reasoning," which is "fast, automatic, effortless, associative, and often emotionally charged," as opposed to "System 2 reasoning," which is "slower, serial, effortful, and deliberately controlled" and typically involves "execution of learned rules." System 1 is clearly adaptive in the main—heuristic reasoning furnishes guidance when lack of time, information, and cognitive ability make more systematic forms of reasoning infeasible—but it remains obviously "error prone" in comparison to the "more deliberative [and] calculative" System 2....

C. The Cultural Evaluator Theory: Emotion as Expressive Perception

Finally there's the cultural evaluator theory of risk perception. This model rests on a view of rational agency that sees individuals as concerned not merely with maximizing their welfare in some narrow consequentialist sense, but also with adopting stances toward states of affairs that appropriately express the values that define their identities. Often when an individual is assessing what position to take on a putatively dangerous activity, she is, on this account, not weighing (rationally or irrationally) her expected utility but rather evaluating the social meaning of that activity. Against the background of cultural norms (particularly contested ones), would the law's designation of that activity as inimical to society's well-being affirm her values or denigrate them?

Like the irrational weigher theory, the cultural evaluator theory treats emotions as entering into the cognition of risk. But it offers a very different account of how—one firmly aligned with the position that sees emotions as constituents of reason....

This account of emotion doesn't see its function as a heuristic one. That is, emotions don't just enable a person to latch onto a position in the absence of time to acquire and reflect on information. Rather, as a distinctive faculty of cognition, emotions perform a unique role in enabling her to identify the stance that is expressively rational for someone with her commitments. Without the contribution that emotion makes to her powers of expressive perception, she would be lacking this vital incident of rational agency, no matter how much information, no matter how much time, and no matter how much computational acumen she possessed.

II. Empirical Evidence
So far, I have outlined three theories of risk perception and the corresponding accounts of emotion they support. I now want to assess how well these theories fit the growing empirical literature on emotion and risk perception.

A. The Cognitive Priority of Emotion to Risk Perception
Among the most important empirical studies on emotion and risk perception are those that demonstrate the cognitive priority of the former. Rather than conform their emotional appraisals of a putatively dangerous activity (say, nuclear power generation) to their assessment of its risks, individuals conform their assessments of its risks to their emotional appraisals....[These studies] are equally compatible with both the cultural evaluator theory's conception of emotion as expressive perception and the irrational weigher theory's conception of emotion as bias.

B. The Effects of Emotion on Information Processing
Another class of studies purports to identify particular characteristics of individuals' risk perceptions that are plausibly viewed as evidence of the impact of emotion on information processing. Studies of this sort, however, also fail to resolve decisively the dispute between emotion as bias and emotion as expressive perception.

One feature of risk perception said to bear the signature of emotion is the unwillingness of individuals to adjust their decisions about the acceptability of risks to changes in information about their probability. System 2 reasoning requires not only that people form unbiased assessments of the magnitude of risks and benefits, but also that they appropriately combine them to determine the expected utility of forgoing or forbearing them. That doesn't happen when people are emotional. Instead they fail to discount a potential harm by its improbability—the phenomenon of "probability neglect"—because "when intense emotions are engaged, people tend to focus on the adverse outcome, not on its likelihood." By the same token, when people "anticipate a loss of what [they] now have, [they] can become genuinely afraid, in a way that greatly exceeds [their] feelings of pleasurable anticipation when [they] look forward to some supplement to what [they] now have." The result is "status quo" bias, the disposition to refrain from action that entails some risks but that nonetheless has a positive expected value. Alternatively, positive emotions—such as hope or pride—can lead to an "overconfidence bias" that induces people to underestimate risks associated with behavior they value.

But an alternative explanation, one in keeping with the cultural evaluator theory, is that individuals' decisions to forgo or forbear risks is based not on the expected utility of those actions but on their social meanings, which are unlikely to be tied in any systematic way to the actuarial magnitude of those risks. The individualist, for example, who continues to worry more about being rendered defenseless than about being shot as the risks of insufficient gun control appear to increase might "not so much [be] afraid of dying as afraid of death without honor." Similarly, for the person who values an activity—say, smoking—precisely because she subscribes to an ethic that prizes the "authenticity of impulse and risk," a cultivated disposition to discount the likelihood of personal harm may be integral to the very form of life that activity helps her to experience. For such persons, moreover, the very idea of conforming their attitudes toward a risk to the results of a cost-benefit calculus might bear a meaning that denigrates their values....

Another supposed sign of the influence of emotion on information processing is the responsiveness of individual risk perceptions to the vividness of information. The irrational weigher theory treats this as further evidence that emotions warp reasoned analysis. Emotionally gripping depictions of harm (e.g., news coverage of a terrorist attack), it is said, are more salient than emotionally sterile ones (e.g., stories about the consequences of global warming). Accordingly, they are more likely to be noticed and recalled, generating the distorted estimation of risks associated with the "availability effect."

But again the cultural evaluator model offers an alternative explanation that fits the data just as well, if not better. The impact of vivid information on risk perceptions is conditional on individuals' cultural worldviews. Shown news of a school shooting spree, egalitarians and communitarians fix on the horrifying image of dead children and revise upward their assessment of the risks of private gun ownership. What captures the attention of hierarchical and individualistic persons, however, is the tragic inability of school personnel to cut the massacre short because they were forbidden by law to bring their own guns onto school premises—a dreaded outcome that causes them to revise upward their assessment of the risk of gun control. Likewise, terrorism risks loom larger than global warming risks only in the imagination of hierarchs [who stress the value of hierarchy and authority] not in the imagination of egalitarians—and in the mind of individualists, neither is particularly worrisome. Because all persons of all cultural persuasions have a stake in forming an evaluation of the incident that appropriately expresses their values, there's no reason to view anyone's response to the vividness of the story as biased rather than rationally informed by emotion.

A similar conclusion can be drawn about one last feature of risk perceptions often presented as evidence of the biasing effect of emotion. This is the tendency of public risk perceptions to reinforce and feed on themselves. Irrational weigher theorists depict this phenomenon as a form of "hysteria" or "mass panic." They link it to emotion by identifying the cause as "highly vivid cases...that receive concentrated media attention" resulting in a distorting "interplay between anxiety, fear, and subjective probabilities."

The problem with this argument is that the power of social influence to amplify perceptions of risk is also known to be highly conditional on individuals' cultural orientations. The view that nuclear power is dangerous and that global warming is a serious threat is uniformly held by egalitarians, but almost uniformly rejected by hierarchs and individualists....

C. Emotion and Systematic Reasoning: Substitutes or Complements?
The experiments I have examined to this point show that emotion matters for risk perception, but they don't address whether emotion is functioning as bias or as a form of expressive perception. A third type arguably does both.

This research relates to how information and emotion interact. The irrational weigher theory treats emotion as an heuristic, System 1 substitute for more considered, System 2 information processing. It follows from this that the situation in which a person is likely to rely most decisively on emotion is when she must form an instantaneous judgment about a risk about which she has little or no information. As people obtain more information on, and have more time to reflect about, a novel risk, their judgments should be less affective or emotional. In this sense, then, the irrational weigher theory hypothesizes a negative interaction between information and emotion.

The cultural evaluator theory suggests something different. According to that theory, emotion enables a person to form an attitude about risk that appropriately expresses her values. Emotion can't reliably perform that function, however, if a person lacks sufficient information to form a coherent judgment about whether crediting it would affirm or denigrate her worldview. On this account, then, emotion can be expected to play a bigger role in the judgment of someone who has had access to information and time to reflect on a relatively novel risk than someone who has not. In this sense, the cultural evaluator theory predicts a positive interaction between information and emotional perception of risk.

Paul Slovic, Don Braman, Geoff Cohen, John Gastil, and I conducted an experiment to test these competing hypotheses. We assessed people's perceptions of the risks of nanotechnology. As we expected, the vast majority of our subjects—about 80%—had heard either "little" or "nothing" about this technology before we conducted our study. Nevertheless, close to 90% had an opinion on whether nanotechnology's potential risks would outweigh its potential benefits. Not surprisingly, their affective responses to nanotechnology exerted a strong influence on their perceptions. But consistent with the prediction of the cultural evaluator theory, and inconsistent with that of the irrational weigher theory, the impact of affect relative to other influences (such as gender, race, or ideology) was significantly larger among persons who knew a modest or substantial amount about nanotechnology before the study. Likewise, we found that affect, as well as cultural worldviews, played an even bigger role in explaining variation among subjects who received information about nanotechnology before their views were elicited than in those who did not receive information first. Again, these findings suggest that emotion is not a heuristic substitute for information, but rather a type of evaluative judgment that depends on access to enough information for a person to evaluate the social meaning of a putatively dangerous activity....

Is this study conclusive in the contest between "emotion as bias" and "emotion as expressive perception"? Definitely not. But as the only study that puts the two squarely in conflict, it underscores the importance of resisting the fallacious inference that because emotion does not perform the role assigned to it by the (discredited) rational weigher model, the function it performs must be an irrational one.

III. Normative and Prescriptive Implications

Only the conceptions of emotion associated with the irrational weigher theory and the cultural evaluator theory fit the data on the relationship between emotion and risk perception. I now want to consider what is at stake as a practical matter in the conflict between them. Whether we see emotion as bias or expressive perception, I will argue, has immense normative and prescriptive implications for risk regulation.

A. Expertise—Scientific and Moral

The normative program associated with the irrational weigher theory has two adversaries. One is a largely anti-interventionist stance that counsels that market forces be trusted to set appropriate levels of risk absent manifest externalities, which themselves should be remedied through regulations that "mimic" the risk-benefit tradeoffs reflected in well-functioning markets. If, as the irrational weigher theory asserts, emotions pervade and distort popular beliefs about risk, then there is little reason to assume that the decisions people make about their own welfare furnish a reliable guide for regulation. The other adversary is a fundamentally "populist" regime that favors reliance on highly participatory democratic processes to identify appropriate levels of risk. That strategy, according to irrational weighers, assures convulsive regulatory responsiveness to the alternating currents of myopia and hysteria that animate popular risk perceptions.

In place of these approaches, the irrational weigher theory advocates delegation of regulatory authority to politically insulated, scientifically trained risk experts. These individuals, it is said, have the information and technical acumen necessary to engage in reflective, System 2 reasoning, free of the biasing effects of emotion. By installing experts in independent regulatory agencies with which politicians cannot (easily) interfere and to which courts are obliged to defer, the law inoculates them from the virus of public irrationality.

Contrary to the objections of the defenders of the pro-market and populist strategies, moreover, irrational weigher theorists argue that this essentially depoliticized mechanism for intervening in private decision making need not be viewed as disrespectful of either individual freedom or self-government. Since ordinary people presumably would disown beliefs that are the product of emotional irrationality, regulating them via standards set by independent experts instead conforms their conduct to the preferences they would hold, as individuals and as a society, if they had the cognitive capacity to form considered and rational beliefs. "When people's fears lead them in the wrong directions," Sunstein explains, this form of "libertarian paternalism can provide a valuable corrective."

The cultural evaluator theory suggests a strong critique of this defense of virtual-representation-by-risk-expert. According to the cultural evaluator model, most of the phenomena that the irrational weigher theory attributes to emotionally biased decision making in fact reflect the use of emotion to form expressively rational stances toward risk. If individuals' factual beliefs are expressive of cultural worldviews, then experts who treat those beliefs as "blunders" unentitled to normative respect in a "deliberative democracy" are necessarily shielding regulatory law from citizens' visions of the good society. In fact, it is quite debatable whether risk experts' judgments are as impervious to emotion as irrational weigher theorists believe. But however much more they know than ordinary members of the public about the actuarial magnitudes of various risks, the scientific experts certainly possess no special insight on the cultural values society's laws should express.

It is exactly this mismatch between the sort of technical expertise possessed by risk experts and the emotional expertise needed to connect stances toward risk to citizens' values that informs unease toward "cost-benefit" and related welfarist modes of policymaking. It's not impossible to imagine the law being coherently informed by such methods. What is impossible to imagine, though, is that the policies will adequately engage the difficult expressive questions that risk conflicts inevitably present. If part of what's troubling (to some) about nuclear power is what it would say about our values to leave to future generations the problem of dealing with ever-accumulating and forever-toxic wastes, then how does it help to treat the likelihood that future generations will in fact find a solution as just another variable in the cost-benefit calculus? If part of what disturbs (some) people about gun control is the condition of servility it expresses to cede protection of themselves and their families exclusively to the state, how responsive is it to print out a regression analysis that shows more lives are saved on net than are lost when handguns are banned? A form of policymaking that deliberately excluded the expressive insight uniquely associated with emotional perception would leave a society in a morally disabled posture analogous to the state of impairment experienced by the emotion-free individuals Damasio describes.

Nevertheless, this objection to deferring to scientific risk experts does not commit the cultural evaluator theory to either the pro-market or populist programs of risk regulation. Recognizing that emotions enable persons to perceive expressive value doesn't imply that the insight it imparts can never be challenged. Indeed, the idea that emotions express cognitive evaluations is historically conjoined to the position that emotions can and should be evaluated as true or false, right or wrong, reasonable or unreasonable, in light of the moral correctness of the values those emotions express.

When we appreciate the expressive contribution that emotions make to risk perception, we are equipped to discern issues of justice that never come into focus under welfarist styles of risk assessment. Should a person about to be operated on be entitled to information about the risk that he could contract HIV from an infected surgeon? Why not, if we think of the decision as reflecting only the interest a prospective patient has in calculating the costs and benefits of her treatment options? But what should our answer be if we know that fear of this risk—at least in those who placidly tolerate many larger risks incident to surgery—expresses commitment to a hierarchical worldview that condemns forms of deviance symbolically associated with AIDS? Is it appropriate for a legislature to limit access to guns in order to avoid the risk of shooting accidents or violent crime? The question is at least a more complicated one if we recognize that part of what motivates aversion to these risks is an egalitarian and communitarian cultural style that despises the individualistic connotations of private gun ownership.

Analogous, and equally difficult, questions arise in other areas of law in which emotions figure. No set of procedures or doctrines, in my view, can ever assure that these issues will be resolved in a just way.

But the normative complexity that the cultural evaluator theory injects into risk regulation is by no means a reason to shy away from it. For if emotion does indeed figure in our risk perceptions in the way that that theory implies, we would certainly be fools not to recognize how dependent risk regulation is on moral, as well as scientific, expertise.

NOTES AND QUESTIONS

1. Kahan's focus is on regulation of risky behavior, but it is easy to see how some similar issues might carry over to natural disasters. For example, some people may view society as having a duty to force people to evacuate and assist them in doing so if necessary. Others may view this as an individual choice and hold people responsible for failing to take disaster precautions for themselves. These perceptions in turn may be tied to cultural differences. Should policy makers attempt to avoid these cultural issues where possible, or should they try to bring them out in the open and discuss them? Or should they try to focus as much as possible on saving as many lives as possible (or preventing as much property damage as possible), regardless of how the public views various risks? For an examination of how Kahan's cultural evaluator theory might be used to help cities prepare for climate change, see Robert R.M. Verchick, *Culture, Cognition, and Climate*, 2016 U. ILL. L. REV. — (forthcoming).

2. Kahan's argument is also relevant to the assignment of decision making. See Molly J. Walker Wilson, *Cultural Understandings of Risk and the Tyranny of the Experts*, 90 Ore. L. Rev. 113 (2011). If accepted, the argument would suggest that experts should play a less central role than some might favor. Could it also suggest that disaster issues should be decided on the state or local level, given that cultural differences are often correlated with geography?

3. These disputes about the nature of risk also relate to prioritization, as discussed in the following excerpt. The author also contests the positions taken in the preceding two excerpts about the nature of risk.

CASS R. SUNSTEIN, WHICH RISKS FIRST?[17]

1997 U. Chi. Legal F. 101, 103-105, 112-114 (1997)

...Some people think that the government should try to maximize the number of total lives saved.[18] If one program would save one hundred lives, and another eighty, the government should (other things being equal) begin with the first program. But other people, referring to pervasive differences between lay and expert evaluations of risk, reject this idea. They say that lay people have more complex, "richer" judgments about which risks are worst and that these judgments should govern regulatory policy. On this view, there is a danger that

---

[17] Copyright © 1997, University of Chicago. Reprinted by permission of the University of Chicago Legal Forum.

[18] This is the tendency in Stephen Breyer, Breaking the Vicious Circle: Toward Effective Risk Regulation (Harvard 1993).

expert judgments will hide controversial ideas about rationality behind a technocratic smokescreen.

...I reject both of these views. A basic assumption is that the American constitutional order is a republic, or a deliberative democracy, in which public representatives are not supposed merely to register existing judgments but "to refine and enlarge the public view." [19] If the issue of risk regulation is seen in these terms, representatives should attend to reflective citizen judgments, but they should not treat those judgments uncritically or accept them regardless of the reasons offered on their behalf....And if we examine the reasons that underlie risk-related judgments, we will conclude that it would be obtuse to say that government should attempt to maximize the number of lives saved, no matter the source and nature of relevant risks. Lives are not fungible with lives; it matters a great deal for what purpose and in what context lives are being put in danger. But it would also be odd to rely entirely on lay judgments, which are frequently based on confusion, ignorance, and selective attention. When those judgments are based on misunderstandings of the facts, they should play no role in policy.

I contend that government should attempt a three-step inquiry. First it should try to estimate *decently-livable life-years saved*, rather than total lives saved. Thus the first step in its analysis should be to see how much aggregate extension of decently-livable years can be brought about by different regulatory initiatives. The second step should incorporate lay judgments to the extent that these are based on reasonable judgments of value rather than factual error or selective attention. In this way, regulators should ask if regulatory priorities should be shifted from the aggregate measure by exploring whether there are important qualities in the context that call for a shift. The key questions here are:

—   Is the risk inequitably distributed?
—   Is it especially dreaded?
—   Is it run involuntarily?
—   How easily can it be controlled by those exposed?

Answers to these questions may call for an adjustment of the first-stage judgment. As we will see, however, the second two questions raise complex issues, for risks are not "voluntary or not" or "uncontrollable or not," but instead come with small or high costs of avoidance. The ordinary criterion of decently-livable life-years should be adjusted upward when the costs of risk avoidance are especially high, and adjusted downward when the costs of risk avoidance are especially low. The third step consists of an incorporation of effects short of mortality, including (but not limited to) morbidity, adverse

---

[19] Federalist 10 (Madison), in Max Beloff ed., The Federalist 45 (Basil Blackwell 2d ed. 1987).

effects on aesthetics and recreation, and mortality effects for plants and animals....

There is considerable crudeness...in the idea of "lives saved" as the regulatory maximand. Of course no program "saves lives"; at best it extends them. Compare two regulations. The first extends the lives of one hundred elderly people, but in doing so, it gives them five additional years, accompanied by considerable pain and distress. The second extends the lives of eighty children, and in doing so, it gives each of them a statistical likelihood of fifty or more years of life. The second policy seems preferable to the first along two important dimensions. *First:* Lives are certainly not fungible, but where regulatory resources are limited and where choices have to be made, it makes sense (other things being equal and as an administrable start) to save as many years as possible. Other things being equal, many years should be chosen over few. *Second:* If government has a choice between preserving lives in a way that ensures decently-livable years and preserving lives in a way that ensures a barely functional and extremely painful continued existence, it should choose the former. To someone who has a choice between death and five years of constant and considerable pain, the latter will probably seem a lot better; but for government regulators, it is preferable to provide five good years rather than five difficult ones if there is a choice. We might conclude, then, that government agencies should shift their attention from "lives saved" to "decently-livable life-years saved."...

An especially controversial issue lurks in the background: it is possible that some lives might be considered not decently-livable because of unjust or highly disadvantageous social conditions. Desperately poor people, for example, may lack decent life prospects already, and a small incremental reduction in their health may seem to push them below the relevant "floor." For purposes of regulatory policy, this ought not to be counted. If it did count, regulatory policy would be devoted to the protection of those already well-off and to the neglect of those in desperate conditions; thus one social injustice would be compounded by another. The question is whether the saved years meet a decent floor, and it should be stipulated that this criterion is met by lives filled with extreme difficulty because of social and economic deprivation alone.

NOTES AND QUESTIONS

1. The elderly are often victims of natural disasters, in part because a higher percentage of the elderly are disabled. Sunstein's analysis suggests that this fact should lessen the amount we would be otherwise willing to invest in precautions. In addition, one might want to zone day care centers away from earthquake faults or flood zones, while worrying less about nursing homes. The same argument would hold for hospices. And in conducting rescue operations, we should similarly prioritize the young and give the lowest priority to the elderly. Is this persuasive?

2. For a fuller presentation of Sunstein's views about risk management, *see* Cass R. Sunstein, Risk and Reason: Safety, Law, and the Environment (2002). In general, he is the paradigm advocate of the "irrational weigher" perspective described by Kahan, while Kahan (like Gillette and Krier) gives more credence to the views of ordinary citizens about risks. Which position do you find more convincing?

3. Sunstein's hope that regulators can be insulated from public "irrationality" does not seem to be supported by the empirical evidence. In a study of Superfund (the federal program for cleaning up hazardous waste sites), two economists concluded that, besides the economically rational factors of expected cancer cases versus clean-up costs, regulatory action "is influenced by many additional factors relating both to risk perceptions and the political nature of the community bearing the risks." *See* W. Kip Viscusi & James T. Hamilton, *Are Risk Regulators Rational? Evidence from Hazardous Waste Cleanup Decisions*, 89 Am. Econ. Rev. 1012 (1999).

4. Regardless of which view we take, the gulf between expert and public understanding of risks poses serious communication problems. Effective risk communication can change attitudes and behavior in ways that cognitive psychology does not account for. See Jeffrey J. Rachlinsky, *Selling Heuristics*, 64 Alabama L. Rev. 389, 407-408 (2012) (using as an example the successful campaign to reduce smoking in the 1990s). On the other hand, rhetoric such as describing natural disasters as "nature at war with humans" may be counterproductive to sensible risk policies. See Justin Pidot, *Deconstructing Disaster*, 2013 BYU L. Rev. 213.

5. Clearly, the numerical information basic to experts may be off-putting or incomprehensible to lay people. For example, people often believe that being in the "100-year flood zone" means that a flood won't happen until a century after the last one or for a hundred years into the future. But it actually means that there's a one percent chance of flood every single year. As an exercise, try to construct a one-sentence statement or put together a slide that will meaningfully inform ordinary people of the magnitude of risk in the 100-year zone.

B. DETERMINING THE APROPRIATE RESPONSE TO RISKS

Once we have evaluated a risk, the next question is how to respond. How much should we invest in disaster precautions, for example? One approach to risk is based on rules of thumb or margins of safety, such as designing structures to survive a 100-year earthquake or building a levee system based on a "standard storm." For instance, in designing a levee, engineers might take the highest water level of the past century and add an extra margin of safety of three feet to the levee. Alternatively, they might compare the expense of building levees of various heights versus the likelihood and harm of the corresponding flood levels – a kind of cost-benefit analysis. Thus, the choice is between rules of thumb and explicit cost-benefit analysis. In this section, we will consider arguments about which approach is better. We begin with an article critiquing the traditional "rule of thumb" approach.

It's worth noting that there is a similar dispute in environmental law, to which some of the excerpts refer. Many environmental statutes require the use of the best available pollution control technology or require that industry eliminate any significant risk of harm. Critics argue that these approaches are clumsy and may require large expenditures for relatively small benefits. These critics advocate the use of cost-benefit analysis as the basis for decisions. In reply, defenders of the current statutes argue that they are simpler to implement and that many important benefits such as preventing cancer deaths or preserving ecosystems cannot be reduced to dollars and cents. This debate mirrors the issues in disaster law about the appropriate level of risk mitigation.

MATTHEW D. ADLER, POLICY ANALYSIS FOR NATURAL HAZARDS: SOME CAUTIONARY LESSONS FROM ENVIRONMENTAL POLICY ANALYSIS

56 Duke L.J. 1 (2006)

Technological availability or feasibility might be a matter of what is physically possible, given current science and engineering, or rather a matter of norms and practices among some group of actors. It is hard to imagine the first sort of approach having much role in natural hazards policy analysis. Consider levee design: the largest physically possible levee would be hundreds of feet high and massively thick and strong. Surely ACE [the Army Corps of Engineers] should (always!) stop well short of this point in building its levees. "Physical possibility" as a goal in levee design would be absurd, and as a putative constraint would be no constraint at all. Parallel points could be made about the construction of hazard-resistant buildings and structures—both ordinary residential and commercial property and more critical infrastructure. The strongest physically possible building would be absurdly expensive. Technology also comes into play in warnings and evacuations. It is technologically possible to evacuate everyone from Florida and the Gulf Coast for all of hurricane season, or to send a government representative to warn every household in person. But these are not serious policy proposals.

Technological availability in the second, norms and practices sense is more thinkable. For example, seismic codes could be specified with reference to current building practices. New construction could be required to be as protective as some percentile of existing construction.

A different sort of technology-based approach to policy analysis, exemplified by ACE practices, employs specific technological rules of thumb. Until the 1990s, ACE traditionally "added 3 feet of freeboard to the design height of its levees, a principle that became a staple of Corps flood damage reduction studies and projects." This three-feet-of-freeboard rule was, in particular, used when ACE built levees to withstand a one hundred-year flood, rather than to maximize net benefits—which occurred when local communities were willing to subsidize the additional levee construction costs needed to reach the one hundred-year mark, so that the area protected by the levee would not be counted as part of the one hundred-year floodplain for purposes of the National Flood Insurance Program. Adding three feet was "a measure to prevent overtopping caused by higher water...than was forecast for the design flood, as some uncertainties may not have been explicitly considered."

Closely related to technology-based policy analysis, and an important tool in current natural hazards decisionmaking, is reliability-based analysis. An excellent example is the approach used by governmental or quasi-governmental bodies in drafting seismic building codes. These bodies typically aim to write codes that will avoid building collapse in the event of any nonextreme earthquake (for example, any earthquake smaller than the 475-year earthquake). The decisional criterion employed by the code drafters is "prevent building collapse in nonextreme earthquakes" rather than "maximize net benefits, including both economic and safety impacts" or "maximize safety benefits." A similar approach has been traditionally used in designing dams, specifically in deciding how low the risk of dam failure (collapse or overtopping) should be. The goal has traditionally been to design the dam so that it will not fail except in an extreme precipitation event. The criterion, here, is "construct the dam so that it will not fail during nonextreme rainfalls" rather than "maximize net benefits," defined inclusively or narrowly.

To sum up: a variety of proxy tests are currently used, or might conceivably be used, by environmental and natural hazards decisionmakers. These are proxy tests insofar as they focus the decisionmaker's attention on some feature of available choices other than their impact on well-being or some of its dimensions. Proxy tests might be technology-based tests (of various kinds), or, a close cousin, reliability tests. Or they might take some other form.

All this is descriptive. But are proxy tests an appropriate policy-analytic tool for environmental or natural hazard regulators? The answer should have a familiar ring: proxy tests are justifiable, if at all, on institutional grounds. And even if proxy tests are justified, their use by administrative agencies simply shifts the locus of welfare-focused, (non-proxy-based) decisionmaking within the governmental process.

To begin, it is clear that proxy tests will, at some rate, select suboptimal policies—policies that are worse than alternatives with respect to overall welfare, equity, and rights. The critical literature on technology-based tests in environmental law makes this point, showing how a requirement that firms employ "feasible" pollution-reducing measures can lead to inefficient overregulation (if, for example, small firms are required to employ high-fixed-cost technologies) or underregulation (if it would be most efficient to reduce pollution beyond the point that is technologically feasible given continued production of the good, for example by shutting down production entirely).

Similar observations can be made about proxy-based criteria for natural hazards policymaking. Consider ACE's three-feet-of-freeboard rule. The rule is meant to provide an extra margin of protection for communities at risk of flooding. But the protection provided by the rule varies from community to community. A recent study by the National Research Council found that the annual probability of flooding in communities protected by levees built to the one hundred-year flood plus three feet of freeboard varied widely, from one in ten thousand to one in one hundred. "[T]his fixed-freeboard approach provided inconsistent degrees of flood protection to different communities and provided substantially different levels of protection in different regions."...

NOTES AND QUESTIONS

1. For an enlightening introduction to how engineers think about risk, *see* Henry Petroski, To Engineer Is Human: The Role of Failure in Successful Design (1982). The "three feet of freeboard" rule is an example of what engineers call a margin of safety.
2. As Adler points out, even if proxy rules (or "rules of thumb" regarding safety margins) are imperfect, they may be justified when more precise analysis is difficult, costly, or subject to political manipulation. Many risk analysts, however, believe that the preferred approach should be cost-benefit analysis. We discuss that approach next.

INTRODUCTORY NOTE ON COST-BENEFIT ANALYSIS

A leading approach to risk management is cost-benefit analysis (CBA). Its use by government began with a statutory mandate to use it for flood control projects. Its use has expanded greatly over the past 30 years. Shortly after taking office, President Reagan signed Executive Order 12,291, 46 Fed. Reg. 13,193 (1981), aimed at improving the efficiency of informal rule making by executive agencies. Section 2 directed that "major" regulations not be promulgated unless, "taking into account affected industries [and] the condition of the national economy," the potential benefits to society outweigh potential costs, and net benefits are at a maximum. Review of the cost-benefit analysis is conducted by the Office of Management and Budget. In various guises, this requirement has survived succeeding presidents. To the surprise of some observers, President Obama's Administration turned out to be a vigorous practitioner of cost-benefit analysis. See Sidney A. Shapiro, *Cost-Benefit Analysis: An Organizational Design Perspective*, 19 NYU L. Rev. 194 (2011).

Whether you favor or are hostile toward this kind of economic analysis, a basic understanding of cost-benefit analysis is invaluable. The "cost" side of CBA is relatively straightforward, since it normally involves immediate economic impacts that (at least in theory) are readily determined. But the "benefit" side can be more complex. In considering safety issues, a key issue is attaching a monetary value to human life, so that the benefits of a proposed risk reduction can be compared directly with the costs.[20]

If people demand $1,000 in return for being exposed to a one in a thousand risk of death, it is conventional to say that the "value of life" is $1 million. This is a bit misleading, since they probably would not be willing to commit suicide for that amount of money! To express this distinction, economists often speak of the value of a statistical (as opposed to individual) life.

Without worrying right now about the technicalities, we could assign monetary values to different levels of risk by looking at how much consumers are willing to pay for safer products, or how much income workers are willing to give up for safer jobs, or how much travel time people are willing to sacrifice for the safety benefits of driving more slowly. All of these would be different ways of determining the market value of safety.

Controversy continues over the correct way to value life. Some suggest that instead of using a single uniform figure, the government should assign a higher value for some risks such as cancer, but that a lower value should often be used for risks that disproportionately affect the poor. *See* Cass R. Sunstein, *Valuing Life: A Plea for Disaggregation*, 54 Duke L.J. 385 (2004). As two critics of the Bush administration's approach note, these disputes have a political dimension:

> In 2000, the U.S. Environmental Protection Agency (EPA) published guidelines that set forth the primary means by which it would value human lives, and determined that each life should be valued at $6.3 million (in year/2000 dollars).

> The use of this $6.3 million figure for the valuation of a human life was challenged by the Bush Administration. Through the inclusion of alternative benefit calculations in environmental cost-benefit analyses, the Administration introduced four questionable techniques that inappropriately lower the value assigned to human life. Following public outcry, the Administration suspended using techniques that undervalued the lives of the elderly relative to those of younger individuals, but it continued to employ other techniques that undervalue all lives, regardless of age. This anti-regulatory approach systematically underestimates the health benefits of environmental regulations.

---

[20] For an economic critique of how the government currently handles discounting and valuation-of-life issues, *see* Richard L. Revesz & Michael A. Livermore, Retaking Rationality: How Cost-Benefit Analysis Can Better Protect the Environment and Our Health (2008).

Laura J. Lowenstein & Richard L. Revesz, *Anti-Regulation under the Guise of Rational Regulation: The Bush Administration's Approaches to Valuing Human Lives in Environmental Cost-Benefit Analyses*, 34 Envtl. L. Rep. 10954 (2004).

Often, the costs and benefits of a regulatory measure occur at different times. When the costs accrue today but the benefits are in the future, we need some method of taking the time factor into account. The technique used by economists is called discounting. On average, if a certain level of flooding has only a 1 percent annual probability (the "hundred-year flood"), then much of the benefit of a levee or dam to control such floods will be received in the future, so discounting is appropriate.

Here is how discounting works. If $1 invested at compound interest today will produce $2 in five years, we "discount" the $2 at the same interest rate, concluding that the "present value" of $2 receivable in five years is $1 today. Making this adjustment allows us to compare different investments whose payoffs have varying time profiles. Because discounting is closely related to compound interest, it can have powerful effects over long time periods. Like looking into the wrong end of a telescope, discounting makes distant objects look smaller.

Suppose you are a cost-benefit analyst faced with the following question: If society is willing to spend $1 million to save a life today, how much should it spend to save a life in 20 years? During the 1980s, the Office of Management and Budget (OMB) would have said $150,000. Until 1992, it used a 10 percent discount rate to convert future regulatory costs and benefits into their "present value." OMB Circular A–94 at 4 (1972). Since 1992, OMB has used a 7 percent rate, which would change the answer to $260,000 (almost twice the earlier figure). OMB Circular A–94, rev. (1992). For example, suppose that we are considering whether to spend $200,000,000 to improve a flood control system to withstand a Category 4 hurricane, that we expect this to save a thousand lives, and that our best estimate of the likely time until the next Category 4 hits is 20 years. Then the flood system upgrade is worth doing if we use a 7 percent discount rate, but not if we use a 10 percent rate.

Over longer time periods, the results of changes in discount rates are even more dramatic, as Cass Sunstein explains:

> If an agency chooses a discount rate of 2%, the outcome will be very different from what it would be if an agency were to choose a discount rate of 10%; the benefits calculation will shift dramatically as a result. If a human life is valued at $8 million, and if an agency chooses a 10% discount rate, a life saved 100 years from now is worth only $581. "At a discount rate of 5%, one death next year counts for more than a billion deaths in 500 years."

Cass R. Sunstein, *Cost-Benefit Default Principles*, 99 Mich. L. Rev. 1651, 1711 (2001). As you can see, in dealing with long-lived infrastructure, it will rarely be worthwhile from an economic point of view to worry about fatalities more than a few decades in the future unless the number will be very large or the cost of precautions is very low.

CBA has been quite controversial, especially as applied to health and safety regulations. The following two excerpts provide contrasting perspectives.

STEVE P. CALANDRILLO, RESPONSIBLE REGULATION: A SENSIBLE COST-BENEFIT, RISK VERSUS RISK APPROACH TO FEDERAL HEALTH AND SAFETY REGULATION[21]

81 B.U. L. Rev. 957 (2001)

Federal health and safety regulations have saved or improved the lives of thousands of Americans, but protecting our citizens from risk entails significant costs. In a world of limited resources, we must spend our regulatory dollars responsibly in order to do the most we can with the money we have. Given the infeasibility of creating a risk-free society, this paper argues that a sensible cost-benefit, risk versus risk approach be taken in the design of U.S. regulatory oversight policy. The goal should always be to further the best interests of the nation, rather than to satisfy the narrow agenda of powerful industry or political forces. This entails designing safety regulations efficiently to maximize society's welfare, choosing the point where their marginal benefits equal their marginal costs—rather than simply asking whether total benefits exceed total costs in the aggregate. Federal regulatory oversight policy should also ask that proposed regulations compare the risks they reduce to the new risks they unintentionally create (substitution risks). Additionally, our citizens should be educated regarding systematic risk misperceptions, and regulatory agencies should make their risk assessments objectively. Moreover, most-likely scenarios must be addressed by responsible regulatory solutions, rather than the current practice of focusing on worst-case estimates. Finally, agencies should publish and justify their regulatory triggers and perform ex-post evaluations of their programs in an attempt to continuously improve the quality of regulatory design.

Efforts by the executive branch, from Presidents Ford, Carter, Reagan and Clinton, have attempted to inject similar common sense into the regulatory oversight process. Unfortunately, the congressional mandates given to government agencies are often silent on the subject of cost-benefit analysis, and recent Supreme Court cases have held that regulatory agencies are not obligated to even consider the costs of their proposals. I will explore several legislative reform bills that are aimed at overriding congressional mandates, but to date, none have been successful.

Finally, this paper will address certain common criticisms to which a marginal cost benefit, risk-risk approach to responsible regulatory reform would

---

[21] Copyright © 2001, Boston University Law Review. Reprinted with permission.

be subject. Most notably, the measurement of costs and benefits is not an exact science, and using "willingness to pay" as a marker of individual and social utility has its limitations. Regulatory reform also faces challenges on moral grounds, as scholars openly decry the explicit tradeoff between human lives and financial resources. While these criticisms contain merit, this paper concludes that to ignore a sensible cost-benefit analysis of federal safety regulations is to divert resources from their most beneficial uses and to settle for second best. In a world of scarcity, we must make regulatory tradeoffs as efficiently as possible in order to do the greatest good for the greatest number, and to save the most lives we can. It would be unethical to do anything less....

"We live in a world of limited resources." "We can't place a dollar value on protecting human life or preserving our environment." Neither statement taken independently strikes the reader as particularly controversial—they both seem perfectly reasonable. Yet there is an inherent and unmistakable tension between the two, for no society has unlimited resources to devote to the protection of human health and the creation of a risk-free world. The questions become: Is it possible to balance the common sense concept of scarce public resources with our deep moral aversion to placing a dollar value on saving human lives? And, more importantly, how do we do it?

We would like to be able to protect every citizen from every harm in our society, but most understand this is neither possible nor financially feasible. Federal environmental and safety regulations aimed at preventing harm have yielded tremendous benefits, but they carry staggering costs—on the order of half a trillion dollars annually! However, despite this reality, there is a startling disconnect between common sense notions of maximizing the effect of scarce resources and of actually putting that notion into practice in carrying out U.S. regulatory programs. Hypothetically, would it be worth tens of millions of dollars to save one person's life if President Bush were to tighten arsenic standards in drinking water to the level proposed by President Clinton in his last days in office? Or would that same money be better spent if it could save thousands of lives by providing subsidized food and prenatal care to low-income mothers and free vaccinations to their babies? If we allocated all our resources to preventing accidental deaths in one area, we would have nothing left over to spend to prevent cancer or to provide food, housing or medical care.

To a large degree, the problem is one of public perception. No politician wants to admit that "we can't save that elderly person's life or institute a proposed environmental protection program, because it will simply cost us too much money to do so." Yet, this cost-benefit rationale is inherent in countless personal decisions made every day, from what career to pursue to what city in which to reside. Similarly, in the regulatory arena, fiscal balancing of the costs against the benefits should play a role in responsible decisionmaking. The tradeoff between costs and results is always present, but we are sometimes gripped by a fear that prevents us from acknowledging it openly. This reluctance limits us as a society because it diverts resources from where they are most needed. Even worse, this diversion is not based on a well-articulated reason, but rather on a fear of the repercussions experienced by those who voice such opinions. For instance, can you imagine a Presidential candidate who said on election-day eve, "I want to do the greatest good for the greatest number, and that means I choose not to help you." Not likely.

This paper proposes that given the reality of limited public resources, America must efficiently reformulate its environmental and health regulatory policies in order to save and improve the most lives possible given the accompanying costs. This is not always going to be politically correct. It entails making tough choices and preferencing certain programs and policies over others, which necessarily implies that some causes will be sacrificed for the greater good. But I urge that given our reality, society must consider carefully how best to structure federal regulatory oversight policy—not how to make it perfect. Perfection is dangerous precisely because it cannot ever be achieved. This paper therefore concentrates on how to efficiently formulate government regulations under the constraint of limited resources, in the hope that such an approach will maximize the overall benefits to our society....

[T]his paper outlines an alternative regulatory approach for America, proposing a sensible cost-benefit, risk versus risk approach to easing the tension between scarce public resources and the deontological value of protecting human lives. In analyzing this tradeoff, we as a caring, thoughtful society should require a cost-benefit analysis of all potential government regulation whether it is aimed at making our environment, air, water, food, or workplace safer. I take this cost-benefit notion one step further than most commentators by suggesting that not only should overall costs and benefits of potential programs be evaluated, but that government agencies must act to set the appropriate regulation at the level where marginal benefits equal marginal costs. Setting our regulatory triggers at this point will have a far greater impact on improving overall social welfare than an absolute cost-benefit comparison would. Most everyone in society should favor a form of regulation that maximizes the benefits minus the costs, and not one that merely asks whether the benefits exceed the costs in the aggregate....

While the achievements made possible by executive oversight have been notable, the success of regulatory reform proposals may also implicitly depend upon rewriting the existing legislative mandates given to government agencies by Congress. Often, the relevant statutory authority governing the mission of U.S. regulatory agencies is oblivious to marginal cost-benefit assessments, or it may even prohibit such comparisons outright. For instance, the Occupational Safety and Health Administration ("OSHA") is charged with assuring "so far as possible [that] every working man and woman in the Nation [have] safe and healthful working conditions." This mandate ignores the fact that nothing can ever be made 100% safe, and that extreme safety precautions necessarily entail extreme costs. Instead, the congressional mandates given to federal regulatory bodies should require, or at a minimum, permit cost-benefit and risk-risk tradeoffs to be made. Such an approach will empower courts to enforce common sense notions about how to best allocate scarce public resources in order to benefit a greater number of our citizens than we do today. Modifying legislative mandates will also force regulatory decisionmakers to be accountable for the policy choices they make....

Moreover, some have raised serious moral criticisms, openly deriding cost-benefit analysis as incurably insensitive to the intrinsic value of life.... This moral resistance also surfaces in the rhetoric of our politicians and in the language of our existing federal regulatory legislation. Our policies often eschew cost-benefit analysis as irresponsible and insensitive to the ultimate goal at hand, and instead opt for a world that should be made as safe as possible—whatever the costs may be.

I am the first to agree that there are serious problems that would make any marginal cost-benefit standard subject to potential manipulation and abuse. But that does not mean we should not try to improve upon what we currently have. The difficulty of measuring these values does not undermine the principle that responsible regulatory programs should focus their efforts where they can save the most lives given limited resources. We as a country would be foolhardy to choose to ignore cost, benefit and risk tradeoffs merely because of the difficulty in their assessment, because we would then be consciously deciding to do something less than the best we can. Thus, despite the valid concerns raised by critics, we must strive to conquer these problems if our ultimate goal is the betterment of society and the maximization of scarce resources.

Finally, we should bear in mind in conducting the foregoing regulatory oversight analysis that it is a matter of common sense that people weigh costs and benefits in making life decisions all the time. American businesses make cost-benefit and cost-effectiveness calculations daily. While individuals are understandably upset by public health and safety decisions that explicitly trade off lives for dollars, no one really wants to spend everything on safety. Policymakers should similarly be able to balance costs, benefits and risks openly in America's regulatory oversight policy. The choice is not between helping all of our citizens or helping none. Given limited resources, the government can only help some. This paper is therefore intended to provoke thought about how responsible, efficient regulatory policy can maximize the number and the value included within that "some."

NOTES AND QUESTIONS

1. The risk of a natural event can often be estimated from the historical record, assuming that the system in question has remained unchanged. The extent and reliability of the historical record may vary, and in some circumstance the system itself may be changing (as with weather events in climate change). In addition, the harm caused by a natural event is partly a function of human siting decisions as well as precaution and response

systems, which may be difficult to assess. All of these issues complicate cost-benefit analysis.

2. If cost-benefit analysis is the standard for making a decision, to what extent should courts review the validity of the analysis? Those who seek regulatory rationality advocate sound science, cost-benefit analysis, and careful judicial review. The result may be to improve the quality of safety regulations and government projects, but it is also likely to decrease their quantity and delay their implementation. Under what circumstances is this a sound strategy?

3. Quite apart from any practical problems with implementing cost-benefit analysis, some authors raise ethical objections to its use in risk management. These objections are the subject of the next article.

FRANK ACKERMAN & LISA HEINZERLING, PRICING THE PRICELESS: COST-BENEFIT ANALYSIS OF ENVIRONMENTAL PROTECTION
150 U. Pa. L. Rev. 1553 (2002)[22]

Many analytical approaches to setting environmental standards require some consideration of costs and benefits. Even technology-based regulation, maligned by cost-benefit enthusiasts as the worst form of regulatory excess, typically entails consideration of economic costs. Cost-benefit analysis differs, however, from other analytical approaches in the following respect: it demands that the advantages and disadvantages of a regulatory policy be reduced, as far as possible, to numbers, and then further reduced to dollars and cents. In this feature of cost-benefit analysis lies its doom. Indeed, looking closely at the products of this pricing scheme makes it seem not only a little cold, but a little crazy as well.

Consider the following examples, which we are not making up. They are not the work of a lunatic fringe, but, on the contrary, they reflect the work products of some of the most influential and reputable of today's cost-benefit practitioners. We are not sure whether to laugh or cry; we find it impossible to treat these studies as serious contributions to a rational discussion.

Several years ago, states were in the middle of their litigation against tobacco companies, seeking to recoup the medical expenditures they had incurred as a result of smoking. At that time, W. Kip Viscusi—a professor of law and economics at Harvard and the primary source of the current $6.3 million estimate for the value of a statistical life—undertook research concluding that states, in fact, saved money as the result of smoking by their citizens.[23] Why?

---

[22] Copyright © 2002, University of Pennsylvania. Reprinted with permission.

[23] W. Kip Viscusi, *Cigarette Taxation and the Social Consequences of Smoking* 47 (Nat'l Bureau of Econ. Research, Working Paper No. 4891, 1994), available at http://papers.nber.org/papers/w4891.pdf.

Because they died early! They thus saved their states the trouble and expense of providing nursing home care and other services associated with an aging population.

Viscusi didn't stop there. So great, under Viscusi's assumptions, were the financial benefits to the states of their citizens' premature deaths that, he suggested, "cigarette smoking should be subsidized rather than taxed."

Amazingly, this cynical conclusion has not been swept into the dustbin where it belongs, but instead recently has been revived: the tobacco company Philip Morris commissioned the well-known consulting group Arthur D. Little to examine the financial benefits to the Czech Republic of smoking among Czech citizens. Arthur D. Little International, Inc., found that smoking was a financial boon for the government—partly because, again, it caused citizens to die earlier and thus reduced government expenditure on pensions, housing, and health care. This conclusion relies, so far as we can determine, on perfectly conventional cost-benefit analysis....

Cost-benefit analysis sets out to do for government what the market does for business: add up the benefits of a public policy and compare them to the costs....Development of environmental regulations has almost always involved consideration of economic costs, with or without formal cost-benefit techniques. What is unique to cost-benefit analysis, and far more problematic, is the other side of the balance, the monetary valuation of the benefits of life, health, and nature itself....

What can it mean to say that saving one life is worth $6.3 million? Human life is the ultimate example of a value that is not a commodity and does not have a price. You cannot buy the right to kill someone for $6.3 million, nor for any other price. Most systems of ethical and religious belief maintain that every life is sacred. If analysts calculated the value of life itself by asking people what it is worth to them (the most common method of valuation of other environmental benefits), the answer would be infinite....

The standard response is that a value like $6.3 million is not actually a price on an individual's life or death. Rather, it is a way of expressing the value of small risks of death; for example, it is one million times the value of a one in a million risk. If people are willing to pay $6.30 to avoid a one in a million increase in the risk of death, then the "value of a statistical life" is $6.3 million.

Unfortunately, this explanation fails to resolve the dilemma. It is true that risk (or "statistical life") and life itself are distinct concepts. In practice, however, analysts often ignore the distinction between valuing risk and valuing life. Many regulations reduce risk for a large number of people and avoid actual death for a much smaller number. A complete cost-benefit analysis should, therefore, include valuation of both of these benefits. However, the standard practice is to calculate a value only for "statistical" life and to ignore life itself.

The confusion between the valuation of risk and the valuation of life itself is embedded in current regulatory practice in another way as well. The Office of Management and Budget, which reviews cost-benefit analyses prepared by federal agencies pursuant to executive order, instructs agencies to discount the benefits of life-saving regulations from the moment of avoided death, rather than from the time when the risk of death is reduced. This approach to discounting is plainly inconsistent with the claim that cost-benefit analysis seeks to evaluate risk. When a life-threatening disease, such as cancer, has a long latency period, many years may pass between the time when a risk is imposed and the time of death. If monetary valuations of statistical life represented risk, instead of life, then the value of statistical life would be discounted from the date of a change in risk (typically, when a new regulation is enforced) rather than from the much later date of avoided actual death.

In acknowledging the monetary value of reducing risk, economic analysts have contributed to our growing awareness that life-threatening risk itself—and not just the end result of such risk, death—is an injury. But they have blurred the line between risks and actual deaths, by calculating the value of reduced risk while pretending that they have produced a valuation of life itself. The paradox of monetizing the infinite or immeasurable value of human life has not been resolved; it only has been glossed over.

...

Finally, the economic valuation called for by cost-benefit analysis is fundamentally flawed because it demands an enormous volume of consistently updated information, which is beyond the practical capacity of our society to generate.

All attempts at valuation of the environment begin with a problem: the goal is to assign monetary prices to things that have no prices because they are not for sale. One of the great strengths of the market is that it provides so much information about real prices. For any commodity that actually is bought and sold, prices are communicated automatically, almost costlessly, and with constant updates as needed. To create artificial prices for environmental values, economists have to find some way to mimic the operation of the market. Unfortunately, the process is far from automatic, certainly not costless, and has to be repeated every time an updated price is needed....

For the reasons we have discussed, there is nothing objective about the basic premises of cost-benefit analysis. Treating individuals solely as consumers, rather than as citizens with a sense of moral responsibility to the larger society, represents a distinct and highly contestable world view. Likewise, the use of discounting reflects judgments about the nature of environmental risks and citizens' responsibilities toward future generations that are, at a minimum, debatable. Because value-laden premises permeate cost-benefit analysis, the claim that cost-benefit analysis offers an "objective" way to make government decisions is simply bogus.

Furthermore, as we have seen, cost-benefit analysis relies on a byzantine array of approximations, simplifications, and counterfactual hypotheses. Thus, the actual use of cost-benefit analysis inevitably involves countless judgment calls. People with strong, and clashing, partisan positions naturally will advocate that discretion in the application of this methodology be exercised in favor of their positions, further undermining the claim that cost-benefit analysis is objective.

Perhaps the best way to illustrate how little economic analysis has to contribute, objectively, to the fundamental question of how clean and safe we want our environment to be is to refer again to the controversy over cost-benefit analysis of the EPA's regulation of arsenic in drinking water. As Cass Sunstein has recently argued, the available information on the benefits of arsenic reduction supports estimates of net benefits from regulation ranging from less than zero up to $560 million or more.[24] The number of deaths avoided annually by regulation is, according to Sunstein, between zero and 112. A procedure that allows such an enormous range of different evaluations of a single rule is certainly not the objective, transparent decision rule that its advocates have advertised....

For many of the same reasons, cost-benefit analysis also generally fails to achieve the goal of transparency. Cost-benefit analysis is a complex, resource-intensive, and expert-driven process. It requires a great deal of time and effort to attempt to unpack even the simplest cost-benefit analysis. Few community groups, for example, have access to the kind of scientific and technical expertise that would allow them to evaluate whether, intentionally or unintentionally, the authors of a cost-benefit analysis have unfairly slighted the interests of the community or some of its members. Few members of the public can participate meaningfully in the debates about the use of particular regression analyses or discount rates which are central to the cost-benefit method.

The translation of lives, health, and nature into dollars also renders decision making about the underlying social values less rather than more transparent. As we have discussed, all of the various steps required to reduce a human life to a dollar value are open to debate and subject to uncertainty. However, the specific dollar values kicked out by cost-benefit analysis tend to obscure these underlying issues rather than encourage full public debate about them.

NOTES AND QUESTIONS

1. One question raised by Ackerman and Heinzerling is whether market valuations should be the basis for government policy. Arguably, the government's determination of the public interest might be based on different criteria than those that individuals use to make private choices. Is it rational for people to use different values as voters than as workers or consumers? Is it paternalistic for the government to impose trade-offs (for

---

[24] Cass R. Sunstein, *The Arithmetic of Arsenic*, 90 Geo. L.J. 2255 (2002).

example, more disaster-resistant structures but higher housing costs) that people would not voluntarily accept in the market?

2. Is it morally offensive to put a dollar value on life? After all, we do make trade-offs between safety and cost all the time. Isn't cost-benefit analysis just a more systematic way of thinking about these trade-offs? Or does the use of cost-benefit analysis depersonalize our approach to these problems?

3. Libertarians may also be critical of cost-benefit analysis because of its focus on increasing total societal well-being, which could involve transfers of wealth from one person to another and perhaps override individual preferences. See Alexander Volokh, *Rationality or Rationalism? The Positive and Normative Flaws of Cost-Benefit Analysis*, 48 Houston L. Rev. 1 (2011).

4. In considering the role of cost-benefit analysis, it is important to ask: compared to what? In terms of the flood control system, for example, some observers might think that use of cost-benefit analysis would increase rather than decrease attention to safety compared with the status quo.

NOTE ON COST-BENEFIT ANALYSIS, CLIMATE CHANGE, AND DISASTER RISKS

Climate change can be considered the granddaddy of all disasters. The question of how much to reduce emissions is not easily answered. Many economists favor gradual emissions reductions for the next few decades, accelerating toward mid-century. Modeling the systemic economic impact of climate change as well as the costs of adaptation and mitigation involves tremendous challenges, particularly if the projection goes out more than a few years.[25] To begin with, the economic model must build on the outputs of climate models, which are themselves uncertain. Then there is the difficulty of forecasting the future trajectory of the economy over future decades. This clearly cannot be done in detail—for example, no forecaster in 1970 would have predicted the explosive growth of personal computers, let alone the Internet, neither of which existed at the time. Even efforts to forecast at a cruder level must rely heavily on the assumption that the future will on average be much like the recent past—for example, that technological progress will continue at something like its current pace, that some unforeseen factor will not cause a population crash, and so forth. The uncertainties go both ways: to the extent that climate change scenarios are based on projections of future emissions, they implicitly make assumptions about future political and economic developments.

---

[25] A good overview of modeling issues can be found in J.C. Haurcade et al., *Estimating the Costs of Mitigating Greenhouse Gases*, in Climate Change 1995: Economic and Social Dimensions of Climate Change: Contribution of Working Group III to the Second Assessment Report of the Intergovernmental Panel on Climate Change 263 (James P. Bruce et al. eds., 1996).

There are multiple models that couple climate change predictions to economic analysis. These models differ in a number of dimensions: whether they focus on the energy sector or rely on a broad macroeconomic analysis, the degree to which they analyze localized versus average global impacts, and their treatment of uncertainty. Models also differ in their assessments of the costs of complying with the Kyoto Protocol, with the range running from negligible losses to at least 1 to 2 percent of GDP annually.[26] The models differ in terms of three critical assumptions about the timing of abatement efforts, the types of policy instruments used, and the likelihood of technological innovation.[27] Other relevant factors include the willingness of economic actors to substitute away from high carbon technologies and trends in energy efficiency.[28]

Among the costs of climate change are increased infrastructure costs to respond to potential weather events. The Stern Review, issued at the request of then-Chancellor of the Exchequer Gordon Brown (later prime minister) by economist Sir Nicholas Stern (head of Britain's Government Economic Service), estimates that

> [i]nfrastructure is particularly vulnerable to heavier floods and storms, in part because OECD economies invest around 20% of GDP or roughly $5.5 trillion in fixed capital each year, of which just over one-quarter typically goes into construction ($1.5 trillion—mostly for infrastructure and buildings). The additional costs of adapting this investment to a higher-risk future could be $15-150 billion each year (0.05-0.5% of GDP), with one-third of the costs borne by the US and one-fifth in Japan. This preliminary cost calculation assumes that adaptation requires extra investment of 1-10% to limit future damages from climate change.[29]

Stern also reports some very preliminary efforts regarding the cost of adaptation in the developing world:

> The most recent estimates come from the World Bank show the additional costs of adaptation alone as $4-37 billion each year. This includes only the cost of adapting investments to protect them from climate-change risks, and it is important to remember that there will be major impacts that are sure to occur even with adaptation. The World Bank estimate is based on an examination of the current core flows of development finance, combined with very rough estimates of the proportion of those investments that is sensitive to climate

---

[26] Jason F. Shogren & Michael A. Toman, *How Much Climate Change Is Too Much?*, in Climate Change Economics and Policy: An RFF Anthology 35, 42 (Michael A. Toman ed., 2001).

[27] *Id.*

[28] *Id.* at 43.

[29] Nicholas Stern, The Stern Review of the Economics of Climate Change 417 (2007).

risk and the additional cost to reduce that risk to account for climate change (5-20% as a very rough estimate).[30]

Another estimate, covering only the least developed countries and the short term, is over a billion dollars for the most urgently needed adaptation measures.[31] The cost of adaptation may or may not be large in comparison with the total world economy, but that comparison will not be relevant to localities that need billions of dollars' worth of expenditures for climate change adaptation. One of the safer predictions about the impact of climate change is that the debate over who will bear those costs is likely to become quite heated.

Cost-benefit analysis certainly is not the only approach to decision making about risks—whether as large as climate change or as small as a flooding creek. The following excerpt defends an important alternative approach.

DOUGLAS A. KYSAR, IT MIGHT HAVE BEEN: RISK, PRECAUTION AND OPPORTUNITY COSTS
22 J. Land Use & Envtl. L. 1 (2006)

This apparent difference in regulatory attitude between the United States and Europe often is said to emerge from the jurisdictions' contrasting stances toward two policymaking paradigms that compete for acceptance within environmental, health, and safety regulation: One—known as cost-benefit analysis (CBA) and increasingly associated with the United States[32]—strives to enhance social welfare by predicting, weighting, and aggregating all relevant consequences of policy proposals in order to identify those choices that represent welfare-maximizing uses of public resources; the other—associated with the precautionary principle (PP) and the European approach to risk regulation—eschews optimization in favor of more pragmatic forms of decisionmaking. One oft-cited articulation of the PP, for instance, seeks to trigger an incremental process of risk regulation through the simple admonition, "When an activity raises threats of harm to human health or the environment, precautionary measures should be taken even if some cause and effect relationships are not fully established scientifically."...

As J.B. Ruhl has observed, "[t]he prevailing schools of environmental policy have described our problem as a series of linear, one-dimensional decisionmaking systems," an approach that assumes "economic conditions can be translated predictably into economic conclusions that call for prescribed economic measures, [and] environmental conditions can be translated predictably into environmental conclusions that call for environmental

---

[30] *Id.* at 502 (footnotes omitted).

[31] *Id.*

[32] *See* Cass R. Sunstein, The Cost-benefit State ix (2002) ("Gradually, and in fits and starts, American government is becoming a cost-benefit state.").

measures." If indeed these prevailing schools are correct that biophysical and sociolegal systems are well-behaved—such that they follow linear operating rules, map onto normal or Gaussian probability distributions, and exhibit stable equilibrium outcomes—then data gaps and other shortcomings of human knowledge need not be viewed as deeply problematic.

If, on the other hand, these systems are complex—such that they exhibit "behaviors such as feedback, emergence, path dependence, and nonlinearity"—then risk regulators face a fundamentally different task. Not only must they assess and manage risks of an uncertain magnitude, but they must do so within the context of numerous, overlapping dynamic systems, each of which is characterized by such perplexing features as extreme sensitivity to minor variations in condition, "fat tail[]" probability distributions [such as the power law distributions discussed earlier in this chapter], and irreducible levels of uncertainty, or chaos. This is a far more intractable problem setting than has tended to be recognized in the risk regulation debate, even by those who critique CBA for its Herculean informational demands. Because complex adaptive systems contain ineliminable uncertainties that cannot be presumed to be insignificant, such systems by their nature are likely to present ill-posed problems—that is, problems whose imperviousness to resolution is not driven by deficiencies in our epistemic position, but rather by features inherent to the problems themselves....

Criticisms of CBA's efforts to grapple with complexity and uncertainty have particular purchase in the case of potentially catastrophic risks. [H]umanity faces a number of threats of uncertain, but possibly monumental consequence, including some threats that might entail the erasure of all life on the planet. In the face of such complete catastrophic threats, conventional approaches to CBA would, first, sum up the total monetary-equivalent worth of the expected human population at the time of potential destruction and, second, discount that number, both for time and for likelihood. The resulting number would, of course, be finite. It might also be quite small, particularly if the anticipated disaster looms far in the future or with minute probability. One could increase the number to reflect a degree of risk aversion, but the result still would be finite and, if cost-benefit analyses of climate change are an indication, not alarmingly large.

The question then arises whether the expectation calculus of CBA is appropriately textured for the type of decision actually being confronted....Put bluntly, either nanotechnology will transform the planet into "gray goo" or it will not. We do not know what the precise probabilities involved are, but given the nature of discontinuity, we do know that the expected utility outcome—the weighted average of these extremes—will not occur. Thus, by displacing context-sensitive discussion of precisely what outcomes are being gambled in favor of what gains and for which winners and losers, the CBA approach tends to understate the challenge posed by long-term catastrophic risks....

In the context of complex, adaptive systems, the deliberate attempt to optimize may not represent simply an imperfect, but useful aid to decisionmaking, as CBA defenders often assert. Rather, it may represent a solution concept that is poorly matched for the problem tasks at hand. In the face of ill-posed problems, we cannot confidently expect that the errors of CBA will cluster around an "optimal" result—indeed, for such problems the very notion of an optimum eludes meaningful description. The errors of CBA therefore are capable of deviating substantially and unpredictably from decision paths that are easily identified as desirable—if not necessarily optimal—through less formalistic decision procedures. In light of such concerns, proponents of the PP consciously part ways with the technocratic paradigm underlying risk assessment and CBA. Rather than insist on quantification as a predicate to decisionmaking, they instead argue that environmental, health, and safety regulation should become infused with a "culture of humility about the sufficiency and accuracy of existing knowledge."

As it turns out, the United States has enjoyed a long and successful experience with precisely this approach. Despite the current prominence of CBA among U.S. policymakers and academics, much of U.S. environmental law and regulation continues to be based instead on policies and procedures that reflect a precautionary approach. In several key pollution control areas, for instance, the United States has forsaken optimization in favor of a precautionary practice of requiring installation of the best available pollution abatement technology, often with opt-out procedures extended to firms that are able to demonstrate achievement of equal abatement levels using alternative technologies. This simple heuristic—in essence, "do the best you can"—implies great collective commitment to the preservation of human life and the environment without requiring satisfaction of Herculean informational demands by regulators.

Realistic but unquantifiable threats of catastrophic loss present an additional case in which heuristic decisionmaking procedures may prove more pragmatically sensible than deliberate cost-benefit optimization. With regard to climate change, for instance, future generations may reflect with marvel on our present day attempts to meticulously calculate the costs and benefits of greenhouse policies. Such studies typically lead to a conclusion that the economic benefits of continued fossil fuel consumption more than outweigh the physical, agricultural, and ecological costs that would be averted by restricting emissions, at least for the next few decades. Accordingly, the optimal carbon reduction policy under CBA is a rather limited one that should not begin any time soon. The important lesson from complexity theory, again, is that the apparent CBA consensus on climate change may not merely be wrong; it may be wildly wrong. Especially in light of the relatively minor cost associated with implementing most proposed carbon emissions abatement policies, uncertain but potentially catastrophic consequences of anthropogenic greenhouse gas emissions should not simply be reduced to an expectation value and included within cost-benefit calculation....

This "safe minimum standards" approach has long been associated with the PP. One also may think of the "safe minimum standards" approach as resembling the maximin principle from decision theory, which counsels minimization of the maximum possible loss when decisionmakers are faced with policy choices that are characterized by true uncertainty. Most famously discussed by John Rawls in the context of elaborating an egalitarian theory of justice, the maximin principle reflects what would be termed an extreme degree of risk aversion if probabilistic information on outcomes were actually available, given that the principle focuses attention exclusively on the worst case outcome from each possible course of action under inspection. For this reason, the principle has attracted a substantial share of criticism. Nevertheless, at least as a preliminary stance, proponents of the PP believe that an extreme level of risk aversion is appropriate for policymaking that concerns unknown but potentially devastating threats to the global climate, the ozone layer, biodiversity, and other natural systems that are thought to be of fundamental and irreplaceable importance to humanity.

Whether characterized as the PP, the best available technology requirement, the safe minimum standard, or the maximin principle, each of these related decisionmaking techniques reflects an awareness that truly rational risk regulation sometimes requires officials to abandon the quest for optimization in favor of less ambitious, more pragmatically sensible approaches. Of course, the extreme conservatism of these approaches begs the questions of when and how to relax their dictates in favor of more permissive standards. According to many PP supporters, however, fostering such an adaptive approach to risk regulation is precisely the point of the PP—something that the principle's critics seem reluctant to acknowledge. Unlike the optimization framework of CBA, which must resort to awkward analytical devices in the presence of imperfectly characterized risks, the PP's incremental approach reflects great sensitivity to the fact that effective decisionmaking in the face of many problems demands procedural rationality....

This potential deliberative deficit of [cost-benefit analysis] is also evident in Judge Posner's recent use of CBA to suggest that the optimal post-Katrina reconstruction plan for New Orleans is one in which "the historic portions of the city (the French Quarter and the Garden District) might be rebuilt and preserved as a tourist site, much like Colonial Williamsburg, without having to be part of a city." Posner may well be right that the United States should not spend billions of dollars reconstructing New Orleans to its former scale, especially in light of projected sea level rises over the next century from climate change that would transform the city into an island. But the reason for this conclusion is not to be found in a CBA premised on the decontextualized preferences of individuals. Whatever pre-Katrina tourist behavior might suggest (for it is their disposable dollars that presumably are driving the conclusion that only the French Quarter and the Garden District are worth rebuilding), it is an open question whether individuals post-Katrina agree that they have little use for a revival of the Ninth Ward and other poor, racially-segregated areas of the city. To say nothing of the deeper issues of environmental justice raised by the Katrina tragedy, we understate the role of citizenship when we assume that shared experiences do not affect the preferences that we hold and the meanings that we attribute to our social world....

As noted above, the contention of PP proponents that environmental, health, and safety decisionmaking is characterized by abiding uncertainty does not commit them to the extreme conservatism of the maximin approach as a general or permanent response. Rather, the PP is intended to commence a program of risk regulation that is both proportionate to the scope of the perceived threat and capable of being updated and adjusted over time. Proponents of the safe minimum standards approach within environmental economics also tend to qualify their position, arguing that fidelity to safe minimum standards should yield when the costs of precaution become "immoderate" or "unacceptably large." Within the legal literature, Dan Farber similarly allows for departure from his strong "environmental baseline" approach to policymaking "when costs would clearly overwhelm any potential benefits" from precautionary regulation...

...Even if we know that the PP's more severe implications will need to be relaxed, the principle nevertheless forces societal discussion regarding the normative status of statistical victims, other societies, and future generations. In that regard, the PP's insistence that human health and the environment deserve constant, anticipatory attention serves as a procedural lever for furthering still-nascent attempts to reason through important questions that lie at the "frontiers of justice"—questions about our responsibilities to members of other nations, other generations, and other species. Such an approach therefore aspires not only to be procedurally rational (e.g., in the sense that dynamic, incremental management approaches are demanded in the face of complexity and uncertainty in biophysical and sociolegal systems) but also to be discursively rational (e.g., in the sense that the PP helps to structure and promote collective deliberation regarding decisions for which our existing, individualized preferences are either ill-formed or ill-suited for the decision under inspection)....

Today, the precautionary approach is derided by U.S. policy elites as a "mythical concept...like a unicorn." Yet if the analysis of the previous Section translates at all smoothly from the individual to the collective context, then the precautionary approach makes a great deal more concrete sense than PP critics appreciate: Even granting the causal optimizer's claim that "risks are on all sides of social situations," that fact alone does not compel the adoption of an optimization standard, such as CBA, in which risks imposed and opportunities foregone are treated as analytically indistinguishable....Instead, something like the "first, do no harm" admonition of Hippocrates may be necessary at the collective level simply for the implicit reminder contained within it, that a political community's actions and decisions carry distinctive moral weight.

NOTES AND QUESTIONS

1. How would Kysar approach a disaster issue such as the appropriate level of hurricane protection for a city such as New Orleans? Would he apply his maximin principle or something different?
2. Protecting New Orleans from hurricanes could be quite expensive, particularly given climate change. Should we abandon the effort and limit ourselves to protecting smaller enclaves such as the French Quarter? Similarly, should some parts of New York such as State Island be abandoned as too expensive to protect given their value? How might this question be addressed:
   a. By a cost-benefit analyst like Sunstein?
   b. By someone applying the precautionary principle like Kysar?
   c. By a culturally attuned analyst like Kahan?
3. A related question is the role of experts in deciding disaster issues. Should Congress delegate major issues of disaster policy to experts or make them legislatively?

NOTE ON CRITICISMS OF THE PRECAUTIONARY PRINCIPLE

The precautionary principle is controversial. There seem to be three main criticisms. The first is its vagueness. Chris Stone observes that the principle is vague in part because of the nature of international diplomacy. Nevertheless, he finds it "increasingly frustrating that there is no convergence as to what it means, or as to what regions of action (environment, public health) it is supposed to apply." [33] In some formulations, the precautionary principle is seemingly a mandate to halt activities when a sufficient level of risk appears, whereas in others it operates to create a presumption against activities potentially harmful to the environment, placing the burden of proof on the advocates of those activities. But none of these formulations is precise, and Stone doubts whether any general rule more specific than "be careful" can be formulated.

A second criticism is that government intervention creates risks of its own.[34] For example, a building code requirement that is designed to limit seismic risks may increase the expense of new housing, leading people to stay in older buildings that are not subject to the code and are highly vulnerable to earthquakes. If the effects of regulation are also uncertain and present

---

[33] Christopher D. Stone, *Is There a Precautionary Principle?*, 31 Envtl. L. Rep. 10790, B (2001).

[34] *See* Jonathan H. Adler, *More Sorry Than Safe: Assessing the Precautionary Principle and the Proposed International Safety Protocol*, 35 Tex. 'Int'l L.J. 194 (2000); Frank B. Cross, *Paradoxical Perils of the Precautionary Principle*, 53 Wash. & Lee L. Rev. 851, 872 (1996).

unforeseen risks to health and environment, then the precautionary principle seems to turn against itself, suggesting that we should not proceed with environmental regulations until we can pin down their effects. As Sunstein explains,

> There is an obvious difficulty with the precautionary principle: Both regulation and nonregulation will often give rise to risks; if so, the principle would seem to be paralyzing, forbidding stringent regulation, inaction, and everything in between. Consider, for example, the case of genetic engineering of food. The precautionary principle might seem to call for stringent regulation of genetic engineering, on the theory that this technology contains at least some risk of causing ecological harm. But such regulation would also create risks of adverse effects, simply because genetic engineering holds out a prospect of producing ecological and health benefits. The precautionary principle would seem both to require and to forbid stringent regulation of genetic engineering. The same can be said for many activities and processes, such as nuclear power and nontherapeutic cloning, simply because risks are on all sides of the situation.[35]

Adding force to the first criticism, this critique argues that the principle is not only vague but also incoherent, since it always, or at least often, generates conflicting directions.

The third criticism adds a charge of irrationality against the precautionary principle. Sunstein argues that when the precautionary principle "seems to offer guidance," it is "often because of the operation of probability neglect," meaning the cognitive incapacity of individuals to attend to the relevant risks.[36]

Considerable debate surrounds these criticisms. The first criticism, based on the principle's vagueness, has prompted various attempts to give it greater content with reference to avoiding irreversible actions, keeping options open, and providing insurance against dangerous risks.[37] Alternatively, some supporters argue that the principle requires a type of case-by-case, common law development.[38] The second criticism, regarding the existence of risks on both

---

[35] Cass R. Sunstein, *Probability Neglect: Emotions, Worst Cases, and Law*, 11 Yale L.J. 61, 93 (2002).

[36] *Id.* at 94. Sunstein further elaborates his critique in Cass R. Sunstein, *Beyond the Precautionary Principle*, 151 U. Pa. L. Rev. 1003 (2003).

[37] *See, e.g.,* Stephen Charest, *Bayesian Approaches to the Precautionary Principle*, 12 Duke Envtl. L. & Pol'y F. 265 (2002); Christian Gollier, Bruno Jullien & Nicolas Treich, *Scientific Progress and Irreversibility: An Economic Interpretation of the "Precautionary Principle,"* 75 J. Pub. Econ. 229 (2000); W. David Montgomery & Anne E. Smith, *Global Climate Change and the Precautionary Principle*, 6 Hum. & Ecological Risk Assessment 399 (2000).

[38] *See* Stephen Toulmin, *The Case for Cosmic Prudence*, 56 Tenn. L. Rev. 29 (1998).

sides of regulatory decisions, is at least partly countered by noting that regulatory decisions may also have unanticipated benefits. The third criticism, as it turns out, may be backwards: a good argument can be made that the precautionary principle is needed to counter defects in the ways people process probability information; rather than being part of the problem of limited human rationality, the precautionary principle may be part of the cure.[39] At this stage, the academic debate is far from settled. For a recent defense of the precautionary principle, see Noah M. Sachs, *Rescuing the Strong Precautionary Principle From Its Critics*, 2011 U. Ill. L. Rev. 1285.

NOTE ON ENVIRONMENTAL IMPACT STATEMENTS, RISK, AND THE "WORST-CASE SCENARIO"

An environmental impact statement (EIS) must be prepared for federal infrastructure projects such as dams and levees, and for projects requiring a federal license, such as nuclear power plants. An EIS does not dictate the substance of regulatory decisions, but it is at least supposed to force the agency to take a "hard look" at the relevant factors.[40]

At one time, mirroring the precautionary principle, agencies were required to deal with such uncertainty by discussing the "worst-case scenario." The history and implementation of this regulation is instructive.

In 1978, the Council on Environmental Quality, the executive agency supervising implementation of the EIS requirement, provided direction to agencies on how to deal with scientific uncertainty.[41] The regulation applied when there were "gaps in relevant information or scientific uncertainty" about a project's environmental impacts.[42] When such information was obtainable at reasonable cost, the agency was instructed to obtain it, but otherwise the agency was told to pursue the following course:

> If (1) the information relevant to adverse impacts is essential to a reasoned choice among alternatives and is not known and the overall costs of obtaining it are exorbitant or (2) the information relevant to adverse impacts is important to the decision and the means to obtain it are not known (e.g. the means for obtaining it are beyond the state of the art) the agency shall weigh the need for the action against the risk and severity of possible adverse impacts were the agency to proceed in the face of uncertainty. If the agency proceeds, it shall

---

[39] David A. Dana, *A Behavioral Economic Defense of the Precautionary Principle*, 97 Nw. U. L. Rev. 1315 (2003).

[40] *See* Robertson v. Methow Valley Citizens Council, 490 U.S. 332 (1989).

[41] *See* Edward A. Fitzgerald, *The Rise and Fall of Worst Case Analysis*, 18 U. Dayton L. Rev. 1 (1992).

[42] 40 C.F.R. §1502.22 (1991).

include a worst case analysis and an indication of the probability or improbability of its occurrence. [43]

In a 1981 guidance document, CEQ explained this rule as mandating "reasonable projections of the worst possible consequences of a proposed action." [44] As an illustration, CEQ said that where a proposed water quality facility would have an unknown impact on juvenile fish, the EIS must include "the possibility of the loss of the commercial or sport fishery." [45] Note that agencies were not directed to avoid taking action in the face of uncertainty, but rather to engage in a balancing test weighing the need for the action against the risk. Worst case analysis was a disclosure requirement, not a decision technique.

Sierra Club v. Sigler [46] was the leading case to apply the worst case requirement. The case involved a controversial proposal to allow oil tankers to operate in an estuary near the Port of Galveston. [47] The EIS concluded that the project would not significantly increase the probability or likely harm of an oil spill. [48] The relevance of oil spills to the decision was unquestioned and the parties agreed that "an analysis of a supertanker oil spill involving a total cargo loss beyond 24 hours after it occurs is beyond the state of the art." [49] The agency had thought this possibility was too remote to warrant discussion. Relying on CEQ's 1981 guidance document, however, the Fifth Circuit held that the EIS was invalid because it "failed to discuss the 'catastrophic impact' of a total cargo loss by a supertanker in the Bay" and the court faulted the agency for failing to consider "that impact and the probability of its occurrence" in deciding to proceed. [50]

The worst-case requirement was criticized as being excessively pessimistic and too intrusive on agency discretion. [51] In 1983, CEQ proposed (but later withdrew) a guidance document that would have required a worst-case analysis only when a risk crossed an "initial threshold of probability" and was reasonably foreseeable but its consequences were uncertain. [52] In the Fifth Circuit's view, the fact that a risk was extremely remote was relevant in assessing its ultimate import for the final decision but not relevant in deciding

---

[43] *Id.* §1502.22(b) (1991).

[44] Vicki O. Masterman, *Worst Case Analysis: The Final Chapter?*, 19 Envtl. L. Rep. 10026, at 10027 n.14 (1989).

[45] *Id.*

[46] Sierra Club v. Sigler, 695 F.2d 957 (5th Cir. 1983).

[47] *Id.* at 962.

[48] *Id.* at 968.

[49] *Id.* at 973.

[50] *Id.*

[51] *See* Charles Weiss, Note, *Federal Agency Treatment of Uncertainty in Environmental Impact Statements under the EPA's Amended NEAP Regulation §1502.22: Worst Case Analysis or Risk Threshold?*, 86 Mich. L. Rev. 777, 807-809 (1988).

[52] *Id.*

whether to include a discussion of it as the worst-case scenario.[53] The court hastened to add, however, that "while remoteness of a possible occurrence does not permit disregarding it in such circumstances as these, where a real possibility of the occurrence has been proved and a database for evaluating its consequences established, the Corps need not concern itself with phantasmagoria hypothesized without a firm basis in evidence and the actual circumstances of the contemplated project, or with disasters the likelihood of which is not shown to be significantly increased by the carrying out of the project." [54]

After withdrawing the 1983 proposal, CEQ called for public comment on possible methods of dealing with uncertainty. It received a laundry list of complaints about the worst-case requirement such as "the limitless nature of the task of conjuring the worst possible case," "the lack of expert support for worst-case analysis in the growing field of risk analysis," and the "minimal value of fanciful worst-case analyses to federal decision-makers who must balance a full range of proven competing interests." [55] CEQ then issued a new regulation dealing with uncertainty, replacing the worst-case scenario requirement. The new regulation, which is still in effect, tells agencies that when important information is not available at a reasonable cost, they must include in the EIS

> (1) a statement that such information is incomplete or unavailable; (2) a statement of the relevance of the incomplete or unavailable information to evaluating reasonably foreseeable significant adverse impacts on the human environment; (3) a summary of existing credible scientific evidence which is relevant to evaluating the reasonably foreseeable significant adverse impacts on the human environment; and (4) the agency's evaluation of such impacts based upon theoretical approaches or research methods generally accepted in the scientific community.[56]

The regulations define "reasonably foreseeable" to include impacts "which have catastrophic consequences, even if their probability of occurrence is low, provided that the analysis of the impacts is supported by credible scientific evidence, is not based on pure conjecture, and is within the rule of reason." [57]

It should be noted that, although the new regulation avoids the term "worst case" and calls for a broader discussion of potential risks, it does still call for discussion of low-probability catastrophes. In effect, it defines "worst case" in terms of the rule of reason rather than completely eliminating the worst case requirement.

---

[53]*Sigler*, 695 F.2d at 974.
[54]*Id.* at 975 n.14.
[55] Masterman, *supra*, note 44.
[56] 40 C.F.R. §1502.22(b).
[57]*Id.*

The Supreme Court upheld this regulation in Robertson v. Methow Valley Citizens Council and held that NEPA does not require a worst-case analysis.[58] In response to a Forest Service decision to allow construction of a private ski resort, the state game department had "voiced a special concern about potential losses to the State's large migratory deer herd, which uses the Methow Valley as a critical winter range and as its migration route." [59] The state agency projected a possible 50 percent reduction in the herd.[60] The Forest Service was more optimistic but admitted that off-site development caused by the project might "noticeably reduce" the herd.[61] Although the court of appeals held that the EIS was invalid because it failed to put forward an explicit worst-case scenario, the Supreme Court held that the CEQ's current regulation was a reasonable interpretation of the statute.[62] Hence, agencies were no longer required to conduct an explicit worst-case analysis after the new regulation went into effect.

PROBLEM ON RISK

The Army Corps of Engineers plans a 300-foot earth fill dam on a California creek, which would create a 3,600-acre lake. (An earth fill dam is made simply by compacting soil, with more sophisticated designs including drainage systems within the dam.) The dam site is located on an inactive fault, but near several active faults. The Corps hired a consultant to conduct a "dynamic analysis" of the dam to test the seismic safety of the design. The consultant concluded that the dam was safe. The process involved constructing a model of the dam in a laboratory and subjecting it to simulated earthquakes that would represent "the maximum credible earthquakes" the dam would be required to withstand. The tests were based on the assumption that the fault that could generate earthquakes having the greatest destructive force on the dam was the San Andreas fault, which is 20 miles from the dam and which could generate an earthquake of a magnitude of 8.3 on the Richter Scale. The consultant did not consider a closer fault (only six miles from the dam), because the fault was thought to be too short to generate a major earthquake.

However, a later study showed that the fault was actually about eight times longer than previously believed. Experts believe that the fault is capable of generating an 8.1 earthquake, which would be more destructive for the dam than an 8.3 on the more distant San Andreas fault. The dam is upstream from a small city with a population of 8,000, many of them immigrant agricultural workers on nearby farms.

---

[58] Robertson v. Methow Valley Citizens Council, 490 U.S. 332 (1989).
[59] Id. at 342.
[60] Id.
[61] Id. at 343.
[62] Id. at 354-355.

Assume the following for purposes of this problem:

- There is a 1 percent chance of an 8.1 earthquake on the fault, and such an earthquake would cause the immediate collapse of the dam.
- If an earthquake does take place, that would happen 20 years after the dam is completed,[63] and it would kill 300-400 people because of the short time that would be available for evacuation. Victims probably would be disproportionately elderly or too poor to own cars.
- The dam will produce net present benefits (not taking into account possible losses due to the earthquake risk) of $7 million in excess of its construction cost and the value of the farmland that would be covered by the reservoir.

Should the Corps abandon the dam project or not? What decision standard would you use—cost-benefit analysis, the precautionary principle, or something else?

Whatever your preferred decision standard, explain what decision-making process you would advise. For instance, would you assign the decision to technical experts or allow local residents to vote on the issue? Should the environmental impact statement discuss the effect of a dam collapse in detail? Would you hold public hearings? Should Congress make the decision or the Corps?

---

[63] Obviously, this assumption is highly artificial, but it is intended to help you think about the temporal dimension of the problem without having to engage in too much complexity. A real problem would involve a much more complicated projection about the range of possible future times for the earthquake during the life of the dam, the amount of harm at those various future times, and the discounted value of those harms. But let's keep things simple!

7

COMPENSATION AND RISK SPREADING

There are limits to how successfully we can prevent harm from disasters. When harm does occur, the next question is compensation. Should we use private insurance, government programs, or the tort system to provide a safety net for victims? Or leave them to their own devices? This subject intersects with the one in the previous chapter: the prospect of compensation may undermine the motivation of potential victims to invest in increased safety. This chapter considers methods of victim compensation and their pitfalls.

FEMA provides grants and loans to disaster victims to help with recovery. Moreover, many victims have insurance of one kind or another. But private insurance often excludes damages from disasters. For instance, coverage is often limited to wind damage as opposed to flood damage. And after floods, FEMA typically requires localities to upgrade their building codes for rebuilding—but the added expenses are not covered by the typical insurance policy, even if the policy covers "replacement cost." An additional problem is that insurance companies tend to withdraw from the market after catastrophes—so people may be very vulnerable if another big catastrophe hits in the next few years. For all of these reasons, designing a system for compensating catastrophe victims involves significant complications.

The issues discussed in this chapter connect with some of the questions of race and class discussed earlier. Of course, the problem of compensation for catastrophic loss cuts across all groups and income levels. But for those groups whose hold on assets may have been the most tenuous in the first place, the problem of compensation may loom even larger.

We will begin with a survey of compensation methods, including an in-depth discussion of tort law. We will then focus on federal flood insurance and on private insurance, before considering innovative approaches in the final part of the chapter.

A. TORT LAW AND OTHER METHODS OF COMPENSATING VICTIMS

Robert L. Rabin & Suzanne A. Bratis, Financial Compensation for Catastrophic Loss in the United States

Financial Compensation for Victims after Catastrophe
(M. Faure & T. Honlief eds., Springer Verlag 2005)

We have selected for closer examination three distinct illustrations of approaches taken by the U.S. legal system to compensation for financial loss in particularly notable instances: 1) the personal injury and death toll stemming from the terrorist attacks on September 11, 2001; 2) the property damage suffered in the single most costly hurricane in recent U.S. history, Hurricane Andrew; and 3) the profile of recovery in the prototypical mass tort disaster, a commercial airline crash.

A. The September 11 Victim Compensation Fund

In the immediate aftermath of September 11, a no-fault compensation plan was enacted that closely reflected the anxieties and emotions stirred up by the horrendous toll of deaths and injuries occurring on that fateful day. The September 11 Victim Compensation Fund (the Fund), signed into law just eleven days after the terrorist attacks, addressed only personal injury and fatality claims. Losses related to property damage, as well as business losses or interruptions, remained compensable only in tort, if at all. Moreover the Fund was part of a broader legislative scheme, the Air Transportation Safety and System Stabilization Act, offering a package of loans and subsidies to the airlines to avoid a potential collapse of the U.S. commercial air transport system.

Within limits, the Fund was meant to create baseline assurance that victims of physical injury and their survivors would receive benefits.[64] More precisely, the Fund established eligibility for individuals "present at [any of the three crash sites] at the time, or in the immediate aftermath, of the terrorist-related aircraft crashes," [65] and who "suffered physical harm or death" as a result of the crashes. For this circumscribed class, the Fund provided benefits for both economic and noneconomic losses on a no-fault basis.

In spelling out those benefits, however, the Fund appeared to be far more generous than earlier-enacted no-fault systems in the United States, virtually all of which follow the traditional model established in the early twentieth century for addressing the toll of industrial injuries: workers' compensation schemes. Under workers' compensation, eligible claimants

---

[64]The description of the Fund and regulations that follows draws in part on an earlier treatment, *see* Robert L. Rabin, *The Quest for Fairness in Compensating Victims of September 11*, 49 Clev. St. L. Rev. 573 (2001).

[65]Air Transportation Safety and System Stabilization Act, Pub. L. No. 107-42, 405(b)(2), 115 Stat. 230, 238 (2001) (codified as amended at 49 U.S.C. §40101 (2004)).

recover medical expenses and a percentage of lost income (generally based on a schedule of awards in cases of permanent disabling conditions and in death benefit cases), subject to a statutory ceiling.

By contrast, under the Fund economic loss was defined to include not just medical expenses and loss of present earnings, but "loss of business or employment opportunities to the extent recovery for such loss is allowed under applicable state law"—presumably, a reference to individual, case-by-case tort principles. And noneconomic loss was broadly defined to include "losses for physical and emotional pain, suffering, inconvenience, physical impairment, mental anguish, disfigurement, loss of enjoyment of life, loss of society and companionship, loss of consortium (other than loss of domestic service), hedonic damages, injury to reputation, and all other non-pecuniary losses of any kind or nature." Interestingly, no parallel to the economic loss definition that referenced "[as] allowed under applicable state law" was included in this latter definition of noneconomic loss. Nonetheless, the pervasive influence of the tort perspective of doing individualized justice—disparaged by critics of the tort system, trumpeted by its advocates—was apparent on the face of both provisions.

But there was one substantial qualification to this apparent generosity of spirit. Under traditional tort principles, there is recovery in tort of out-of-pocket expenses even if they have been reimbursed by "collateral" sources such as health and disability insurance. Under the Fund, there is no recovery for these items. Indeed, the restriction on "double recovery," as tort critics would put it, was written in exceedingly broad terms to cover "all collateral sources, including life insurance, pension funds, death benefit programs, and payments by Federal, State, or local governments related to the terrorist-related aircraft crashes...."

Thus, the Fund steered a somewhat uncertain course between collective principles that would emphasize timely compensation and filling the gaps of unmet need, on the one hand, and individualized recovery that would pull in the direction of the tort model, on the other. Before examining this tension in somewhat more detail, however, consider the escape hatch provided in the Act: the prospect of lodging a tort claim instead of proceeding under the Fund.

One can only speculate about why a statutory tort cause of action for claimants was established in the Fund legislation; perhaps in recognition of the fact that some victims with substantial collateral source recoveries—most notably, victims with major life insurance holdings, accrued pension benefits, or accidental death coverage—might well have anticipated no recoverable benefits under the Fund. Or realistically, Congress may have simply recognized that substantial categories of September 11 victims—most clearly, those suffering property damage and psychological harm without accompanying physical injury—were simply not covered by the Fund. Of course, tort, as the default system, would have been available for addressing these claims—how successfully is another matter—without the need for establishing a federal cause of action under the Act. But this would arguably have created the appearance of treating Fund beneficiaries as second-class citizens if they were offered no tort option.

Whatever the case, Congress's ambivalent embrace of tort is highlighted by the title of section 408, which created the federal cause of action: "*Limitation* on Air Carrier Liability." If Congress was determined to leave tort as an option, it was equally determined to constrain tort along lines familiar to observers of late twentieth-century U.S. tort reform. The Act established a ceiling on tort liability of the air carriers, providing that liability "shall not be in an amount greater than the limits of the liability coverage maintained by the air carrier." [66] In subsequent legislation, this protective cap on liability, linking it to the limits of insurance coverage, was carried over to aircraft manufacturers, property owners in the World Trade Center, airport owners, and governmental entities.

Ceilings aside, exclusive jurisdiction to hear "all actions brought for any claim (including any claim for loss of property, personal injury, or death) resulting from or relating to the terrorist-related aircraft crashes" was located in the federal district court for the Southern District of New York. But no federal common law was created; rather, the court was to apply the substantive law of the state in which the crash occurred. Finally, just to leave no doubt about it, section 408(b)(1) declared that the federal cause of action was to be "the exclusive remedy for damages arising out of the hijacking and subsequent crashes of such flights."

Thus, claimants eligible under the Fund were put to a choice—they had either to elect a claim for benefits under the Fund or to waive their rights and pursue a tort claim. At the same time, for those falling outside the eligibility limits of the Fund—such as those claiming solely economic loss—tort, as circumscribed in the Act, remained available. Interestingly, the tort option provided in the Fund legislation is not found in the traditional workers' compensation model, which precludes recourse to tort altogether (other later-enacted, no-fault schemes vary in this regard). Nonetheless, in its benefit provisions, as indicated, the Fund was far more generous than any other existing no-fault scheme in the United States.

These singular aspects of the Fund were not lost on the Special Master, appointed under the Act, who faced the immediate task of developing a concrete program for determining benefit awards for victims of September 11. His efforts offer an alternative vision of how one might design a no-fault model for future victims of terrorism, or catastrophic loss more broadly conceived.

---

[66] *Id.* §408(a). The amount of insurance coverage was reported to be $1.5 billion per plane. *See* Jim VandeHei & Milo Geyelin, *Economic Impact: Bush Seeks to Limit Liability of Companies Sued as Result of Attacks*, Wall St. J., Oct. 25, 2001, at A6.

When the Special Master, Kenneth Feinberg, was appointed on November 26, 2001, his initial task was to promulgate regulations resolving the principal tensions in the Act and filling in some important blanks. He issued a set of draft regulations ("Interim Final Rule") for commentary on December 21, 2001, and subsequently, on March 8, 2002, he issued final regulations ("Final Rule"), spelling out his interpretations of Fund provisions.

Feinberg's reading of the main provisions of the Fund reveals an interesting effort to strike a balance between understanding the Act in traditional no-fault terms that would have emphasized meeting scheduled basic loss of victims, and interpreting the Act in an open-ended fashion that essentially would have offered tort-type, individualized compensation in a no-fault setting. His manner of resolving this tension is evident in the approach taken to the three key substantive benefit provisions already discussed: collateral source offset, economic loss, and noneconomic loss.

As mentioned earlier, the Act explicitly called for the offset of life insurance and pension benefits. These provisions raised a firestorm of criticism from victims' families (in particular, the well endowed), concerned that they were likely to receive nothing in Fund benefits because of the foresight of the deceased, who it was argued, had earned or set aside funds for just such a contingency as occurred. These protests were sharpened to a fine point by prospective claimants observing that unconstrained tort—the absence of a Fund—would be a superior option, since life insurance and pension benefits traditionally are not offset under the tort system.

The Special Master responded to these criticisms in the Final Rule, by interpreting the Act to allow reduction of the offset to the extent of victims' self-contributions. More generally, Feinberg announced that it would be "very rare" for *any* eligible claimant to receive less than $250,000. It should be noted that neither of these interpretive moves is grounded in the language of the act.

Rather, the Special Master's actions reflected a fundamental philosophical difference buried in the esoteric legal language of collateral offset. On the one hand, a need-based approach to compensation would point to full offset of all collateral sources, as the Act appeared to require, since these outside benefits do contribute to meeting basic needs. On the other hand, under an individual claimant-focused, tort-type inquiry as to the "deserving" status of the victim, offsets arguably would be ignored entirely. In the end, the Special Master arrived at something of a compromise, liberalizing the statute from the victims' perspective by reducing the offset through recognition of victims' contributions and ignoring entirely outside private charity received by Fund-eligible claimants, as well as establishing a quite substantial presumptive minimum recovery.

As indicated, in addressing economic loss the Act appears to be at cross-purposes with the literal terms of the collateral source offset provision, in referring to recovery of "loss of business or employment opportunities" as defined in state tort law. On its face, this would seem to suggest an individualized inquiry in every case into the lifetime earnings prospects of each deceased victim, entirely at odds with the traditional no-fault approach of scheduled benefits.

In the Final Rule, the Special Master again crafted a compromise. Although there is no mention of scheduling in the statute, Feinberg established a grid applicable to the range of potential claimants—a "presumed economic loss" schedule—based on age, size of family, and recent past earnings, along with a presumptive cap applicable to the upper 2 percent of income earners. In devising this strategy, he provided for awards that recognized very considerable future earnings disparities, an announced range of $250,000 to between $3 and $4 million. But at the same time, he rejected an approach that would have recognized entirely open-ended, case-by-case speculation about future earnings prospects.

Although there are exceptions, no-fault schemes typically do not provide for pain and suffering loss, apart from optional or supplemental recourse to tort. In fact, tort law itself, as encapsulated in wrongful death statutes, did not traditionally provide any pain and suffering loss for survivors— that is, loss of companionship. Indeed, many states still do not recognize nonpecuniary loss as compensable to survivors in tort, limiting recovery to economic loss. And some other states, such as California, refuse to recognize pain and suffering of the deceased *victim* prior to death as recoverable in tort.

Nonetheless, the Special Master provided for *scheduled* noneconomic benefit awards under the Fund, for each victim and every surviving eligible family member. In the Interim Final Rule, $250,000 was to be awarded for each victim; a figure that remained unchanged in the Final Rule. With respect to survivors, the Interim Final Rule provided $50,000 for the spouse and each dependent, a figure that was increased to $100,000 each in the Final Rule. Thus, a surviving spouse with two children would receive benefits of $550,000 for noneconomic loss in a claim under the Fund....

B. Compensating Hurricane Damage: Hurricane Andrew

On August 24, 1992, Hurricane Andrew made landfall in the United States. This Category 4 hurricane struck just east of Homestead Air Force Base in Florida, passed through the southern Florida peninsula and moved onto south-central Louisiana. When it hit Florida, the storm had sustained wind speeds of approximately 145 mph, with gusts of at least 175 mph, and storm surges up to 16.9 feet.

Natural events only become "disasters" because of the impact that they have on human settlements. And disaster events are typically ranked relative to one another based on the costs associated with the damage that they cause. When it struck, Hurricane Andrew became the costliest natural disaster in U.S. history, both in terms of the FEMA relief required and total estimates of property damaged. Total property damage was estimated to be more than 25 billion dollars. Florida witnessed 28,066 of its homes destroyed and another

107,380 damaged. 180,000 people were left homeless, 82,000 businesses were destroyed or damaged, 1.4 million residents were left without power and 32,000 acres of farmland were damaged. In addition, twenty-six deaths were found directly attributable to the hurricane's impact and another 39 lives were lost as an indirect result of the storm.

Hurricane Andrew caused $17 billion in insured damage. Homeowner policy holders in Florida submitted 280,000 claims and recovered over $11 billion or 65% of total insured losses resulting from Andrew. The other types of insurance coverage triggered by the event included commercial multiperil ($3.767 billion), commercial fire ($1.062 billion), automobile/physical damage ($365 million), mobile-home owners ($204 million), and farm owners ($16 million).

The size of the disaster caught many insurance companies unprepared, which affected the efficiency of claims processing. First, insurers were, themselves, victims of the disaster. Many of the insurers' employees who lived in the south Florida area suffered property damage, making it difficult for them to attend to their business duties and their own home crises. Additionally, the storm damaged office buildings, communications services, and data storage facilities of the insurance companies. This damage created hurdles for efficient operation of business.

There was also simply a dearth of claims adjusters in relation to the magnitude of claims filed. Florida's Department of Insurance streamlined its process of licensing claims adjusters in the days following the storm, enabling insurers to use emergency adjusters to deal with the volume of claims. Some insurers did not take advantage of this emergency provision, and the shortage of adjusters introduced delays in the system. With so many policyholders left homeless or severely in need in the first few days after the storm, these delays resulted in many people having to wait for the temporary living expense funds they needed to pay for basic necessities like food, shelter, and clothing.

In 1992, property insurers in Florida collected $1.5 billion in premiums. They paid out about 10 times that amount to victims of Hurricane Andrew. The costs of the hurricane were greater than any company expected and forced members of the Florida insurance industry to recalculate their risks. In the aftermath of Hurricane Andrew, the landscape of Florida's insurance industry changed dramatically. Before Andrew struck, nearly 300 insurers provided a variety of coverage options to Florida's citizenry. As a result of the losses caused by Andrew, seven small insurers became insolvent, 34 insurers informed Florida's Department of Insurance of their intent to withdraw from the market entirely, and 29 reduced their coverage options in the state. Reinsurers also contributed to the situation. Primary insurers are restricted in the coverage that they can offer by the reinsurance available to them and many reinsurers became reluctant to provide coverage after the events of Hurricane Andrew.

The Florida Legislature responded to the state's insurance crisis by creating the Residential Property and Casualty Joint Underwriting Association and the Florida Hurricane Catastrophe Fund, which are currently of major importance....

The risk of hurricane events occurring in Florida is continuous. If anything, climate change studies indicate that the frequency and severity of such storms will increase in the future. And the potential damage that a storm of Andrew's caliber could inflict today far exceeds the destruction that occurred in 1992. One study estimated that if Hurricane Andrew hit with the same force in the same location today, it would cause close to $70 billion in damage, nearly twice the 1992 figure. As coastal area populations continue to increase and infrastructure continues to grow denser, the potential impact of future hurricanes becomes more devastating.

The catastrophe-response infrastructure of both Florida and FEMA were heavily analyzed in the aftermath of the storm. Since 1992, FEMA has updated the Federal Response Plan twice, attempting to strengthen federal coordination, management, and leadership. Likewise, Florida's insurance industry underwent a major overhaul, along the lines discussed above.

The 2004 summer hurricane season put both the national and the state relief reforms to an unprecedented test. Beginning with Hurricane Charley, the southeast coastal states suffered through four significant hurricanes between August and October. As of late October, 2004, combined state and federal disaster aid for Florida alone reached more than $2 billion.

This cluster of hurricanes will provide a test for Florida's insurance industry, as well as FEMA. Florida's government will be challenged both in its role as a primary catastrophe insurer, through the state's newly formed Citizens Property Insurance Corporation, and as a reinsurer, through the Florida Hurricane Catastrophe Fund. These programs were created by the state in direct response to the lessons learned from Hurricane Andrew. As the state cleans up from Hurricane Charley and its three successors, and Florida's residents begin rebuilding their homes and their lives, onlookers will have the opportunity to assess whether Andrew's lessons were well-heeded.

Whatever the doctrinal limitations, tort is frequently criticized from the broader perspectives of economic efficiency, distribution of risk, and fairness. Certainly from a compensation vantage point, the latter two concerns loom large. Tort only provides compensation: 1) when the *wrongdoing* of a defendant can be established, and 2) when the defendant is *solvent*....These limitations, along with the no-duty rules..., mean that it is often the case that victims suffering similar injuries are not treated in a like fashion—and indeed that the disparities are sometimes glaring (ranging from no recovery to millions of dollars for similar accidental injuries or deaths). Thus, both in terms of risk distribution and fairness, it can be argued that tort leaves much to be desired.

Moreover, these limitations spill over into a critique from an economic, deterrence-oriented perspective, as well: No-duty rules, as well as insolvency, that insulate risk generators from bearing the cost of accidents for which they are responsible, translate into inadequate incentives on risk generators to provide safety precautions. In addition, the high administrative cost of shifting losses in tort is frequently invoked as an independent shortcoming of the system—undermining both its deterrence function and its efficacy from a risk-distribution and fairness perspective.[67]

As indicated in the section on insurance, the limitations of tort do not mean that those suffering personal injury loss as a consequence of catastrophic harm go entirely uncompensated.[68] About 85% of the U.S. population is covered to some extent by private health insurance, and Medicare offers public health insurance coverage to those over 65 years of age. The resulting gap in medical coverage—while still fairly substantial—is not as wide as the shortfall in coverage for wage loss. Private disability insurance coverage in the U.S. is quite uncommon, and while state disability and unemployment insurance benefits provide short-term partial relief, they do not fill the gap in cases of longer-term or very serious injuries. On this latter score, the federal SSDI insurance program, as indicated earlier, does offer scheduled benefits—although considerably short of full economic restoration—to those experiencing permanent total disability. In sum, the public welfare schemes in the U.S. leave quite large gaps in coverage for the economic consequences of personal injury, and private insurance sources fill only part of the gap, primarily for those carrying generous health insurance.

With regard to residential and commercial property and casualty loss, private insurance is the avenue of recourse. In the case of residential property, it is likely to be held by homeowners; much less likely to be held by renters. There are no general exclusions in the standard policies that would apply to catastrophic loss—just as there is none for third-party liability in the personal injury setting.

NOTES AND QUESTIONS

1. The 9/11 compensation fund has not been seen as a model for compensating for death or injury of disaster victims. Most of the attention regarding disasters such as Katrina has been on compensation for property loss. Should we consider a fund to compensate the families of those who were killed, or was 9/11 a unique event because of its national security dimension? Of course 9/11 was different in other

---

[67] It is generally thought that injury victims in tort receive roughly 50% of total expenditures by tort defendants. *See* J. Kakalik & N. Pace, RAND Inst. Civ. Just., Costs and Compensation Paid in Tort Litigation (1985).

[68] Indeed, a 1991 study conducted by RAND Institute for Civil Justice found that overall areas of personal injury, payments in tort comprised 11% of total benefits received by accident victims—although the percentage would almost certainly be higher for victims in catastrophic loss cases. D. Hensler et al., RAND Inst. Civ. Just., Compensation for Accidental Injuries in the United States (1991).

ways: the harm was caused by an identifiable enemy, possible liability by the airlines could have had devastating economic effects, and the families of the victims were often affluent and legally sophisticated. Should those differences matter? Note that an administered fund was used for compensation after the BP Deepwater Horizon Spill. See Myriam Gilles, *Public-Private Approaches to Mass Tort Victim Compensation: Some Thoughts on the Gulf Coast Claims Facility*, 61 Depaul L. Rev. 419 (2012) (with the same person, Ken Feinberg, who administered the 9/11 fund). It's not hard to imagine that, as in the Fukushima nuclear meltdown following a Japanese tsunami, a natural disaster could combine with design flaws to cause widespread harm. Is there some reason why an administered fund is more appropriate for the harms mediated by technology failure than the harms caused directly by a natural disaster?

2. Could the federal government be held liable for defectively designing or constructing the New Orleans flood control system? Could state or local governments be held liable for similar problems with nonfederal levees or for failing to inspect and maintain federal levees? Consider your answers in light of the next three cases.

PATERNO V. STATE OF CALIFORNIA

113 Cal. App. 4th 998; 6 Cal. Rptr. 3d 854; 2003 (2003)

MORRISON, J. The environmental aftermath of the Gold Rush continues to plague California. Hydraulic mining debris caused flooding which led to the building of levees at the confluence of the Yuba and Feather Rivers. Almost a century ago the Linda levee was built with uncompacted mining debris, and the use of that debris caused the levee to collapse on February 20, 1986.

About 3,000 plaintiffs sued the State of California (State), Reclamation District 784 (District) and others not now parties, seeking damages. In Paterno v. State of California (1999), 74 Cal. App. 4th 68 [87 Cal. Rptr. 2d 754] (*Paterno I*), we affirmed a defense jury verdict finding no dangerous condition of public property and reversed an inverse condemnation liability finding against defendants, and remanded for another trial on inverse liability. A new coordination judge (Hon. John J. Golden), conducted a lengthy court trial and issued a defense judgment against sample plaintiffs (collectively, Paterno) who filed this appeal.

Paterno embraces Judge Golden's factual findings, which in his view, create inverse liability on the part of the State as a matter of law. We agree. When a public entity operates a flood control system built by someone else, it accepts liability as if it had planned and built the system itself. A public entity cannot be held liable for failing to upgrade a flood control system to provide additional protection. But the trial court found the levee was built with porous, uncompacted mining debris, in a location which encouraged seepage, leading directly to the failure of the levee, and that long before the failure, feasible cures could have fixed the problems. Use of such technology would not have been an upgrade, but would have ensured the planned flood control capacity was achieved.

.. . . Inverse liability stems from the California Constitution and is not dependent on tort or private property principles of fault. California Supreme Court precedent dictates that a landowner should not bear a disproportionate share of the harm directly caused by failure of a flood control project due to an unreasonable plan. Whether the plan is unreasonable is not measured by negligence principles, as in a tort case alleging a dangerous condition of public property, but by balancing a number of specific factors referred to as the *Locklin* factors. (Locklin v. City of Lafayette (1994) 7 Cal. 4th 327 [27 Cal. Rptr. 2d 613, 867 P.2d 724] (*Locklin*).) Based on the facts found by the trial court and application of the *Locklin* factors, we conclude Paterno's damages were directly caused by an unreasonable State plan which resulted in the failure of the Linda levee and the State is liable to pay for Paterno's damages. In large part our conclusion is based on the fact that the levee system benefited all of California and saved billions of dollars, and to require Paterno to bear the cost of the partial failure of that system—a failure caused by construction and operation of an unstable levee—would violate *Locklin*. A basic part of the State's flood plan was to accept existing levees as much as possible, to reduce the cost of an extensive, coordinated, flood control system. The People benefited from that cost-saving feature. However, the record shows the State never tested the Linda levee, or reviewed the records of its construction, to see if it was as strong as the global plans assumed it was, and the State even ignored specific warnings about the levee's weaknesses. In such circumstance, the costs of the levee failure must be deemed part of the deferred costs of the project. We do not separately address an alternate theory that the State is liable because of an inadequate levee inspection plan, although we discuss the lack of any plan to examine the heart of the levee.

Although in some ways the District is a coparticipant with the State in operating the levee, we conclude it is entitled to judgment. The District was responsible for and only for ordinary maintenance and could not alter the structure of the levee, even if it had the financial means to do so.

We will affirm the judgment in favor of the District, reverse the judgment in favor of the State with directions to enter judgment in favor of Paterno, and remand for further proceedings. In making this order, we realize this case is as hoary as Jarndyce v. Jarndyce. We expedited this appeal, and counsel assisted this court by providing much of the record and the briefs in computerized format. We will direct that this case be given priority in the trial court and that all available means to expedite the remaining triable issues be implemented....

In 1904 Yuba County adopted a resolution authorizing construction of a levee known as the Morrison Grade, which became the Linda levee. It was built by men and horses using scrapers to borrow nearby material, mostly mining debris. The trial court found: "In the process, little or no compaction of the material was attempted or achieved. As built, Morrison Grade was highly susceptible to seepage failure because of its siting on top of fifteen feet of porous hydraulic mining debris, the porosity of the material of which it was constructed, and the absence of any compaction of that material during construction." The Linda levee was part of the District, formed in 1908, and incorporated into the SRFCP.

Pursuant to the Grant Report the Corps improved the levee in 1934 and 1940 but the trial court found "the existing levee was incorporated into the finished work" without change. The floods of 1955 sorely tested the SRFCP and exposed many deficiencies, but no problems were revealed in the Linda levee, in particular the south levee on the Yuba between the Southern Pacific Railroad and the E Street Bridge (before the Feather confluence). Although the flood stage *exceeded* design capacity and water came within a foot of the top, it held. In the 1964 flood year the Linda levee was also subjected to higher waters than in 1986, yet held.

In February 1986, a tropical weather system brought much warm rain, which in turn caused snow melt triggering massive flooding in California. For three days the Linda levee held water reaching to 76 feet (U.S. Engineering Datum), but it failed when the water had receded to about 74.3 feet; it is designed to hold up to 80 feet. The State concedes the levee failed at about *half* its designed capacity. The trial court found "the resulting 150 foot gap in the embankment allowed roughly 20,000 acre-feet of water...to inundate some 7,000 acres of land situated in the communities of Linda and Olivehurst, lying across the river south of Marysville in a territory which had been protected by the [levee] from flooding for many years. The flooding resulted in damage...estimated to be in the range of one hundred million dollars." "By 1986, the value of property protected by the levee...was about $409,400,000. There was evidently no general perception that the area was not a safe place for urban development."

...

On appeal the State (but not the District) asserts the levee broke due to unforeseeable causes (e.g., "hydro-consolidation") and therefore the State cannot be liable to Paterno. We tend to agree with Paterno that the State has waived this argument. At trial the State objected to the trial court's proposal that it consider the Albers factors, which included foreseeability. Elsewhere at trial the State asserted it "has never contended that foreseeability was an issue in this case, ever." The State appears to be improperly changing its theory on appeal by claiming lack of foreseeability as a defense. But the point is important and raises no new factual issues, so we will address it.

The State misapprehends the role of foreseeability. As Paterno points out, foreseeability plays no role in the causation analysis and is not determinative in the balancing step, only informative. This is not a case involving a dangerous condition of public property, and we are not applying tort or water law standards of liability. We are implementing the constitutional command that the State must compensate landowners when it damages their property. As Paterno points out, "Even if the State failed to appreciate the risk of failure, this is not a defense to proximate cause. In other words, the levee's planned design and construction throughout its life 'endangered the levee in a way not adequately valued by the planners.'" We agree with Paterno's interpretation and the point has been made elsewhere.

The "reasonableness" balanced here is not a negligence standard of care, which might turn on foreseeability, but is "determined by balancing the public benefit and private damage in each case." The causation element is restated with greater precision in terms of 'substantial causation.' "

Thus, while foreseeability may weigh in favor of the landowner, lack of foreseeability does not defeat the claim.

In this case the evidence overwhelmingly shows the failure of the levee was foreseeable. The State says "There were no events that reasonably put the State on notice before Linda levee failed that its capability to safely carry flood flows was or was becoming compromised." Paterno does not argue the State actually foresaw the levee failure. But the State must be charged with knowledge of how the levee was built. It operated the levee for decades and had ample opportunity to examine it. If it chose not to do so for fiscal reasons, that would indicate the loss should be absorbed by the State.

NOTES AND QUESTIONS

1. What about tort actions by FEMA against state and local governments to recover for its expenditures? In United States v. Parish of St. Bernard, 756 F.2d 1116 (5th Cir. 1985), the Fifth Circuit affirmed the district court's grant of summary judgment to various local governments and public entities. FEMA had sued to recover over $100 million from the defendants for noncompliance with the National Flood Insurance Program. The court held that Congress had not expressly authorized a contract theory for a right of action under the NFIP, but the federal government could pursue common-law claims to recover the defendants' NFIP-insured property. The NFIP will be discussed in more detail in the next section.

   Would it be helpful for the federal government to have a cause of action against local governments for negligently maintaining levees or failing to implement measures required by federal law? Would this provide an incentive for improved performance at the local level? Or would it just saddle already battered municipalities with a heavy litigation burden?

2. The next case considers the potential liability of the federal government itself for flood damages. Note that while the California constitution requires compensation whenever the government "damages" property, the federal Constitution does not impose such a requirement. Instead, it merely provides liability when property is deliberately "taken" by the government. Thus, any recovery for the failure of federal flood control projects must be based on tort rather than on inverse compensation.

IN RE KATRINA CANAL BREACHES LITIGATION
U.S. Court of Appeals for the Fifth Circuit
696 F.3d 436 (2012).

JERRY E. SMITH, Circuit Judge:

[An earlier opinion by the same Fifth Circuit panel had ruled in favor of one set of plaintiffs that the government was liable for damage caused by the MRGO canal (described later in the opinion). The government petitioned for rehearing en banc.]

Treating the petition for rehearing en banc as a petition for panel rehearing, the petition for panel rehearing is GRANTED. We withdraw our opinion, In re Katrina Canal Breaches Litig., 673 F.3d 381 (5th Cir.2012), and substitute the following:

Decades ago, the Army Corps of Engineers (the "Corps") dredged the Mississippi River Gulf Outlet ("MRGO"), a shipping channel between New Orleans and the Gulf of Mexico, and levees alongside the channel and around the city. When Hurricane Katrina struck in 2005, MRGO's size and configuration greatly aggravated the storm's effects on the city and its environs.

Claimants alleging damage from Katrina filed hundreds of lawsuits, many of which were consolidated before the district judge a quo. That court worked with plaintiffs' litigation committees to identify several categories of plaintiffs and individual "bellwether" plaintiffs. This opinion concerns three groups of bellwether plaintiffs, all suing the United States for flood damages. One group of seven plaintiffs went to trial; three prevailed on all claims, and four did not. Another group was dismissed before trial when the government was found immune. The third has survived motions to dismiss and is proceeding to trial.

All losing parties have appealed; the government has also petitioned for a writ of mandamus to stay the third group's trial pending issuance of this opinion. We REVERSE each judgment for the plaintiffs, AFFIRM each judgment for the government, and DENY the petition as moot.

I. Background.

In 1943, Congress requested a report from the Chief of Engineers, Secretary of the Army, investigating ways to make the Port of New Orleans more accessible for maritime and military use. That request led to the authorization of MRGO in 1956. The channel was built to its full dimensions by 1968 and afforded a shorter shipping route between the Gulf of Mexico and New Orleans. As the district court noted, the channel, as originally designed, "was to be 36 feet deep and 500 feet wide, increasing at the Gulf of Mexico to 38 feet deep and 600 feet wide." MRGO was cut through virgin coastal wetlands at a depth that exposed strata of so-called "fat clay," a form of soil soft enough that it will move if made to bear a load. The channel's original designers considered and rejected armoring its banks with foreshore protection, leaving them vulnerable to erosion.

During the design and construction of MRGO, the Corps also implemented the Lake Pontchartrain and Vicinity Hurricane Protection Plan ("LPV"). Pursuant to that plan, the Corps constructed, inter alia, the New Orleans East Unit, levees protecting New Orleans East; the Chalmette Area Unit, levees protecting the Ninth Ward and St. Bernard Parish; and higher floodwalls in the outfall canals at 17th Street, Orleans Avenue, and London Avenue. Separately from MRGO, between 1967 and 1985 the Corps also "lifted" and enlarged portions of the levee paralleling Reach 2 of the channel.

Reach 2 of MRGO runs southeasterly from a point near Michoud in eastern New Orleans along the south shore of Lake Borgne and through the marshes to and across Chandeleur Sound to the Gulf of Mexico. Its south shore parallels the Reach 2 levee (later breached during Katrina, resulting in massive flooding). Foreshore protection was authorized for that shore in 1967 and costs charged to the MRGO project in 1968. From 1968 until 1980, it is not evident why the protection was not implemented. In March 1980, the Corps scrapped its original design for further study, which it continued for the next two years. In 1982, it began testing foreshore protection along the south shore; the study was completed in early 1983. A contract was awarded in 1985, and the foreshore protection was finished in 1986.

For the north shore of Reach 2—that shore which abuts Lake Borgne and its wetlands—the district court found that, by the early 1970s, erosion of the channel had threatened the wetlands, in particular the land bridge that prevented Lake Borgne from flowing directly into the MRGO. In the early 1980s, the Corps was directed to study the feasibility of protection along the north shore. In 1984 and 1988, the Corps reported studies recognizing that erosion from wave wash had widened the channel and that the north shore was close to being breached, thereby exposing development and inhabitants to the southwest to hurricanes from Lake Borgne.

The Corps outlined two erosion-control plans in the 1984 report. The 1988 report concluded that the bank-erosion problem threatened to increase dredging costs sixfold, a problem Corps engineers with the New Orleans Division attempted to address via a supplement to MRGO's Design Memorandum, which would encompass further studies and bypass any requirements for local cost-sharing. That attempt was rejected by the Lower Mississippi Valley Division, which criticized the modeling used and the estimated costs of dredging.

The Corps took the position that design modification was not warranted under the cost-benefit ratio: "[U]ntil the cost of providing foreshore protection proved to be less expensive than the continued need for dredging to maintain the channel's navigability, the Corps did not actively pursue funding for this protection." Id. at 662. The Corps refused to undertake the cost of foreshore protection unless there was local cost participation under the Water Resources Development Act, 33 U.S.C. § 2201 et seq. Furthermore, the district court noted, the Corps did not prioritize protecting the north shore, because there was no levee to protect, and the primary mission of the Corps was to keep the channel navigable.

In 1994, the Corps issued another report in which it still proceeded under the assumption that the cost of foreshore protection was greater than it proved to be; the Corps took the position that costs for bank stabilization should be shared by the local population. Finally, in the mid–1990s, the Corps realized that the actual costs of maintaining the foreshore protection were less than estimated in the 1988 report, so a "re-analysis of the benefits and costs based on this new cost information was the genesis for an April 1996 Evaluation Report." That report recommended funding for protection along five sections of the north shore of Reach 2, and that same year, Congress instructed the Corps to use its available operations and maintenance funds to protect the shore to minimize future dredging costs and preserve the wetlands.

The Corps' delay in armoring MRGO allowed wave wash from ships' wakes to erode the channel considerably, destroying the banks that would have helped to protect the Reach 2 levee (in the Chalmette Area Unit) from front-side wave attack and loss of height. The increased channel width added more fetch2 as well, allowing for a more forceful frontal wave attack on the levee.

MRGO's expansion thus allowed Hurricane Katrina to generate a peak storm surge capable of breaching the Reach 2 levee and flooding the St. Bernard polder. Separately from MRGO, the hurricane also caused the 17th Street, Orleans Avenue, and London Avenue levees to breach. ...

Over four hundred plaintiffs sued in federal court to recover for Katrina-related damages, many naming the federal government as a defendant. Seven of those (the "Robinson plaintiffs") went to trial. The court issued its impressive rulings in thorough opinions. The court found that neither the Flood Control Act of 1928 ("FCA"), 33 U.S.C. § 702, nor the discretionary-function exception ("DFE") to the Federal Tort Claims Act ("FTCA"), 28 U.S.C. § 2680(a), protected the government from suit; after nineteen days of trial, the court found that three plaintiffs had proven the government's full liability and four had not. Another group of plaintiffs (the "Anderson plaintiffs") had their cases dismissed on the government's motion, the court finding both immunities applicable. Still a different group (the "Armstrong plaintiffs") are preparing for trial of their own case against the government.

The government appeals its losses in *Robinson*; the losing *Robinson* plaintiffs cross-appeal. The Anderson plaintiffs have appealed as well. On the theory that a favorable ruling here might moot the pending *Armstrong* trial, the government petitions this court for a writ of mandamus to order the district court to stay trial until we issue an opinion in Robinson. The three cases have been consolidated on appeal. . . .

III. The FCA: Construction and Application.

Under the *Central Green–Graci* test,[69] the government enjoys immunity only from damages caused by floodwaters released on account of flood-control activity or negligence therein. Some Katrina-related flooding was caused not by flood-control activity (or negligence therein) but by MRGO, a navigational channel whose design, construction, and maintenance cannot be characterized as flood-control activity. Therefore, the FCA does not immunize the government against liability for that flooding. . . .

A. The Scope of FCA Immunity.

The FCA "was the Nation's response to the disastrous flood in the Mississippi River Valley in 1927." *United States v. James,* 478 U.S. 597 (1986). The law enacted "a comprehensive ten-year program for the entire [Mississippi River] valley, embodying a general bank protection scheme, channel stabilization and river regulation, all involving vast expenditures of public funds." Staggering in scope, the FCA's flood-control program was "the largest public works project undertaken up to that time in the United States."

The FCA predated the FTCA [Federal Torts Claims Act] and the latter's abrogation of sovereign immunity from tort liability, but Congress nonetheless included Section 702c in the FCA, 33 U.S.C. § 702c, which affirms the government's sovereign immunity in the flood-control context: "No liability of any kind shall attach to or rest upon the United States for any damage from or by floods or flood waters at any place." The Supreme Court has read Section 702c's legislative history as reflecting Congress's "consistent concern for limiting the Federal Government's financial liability to expenditures directly necessary for the construction and operation of the various projects" funded by the FCA. ...

The government proposes a broader interpretation of FCA immunity that would hold it immune where plaintiffs allege damage caused by flood waters that a federal flood-control project had failed to contain. If the flood waters at issue are connected to a flood-control project, the government

---

[69] See Cent. Green Co. v. United States, 531 U.S. 425, 121 S.Ct. 1005, 148 L.Ed.2d 919 (2001); Graci v. United States, 456 F.2d 20 (5th Cir. 1971).

argues, the claim is barred. Language in *James* supports the government's position: The Court read Section 702c's "plain language" and defined the phrase "floods or flood waters" to mean "all waters contained in or carried through a federal flood control project for purposes of or related to flood control, as well as to waters that such projects cannot control." The issue in *James*, however, was whether Section 702c's reference to " 'damage' encompassed not just property damage, but also personal injuries and death."

In *Central Green*, the Court most recently considered the scope of Section 702c immunity and the meaning of the phrase "floods and flood waters." The Ninth Circuit—purporting to follow *James*'s definition of "floods and flood waters"—had focused on whether the source of water that caused the complained-of damage was part of a federal flood-control project; that court ultimately concluded that immunity attached " 'solely because [the Madera Canal] is a branch of the Central Valley Project.' " In so holding, the Ninth Circuit "recognized that the Government would probably not have enjoyed immunity in at least three other Circuits where the courts require a nexus between flood control activities and the harm done to the plaintiff." The Court granted certiorari to resolve that circuit split and framed the issue as "whether ['floods or flood waters'] encompass all the water that flows through a federal facility that was designed and is operated, at least in part, for flood control purposes."

With the meaning of the phrase "floods and flood waters" squarely before it, the Court rejected *James*'s definition as "confusing dicta ... that, if read literally, ... sweeps so broadly as to make little sense"; the *Central Green* Court set about narrowing the scope of Section 702c immunity by shifting the analytical focus away from the water's presence in a federal flood-control project. Under the Ninth Circuit's interpretation of *James*, waters constituted "floods or flood waters," and immunity applied where the government was linked to the waters through the mere presence of a federal flood-control project. In *Central Green*, the Court noted that "the text of the statute does not include the words 'flood control project,' " so the scope of Section 702c is not determined "by the character of the federal project or the purposes it serves, but by the character of the waters that cause the relevant damage and the purposes behind their release." Waters that constitute "floods or flood waters" within the meaning of Section 702c, therefore, are not all waters that pass through a federal flood-control project, but are instead waters of a certain "character." ...

... Thus, after *Central Green*, waters have the immune character of "flood waters" if the government's link to the waters is through flood-control activity. That is to say, the government's acting upon waters for the purpose of flood control is flood-control activity, and flood-control activity is what gives waters an immune "character." We therefore reject the government's interpretation of the scope of Section 702c and conclude, instead, that the

United States enjoys immunity under that section only where damages result from waters released by flood-control activity or negligence therein.

B. The MRGO–St. Bernard Polder Plaintiffs: No Immunity.

Plaintiffs ...allege that the operation and maintenance of MRGO caused the levee along Reach 2 of MRGO to be breached, resulting in the flooding of the St. Bernard polder. The district court found that a combination of erosion caused by MRGO (which could have been prevented through timely foreshore protection) and destruction of wetland vegetation caused by increased salinity levels on account of MRGO's operation led to the breaches in the Reach 2 levee. The court concluded that MRGO was a navigational, not flood-control, project and, unlike the canals in Anderson, wholly extrinsic to the LPV.

The court analogized MRGO to a Navy vessel that, as a result of negligent operation, crashes through a levee, causing a flood: Though the levee would be a flood-control project, the cause of the waters' release—negligent operation of a Navy vessel—would not be the flood-control project or its negligent operation, but rather the negligence in a wholly extrinsic government action. Thus, the government would be afforded no immunity under Section 702c. Similarly, the court ruled, the negligently maintained MRGO acted upon the levees in a way that caused them to be breached during Hurricane Katrina, and, because MRGO was not a flood-control project and was separate from the LPV, no immunity should attach under Section 702c.

But the government maintains that, instead of being distinct from one another, MRGO and the LPV were intertwined. Because the failure to implement timely foreshore protection (as opposed to continued dredging of MRGO) caused the levee breach, the government argues that foreshore protection would have been done solely to benefit the levee system, a flood-control project. Thus, the government argues, the Corps's actions with respect to MRGO were relevant precisely because of their asserted impact on the Reach 2 levees; the government describes the plaintiffs' claim as an assertion that "the government did not take adequate measures to ensure that the Reach 2 levee would be able to restrain flood waters." Consequently, the government says that the claim should be barred by Section 702c. ...

Our interpretation of Section 702c and the caselaw, however, provides a rule slightly different from the district court's. Instead of its strictly categorical approach, which would have immunity attach only where a flood was caused by a project that had the purpose of flood control, we recognize immunity for any flood-control activity engaged in by the government, even in the context of a project that was not primarily or substantially related to flood control. Thus, for example, if the government had attempted foreshore protection inside MRGO, but that protection (whether by design or negligence) caused or exacerbated flood damage, the district court's rule would grant the Corps no immunity, because MRGO was not a flood-control project. Our rule, by contrast, attaches immunity if the foreshore protection had flood control as its purpose—that is, if installing and maintaining foreshore protection was a flood-control activity regardless of the nature of MRGO, the overall project.

To assess the St. Bernard plaintiffs' argument, then, we must determine whether the Corps's decision to dredge MRGO instead of implementing foreshore protection constitutes flood-control activity qualifying for Section 702c immunity. The government would contend that, because foreshore protection would have been done instead of dredging for the sole purpose of protecting the levees, the decision to dredge was flood-control activity protected by Section 702c. Even under our formulation instead of the district court's, the government's defense fails.

The district court found that "the Corps clearly took the position that its primary mission was to keep the shipping channel open to deep draft traffic regardless of the consequences." Accordingly, the Corps chose to dredge MRGO to keep it navigable rather than promptly implement costlier foreshore protection, which would have had the dual purpose of keeping MRGO navigable and protecting the levees. Thus, even in the context of MRGO, the Corps took no action that could be characterized as flood-control activity. The only conceivable flood-control activity is the failure of the government to implement timely foreshore protection, the very omission complained of by the plaintiffs. Such an omission cannot provide the basis for immunity under Section 702c, lest all flood damage caused by government activity be regarded as a result of (a lack of) flood-control activity.

The district court's naval analogy is apt. There, a negligent government activity (operating a ship) wholly unrelated to flood control causes a flood, destroying another government project (a levee). Though one could imagine a plaintiff's saying that the Navy was negligent in not creating an onboard warning system preventing its ship from running into the levee, that hypothetical system does not transform the operation of the Navy vessel into a flood-control activity. To use another analogy, suppose the government builds an Army base on the banks of the Mississippi River. Because of soft soil, the weight of its structures depresses the land and causes flooding to nearby farms during a heavy rain. Although the government might argue that the Army could have built dikes to prevent the flooding, that hypothetical solution does not transform the building of a base into a flood-control activity, or the failure to build dikes into negligence in flood-control activity. In each example, the government is negligent, but in nautical or construction activity, not flood control.

Thus, the government cannot claim Section 702c immunity for MRGO's role in breaching the Reach 2 levee. The dredging of MRGO was not a flood-control activity, nor was MRGO so interconnected with the LPV as to make it part of the LPV. Therefore, the flood waters that destroyed the plaintiffs' property were not released by any flood-control activity or negligence therein. . . . [The Court found that the *Robinson* plaintiffs were not entitled to recover for unrelated reasons, and the *Anderson* plaintiffs could not recover because their claims related to the breach of the city's levees, which *were* flood control projects.]

IV. Construction and Application of the DFE.

The DFE bars suit on any claim that is "based upon the exercise or performance or the failure to exercise or perform a discretionary function or duty on the part of a federal agency or an employee of the Government, whether or not the discretion involved be abused." The purpose of the DFE "is to prevent judicial second-guessing of legislative and administrative decisions grounded in social, economic, and political policy through the medium of an action in tort."

"The Supreme Court has developed a two-part test for determining whether the federal government's conduct qualifies as a discretionary function or duty." First, the conduct must involve "an element of judgment or choice." "If a statute, regulation, or policy leaves it to a federal agency or employee to determine when and how to take action, the agency is not bound to act in a particular manner and the exercise of its authority is discretionary." "On the other hand, [t]he requirement of judgment or choice is not satisfied and the discretionary function exception does not apply if a federal statute, regulation, or policy specifically prescribes a course of action for an employee to follow, because the employee has no rightful option but to adhere to the directive."

Second, the DFE "protects only governmental actions and decisions based on considerations of public policy." Id. (citations omitted). The "proper inquiry" is not whether the decisionmaker "in fact engaged in a policy analysis when reaching his decision but instead whether his decision was susceptible to policy analysis." "[T]he very existence" of a law or regulation allowing a government employee discretion . . . "creates a strong presumption that a discretionary act authorized by the regulation involves consideration of the same policies which led to the promulgation of the regulations."

[The *Robinson* plaintiffs made three arguments against applying the DFE. First, they claimed that the Corps' failure to prepare adequate environmental impact statements eliminated its immunity, but the court concluded that this was merely a procedural error. Second, they argued that the Corps had a non-discretionary duty to armor the banks of MRGO under various appropriations acts describing the dimensions of the canal, but the court did not read that statutory language as imposing a duty to armor the channel. Finally, they argued that "the critical calculation made by the Corps in waiting to armor MRGO was an erroneous scientific judgment, not a decision susceptible to public-policy considerations." This argument is discussed below.]

In their attempt to negate the second DFE prong, the *Robinson* plaintiffs allege that the critical calculations made by the Corps in waiting to armor MRGO were only erroneous scientific judgments, not decisions susceptible to public-policy considerations. If the government's discretion is "grounded in the policy of the regulatory regime," the decision is immune under the DFE, even if it also may entail application of scientific principles. If it is susceptible only to the application of scientific principles, however, it is not immune.

For the government to enjoy DFE immunity, the deciding agent need not have actually considered any policy implications; instead, the decision must only be "susceptible to policy analysis." Under *Gaubert*, "the very existence" of a law or regulation allowing a government employee discretion (satisfying *Berkovitz*'s first prong) "creates a strong presumption that a discretionary act authorized by the regulation involves consideration of the same policies which led to the promulgation of the regulations." The relevance of the grounds for the decision is strictly limited: "Evidence of the actual decision may be helpful in understanding whether the 'nature' of the decision implicated policy judgments, but the applicability of the exemption does not turn on whether the challenged decision involved such judgments."

As discussed above, there is ample record evidence indicating the public-policy character of the Corps's various decisions contributing to the delay in armoring Reach 2. Although the Corps appears to have appreciated the benefit of foreshore protection as early as 1967, the record shows that it also had reason to consider alternatives (such as dredging and levee "lifts") and feasibility before committing to an armoring strategy that, in hindsight, may well have been optimal. The Corps's actual reasons for the delay are varied and sometimes unknown, but there can be little dispute that the decisions here were susceptible to policy considerations. Whatever the actual reasons for the delay, the Corps's failure to armor timely Reach 2 is shielded by the DFE.

NOTES AND QUESTIONS

1. The Flood Control Act was passed in a different era, when the federal government was generally immune from liability for negligence. It was also an era when federal involvement in flood control was considered quite extraordinary. Thus, it may not be surprising that the courts are applying the FCA's immunity provision somewhat sparingly. The FTCA provides the basis for tort suits against the government, but as the main case indicates, its "discretionary function" exception has proved troublesome and difficult to apply. Policy considerations are relevant to all but the most routine functions of low-level employees, so it is not easy to locate the point where the policy element becomes significant enough to trigger the exemption. As we saw in the *Paterno* case, California takes a more generous view of government liability for flooding than the federal government. Which approach is preferable?

2. For another illustration of the FCA, consider Mocklin v. Orleans Levee District, 877 F.2d 427 (5th Cir. 1989). The plaintiffs brought suit against several defendants, including the Army Corps of Engineers, for the wrongful death of their son and sought damages under the Federal Torts Claim Act. The child had drowned when he slipped from a sand

bar caused by the dredging into one of the flotation channels used to prevent further flood damage; the Corps had dredged the lake (Lake Pontchartrain) to make flotation channels during the construction phase of levees. The government's defense relied on §702c. The Court concluded that the child died "from or by" flood water within the meaning of the FCA, because the flotation channel where the plaintiffs' son died contained water related to flood control; the flood channels were "inescapably" part of the flood control project.

3. For other examples of the difficulty of suing the federal government for disaster-related activities, *see* Ames Farms v. United States, 1995 U.S. Dist. LEXIS 9827, 94-1448-Civ-Moreno (S.D. Fla. 1995) (dismissing suit for damages to property as a result of debris placement and removal after Hurricane Andrew); B & D Farms Inc. v. United States, 94-1449-Civ-Marcus (S.D. Fla. Dec. 21, 1994) (dismissing suit for damages to property as a result of debris removal after Hurricane Andrew); Dureiko v. Phillips & Jordan, Inc., 1996 U.S. Dist. LEXIS 22365 (S.D. Fla. 1996) (dismissing suit for damages following a claim against government for negligent supervision of contractor which performed cleanup after Hurricane Andrew); Kirchmann v. United States, 8 F.3d 1273 (8th Cir. 1993) (affirming trial court's ruling that federal government was not liable for negligent supervision of a contractor who failed to safely dispose of hazardous waste in farmland).

4. Despite the Court's ruling in In re *Katrina Canal Breaches Litigation,* the dispute over government liability for damages arising from Hurricane Katrina remains unsettled. In a dispute relying on much of the same evidence, the U.S. Court of Federal Claims found that the Army Corps' negligence in maintaining MRGO caused flooding of such consequence that it amounted to a "taking" of homeowners' property under the Fifth Amendment of the U.S. Constitution, thus requiring the payment of "just compensation." *St. Bernard Parish Government v. United States* (Fed. Cl., May 1, 2015, 05-1119) 2015 WL 2058969, at *1. Legal experts expect the government to appeal the ruling.

B. FLOOD INSURANCE

FEMA has succinctly summarized the basics of federal flood insurance program, which combines insurance, land use management, and public disclosure.

FEDERAL EMERGENCY MANAGEMENT AGENCY, NATIONAL FLOOD INSURANCE PROGRAM—
PROGRAM DESCRIPTION

http://www.fema.gov/library/viewRecord.do?id=1480
(August 1, 2002, July 6, 2009)

Section 1315 of the 1968 Act is a key provision that prohibits FEMA from providing flood insurance unless the community adopts and enforces floodplain management regulations that meet or exceed the floodplain management criteria established in accordance with Section 1361(c) of the Act. These floodplain management criteria are contained in 44 Code of Federal Regulations (CFR) Part 60, Criteria for Land Management and Use. The emphasis of the NFIP floodplain management requirements is directed toward reducing threats to lives and the potential for damages to property in flood-prone areas. Over 19,700 communities presently participate in the NFIP. These include nearly all communities with significant flood hazards.

In addition to providing flood insurance and reducing flood damages through floodplain management regulations, the NFIP identifies and maps the Nation's floodplains. Mapping flood hazards creates broad-based awareness of the flood hazards and provides the data needed for floodplain management programs and to actuarially rate new construction for flood insurance.

When the NFIP was created, the U.S. Congress recognized that insurance for "existing buildings" constructed before a community joined the Program would be prohibitively expensive if the premiums were not subsidized by the Federal Government. Congress also recognized that most of these flood-prone buildings were built by individuals who did not have sufficient knowledge of the flood hazard to make informed decisions. Under the NFIP, "existing buildings" are generally referred to as Pre-FIRM (Flood Insurance Rate Map) buildings. These buildings were built before the flood risk was known and identified on the community's FIRM. Currently about 26 percent of the 4.3 million NFIP policies in force are Pre-FIRM subsidized compared to 70 percent of the policies being subsidized in 1978....

The NFIP would not be able to offer insurance at affordable rates without the existence of risk management (floodplain management) to reduce flood losses. In order to assess and manage the flood risk, a national standard was needed. The U.S. Department of Housing and Urban Development, which initially administered the NFIP before FEMA was created, began its administration of the NFIP by calling on a group of experts to advise the agency as to the best standard to be used as the basis for risk assessment, insurance rating, and floodplain management for the Program. After extensive study and coordination with Federal and State agencies, this group recommended the 1-percent-annual-chance flood (also referred to as the 100-year or "Base Flood") be used as the standard for the NFIP.

The 1-percent-annual-chance flood was chosen on the basis that it provides a higher level of protection while not imposing overly stringent requirements or the burden of excessive costs on property owners. The 1-percent-annual-chance flood (or 100-year flood) represents a magnitude and frequency that has a statistical probability of being equaled or exceeded in any given year, or, stated alternatively, the 100-year flood has a 26 percent (or 1 in 4) chance of occurring over the life of a 30-year mortgage....

Section 1304 of the 1968 Act authorizes the Director of FEMA to establish and carry out *"a national flood insurance program which will enable interested persons to purchase insurance against loss resulting from physical damage to or loss of real property or personal property "* resulting from flood. Flood insurance provides the mechanism by which floodplain occupants are compensated for flood damages. Flood insurance also provides a way for some of the financial burden of flood losses to be removed from taxpayers, such as for Federal disaster assistance and casualty loss deductions under Federal income taxes.

The number of policies in force in the United States has increased from about 95,000 before the Flood Disaster Protection Act of 1973, to 2.2 million in 1989, to over 4.3 million currently. Any property owner of insurable property may purchase flood insurance coverage, provided that the community in which the property is located is participating in the NFIP. The amount of flood insurance coverage in force as of March 31, 2002 is over $606 billion.

NOTES AND QUESTIONS

1. Flood insurance presents a tricky set of problems. If it is priced too high, people simply may fail to insure. If it is priced too low, society is in effect subsidizing individuals to build in high-risk areas. Obviously, the solution is to price it "just right"—but finding the right level may not be easy, especially because there is no private market to use as a benchmark.
2. Despite all these failings, the flood control program has had some successes, as the following excerpt discusses.

OLIVER A. HOUCK, RISING WATER: THE NATIONAL FLOOD INSURANCE PROGRAM AND LOUISIANA

60 Tul. L. Rev. 61-164 (1985)

One of the surprises of this research, notwithstanding its negative findings, has been the extent to which the NFIP, in fact, works. It would be hard to find a program which cuts against more fundamental grains: freedom to choose where to live and build, freedom from government restriction (the federal government, at that), and freedom to maximize a profit from the land, buyer beware. Yet, without a strong economic constituency, this program has managed to survive in Congress and to have evolved at least to the flood-map and local-ordinance phase in thousands of communities. The NFIP is a remarkable phenomenon in American politics—an unpopular, grudgingly accepted program making its modest way. The conclusions and criticisms which follow should be taken in that light. This program undertakes a terribly difficult job. One has to remember that doughnut when looking at the hole.

The first impression one carries away from this research is that Congress, for all of its support for the NFIP, has yet to commit fully to making the NFIP's approach to the flood control problem work. The nation can approach flooding in only a few ways: (1) ignore it, (2) keep the water away from the people, (3) pay the people who get wet, or (4) keep the people away from the water. For one hundred years we tried option (1). As a matter of politics and humanity, (1) is no longer an option; given enough disasters—and flood disasters continue on a rising curve—the nation will respond. Options (2) and (3) represent the historic responses, and they are both attractive. Their difficulty is that they are both expensive, and their spectacularly unsuccessful history proves that they can never solve the problem. One is left with option (4). So is Congress, but with a more than wistful eye on the never-ending dams and levees and politically attractive disaster relief grants of (2) and (3)....

Congress appears to have made the reasonable choice of the means available under option (4) to guide development away from floodplains. The NFIP is, to the maximum extent imaginable, a local program. One could scarcely think of a lesser federal presence short of, perhaps, simply mailing the insurance checks. Unfortunately, insurance checks will not avert future losses. Indeed, as predicted early on in the testimony which gave birth to the NFIP, insurance payments can encourage future losses. It is up to FEMA, with congressional support, to make the guided development part work. Congress can do more to provide that support, and FEMA can do considerably more to implement it.

Recommendations for action at the congressional level, while unconstrained by existing legislation, are limited by the art of the possible. Congress is not about to forgo new water project construction, or to withhold future disaster relief, nor should it. It should, however, structure these two programs so that they aid rather than frustrate the NFIP. With regard to water projects, it should require, as a condition for authorization of flood control dams, levees, and other structures, evidence that they be: (1) limited to that protection which could not be afforded by full NFIP compliance, (2) authorized only upon a demonstration that no other means of protection are feasible or prudent, and (3) conditioned, even then, upon binding agreements to discourage new development in surrounding flood-hazard areas. No flood-protection rationale for a structural project should be eligible for inclusion in any cost/benefit ratio absent these showings.

Congress should also examine other federal assistance and disaster relief benefits to flood-prone areas. The 1977 amendments to the NFIP, which permitted federally insured financing of development in nonparticipating communities, should be re-examined and repealed. No compelling argument—other than the profits to be made by individual developers—supports federal facilitation of new floodplain development that will lead to inevitable flood losses. Similarly, the more recent amendments proposed to limit disaster relief to participating communities should be adopted. The motives here are neither punitive nor even fiscal. Federal funds simply should be distributed in a way which maximizes local prevention of local flood losses, and the NFIP presents the means to that end.

Lastly, Congress should mandate a study of the degree to which upstream levees and channelization affect water stages downstream. Information on increased stages is available only from small, isolated watersheds. The analysis which accompanies an individual project goes no further. The cumulative effects of thousands of these projects, in virtually every watershed from Ohio to Montana, are largely unrecognized. Decisionmakers at all levels should be aware of the true costs of local, structural strategies to communities downstream, including, of course, the ultimate downstream community, Louisiana.

Turning to improvements available to FEMA and to local authorities within the existing NFIP, there is no part of the program which could not be better performed. In its most jaundiced light, the Emergency Program lags, the mapping is dubious, and the requirements of even the Regular Program are misunderstood, misapplied, and ignored. The deficiencies noted in this report are not new to FEMA: they confirm findings by the Comptroller General on at least two occasions, as well as an independent survey of the National Science Foundation. What may be new to FEMA is the scale of these deficiencies and, as illustrated in *United States v. Parish of St. Bernard*—and Hurricane Juan—their potential consequences. Rather than repeating these findings in full, two bear mention because of their particular significance to Louisiana: the treatment of coastal high-hazard areas and the adequacy of enforcement.

The effect of the NFIP on coastal development remains, to this observer, quite uncertain. In Louisiana, the program has only recently begun to be applied to coastal areas in a way that reflects actual storm damages. The accuracy of mapping remains contested, and there is virtually no experience by which to measure the success of local ordinances. From a purely analytical perspective, no good reason appears for providing federal assistance of any kind to high-hazard coastal development. There is every chance that, over a life of the structure, it will meet hurricane forces and will come off second best. Coastal high-hazard areas are as dynamic and storm-threatened as the barrier islands, and the same logic which led to legislation barring federal assistance to barrier island development should bar federal assistance in these areas as well. From Louisiana's perspective, coastal prospects look particularly bleak given the phenomenal rate of coastal subsidence, the addition of sea-level rise, and FEMA's reluctance to take either into account. At the least, the structural elevation and storm-proofing requirements for insurance eligibility should reflect the anticipated conditions over the life of the structure. Maps updated at a later time provide no remedy; construction will at that point already be grandfathered into the program. The cure starts only when future conditions are looked squarely in the eye. For much of coastal Louisiana they are a grim sight. However, they are no grimmer than the sight of evacuees.

The last word is reserved for enforcement. It is difficult to speak harshly of the efforts of an agency with so much to oversee and so little means. FEMA's regional staff has been decimated in recent years. Here more than anywhere, the unavoidable question is whether Congress and the administration really want the program to work. If they do, they will need to provide resources for the program on the theory that, over time, the enforcement of realistic ordinances will ultimately save the government money....

The NFIP is not a glamorous program. It is also not an easy program to understand. One tends to approach it, as this researcher did several years ago, with high skepticism. One tends to emerge, or at least this researcher did, with the conviction that, perversely, its implementation is successful in almost inverse proportion to the risk of flooding in a given area. Where the risk is low, compliance is generally good; no one's shoe is pinched. Where the risk is high, however, as in much of South Louisiana, tomorrow's development still overrides next year's inevitable losses. We know this much from the positive side: the program can work. What is still unknown is whether Congress will support the program sufficiently to allow it to work in those very places where making it work is the most difficult, and the most necessary.

NOTES AND QUESTIONS

1. Flood insurance covers property loss, but not loss of life. Should the federal government try to fill that gap?
2. Should the government protect people from the consequences of their own choices? When individuals knowingly build in flood-prone areas, should they be held responsible for the risks they are taking?

A NOTE ON FLOOD INSURANCE REFORM LEGISLATION

A 2008 GAO report criticized the government's rate-setting methods:

> FEMA's method for setting full-risk rates may not ensure that the rates accurately reflect the actual risk of flood damage. FEMA's model for setting these rates incorporates data on flood risks generated by a hydrologic model that is based on largely the same principles as hazard risk models used by private insurers and other federal agencies. More specifically, FEMA generates rates for flood insurance according to estimates of flood risk and expected flood damage. However, a number of factors may affect the accuracy of rates generated by the process. First, the data that FEMA uses to define flood probabilities are outdated or inaccurate. For example, some of the data used to estimate the probability of flooding have not been updated since the 1980s.

Similarly, the claims data used as inputs to the model may be inaccurate because of incomplete claims records and missing data. Further, the maps FEMA uses to set premium rates remain substantially out of date despite recent modernization efforts. In addition, an NFIP policy decision allows certain properties remapped into riskier flood zones to keep their previous lower rates, which, like subsidized rates, do not reflect the actual risk of flooding to the properties and do not generate sufficient premiums to cover expected losses. Moreover, FEMA does not collect data on these properties—known as grandfathered properties—or measure their financial impact on the program and does not know how many of these properties exist, their exact location, or how much they generate in losses. FEMA's rate-setting process also does not fully take into account ongoing and planned development, long-term trends in erosion, or the effects of global climate change, although private sector models are incorporating some of these factors. Finally, FEMA sets flood insurance rates on a nationwide basis, combining and averaging many topographic factors that are relevant to flood risk, so that these factors are not specifically accounted for in setting rates for individual properties. Moreover, some patterns in historical claims and premium data suggest that NFIP's rates may not accurately reflect differences in flood risk. Collectively, these factors increase the risk that full-risk premiums may be insufficient to cover future losses, adding to concerns about NFIP's financial stability.

Government Accountability Office, FEMA's Rate-Setting Process Warrants Attention (GAO-09-12 2008), Oct. 2008, *available at* http://www.gao.gov /assets/290/283035.pdf.

In response to these concerns, Congress passed the Biggert-Waters Flood Insurance Reform Act of 2012 (BW12). BW12 raised premiums substantially (25 percent annually) for certain categories of property: non-primary residences, businesses, and severe repetitive loss properties. Outside of those categories, rates would also increase, but could not exceed 18 percent annually. A grandfather provision in the 1968 program had allowed owners to continue to use obsolete flood maps as the basis for calculating their premiums. BW12 eliminated that practice and instituted a five-year phase-in of the more accurate risk appraisals. BW12 also required that new flood maps use the most accurate topography and elevation data available, a move that will probably require climate change data to be integrated into future maps.

Nearly two years later, Congress passed the Homeowner Flood Insurance Affordability Act of 2014, which repealed and modified some of BW12's most important provisions. Some aspects of BW12 (like the new mapping requirements) were left intact. But overall, lawmakers were back-pedaling at full speed. The 2014 act made these major changes:

1. The original 1968 act had provided subsidized rates for buildings that were in existence when an area became covered by the flood insurance

program. BW12 intended to eliminate those subsidies over time. The 2014 law restored some but not all of those subsidies. (For instance, the 2014 act appears to have retained BW12's premium increases for non-primary residences, businesses, and severe repetitive loss properties.)

2. BW12 required that premiums increase when new flood maps showed higher risk levels than older ones did. The new law allows the continued use of obsolete maps to calculate premiums on existing buildings.

3. The original 1968 act had allowed subsidies to follow the property even after it was sold to a new owner. BW12 ended that practice and required new owners to pay market rates. The 2014 act reversed BW12 on this issue, returning to the original 1968 rule.

4. Increased costs from the 2014 act are to be offset by a flat assessment against all holders of flood insurance ($25 for homeowners, $250 for others), with exceptions for some homeowners who are paying the non-subsidized insurance rate.

In addition, the 2014 law reinstated the grandfather provision for obsolete flood maps that had been repealed by BW12. Another provision of the 2014 act gradually phases in full actuarial rates on property that is newly included in a 100-year-flood zone and does not qualify for subsidized rates. But property that was already in a flood zone will continue to pay premiums based on obsolete maps.

Should the flood insurance program be abandoned, in favor of reliance on private insurance? You may want to consider that question in light of the next section.

C. PRIVATE INSURANCE

We begin with an excerpt that discusses the impact of Hurricane Katrina on the insurance industry, and some possible legislative solutions for the problems of insuring against catastrophic disasters. We will then look more carefully at some insurance issues raised by hurricanes and floods, before turning in the next section to the question of legislation.

HURRICANE KATRINA: INSURANCE LOSSES AND NATIONAL CAPACITIES FOR FINANCING DISASTER RISK

Congressional Research Service (Sept. 15, 2005)

[Private] insurer losses from Hurricane Katrina are estimated to be $40-$60 billion. This would make the tropical storm the costliest natural disaster in U.S. history, exceeding Hurricane Andrew in 1992 and the September 2001 terrorist attacks. These insured loss figures include damages caused by storm's landfall in Florida on August 25, 2005, that led to an estimated $600 million to $2 billion in insured losses, as well as dozens of offshore oil and gas platforms reported either lost, damaged, or missing and believed sunk. Total damages are expected to exceed $200 billion, with the federal government expected to spend over $100 billion for response and recovery efforts associated with Hurricane Katrina in Alabama, Florida, Louisiana, Mississippi, and other affected areas. These amounts will exceed the initial cost for recovery from the September 11 terror attacks....

Insured loss estimates are likely to change as the extent of losses becomes better known. Disaster experts and modeling firms expect the numbers to change as more is known about the levels of water contamination and economic losses from business interruption and displacement of residents in New Orleans, Biloxi, Pascagoula, and Gulfport. These figures will also change when more accurate information about the economic costs of interruption of oil supply and exports of commodities such as grain becomes available. Most of the U.S. energy operations are in the Gulf Coast region.

Most insurance market analysts would agree that insurers will be able to pay all Katrina-related claims without triggering insurer insolvencies or market disruption. Despite the severity of damages, insurers are well-equipped to manage the financial impact of a catastrophe of this scale. The U.S. personal lines insurers have benefited from recent favorable market conditions and have built up policyholder surplus for an unexpected event like Katrina. [T]he industry as a whole earned $38.7 billion in net after-tax income in 2004, and policyholder surplus increased by 13.4%, or $46.5 billion, to a record $393.5 billion for the same year. A.M. Best, an insurance rating and information agency, reports that almost all rated companies will be able to meet their commitments. A few individual companies' ratings may, however, be lowered.

Although the insurance industry will emerge largely intact from Hurricane Katrina and is better capitalized now than ever, the industry simply does not have sufficient capital to fund a mega-catastrophe. This fact is not new. Insurers and financial market experts knew after Hurricane Andrew in 1992 that outside capital was needed to supplement industry capacity. Since then, new capital entered the catastrophe insurance market.

Insurers learned important lessons from Hurricane Andrew that prompted them to make changes to both protect the industry's balance sheets and stabilize the property insurance markets in the aftermath of a small-to-moderate hurricane. For example, after Hurricane Andrew, the Florida state legislature worked with insurers and regulators to create a hurricane catastrophe system designed to mitigate losses to the insurance industry and prevent insurers from withdrawing from the Florida insurance market. The Florida Hurricane Catastrophe Fund was created as a reinsurance-like entity funded by a portion of insurance premiums and managed by the Florida State Board of Administration. Florida also began using percentage deductibles tied to the value of homes instead of a dollar amount such as $500 per claim. Florida created a state-regulated insurer of last resort to provide insurance when no company is willing to underwrite disaster risks. These measures saved the property insurance industry from financial disaster after the four major hurricanes in 2004. Neither Louisiana, Mississippi, nor Alabama, however, ha[s] a similar catastrophe fund to compensate hurricane victims at a level comparable to what is available in Florida.

Most insurance analysts predict that Hurricane Katrina will likely result in higher pricing and restricted coverage in the hardest-hit areas. Insurers who specialize in coverage for offshore oil rigs and platforms, for example, have already announced 50% increases in premium prices. In addition, insurance rating agencies are now comparing their insurers' modeled catastrophe exposures to the potential market share exposure to determine the need for rating action. Insurance market analysts note that insurers with accurate loss exposure projections will be able to manage their losses within their capital base. Those that are shown to not have accurate loss exposure projections could suffer a rating downgrade.

When claims adjusters are finally able to assess the hundreds of thousands of damaged structures, they will likely face major challenges in distinguishing the portion of damage attributable to wind or flood. What was the wind damage before the levees broke and flooding began? This is important because wind damages are covered under standard commercial and residential property insurance policies, but floods are not. The central question of when the wind-driven rain or rising floodwater came in and when the wind came in will determine how flood claims are apportioned among the National Flood Insurance Program (NFIP), private insurers, and individuals.

It is quite likely that policyholders who lack federal flood insurance coverage might take advantage of vague policy language in their homeowners insurance policies to argue that the ultimate cause of damage was not flooding, but breaches of the New Orleans levees. Insurers are likely, however, to argue that they did not price the flood risk in the homeowners policy, and hence did not set aside reserves to pay such claims.

Although the purchase of federal flood insurance is mandatory for certain property owners as a condition of eligibility for loans from federally regulated lending institutions, many residents in flood-prone areas impacted by Katrina did not have flood insurance. According to the Insurance Information Institute, only about 30% of homes in Louisiana are protected by flood coverage, and even fewer homeowners in Mississippi and Alabama purchased the coverage. A problem is that, although mortgage lenders required homeowners in flood zones to buy flood coverage, these institutions reportedly have no system in place to ensure that homeowners keep the coverage in force. In addition, banks that provide mortgage loans on property found to be uninsured for flood damage might incur losses should homeowners who cannot afford reconstruction abandon both the property and the mortgage commitment....

The increasing magnitude of both insured and uninsured losses from natural disasters represents an ongoing challenge for both governments and the private sector. Natural disasters typically result in large government outlays for disaster relief assistance, and they place a financial strain on private disaster insurance markets. The federal government alone, facing fiscal constraints to cover the losses to the private sector, will find it costly and challenging to meet long-term disaster related spending. In addition, insurers have been and will continue to be reluctant to cover properties in high-risk areas because of high long-run costs (which translates into high prices for disaster insurance) and low demand for disaster insurance.

Most insurance market analysts note that there is no state in the Union that is not subject to catastrophe exposure, and the current situation suggests that the projected exposures are far greater than the insurance industry is currently prepared to handle. The insurance industry's financial capacity and surplus to underwrite a $100 billion-plus mega-catastrophic event remains in doubt.

NOTES AND QUESTIONS

1. Hurricane Sandy also put significant stress on the flood insurance system:

> Government payouts under the National Flood Insurance Program (NFIP) are estimated to be between $12 billion and $15 billion in flood insurance claims. In the immediate aftermath of Sandy, this amount quickly exceeded the $4 billion in cash and remaining borrowing authority from the Treasury Department. By January 2013, the NFIP had processed more than 140,000 claims for Sandy-related damages totaling about $1.7 billion. To protect the financial integrity of the NFIP and ensure that the NFIP has the financial resources to cover its existing commitments following the devastation caused by Sandy, the Obama Administration requested that Congress pass legislation to increase the NFIP's borrowing authority. On January 4, 2013, Congress passed, and the President two days later signed into law, H.R. 41 to provide a $9.7 billion increase in the NFIP's borrowing authority, from $20.725 billion to $30.425 billion, to pay flood claims related to Hurricane Sandy.
>
> Rawle King, *The National Flood Insurance Program: Status and Remaining Issues for Congress* (Congressional Research Serv. 2013) (summary section; unpaginated).

2. We will discuss in more detail in the next section the problems confronted by the insurance industry in covering catastrophic losses as well as possible policy responses.

3.   Floods often involve large numbers of highly correlated losses, which are an unappealing subject for insurance companies. The companies may also be reluctant to offer coverage for flood losses in competition with the federal government's insurance program. Consequently, private insurers generally seek to exclude flood damages from insurance coverage even of "all risks" policies.

In theory, individuals should know that their insurance does not cover flooding, but consumer knowledge on this point may be somewhat spotty. Should this affect the insurance company's liability? At a press conference immediately after Katrina, Mississippi State Attorney General Jim Hood stated, "All that the people have left is hope and I'm not going to allow an insurance company to wrongfully take that hope away. Although some insurance companies are trying to do the right thing, I won't allow the others to take advantage of people hurt by Hurricane Katrina." He unsuccessfully attempted to have the courts declare unenforceable contract provisions that exclude from coverage loss or damage caused directly or indirectly by water, whether or not driven by wind. The complaint stated that these provisions should be strictly construed against the insurance companies who drafted the insurance policies and their exclusions. The complaint also stated that the issuance of such insurance policies violates the Mississippi Consumer Protection Act. "I'm hopeful that next week we will be able to stop unscrupulous insurance adjusters from requiring people to sign away their rights to 'flood damage' claims in exchange for a significantly smaller amount which will be used for immediate living expenses. I want to encourage the people to continue to fight and I'll do everything I can to make sure that insurance companies pay what they owe," Hood said. Similar claims were made in private litigation between insurers and their customers, as exemplified by the following case.

LEONARD V. NATIONWIDE MUTUAL INSURANCE CO.
United States Court of Appeals for the Fifth Circuit, 499 F.3d 419 (2007)

EDITH H. JONES, Chief Judge:

This homeowner's policy coverage dispute arose from the destruction wrought by Hurricane Katrina along the Mississippi Gulf Coast....

The Leonards' home lies twelve feet above sea level on the southmost edge of Pascagoula, Mississippi, less than two hundred yards from the Mississippi Sound. Hurricane Katrina battered Pascagoula with torrential rain and sustained winds in excess of one hundred miles per hour. By midday, the storm had driven ashore a formidable tidal wave—also called a storm or tidal surge—that flooded the ground floor of the Leonards' two-story home....

Like most homeowner's policies, the Leonards' policy unambiguously excludes damage caused by water—including flooding—in a broadly worded exemption clause (the "water-damages exclusion"):

> (b) Water or damage caused by water-borne material. Loss resulting from water or water-borne material damage described below is not covered even if other perils contributed, directly or indirectly, to cause the loss. Water and water-borne material damage means:
>
> > 1. flood, surface water, waves, tidal waves, overflow of a body of water, spray from these, whether or not driven by wind....

When the Leonards annually renewed their policy, they received the following notice from Nationwide informing them that flood losses would not be covered, but that additional flood coverage was available upon request:

> *IMPORTANT INFORMATION*
>
> A Message From Your Nationwide Agent:
>
> Your policy does not cover flood loss. You can get protection through the National Flood Insurance Program. If you wish to find out more about this protection, please contact your Nationwide Agent.

The Leonards never purchased additional flood coverage under the federally subsidized National Flood Insurance Program ("NFIP").

3.   Concurrent Action by Wind and Water

The prefatory language introducing the water-damages exclusion addresses situations in which damage arises from the synergistic action of a covered peril, e.g., wind, and an excluded peril, e.g., water:

> 1.   We do not cover loss to any property resulting directly or indirectly from any of the following. *Such a loss is excluded even if another peril or event contributed concurrently or in any sequence to cause the loss....*

Commonly referred to as an "anticoncurrent-causation clause," or "ACC clause," this prefatory language denies coverage whenever an excluded peril and a covered peril combine to damage a dwelling or personal property. The inundation of the Leonards' home was caused by a concurrently caused peril, i.e., a tidal wave, or storm surge—essentially a massive wall of water—pushed ashore by Hurricane Katrina's winds. Accordingly, argues Nationwide, losses attributable to storm surge-induced flooding are excluded under the ACC clause.

The validity of the ACC clause is the key interpretive battleground of this appeal....

Paul Leonard testified that when he first bought his policy in 1989, he asked Nationwide's agent Jay Fletcher whether the Nationwide policy covered hurricane-related losses. According to Leonard, Fletcher responded that all hurricane damage was covered. Fletcher stated in his deposition testimony that he did not recall this conversation; the district court deemed it irrelevant to the case.

Leonard claims he spoke again with Fletcher ten years later to discuss a proposed increase in the wind/hail deductible that Nationwide was instituting on its homeowner's policies. Leonard called Fletcher after seeing advertisements for additional NFIP coverage in the wake of Hurricane Georges, which struck the Mississippi coast in 1998. Fletcher allegedly assured Leonard that he did not need additional flood coverage because Leonard did not live in an area classified Zone A for flood risk by the Federal Emergency Management Agency ("FEMA"). Fletcher purportedly added that his own property was not insured under the NFIP. Leonard does not allege that Fletcher told him the Nationwide policy covered flooding caused by a hurricane; Leonard merely inferred from Fletcher's comments that such coverage existed....

Inspection of the Leonards' residence following the storm revealed modest wind damage. The roof suffered broken shingles and loss of ceramic granules, but its water-tight integrity was not compromised. The non-load-bearing walls of the garage and the garage door were severely damaged; doors in the house and garage had been blown open. Finally, a "golf-ball sized" hole in a ground-floor window was likely caused by a wind-driven projectile. Water damage, in contrast, was extensive. The Leonards' neighborhood had suffered a seventeen-foot storm surge, causing the entire ground floor of their residence to become inundated under five feet of water blown ashore from the Mississippi Sound. Walls, floors, fixtures, and personal property sustained extensive damage. The second floor of the house remained unscathed.

Nationwide's adjuster evaluated the storm damage and, after applying the Leonards' five hundred dollar deductible, tendered a check for $1,661.17—the amount determined attributable solely to wind. Nationwide informed the Leonards that damages caused by water and the storm surge's concurrent wind-water action were barred, respectively, by the water-damages exclusion and the ACC clause.

At trial, the Leonards offered expert testimony that the total damages actually exceeded $130,000, but this figure did not apportion damages caused by different perils. The Leonards' wind-specific assessment claimed $47,365.41, including costs for roof replacement and structural repairs to the garage.

The district court found the ACC clause ambiguous, leading it to conclude: "Thus, [the ACC] language does not exclude coverage for different damage, the damage caused by wind, a covered peril, even if the wind damage occurred concurrently or in sequence with the excluded water damage. The wind damage is covered; the water damage is not." The court applied "established Mississippi law" dating from the Hurricane Camille cases and explicitly held that a Mississippi policyholder could parse out and recover for loss due to covered wind damage that combined with excluded water damage in a concurrently caused peril. Consequently, as a matter of Mississippi law, Nationwide's ACC clause is invalid. That such rulings vitally affect Nationwide's rights in subsequent litigation involving its homeowner's policy would seem to be emphasized by the Leonards' determination to render the rulings unassailable on appeal.

Although the district court granted the Leonards only a meager monetary recovery for losses proven to have been caused by wind, it also summarily invalidated the ACC clause, stating that "[t]he provisions of the Nationwide policy that purport to exclude coverage entirely for damages caused by a combination of the effects of water (an excluded loss) and damage caused by the effects of wind (a covered loss) are ambiguous." Contrary to the district court's ruling, Nationwide's ACC clause is not ambiguous, nor does Mississippi law preempt the causation regime the clause applies to hurricane claims.

Eschewing a text-based analysis, the district court opines that the clause does not affect the coverage for other losses (covered losses), i.e., damage caused by wind, that occur at or near the same time. Thus, [the ACC clause] does not exclude coverage for different damage, the damage caused by wind, a covered peril, *even if the wind damage occurred concurrently or in sequence with the excluded water damage.* The wind damage is covered; the water damage is not. This conclusion is unjustifiable when read against the clause's plain language....

The clause unambiguously excludes coverage for water damage "even if another peril"—e.g., wind—"contributed concurrently or in any sequence to cause the loss." The plain language of the policy leaves the district court no interpretive leeway to conclude that recovery can be obtained for wind damage that "occurred concurrently or in sequence with the excluded water damage." Moreover, in the past we have not deemed similar policy language ambiguous. Nationwide's assertion that the district court "simply read the clause out of the contract," is not at all wide of the mark. The clause is not ambiguous.

The fatal flaw in the district court's rationale is its failure to recognize the three discrete categories of damage at issue in this litigation: (1) damage caused exclusively by wind; (2) damage caused exclusively by water; and (3) damage caused by wind "concurrently or in any sequence" with water. The classic example of such a concurrent wind-water peril is the storm-surge flooding that follows on the heels of a hurricane's landfall. The only species of damage covered under the policy is damage caused *exclusively* by wind. But if wind and water synergistically caused the *same* damage, such damage is excluded. Thus, the Leonards' money judgment was based on their roof damages solely caused by wind. Contrary to the court's damage matrix, however, had they also proved that a portion of their property damage was caused by the concurrent or sequential action of water—or any number of other enumerated water-borne perils—the policy clearly disallows recovery.

The district court seemed to fear that enforcement of the policy's concurrent causation exclusion would render *any* recovery for hurricane damage illusory. Observing that the policy denies coverage whenever a "windstorm[] combined with an excluded cause of loss, e.g., flooding," the court hypothesized that "an insured whose dwelling lost its roof in high winds and at the same time suffered an incursion of even an inch of water could recover nothing...." That fear is unfounded, with regard to the policy's wind-coverage clause....If, for example, a policyholder's roof is blown off in a storm, and rain enters through the opening, the damage is covered. Only if storm-surge flooding—an excluded peril—then inundates the *same* area that the rain damaged is the ensuing loss excluded because the loss was caused concurrently or in sequence by the action of a covered and an excluded peril. The district court's unsupported conclusions that the ACC clause is ambiguous and that the policyholder can parse out the portion of the concurrently caused damage that is attributable to wind contradict the policy language.

Like the district court, the Leonards provide no support for their argument that the ACC clause is ambiguous. Instead, they adopt the district court's reliance on venerable Mississippi authorities regarding proximate causation of damage caused by hurricanes. Because the ACC clause is unambiguous, the Leonards can prevail only if they can demonstrate that the clause is prohibited by Mississippi caselaw, statutory law, or public policy. None of these sources of state law restricts Nationwide's use of the ACC clause to preclude recovery for concurrently caused hurricane losses.

Contrary to the Leonards' contention, Mississippi courts have not conclusively resolved whether an insurance policy may preclude recovery for damages caused by the concurrent action of the wind and water of a hurricane. Accordingly, this court, applying state substantive law, must make an educated "*Erie* guess" as to how the Mississippi Supreme Court would resolve the issue. The default causation rule in Mississippi regarding damages caused concurrently by a covered and an excluded peril under an insurance policy is that the insured may recover if the covered peril was the "dominant and efficient cause" of the loss. This rule is typically referred to as the doctrine of efficient proximate cause. To recover under the doctrine in the context of a homeowner's policy that covers wind damage but excludes damage by water, "it is sufficient to show that wind [i.e., the covered peril] was the proximate or efficient cause of the loss...notwithstanding other factors [i.e., excluded perils like water] contributed...."

The Mississippi Supreme Court frequently employed this default rule in the welter of insurance coverage cases that surfaced in the aftermath of Hurricane Camille. It is also the rule the district court and the Leonards contend must apply here. However, although the Mississippi Supreme Court often premised recovery for policyholders on the application of the efficient proximate cause rule, in actuality, in many of the Camille cases the court did little more than uphold jury findings that the damages suffered by policyholders were caused *exclusively by wind*, not by concurrent wind-water action. Such cases thus do not support the Leonards' argument that the Mississippi default rule in hurricane cases is always to allow recovery for covered damages even if they are concurrent with excluded damages and irrespective of contrary policy language. In fact, the Mississippi Supreme Court intimated in one case that even if a covered peril is the efficient proximate cause of damage, a concurrently contributing cause that is excluded under a homeowner's policy may preclude recovery.

Whatever the effect of the efficient proximate cause doctrine in the Hurricane Camille cases, those decisions do not control the current case because none of the policies they involve contain ACC clauses similar to the one at issue here, nor do those cases purport to enshrine efficient proximate causation as an immutable rule of Mississippi insurance policy interpretation. The Fifth Circuit long ago explicitly recognized that efficient proximate causation does not necessarily control Mississippi contracts for hurricane damage.

Two federal appellate courts and many state and district courts have endorsed using ACC clauses to circumvent default causation rules like efficient proximate cause. A majority of states that have considered the matter enforce ACC exclusion clauses. Only Washington and West Virginia do not allow abrogation of the default rule via an ACC clause. California and North Dakota require efficient proximate causation by statute....

For all these reasons, we conclude that use of an ACC clause to supplant the default causation regime is not forbidden by Mississippi caselaw (including the Camille cases which antedate such clauses), statutory law, or public policy. Because the ACC clause is unambiguous and not otherwise voidable under state law, it must stand....

Finally, the Leonards claim that misrepresentations Fletcher made during two conversations in 1989 and 1999 effected an oral modification of their policy, enabling recovery for all Katrina-related losses. The district court allowed litigation of the question whether Fletcher negligently misrepresented the policy's terms, but found that none of Fletcher's statements "could be reasonably understood to alter the terms of the Nationwide policy," and that any inferences that Paul Leonard drew from the conversations were inconsistent with the policy exclusion for water damage.

The Leonards fail to present an actionable claim of negligent misrepresentation because they cannot prove two of the elements required to show apparent authority. First, Nationwide's conduct in no way indicated that Fletcher was authorized to orally modify policies he sold. The Form HO-23-A has an integration clause specifically disclaiming the agent's ability to do so....Paul Leonard admits to having read the policy. Even had he not, knowledge of the integration clause is imputed to him under state law. Only "[t]hose dealing with agents without notice of restrictions upon the agent's authority have a right to presume that their authority is there."

Second, the Leonards' reliance on Fletcher's statements was objectively unreasonable in light of the policy language clearly excluding water damage, including damage caused by a flood.

NOTES AND QUESTIONS

1. From the point of view of the property owner, whether property is destroyed by wind or water is largely irrelevant. But insurers have not wanted to participate in the market for flood insurance, and exclusions for damages caused by water are their effort to avoid coverage for flood risks. Thus, there is a mismatch between the insured's expectation that insurance will cover major risks and the insurer's desire to manage risk exposure.

2. Following Hurricane Sandy, similar issues have arisen in the Northeast and are expected to lead to substantial litigation. New York and New Jersey seem to take somewhat different approaches to cases involving concurrent causes. See Abrams Gorelick, *White Paper: Superstorm Sandy: Emerging Coverage Issues,* http://www.agfjlaw.com/gendocs/Sandy%20Whitepaper%2012-4-12.pdf. The issue of "wind versus water" can arise in many different settings. Consider the following factual scenarios:

   a. The roof is blown off the house by wind. Some water also entered the house from flooding. It is unclear how much of the flooding was due to wind and how much to rain. Who has the burden of proof, the insured or the insurer?

   b. A house is flooded first, but then the roof blows off, so the house would have suffered the same water damage even without the flood. Should the fact that the flooding occurred first relieve the insurer from liability, considering that the same damage would have resulted from wind anyway?

   c. Rain first floods a lake, but then wind drives the flood waters against levees, bursting the levees and resulting in water damage to a house. Is the proximate cause wind or water?

4. In addition to the "wind versus water" issues, another frequent insurance issue involves the "ordinance or law" exclusion:

   > A typical Ordinance or Law exclusion clause reads: "We do not cover loss...resulting in any manner from...enforcement of any ordinance or law regulating the construction, reconstruction, maintenance, repair or demolition of buildings or other structures." The insurance industry has articulated several reasons for the exclusion.

Insurance companies most frequently state that the purpose of the exclusion is to prevent an insured from obtaining a "windfall" through the enforcement of a local or state ordinance or law. For example, in Bradford v. Home Insurance Co.,[70] the insured sustained damage to his leaching field. The cost of replacing the field with material similar to the original would have been $1,000. However, a local ordinance required that the insured also install a septic tank at a cost of $2,300. The insurer denied coverage for the cost of the tank based on an Ordinance or Law exclusion in the insured's policy and the court upheld the insurer's decision. Another court articulated the purpose of the exclusion as follows:

> [T]he insurer is required...to indemnify the insured for the cost of repairing or replacing a building which was lost or destroyed by fire with materials of like kind and quality, but it is not required to assume repair or replacement costs which would provide the insured with a more structurally valuable building than the one that was damaged or destroyed....The owners of new buildings which conform with state or local building laws are merely reimbursed for costs which they actually incurred. On the other hand, the owner of buildings which do not conform with such laws are not permitted to recover costs which they never assumed in the first place.[71]

Such windfalls, however, are inherent in "replacement cost" policies, which obligate insurers to reimburse the insured for the actual cost of repairs and construction without deducting any amount for depreciation. For example, if an insured needed to replace a damaged roof, the insurer would be liable for the cost of the entire new roof, even if the damaged roof had been ten years old. This begs the question: Why is paying to replace a ten-year-old roof with a new roof less objectionable than paying to replace a home built under an old building code with a home that complies with a current building code?

Insurers also justify the exclusion by stating that they must limit their exposure to the risk of having to pay for costs that are uncertain. Moreover, insurers claim that it is expensive to keep track of, and properly estimate, the impact of building codes. Ironically, uncertainty created the need for insurance in the first place and inspires many homeowners to purchase insurance. The basic purpose of insurance is to pool and distribute the risk of uncertain losses over a large number

---

[70]384 A.2d 52 (Me. 1978).

[71]Breshears v. Indiana Lumbermens Mut. Ins. Co., 63 Cal. Rptr. 879, 883 (Cal. Ct. App. 1967).

of people so that an individual will not bear the entire impact of a loss. Who better to evaluate and spread risk than insurance companies?

Because insurance companies have the knowledge and ability to pool and spread risk, and because ordinances and laws—e.g., building codes—are enacted for the health, safety, and welfare of the public, the following questions must be asked: Why is coverage of building code upgrades not automatically included in insurance policies? Why have insurance companies fought so ardently to support the exclusions despite the fact that courts have been ambivalent toward the exclusions? The fact that some individuals may benefit from an increase in the value of their property because of an upgrade required by an ordinance or law is unimportant when weighed against the potentially devastating effect the exclusions can have when they are enforced.[72]

2. Apart from the substance of insurance claims, their sheer number may overwhelm the litigation system. Consider the following alternative:

In response to Hurricanes Katrina and Rita and the devastation left in their wake, the AAA has developed AAA Disaster Recovery Claims Resolution Services, a permanent program to address insurance claim disputes quickly and fairly. At present, more than 400 neutrals have agreed to serve at reduced rates on the panel for this special dispute management program. The insurance providers have agreed to pay the AAA's case administration fees and the neutral's compensation and expenses. Information about this program can be found at www.adr.org/sp.asp?id=26808/; www.adr.org/si.asp?id=2025; and adr.org/si.asp?id=2024/(Guide to AAA Disaster Recovery Claims).

The AAA previously helped victims of Hurricanes Andrew and Iniki, the Northridge earthquake, and the Grand Forks flood resolve insurance disputes. However, unlike those temporary programs, the new program is permanent. It will have its own formal set of procedures, available at www.adr.org/sp.asp?id=26802/. Under these procedures, the AAA will assist individuals with their property claims regardless of the amount involved. It will also assist businesses with claims under $75,000. This program will use telephone and in-person mediations to resolve disputes.[73]

---

[72]Hugh L. Wood, Jr., Comment *The Insurance Fallout Following Hurricane Andrew: Whether Insurance Companies Are Legally Obligated to Pay for Building Code Upgrades despite the "Ordinance or Law" Exclusion Contained in Most Homeowners Policies*, 48 U. Miami L. Rev. 949 (1994).

[73]*AAA OFFERS New Disaster Recovery Services*, 60-JAN Disp. Res. J. 4 (2005).

D. DESIGNING INSURANCE FOR CATASTROPHIC RISKS

STEPHEN D. SUGARMAN, ROLES OF GOVERNMENT IN COMPENSATING DISASTER VICTIMS

Issues in Legal Scholarship, http://www.bepress.com/ils/iss10/art1 (2007)

The financial consequences of many of the losses that result from catastrophic events may be ameliorated by the advance purchase of private insurance that covers the peril in question. Life insurance, health insurance, disability insurance, and accidental death and dismemberment insurance are all examples of privately sold policies that provide compensation for individuals suffering casualty losses to the person. Property insurance (covering fire and all sorts of other perils) is a private mechanism that provides compensation to those who suffer covered losses to physical property (both real property and personal property); and homeowner's insurance, for example, will often pay, not only for the rebuilding or repair of one's home, but also for temporary living costs. Business interruption insurance can serve as at least a partial substitute for temporarily lost income or pay for temporarily higher expenses. And while these sorts of insurance policies are primarily used to cover the risk of individual loss in non-disaster settings, they can indeed come into play in the event of a disaster. Yet, one problem with private insurance solutions is that there is sometimes no private insurance available for certain types of catastrophic risks to which people are subject. Indeed, it is precisely the dramatically large event that leads to widespread disastrous consequences that is frequently specifically excluded from certain standard private insurance policies. For example, the destruction of one's home or other buildings is generally not covered by ordinary property insurance (or homeowners') policies if the harm is caused by things like war, nuclear radiation, floods, and, at least in some places, earthquakes.

Sometimes those catastrophic risks may be specially insured against through privately purchased policies that are narrowly tailored to specific potentially catastrophic events (although sometimes the availability of these private policies requires governmental intervention, as discussed later). But often, no private insurance market exists for these risks. While this insurance unavailability might be viewed as a market failure, there are usually understandable reasons why insurers won't underwrite certain risks. First of all, they find themselves unable to sensibly price the insurance, both because the precipitating event too infrequently occurs and when it does the amount of harm it will cause is not really predictable. Moreover, it is especially worrying to insurers that the catastrophe might occur markedly earlier than expected, so that not enough premiums would yet have been accumulated, thereby putting an insurer at risk of insolvency. Even if the timing and scale of the risk were reasonably predictable, however, insuring against infrequent disasters would require a long accumulation and investment of premium income in a way that is not altogether attractive to insurers (and re-insurers who might be enticed to spread the risk beyond the insurer who initially sold coverage to its customers). Among other things, U.S. tax law rules discourage insurance lines that involve premium collection without payouts, even if funds are set aside for eventual losses. Besides, when the gigantic-loss event finally occurs, insurers could be swamped by the claims-handling process, having to rely on out-of-area and/or inexperienced staff who are likely to be more costly and less efficient. As a result, catastrophic risk coverage might simply be an unattractive product for mainstream insurers to offer.

Two common reasons why underwriters typically don't cover certain risks are also relevant in the disaster setting. One is moral hazard, by which I mean that the insured may do something (or fail to do something) that precipitates the insurable event or the level of its consequences. The other is adverse selection, by which I mean the insurer is not easily able to screen out, or charge more to, those customers with higher than average risks. For example, suppose that a lot of people don't take care of their property in a way to minimize the risk of landslide damage and that insurers cannot monitor this failure to take sufficient precautions. Then, not only are landslide damage claims likely to be larger than predicted, but also insurers may find it infeasible to charge different premiums to those who are more and less at risk, thereby forcing them to set premiums at a rate that discourages purchase by responsible owners. In such a setting, especially given the possibility of enormous landslide claims made by lots of customers in one location, who are all harmed by a single major storm, insurers may prefer simply to exclude this risk.

Not all insurance against catastrophic harm is subject to this sort of exclusion, however. For example, "major medical" insurance is designed to cover personally catastrophic risks that would cause the insured to need a great deal of expensive medical care. And this sort of health insurance generally will cover medical costs incurred in connection with any sort of societal disaster. One reason for the availability of this coverage is that, even a major disaster is not likely to cause a large share of any insurer's customer base to file claims.

So, too, large amounts of life insurance are generally available for purchase and proceeds of the policy are normally payable regardless of whether the person died from a societal catastrophe or not. To be sure, in some policies some causes of death are excluded from coverage. These may include suicide for a moderate period of time after the policy is obtained, as well as death from sky diving, bungee jumping, and other specifically listed perils—i.e., what are viewed as extraordinarily dangerous activities that the insured party voluntarily undertakes. But deaths from earthquakes, floods, or terrorism, for example, are generally covered by standard life insurance policies. Again, even a major earthquake is likely to kill only a small share of any one life insurer's clients, and the amount of the insurance payout has been specified (and specifically priced) in advance....

As noted already, sometimes the private insurance market by itself will not provide insurance coverage for the consequences of certain disasters. In that case, government might act, either by becoming an insurer itself and offering (or even mandating purchase of) the missing coverage or by working with insurers to get (or force) them to provide the coverage.

The latter could involve getting each insurer of similar risks (e.g. property insurers) to take on its "fair share" of the target risk (like earthquakes). Or it could involve creating of [sic] a fund paid for by insurers (presumably from extra premiums collected from its customers) that covers the target risk (like earthquakes). Alternatively, government may become the actual insurer of the risk (like earthquakes) although even there government might yet enlist private insurers in the roles of selling the product, collecting the premiums, and perhaps even processing the claims were the covered risk to occur.

The regime supervised by California's current California Earthquake Authority is one example of how government can get involved with creating a market for insurance coverage for a risk that is not covered by nearly all basic property insurance policies sold in California. A somewhat different role is played by the state of Florida under the Florida Hurricane Catastrophe Fund that was created in 1993 in the wake of Hurricane Andrew. The National Flood Insurance Program is an example of how the federal government stepped in to create coverage for a risk that private insurers were generally unwilling to underwrite on their own. Recent governmental interventions designed to assure the availability of insurance against the consequences of terrorism (most importantly, a temporary agreement by the federal government to pay for a share of covered losses) is yet another. These schemes are all aimed at physical property damage. Although not now in place, it is imaginable that, with the help of government, the insurance industry could provide property insurance against the full range of natural disasters.

An important issue confronting any such arrangement—either a comprehensive scheme or one aimed at a specific disaster risk—is the premium structure. Is the government-arranged scheme, on average, charging the equivalent of "market" rates, or are taxpayers subsidizing those who buy the insurance? A justification for subsidy might be the otherwise low-income status of the victims. A second-best sort of justification might be that, if, after the disaster, political realities would require government to come in with taxpayer money and help out anyway, it might be socially desirable to get at least some contribution in advance from those who are specifically at risk.

Additional critical pricing issues are (1) whether individual or classes of buyers will be charged differently because they run different risks, and (2) to what extent will underwriting investigations be carried out and underwriting conditions be attached so as to promote efficient precautions by those who are at risk. Failure to differentiate among insureds in the way a private market would results in subsidies. To be sure, sometimes these seeming subsidies are justified because price classification is simply too costly to engage in. Other times, failure to discriminate in pricing may reflect a positive choice to favor certain parties who are at risk, such as low (or high) income people. In any event, the absence of actuarially sensible risk-related premiums can discourage both insurance companies and certain property owners from participating, and it can cause some people to incur risks they would not run were their insurance costs actuarially fair.

SEAN HECHT, CLIMATE CHANGE AND THE TRANSFORMATION OF RISK: INSURANCE MATTERS
55 UCLA L. Rev. 1559 (2008)

Some insurance industry leaders have noted that the industry has a significant financial stake in climate change, and some have asserted that the insurance sector can and should play an active role in solving our society's climate change-related problems. This awareness has encouraged significant recent activity among insurance companies to attempt to assess and to react to climate change. Trevor Maynard, Manager of Emerging Risks for the massive surplus insurer Lloyd's of London, has stated that "[c]limate change is already affecting the global insurance industry," and has argued that "[a]ll aspects of an insurer's balance sheet, its liabilities, capital requirements and assets may be affected." And a report issued recently by the major financial services firm Ernst and Young identified climate change as the "top insurance risk in 2008," noting that it is a "long-term issue with broad-reaching implications that will significantly impact the industry."...

Climate change will affect, and in some cases is already affecting, most major types of insurance products. First, insurers will feel the impact of climate change on property and casualty insurance, where the insurer bears the risk of a loss suffered directly by the policyholder. These property and casualty claims include not only damage to insured property as a direct result of weather, but also claims for business interruptions and other consequences of weather-induced events. Second, health and life insurers will face increasing costs. Third, insurers will face claims based on liability insurance, where the insurer pays for legal claims brought by third parties against the policyholder. Depending on the risk involved, all these types of insurance may be particularly affected by climate change-related losses or present unique opportunities to encourage the mitigation of such losses. And insurers will face challenges to insurability that may deeply impact the industry's ability to spread risk. This Part will discuss the impact that climate change is likely to have on both loss trends and insurability.

The direct risks to insurers from climate change are primarily catastrophe related. Catastrophes are the single largest threat to insurer solvency. Catastrophes, defined by the American Academy of Actuaries as "infrequent events that cause severe loss, injury or property damage to a large population of exposures," pose a unique, complex, and significant set of risks to insurer solvency. Catastrophes—particularly catastrophes that are stochastic in nature, such as severe weather events, earthquakes, or terrorism—pose challenges of risk magnitude, uncertainty, and correlation, "complicat[ing] the fundamental actuarial and pricing processes that underlie well-functioning insurance markets." Weather-related catastrophes have disrupted insurance markets in the past—for example, after Hurricane Andrew in 1992, and after the 2005 hurricane season in the Gulf of Mexico—and are likely to do so again in the future. According to a 2007 Congressional Research Service report, "[m]ost insurance market analysts note that there is no state in the Union that is not subject to catastrophe exposure, and the current state of affairs suggests that the exposures are far greater than the insurance industry is now currently prepared to handle." And there is significant evidence that climate change will increase both the risks borne by insurers from catastrophic events and the uncertainties associated with these risks. These risks include both first-party risk (the risk of loss by an insured) and third-party risk (the risk that an insured's actions will result in losses to others). In addition, climate change may significantly affect risks and uncertainties from other, noncatastrophic insured losses.

A. Climate Change and Insurance Losses

Insurers' underwriting is affected directly by the risks to which their policyholders are exposed. The insurance industry recognizes that "[f]or many industries, [weather] is the greatest risk to earnings: a risk that cannot be prevented, avoided or isolated." Swiss Re, a surplus insurer that has been aggressive in identifying climate change as a major risk to businesses internationally, has noted that "[v]ariable weather affects supply and demand in almost every industry: evidently in such sectors as energy or agriculture; more subtly, but still significantly, in others, for example retail, clothing, or entertainment." According to a researcher for leading surplus insurer Lloyd's of London, "[c]limate change is already affecting the global insurance industry. There are clear trends in past climate data that have translated into trends in insurance claims," including rising sea levels and consequent storm surges and longer and more frequent forest fires. Since an estimated $3 trillion of the U.S.'s $11 trillion economy is directly affected by weather, it is essential that the insurance industry retain the capacity to buffer businesses' exposure to weather-related losses....

Extreme weather trends will deeply affect the insurance industry. Swiss Re has noted that "extreme events [are] expected to increase both in frequency and severity due to climate change." The Association of British Insurers also believes that climate change has caused extreme weather trends, noting that "climate change is making it likely that storm surges will occur more frequently, and that they will be more destructive when they do." And Lloyd's of London has expressed concerns about the effects of climate change on weather volatility, and on the implications that uncertainties surrounding these effects may have on insurability. Accordingly, some insurers have developed products to meet the "increasing demand for protection against adverse weather" and weather volatility due to climate change.

Unexpected catastrophe losses have already rocked the sector. Researchers Howard Kunreuther and Erwann Michel-Kerjan note that some insurers were taken by surprise at the size of losses from Hurricane Andrew and the Northridge earthquake in 1992 and 1994, respectively. "[F]ollowing Hurricane Andrew, many insurers only marketed coverage against wind damage in Florida because they were required to do so and state insurance pools were formed to limit their risk. In California, insurers refused to renew homeowners' earthquake policies after the 1994 Northridge earthquake, and in their place the California Earthquake Authority was formed by the state in 1996 with funds from insurers and reinsurers." In 2003, natural catastrophes worldwide caused $15 billion in insured losses ($8 billion of which were caused by storms). In 2005, Hurricane Katrina and other weather catastrophes caused insured losses of almost $80 billion worldwide, causing some companies' payouts to exceed insurance premiums. According to a recent report, "Louisiana property insurer losses following Hurricane Katrina were $3 billion more than all premiums collected in the state for the preceding 22 years [and] Lloyd's posted...a loss of $180 million in 2005 which equates to $1.12 paid out for ever[y]$1.00 in premium revenues, thanks largely to hurricane losses."

Whether or not current weather patterns already reflect climate change's impacts, insured losses from catastrophic weather events are increasing and are expected to continue to increase. According to a recent study, socioeconomic factors, including the "degree of urbanization and value at risk," "directly influence the level of economic losses due to weather-related events." These factors, in synergy with changing weather patterns, are likely to affect the insurance industry's covered losses significantly over time. And aside from extreme weather events, other adverse effects of climate change should concern the insurance industry because of their potential costs. As insurers' costs rise, the premium levels necessary for an insurer to make a profit rise, shrinking the potential market for the insurance. If costs are high enough, there will be no price point that satisfies both the insurer and the consumer, and there will be no market for the insurance, rendering the risk effectively uninsurable.

Climate change-related risks are likely to affect all major insurance types: property/casualty, health, life, and liability. Property and casualty insurance lines are likely to be affected by climate change, even aside from extreme weather. For example, coastal and sea-level property losses due to flooding from a higher sea level are expected. According to the Intergovernmental Panel on Climate Change, "[m]any millions more people are projected to be flooded every year due to sea-level rise by the 2080s." A report commissioned by the Association of British Insurers predicts that if no action to mitigate climate change is taken, the annual losses from coastal flooding in England and Wales "could increase by between £1.0 billion and £13.5 billion by the end of the century." In addition, property-damaging wildfires may increase in number and in intensity, in part because of climate change-related droughts, changes in wind and vegetation patterns, lightning strike increases, and reduced moisture content in vegetation. As an example of wildfires' potential cost to the insurance industry, one 1991 wildfire that reached the urban Oakland and Berkeley areas in northern California caused $2.4 billion in insured losses, including the loss of 3,400 buildings and 2,000 cars. Swiss Re and Lloyd's of London believe that climate change may have increased the magnitude of losses from the Oakland-Berkeley fire and other wildfires.

> ...

Because of the potential for large losses associated with a single event and other correlated losses, all these climate change-related risks deeply affect the reinsurance industry. Retail insurers transfer large amounts of risk to large companies that specialize in reinsurance and surplus insurance, such as Lloyd's, Swiss Re, and Munich Re. Often, those insurers serve as the primary insurers for risks that are seen as uninsurable by smaller insurers, both because of the deep access to capital that the surplus insurers enjoy and because the surplus insurers are subject to less regulation since they are typically nonadmitted in jurisdictions, such as U.S. states, that maintain strict regulatory requirements on underwriting.

In all, the changing climate is likely to have a wide-ranging and deep impact on the insurance industry. The attention that insurers—including large international insurers such as Swiss Re, Munich Re, AIG, and Lloyds of London, and an increasing number of domestic insurers—have placed on climate change is itself evidence that the industry expects climate change to transform its business practices.

B. Climate Change and Insurability of Risks

Climate change presents significant risks to insurability. These risks, in turn, may limit the insurance industry's ability to continue to grow and to be profitable in those insurance lines affected by climate-related risk, unless insurers adapt to the changing conditions—itself a challenge because of the uncertainties inherent in climate change-related risk. Reinsurers will be affected disproportionately, since they bear such a high proportion of catastrophic risk. But innovations in capital markets and the reinsurance industry may enable the insurance sector to continue to manage risks effectively.

1. Climate Change's Threat to Insurability: Uncertainty, Potential for Losses High Enough to Threaten Solvency, and Correlated Risks

Climate change presents a particularly challenging type of risk for insurers because its effects may impact the insurability of a significant number of risks across various insurance product lines. This is especially true to the considerable extent that climate change-related losses are catastrophe-related....

First, climate change's relationship to global weather patterns increases the potential for losses so large that they threaten the solvency of insurers as more severe weather becomes more common and overall variability of conditions increases.

Second, uncertainties in assessing climate change's impacts are high, affecting property and casualty, business interruption, health, and liability insurance, among others. As a result, where a risk has significant ambiguous components, insurers are both more likely to charge a significantly higher premium and more likely to avoid insuring the risk entirely than where a risk is more well-defined. Current catastrophe models, epidemiological assessments, and litigation risk models are likely not adequate to predict future risks.

Third, it is likely that many climate change-related risks are correlated, creating a skewed risk pool and exacerbating the risk of extremely large losses, and that some of these risks are not well-distributed across existing insureds. Severe weather-related losses, in particular, raise these issues, as does sea-level rise.

Finally, as a result of insurers' uncertainty aversion and need to protect against extremely large losses from single or related events, it is not clear that insurers will be willing to insure against some climate change-related risks at a price that policyholders are willing to pay.

Thus, many of the basic criteria of insurability are threatened by climate change. Moreover, the higher the magnitude of climate change in store for the Earth, the greater each of these challenges becomes. There is remarkable uncertainty about conditions around the globe at levels of future global warming that are considered extreme but possible even as soon as 2100.

2. Implications for the Insurance Industry of Climate Change's Threat to Insurability

Under these conditions, climate change poses a potential threat to the stability of the insurance industry over the next several decades if insurers do not take the necessary steps to adapt. One clear consequence of this situation is that insurers should be motivated to conduct research to help to better understand climate change's likely impacts. Insurers are already doing this. But it is less clear that insurers will work hard to adapt their basic products to a world in which the climate is changing. Uncertainty aversion and the possibility of enormous losses can motivate insurers either to attempt to create a business model that addresses climate change-related risk, or alternatively to withdraw from markets entirely.

This latter course of action unfortunately may be the most likely course of action for many insurers, at least in the short term. Insurers often will react to unanticipated losses or to significant changes in risk profile or uncertainty by limiting their underwriting. Regulated insurers, who have relatively less ability to price novel risks at a comfortable premium, are more likely to react this way than nonadmitted insurers such as large reinsurance companies. But even nonadmitted insurers have difficulty assuming risks that are too uncertain or novel, or that cannot be priced at a level that is marketable. So, for example, even large surplus insurers withdrew from the pollution insurance market in 1984 when they judged underwriting environmental liability insurance at marketable rates untenable. Similar problems occurred in the reinsurance market after the insurance industry grossly underestimated potential losses from Hurricane Andrew in 1992.

Climate change is likely to result in a combination of unanticipated losses and increased uncertainty that could create a similar, or even greater, potential for contraction of the insurance industry's overall coverage. But in the long run, such contraction will hurt the industry, and so innovative insurers will be looking for ways to make risks insurable.

Climate change should also provide an incentive for the insurance industry to work to reduce our society's overall greenhouse gas emissions. The difference between the more pessimistic end of the predicted climate spectrum in the future and the more optimistic end—the difference between the real chance of a scenario where "an entirely new planet is coming into being, one largely unrecognizable from the Earth we know today"—and the likelihood of a more manageable set of societal risks will involve dramatic cuts in greenhouse gas (GHG) production worldwide. To the extent that climate change's impacts can be limited, they will be more predictable and thus more insurable, creating business opportunities for insurers.

Climate change thus poses a challenge to the insurance industry's long-term stability, if insurers do not adapt. But taking action to address climate change will better enable the industry to manage its future successfully. This appears to be a primary motivation for the engagement of companies such as Lloyds, Munich Re, and Swiss Re in research, lobbying, and public education about climate change. These initiatives reflect the reality that the entire industry could be harmed by the increasing uncertainty that climate change will bring.

3. The Role of Reinsurance and Other Risk Transfer Instruments in Helping Insurers Cope with Climate Change

Insurers' ability to cope with the dramatic and significant risks posed and exacerbated by climate change is dependent in large part on their ability to transfer risk to reinsurers or other parties. Reinsurance and other vehicles that allow insurers to spread their own risk play a crucial role in allowing insurers to take on risks of large losses. These vehicles allow insurers to reduce both their average loss and maximum possible loss, increasing their capacity to cover risks. In an era in which catastrophe exposure is growing and the limits of insurability of catastrophic loss coverage may be increasingly uncertain, reduction of insurers' average and maximum losses will be even more central to future insurability of these risks.

Unfortunately, the reinsurance market has historically faced challenges covering catastrophic losses. Some losses strain the reinsurance market's liquidity and functionality. As a result, limitations on reinsurance capacity have limited the catastrophe insurance market. Companies and individuals exposed to catastrophe risk have had to turn to other avenues to preserve their capital and reduce this risk. Insurers and other financial institutions are looking to alternative risk-spreading instruments in order to accomplish this goal. Insurance-linked securities (ILSs) and "special-purpose vehicles" are the chief instruments being developed and implemented for this purpose. These instruments allow insurers and other companies to hedge climate risk. They include catastrophe bonds, industry loss warranties, weather derivatives, and "sidecar" companies whose purpose is to issue securities that hedge insurers' and reinsurers' risk. These instruments all allow an insurer or reinsurer to obtain access to capital if a specified set of conditions arises (for example, low rainfall, high temperatures, or a storm of a particular size making landfall). The sellers of the securities are, in essence, betting that the condition will not happen; they receive a premium that they are entitled to keep in the event that the condition is not met. If the condition is met, the sellers agree to pay a much higher, specified amount to the purchaser. Major reinsurers are developing these products. Their market has increased dramatically over the past few years, though it has not yet reached the level that researchers believe will be necessary to sustain a robust catastrophe insurance market.

The huge amount of risk held by a comparatively small number of reinsurers may explain why those companies have been the most proactive in addressing climate risks. Moreover, because reinsurers also often act as nonadmitted insurers, they may be doubly exposed to these risks to the extent they act as primary insurers of significant risks associated with climate change.

In short, the success of reinsurance and similar vehicles in allowing insurers and large businesses to spread catastrophic risks will be essential to our society's ability to address climate change. Because insurers rely on risk-spreading instruments to manage their own exposure to high-magnitude or correlated losses, the supply of insurance for catastrophic events depends on the availability of these instruments.

ROBERT L. RABIN & SUZANNE A. BRATIS, FINANCIAL COMPENSATION FOR CATASTROPHIC LOSS IN THE UNITED STATES

Financial Compensation for Victims after Catastrophe (M. Faure & T. Honlief eds., Springer Verlag 2005)

The Terrorism Risk Insurance Act of 2002 (TRIA) exemplifies the federal government assuming the role of excess liability insurer, in effect providing a cap on the losses for which the private insurance industry will be responsible in the event of a major act of terrorism.

In terms of insurance losses, the terrorist attacks on the World Trade Center and Pentagon on September 11, 2001, rank as the most costly catastrophe in U.S. history. This is without reference to the personal injury claims compensated under the Victim Compensation Fund, totaling nearly $7 billion, discussed in a separate section of this report. By the middle of October 2003, private insurance companies had received 35,094 claims related to the September 11 attacks on the World Trade Center alone, representing a total of $19.07 billion, including massive numbers of personal property and business interruption claims (the latter including claims for lost income and expenses related to restarting or reinvigorating affected businesses). Workers compensation claims paid by the industry came to 5,660. These aggregate costs far exceeded past terrorism-related damage claims in the U.S.

In the aftermath of the attacks, even before massive numbers of claims began to be filed, the U.S. Congress was faced with widespread concern about the solvency of the American insurance industry. On November 26, 2002, President George W. Bush signed into law the Terrorism Risk Insurance Act of 2002. TRIA was created to ensure the continuing availability of insurance for terrorism risk. Its goals encompassed both protecting the American public, by ensuring continued insurance coverage, and protecting the insurance industry as it rebuilt after the losses caused by September 11. The Act created a mechanism by which the federal government and private insurance providers would share the burden of property and casualty losses resulting from any future terrorist attacks.

Essentially, all commercial insurers doing business within the U.S are required to participate in the program. Under the Act's provisions, insurers are required to make available coverage for insured losses resulting from acts of terrorism in all of their commercial property and casualty insurance policies. The coverage cannot differ materially from the terms, amounts, and other limitations of policies written to cover losses arising from nonterrorist causes. In addition to the continued availability of coverage, insurers must inform policyholders of the premium charged for coverage and the federal share of compensation provided for under the Act.

In return for such actions on the part of insurers, the federal government assumes a percentage of an insurer's losses from compensating claims arising from terrorist acts. Each insurer is responsible for a deductible amount. But once that threshold is reached, federal funds are used to reimburse the insurer 90% of the insured losses in excess of the deductible. Importantly, the Act imposes a $100-billion annual industry-aggregate limit on federal reimbursements.

The program's reimbursement provision is triggered only by the occurrence of an "act of terrorism." To qualify, an event must meet a three-part definition, in addition to a threshold dollar amount of $5 million. The act must: (1) be "a violent act or an act that is dangerous to human life, property or infrastructure"; (2) result in damage within the U.S. (or outside of the United States in the case of air carriers, vessels, and U.S. missions), committed by one or more individuals, on behalf of foreign interests, in an "effort to coerce the civilian population of the United States or to influence the policy or affect the conduct of the United States Government by coercion"; and (3) be certified as an "act of terrorism" by the secretary of the treasury in concurrence with the secretary of state and the attorney general. Reimbursement of the insured (including the federal contribution), and risk management administration, remains in the hands of the private insurer.

In addition to providing for reimbursement, the act also contains provisions for managing litigation arising out of certified acts of terrorism. Once an act of terrorism is certified, the Act creates an exclusive federal cause of action and remedy for property damage, personal injury, or death arising out of or relating to the terrorist act. The federal cause of action preempts certain state law claims and provides for the consolidation of all civil claims. Additionally, the Act provides that punitive damages awarded in actions for property damage, personal injury, or death are not to be counted as "insured losses" and are not paid under the Program. Finally, the United States is provided the right of subrogation with respect to any payment made by the United States under the Program.

The provisions of the Act make it clear that Congress did not intend the program to be a primary source of compensation. Compensation provided for by other federal programs cannot be duplicated by funds from the Program. For example, disaster relief provided under FEMA or benefit awards under the September 11th Victim Compensation Fund must be deducted from the total amount otherwise payable under TRIA. Moreover, the TRIA program is a stopgap measure. The Act expires in 2005 [but was later renewed] and the deductible amount attributed to the insurers increases annually until that point to reduce the total amount of losses subject to federal reimbursement.

RAWLE O. KING, HURRICANE KATRINA: INSURANCE LOSSES AND NATIONAL CAPACITIES FOR
FINANCING DISASTER RISKS

Congressional Budget Office (January 31, 2008)

Despite billions invested in flood management, the United States has not been able to curb the rising costs of flood damage and public and private development in flood risk areas. This was the conclusion of the Gilbert F. White National Flood Policy Forum held in November 2007 at George Washington University. 68 The forum brought together 92 diverse experts to consider the future of floodplain management under a "business-as-usual scenario" and under an alternative scenario of aggressive action to address increasing flood risk in the nation. The experts at the forum concluded that an unprecedented set of conditions (e.g., population growth and migration, Despite billions invested in flood management, the United States has not been able to curb the rising costs of flood damage and public and private development in flood risk areas. This was the conclusion of the Gilbert F. White National Flood Policy Forum held in November 2007 at George Washington University. The forum brought together 92 diverse experts to consider the future of floodplain management under a "business-as-usual scenario" and under an alternative scenario of aggressive action to address increasing flood risk in the nation. The experts at the forum concluded that an unprecedented set of conditions (e.g., population growth and migration, changes in climate, and degradation of water-based resources) now faces the United States that could increase flood losses more rapidly in the future. Several policy options emerged, and are listed below.
Long-Term Flood Insurance Contracts

Long-term flood insurance contracts (LTFIC) coupled with mitigation loans arguably would encourage investment in risk-reduction measures. The idea is for private insurers to offer 5-, 10- or 20-year flood insurance contracts combined with long-term mitigation loans (e.g., for retrofitting, elevation, and flood-proofing of structures) tied to the mortgage. Mitigation loans would be offered to help finance the high upfront costs associated with investing in mitigation measures. The long-term flood insurance policies would have a maturity that corresponds to the length of the mortgage on the property and the policy would not terminate when the property owner sells the property.

The economic rationale for using LTFI to pre-fund disaster costs is that insurers, generally, need guaranteed premiums for a long time period if rates are to be based on expected losses. By lengthening the term of the property insurance contract, and spreading the risk through a mandatory purchase requirement, LTFI contracts could implicitly permit insurers to compensate for their present inability to prepare adequately for rare and unpredictable flood events.

Privatization of Flood Risk

FEMA has a responsibility to examine the NFIP's contingent liabilities and recommend ways to provide financial stability to the federal flood insurance program. This activity is performed in conjunction with the program's annual rate-setting process. In 2000, FEMA undertook a study with the assistance of accounting firm Deloitte & Touche to explore alternative financing arrangements to reduce the need for U.S. Treasury borrowing. FEMA was concerned about the NFIP's erratic cash flow and the potential for catastrophic losses within a short period of time.

Since Hurricane Katrina in 2005, recognizing the shortcomings of the current financing arrangement under the NFIP, two basic alternatives have emerged: a multi-peril insurance approach and a reinsurance pool approach (i.e., standing facility provided for in the original 1968 act) that would expand the private-sector involvement in the NFIP. With the development of computer simulation catastrophe risk models and remote sensing technologies, some private- sector firms have argued that reinsurance and catastrophe bonds are good ideas that should be explored.

In this context, FEMA could require private insurers to "make available" private flood insurance policies at actuarially determined prices in flood-prone areas with the federal government providing federal reinsurance (see discussion on "Multi-peril Insurance" below). The Flood Insurance Reform Act of 2012 requires FEMA and GAO to study the option of privatizing the program and to report to Congress within one year of enactment. The new law also mandated the director of the Federal Insurance Office to study the current state of the market for natural disaster insurance in the United States.

Multi-Peril Homeowners Policies Covering the Flood Peril

Along the lines of privatization, Congress might choose to encourage private insurers to offer multiple-peril insurance policies covering the flood peril, and to have this risk segmented for the insurers' other book of business and transferred through reinsurance transactions to the federal government. Under this arrangement, the federal government would operate as a reinsurer, rather than a direct writer as it does currently under the Write Your Own Program. The underwriting of flood risk by private insurers would be exempt from state insurance law. Rates, flood maps, and the criteria (regulation) for land management and use would continue to be the responsibility of the federal government. States and local communities would continue to enforce floodplain management regulations developed by the federal government. Lending institutions would continue to enforce the NFIP mandatory flood purchase requirement.

In theory, the main benefits of the "multi-peril policy" option would be enhanced efficiency in risk financing through greater pooling and diversification of flood risk. The flood coverage would be distributed more broadly through the larger homeowners' insurance market, resulting presumably in more contracts issued, and losses spread more broadly among all insurers.

On the other hand, this option could give rise to questions of fairness, the potential for new liabilities for federal taxpayers, and institutional and practical issues surrounding the way private and social risks are managed and financed (e.g., rate setting processes, data quality, coverage for catastrophic losses, oversight, and "who benefits and who pays for development at risk").

Community-Based Flood Insurance Policy Contracts

Congress might choose to explore the feasibility of group flood insurance either for entire communities, identified-floodplain areas, or residual-risk areas behind levees. The group policy would be purchased by the community on behalf of all residents. Premiums would be collected either through property taxes or as a utility-type payment. In the 112th Congress, the House of Representatives passed H.R. 6186 to require FEMA to undertake a study of the feasibility of voluntary community-based flood insurance options and how such options could be incorporated into the NFIP. The bill required the GAO to review and provide an analysis of the FEMA study and to report its findings and recommendations to Congress within one year. To address the affordability of insurance for low-income property owners, Congress might also explore the feasibility of providing means-tested flood insurance vouchers.

Integrated Watershed-Based Risk Management Strategy

In recent years, FEMA has undertaken a long-term flood risk management strategic planning effort. This effort included studying the feasibility of a more integrated watershed-based risk management strategy designed to weave flood hazard data developed in support of the NFIP into watershed-based risk assessment. The goal has been to increase the public's awareness and understanding of risk management and to address the nation's increasing vulnerability to flood risk and water resources management challenges. This integrated (some call it "holistic") approach to flood risk management draws on floodplain management with natural resources (i.e., water resources and waste water) management; it requires coordination among federal, state, and local authorities, businesses, and individuals homeowners.

Many disaster experts believe effective flood risk management policy will require intergovernmental coordination of natural resources management with floodplain management activities that reduce the vulnerability of people and economic assets to catastrophic flooding. Policymakers have been moving in this direction for several years.

Technological Innovation in Financing Large-Scale Natural Disasters

The series of extreme weather events since 2005 underscores some social and economic challenges to U.S. disaster risk management policy. The costs of reconstruction and compensation for flood victims are financed through tax revenue, dedicated disaster funds, and, to a lesser extent, private insurance payments. Private disaster insurance, however, has become less available and affordable because of insurability problems posed by uncertainties surrounding extreme risks, such as catastrophic flood events.

The Biggert-Waters Flood Insurance Reform Act of 2012 authorized FEMA to study the capacity of private insurers, reinsurers, and financial markets to assist communities in managing financial risk associated with flooding.73 One possible public-private initiative for financing catastrophic flood risk is for the government to encourage private-sector technological innovation—through tax and regulatory policy changes—in financing recovery from large-scale natural disasters. Given the nation's increasing flood exposure, and the desire to alleviate taxpayers' responsibility for flood losses (i.e., post-disaster relief), some disaster experts have expressed an interest in finding alternative ways to finance residual flood risk through the standardization of insurance- linked securities that transfer flood risk on an electronic platform to the capital markets. This approach would reduce the government's current role under the NFIP.

In November 2012, at an annual meeting of the National Association of Insurance Commissioners, Center for Insurance Policy Research (NAIC/CIRP), regulators and stakeholder groups with an interest in catastrophe risk financing explored new standards for transparency, compliance, and accountability with respect to two kinds of large scale disasters: environmental (i.e., catastrophe risk) and financial (i.e., residential mortgage back securitization). One speaker at the meeting, David M. Rowe, concluded that in order to efficiently transfer risk to capital markets via the issuance of financial instruments, two obstacles must be overcome: (1) a computer system challenge that involves data storage, communication issues, and computer processing analytics and (2) finding ways to make risk exchanges and transaction platforms more efficient. Eric Ordman, director of Research for the NAIC, and coordinator of the study released at the 2012 NAIC/CIRP meeting, suggested that the two risk management challenges identified by David M. Rowe could be addressed through regulatory changes in the way insurance companies invest in certain financial instruments, including residential mortgage-backed securities.

During the NAIC/CIRP panel discussion, Michael Erlanger, managing principal of Marketcore, a company that developed an electronic system architecture for aggregating risk elements in a way that facilitates valuations for complex risk transfers, stated that legislation introduced in previous Congresses, the Homeowners Defense Act,76 had, among other things, called for a change in regulatory structures that deliver consistent micro-to-macro risk-detailing views in near real time, assuring transparency in the market for catastrophe risk, including flood risk. He pointed out that the act called for the creation of a National Catastrophe Risk Consortium to (1) encourage data capture that leads to catastrophe risk differentiation and (2) expand the ability of private-sector financial and capital market firms and state residual property insurance pools to underwrite and bear the risk of an extreme event, such as a catastrophic flood event.

The Consortium, Erlanger stated, could, in theory, establish a holistic risk assessment framework that results in ever more granular market information induced by financial and strategic incentives for risk disclosure by all market participants. The standardized "granular risk data" at the contract level could be aggregated and the risk transferred via the Consortium's electronic platform to investors in the capital markets. This structure arguably would induce transparency, provide market liquidity for catastrophe risk financing, and track all changes in the underlying contracts (e.g., flood policies) in real time.

In theory, driving transaction volume and associated liquidity to a new exchange by leveraging the most valuable thing the new exchange provides, namely, the reliable, timely, and detailed information it creates, could enable financial markets to supply the necessary pressure for sellers (private insurers, reinsurers, and capital markets participants) to make their offerings increasingly more transparent.

Opposition to the Homeowners' Defense Act of 2010 in the 111th Congress had come from representatives of insurance and reinsurance groups, and several organizations including the National Fire Protection Association, National Flood Determination Association, National Wildlife Federation, Heartland Institute, Taxpayers for Common Sense, and Competitive Enterprise Institute. These groups argued the legislation would encourage coastal development in environmentally sensitive areas by lowering costs, bail out wealthy owners of beachside vacation homes, and crowd out the private insurance market.

Concluding Observations

The current system of managing and financing flood risk (NFIP) is more than $20 billion in debt. The Flood Insurance Reform Act of 2012 made significant changes in the financial, operational, and management structures of the NFIP. Specifically, this law would work to achieve several outcomes: (1) implement a phase out of premium rate subsidies that have undermined the financial viability of the program; (2) ensure that flood risk maps are updated and accurate and take into account anticipated sea-level rise and residual risk behind levees so that people understand and can better prepare for their risks; (3) encourage broad participation in the NFIP; and (4) streamline and strengthen federal mitigation programs to protect flood-exposed homes, businesses, and communities better, which helps to decrease future flood losses.

Some experts question whether the NFIP still provides appropriate protection against the peril of flood losses and helps build resilient communities. The success of the NFIP will be judged in part by how it handles five major challenges:

- Extreme weather events and coastal flooding. Most experts expect coastal storm surge and storm impacts will intensify as sea levels continue to rise. According to FEMA, flood and flood damage associated with extreme rainfall events have risen from $6 billion to $10 billion each year, despite billions spent on flood control.

- Accurate Flood Risk Maps. The accuracy and reliability of FEMA's flood mapping process. FEMA's Risk Mapping, Assessment, and Planning (Risk MAP) provides flood hazard data and tools to increase public awareness and help people make better decisions to protect themselves and communities to enforce floodplain management regulations that support the building of sustainable and resilient communities.77
- Financial Sustainability of the NFIP. The financial soundness of the NFIP requires flood insurance premiums to fully reflect a building's actuarial risk. Some experts have argued that subsidized insurance rates facilitate development in flood-prone areas that put people and property at risk. Compensating flood victims with federal disaster relief is costly and a potential burden on federal taxpayers. But requiring property owners to pay full actuarial rates that reflect actual risk could make flood policies less affordable.
- Residual Flood Risk from Levees. The existing regulatory framework for residual flood risk behind certified 100-year levees has created a perceived safety zone that spurs development behind the levee systems.78 Individuals might think a flood occurring once in a 100-year period could not harm them and, therefore, choose not to seek financial protection against this risk. Most disaster experts would agree that resolution of the nation's flood management challenge must involve hazard-mitigation measures that get people and communities to retreat or avoid living in flood-prone areas while supporting the building of hazard-resilient coastal communities.
- Distributional Effects of the NFIP. There is a perception of the inequitable distribution of the NFIP's costs and benefits across income groups and geographic regions.

NOTES AND QUESTIONS

1. There have been some important changes in catastrophic risk insurance since Hurricane Andrew first showed the potential scale of losses:
   - *Hurricane Insurance Deductibles.* Seventeen states (Alabama, Connecticut, Florida, Georgia, Hawaii, Louisiana, Maine, Maryland, Massachusetts, Mississippi, New Jersey, New York, North Carolina, Rhode Island, South Carolina, Texas, and Virginia) and the District of Columbia require property owners to pay hurricane or windstorm deductibles from 1 percent to 15 percent of the insured value of the property, depending on the type of home (e.g., mobile homes carry a higher percentage deductible) and where the property is located, rather than traditional dollar deductibles used for other types of claims,

such as fire damage and theft. Higher deductibles have also
been imposed for wind damage. These deductibles allow private
insurers to shift the risk onto homeowners while also providing
an incentive for risk mitigation.

o *State Governments.* State governments in a number of states
have established insurers of last resort or entities that simply
provide insurance against particular risks such as earthquakers
or hurricane damage that are excluded from private policies.
For discussion, see Carolyn Kousky, *Managing the Risk of
Natural Catastrophes: The Role and Functioning of State
Insurance Programs* (Resources for the Future Discussion Paper
10-39, 2010).

o *Capital Market for Catastrophe Securities.* Starting in the late
1980s, insurers, reinsurers, and investment banks began
offering catastrophe securities (sometimes known as insurance-
linked securities, or ILS) that transfer risk of natural calamities
to the capital market. These securities sell because they offer
unusually high returns and because the rates of return are not
correlated with returns in the stock and bond markets. See
Georgia Levenson Keohane, *Preparing for Disaster While Betting
Against It,* N.Y. Times, Feb. 12, 2014.

o *Building Codes and Construction Standards.* In hurricane-prone
areas, home insurance rates are now linked to new building
codes and structural standards based on a building's ability to
withstand wind damage. Following Hurricane Andrew, the
Insurance Institute for Property Loss Reduction (IIPLR) launched
a study to develop better wind and seismic building codes so
structures could better withstand the force of storms and
earthquakes. This led to the Building Code Effectiveness Grading
Schedule (BCEGS), which takes into account many factors such
as the skill of building inspectors and the budgets of
communities. The Florida legislature requires insurers to take
into account the BCEGS system when pricing rates.

2. *Flourishing of Catastrophe Simulation Modeling after Hurricane Andrew.*
These models allow insurers to better predict future windstorm losses
based on current demographics and construction methods than reliance
on historical data. However, the damage forecasts from these models
are often wrong by many orders of magnitude. Climate change is likely
to increase the severity of flood risks, both inland due to larger peak
precipitation events and in coastal areas due to sea level rise. In
addition, there are some indications that hurricane intensity could
increase. Thus, it will become increasingly urgent to provide incentives
to avoid building in flood zones and to make infrastructure resilient.
Somewhat at cross-purposes, there will be a growing need for an

effective insurance system covering unavoidable losses. The 2014 amendments to the flood insurance program require Congress to revisit the issue in 2017. What should Congress do then to make the program more conducive to climate adaptation efforts? For some thoughts on this, see Robert R.M. Verchick & Lynsey Rae Johnson, *When FEMA Heads for the Hills: Climate Retreat and the Flood Insurance Reform Act*, 47 J. Marshall L. Rev. 695 (2014).

8

RECOVERING FROM
DISASTER

After a disaster has occurred, the task becomes rebuilding. A city on its knees must confront a host of questions: How much of the old city should be restored? How should land uses be changed from residential to other uses? How can redevelopment be effective and fair at the same time? How can a city minimize the risk of future devastation? This chapter confronts some of those issues.

A. FEDERAL POLICY ON DISASTER RECOVERY AND CLIMATE RESILIENCE

In response the Post-Katrina Emergency Management Reform Act of 2006, FEMA released the 2008 National Response Framework (NRF), which clarified the response roles of key agencies and levels of government during an emergency and identified the resources available. (The NRF is discussed in Chapter 4.) Three years later, the Obama administration released a parallel National Disaster Recovery Framework (NDRF) to guide the recovery stage of disaster management. This framework—which applies to all presidentially-declared major "disasters," and is relevant to lesser emergencies too—is the first all-hazards recovery policy ever advanced at the federal level. The framework seeks to empower recovering states and localities by making sure federal programs are activated early and across a broad range of needs. Perhaps the most notable feature of the design is the plan's insistence that recovery efforts are not *separate* from immediate response efforts, but are rather a culmination of those initial endeavors. The NRF and NDRF are two acts in the same play.

In reading the excerpt below, pay attention to the framework's governing principles, particularly its commitment to building back smarter and involving all members of the community. Note how leadership roles are to be transferred from emergency response officials to recovery officials within a single "unified coordination group." And note the key role played by the so-called Recovery Support Functions (RSFs), federal advisory groups designed to help communities solve logistical problems, access federal resources, and coordinate gaggles of public and private stakeholders.

FEDERAL EMERGENCY MANAGEMENT AGENCY, NATIONAL DISASTER RECOVERY FRAMEWORK: STRENGTHENING DISASTER RECOVERY FOR THE NATION

http://www.fema.gov/pdf/recoveryframework/ndrf.pdf (Sept. 2011)
(footnotes omitted)

Introduction

The *National Disaster Recovery Framework (NDRF)* describes the concepts and principles that promote effective Federal recovery assistance. It identifies scalable, flexible and adaptable coordinating structures to align key roles and responsibilities. It links local, State, Tribal and Federal governments, the private sector and nongovernmental and community organizations that play vital roles in recovery….Importantly, the NDRF is intended to address disasters of all kinds and sources, whether it is a major Presidentially-declared disaster or a non-Presidentially declared incident. The NDRF is a companion document to the *National Response Framework (NRF)*….

Relationship to the National Response Framework

…As response, short-term and intermediate recovery activities begin to wind down, recovery needs gradually take on a more critical role….The NRF fully transitions to the NDRF when the disaster-specific mission objectives of the [federal advisory groups called,] Emergency Support Functions (ESFs), are met and all ESFs demobilize….

Recovery Continuum

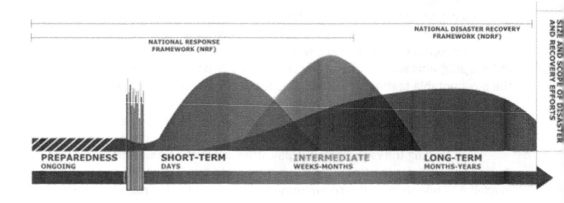

Core Principles

The *National Disaster Recovery Framework (NDRF)* is guided by nine core principles that, when put into practice, maximize the opportunity for achieving recovery success.

Individual and Family Empowerment. All community members must have equal opportunity to participate in community recovery efforts in a meaningful way. Care must be taken to assure that actions, both intentional and unintentional, do not exclude groups of people based on race, color, national origin (including limited English proficiency), religion, sex or disability. Care must be taken to identify and eradicate social and institutional barriers that hinder or preclude individuals with disabilities and others in the community historically subjected to unequal treatment from full and equal enjoyment of the programs, goods, services, activities, facilities, privileges, advantages and accommodations provided. A successful recovery is about the ability of individuals and families to rebound from their losses in a manner that sustains their physical, emotional, social and economic well-being....

Leadership and Local Primacy. Successful recovery requires informed and coordinated leadership throughout all levels of government, sectors of society and phases of the recovery process. It recognizes that local, State and Tribal governments have primary responsibility for the recovery of their communities and play the lead role in planning for and managing all aspects of community recovery....The Federal Government...is prepared to vigorously support local, State and Tribal governments in a large-scale disaster or catastrophic incident.

The Pre-Disaster Recovery Process. The speed and success of recovery can be greatly enhanced by establishment of the process and protocols prior to a disaster for coordinated post-disaster recovery planning and implementation. All stakeholders should be involved to ensure a coordinated and comprehensive planning process, and develop relationships that increase post-disaster collaboration and unified decisionmaking. Another important objective of pre-disaster recovery planning is to take actions that will significantly reduce disaster impacts through disaster-resilient building practices....

Partnerships and Inclusiveness.....Partnerships and inclusiveness are vital for ensuring that all voices are heard from all parties involved in disaster recovery and that all available resources are brought to the table. This is especially critical at the community level where nongovernmental partners in the private and nonprofit sectors play a critical role in meeting local needs. Inclusiveness in the recovery process includes individuals with disabilities and others with access and functional needs, advocates of children, seniors and members of underserved populations. Sensitivity and respect for social and cultural diversity must be maintained at all times. Compliance with equal opportunity and civil rights laws must also be upheld.

Public Information. Clear, consistent, culturally appropriate and frequent communication initiatives promote successful public information outcomes. These incorporate a process that is inclusive and ensures accessibility to all, including those with disabilities, persons who are deaf or blind and those with limited English proficiency....

Unity of Effort. A successful recovery process requires unity of effort, which respects the authority and expertise of each participating organization while coordinating support of common recovery objectives....

Timeliness and Flexibility. A successful recovery process upholds the value of timeliness and flexibility in coordinating and efficiently conducting recovery activities and delivering assistance. It also minimizes delays and loss of opportunities....

Resilience and Sustainability. A successful recovery process promotes practices that minimize the community's risk to all hazards and strengthens its ability to withstand and recover from future disasters, which constitutes a community's resiliency. A successful recovery process engages in a rigorous assessment and understanding of risks and vulnerabilities that might endanger the community or pose additional recovery challenges....Resilience incorporates hazard mitigation and land use planning strategies; critical infrastructure, environmental and cultural resource protection; and sustainability practices to reconstruct the built environment, and revitalize the economic, social and natural environments.

Psychological and Emotional Recovery. A successful recovery process addresses the full range of psychological and emotional needs of the community as it recovers from the disaster through the provision of support, counseling, screening and treatment when needed. These needs range from helping individuals to handle the shock and stress associated with the disaster's impact and recovery challenges, to addressing the potential for and consequences of individuals harming themselves or others through substance, physical and emotional abuses. Successful recovery acknowledges the linkages between the recovery of individuals, families and communities.

Achieving Recovery

Each community defines successful recovery outcomes differently based on its circumstances, challenges, recovery vision and priorities....Although no single definition fits all situations, successful recoveries do share conditions in which:

- The community successfully overcomes the physical, emotional and environmental impacts of the disaster.
- It reestablishes an economic and social base that instills confidence in the community members and businesses regarding community viability.
- It rebuilds by integrating the functional needs of all residents and reducing its vulnerability to all hazards facing it.

- The entire community demonstrates a capability to be prepared, responsive, and resilient in dealing with the consequences of disasters.

Recovery is more than the community's return to pre-disaster circumstances, especially when the community determines that these circumstances are no longer sustainable, competitive or functional as shown by the community's post-disaster condition. A successful recovery in this case may include a decision to relocate all or some portion of the community assets and restoration of the affected area to a more natural environment. In these circumstances, the community recovery decisionmaking is informed by evaluating all alternatives and options and avoiding simple rebuilding or reconstructing of an area that continues to be vulnerable....

Recovery Roles and Responsibilities
...

Individuals and Households. Individuals and families need to plan and be prepared to sustain themselves in the immediate aftermath of a disaster. Those who prepare reduce personal stress, and they enhance their ability to undertake their own recovery and shape the future of their community's recovery....

Private Sector. The private sector plays a critical role in establishing public confidence immediately after a disaster....If local leadership and the business community work together pre-disaster and develop a conceptual recovery plan, the public is more likely to be optimistic about the community's ability to recover post-disaster.

Additionally, the private-sector owns and operates the vast majority of the Nation's critical infrastructure, such as electric power, financial and telecommunications systems....

Major players in recovery efforts, businesses and critical infrastructure owners and operators have an important responsibility to improve disaster resilience by mitigating risks and increasing disaster preparedness. Businesses should adopt and exercise business continuity plans to minimize costly operational disruptions and purchase adequate all-hazards insurance policies. Businesses that plan for disruption are less likely to go out of business after a disaster than those that do not.

Nonprofit Sector....Nonprofit-sector support is provided by a range of organizations from small locally-based nonprofits to national organizations with extensive experience in disaster recovery. Nonprofits directly supplement and fill gaps where government authority and resources cannot be applied. Resourceful fundraisers, grantors and investors inject needed financial resources to meet recovery needs and obligations that otherwise are not funded by a government program....Nonprofit organizations are critical for ensuring participation and inclusion of all members of the impacted community.

Local Government. The local government has the primary role of planning and managing all aspects of the community's recovery. Individuals, families and businesses look to local governments to articulate their recovery needs....

The majority of mitigation measures are adopted, codified and enforced at the local level. While there are State and Federal standards, it is often up to the local government to adopt and enforce them. Examples include participating in the *National Flood Insurance Program (NFIP)* and enforcing building codes. Local governments also lead the community in preparing hazard mitigation and recovery plans, raising hazard awareness and educating the public of available tools and resources to enhance future resilience....

State Government. States lead, manage and drive the overall recovery process and play the central role in coordinating recovery activities that include providing financial and technical support....

Tribal Government. Tribal governments, as sovereign nations, govern and manage the safety and security of their lands and community members. Many Tribal government borders cross multiple counties and States, presenting a unique challenge in planning response and recovery efforts. While resources in other communities and governments maybe available and easily accessible, this is not the case in many Tribal government communities....[Under Executive Order 13175, *Consultation and Coordination with Indian Tribal Governments,*] the Federal Government is required to engage in meaningful consultation with Tribal governments prior to the finalization of policy or program implementation Local and State governments are encouraged to engage with Tribal governments as well.

Federal Government.... When a disaster occurs that exceeds the capacity of State and Tribal resources—or impacts Federal property, other areas of primary Federal jurisdiction or national security interests—the Federal Government may use the [NDRF] to engage necessary and available department and agency capabilities to support local recovery efforts....The duration and extent of Federal support is determined in part by the scale and enduring impacts of the disaster....

Prior to a disaster, the Federal Government has a responsibility to assist local, State and Tribal governments to prepare for recovery by providing guidance and tools for planning and preparedness activities.

From the Federal perspective, a successful recovery optimizes the return on Federal investment. This includes reducing future risk from hazards and increasing resilience while adopting courses of action consistent with national laws and policies. The Federal Government requires that all recipients of Federal assistance comply with civil rights obligations under Section 504 of the *Rehabilitation Act* and *Title VI of the Civil Rights Act of 1964*, and the *Age Discrimination Act of 1975*. Government agencies also play roles as employers and need to have their own plans to protect and assist their employees during emergencies.

Leadership

The [NDRF] strongly recommends that State governors as well as local government and Tribal leaders prepare as part of their disaster recovery plans to appoint Local Disaster Recovery Managers (LDRMs) and State/Tribal Disaster Recovery Coordinators (SDRCs/TDRCs) to lead disaster recovery activities for the jurisdiction....

In large-scale disasters...where a Federal role may be necessary, the SDRC and/or TDRC is the primary interface with the Federal Disaster Recovery Coordinator (FDRC).

Recovery Support Functions

The Recovery Support Functions (RSFs) [embody] the [NDRF's] coordinating structure for key functional areas of assistance....The RSFs bring together the core recovery capabilities of Federal departments and agencies and other supporting organizations—including those not active in emergency response—to focus on community recovery needs....Through the RSFs, relevant stakeholders and experts are brought together during steady-state planning and when activated post-disaster to identify and resolve recovery challenges....

Recovery Functions within the Joint Field Office Chain of Command

JFO organizational structure for the newly developed positions of FDRC and SDRC and the six RSFs established within the NDRF

In all actions, FDRCs and RSFs strive for affected residents to have a voice; for services to reach those who need them most; for equitable distribution of resources; and for recovery programs appropriate for the socioeconomic and cultural makeup of the community.

NOTES AND QUESTIONS

1. The NDRF envisions a federal government that is "on tap," not on top. The document recognizes the "primary responsibility" of local, state, and tribal governments, pledging a federal role of "vigorous[] support." Is it realistic to think that a partner, like the federal government, with all its cash and technical resources, will sit quietly while locals call the shots? Is it desirable? What is the federal role in making sure taxpayer dollars are spent sensibly, free of undue political influence, and that they are used in the way originally intended? Local primacy is a hallmark of U.S. recovery policy. But it is not the only model. Keep this in mind when reviewing the rebuilding efforts in Christchurch, New Zealand, later in this chapter.

2. How do you measure the success of a recovery? The NDRF takes on this difficult issue, suggesting it be based on outcomes embraced by the community itself. Economic well-being is one important measure. But the document gives equal attention to overcoming "the physical, emotional and environmental impacts of the disaster." The NDRF also stresses long-term resilience. It is not enough to build back. One must build back better.

3. Did somebody say, "retreat"? Not directly. But removing development from risky areas is surely on the table. Or, as the drafters put it, "[a] successful recovery" may entail "restoration of the affected area to a more natural environment." In the last decade, the federal government, through FEMA, appears to have encouraged retreat-based options more than in the past. Robert R.M. Verchick and Lynsey Rae Johnson, *When FEMA Heads for the Hills: Climate Retreat and the Flood Insurance Reform Act*, 47 J. Marshall L. Rev. 695 (2014). .The decision of whether to build back or relocate is a thorny issue, which we examine later in this chapter.

4. The NDRF, released in September 2011, was first fully implemented a year later in response to Hurricane Sandy. Later in this chapter, we'll look at post-Sandy recovery efforts and consider what effect the NDRF is having.

On June 25, 2013, President Obama introduced his Climate Action Plan to reduce greenhouse gas pollution, advance clean energy sources, and make the United States more resilient in the face of climate change. This last goal, "climate resilience," has become a central concern for many federal agencies whose missions—defending public health, maintaining roads and bridges, protecting forests and wetlands—will be severely challenged by hotter temperatures, rising seas, downpours and drought, and increased flooding. All of these things, of course, seriously affects disaster planning. When assessing the long-term risks faced by recovering community, it is not enough to know what has come before, because our future may not look like the past. For this reason, President Obama's Climate Action Plan has become a feature of federal disaster recovery policy. In the aftermath of the Hurricane Sandy, the NDRC has been implemented with reference to action plan principles, as has the federal Hurricane Sandy Rebuilding Strategy (excerpted later in this chapter).

PRESIDENT OBAMA'S CLIMATE ACTION PLAN

http://www.whitehouse.gov/sites/default/files/image
/president27sclimateactionplan.pdf (June 2013)

As we act to curb the greenhouse gas pollution that is driving climate change, we must also prepare for the impacts that are too late to avoid....The federal government has an important role to play in supporting community-based preparedness and resilience efforts,...supporting science and research germane to preparedness and resilience, and ensuring that federal operations and facilities continue to protect and serve citizens in a changing climate....

Going forward, the Administration will expand these efforts into three major, interrelated initiatives to better prepare America for the impacts of climate change:

I. Building Stronger and Safer Communities and Infrastructure
Promoting on-the-ground planning and resilient infrastructure will be at the core of our work to strengthen America's communities....Specific actions will include:

Directing Agencies to Support Climate-Resilient Investment: The President will direct federal agencies to identify and remove barriers to making climate-resilient investments; identify and remove counterproductive policies that increase vulnerabilities; and encourage and support smarter, more resilient investments, including through agency grants, technical assistance, and other programs, in sectors from transportation and water management to conservation and disaster relief....

Supporting Communities as they Prepare for Climate Impacts: Federal agencies will continue to provide targeted support and assistance to help communities prepare for climate-change impacts....The Administration will continue to assist tribal communities on preparedness through the Bureau of Indian Affairs, including through pilot projects and by supporting participation in federal initiatives that assess climate change vulnerabilities and develop regional solutions. Through annual federal agency "Environmental Justice

Progress Reports," the Administration will continue to identify innovative ways to help our most vulnerable communities prepare for and recover from the impacts of climate change. The importance of critical infrastructure independence was brought home in the Sandy response. The Federal Emergency Management Agency and the Department of Energy are working with the private sector to address simultaneous restoration of electricity and fuels supply....

Rebuilding and Learning from Hurricane Sandy: In August 2013, President Obama's Hurricane Sandy Rebuilding Task Force will deliver to the President a rebuilding strategy to be implemented in Sandy-affected regions and establishing precedents that can be followed elsewhere....In the transportation sector, the Department of Transportation's Federal Transit Administration...is dedicating $5.7 billion to four of the area's most impacted transit agencies, of which $1.3 billion will be allocated to locally prioritized projects to make transit systems more resilient to future disasters....[W]ith partners, the U.S. Army Corps of Engineers is conducting a $20 million study to identify strategies to reduce the vulnerability of Sandy-affected coastal communities to future large-scale flood and storm events, and the National Oceanic and Atmospheric Administration will strengthen long-term coastal observations and provide technical assistance to coastal communities.

II. Protecting our Economy and Natural Resources

Climate change is affecting nearly every aspect of our society, from agriculture and tourism to the health and safety of our citizens and natural resources. To help protect critical sectors, while also targeting hazards that cut across sectors and regions, the Administration will mount a set of sector- and hazard-specific efforts to protect our country's vital assets, to include:

Identifying Vulnerabilities of Key Sectors to Climate Change: The Department of Energy will soon release an assessment of climate-change impacts on the energy sector, including power-plant disruptions due to drought and the disruption of fuel supplies during severe storms, as well as potential opportunities to make our energy infrastructure more resilient to these risks....

Promoting Resilience in the Health Sector: The Department of Health and Human Services will launch an effort to create sustainable and resilient hospitals in the face of climate change. Through a public-private partnership with the healthcare industry, it will identify best practices and provide guidance on affordable measures to ensure that our medical system is resilient to climate impacts....

Conserving Land and Water Resources:...The Administration has invested significantly in conserving relevant ecosystems, including working with Gulf State partners after the Deepwater Horizon spill to enhance barrier islands and marshes that protect communities from severe storms....[T]he President is also directing federal agencies to identify and evaluate additional approaches to improve our natural defenses against extreme weather, protect biodiversity and conserve natural resources in the face of a changing climate, and manage our public lands and natural systems to store more carbon. . . .

Managing Drought: Leveraging the work of the National Disaster Recovery Framework for drought, the Administration will launch a cross-agency National Drought Resilience Partnership as a "front door" for communities seeking help to prepare for future droughts and reduce drought impacts. By linking information (monitoring, forecasts, outlooks, and early warnings) with drought preparedness and longer-term resilience strategies in critical sectors, this effort will help communities manage drought-related risks....

Reducing Wildfire Risks:...Federal agencies will expand and prioritize forest and rangeland restoration efforts in order to make natural areas and communities less vulnerable to catastrophic fire.

Preparing for Future Floods: To ensure that projects funded with taxpayer dollars last as long as intended, federal agencies will update their flood-risk reduction standards for federally funded projects to reflect a consistent approach that accounts for sea-level rise and other factors affecting flood risks....

III. Using Sound Science to Manage Climate Impacts

...The Administration will continue to lead in advancing the science of climate measurement and adaptation and the development of tools for climate-relevant decision-making by focusing on increasing the availability, accessibility, and utility of relevant scientific tools and information....

NOTE

1.	While a full discussion of climate change goes beyond the scope of this book, readers wanting to know more about climate impacts and climate change adaptation might start with Climate Change 2014: Impacts, Adaptation and Vulnerability (Intergovernmental Panel on Climate Change Fifth Assessment Report) (2014) (Final Draft), *available at* https://www.ipcc.ch /report/ar5/wg2/, Climate Change Impacts in the United States: The Third National Climate Assessment (U.S. Global Change Research Program) (Jerry M. Melillo, et al., eds., 2014), *available at* http://nca2014.globalchange.gov/ downloads, and The Law of Adaptation to Climate Change: United States and International Aspects (Michael B. Gerrard & Katrina Fischer Kuh, eds., 2012).

B. RESILIENCE THROUGH LOCAL ACTION

Practically speaking, some of the most important aspects of reducing disaster risk must be implemented at the local level. Planning experts Anna Schwab and David J. Brower establish some principles for building resilience at the local level and discuss ways in which municipalities can use their basic police powers to make communities less vulnerable.

Anna K. Schwab & David J. Brower, Increasing Resilience to Natural Hazards: Obstacles and Opportunities for Local Governments under the Disaster Mitigation Act of 2000

Losing Ground: A Nation on Edge, 281, 283-301 (John Nolon & Daniel Rodriguez eds., 2007) (footnotes omitted)

[L]ocal communities have at their disposal many ways to increase resilience, methods that fall well within the police power delegated to [them] from their respective states. In the effort to become more resilient to the impacts of natural hazards, communities should adhere to a few basic principles....

The first...principle...involves awareness and acceptance. Community members must be aware of the natural hazards they face, and must accept that they are capable of and responsible for addressing their hazard risks....

The second principle...is an articulation of values among the citizenry and elected officials. A "mitigation ethic" must be infused into community policies and integrated into the mainstream of community decision making, so that hazard resilience is addressed as an important and valid concern worthy of public attention....

A third principle...involves full public engagement in the process of mitigation planning and goal formulation. Although public participation can be a bulky and time-consuming activity,...the end result is worthwhile....

The fourth...principle...is a willingness to invest in the community's capacity for developing and carrying out mitigation policies and programs. There are many components to a community's capacity to engage in mitigation, including:

- *fiscal capability* (the ability to fund or to seek funding for mitigation projects and activities);
- *technical capability* (the ability to carry out hazard identification and vulnerability analyses to produce accurate information regarding where and to what extend hazards are likely to impact the community);
- *legal capability* (the ability and willingness to use the local police power to enact necessary land use and other regulations that restrict the use of hazardous lands for building purposes while respecting the rights of

private property owners to realize their investment-backed
expectations);
- *institutional capacity* (the ability to create the institutional framework
  or to designate responsible positions within the existing institutional
  framework to implement and sustain mitigation policies); and
- *political capacity* (the willpower to propose and carry out enduring
  mitigation strategies notwithstanding the shortened horizon of some
  elected positions).

Capacity building [implies] that the knowledge base necessary to plan
for and implement hazard mitigation measures must primarily reside within the
community itself....Of course, consultants often play a vital role in mitigation
programming at the local level....Yet while consultants (for a price) can perform
many of the activities involved in generating and analyzing important
background data, the real action of devising strategies, adopting goals and
implementing policies must be carried out by those with a lasting stake in the
ultimate resilience of the community.

Action Strategies for Local Governments
Broadly speaking, there are five interrelated approaches to reducing
vulnerability at the local level. Within these categories is a wide selection of
specific mitigation strategies and actions, many if not all of which are well within
the police power of local governments....[I]n general terms mitigation
techniques can be classified as follows:
- structural engineering projects
- hazard avoidance
- property protection
- environmental preservation
- education and outreach

...

Structural Engineering Projects
Structural mitigation projects are intended to lessen the impact of a hazard by
modifying the environment or by interfering with the natural progression of the
hazard event. As mentioned earlier, large-scale armoring against nature is
expensive (usually beyond what local government acting alone can afford) and
may encourage development in unsafe areas....

On a smaller scale,...structural projects are usually designed by
engineers and managed or maintained by public works staff, and include such
necessary actions as the construction and maintenance of storm sewers and
drainage infrastructure. In most states, storm drainage is provided by counties
and municipalities as one of the services required to maintain healthy and safe
living conditions. The spending power of local governments allows public
monies to be directed to these essential services, and the power of acquisition

allows local governments to purchase or condemn land and rights-of-way for stormwater management....

Hazard Avoidance

Over the long term, the most straightforward and cost-effective strategy to minimize or prevent damages and losses from natural hazards is to guide development away from hazard-prone areas....The most direct way of achieving avoidance objectives is through acquisition of hazard areas, accompanied by demolition or relocation of hazard-prone structures when homes and businesses are present. A second means...involves land use planning and regulation, including the enactment of zoning and subdivision ordinances. A third method...invokes the local jurisdiction's powers of spending and taxation....The hazard avoidance approach is most appropriate when alternative locations within the community are available for development. Communities that are at or close to build-out have more limited options for hazard avoidance, although encouraging higher density building and in-fill development in safe locations can help alleviate the constraints imposed by a scarcity of land.

Acquisition and Relocation

Enabling legislation typically empowers local governments to acquire and hold property for public purpose. By acquiring lands in hazard-prone areas, a community can ensure that the land will be put only to those uses that are compatible with the nature of the hazard risk. Picnic shelters and ball fields, for instance, are more appropriate uses of land in the floodplain than homes and businesses. Although acquisition is typically one of the most expensive mitigation tactics, in the long run it is often less expensive to acquire and demolish a building than to repeatedly provide for its reconstruction.

While the power of eminent domain is a necessary tool for acquiring land for certain community needs (schools and road rights-of-way are typical uses of condemnation), it is rarely invoked for hazard mitigation purposes. More common is the acquisition of land from a willing seller. Owners of properties that have experienced repetitive losses and who face probable future flooding are often very willing to sell, so long as the benefits are explained fully, and a viable alternative is made available to them.

On the downside, since title to the property is transferred to the public domain, acquisition may remove properties entirely or in part from the local government's property tax rolls, depending upon the type of acquisition program used. However, the cost of losing tax revenues from these properties is often lower compared to the cost of providing services to properties in hazard areas and the periodic costs of rescue and recovery from disasters. Another disadvantage with acquisition projects in some communities, particularly in rural or impoverished areas, is that the local government becomes the responsible party with respect to maintaining and preserving the acquired land as open space in perpetuity. However, local governments may transfer title to acquired land to other government agencies or to a nonprofit agency, such as a conservation or environmental organization....

Communities have used various methods to fund acquisitions using local financial resources, including bond referendums, taxes and fees, or partnerships with nonprofit organizations. However, the vast majority of buy-out programs are financed with federal funds, such as the Hazard Mitigation Grant Program and the Pre-Disaster Mitigation program administered by [FEMA]. Counties and municipalities have also made use of Community Development Block Grant funds from the U.S. Department of Housing and Urban Development, which are available for projects that benefit low- and moderate-income persons by removing slum and blighted conditions, or that address conditions of urgent need.

Reuse of acquired properties varies....Local governments have created public parks, incorporated land into open space systems, and let the land revert to its natural vegetative state as experimental or communal gardens. Some communities have built picnic shelters, tennis courts, ball fields, and bicycle or jogging paths on acquired land to encourage public uses. Acquisition has also been used to increase floodplain storage capacity, preserve wetlands, maritime forest, estuaries and other natural habitats, and protect aquifer recharge zones and riparian buffers....

Land Use Regulation

Local governments are authorized under the police power to regulate the use of private property to safeguard the physical environment, to encourage economic development, and to protect the public's health and safety....Through various land use regulatory powers, a local government can control the amount, timing, density, quality, and location of new development. All these characteristics of growth are determinants of local vulnerability to natural hazards....

Zoning is the traditional and nearly ubiquitous tool available to local governments to control the use of land. Some communities have made good use of their zoning ordinances for mitigation purposes by delineating hazard areas on the local zoning map. The corresponding text of the ordinance may designate these areas for low-intensity uses such as recreation, open space, conservation, or agriculture. Zoning can also be used to prohibit environmentally hazardous uses, such as junkyards and chemical storage facilities in areas vulnerable to flooding or earthquake. A zoning ordinance may encourage development in safe areas, by allowing greater density in hazard-free zones.

When a community uses the local zoning ordinance as a hazard mitigation tool, the phrasing of its nonconforming use provisions is critical. The rules must be very clear as to whether or not reconstruction will be allowed if buildings are severely damaged or destroyed by a storm or other natural hazard event....

Subdivision ordinances control land that is being divided into parcels for sale by establishing standards for infrastructure and lot layout. Subdivision regulations are used to prevent new construction on land that is not suitable for development, and to ensure that infrastructure is provided to adequately support the development. In terms of their effectiveness for hazard mitigation purposes, studies have shown that subdivision controls, although more widely used than zoning, are not well tied to hazard mitigation aims....

Local Spending Policies

...When making decisions about expenditures for new facilities such as schools, fire stations, sewer treatment plants and other public necessities, local governments can choose to locate these critical facilities in areas with lowered risk of damage from natural hazards. Careful siting can protect lifelines during a disaster, reduce public outlays for repair, and minimize the time and expense for reconstruction following a hazard event. Local governments can also use capital improvement and maintenance programs to prescribe standards for the design and construction of new public facilities with hazard mitigation components, or to retrofit existing public structures....[T]here is a persistent disincentive to protect critical facilities from natural hazards because the damage costs are typically passed on to the federal government through various disaster assistance programs.

...[L]ocal governments can also use their spending power to discourage private development in hazardous areas, while directing new growth to designated nonhazard areas. By limiting the availability of public services such as roads, schools, utility lines, and other supporting infrastructure, the municipality can steer development appropriately. However, studies indicate that jurisdictions tend to ignore their own capital programs, and that policies designed to locate public facilities outside of hazard areas to discourage growth do not alter the basic spatial pattern of development. Furthermore, capital improvement programs are generally ineffective for controlling development in communities that have already reached [their capacity for] build-out, or where private developers are able to provide the infrastructure necessary to support new construction....

Local Taxation and Fee Policies

The power of taxation can have a profound impact on the pattern of development....By assessing differential tax rates in certain districts, the local government can influence which lands are relatively affordable to develop. The community can then direct growth to desirable, safe areas, while providing disincentives for developers to build on lands identified as hazardous....

...Tax abatements can encourage homeowners and developers to integrate mitigation measures into new structures and to retrofit existing properties, much like tax credits and allowances have been used to encourage the construction of energy efficient homes and office buildings. Tax incentives have been applied to storm proofing, flood proofing, wind strengthening, and seismic retrofitting, among other hardening construction techniques....The village of South Holland, Illinois, has a rebate program to help property owners fund retrofitting projects to protect against surface and subsurface flooding. If a project is approved, installed, and inspected, the village will reimburse the owner 25% of the cost up to $2500. About 650 flood-proofing and sewer backup protection projects have been completed under the program. Perhaps not surprisingly, local contractors have become some of the best agents to publicize the program.

Impact fees and special assessments are often levied against property owners to more equitably distribute the financial burden of development to those who directly benefit. Special assessments can be used for mitigation purposes to raise revenue for specific improvements, such as a flood retention pond, or to fund ongoing services such as maintenance of stormwater management systems. These charges do not usually discourage development in the assessment district, but they do transfer some of the cost of living or doing business in a hazard-prone area to those who choose to do so....

Property Protection

In a perfect world, communities would be built in locations that are never exposed to the impacts of natural hazards. Hazard avoidance, however, is an impractical approach to mitigation in areas where development is warranted on economic grounds, where hazard risk is uniformly experienced across the jurisdiction, or where the hazard area itself is integral to the community's identity. In these places, the most appropriate strategy to reduce potential disaster losses is to strengthen buildings and facilities so that they are able to withstand hazard impacts.

Property protection involves physical or structural measures applied to individual buildings and facilities to make them more resilient to identified hazard impacts....

Elevation is one of the most widely used property protection techniques and has successfully reduced future flood losses while keeping neighborhoods intact in communities nationwide. Elevation involves raising the lowest habitable floor above the 100-year or base flood elevation (BFE). Alternatively, elevation entails raising critical components of a building above expected flood levels, including, for example, the [heating, ventilating, and air conditioning], electrical circuitry or other systems that can be damaged by contact with water....

Flood-proofing techniques can provide protection to certain types of buildings. Although the [National Flood Insurance Plan] does not allow flood proofing of new residential structures..., it is a reasonable mitigation tool for some other types of buildings. Nonresidential buildings can be constructed to withstand anticipated flood forces, and in some instances, older buildings can be retrofitted with flood-proof materials.

Seismic retrofit programs can be cost-effective approaches to reducing earthquake vulnerability. The objective is to make buildings and infrastructure resistant to the effects of ground shaking and liquefaction [of underlying soils]. Both structural and nonstructural retrofit techniques can be adopted to minimize casualties and reduce damages. Low-cost techniques include securing suspended ceilings, bolting bookcases to the walls, or fastening heavy equipment like computers to prevent injury to occupants during earthquake tremors....

...[T]he most effective way to promote structural mitigation is through the creation, implementation, and enforcement of *building codes* that reflect adequate standards of protection for specific hazard risks.

Strict compliance with the letter as well as the spirit of the building code is especially critical in the aftermath of a disaster. It is understandable that residents and property owners want to rebuild their homes and businesses as quickly as possible following a hurricane or other large-scale event....However, the urge to return to normalcy must not be indulged at the sacrifice of public health and safety. Nor should the rebuilding process take place so quickly that valuable mitigation opportunities are lost.

Some local jurisdictions have moratoria that can be activated during a state of emergency following a natural hazard event. Moratoria provide local officials the time needed to assess the extent of site-specified hazard impacts and to re-map high-hazard areas to reflect actual damages. Moratoria can also help local decision makers set priorities for response and long term recovery efforts and to consider mitigation measures to reduce the risk of future disasters. Moratoria are often used to prevent property owners from rebuilding damaged structures before an acquisition program can be put in motion, or to activate new regulations for elevation and other property protection measures.

The town of Nags Head, located on the hurricane prone Outer Banks of North Carolina, has building moratoria of various lengths that can be activated following a disaster. An initial, 48-hour moratorium goes into effect immediately. Replacement of destroyed structures is halted for 30 days. In the meantime, planners and the Board of Commissioners may adjust the zoning code to reflect new inlets or eroded areas or to incorporate mitigation standards. All replacement construction must comply with the new ordinances established during the 30-day moratorium. Building permits issued prior to the storm are revoked for at least 30 days. These moratoria have proved useful to local officials in the post-disaster phase to restructure the regulatory regime according to damage actually sustained and newly identified hazard risks.

Environmental Preservation

...[W]etlands, hillsides, shorelines, floodplains, riparian areas, forests, and habitats can provide important and cost-effective natural services and benefits, not the least of which is hazard mitigation. A sustainability approach to natural hazards understands that frequently the most effective way to reduce vulnerability of people and property is to preserve a healthy, well-functioning ecosystem.

Many communities have initiatives to protect and manage these [systems]. Soil conservation and steep slope preservation measures typically place restrictions on the grading of hillsides and prohibit development on landslide-prone slopes. Oceanfront setbacks establish a minimum distance between the existing shoreline and the buildable portion of a lot. Dune preservation laws help protect development against storm surge flooding by restricting pedestrian and vehicular access, and by prohibiting the leveling or lowering of dunes for visual access. Wetland protection and restoration can be effective for stormwater management and floodwater retention. These and other measures are implemented through regulation, acquisition, incentives for private landowners, or partnerships with nonprofit conservation and land trust agencies.

...[I]n general, these measures are most successful when used in concert with state and federal management programs....

Education and Outreach

The key to [instilling a] "mitigation ethic" often depends on community consciousness....An array of innovative approaches to foster community support for hazard mitigation and disaster preparedness is available to local government's intent on generating a well-informed citizenry. Hazard mapping, disclosure laws, disaster warning, and public awareness campaigns are some of the more commonly used measures to disseminate information to citizens about their hazard risks....

Financing Local Mitigation Strategies

Local elected officials must balance many competing interests when allocating limited local resources....However, many local governing boards have come to realize that money invested in hazard mitigation activities can protect the community's tax base, saving millions of dollars in property damage by reducing losses from inevitable natural hazards. The economic value of mitigation is particularly evident in communities that have carried out acquisition projects involving repetitive flood structures. Although the initial outlays are steep, it has proven to be a cost-effective strategy over the long term to remove families from flood-hazard properties. Keeping businesses open, residents in their homes, and basic services operating following an emergency results in economic security and social stability for local communities.

State and federal aid is a large part of many local governments' revenue stream. Grants and other aid programs help local governments meet specific needs, including emergency preparedness, disaster recovery, and hazard mitigation. States that experience multiple disaster declarations have been able to funnel money to local governments to carry out large mitigation projects, such as massive buyouts of repetitively flooded structures and elevations of homes in entire neighborhoods.

While outside sources of funding pay for the bulk of large-scale mitigation projects, many creative local governments are becoming more self-reliant when it comes to financing mitigation activities. Local governments have used capital improvement funding, taxes and special assessments, utility fees, municipal bonds, regulatory fees, and other methods of raising revenue to pay for mitigation....Some of the most effective mitigation strategies may require no additional money at all, just a shift in thinking, particularly with regard to land use planning and growth management.

NOTES

1. Local planning is an essential part of hazard mitigation. Some federal laws encourage (and sometimes require) states, tribes, and local governments to have mitigation strategies for natural hazards. Examples include the Coastal Zone Management Act, the Community Rating System of the National Flood Insurance Program, the Safe Drinking Water Act, and the Water Resources Planning Act. Also, many federal programs, such as the National Landslide Hazards Mitigation Strategy, recommend closer partnerships between states and their local governments, where most mitigation necessarily occurs.

2. More specifically, the Disaster Mitigation Act of 2000, U.S.C. §5112 et seq., sometimes called DMA2K, encourages states and local governments to identify natural hazards in their areas and develop plans to reduce the risk. State and local governments that have an approved mitigation plan are eligible to receive increased financial assistance under the Hazard Mitigation Grant Program. Although approved plans need only account for natural disasters, FEMA encourages plans to address "manmade hazards" too.

   State mitigation plans require significant public involvement and must address five basic elements: (1) a description of the planning process; (2) an assessment of the risks faced; (3) a strategy for reducing risks; (4) coordination; and (5) maintenance.

Local mitigation plans are similar to state plans. One difference is that local plans must also incorporate multijurisdictional plans to allow local governments to work together to address large regional hazards. The process of creating local and multijurisdictional plans will typically include members of communities, businesses, universities, public agencies, and nonprofit organizations. For more on the contours of planning and disaster resilience, see Lisa Grow Sun, *Smart Growth in Dumb Places: Sustainability, Disaster, and the Future of the American City,* 2011 B.Y.U. L. Rev. 2157 (2011) and Patricia E. Salkin, *Sustainability at the Edge: The Opportunity and Responsibility of Local Governments to Effectively Plan for Natural Disaster Mitigation, in* Losing Ground: A Nation on Edge 125 (John Nolon & Daniel Rodriguez eds., 2007).

3. Some hazard-mitigation planning now incorporates climate change. Following the 2008 Iowa floods that inundated Iowa City, Cedar Rapids, and many smaller towns, the EPA launched a pilot project to consider how the latest climate science could be integrated into planning efforts in the state, including local hazard mitigation plans. *See* Robert R.M. Verchick & Abby Hall, *Adapting to Climate Change while Planning for Disaster: Footholds, Rope Lines, and the Iowa Floods,* 2011 B.Y.U. L. Rev. 2201 (2011). In 2010, FEMA and the EPA entered a Memorandum of Agreement, making it easier for the two agencies to help communities integrate climate-change data and sustainability principles into their planning efforts. *See* Memorandum of Agreement between the Dep't of Homeland Sec. (DHS), Fed. Emergency Mgmt. Agency (FEMA), and the Envtl. Prot. Agency (EPA) (May 12, 2010), *available at* http://www.epa.gov/dced/pdf/2011_0114_fema-epa-moa.pdf.

C. A COMMON SNAG: LAND ACQUISITION

After a major disaster, it is common for a municipality to acquire land for reasons of safety or redevelopment. Officials generally prefer voluntary "buyouts" or other arms-length transactions. They are often faster and, of course, more politically acceptable. But sometimes voluntary transactions are not possible, either because of "holdout" problems or because the owners cannot be found. Is it appropriate for local government to use eminent domain to acquire property from current landowners and then turn it over to developers for reuse? Consider the opinions in the following case.

545 U.S. 469, 125 S. Ct. 2655, 162 L. Ed. 2d 439 (2005) (footnotes omitted)

Justice STEVENS delivered the opinion of the Court.

In 2000, the city of New London approved a development plan that, in the words of the Supreme Court of Connecticut, was "projected to create in excess of 1,000 jobs, to increase tax and other revenues, and to revitalize an economically distressed city, including its downtown and waterfront areas." In assembling the land needed for this project, the city's development agent has purchased property from willing sellers and proposes to use the power of eminent domain to acquire the remainder of the property from unwilling owners in exchange for just compensation. The question presented is whether the city's proposed disposition of this property qualifies as a "public use" within the meaning of the Takings Clause of the Fifth Amendment to the Constitution....

Two polar propositions are perfectly clear. On the one hand, it has long been accepted that the sovereign may not take the property of A for the sole purpose of transferring it to another private party B, even though A is paid just compensation. On the other hand, it is equally clear that a State may transfer property from one private party to another if future "use by the public" is the purpose of the taking; the condemnation of land for a railroad with common-carrier duties is a familiar example. Neither of these propositions, however, determines the disposition of this case.

As for the first proposition, the City would no doubt be forbidden from taking petitioners' land for the purpose of conferring a private benefit on a particular private party. Nor would the City be allowed to take property under the mere pretext of a public purpose, when its actual purpose was to bestow a private benefit. The takings before us, however, would be executed pursuant to a "carefully considered" development plan. The trial judge and all the members of the Supreme Court of Connecticut agreed that there was no evidence of an illegitimate purpose in this case.

On the other hand, this is not a case in which the City is planning to open the condemned land—at least not in its entirety—to use by the general public. Nor will the private lessees of the land in any sense be required to operate like common carriers, making their services available to all comers. But although such a projected use would be sufficient to satisfy the public use requirement, this "Court long ago rejected any literal requirement that condemned property be put into use for the general public." Indeed, while many state courts in the mid-19th century endorsed "use by the public" as the proper definition of public use, that narrow view steadily eroded over time. Not only was the "use by the public" test difficult to administer (e.g., what proportion of the public need have access to the property? at what price?), but it proved to be impractical given the diverse and always evolving needs of society. Accordingly, when this Court began applying the Fifth Amendment to the States at the close of the 19th century, it embraced the broader and more natural interpretation of public use as "public purpose." Thus, in a case upholding a mining company's use of an aerial bucket line to transport ore over property it did not own, Justice Holmes' opinion for the Court stressed "the inadequacy of use by the general public as a universal test." We have repeatedly and consistently rejected that narrow test ever since.

The disposition of this case therefore turns on the question whether the City's development plan serves a "public purpose." Without exception, our cases have defined that concept broadly, reflecting our longstanding policy of deference to legislative judgments in this field.

In Berman v. Parker, 348 U.S. 26 (1954), this Court upheld a redevelopment plan targeting a blighted area of Washington, D.C., in which most of the housing for the area's 5,000 inhabitants was beyond repair. Under the plan, the area would be condemned and part of it utilized for the construction of streets, schools, and other public facilities. The remainder of the land would be leased or sold to private parties for the purpose of redevelopment, including the construction of low-cost housing.

The owner of a department store located in the area challenged the condemnation, pointing out that his store was not itself blighted and arguing that the creation of a "better balanced, more attractive community" was not a valid public use. Writing for a unanimous Court, Justice Douglas refused to evaluate this claim in isolation, deferring instead to the legislative and agency judgment that the area "must be planned as a whole" for the plan to be successful. The Court explained that "community redevelopment programs need not, by force of the Constitution, be on a piecemeal basis—lot by lot, building by building." The public use underlying the taking was unequivocally affirmed:

> We do not sit to determine whether a particular housing project is or is not desirable. The concept of the public welfare is broad and inclusive....The values it represents are spiritual as well as physical, aesthetic as well as monetary. It is within the power of the legislature to determine that the community should be beautiful as well as healthy, spacious as well as clean, well-balanced as well as carefully patrolled. In the present case, the Congress and its authorized agencies have made determinations that take into account a wide variety of values. It is not for us to reappraise them. If those who govern the District of Columbia decide that the Nation's Capital should be beautiful as well as sanitary, there is nothing in the Fifth Amendment that stands in the way.

In Hawaii Housing Authority v. Midkiff, 467 U.S. 229 (1984), the Court considered a Hawaii statute whereby fee title was taken from lessors and transferred to lessees (for just compensation) in order to reduce the concentration of land ownership. We unanimously upheld the statute and rejected the Ninth Circuit's view that it was "a naked attempt on the part of the state of Hawaii to take the property of A and transfer it to B solely for B's private use and benefit." Reaffirming *Berman*'s deferential approach to legislative judgments in this field, we concluded that the State's purpose of eliminating the "social and economic evils of a land oligopoly" qualified as a valid public use. Our opinion also rejected the contention that the mere fact that the State immediately transferred the properties to private individuals upon condemnation somehow diminished the public character of the taking. "[I]t is only the taking's purpose, and not its mechanics," we explained, that matters in determining public use....

Viewed as a whole, our jurisprudence has recognized that the needs of society have varied between different parts of the Nation, just as they have evolved over time in response to changed circumstances. Our earliest cases in particular embodied a strong theme of federalism, emphasizing the "great respect" that we owe to state legislatures and state courts in discerning local public needs. For more than a century, our public use jurisprudence has wisely eschewed rigid formulas and intrusive scrutiny in favor of affording legislatures broad latitude in determining what public needs justify the use of the takings power.

Those who govern the City were not confronted with the need to remove blight in the Fort Trumbull area, but their determination that the area was sufficiently distressed to justify a program of economic rejuvenation is entitled to our deference. The City has carefully formulated an economic development plan that it believes will provide appreciable benefits to the community, including—but by no means limited to—new jobs and increased tax revenue. As with other exercises in urban planning and development, the City is endeavoring to coordinate a variety of commercial, residential, and recreational uses of land, with the hope that they will form a whole greater than the sum of its parts. To effectuate this plan, the City has invoked a state statute that specifically authorizes the use of eminent domain to promote economic development. Given the comprehensive character of the plan, the thorough deliberation that preceded its adoption, and the limited scope of our review, it is appropriate for us, as it was in *Berman*, to resolve the challenges of the individual owners, not on a piecemeal basis, but rather in light of the entire plan. Because that plan unquestionably serves a public purpose, the takings challenged here satisfy the public use requirement of the Fifth Amendment.

To avoid this result, petitioners urge us to adopt a new bright-line rule that economic development does not qualify as a public use. Putting aside the unpersuasive suggestion that the City's plan will provide only purely economic benefits, neither precedent nor logic supports petitioners' proposal. Promoting economic development is a traditional and long accepted function of government. There is, moreover, no principled way of distinguishing economic development from the other public purposes that we have recognized....It would be incongruous to hold that the City's interest in the economic benefits to be derived from the development of the Fort Trumbull area has less of a public character than any of those other interests. Clearly, there is no basis for exempting economic development from our traditionally broad understanding of public purpose.

It is further argued that without a bright-line rule nothing would stop a city from transferring citizen A's property to citizen B for the sole reason that citizen B will put the property to a more productive use and thus pay more taxes. Such a one-to-one transfer of property, executed outside the confines of an integrated development plan, is not presented in this case. While such an unusual exercise of government power would certainly raise a suspicion that a private purpose was afoot, the hypothetical cases posited by petitioners can be confronted if and when they arise. They do not warrant the crafting of an artificial restriction on the concept of public use.

Alternatively, petitioners maintain that for takings of this kind we should require a "reasonable certainty" that the expected public benefits will actually accrue. Such a rule, however, would represent an even greater departure from our precedent. "When the legislature's purpose is legitimate and its means are not irrational, our cases make clear that empirical debates over the wisdom of takings—no less than debates over the wisdom of other kinds of socioeconomic legislation—are not to be carried out in the federal courts." *Midkiff*.…The disadvantages of a heightened form of review are especially pronounced in this type of case. Orderly implementation of a comprehensive redevelopment plan obviously requires that the legal rights of all interested parties be established before new construction can be commenced. A constitutional rule that required postponement of the judicial approval of every condemnation until the likelihood of success of the plan had been assured would unquestionably impose a significant impediment to the successful consummation of many such plans.

Justice KENNEDY, concurring.

A court applying rational-basis review under the Public Use Clause should strike down a taking that, by a clear showing, is intended to favor a particular private party, with only incidental or pretextual public benefits, just as a court applying rational-basis review under the Equal Protection Clause must strike down a government classification that is clearly intended to injure a particular class of private parties, with only incidental or pretextual public justifications.

A court confronted with a plausible accusation of impermissible favoritism to private parties should treat the objection as a serious one and review the record to see if it has merit, though with the presumption that the government's actions were reasonable and intended to serve a public purpose. Here, the trial court conducted a careful and extensive inquiry into "whether, in fact, the development plan is of primary benefit to…the developer [i.e., Corcoran Jennison], and private businesses which may eventually locate in the plan area [e.g., Pfizer], and in that regard, only of incidental benefit to the city.″...Even the dissenting justices on the Connecticut Supreme Court agreed that respondents' development plan was intended to revitalize the local economy, not to serve the interests of Pfizer, Corcoran Jennison, or any other private party. This case, then, survives the meaningful rational basis review that in my view is required under the Public Use Clause.

Petitioners and their *amici* argue that any taking justified by the promotion of economic development must be treated by the courts as *per se* invalid, or at least presumptively invalid. Petitioners overstate the need for such a rule, however, by making the incorrect assumption that review under *Berman* and *Midkiff* imposes no meaningful judicial limits on the government's power to condemn any property it likes. A broad *per se* rule or a strong presumption of invalidity, furthermore, would prohibit a large number of government takings that have the purpose and expected effect of conferring substantial benefits on the public at large and so do not offend the Public Use Clause.

My agreement with the Court that a presumption of invalidity is not warranted for economic development takings in general, or for the particular takings at issue in this case, does not foreclose the possibility that a more stringent standard of review than that announced in [earlier cases] might be appropriate for a more narrowly drawn category of takings. There may be private transfers in which the risk of undetected impermissible favoritism of private parties is so acute that a presumption (rebuttable or otherwise) of invalidity is warranted under the Public Use Clause. This demanding level of scrutiny, however, is not required simply because the purpose of the taking is economic development.

This is not the occasion for conjecture as to what sort of cases might justify a more demanding standard, but it is appropriate to underscore aspects of the instant case that convince me no departure from [precedent] is appropriate here. This taking occurred in the context of a comprehensive development plan meant to address a serious city-wide depression, and the projected economic benefits of the project cannot be characterized as *de minimis*. The identity of most of the private beneficiaries were unknown at the time the city formulated its plans. The city complied with elaborate procedural requirements that facilitate review of the record and inquiry into the city's purposes. In sum, while there may be categories of cases in which the transfers are so suspicious, or the procedures employed so prone to abuse, or the purported benefits are so trivial or implausible, that courts should presume an impermissible private purpose, no such circumstances are present in this case.

Justice O'CONNOR, with whom Chief Justice REHNQUIST, Justice SCALIA, and Justice THOMAS join, dissenting.

This case returns us for the first time in over 20 years to the hard question of when a purportedly "public purpose" taking meets the public use requirement. It presents an issue of first impression: Are economic development takings constitutional? I would hold that they are not. We are guided by two precedents about the taking of real property by eminent domain....

The Court's holdings in *Berman* and *Midkiff* were true to the principle underlying the Public Use Clause. In both those cases, the extraordinary, precondemnation use of the targeted property inflicted affirmative harm on society—in *Berman* through blight resulting from extreme poverty and in *Midkiff* through oligopoly resulting from extreme wealth. And in both cases, the relevant legislative body had found that eliminating the existing property use was necessary to remedy the harm. Thus a public purpose was realized when the harmful use was eliminated. Because each taking *directly* achieved a public benefit, it did not matter that the property was turned over to private use. Here, in contrast, New London does not claim that Susette Kelo's and Wilhelmina Dery's well-maintained homes are the source of any social harm. Indeed, it could not so claim without adopting the absurd argument that any single-family home that might be razed to make way for an apartment building, or any church that might be replaced with a retail store, or any small business that might be more lucrative if it were instead part of a national franchise, is inherently harmful to society and thus within the government's power to condemn.

In moving away from our decisions sanctioning the condemnation of harmful property use, the Court today significantly expands the meaning of public use. It holds that the sovereign may take private property currently put to ordinary private use, and give it over for new, ordinary private use, so long as the new use is predicted to generate some secondary benefit for the public—such as increased tax revenue, more jobs, maybe even aesthetic pleasure. But nearly any lawful use of real private property can be said to generate some incidental benefit to the public. Thus, if predicted (or even guaranteed) positive side-effects are enough to render transfer from one private party to another constitutional, then the words "for public use" do not realistically exclude *any* takings, and thus do not exert any constraint on the eminent domain power....

Any property may now be taken for the benefit of another private party, but the fallout from this decision will not be random. The beneficiaries are likely to be those citizens with disproportionate influence and power in the political process, including large corporations and development firms. As for the victims, the government now has license to transfer property from those with fewer resources to those with more. The Founders cannot have intended this perverse result. "[T]hat alone is a *just* government," wrote James Madison, "which *impartially* secures to every man, whatever is his *own.*"

Justice THOMAS, dissenting.

The most natural reading of the [Takings] Clause is that it allows the government to take property only if the government owns, or the public has a legal right to use, the property, as opposed to taking it for any public purpose or necessity whatsoever. At the time of the founding, dictionaries primarily defined the noun "use" as "[t]he act of employing any thing to any purpose." 2 S.

Johnson, A Dictionary of the English Language 2194 (4th ed. 1773) (hereinafter Johnson). The term "use," moreover, "is from the Latin *utor*, which means "to use, make use of, avail one's self of, employ, apply, enjoy, etc." J. Lewis, Law of Eminent Domain §165, p. 224, n.4 (1888) (hereinafter Lewis). When the government takes property and gives it to a private individual, and the public has no right to use the property, it strains language to say that the public is "employing" the property, regardless of the incidental benefits that might accrue to the public from the private use. The term "public use," then, means that either the government or its citizens as a whole must actually "employ" the taken property....

Our current Public Use Clause jurisprudence, as the Court notes, has rejected this natural reading of the Clause. The Court adopted its modern reading blindly, with little discussion of the Clause's history and original meaning, in two distinct lines of cases: first, in cases adopting the "public purpose" interpretation of the Clause, and second, in cases deferring to legislatures' judgments regarding what constitutes a valid public purpose. Those questionable cases converged in the boundlessly broad and deferential conception of "public use" adopted by this Court in *Berman* and *Midkiff*, cases that take center stage in the Court's opinion. The weakness of those two lines of cases, and consequently *Berman* and *Midkiff*, fatally undermines the doctrinal foundations of the Court's decision. Today's questionable application of these cases is further proof that the "public purpose" standard is not susceptible of principled application. This Court's reliance by rote on this standard is ill advised and should be reconsidered....

The Court relies almost exclusively on this Court's prior cases to derive today's far-reaching, and dangerous, result....When faced with a clash of constitutional principle and a line of unreasoned cases wholly divorced from the text, history, and structure of our founding document, we should not hesitate to resolve the tension in favor of the Constitution's original meaning.

NOTES AND QUESTIONS

1. Justice Thomas noted in his dissent that "[o]ver 97 percent of the individuals forcibly removed from their homes by the 'slum-clearance' project upheld by this Court in *Berman* were black." Of course, if economic development programs are successful, the beneficiaries from increased employment and better-funded government services might also be poor and minority. How, if at all, should the Court take into account potential racial and class dimensions of the problem?

2. Are you persuaded by Justice O'Connor's effort to distinguish prior cases (including the *Midkiff* decision, which she authored)? Under her proposed approach, how would efforts to assemble land for new development fare in a city that had been destroyed in a flood or

earthquake? What would it take to satisfy the test suggested by Justice
Kennedy in his concurrence?

3. There is serious political opposition to the use of eminent domain for
   private development. After *Kelo*, 42 states enacted legal reforms to limit
   the state use of eminent domain in response to that decision. In 2006,
   barely a year after Hurricane Katrina, citizens of Louisiana approved two
   amendments to the state constitution in response to *Kelo*. *See* 2006 La.
   Acts 851 (amending La. Const. art. I, §§4(B), 21(A), and adding art. VI,
   §21(D)); 2006 La. Acts 859 (adding La. Const. art. I, §4(H)). The
   amendments put limits on the state's ability to transfer expropriated
   property and restricted the state's eminent domain power to traditional
   public uses such as transportation, flood control, and the construction
   of public buildings. One provision holds that neither "economic
   development" nor "any incidental benefit to the public" can be
   considered in assessing a state's "public purpose." *See* La. Const. art. I,
   §4(B). Law professor Frank Alexander argues that these restrictions
   slowed recovery efforts in New Orleans by making it harder to condemn
   damaged structures that had been abandoned by their owners.
   (Although Louisiana allows expropriation to eradicate blight, the
   meaning of that term is often debated and disputes cause delay.) *See*
   Frank S. Alexander, *Louisiana Land Reform in the Storm's Aftermath*, 53
   Loy. L. Rev. 727 (2007). Because of the states' reaction to *Kelo*, some
   commentators argue the decision has ironically resulted in an overall
   reduction in economic-development takings authority in the United
   States. *See* Gregory J. Robson, *Kelo v. City of New London: Its Ironic
   Impact on Takings Authority*, 44 Urb. Law. 865 (2012).

D. LEARNING FROM THE RECENT PAST

Perhaps the best way to understand how law and politics affect disaster
recovery is to see them in action. This section studies communities that have
taken notable, and often controversial, steps on the road to recovery. We begin
with a retelling of recovery efforts in Kobe, Japan, following the 1995 Hanshin
Earthquake. This piece appeared in the New Orleans *Times-Picayune* less than
three months after Katrina, when residents of the Crescent City were thirsting
for ideas and inspiration.

1. KOBE, JAPAN

Jed Horne, Carving a Better City

Times-Picayune (New Orleans), Nov. 13, 2005, A1

Three months after [the Hanshin Earthquake]...Japan's sixth-largest city was still in ruins. Hundreds of acres of a once teeming metropolis had been reduced to rubble. Gas and water service was spotty. Roads and public transportation had collapsed, as had the morale of hundreds of thousands of evacuees still fighting for space in trailer-like emergency housing....

Ten years later, one can stand on Flower Road across from Kobe's city hall and have no clue that a little after dawn on a frigid January morning in 1995, the building's fifth floor pancaked and suddenly became the fourth floor. Hulking office towers broke ranks and lurched into the street. A walk past the busy casbah of shops in the shadow of the elevated Hanshin Expressway near Kobe's eastern boundary offers no hint that hundreds of yards of the elevated superhighway shuddered on massive concrete columns and crashed sideways onto the ground. The port has repaired its caved-in wharves and the towering derricks that pluck shipping containers the size of small houses from freighter decks. Electrified trains come and go with clockwork precision over track that coiled like concertina wire during the quake. The screams of the elderly echo only in the memory of those who tried to free them from shattered cottages before they burned to death. A decade after the Great Hanshin Disaster killed 6,400 people—90 percent of them in the 20 seconds the quake lasted—and charred hundreds of acres of once densely urban landscape, Kobe largely has healed. The skyline is studded with glistening new apartment towers. Low-rise neighborhoods have been replotted with wider, straighter streets and housing has been rebuilt with fireproof materials.

The comeback attests to what Lawrence Vale [of the Massachusetts Institute of Technology] calls the "resilience" of cities, and it is a mighty if not quite unstoppable force. Urban resilience brought back London after the blitz and downtown New York after Sept. 11. It restored Mexico City, a colossus, after the pulverizing 1985 earthquake, and smaller cities—Tulsa, [Oklahoma], Grand Forks, [North Dakota]—after terrible floods....

The quake, which registered 7.3 on the Richter scale, damaged hundreds of thousands of buildings and destroyed 79,283 Kobe housing units, a figure roughly identical to estimates of New Orleans' eventual loss [after Hurricane Katrina].

About 300,000 victims of the earthquake took refuge in schoolhouses, gymnasiums and other makeshift shelters under deteriorating conditions as vile as the post-Katrina Superdome. Trapped there for weeks, they were then assigned, in some cases for years, to trailer camps.

Immediate Moratorium

The quake struck at 5:46 a.m. and within the hour Mayor Kazutoshi Sasayama had been picked up at his home by the vice mayor, his right-hand man and political heir apparent. In the 45 minutes it took to weave their way through streets not choked by fallen buildings and jumbled cars and buses, Sasayama tried to assess the damage....

"Forty-five minutes of direct observation gave him enough information to start in on the whole thing," said Haruo Hayashi, a Kyoto University professor who specializes in earthquake mitigation. From the destruction he witnessed first-hand, Sasayama could roughly estimate the destruction he had not gotten close enough to see. In his head he adjusted the master plan accordingly, Hayashi said....

Sasayama's first and most aggressive step[] in rebuilding Kobe was to impose a moratorium on rebuilding anything at all. The goal was simple: to prevent Kobe from following in the footsteps of post–World War II Tokyo and winding up with endless miles of shantytowns cobbled together by homeowners guided only by urgent need, limited resources and no central planning....Sophisticated members of the Kobe intelligentsia, Hayashi among them, understood what Sasayama was up to and took heart in his tough stance as an early sign that Kobe was going to come back and come back better. But the grassroots political repercussions were toxic. The government was accused of exploiting the disaster to ram through a redesign of Kobe that otherwise would have been politically impossible. Planners were dubbed kajibadorobo by critics, using a Japanese term that translates more or less as "thieves at the scene of a fire." The vice mayor was undone by the intense hostility, which also took the form of lawsuits to stop City Hall. He committed suicide on the first anniversary of the quake. Sasayama rode out the firestorm and two years later was rewarded for the recovery's slowly emerging promise with an overwhelming re-election margin.

Strong Planning

For Sadaharu Ueno, who owned his home but, like many Japanese, not the land underneath it, being denied permission to rebuild seemed like being stripped of his only material asset of real worth....

Ueno and his wife lived in their car for a day or two until they could get to a daughter's place in Osaka. They were eventually able to secure temporary housing in a box about the size of a shipping container set up by Ueno's employer, a manufacturer of metal processing machinery. It was their home for five years and far from [the Rokkomichi district, where they used to live]. But Ueno stayed in touch with old neighbors through their machizukuri kyogikai, or town-building organization. In due course the group, like others throughout Kobe, would demand—and get—a role in the process that led to the redevelopment of the area from a warren of traditional one- and two-story houses vulnerable to both quakes and fire, into a cluster of high-rise towers.

They surround a small, well-tended park and playground popular with skateboarding adolescents, small children and mothers.

Ironically, the park was one of the features of the redevelopment most bitterly opposed by the machizukuri. The government held its ground, insisting that open space was a life-saving necessity in the event of a future quake and fire: a place of refuge for victims and a staging ground for recovery....

Some of Ueno's neighbors gave up on Rokkomichi and moved away before the elaborate $840 million reconstruction plans could be implemented through a mix of public and private funding. But by riding herd on the government as a member of the machizukuri organization and refusing to relinquish his rights as a stakeholder in the community—albeit the lowly rights of a mere tenant—Ueno eventually secured compensation in the form of a rent-subsidized two-bedroom apartment on the fifth floor of one of the towers. It's a decent place, but not as big as the house destroyed in the earthquake, and the subsidy lasts for only five years. After that, the Uenos are on their own....

Moving Quickly

Mayor Sasayama's planners had raced furiously to create a vision for Kobe's recovery in time for their funding request to be included in the national budget.

They were ably assisted by other professionals. Kazuyoshi Ohnishi, an architect and professor at Kobe University, mustered 1,000 student volunteers and within weeks they had completed a building-by-building assessment of the damage....Tokyo responded with $58 billion, chiefly to repair infrastructure throughout the prefecture centered around Kobe, in the first three years after the quake. In seeking money to rebuild burned-out cityscapes, Kobe proposed "land readjustments," a mechanism in place since the end of World War II that encouraged replacing narrow winding streets and wooden houses with wider avenues and fewer structures, all of them built with fire-resistant materials....

Some properties were expropriated outright to make room for the improved street grid, and most lots were trimmed. The tradeoff was the higher property values that would be realized in a better-built community, city officials argued. All told, 11 ravaged neighborhoods were subjected to the land-readjustment process. In Rokkomichi and two other more drastically overhauled communities, the government built the new housing—mostly high-rise condominiums—and moved residents into them. To generate additional money, they added floors over and above what was needed to accommodate the original population. The extra space was sold on the open market to offset construction costs....

Kobe's grand plan cost Rokkomichi some of its residents. As the plans made their way through the Japanese legislature, the residents with the most at stake in their outcome were kept in the dark for months, an interval during which many of them gave up. Today, only a third of the original community abides in Rokkomichi. The rest are newcomers....

The earthquake response required different thinking, Tarumi came to realize. Neighborhoods were not just about bricks and mortar and money. Their vigor and resilience hinged on flesh-and-blood people, many of whom— including Ueno and even a pillar of the business establishment like Kusuba— were turning up at City Hall to wave placards in the faces of Tarumi's staff as the bureaucrats arrived at work. Eventually, the government not only yielded to community input but came to see positive value in formalizing relations with the machizukuri organizations....

But Tarumi makes no apologies for the goals of the planning process: the mix of earthquake- and fire-proof towers and low-rise structures that replaced the rickety traditional neighborhoods all across Kobe, 110,000 units of public and private housing that were created in short order. Not only was haste necessary to secure funding in the upcoming fiscal year, Tarumi saw himself in a race against the dangerous hodge-podge that would result if homeowners simply rebuilt what they had lost, with gaping holes left by those who chose not to return. Kobe needed a guiding vision of its future both to mitigate future earthquake disaster and the equally costly economic blight that had set in when planning principles were ignored. The alternative was chaos and further degradation as already traumatized communities came back partially or not at all....

Opposed to Handouts

Unlike FEMA in the United States, the central government apparatus responsible for emergency management in Japan is philosophically opposed to direct handouts. While Kobe's postquake infrastructure was being upgraded, private business and individual householders were accorded tax breaks and temporary exemptions, but otherwise left to fend for themselves. Eighty percent of Kobe's 2,000 small-to-medium-size businesses failed....

Eventually funded to the tune of $9 billion by the central government, a Special Fund for the Great Hanshin Disaster was used to provide low-interest loans to Kobe city government, which in turn passed along some of the money in the form of rent subsidies, aid to the elderly and handicapped, and the like. At heart, these were violations of the ban on direct subsidies to quake victims, but the central government had the good sense to look the other away.

Still Recovering

[While Kobe's recovery is impressive, there is below the surface a more complicated reality.] The port, for example, has not come all the way back and schemes to reorient Kobe's economy toward tourism, robotics and information technology remain nascent. At the local level, Nagata, to cite just one laggard community, has not rebounded to its prequake vitality.

Private-sector investment has been inattentive to the needs of the working poor and instead has followed well-to-do residents to the east end of the city, closer to Osaka, epicenter of the megalopolis of 15 million to 20 million people that includes Kobe and provides a source of work for many of its residents.

Nagata's population is still off by almost 20 percent. Huge apartment towers have gone up along the edges of the community, but many apartments are empty, as are a goodly number of storefronts in the enormous triple-decker shopping plaza that replaced the Taisho Suji arcade, a covered street market that became an inferno after the quake.

Kobe remains...vulnerable to another quake...but no one seriously proposed abandoning the city. The consensus that immediately prevailed within the governing class was to rebuild, not as it was but as it needed to be to assure greater public safety in the future.

NOTES AND QUESTIONS

1. Kobe is one of the most-studied examples of urban recovery in disaster literature. The take-home lesson is often said to be that successful recovery depends on fast action and decisive leadership. In what ways did those elements benefit Kobe's recovery? In what ways did they create barriers and hardship?

2. Jed Horne writes that after the Hanshin Earthquake demolished Kobe, "no one seriously proposed abandoning the city." Should that option have been on the table? If so, how should the decision whether to abandon or rebuild have been reached? Would a cost-benefit approach to the question be helpful? *See* Robert W. Hahn, *The Economics of Rebuilding Cities: Reflections after Katrina*, The Economists' Voice, Vol. 2 (2005), No. 4, Article 1, http://www.bepress.com/ ev/vol2/iss4/art1 (arguing that cost-benefit analysis provides a starting point for deciding whether to abandon a city after it has been destroyed by "nature (or an enemy)").

3. The truth is that after a major city is ruined by catastrophe, whether natural or manmade, it is almost always rebuilt. Lawrence J. Vale & Thomas J. Campanella, *Introduction: The Cities Rise Again*, in The Resilient City: How Modern Cities Recover from Disaster 3, 4 (Lawrence J. Vale & Thomas J. Campanella eds., 2005) (offering first-century Pompeii as an exception to the rule). After the San Francisco earthquake and fire of 1906, city leaders sought to quell debates about development in an earthquake zone by downplaying the role of the earthquake and instead emphasizing the more destructive role played by the ensuing fires. That the earthquake *caused* the fires was a point, it was hoped, many outside investors would miss. *See generally*, Philip L. Fradkin, The Great Earthquake and Firestorms of 1906: How San Francisco Nearly Destroyed Itself (2005). Today it is much the same. When, in 1993, Hurricane Andrew walloped Dade County, Florida, politicians clamored to provide an $8 billion aid package to resurrect

damaged communities; no one seriously considered letting it all go. But the question of abandonment did arise—however fleetingly—when a failed levee system flooded New Orleans after Hurricane Katrina.

2. NEW ORLEANS

RICHARD CAMPANELLA, BIENVILLE'S DILEMMA: A HISTORICAL GEOGRAPHY OF NEW ORLEANS
351-354 (2008)

Various philosophies have emerged on the rebuilding of New Orleans, each with its own logic, passion, experts, and dogma. But all can be boiled down to a simple line on a map, separating areas recommended for rebuilding from those deemed best returned to nature. Where people locate their build/no-build line says as much about them—and how they view and weigh science, economics, social, and humanistic values—as it says about the geographical future of New Orleans.

One philosophy recommends the total abandonment of the metropolis. Its advocates essentially draw the build/no-build line at the metropolis' upper boundary...or above [the northern shore of Lake Pontchartrain, whose southern shore forms the upper boundary of new Orleans]. St. Louis University geologist Timothy M. Kusky first voiced the "abandonist" philosophy in a *Boston Globe* editorial entitled "Time to Move to Higher Ground" which later earned him a national audience on CBS *60 Minutes.* He readily acknowledged:

> New Orleans is one of America's great historic cities, and our *emotional response* to the disaster is to rebuild it grander and greater than before. However this may not be the *most rational* or *scientifically sound* response and could lead to *even greater human catastrophe* and *financial loss* in the future.

Abandonists like Kusky tend to be pragmatic and fiscally conservative; for them it is a rational question of hard science, hard dollars, and body counts. In making their case, they cite only the gloomiest scientific data on subsidence, coastal erosion, and sea-level rise, and dismiss humanist and cultural arguments as "emotional" or "nostalgic." Abandonists almost always have nothing to lose personally if the city does disappear, and feel no obligation to propose financial compensation plans for those who do. They are loathed in New Orleans, but occupy a seat at the table in the national discourse.

At the opposite end are those who advocate maintaining the urban footprint at all costs. Unlike abandonists, "maintainers" see this as primarily a humanist and cultural question, rather than a scientific or engineering one. To be against maintaining all neighborhoods is to be against people and against culture—worse yet, against *certain* peoples and *certain* cultures.

Maintainers tend to be passionate, oftentimes angry, and for good reason: many are flood victims and have everything to lose if the build/no-build line crosses their homes. If a levee can be built well enough to protect *them*, they reason, why not extend it around *us?* Among the most outspoken maintainers are social activists who interpret any postdiluvian adjustment to the urban perimeter as a conspiracy of "politically conservative, economically neoliberal power elites" who "are doing everything in their power to prevent (working-class African Americans) from returning." Ignoring scientific data and fiscal constraints, maintainers push the build/no-build line beyond the rural fringes of St. Bernard Parish, even all the way to the Gulf of Mexico.

In between fall the "concessionists," usually aficionados of the city, particularly its historical heart, and often residents of its unflooded sections. Concessionists struggle to balance troubling scientific data with treasured social and cultural resources. Their answer: concede certain low-lying modern subdivisions to nature—areas which, incidentally, they never found structurally appealing in the first place—and increase population density and flood protection in the higher, historically significant areas. Concessionists argue that, in the long run, this would reduce costs, minimize grief, protect the environment, and save lives. Concessionists sometimes failed to recognize, however, that footprint shrinkage itself costs money, in the form of fair and immediate compensation to homeowners.

Sensitive to accusations of elitism, concessionists soften their message with careful wordsmithing and confusing maps. They place their build/no-build line somewhere between those of the abandonists and the maintainers—sometimes near the Industrial Canal [east of the city's core] and the lakefront, usually to the exclusion of the distant, charmless, low-lying subdivisions of New Orleans East [a mainly African American part of the city]. Concessionists enjoy widespread support among many educated professionals who live on high ground, but encounter fierce resistance among maintainers, who often accuse them [of] being, at best, unrealistic utopian dreamers, and at worst, elitist, classist, racist land-grabbers.

Reports that rural, isolated lower Plaquemines Parish—home to only 14,000 people, or 2 percent of the region's population—may not receive full funding for levee maintenance seems to have spawned a fourth philosophy: push the build/no-build line down just past Belle Chasse, the only major community in upper Plaquemines Parish that adjoins the metropolitan area. Advocates include city dwellers, both concessionists and maintainers, who stand to benefit from the abandonment of lower Plaquemines because it would clear the path for aggressive coastal restoration while reducing the price tag on their own protection. Let the sediment-laden waters of the Mississippi River replenish those eroding marshes, they might contend; we need to restore them to buffer the metropolis against storm surges. What about the rural peoples who have called those marshes home for over a century? Well, as geologist Kusky put it in his now-famous abandonist editorial, it's "time to move to higher ground."

Thus, social, cultural, and humanistic values, plus a sense of personal investment, tend to push the build/no-build line in a downriver direction, while scientific and financial values nudge the line upriver. What to make of all this?

First, even the most ardent lovers of New Orleans should refrain from loathing the abandonists. After all, concessionists (and those maintainers willing to sacrifice lower Plaquemines) are essentially making the same abandonist arguments that earned Kusky the enduring hatred of many New Orleanians. They're just applying them below different lines on the map.

Second, we should probably only pencil in whatever build/no-build lines we draw, because we may well wish to change them if the going gets rough. Others have. Illinois Republican Rep. J. Dennis Hastert was among the first to hint at abandonment when he said rebuilding New Orleans "doesn't make sense to me. And it's a question that certainly we should ask." Shaken by angry responses, he later clarified his statement: "I am not advocating that the city be abandoned or relocated...." Wallace, Roberts & Todd, a design firm hired to advise the [Bring New Orleans Back] Commission, at first professed a bold maintainer philosophy ("If you plan on shrinkage, shrinkage is what you'll get") but ended up recommending concessions in their final report to the Commission. Even Kusky softened his abandonist advice and suggested the possibility of "newer, higher, stronger seawalls" for "the business and historic parts of the city."

I, too, as a geographer with both physical and cultural interests, have grappled with my concessionist recommendations when confronted by the tragic personal stories of individuals who desperately want to maintain the world they once knew and loved. Should another hurricane of the magnitude of Katrina strike New Orleans, we may see build/no-build lines erased and redrawn *en masse:* maintainers may become concessionists, concessionists may be willing to concede more, and abandonists will increase their ranks.

Finally, beware of those who claim to speak solely "for science," or "for the people." This is a complicated, interdisciplinary dilemma. The social scientist needs to be at the table as much as the physical scientist; the humanist deserves a voice as much as the economist; the poor renter of a shotgun house should be heard as much as the rich owner of a mansion. We should acknowledge that a tangle of personal, cultural, financial, nostalgic, emotional, practical, and scientific factors underlie which philosophy—abandon, maintain, or concede—we uphold for the future of New Orleans, and that *this is OK; this is acceptable.*

Postscript: Who Prevailed?

[Mayor Ray Nagin of New Orleans,] supported by most flooded homeowners and a vociferous cadre of local officials, opted for a politically safe *laissez-faire* repopulation and rebuilding policy. Abetting their victory, more through passivity than active support, was the federal government: FEMA's revised Advisory Base Flood Elevation maps, released in 2006, continued to make flood insurance available to heavily flooded areas, thus encouraging their rebuilding. And no federal buy-out plan promised compensation to homeowners and business owners who would be forced off their land in a concessionist (eminent domain) mandate coming from city, state, or federal levels. No sane person "concedes" his or her major life investment without fair compensation.

The apparent outcome: *Let people return and rebuild as they can and as they wish, and we'll act on the patterns as they fall in place.* The maintainers prevailed in drawing the build/no-build line along the existing, pre-Katrina urban edge (though the possibility of a lower-Plaquemines concession remains). Whether that line gets erased and redrawn again—by concessionists or by abandonists—will be determined by the insurance industry, by mortgage companies, by property values, by federal intervention, by disappointed residents forced to re-address their initial post-Katrina rebuilding stance, and ultimately, by nature.

NOTES AND QUESTIONS

1. Ed Blakely, an expert in planning and public redevelopment, served as an adviser both to New York City after the 9/11 attacks and to the city of Kobe, Japan, after the Hanshin Earthquake. As the preceding essay notes, he also served as Executive Director of Recovery Management for the City of New Orleans from January 2007 to May 2009. An iron-willed and outspoken figure, Blakely's tenure was often marked with controversy and questions about his effectiveness. In 2011, Blakely published a memoir about Katrina, titled, *My Storm: Managing the Recovery of New Orleans in the Wake of Katrina (The City in the Twenty-First Century)*; but not everyone was impressed. In a review, New Orleans journalist James Gill wrote, "it would take another book to list all the errors in Blakely's." James Gill, *Ed Blakely Can't Get Anything Right*, Times-Picayune (New Orleans), Jan. 18, 2012, http://www .nola.com/opinions/index.ssf/2012/01/ed_blakely_cant_get _anything_r.html.

2. Louisiana used millions of dollars in special federal Community Development Block Grants and tax credits to develop programs to rebuild the housing stock. These included two programs to promote the repair of large and small rental properties, and one, known as the Road Home program, to compensate homeowners for the costs of rebuilding. Although these programs greatly accelerated the rebuilding process, they have been criticized for not doing enough for the city's vulnerable populations. Because of funding limitations, the rental repair programs were only able to support the repair of less than one-third of the 82,000 rental units lost to hurricanes Katrina and Rita. PolicyLink, "A Long Way Home: The State of Housing Recovery in Louisiana," 6 (2008), www.policylink.org (December. 1, 2008). As for homeowners, nearly

three-quarters of Road Home applicants had gaps between the received rebuilding resources and the actual costs of repair. The average shortfall for African Americans ($39,082) was roughly $8,000 more than it was for Whites ($30,863). *Id.* at 42. In the Lower-Ninth Ward, which was almost entirely African American, the gap between a household's average damage estimate and the average government grant exceeded $75,000. *Id.* at 47. The reason for the inequality is that the formula for grant awards was based on a home's pre-storm value rather than the cost of repair. Because homes in African-American neighborhoods had lower average pre-storm values, their owners received less even when repair costs were similar to those in other neighborhoods.

3. Some residents had feared that after Katrina, New Orleans would lose its African-American identity. But two years after the storm, the city's racial profile was pretty close to what it had been before the storm. According to estimates from the U.S. Census Bureau, "the proportion of the New Orleans population that is African American fell from 66.7 percent in 2000 to 60.2 percent in 2007. The proportion of the city's population that is Asian increased from 2.3 percent in 2000 to 3.0 percent in 2007 and the proportion that is Hispanic (of any race) increased from 3.1 percent to 4.5 percent." Allison Plyer & Joy Bonaguro, Demographic Profiles of New Orleans & the Metro Area, May 21, 2009, http://www.gnocdc.org/2007Demographics/index.html (June 17, 2009). Demographers expect the percentage of African Americans and Hispanics to continue growing at a gradual rate. *See* Michelle Krupa, "Black, Hispanic Numbers Jump," Times-Picayune (New Orleans), May 14, 2009, at A1.

3. TUSCALOOSA AND JOPLIN

DAVID BEITO & DANIEL J. SMITH, TORNADO RECOVERY, HOW JOPLIN IS BEATING TUSCALOOSA

Wall Street Journal, April 13, 2012, http://online.wsj.com/news/articles/ SB10001424052702303404704577309220933715082

[On April 27, 2011], one of the worst tornadoes in American history tore through Tuscaloosa, Ala., killing 52 people and damaging or destroying 2,000 buildings. In six minutes, it put nearly one-tenth of the city's population into the unemployment line. A month later, Joplin, Mo., suffered an even more devastating blow. In a city with half the population of Tuscaloosa, a tornado killed 161 and damaged or destroyed more than 6,000 buildings.

More than 100,000 volunteers mobilized to help the stricken cities recover. A "can-do" spirit took hold, with churches, college fraternities and talk-radio stations leading the way. But a year after the tragedies, that spirit lives on far more in Joplin than in Tuscaloosa. Joplin is enjoying a renaissance while Tuscaloosa's recovery has stalled.

In Joplin, eight of 10 affected businesses have reopened, according to the city's Chamber of Commerce, while less than half in Tuscaloosa have even applied for building permits, according to city data we reviewed. Walgreens revived its Joplin store in what it calls a "record-setting" three months. In Tuscaloosa, a destroyed CVS still festers, undemolished. Large swaths of Tuscaloosa's main commercial thoroughfares remain vacant lots, and several destroyed businesses have decided to reopen elsewhere, in neighboring Northport.

The reason for Joplin's successes and Tuscaloosa's shortcomings? In Tuscaloosa, officials sought to remake the urban landscape top-down, imposing a redevelopment plan on businesses. Joplin took a bottom-up approach, allowing businesses to take the lead in recovery.

"Out of the heartbreak of disaster," declared Tuscaloosa Mayor Walt Maddox several days after his city's tornado, "rises an extraordinary opportunity to comprehensively plan and rebuild our great city better than ever before." In this transformative spirit, Tuscaloosa's city council imposed a 90-day construction moratorium in the disaster area, restricting commercial and residential redevelopment until officials could craft and adopt a long-term master plan. Many of the restrictions remained long after the moratorium officially expired. Joplin, by contrast, passed a 60-day moratorium that applied only to single-family residential structures and was lifted on a rolling basis, as each section of the city saw its debris cleared, within 60 days.

The Alabama city's recovery plan, "Tuscaloosa Forward," is indeed state-of-the-art urban planning—and that's the crux of the problem. It sets out to "courageously create a showpiece" of "unique neighborhoods that are healthy, safe, accessible, connected, and sustainable," all anchored by "village centers" for shopping (in a local economy that struggles to sustain current shopping centers). Another goal is to "preserve neighborhood character" from a "disproportionate ratio of renters to owners." The plan never mentions protecting property rights.

In Joplin, the official plan not only makes property rights a priority but clocks in at only 21 pages, compared with Tuscaloosa's 128. Joplin's plan also relied heavily on input from businesses (including through a Citizen's Advisory Recovery Team) instead of Tuscaloosa's reliance on outside consulting firms. "We need to say to our businesses, community, and to our citizens, 'If you guys want to rebuild your houses, we'll do everything we can to make it happen,'" said Joplin City Council member William Scearce in an interview.

Instead of encouraging businesses to rebuild as quickly as possible, Tuscaloosa enforced restrictive zoning rules and building codes that raised costs—prohibitively, in some cases. John Carney, owner of Express Oil Change, which was annihilated by the storm, estimates that the city's delays and regulation will cost him nearly $100,000. And trying to follow the rules often yielded mountains of red tape, as the city rejected businesses' proposals one after another.

"It's just been a hodgepodge," says Mr. Carney. "We've gotten so many mixed signals from the get go. The plans have been ever-changing." Boulevard Salon owner Tommy Metrock, one of the few business owners to rebuild on Tuscaloosa's main thoroughfare, McFarland Boulevard, says the restrictions created "chaos" as people put their livelihoods on hold while the city planned.

Joplin took a dramatically different approach. According to interviews with local business owners, right after disaster struck the city council formally and informally rolled back existing regulations, liberally waving licensing and zoning mandates. It even resisted the temptation to make "safe rooms" a condition of rebuilding.

The owner of one Joplin construction company told us that when it came to regulations, the "city just sort of backed out....We had projects that we completed before we got building permits." Said another Joplin resident: "When you have the magnitude of that disaster, really the old ways of doing things are suspended for a while until you create whatever normal is....The government was realistic to know that there is a period of time when common sense, codes and laws that are in place to protect people are suspended for the sake of the greater good."

Despite it all, Tuscaloosa officials are determined to stick to their plan. The final version of Tuscaloosa Forward is on track for approval by the City Council. The city is banking on defraying its costs through as-yet-unreceived funding from the Federal Emergency Management Agency (FEMA), the Department of Housing and Urban Development, and other federal bodies. As Tuscaloosa Forward bluntly acknowledges, full implementation of the plan is impossible without "public subsidies to leverage private capital."

Last year's decentralized volunteer response seems to be entirely forgotten by city officialdom. As Mayor Maddox recently said: If Tuscaloosa "had a trained FEMA corps on the ground" when the tornado struck, "they could have taken over organizing the volunteers immediately."

In an age of mounting deficits and limited federal attention spans, hoping for more subsidies from Washington, D.C. is a risky bet at best. Joplin's safer wager is in the good sense and independently generated resources of those individuals and businesses most directly affected by nature's fury.

NOTES AND QUESTIONS

1. Tuscaloosa's mayor, Walt Maddox, did not take kindly to the unflattering comparison between his city and Joplin. Maddox argued the situations were not parallel, noting that Tuscaloosa had a higher percentage of small businesses that were destroyed and more older buildings whose weaker construction standards had been grandfathered in. *See* Patrick Rupinski,

Opinions Divided on Tuscaloosa's Recovery Progress, Tuscaloosa News, Apr. 29, 2012, http://www.tuscaloosanews.com/article /20120429/ news/120429671?p=1&tc=pg. Do you think the comparison is fair? What is the lesson?

2.   Note that Tuscaloosa apparently had no recovery protocol in place before the tornado. As with planting a tree, the time to adopt a recovery plan is *yesterday*.

4. CHRISTCHURCH, NEW ZEALAND

CHARLES ANDERSON, CHRISTCHURCH: AFTER THE EARTHQUAKE, A CITY REBUILT IN WHOSE IMAGE?

The Guardian (London) Jan. 27, 2014, http://www.theguardian.com/cities/2014/jan/27/ christchurch-after-earthquake-rebuild-image-new-zealand

A recent international visitor to New Zealand's second largest city asked Coralie Winn why there were so many diggers in its centre tearing down buildings. It seemed they had little notion that less than three years earlier, Christchurch had endured a series of earthquakes that destroyed the city's infrastructure, homes and communities.

The most violent quake, on 22 February 2011, killed 181 people. Thousands more were made homeless, and an area more than four times the size of London's Hyde Park was deemed uninhabitable. Less than three years on, the diggers that rattle about Christchurch's gridded streets are a constant reminder of how far there is to go to recreate what was once there. "People don't comprehend," Winn said. "Rebuilding a city is complicated."

In the wake of the earthquake, Winn helped found an organisation devoted to creatively inhabiting the vacant gaps where those buildings once stood. Gaps are expected to keep opening up for at least another five years, as 70% of the central business district's (CBD) buildings come down.

Many locals cannot remember what the central city used to look like. Gravel quadrants have replaced multi-storey buildings, creating lines of sight through the city that never existed before. Many of the buildings that still stand are boarded up, with steel fencing around them as they wait to be sold or demolished. The main strip of bars and restaurants that lined the river, and was the site of the city's main entertainment hub, is now an empty lot.

Until recently, you could look through the dusty windows of a closed down cafe and still see an untouched 22 February 2011 edition of the local newspaper. And while creative novelties such as a retail mall made entirely out of steel shipping containers draw increasing numbers of visitors, the city's other main attraction is the battered and broken cathedral in the middle of the main square – a monument to what was endured.

The new Christchurch, which is being marketed as "greener, more compact, more accessible and safer," will cost in the region of NZ$40bn [US$34bn] – almost 20% of New Zealand's annual GDP. In the immediate aftermath of the earthquake, central government moved to triage the most important parts of a functioning city. Infrastructure like roads and bridges had been shattered. Silt that had bubbled up from the earth clogged sewerage systems. Powerlines were down. Homes were without working toilets for weeks, sometimes months.

The government's response was to establish a single body, the Canterbury Earthquake Recovery Authority (Cera). It was solely responsible for managing the rebuild. "If you look around the world at cities which have experienced disasters, it is single-purpose organisations that are the most efficient," said Cera's chief executive, Roger Sutton. This one was tasked with managing the complete project—from the demolition of commercial buildings and residential homes to planning the next phase of rebuilding. In the early period, almost 8,000 of the area's 180,000 homes were "red zoned", meaning land was so badly damaged that it was unlikely it could ever be rebuilt on. A further 9,100 properties were reckoned to be uninhabitable because they required such major repairs. From June 2010 to June 2012, the population for the greater Christchurch area declined by 9,200 (2%).

In times of crisis, Sutton said, it is better to be 90% right and get a message out quickly than 99% right and issue it slowly. The risk to this strategy, however, is that the missing 9% comes back to bite you. In some instances, it has. There have been protests over the way Cera has handled the red zoning of residential areas. Last November, some homeowners living in the city's hills were told their properties were too dangerous to inhabit—after being told the contrary for more than a year. Many saw this as an example of top-down leadership gone wrong.

The city's newly installed mayor, Lianne Dalziel, hopes to usher in a new era of governance that focuses on empowering community organisations to do things for themselves. "Building a resilient city starts at the grassroots, so that bottom-up meets top-down halfway," she wrote recently.
The ability to plan for, absorb, recover from and adapt to events is surely key to becoming a more resilient city. At a conference on "resilient futures", which was held in the city soon after the earthquake, Massey University's Prof Bruce Glavovic, the country's top recovery expert, criticised the purely top-down approach. "How is [Cera] going to capitalise on local culture and knowledge? How is it going to mobilise local capacity to rebuild? How is it going to enable local communities to make choices that will build safer and more sustainable communities?" he asked.

Despite such sentiment, a division of Cera was tasked with developing the city's first urban blueprint plan. Taking in 106,000 ideas from across the community, it was launched in July 2012 after a 100-day deadline. "We want this city to be distinctive with an active urban edge," said the division's general manager, Don Miskell. A team of local and international architects and designers created the plan, which involved 70 projects being constructed over the next 20 years. It imagined a compact central business district dominated by low-rise buildings. A "green frame" around the CBD would blend in with the Avon river that was being developed as a corridor of parkland through the city. It also emphasised environmentally sensitive transport, including a new light rail network, pedestrian boardwalks and cycle lanes.

Before the earthquakes, the centre's retail areas were not competing well against the rise of suburban malls: "It was clear," Miskell said, "the rebuild following the 2011 earthquake provided a great opportunity to make Christchurch better than it ever was." But some have questioned parts of that vision. While certain building codes had been changed to include height restrictions, there was no legislation to enforce building "greener." Sir Mark Solomon, the head of the local Maori tribe Ngai Tahu, recently remarked that the rebuild had not put enough emphasis on sustainability. "It was certainly one of my visions that we would adopt full green technology across the city," he told a televised panel discussion. "But if you go through the subdivisions—including our own—it's the same old, same old."

There is still debate about what Christchurch should become. The earthquake recovery minister, Gerry Brownlee, has suggested that the region's sporting heritage makes it a perfect location to become a world leading sports hub, with state-of-the-art facilities and stadia. But at grassroots level, some feel this idea is too narrow and does not represent the greater Christchurch.

"Unless people in communities understand what is happening and can relate that to their own situation, there can be a sense of anger and frustration," said community organiser Evan Smith, whose own house was red-zoned soon after the February quake. Smith advocates a return to "village values," with the city being made up of many smaller residential areas. "One thing the earthquake taught us is that you can't always rely on central services to survive," he said. "You have to rely on things within walking distance, without a car or a laptop. If you build with that in mind, you build in a lot of resilience."

With precisely this in mind, dozens of community organisations, manned by people like Smith, popped up after the earthquake. They became the voice of people on the ground while government attempted to gain an overall picture of the disaster (often the information that government had and the reality depicted by these organisations were vastly different).

These were the seeds of what Smith hoped would become more of a participatory democracy. Furthermore, he said, the opportunity to rebuild on the basis of the best modern urban planning (as opposed to the city's previous grid system, which evolved without a great deal of control) also throws up exciting possibilities. "Very few have the opportunity to do that retrospectively. It's the one shot and we have to get it right."

Smith is working on a proposal to turn the entire 11km (7 mile) red zone along the Avon river into an ecological and recreational reserve for the community. It will turn a "scar on the landscape" into a source of hope for the city, he said.

Coralie Winn's temporary projects have also helped spur that hope. Restaurant areas, innercity dance floors and music sites, she said, have all encouraged a creative rethink about what makes up a vibrant and resilient city. "We'd really like to see more of an intersection between the blueprint style and the temporary," Winn added. "They both need to one another and work together."

In the meantime, tourists with high-powered digital cameras stop and stare at machinery continuously tearing down buildings. More recently, though, another trend has emerged: tourists are also watching with curiosity as more and more buildings slowly go up.

NOTES AND QUESTIONS

1. While the mayor describes Christchurch's recovery as "bottom-up meets top-down halfway," the power of the national Canterbury Earthquake Recovery Authority (Cera) is still considerable. The agency has the ability to acquire, hold, manage, and dispose of property seemingly at will, and may relax, suspend, or extend laws for the purpose of earthquake recovery. (A review panel and appeals system does exist.) *See, generally,* Cera: Canterbury Earthquake Recovery Authority, http://cera.govt.nz. What are the advantages and pitfalls of such an approach?

2. In an annual review of the recovery process published in 2013, Cera received generally good marks for management, community engagement, and urban development, although the review suggested there was room for improvement in the area of public transparency. *See* Simon Murdoch, Annual Review of Canterbury Earthquake Recovery Act 2011, August 2013, *available at* http://cera.govt.nz/sites/cera.govt.nz/files/common/canterbury-earthquake-recovery-act-2011-annual-review-2013.pdf.

5.   NEW YORK AND NEW JERSEY

Hurricane Sandy Rebuilding Taskforce, Hurricane Sandy Rebuilding Strategy: Stronger Communities, A Resilient Region

http://portal.hud.gov/hudportal/HUD?src=/sandyrebuilding (Aug. 2013)

On October 29, 2012 multiple weather systems—including Hurricane Sandy—collided over the most densely populated region in the nation, with devastating and tragic results. At least 159 people in the United States were killed as either a direct or indirect result of Sandy.

More than 650,000 homes were damaged or destroyed and hundreds of thousands of businesses were damaged or forced to close at least temporarily. The power of nature was set loose on our nation's largest city and some of our smallest coastal towns, with results that would have previously seemed unimaginable. Lives were lost, millions of homes were upended, families were made homeless in a single night, and entire communities were in shock at the scale of the loss....

Hurricane Sandy affected twenty-four states across the northeastern and mid-Atlantic United States....Much of the destruction inflicted by Hurricane Sandy centered in the densely populated coastal areas of New Jersey and the New York metropolitan area...

Hurricane Sandy by the Numbers

$65 BILLION in damages and economic loss	
200,000	Small business closures due to damage or power outages
2 million	Working days lost
$58 million	In damages to the recreational fishing sector
100 million	Gallons of raw sewage released in Hewlett Bay 2 days after Sandy
70	National Parks impacted

At least 159 FATALITIES caused by Hurricane Sandy	
72	U.S. fatalities directly caused by the storm
87	U.S. fatalities caused by circumstances indirectly associated with the storm

8.5 MILLION customers left without power	
48,000	Number of trees removed or trimmed to restore power in New Jersey
$1 billion	Estimated cost of power and gas line repairs in New Jersey

650,000 HOMES damaged or destroyed	
6,477	Storm survivors in shelters at the peak of the disaster
43%	Portion of those registered for FEMA assistance that were renters
64%	Portion of renter registrants from NYC that were low-income
67%	Portion of renter registrants from NJ that were low-income

Portion of workers who commute using public transportation in the Tri-state area: 30.5 PERCENT	
8	Flooded tunnels
42 minutes	Average commute time in Brooklyn before Sandy
86 minutes	Average commute time in Brooklyn after Sandy

Disasters or emergencies declared in 13 STATES	
CT DC DE MA MD NH NJ NY PA RI VA WV	States with emergency declarations
CT DC DE MA MD NH NJ NY OH PA RI VA WV	States with Major Disaster Declarations

In January 2013, Congress passed and the President signed the Disaster Relief Appropriations Act, 2013, which provided about $50 billion in funding to support rebuilding in the region.

This Rebuilding Strategy establishes guidelines [and recommendations] for the investment of the Federal funds made available for recovery and sets the region on the path to being built back smarter and stronger.

Incorporating Projections of Current and Future Risk

Even a moderate amount of sea level rise will increase the flooding that coastal storm events cause….

When determining the level of acceptable risk-tolerance, decision makers must assess the potential for catastrophic loss of life, damage to infrastructure, interruption to local economy, and threats to ecosystem functions. In addition, these decision makers must consider issues of perceived fairness and the voluntary nature of risks. Finally, the decision makers must take into account human vulnerability and the adaptive capacity of a system or community to respond successfully to a coastal flooding event, including adjustments to behavior, resources, and technologies….

> *Recommendation*:[*] Facilitate the incorporation of future risk assessment, such as sea level rise, into rebuilding efforts with the development of a sea level rise tool….
>
> *Recommendation:* Develop a minimum flood risk reduction standard for major Federal investment that takes into account data on current and future flood risk.

Energy Infrastructure

Extensive power outages during Sandy affected millions of residents and resulted in substantial economic loss to communities. [R]esilient energy solutions could have helped limit power outages. In addition, improvements in and hardening of, the liquid fuel supply chain would have prevented some of the most visible impacts of the storm….

> *Recommendation*: Mitigate future impacts to the liquid fuels supply chain like those experienced during the Sandy recovery.
>
> *Recommendation*: Encourage Federal and State cooperation to improve electric grid policies and standards.

Successes in Hazard Mitigation through Green Infrastructure during Hurricane Sandy

Green infrastructure includes natural and/or restored features (e.g., wetlands or sand dune ecosystems), that incorporate the natural processes (e.g., flood protection, water filtration) that are recognized as integral to community, economic, and environmental resilience. These approaches have proven successful in other regions, and it appears they reduced flood damage where applied in the region impacted by Sandy.

During Sandy, an example of effective hazard mitigation through green infrastructure was demonstrated at the Alligator River National Wildlife Refuge in North Carolina. As part of a climate change adaptation project, oyster reefs were installed several years ago parallel to the Pamlico Sound shoreline near Point Peter Road and the canal that ends at the Sound. The oyster reefs absorbed some of the energy of storm-generated waves and decreased the amount of erosion at the end of Point Peter Road and along the shoreline adjacent to the road. The water control structure installed in the canal next to the road as part of this project likely slowed erosion by adapting the flow of storm flood waters from a channelized system to a sheet flow system which emulated natural processes.

Recommendation: Consider green infrastructure options in all Sandy infrastructure investments....

Water Infrastructure

Hurricane Sandy overwhelmed, compromised, and in some cases destroyed much of the region's water infrastructure. Beaches were washed onto roads, houses, rivers, and even across barrier islands. Flood walls were breached and overtopped and stormwater systems were inundated. The flooding and loss of power caused wastewater and drinking water systems to fail, impacting hundreds of thousands of people and causing untold ecological damages to waterways and sensitive habitats.

Recommendation: Ensure Sandy recovery water infrastructure investments are timely, resilient, sustainable, and effective.

FEMA will spend more than a billion dollars on repairs...and improvements [to wastewater and drinking water facilities damaged by Sandy] to ensure they are prepared for threats posed by future sea level rise and other impacts of climate change....

Building Codes

Using disaster-resistant local building codes is the most effective method to ensure new and rebuilt structures are designed and constructed to a more resilient standard....

The International Code Council [a nonprofit association made up of thousands of federal, state, and local experts] publishes [model building codes for commercial and residential construction,] which all fifty states and the District of Columbia have adopted. While [these codes] have been adopted in the States most impacted by Sandy, the most current version of the model building codes (2012) have only been adopted in Rhode Island and Maryland: New Jersey has adopted the 2009 version, New York the 2006 version, and Connecticut the 2003 version. Both New York and New Jersey, however, are currently in the process of adopting the current editions of the codes.

> *Recommendation*: States and localities should adopt and enforce the most current version of [commercial and residential construction codes].

> While the [International Codes for commercial and residential construction] have been adopted in the States most impacted by Sandy, the most current version[s] of the model building codes (2012) have only been adopted in Rhode Island and Maryland.

NOTES AND QUESTIONS

1. In February 2014, the Congressional Research Service (CRS) evaluated the Hurricane Sandy Rebuilding Strategy (HSRS) and assessed its implementation thus far. The CRS found that 52 of the 69 of the strategy's recommendations had already been put into place or soon would be. The remaining 17 recommendations were reported as being "in process" or "underway"— "generally meaning that they required significant further action." Jared T. Brown, The Hurricane Sandy Rebuilding Strategy: In Brief at 2, Congressional Research Service, Feb. 10, 2014, available at http://www.fas.org/sgp/crs/misc/R43396.pdf.

   Items left on the back burner relate mainly to infrastructure investment, residential safety, and support for small businesses. *Id*. at 4-5, Table 1. Some recommendations would require executive-branch overhauls. A uniform flood-elevation standard for federal facilities sounds good, but would probably entail "significant revisions of existing rulemakings and internal policy guidance across several federal agencies." *Id*. at 7. Other suggestions might involve Congressional action. "For instance," the report explains, "the HSRS recommends that federal agencies work to 'Mitigate future impacts to the liquid fuels supply chain like those experienced during the Sandy recovery.' As the Administration implements this recommendation for future disasters, Congress may determine that new statutory authorities are required to encourage investments by the private sector to protect the liquid fuel supply, or that more grant funding is required to invest in mitigation measures for the supply chain, or that there are existing statutory impediments to the development of mitigation measures." *Id.* at 8. Finally, some recommendations, like those for updated building codes, depend on local initiative. Our government's horizontal and vertical latticework is the structure on which everything else depends.

2.   As discussed earlier in this chapter, the Obama administration stresses climate resilience in disaster recovery. In their review of Congress's $50.7 billion Sandy relief package, policy analysts Nicole Smith and Jessica Grannis noted several mechanisms that could help communities prepare for the impacts of climate change. See Nicole Smith & Jessica Grannis, Understanding the Adaptation Provisions of the Sandy Disaster Relief Appropriations Act (H.R. 152) (Georgetown Climate Center) (Discussion Draft, May 2013), http://www.georgetownclimate .org/sites/default/files/GCC_Sandy_Relief_Act_Analysis.pdf.

The governors of the two hardest hit states, New York and New Jersey, each promised a vibrant recovery from the ruin of Hurricane Sandy. But they set off on two different paths, which later converged.

SHAWN BOBURG, REBUILD V. RETREAT: CHRISTIE AND CUOMO OFFER CONTRASTING PLANS IN WAKE OF SANDY

The Record (Bergen County), March 15, 2013, http://www.northjersey.com/news/rebuild-vs-retreat-christie-and-cuomo-offer-contrasting-plans-in-wake-of-sandy-1.589124

In New Jersey, owners of damaged coastal homes would get cash to stay put and rebuild. In New York, those on the water's edge would get generous incentives to walk away.

It's a difference that could mean divergent futures for both states' shorelines. And the calculus that goes into the two approaches—by Governor Christie in New Jersey and Gov. Andrew Cuomo in New York—has set off a complex debate among environmentalists, planners, economists and government officials about which is a bigger threat: rising sea levels that could pose a future risk to rebuilt communities, or the economic and emotional impact of peeling back development from the coast....

Christie, a Republican who said immediately after superstorm Sandy struck in October that climate change was not his "main concern," is offering owners of flood-damaged homes $10,000 in exchange for a promise to do repairs and stay in their homes for at least two years. The administration expects 20,000 residents to accept the offer....

In contrast, Cuomo, a Democrat who has said Sandy showed the need to aggressively prepare for rising sea levels, is offering homeowners pre-storm market value for their properties, which would be cleared and left fallow. But New York's proposed . . . voluntary buyback program...is also complicated by questions about whether neighborhoods will become checkerboards of vacant and occupied lots, as neighbors weigh their options.

Both plans were unveiled this week, part of each state's proposal for how to spend an initial piece of the $60 billion in Sandy aid approved by Congress in January....

[T]he differences in incentives have prompted environmentalists to criticize Christie for missing an opportunity.

"It seems that the administration is more concerned about people rebuilding even if they get flooded again and it costs us more money down the road," said Jeff Tittel, director of New Jersey's Sierra Club....

Cuomo, who has said "climate change is a reality," suggested in his January State of the State address that residents abandon flood prone areas. "There are some parcels that Mother Nature owns," he said. "She may visit once every few years, but she owns the parcel and when she comes to visit, she visits."

In New Jersey, where the Shore and its summer tourism industry bring in significant tax revenues, the issue of whether to build or buy out holds implications for the state economy. Experts say most Shore residents don't want to give up their homes — and towns don't want to lose tax dollars....

"We have to get people rebuilt," said Borough Administrator Jennifer Maier, who added that most residents want to stay. "To create more open space, it's nice as a concept, but it's just not an option."

But some experts say a focus on the short-term financial recovery masks a long-term threat.

"In terms of hazards, it makes more sense to buy people out rather than rebuilding in certain areas, but then you begin to turn off the economic engine, and who would argue against pumping more money into the system?" said Karl Nordstrom, a professor of marine and coastal sciences at Rutgers University who favors restoring natural dunes along the coast, a process that will takes years. "The biggest problem now is if the houses stay where they are, the space is so restricted, there's almost nothing we can do to make things better in that restricted space."...

And there is plenty of interest in coastal buyouts, said Alex Dubrovsky, a member of a newly formed resident group [in Staten Island, New York]. Dubrovsky said neighbors are starting to realize it's impractical and prohibitively expensive to raise the 90-year-old bungalows that line his block. Many would need to be lifted an addition 8 to 15 feet to avoid flood insurance rate hikes that are expected in the next few years as new flood maps become official, and push premiums in the most vulnerable areas up to $31,000 per year.

"No one in my neighborhood is elevating anything," he said. "And when people start realizing they'll be paying more in flood insurance than their mortgages, they get panicked."...

Judd Schechtman, a lecturer and doctoral candidate at Rutgers University's Edward J. Bloustein School of Planning and Public Policy, said buyouts are an option that New Jersey "should have on the table now."...

Schechtman advocates a system in New Jersey in which developers could buy rights to increase housing density in less flood-prone areas in exchange for agreeing not to rebuild in more vulnerable areas. Decisions ultimately have to be made at the local level with sound guidance from the state, he said.

"Certainly there are many strategies that work for different communities, but we're talking about ecological restoration in certain areas where human settlement is not feasible in the long term."

NOTES AND QUESTIONS

1. New York's "buyout and acquisition" plan may be the largest residential buyout scheme ever attempted in the United States. The program, intended for homes damaged or destroyed during Hurricane Sandy, Hurricane Irene and Tropical Storm Lee, serves three districts in Staten Island and one on Long Island. Under the plan, the state agrees to purchase homes in areas of "highest risk" for 100 percent of pre-storm fair market value (FMV), with added incentives for owners who agree to relocate en masse, agree to relocate within the county, or both. For eligible homes in areas of lower risk, the state will pay the *post-storm* FMV with added incentives. Purchased homes in "highest risk" areas must be maintained in perpetuity as coastal buffer zones—a version of what land-use planners call "managed retreat." Properties in lower-risk areas are eligible for redevelopment. Governor's Office of Storm Recovery, NY Rising Buyout and Acquisition Programs, http://stormrecovery.ny.gov/ny-rising-buyout-and-acquisition-programs (last visited May 7, 2014).

   Interest in the program has been high, particularly in Staten Island, where several shoreline neighborhoods jockeyed for the chance to participate. By some estimates, the cost of the program could top $400 million. Hillary Russ, *New York's Post-Sandy Buyouts Could Cost $400 Mln*, Reuters, Feb. 4, 2013, http://www.reuters.com/article/2013/02/05/storm-sandy-newyork-buyouts-idUSL1N0B4D1T20130205.

2. In May 2013, Governor Christie announced a voluntary buyout plan of his own. Press Release, "Governor Christie Announces $300 Million Buyout Plan To Give Homeowners The Option To Sell Sandy-Damaged [Homes]," May 16, 2013, http://www.nj.gov/governor/news/news/552013/approved/20130516a.html. The program, supported by $300 million in federal funds,

focuses on roughly 1,000 homes harmed by Sandy in the state's tidal areas and on another 300 repetitively flood-damaged homes located in the Passaic River Basin. *Id.*

In contrast to the New York experience, most properties acquired under the New Jersey plan have been located inland. That's because property on the shore is more valuable, and many shoreline owners are apparently holding out for a rebound in the real estate market. *See NJ Eyes Nearly 700 Homes for Post-Sandy Buyouts*, Associated Press, Apr. 22, 2014, http://www.nj.com/news/index.ssf/2014/04/nj_eyes_nearly_700_homes_for_post-sandy_buyouts.html.

Are shoreline owners acting rationally? How might the state further encourage owners of high-risk property to sell out? Could it provide better incentives? More persuasive information? Could the state condemn properties and effectively force owners to sell? Under what circumstances, if any, should a state do that?

3. The recovery plans in New York and New Jersey continue to differ on what to do about climate change. New York, for example, now offers a planning "toolkit" that assesses flood risks based on climate projections over the next hundred years. *See* Guidance for New York Rising Community Reconstruction Plans (undated), *available at* http://stormrecovery.ny.gov/sites/default/files/documents/Guidance_for_Community_Reconstruction_Plans.pdf. Journalist Scott Gurian explains the logic: "[W]hile homeowners might spend tens of thousands of dollars to elevate their house to bring themselves into compliance with the new FEMA flood maps, those maps are based on current conditions, and do not take sea-level rise projections into account. Given that the average life expectancy of a house is one hundred years or more, homeowners who are simply raising their structures to the minimum required height might have to go through the trouble and expense of elevating them again in a few decades, if sea levels continue to rise." Scott Gurian, *NJ Sandy Recovery Fails to Consider Long-Term Climate Predictions*, NJ Spotlight, Nov. 12, 2013, http://www.njspotlight.com/stories/13/11/11/nj-sandy-recovery-fails-to-consider-long-term-climate-predictions/?p=all. Connecticut, Delaware, and Maryland have also incorporated climate information into their recovery efforts.

In contrast, the Garden State has no statewide policy for considering climate change in planning, although some towns have independently adopted such policies. *Id.* What explains this difference in approach?

E. PROBLEM

Below is a problem designed to encourage you to think more about the many issues and diverse interests involved in rebuilding a city. The facts are fictional, but they are based on accounts of real hurricanes that have hit the United States in the last twenty-five years. The problem may be used as a class exercise in which students act as advocates for particular interest groups, or, more simply, as a launch pad for more general classroom discussion.

RISING FROM THE RUBBLE: THE CITY OF WILD PALMS

Wild Palms is a coastal city of about 100,000 people, located on the Gulf of Mexico. Incorporated in the 1800s, Wild Palms is known for its beach resorts, good fishing, and historical Spanish and Caribbean architecture. The city is also occasionally visited by tropical storms and hurricanes.

A month ago Wild Palms was raked by Hurricane Addie, a Category 4 storm with winds near 140 mph and a surge of more than eighteen feet. Twenty people died in the storm and hundreds more were injured. Addie's winds flattened buildings throughout the city, including schools, houses of worship, and tens of thousands of homes. Because of high insurance rates, at least one-third of the damaged households were not insured for wind damage. In one of the most dramatic events, storm winds demolished a privately owned mobile home park on the outskirts of town. The facility provided housing for more than 300 agricultural laborers and their families. Nearly all park residents were Latino with household earnings at or below the federal poverty line. This agricultural workforce is essential to the farm economy of the surrounding county, which provides almost a quarter of the nation's tomatoes, green beans, and squash. Many farm operators are concerned that worker housing will not be replaced in time for the upcoming winter harvest.

In addition, Hurricane Addie's eighteen-foot surge flooded several square miles of low coastal land. Among the areas worst hit was the city's East Side neighborhood, a working-class, traditionally African-American neighborhood filled with handsome century-old architecture. East Side was sliding into disrepair even before the storm, and some privately wonder if it is even worth bringing back. Despite federal requirements, officials estimate that a quarter of damaged homes lacked flood insurance.

Addie was one of the most powerful storms known to have hit this part of the coast. Experts loosely describe it as a "400-year storm," that is, a storm that has a 0.25 percent chance of striking in any given year. (As a comparison, Hurricane Katrina is considered a 400-year storm.)

The city is really struggling. Most small businesses have yet to reopen. The local university closed its classrooms and dormitories for the semester, leaving thousands of students in limbo. The nearby Air Force base—an important source of employment that was already slated to close down—now plans to accelerate its departure. And the major league baseball team that had kept its spring training camp in Wild Palms (thus generating tourism and national publicity) recently announced plans to permanently move its facilities to another Southern city.

Officials in Wild Palms estimate that its population has dropped from 100,000 to about 70,000. The city's morale is falling rapidly. "It's so ugly here, it's hard to get anyone to think about tomorrow," one resident told a Washington journalist. "There isn't a leaf left. There isn't a bird in the sky."

To address rebuilding efforts, the mayor of Wild Palms has planned several meetings of government and civic leaders. Although nearly everyone wants a safer and more resilient city, the course is not clear. The city will always be prone to violent storms. And in an era of accelerated climate change, no one can accurately predict the effects of future sea level rise or the cycle and intensity of future tropical storms.

Imagine you represent one of the three parties below. How would you address the following issues and questions?

1. The Mayor's Office
2. The Wild Palms Chamber of Commerce, a nonprofit organization interested in promoting local and regional business and development
3. Disaster Justice Now!, a local nonprofit organization promoting the interests of poor communities and communities of color

Rebuilding Homes. Wild Palms hopes to benefit from a package of federal Community Development Block Grants that will be given to the state and used to help rebuild devastated areas. (Though many owners had insurance, such coverage is usually not enough to completely rebuild a home.) As a first step, Congress has asked the state and the city of Wild Palms to propose a detailed plan for how the money will be managed and spent. Although funds for the city are expected to be significant, everyone understands there will not be enough to satisfy every need. Priorities must be set. If the money is spread broadly, but too thin, there is a chance that no group will be able to successfully rebound. The mayor has assembled a meeting of government and civic leaders to address the following fundamental questions.

1. How should individual grants be allocated? Should they be available to owners of homes, owners of rental units, the owner of the mobile home park? In what proportions? What about vacation homes? Should uninsured owners be eligible?
2. How should an individual grant amount be determined? Should calculations be based on pre-storm value, the cost of rebuilding, financial need, or some other factor(s)?
3. How should the grants be used? In addition to rebuilding, some propose that owners be allowed to sell their damaged property to the city or state in exchange for grant money; recipients could then use the funds

to relocate to a safer part of town. If adopted, should this buyout program be limited to owners who plan to relocate *within* the city? Or should it apply to those relocating outside the city? What about those relocating outside the state?

Increasing Resilience. In the short time after the storm, the city's mayor has become a quasi-expert in the history of municipal disaster recovery. She is particularly inspired by the recovery of Kobe, Japan. With that in mind, the mayor immediately imposed a building moratorium in Wild Palms, which is to remain in effect until officials decide what to do. The mayor has assembled a meeting of government and civic leaders to address the following questions related to disaster mitigation.

1. What new building code should be imposed and how should it be enforced? Some experts recommend a code similar to the state-of-the-art regulations of Florida's Miami-Dade County. That code requires special "hurricane clips" that fasten a house's roof to the frame and insists that a roof's surface be attached with screws rather than nails. In addition, the code mandates storm shutters and glass that can withstand winds of up to 146 mph. But the requirements are expensive and can increase building costs by more than 33 percent. Assuming the city adopts a new code, when should it be required? The traditional "50 percent Rule" holds that any structure with damage amounting to 50 percent or more must comply with an updated code. But this leaves out many buildings. In addition, avoidance of compliance is common. In New Orleans many homeowners were able to circumvent new rules by convincing sympathetic officials to assess their damages at 49 percent.

2. What should the city's new footprint look like? With a smaller population, keeping the old footprint might result in a city that is too spread out. Providing services such as police and fire protection to outlying areas might become too costly. Some city planners warn of a "jack-o'-lantern effect" in which residential streets are dotted intermittently with blighted properties, like the missing teeth of a Halloween pumpkin. On the other hand, people are attached to their communities and benefit significantly from the social relationships they have nurtured over the years, including those linked by culture, geography, religion, commerce, and recreation. For many people, the largest asset they own is the residential lot in their neighborhood. Assuming a smaller footprint is desirable, how should the new contours be implemented? Should the city prevent rebuilding in some neighborhoods? Would that be constitutional under Lucas v. South Carolina Coastal Council (Chapter 2)? Or should the city use targeted investment and economic incentives to encourage people to develop in desired areas? For a city strapped for cash, how can that be accomplished?

3. How long should the city's building moratorium remain in effect? Residents are understandably anxious to rebuild their lives. Some argue that the moratorium has already discouraged many evacuees from moving back. Should

the mayor now lift the moratorium entirely? Should the mayor lift the moratorium in some areas, but retain it in the more vulnerable areas, such as East Side or the site of the demolished mobile home park? At what point does a moratorium in such circumstances become a regulatory taking? *See* Tahoe-Sierra Preservation Council, Inc. v. Tahoe Regional Planning Agency, 535 U.S. 302 (2002) (thirty-two-month moratorium in Lake Tahoe Basin while scientists studied environmental effects of development was not a per se taking).

Revitalizing the Economy. One of the most controversial issues involves the East Side neighborhood. Residents have been adamant about rebuilding their community. Various historic preservation groups also support this effort. The area is obviously prone to dangerous flooding, but civil engineers say it could be made much safer if new houses were built on raised foundations and artificial barriers were created to protect especially vulnerable parts of the neighborhood.

In contrast, the mayor is wondering if it might be more sensible to buy out East Side residences, clear the area, and build a waterfront park that could be used year-round for public events, festivals and other activities. The park would be designed to absorb the shock of a storm surge and to drain invading water away from residential communities. The park could be partially funded by selling three-quarters of the reclaimed land to a private developer for use as a high-rise resort with a hotel and casino. The plan would not only move East Side residents out of harm's way, the mayor reasons, but also revitalize the city's threatened economy.

East Side residents, of course, oppose the plan. They claim that the mayor is just trying to oust the community from a valuable swath of land. They believe that such an expropriation would amount to an unconstitutional taking under the federal constitution. But to be absolutely sure, an East Side advocacy group is working to add an amendment to the state constitution, patterned after the post-*Kelo* amendment adopted in Louisiana. The amendment would limit the state's use of expropriation to traditional public purposes and hold that enhanced tax revenues or economic development could not be considered in determining "public use."

Is expropriation a good idea? What are the alternatives? Could the mayor's plan survive a challenge under *Kelo*? What are the long-term implications of the proposed amendment to the state constitution?

9

INTERNATIONAL DISASTER LAW & POLICY

Disasters in the United States are in many ways not so different from those occurring in other countries. Both types are driven by a combination of environmental hazards, human development, and human vulnerabilities. Reducing the risk, responding to victims, and reimagining the future all pose enormous political and psychological challenges. Every country, when planning for or responding to disaster must find the right balance between local rule and national rule, autonomy and order, fairness and efficiency.

But two factors set many foreign disasters apart: intensity and complexity. This is particularly so in poorer countries. By intensity, we mean the power with which a disaster disables a country's political and economic institutions, its access to natural resources, and its morale. When hurricanes Katrina and Rita ripped through the Gulf Coast, lives and property were lost and a city fell to its knees, but the United States as a whole carried on almost as before. In terms of our Gross Domestic Product, those storms were barely a blip on the radar screen. But when a cyclone swamps half of Bangladesh, or an earthquake shatters a Pakistani city, tens of thousands of lives can be lost; in terms of economic development, such countries can be set back months or even years. In addition, things get much more complex. Many developing countries, for instance, have inefficient or even dysfunctional political institutions. Because they are poor, they must rely much more on outside aid (from other countries and outside organizations), which brings along its own bureaucracies. Add to this extreme differences in wealth, strong religious and ethnic tensions, and (in some cases) antidemocratic political institutions, and you have a witch's cauldron of logistical issues.

This chapter gives you a brief look at the legal and political elements associated with disaster in the international context, paying special attention to issues in developing countries. We will first look at the distribution of disaster risk around the world. We will then look at the combination of causes, primarily ecological exposure and social vulnerability. Next, we will introduce some of the most important international agreements relevant to disaster risk, including incentives for better planning and agreements addressing discrimination. Finally, we conclude with a discussion exercise that hopes to pull together many concepts presented in this chapter as well as in the rest of the book.

A. THE GEOGRAPHY OF DISASTER

UNITED NATIONS INTERNATIONAL STRATEGY FOR DISASTER REDUCTION, GLOBAL ASSESSMENT REPORT ON DISASTER RISK REDUCTION

3-12 (2009)

In 2008, numerous major disasters provided a stark reminder of the massive concentrations of disaster risk that threaten human development gains across the world. In May, the tropical cyclone Nargis caused an estimated 140,000 mortalities in Myanmar, primarily due to a storm surge in the low-lying, densely populated Irrawaddy River delta.

In May, China's most powerful earthquake since 1976 affected Sichuan and parts of Chongqing, Gansu, Hubei, Shaanxi and Yunnan killing at least 87,556 people, injuring more than 365,000 and affecting more than 60 million people in ten provinces and regions. An estimated 5.36 million buildings collapsed and more than 21 million buildings were damaged....

Also in August 2008, the Kosi River in Bihar, India, broke through an embankment and changed its course 120 km eastwards, rendering useless more than 300 km of flood defences that had been built to protect towns and villages. Flowing into supposedly flood safe areas, the river affected 3.3 million people in 1,598 villages located in 15 districts. It was characterized as the worst flood in the area for 50 years, prompting the Prime Minister of India, Manmohan Singh, to declare a "national calamity" on 28th August.

Internationally reported disaster loss is heavily concentrated in a small number of infrequently occurring events. Between January 1975 and October 2008 and excluding epidemics, the International Emergency Disasters Database EMDAT recorded 8,866 events killing 2,283,767 people. Of these, 23 mega-disasters...killed 1,786,084 people, mainly in developing countries. In other words, 0.26 percent of the events accounted for 78.2 percent of the mortality.

In the same period, recorded economic losses were US$1,527.6 billion. [Twenty-five] mega-disasters...represented only 0.28 percent of the events, yet accounted for 40 percent of that loss, mainly in developed countries. Of the ten disasters with the highest death tolls since 1975, no fewer than half...have occurred in the five year period between 2003 and 2008. [L]ikewise...four of the ten disasters with the highest economic losses occurred in the same period.

Nationally reported disaster loss is similarly highly concentrated. Losses reported between 1970 and 2007 at the local government level in a sample of 12 Asian and Latin American countries showed that 84 percent of the mortality and 75 percent of the destroyed housing was concentrated in only 0.7 percent of the loss reports. Destruction in the housing sector usually accounts for a significant proportion of direct economic loss in disasters.

At whatever scale disaster losses are viewed, therefore, mortality and direct economic loss appear to be highly concentrated geographically and associated with a very small number of hazard events. These are areas where major concentrations of vulnerable people and economic assets are exposed to very severe hazards....

In contrast, and at whatever scale disaster losses are viewed, wide regions are exposed to more frequently occurring low-intensity losses. These widespread low-intensity losses are associated with other risk impacts such as a large number of affected people and damage to housing and local infrastructure, but not to major mortality or destruction of economic assets. For example, 99.3 percent of local loss reports in the 12 countries mentioned accounted for only 16 percent of the mortality but 51 percent of housing damage. These losses are pervasive in both space and time. In the country sample, 82 percent of local government areas reported disaster losses at least once between 1970 and 2007, 48 percent reported disaster losses six or more times and there was an average of nine local loss reports per day....

The fact that disasters have a disproportionate impact on the poor in developing countries has been highlighted in research for at least 30 years....

This Report confirms that poorer countries have disproportionately higher mortality and economic loss risks, given similar levels of hazard exposure. For example, globally, high-income countries account for 39 percent of the exposure to tropical cyclones but only 1 percent of the mortality risk. Low-income countries represent 13 percent of the exposure but no less than 81 percent of the mortality risk.

For example, gross domestic product (GDP) per capita in Japan is US$31,267 compared to US$5,137 in the Philippines, and Japan has a human development index of 0.953 compared to 0.771 in the Philippines. Japan also has about 1.4 times as many people exposed to tropical cyclones than the Philippines. However, if affected by a cyclone of the same magnitude, mortality in the Philippines would be 17 times higher than that in Japan.

Countries with small and vulnerable economies, such as many Small Island Developing States and Land-Locked Developing Countries not only suffer higher relative levels of economic loss, with respect to the size of their GDPs. They also have a particularly low resilience to loss, meaning that disaster losses can lead to major setbacks in economic development. The countries with the highest economic vulnerability to natural hazards and the lowest resilience are also those with very low participation in world markets and low export diversification.

At the local level, there is also empirical evidence to show that poor areas suffer disproportionately high levels of damage in disasters and that this is related to factors such as unsafe housing. Case study evidence from particular cities also shows that both disaster occurrence and loss are associated with processes that increase the hazard exposure of the poor—for example, the expansion of informal settlements in hazard prone areas....

Disaster risk is now widely recognized as an integral part of a wider constellation of risks related to food and energy insecurity, financial and economic instability, global climate change, environmental degradation, disease and epidemics, conflict and extreme poverty....

[R]eports by the United Nations Department for Social and Economic Affairs and by the World Economic Forum have argued that different kinds of risk now form an interlocked system, implying that impacts in one sphere spill over into other areas, and that actions to reduce one risk may imply trade-offs in reducing others. The [Fourth Assessment Report of the U.N. Intergovernmental Panel on Climate Change in 2007] dispelled any remaining doubt that climate change is a catastrophic threat on a global scale.

These interlinkages are becoming increasingly visible. In 2008, successive global crises hit the headlines as the prices of grain and energy sources fluctuated wildly and the global financial system threatened to collapse, all in the context of ongoing concerns about global climate change, conflict, security and extreme poverty. These systemic risks now pose a very serious threat to global security and sustainability. Ongoing disaster losses undermine resilience to other kinds of threats, while major impacts in mega-disasters can trigger reactions in other risk spheres.

The way disaster risk is magnified by other kinds of global risk, and in turn feeds back into them, can be illustrated by a hypothetical but plausible example. If global climate change magnifies the severity of drought in a key grain producing region causing harvest failure, this could feed back into speculative increases in food prices. The most affected will not only be those living in the region but poor households in other parts of the world who spend a large proportion of their income on food. Faced with chronic food insecurity and with their resilience undermined by other hazards such as poor health or conflict, poor rural households may then migrate to urban areas. In many towns and cities across developing countries migration from rural areas is absorbed through the growth of informal settlements in areas prone to hazards such as floods. Flood risk in turn may also be further magnified by climate change.

Other examples of the interlocked nature of risk include the increase of oil prices when hurricanes threaten the Gulf of Mexico at the same time as conflict threatens oil production in Nigeria. As the credit crisis in developed countries is pushing economies into recession, the construction boom in the

Persian Gulf is faltering, leading to a decrease in remittances from migrant workers to relatives in the Indian sub-continent. This in turn may lead to decreasing economic resilience in poor households in that region, increased rural-urban migration and subsequent increases in the population exposed to weather-related hazards in cities.

The linkages between disaster risk, poverty and climate change, described above, form a particularly tightly interlocked group of global challenges, in which impacts in any one sphere spill over into the other two and which have to be addressed in a way that recognizes their inter-connectedness.

Table 1.1: Disasters with more than 10,000 fatalities, January 1975 – June 2008[4]

(Highlighting denotes disasters within the five-year period, 2003–2008.)

Source: EMDAT; Analysis by ISDR, 2008 (data as of September 2008)

Year	Country	Disaster	Fatalities
1983	Ethiopia	Ethiopian drought	300,000
1976	China	Tangshan earthquake	242,000
2004	South Indian Ocean	Indian Ocean tsunami	226,408
1983	Sudan	Sudan drought	150,000
1991	Bangladesh	Cyclone Gorky	138,866
2008	Myanmar	Cyclone Nargis	133,655
1981	Mozambique	Southern Mozambique drought	100,000
2008	China	Sichuan earthquake	87,476
2005	India, Pakistan	Kashmir earthquake	73,338
2003	Europe	European heat wave	56,809
1990	Iran	Manjil-Rudbar earthquake	40,000
1999	Venezuela	Vargas floods	30,000
2003	Iran	Bam earthquake	26,796
1978	Iran	Tabas earthquake	25,000
1988	Soviet Union	Spitak earthquake	25,000
1976	Guatemala	The Guatemala earthquake	23,000
1985	Colombia	Nevado Del Ruiz volcano	21,800
2001	India	Gujarat earthquake	20,005
1999	Turkey	Izmit earthquake	17,127
1998	Honduras	Hurricane Mitch	14,600
1977	India	Andhra Pradesh cyclone	14,204
1985	Bangladesh	Bangladesh cyclone	10,000
1975	China	Haicheng earthquake	10,000

	Year	Country	Hazard	Total loss (billion US$)
Table 1.2: Disasters leading to losses of more than US$ 10 billion, January 1975 – June 2008	2005	United States of America	Hurricane Katrina	125
	1995	Japan	Kobe earthquake	100
	2008	China	Sichuan earthquake	30
	1998	China	Yangtze flood	30
	2004	Japan	Chuetsu earthquake	28
	1992	United States of America	Hurricane Andrew	26.5
	1980	Italy	Irpinia earthquake	20
(Highlighting denotes disasters within the five-year period, 2003–2008.)	2004	United States of America	Hurricane Ivan	18
	1997	Indonesia	Wild fires	17
	1994	United States of America	Northridge earthquake	16.5
Source: EMDAT; Analysis by ISDR, 2008 (data as of September 2008)	2005	United States of America	Hurricane Charley	16
	2004	United States of America	Hurricane Rita	16
	1995	Democratic People's Republic of Korea	Korea floods	15
	2005	United States of America	Hurricane Wilma	14.3
	1999	Taiwan (China)	Chichi earthquake	14.1
	1988	Soviet Union	Spitak earthquake	14
	1994	China	China drought	13.8
	1991	China	Eastern China floods	13.6
	1996	China	Yellow River flood	12.6
	2007	Japan	Niigataken Chuetsu-oki earthquake	12.5
	1993	United States of America	Great Midwest flood	12
	2002	Germany	River Elbe floods	11.7
	2004	United States of America	Hurricane Frances	11
	1991	Japan	Typhoon Mireille	10
	1995	United States of America	Major west coast wind storm	10

Reprinted from UNISDR, Global Assessment Report on Disaster Risk Reduction (2009).

NOTES AND QUESTION

1. Maps can help us see information in new ways. The map below is called a "density equalizing map," or "cartogram." Through calculated distortion, it shows the proportion of people affected by disasters from 1975 to 2004 in terms of "resized" territorial space. (In this case, being "affected" includes requiring emergency assistance for basic survival or catching a disease not usually found in the area.) What role should geographic and economic distribution of risk play in shaping disaster policy? For more cartograms on a variety of topics, see http://www.worldmapper.org.

Affected by Disaster

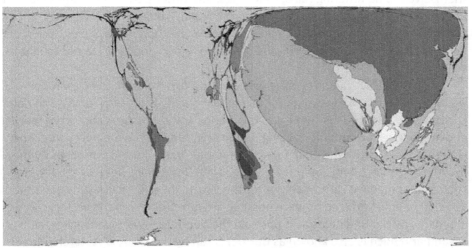

Source: Social and Spatial Inequalities Group, University of Sheffield, and Mark Newman, University of Michigan.

C. SOCIAL VULNERABILITY

ROBERT R.M. VERCHICK, ENVIRONMENTAL ACTION FOR A POST-KATRINA WORLD
112-16 (2010) (footnotes omitted)

[In developing countries,] the relatively poor and the socially excluded endure special burdens. As in industrialized countries, poverty and bigotry push settlements into cheap and dangerous areas like flood plains or landfills. The grass huts and tin-roof shanties that tens of millions of people call home provide little protection. Disaster aggravates engrained patterns of discriminatory treatment. In southern India, after the Asian Tsunami, human rights advocates reported widespread discrimination against lower-caste *dalits*, in the distribution of supplies, the removal of bodies, and the availability of shelters.

Women and girls also face disproportionate harm. Poring over international surveys, one confronts the alarming fact that in the developing world women and girls are much more likely to die during naturally triggered disasters. The Asian Tsunami [of 2004] claimed the lives of twice as many women than men in two hard-hit districts in the Indian state Tamil Nadu. In one district of Sri Lanka, women and girls accounted for 80 percent of fatalities. In both the 2005 Kashmir Earthquake and India's 1993 Latur Earthquake, many more women died than men. The disparity is attributable to many factors. As primary care-givers, women are more likely to be home during a disaster; and these homes are often poorly constructed or in a vulnerable area. Women are usually the first ones to search for missing family members, exposing themselves to hammering rains, mudslides, and other perils. Sometimes women are constrained by social norms. During the Asian Tsunami many women drown[ed] because they were "ashamed" to run to shore after waves ripped away parts of their clothing. In some cultures women and girls are not taught to swim.

On May 3, 2008, a cyclone called Nargis tore through the Irawaddy Delta of Myanmar, a low-lying coastal nation roughly the size of Texas. The delta is laced with hundreds of rivers and tributaries and rarely rises above ten feet above sea level. Communities living on those muddy flats were pulverized. The United Nations estimates that 2.4 million people were severely affected by the cyclone and that 1.4 million people were left in immediate need of food, water, shelter, and medical care. Weeks after the storm, local officials estimated that 134,000 people had died or were missing, a figure that comports with early estimates by the Red Cross. It is possible the death toll was much higher, as Myanmar (which is also known as Burma) is run by a military dictatorship that is notorious for secrecy and a myriad of human rights abuses.

The events of the storm, which played out in news reports around the world, offer a shocking glimpse at yet another category of people especially vulnerable to natural hazards: citizens of oppressive, non-democratic regimes that simply don't care. Myanmar's military government, for instance, had never bothered to draft a disaster relief plan for a major cyclone although the threat was well known. And even after India's meteorological department notified Burmese officials of the cyclone's approach two days in advance, the government did little to warn its citizens on the Irrawaddy. In the aftermath, Myanmar denied access to international aid workers and frustrated attempts to deliver supplies into the region, at one point leading the United States to accuse the government of "criminal neglect."

There were also powerful aspects of ethnicity and class in this story, which were nearly ignored in America's mainstream media. Myanmar has more than 100 different ethnic groups and sub-groups within its borders, making it one of the most ethnically diverse populations in South East Asia. The largest minority group, the Karens, live mainly on the Irrawaddy Delta where the cyclone hit. The Karens have suffered persecution from the governing junta since the country's early days of independence more than a half century ago.

After the storm, there were many reports of government officials hording supplies or selling them to victims at inflated prices. Some journalists described soldiers forcing survivors into hard labor, forcing them to "break up large boulders into pieces of rock for road construction" for less than a dollar a day. Those in the area reported that Karens, in particular, were being discriminated against. Human rights workers cited unconfirmed reports that boatmen helping with the evacuation were taking ethnic Burmese from the delta but leaving Karens behind. Such reports are consistent with a historic pattern of discrimination against Karens by the Burmese government, which includes violent attacks, property seizures, and forced labor. Some human rights observers believed such discrimination was "really the root of the [aid distribution] problem." This can be seen as an extension of political and ethnic oppression that had been occurring for decades, just as violence toward blacks during America's [Great Mississippi River Flood of 1927] can be seen as an extension of generations of continued government-supported racial oppression.

Discriminatory abuse appeared to have spilled over against other ethnic groups on the delta, including the Mon, Muslim Indians, aboriginal groups, and even the ethnic Burmese. A relatively wealthy class of Chinese landowners on the delta feared the government would use the evacuation as an opportunity to seize their land. Hardship...affects some [groups] more acutely because of past discrimination and other violations of human rights. For instance, millions of storm survivors were left homeless and denied interim shelter by even their own government. The homeless crisis in Myanmar thus equals the scale of the Asian Tsunami in 2004. But the tragedy is compounded by the fact that before the cyclone, an estimated one million people were *already* internally displaced—most of them, members of ethnic minorities—whose homes had been seized or destroyed by soldiers in "counterinsurgency" efforts or to make way for dams, oil pipelines, and mining operations. In the half-century before the storm, some delta communities had relocated more than 100 times—often at the point of a gun.

Children were particularly harmed. The United Nations Children's Fund (UNICEF) estimates that 40 percent of those who died in the cyclone and accompanying floods were children. Those children lucky enough to survive faced another set of struggles. Because of small body size, many were at special risk to disease and starvation. Children are also at much higher risk of protracted trauma and psychological problems, especially those who lost parents or other family members. Some independent relief centers, like those operated by UNICEF, provided "child-friendly" programs in which children played and made drawings as a means of coping with loss and trauma. Hundreds, perhaps even thousands, of children were separated from their parents during the storm or, perhaps, orphaned. They now face the prospects of living in dour state-run orphanages or, worse, being swept up in the global slave trade. Myanmar has long been a "source country" for human trafficking, including domestic servitude, bonded labor, and forced prostitution. Less than two weeks after the cyclone, the United Nations had already reported an incident of two "brokers" entering a relief center in Yangon (also known as Rangoon) and trying to recruit orphaned children. The pair was arrested, but in the wake of the storm, the trend of child abductions and trafficking appeared likely to increase.

The earthquake that shook China's Sichuan province in 2008 occurred in the same month as Cyclone Nargis. In contrast to that painful fiasco, Chinese leaders generally won praise for the efficiency and relative transparency of their relief efforts. Still, one can find evidence of distributional unfairness. As in

Myanmar—or, for that matter, the United States—social problems that exist before a catastrophe are thrown into sharp relief when all hell breaks loose.

At a magnitude of 7.9, the Sichuan Earthquake was the strongest earthquake China had seen in thirty years. It killed more than 70,000 people and left almost 5 million homeless. After the quake, tours of affected communities revealed the poor had suffered most. In some poorer villages, where homes are made of cheap material and families live on $100 per month, nearly every building lay in ruins. As is common, most residents in these communities lacked insurance. Although China's central government set aside $772 million for relief aid, many villagers reasonably feared there would not be enough to go around. "The government has never helped us," said one villager to an American news service, "We don't trust that they will help us now." Before the earthquake, government statistics showed that 2.1 million people in Sichuan province lived in poverty. Weeks after the quake, the Chinese government reported that an additional 1.4 million farmers in 4,000 villages had fallen into poverty because of the destruction.

In Beijing political circles, class is a sensitive topic. President Hu Jintao had based much of his public legitimacy on efforts to shrink China's widening economic gap, which is most noticeable when comparing urban and rural populations. Days after the earthquake an article in the *Wall Street Journal* contrasted two areas in the strike zone. In one, a rural village called Yinhua, [b]oulders loosed by [the] quake, some as big as vans, littered the main road...along with the vehicles they knocked over or crushed." Nearly every home was destroyed. Meanwhile, roughly 55 miles away in Sichuan's capital city, Chengdu, conditions were very different. "The glitzy new office towers and hotels...were still standing and largely intact. The city suffered relatively little in [the] quake, despite its proximity to the epicenter."

The collapse of nearly 7,000 school buildings in Sichuan heaped more attention on China's economic inequality. At least 10,000 children perished in school buildings that many believe were poorly constructed and out of compliance with building codes. Thousands of enraged parents demanded government inquiries and protested what they called "tofu buildings." Many parents were "especially upset that some schools for poor students crumbled into rubble even though government offices and more elite schools not far away survived the May 12 quake largely intact." Public outcry over such disparities appeared to knock the Chinese leadership on its heels. They were, after all in the midst of preparing for Beijing's much-anticipated [2008 Summer] Olympic Games, which, with its "Water Cube" and stylish stadium, would prove to be one of the most expensive and lavish celebrations the world had ever seen. Weeks after the quake, Chinese officials were seen buying the silence of angry parents who had lost children in the calamity, offering them anywhere from $5,600 to $8,800 in cash in exchange for a signed promise to avoid protests and "maintain social order."

NOTES AND QUESTIONS

1. The social vulnerabilities described in Myanmar and China are made worse by the lack of government transparency, democratic processes, and civil liberties. How do such features help vulnerable populations in times of disaster? To what degree should values such as transparency or autonomy be limited by the need for efficiency and quick response? Who should decide that balance?

2. In the aftermath of Cyclone Nargis, news reports generally praised the swift and generous response of the international community, while properly condemning Myanmar's callous government. Although the Burmese junta bears ultimate responsibility for the government's repression, corruption, and mismanagement, some observers have suggested that the international community made matters worse by restricting foreign aid except in times of catastrophic emergency. Soon after the Myanmar disaster, a well-respected, nonpartisan think tank called the International Crisis Group offered this view:

   > Twenty years of aid restrictions—which see Myanmar receiving twenty times less assistance per capita than other least-developed countries— have weakened, not strengthened, the forces for change. Bringing about peace and democracy will require visionary leaders at all levels, backed by strong organisations, who can manage the transition and provide effective governance. These are not common attributes of an isolated and impoverished society. As the country's socio-economic crisis deepens and its human resources and administrative capacity decline, it will become harder and harder for any government to turn the situation around.

   International Crisis Group, Burma/Myanmar After Nargis: Time to Normalise Aid Relations (Asia Report No. 161), Oct. 20, 2008, at i, http://www.crisisgroup.org/home/index.cfm?id=5734 (Aug. 25, 2009). What responsibility do nations have to address social vulnerabilities within foreign countries *before* disaster strikes? What is the best way to accomplish this? Do you agree with the view expressed above?

3. Does a country have the right to refuse emergency response aid when it is offered? Following Cyclone Nargis, Burmese authorities not only failed to provide adequate food, water, and shelter to survivors; they actively *obstructed* private relief efforts, confiscating goods and arresting volunteers trying to help. *See* Voravit Suwanvanichkij, Mahn Mahn, Cynthia Maung, Brock Daniels, Noriyuki Murakami, Andrea Wirtz, Chris Beyrer, *After the Storm: Voices from the Delta* (March 2009), *available at* www.jhph.edu/humanrights. The Burmese government also barred foreign soldiers from delivering aid to the Irawaddy Delta. Jürgen Haacke, Myanmar, the Responsibility to Protect, and the Need for

Practical Assistance, 1 *Global Responsibility to Protect* 156, 157 (2009). In response to that policy, then-French Foreign Minister Bernard Kouchner urged the United Nations to ignore protests from Myanmar's military government and *impose* the delivery of foreign aid. Kouchner argued that such an action could be justified under the Responsibility to Protect (R2P), an international norm that obligates a state to protect its population from genocide, war crimes, crimes against humanity, and ethnic cleansing, and that obligates the international community to intervene in a country's affairs when that job is not being done. *See* International Coalition for the Responsibility to Protect, *The Crisis in Burma*, http://www.responsibilitytoprotect.org/index.php/crises/crisis-in-burma#Cyclone. Edward Luck, then-Special Adviser to the Secretary General on the Responsibility to Protect, criticized that approach and characterized Kouchner's reasoning as "a misapplication of the [R2P] doctrine." *Id.* (quoting Luck). The organization charged with building international consensus on R2P—then called, Responsibility to Protect-Engaging Civil Society (now, International Coalition for the Responsibility to Protect)—weighed in on the controversy at least twice. In its final analysis, the organization concluded that if it could be shown that the Burmese government's actions would lead to crimes against humanity, the global community would have not only the authority, but the responsibility to act—first through peaceful means, and then, if unsuccessful, through force. *See id.* In the end, the international community did not forcefully intervene in Myanmar and R2P was never invoked.

4. Poor governance and sectarian violence continue to impair disaster response in Myanmar. In May 2013, in the face of an oncoming cyclone, 140,000 people living in low-lying camps refused government orders to evacuate. Most of the residents were members of the Rohingya, a Muslim minority group. The Rohingya have long distrusted Burmese authorities, accusing them of decades of discrimination and property theft. *See Distrustful Rohingya Dig in as Burma Braces for Cyclone Mahasen*, The Guardian, May 15, 2013, http://www.theguardian.com /world/2013/may/15/rohingya-cyclone-mahasen-burma-rakhine (last visited June 4, 2014).

C. INTERNATIONAL LAW AND INTERNATIONAL AID

1. THE HYOGO FRAMEWORK AND MITIGATION PROJECTS

In January 2005, government officials from around the globe met in Kobe, Japan, to discuss disaster preparation and response. By an odd coincidence, only days before, an enormous earthquake off the west coast of Sumatra had triggered the devastating Asian tsunami that battered the coasts of eleven countries and killed more than 225,000 people. At that international meeting, called the World Conference on Disaster Reduction, all member states of the United Nations agreed to reduce disaster loss by strengthening the resilience of nations and communities at risk. One product of the conference, reported widely by the press, was a plan to establish an international early warning system to identify coastal storms and tsunamis in time for people to evacuate. A related and even more ambitious product was an international framework intended to guide the world's disaster initiatives through 2015. The document was called the Hyogo Framework for Action (HFA), named after the prefecture, or political district, in which Kobe is located. An excerpt from this document is reprinted below.

HYOGO FRAMEWORK FOR ACTION 2005-2015: BUILDING THE RESILIENCE OF NATIONS AND COMMUNITIES TO DISASTERS

(A/CONF.206/6)

I. Preamble

...

A. Challenges Posed by Disasters

...

There is now international acknowledgement that efforts to reduce disaster risks must be systematically integrated into policies, plans and programmes for sustainable development and poverty reduction, and supported through bilateral, regional and international cooperation, including partnerships. Sustainable development, poverty reduction, good governance and disaster risk reduction are mutually supportive objectives, and in order to meet the challenges ahead, accelerated efforts must be made to build the necessary capacities at the community and national levels to manage and reduce risk....

III. Priorities for Action 2005-2015

A. General Considerations

In determining appropriate action to achieve the expected outcome and strategic goals, the Conference reaffirms that the following general considerations will be taken into account:...

(b) Taking into account the importance of international cooperation and partnerships, each State has the primary responsibility for its own sustainable development and for taking effective measures to reduce disaster risk....

(c) An integrated, multi-hazard approach to disaster risk reduction should be factored into policies, planning and programming....

(d) A gender perspective should be integrated into all disaster risk management policies....

(e) Cultural diversity, age, and vulnerable groups should be taken into account when planning for disaster risk reduction, as appropriate;

(f) Both communities and local authorities should be empowered to manage and reduce disaster risk by having access to the necessary information, resources and authority to implement actions for disaster risk reduction;

(g) Disaster-prone developing countries, especially least developed countries and small island developing States, warrant particular attention in view of their higher vulnerability and risk levels, which often greatly exceed their capacity to respond to and recover from disasters;

...

B. Priorities for Action

...

The Conference has adopted the following five priorities for action:

1. Ensure that disaster risk reduction is a national and a local priority with a strong institutional basis for implementation

...

Key activities:

(i) National institutional and legislative frameworks

(a) Support the creation and strengthening of national integrated disaster risk reduction mechanisms, such as multi sectoral national platforms, with designated responsibilities at the national through to the local levels to facilitate coordination across sectors....

(b) Integrate risk reduction, as appropriate, into development policies and planning at all levels of government, including in poverty reduction strategies and sectors and multi sector policies and plans....

(d) Recognize the importance and specificity of local risk patterns and trends, decentralize responsibilities and resources for disaster risk reduction to relevant sub-national or local authorities, as appropriate.

(ii) Resources

(e) Assess existing human resource capacities for disaster risk reduction at all levels and develop capacity-building plans and programmes for meeting ongoing and future requirements....

(g) Governments should demonstrate the strong political determination required to promote and integrate disaster risk reduction into development programming.

(iii) Community participation

(h) Promote community participation in disaster risk reduction through the adoption of specific policies, the promotion of networking, the strategic management of volunteer resources, the attribution of roles and responsibilities, and the delegation and provision of the necessary authority and resources.

2. Identify, assess and monitor disaster risks and enhance early warning

...

Key activities:
(i) National and local risk assessments
(a) Develop, update periodically and widely disseminate risk maps and related information to decision makers, the general public and communities at risk in an appropriate format....
(ii) Early warning

...

(d) Develop early warning systems that are people centered, in particular systems whose warnings are timely and understandable to those at risk, which take into account the demographic, gender, cultural and livelihood characteristics of the target audiences, including guidance on how to act upon warnings, and that support effective operations by disaster managers and other decision makers.
(iii) Capacity
(i) Support the development and sustainability of the infrastructure and scientific, technological, technical and institutional capacities needed to research, observe, analyse, map and where possible forecast natural and related hazards, vulnerabilities and disaster impacts....
(iv) Regional and emerging risks

...

(n) Cooperate regionally and internationally, as appropriate, to assess and monitor regional and trans-boundary hazards, and exchange information and provide early warnings through appropriate arrangements, such as, *inter alia*, those relating to the management of river basins....
3. Use knowledge, innovation and education to build a culture of safety and resilience at all levels

...

Key activities:
(i) Information management and exchange
(a) Provide easily understandable information on disaster risks and protection options, especially to citizens in high-risk areas, to encourage and enable people to take action to reduce risks and build resilience....
(ii) Education and training
(h) Promote the inclusion of disaster risk reduction knowledge in relevant sections of school curricula at all levels and the use of other formal and informal channels to reach youth and children....
(i) Promote the implementation of local risk assessment and disaster preparedness programmes in schools and institutions of higher education....
(m) Ensure equal access to appropriate training and educational opportunities for women and vulnerable constituencies; promote gender and cultural sensitivity training as integral components of education and training for disaster risk reduction.

(iii) Research

(n) Develop improved methods for predictive multi-risk assessments and socioeconomic cost—benefit analysis of risk reduction actions at all levels; incorporate these methods into decision-making processes at regional, national and local levels.

...

4. Reduce the underlying risk factors
Key activities:
(i) Environmental and natural resource management

(a) Encourage the sustainable use and management of ecosystems, including through better land-use planning and development activities to reduce risk and vulnerabilities.

(b) Implement integrated environmental and natural resource management approaches that incorporate disaster risk reduction, including structural and non-structural measures, such as integrated flood management and appropriate management of fragile ecosystems.

(c) Promote the integration of risk reduction associated with existing climate variability and future climate change into strategies for the reduction of disaster risk and adaptation to climate change, which would include the clear identification of climate-related disaster risks, the design of specific risk reduction measures and an improved and routine use of climate risk information by planners, engineers and other decision makers.

(ii) Social and economic development practices

(d) Promote food security as an important factor in ensuring the resilience of communities to hazards, particularly in areas prone to drought, flood, cyclones and other hazards that can weaken agriculture-based livelihoods....

(f) Protect and strengthen critical public facilities and physical infrastructure, particularly schools, clinics, hospitals, water and power plants, communications and transport lifelines, disaster warning and management centres, and culturally important lands and structures through proper design, retrofitting and re-building, in order to render them adequately resilient to hazards.

(g) Strengthen the implementation of social safety-net mechanisms to assist the poor, the elderly and the disabled, and other populations affected by disasters. Enhance recovery schemes including psycho-social training programmes in order to mitigate the psychological damage of vulnerable populations, particularly children, in the aftermath of disasters....

(j) Promote diversified income options for populations in high-risk areas to reduce their vulnerability to hazards, and ensure that their income and assets are not undermined by development policy and processes that increase their vulnerability to disasters....

(iii) Land-use planning and other technical measures

(n) Incorporate disaster risk assessments into the urban planning and management of disaster-prone human settlements, in particular highly populated areas and quickly urbanizing settlements....

(q) Incorporate disaster risk assessment into rural development planning and management, in particular with regard to mountain and coastal flood plain areas....

5. Strengthen disaster preparedness for effective response at all levels...
Key activities:

...

(d) Prepare or review and periodically update disaster preparedness and contingency plans and policies at all levels, with a particular focus on the most vulnerable areas and groups. Promote regular disaster preparedness exercises, including evacuation drills, with a view to ensuring rapid and effective disaster response and access to essential food and non-food relief supplies, as appropriate, to local needs.

...

IV. Implementation and Follow-Up

States, within the bounds of their financial capabilities, regional and international organizations, through appropriate multilateral, regional and bilateral coordination mechanisms, should...

(a) Mobilize the appropriate resources and capabilities of relevant national, regional and international bodies, including the United Nations system;

(b) Provide for and support, through bilateral and multilateral channels, the implementation of this Framework for Action in disaster-prone developing countries, including through financial and technical assistance, addressing debt sustainability, technology transfer on mutually agreed terms, and public–private partnerships, and encourage North–South and South–South cooperation;

(c) Mainstream disaster risk reduction measures appropriately into multilateral and bilateral development assistance programmes including those related to poverty reduction, natural resource management, urban development and adaptation to climate change;

(d) Provide adequate voluntary financial contributions to the United Nations Trust Fund for Disaster Reduction, in the effort to ensure the adequate support for the follow-up activities to this Framework for Action.

NOTES AND QUESTIONS

1. Although the HFA was not the first international agreement to address disaster mitigation, it is the most comprehensive. For instance, the Yokohama Strategy for a Safer World: Guidelines for Natural Disaster Prevention, Preparedness and Mitigation and its Plan of Action (1994) established many of the principles expanded upon in Hyogo. The Agenda for Humanitarian Action adopted by the International

Conference of the Red Cross and Red Crescent in December 2003 set forth goals and actions to "reduce the risk and impact of disasters and improve preparedness and response mechanisms."

Many international environmental agreements also address disaster risk. The U.N. Convention to Combat Desertification in Those Countries Experiencing Serious Drought and/or Desertification, Particularly in Africa, adopted in 1994, specifically targeted issues of water scarcity. The U.N. Millennium Declaration of 2000 listed among its key objectives, "[p]rotecting the vulnerable" and "[p]rotecting our common environment"; the parties also resolved to "intensify cooperation to reduce the number and effects of natural and man-made disasters." The Johannesburg Plan of Implementation of the World Summit on Sustainable Development, held in 2002, urged that "[a]n integrated, multi-hazard, inclusive approach to address vulnerability, risk, assessment and disaster management, including prevention, mitigation, preparedness, response and recovery, is an essential element of a safer world in the 21st century." The Johannesburg Plan also requested the Intergovernmental Panel on Climate Change (IPCC) to "improve techniques and methodologies for assessing the effects of climate change, and encourage the continuing assessment of those adverse effects." Similarly, the U.N. General Assembly has encouraged the IPCC to continue to assess the adverse effects of climate change on the socioeconomic and natural disaster reduction systems of developing countries.

2. The HFA emphasizes the broad interdisciplinary nature of disaster planning and response. Note the attention paid to scale of government (federalism), identity and culture, poverty, land use planning, environmental protection, risk analysis, and education. The document also emphasizes systemic integration—the idea that disaster policies should be "mainstreamed" into more general initiatives having to do with economic development, environmental protection, land use planning, scientific research, and other concerns. What are the challenges in mainstreaming disaster policy in this way? Why not encourage a nation or the international community to concentrate on a *single* initiative or agreement that would address disaster mitigation in all aspects?

3. Another obvious, but less prominent, theme is the need for resources: information, technology, training, and, of course, money. Many of the resources needed for disaster mitigation and the inevitable emergency response are simply beyond reach in places such as Haiti, Bangladesh, or Pakistan. For this reason, the HFA urges wealthier nations to offer "financial and technical assistance" to poorer countries and to provide "adequate voluntary financial contributions" to the United Nations disaster reduction fund. But charity is a weak foundation for long-term

development efforts such as this. How would you persuade a wealthy government to invest in disaster mitigation for developing countries? Could such investment be justified in terms of national or economic security? Is there something recipient nations could offer in return?

4. As of 2014, 79 countries have established "national platforms" for implementing the HFA's strategic goals. More than 100 countries have some agency or other body responsible for implementing and monitoring progress toward these goals. HFA-inspired risk reduction strategies have already been designed or implemented in the Andes region, Central America, the Caribbean, the Pacific, Asia, Africa, and Europe. In earthquake-prone Kazakhstan, for instance, the U.N. Development Programme is helping to incorporate disaster response information in grade school curricula as a way of building resilience in poorer communities. Nigeria, whose people sometimes endure heavy rains and dangerous floods, has integrated risk reduction into its regional planning budgets and antipoverty initiatives. In Vietnam, a special partnership of government offices, private donors, and NGOs is promoting disaster management for the country's storm-swept jungles and shores; the effort focuses on *both* lifting villagers out of poverty *and* protecting river basins, swamps, and coastal beaches.

   For more information on the HFA and its global implementation, see U.N. International Strategy for Disaster Reduction, *Global Assessment Report on Disaster Risk Reduction: Revealing Risk, Redefining Development* (2011), available at http://www .preventionweb.net/english/hyogo/gar/?pid:222&pil:1.

5. To see how disaster mitigation unfolds on the ground, read the following case study from Gaibandha, a remote part of Bangladesh located at the confluence of the Tista and Brahmaputra rivers. The project was implemented by a nonprofit organization called Practical Action and funded by the British government.

U.N. INTERNATIONAL STRATEGY FOR DISASTER REDUCTION, LINKING DISASTER RISK REDUCTION AND POVERTY REDUCTION: GOOD PRACTICES AND LESSONS LEARNED

3-4 (2008)

Gaibandha District is located in northern Bangladesh at the confluence of two major rivers: Tista and Brahmaputra. This location makes the area vulnerable to disasters, due to flooding and river erosion. Frequent disasters make life in the area much more difficult than in the rest of country, depriving residents of land, employment opportunities and basic services.

As a result, local populations live below subsistence level. They often have to live where there are minimal or no basic services, such as safe water, sanitation, health and education. Communications are extremely poor. The remoteness of the district and the complexity of its problems result in a high degree of social marginalization, child labour, exploitation, child marriage, early pregnancies and violation of human rights. Women and children are the most vulnerable, as men migrate in large numbers in search of employment and livelihood security.

To cope with their situation of both extreme poverty and disaster risk, the communities generally depend on external relief and rehabilitation after a disaster. Vulnerable community members are also forced to engage in indentured labour for their survival.

The 20,000 households targeted by the project were a highly disadvantaged segment of the community. After losing their lands and shelters permanently in the river, the communities relocated to the flood protection embankment where there were no basic services, employment opportunities or secure livelihood options. The project's comprehensive approaches have helped them secure access to income and basic services such as shelter, health, education and food. Highly diversified and alternative risk reduction strategies and income opportunities have been explored throughout the command areas (over 1,600 km^2) with proven results and visible impacts on the communities' lives and livelihoods. The project beneficiaries now have a range of innovative mechanisms to cope sustainably with disaster risk and poverty, which has significantly reduced migration.

To help manage and minimize disaster risk, the project has developed participatory technologies all over the command areas and in the district. The major risk reduction and livelihood strategies are:

- Providing access to improve livelihood knowledge, skills and information through capacity building training and demonstrations of off-farm and on-farm based technologies.
- Developing infrastructure services and facilities such as multi-purpose shelters, cluster villages, community clinics, schools, safe water and sanitation.
- Establishing community-based early warning and rapid evacuation systems.
- Ensuring better access to common property resources, and to social, civil and political rights.
-

The project works directly with the communities to reduce poverty, disaster risk and vulnerability, by building capacity through technological and social interventions. The interventions include:

- Flood-friendly agriculture, fisheries and livestock resource management.
- Flood-resistant housing and multi-purpose shelter development.
- Alternative income generation through light engineering training.

- Small enterprise development through small businesses, and agro-processing for added value (which has created better access to common property resources, ensuring legal rights).
- Influencing policy makers to recognize successful practices for national and international dissemination.

In combining disaster risk reduction with poverty reduction, the project has used comprehensive disaster risk reduction strategies, shifting relief-dependent attitudes towards long-term disaster risk reduction, management and planning. Additionally, the project worked to motivate local, national and international agencies to mainstream disaster issues into development practices for the sake of effective and long-term sustainable solutions. In a nutshell, the project has demonstrated a number of ways to help communities reduce their vulnerability to disasters, which also help them overcome chronic poverty and social problems. It has also developed people's capacity to cope with frequent natural hazards, and to adapt to climate change....

The project can be described as good practice because it has developed a very effective risk reduction and management model, as well as a number of innovative pro-poor-based natural resource management technologies. These technologies were designed for wider impact on the poor and naturally disadvantaged communities not only in the project areas, but also in other districts and regions.

The project also developed innovative ideas and models on risk reduction and management, climate change adaptation and natural resource management issues. Innovative ideas included:

- The development of a model cluster village to resettle communities displaced by river erosion.
- The development of multi-purpose shelters to accommodate affected communities hit by flood disasters.
- The establishment of a community-based rapid evacuation system to minimize community risk and vulnerability.
- The development of unique, low-cost and pro-poor technologies such as agricultural production on barren sand bars, floating gardens and cage aquaculture.
- Improved access of marginalized people to basic rights (health, education, sanitation and legal rights), particularly for women and children.

All the above ideas, innovations, knowledge and learning strongly motivated community members, policy makers, development practitioners, donors and other stakeholders both at the local, national and international levels. The project also influenced the development of a new policy for poor people living on the edge of mighty rivers in Bangladesh.

The project was shared at a number of international forums to influence policy makers and development practitioners in building awareness of climate change issues. These included World Water Week 2007 and the House of Lords event for the Oxfam "Make Poverty History" campaign in the United Kingdom, as well as other events at Sheffield University (UK), the British parliament, the German and Belgian parliaments, and the Plenary Meeting of the Asia-Pacific Forum for Environment and Development (APFED) in China....

The project has initiated a very comprehensive disaster risk and poverty reduction strategy, aiming to develop a sustainable model for replication in other parts of Bangladesh, particularly among disadvantaged communities living on the edge of mighty rivers. Replication could be easily achieved in other parts of the country with a tiny amendment to national policy, and channeling of national and donor funding to relevant development initiatives.

NOTES AND QUESTIONS

1. The U.N. International Strategy for Disaster Reduction (UNISDR) is the U.N. agency charged with overseeing the implementation of the HFA. At the request of the U.N. General Assembly, the UNISDR is now working on a successor framework that would take effect in 2015, the year the HFA expires. *See,* U.N. International Strategy for Disaster Reduction, *Towards a Post-2015 Framework for Disaster Risk Reduction,* March 2012, *available at* http://www.unisdr.org/files/25129_ towardsapost2015frameworkfordisaste.pdf; U.N. International Strategy for Disaster Reduction, *Synthesis Report: Consultations on a Post-2015 Framework on Disaster Risk Reduction (HFA2),* April 2012.

2. In assessing the HFA, the UNISDR finds that the HFA has "proved effective in galvanizing and bringing together the many stakeholders in disaster risk reduction including national and local governments, parliamentary forums, inter-government organizations, non-government organizations, community-based organizations and practitioners, the private sector, academic and technical institutions, the media and international organizations. UNISDR, *Towards a Post-2015 Framework, supra,* at 6. The framework also assisted governments in passing disaster risk reduction legislation. *Id.* And "parties to the U.N. Framework Convention on Climate Change have identified the HFA as a pillar of their efforts to adapt to climate change." *Id.* But more remains to be done. In the post-2015 era, the UNISDR sees the need for "a set of normative standards," as well as a timeline for implementation. *Id.* According to the agency, a successor framework should also focus more on the underlying

risk factors of vulnerability and place more emphasis on the perspectives of women. *Id.* at 6-7. What would you add to the list? How much should we expect from global frameworks like HFA, which, necessarily govern from the top down?

2. PROTECTING AGAINST DISCRIMINATION

Of international agreements important to disaster management, many focus on human rights. These include the International Covenant on Civil and Political Rights, the Convention on the Elimination of All Forms of Racial Discrimination (CERD), and the Protocol Relating to the Status of Refugees, all of which the United States has ratified. Other relevant treaties, but which the United States has not ratified, include the International Covenant on Economic, Social and Cultural Rights; the Convention on the Elimination of All Forms of Discrimination against Women (CEDAW); and the Convention on the Rights of the Child. For the most part these agreements were not written with disaster management specifically in mind. And although aggrieved individuals have the right to issue complaints with the United Nations, none of these conventions creates individual rights legally enforceable in the traditional sense. Consider these excerpted provisions of two important antidiscrimination agreements, CERD and CEDAW.

INTERNATIONAL CONVENTION ON THE ELIMINATION OF ALL FORMS OF RACIAL DISCRIMINATION
660 U.N.T.S. 195 (1965)

Article 1
1. In this Convention, the term "racial discrimination" shall mean any distinction, exclusion, restriction or preference based on race, color, descent, or national or ethnic origin which has the purpose or effect of nullifying or impairing the recognition, enjoyment or exercise, on an equal footing, of human rights and fundamental freedoms in the political, economic, social, cultural or any other field of public life.

2. This Convention shall not apply to distinctions, exclusions, restrictions or preferences made by a State Party to this Convention between citizens and non-citizens.

3. Nothing in this Convention may be interpreted as affecting in any way the legal provisions of States Parties concerning nationality, citizenship or naturalization, provided that such provisions do not discriminate against any particular nationality.

...

Article 2

1. States Parties condemn racial discrimination and undertake to pursue by all appropriate means and without delay a policy of eliminating racial discrimination in all its forms and promoting understanding among all races...

Article 5

In compliance with the fundamental obligations laid down in article 2 of this Convention, States Parties undertake to prohibit and to eliminate racial discrimination in all its forms and to guarantee the right of everyone, without distinction as to race, colour, or national or ethnic origin, to equality before the law, notably in the enjoyment of the following rights:

(a) The right to equal treatment before the tribunals and all other organs administering justice;

(b) The right to security of person and protection by the State against violence or bodily harm, whether inflicted by government officials or by any individual group or institution;

(c) Political rights, in particular the right to participate in elections—to vote and to stand for election—on the basis of universal and equal suffrage, to take part in the Government as well as in the conduct of public affairs at any level and to have equal access to public service;

(d) Other civil rights, in particular:
  (i) The right to freedom of movement and residence within the border of the State;
  (ii) The right to leave any country, including one's own, and to return to one's country;
  (iii) The right to nationality;
  (iv) The right to marriage and choice of spouse;
  (v) The right to own property alone as well as in association with others;
  (vi) The right to inherit;
  (vii) The right to freedom of thought, conscience and religion;
  (viii) The right to freedom of opinion and expression;
  (ix) The right to freedom of peaceful assembly and association;

(e) Economic, social and cultural rights, in particular:
  (i) The rights to work, to free choice of employment, to just and favourable conditions of work, to protection against unemployment, to equal pay for equal work, to just and favourable remuneration;
  (ii) The right to form and join trade unions;
  (iii) The right to housing;
  (iv) The right to public health, medical care, social security and social services;
  (v) The right to education and training;
  (vi) The right to equal participation in cultural activities;

(f) The right of access to any place or service intended for use by the general public, such as transport, hotels, restaurants, cafes, theatres and parks....

CONVENTION ON THE ELIMINATION OF ALL FORMS OF DISCRIMINATION AGAINST WOMEN

1249 U.N.T.S. 13 (1979)

Article 1

For the purposes of the present Convention, the term "discrimination against women" shall mean any distinction, exclusion or restriction made on the basis of sex which has the effect or purpose of impairing or nullifying the recognition, enjoyment or exercise by women, irrespective of their marital status, on a basis of equality of men and women, of human rights and fundamental freedoms in the political, economic, social, cultural, civil or any other field.

Article 2

States Parties condemn discrimination against women in all its forms, agree to pursue by all appropriate means and without delay a policy of eliminating discrimination against women....

Article 3

States Parties shall take in all fields, in particular in the political, social, economic and cultural fields, all appropriate measures, including legislation, to ensure the full development and advancement of women, for the purpose of guaranteeing them the exercise and enjoyment of human rights and fundamental freedoms on a basis of equality with men.

Article 4

1. Adoption by States Parties of temporary special measures aimed at accelerating de facto equality between men and women shall not be considered discrimination as defined in the present Convention...

2. Adoption by States Parties of special measures, including those measures contained in the present Convention, aimed at protecting maternity shall not be considered discriminatory....

Article 5
States Parties shall take all appropriate measures:

(a) To modify the social and cultural patterns of conduct of men and women, with a view to achieving the elimination of prejudices and customary and all other practices which are based on the idea of the inferiority or the superiority of either of the sexes or on stereotyped roles for men and women;

(b) To ensure that family education includes a proper understanding of maternity as a social function and the recognition of the common responsibility of men and women in the upbringing and development of their children, it being understood that the interest of the children is the primordial consideration in all cases.

Article 6
States Parties shall take all appropriate measures, including legislation, to suppress all forms of traffic in women and exploitation of prostitution of women.

Article 7
States Parties shall take all appropriate measures to eliminate discrimination against women in the political and public life of the country and, in particular, shall ensure to women, on equal terms with men, the right:

(a) To vote in all elections and public referenda and to be eligible for election to all publicly elected bodies;

(b) To participate in the formulation of government policy and the implementation thereof and to hold public office and perform all public functions at all levels of government;

(c) To participate in non-governmental organizations and associations concerned with the public and political life of the country.

...

Article 11
1. States Parties shall take all appropriate measures to eliminate discrimination against women in the field of employment in order to ensure, on a basis of equality of men and women, the same rights, in particular:

(a) The right to work as an inalienable right of all human beings;

(b) The right to the same employment opportunities, including the application of the same criteria for selection in matters of employment;

(c) The right to free choice of profession and employment...

(d) The right to equal remuneration, including benefits, and to equal treatment in respect of work of equal value...

(f) The right to protection of health and to safety in working conditions, including the safeguarding of the function of reproduction.

...

Article 12

1. States Parties shall take all appropriate measures to eliminate discrimination against women in the field of health care in order to ensure, on a basis of equality of men and women, access to health care services, including those related to family planning.

2. Notwithstanding the provisions of paragraph I of this article, States Parties shall ensure to women appropriate services in connection with pregnancy, confinement and the post-natal period, granting free services where necessary, as well as adequate nutrition during pregnancy and lactation.

Article 13

States Parties shall take all appropriate measures to eliminate discrimination against women in other areas of economic and social life in order to ensure, on a basis of equality of men and women, the same rights, in particular:

(a) The right to family benefits;

(b) The right to bank loans, mortgages and other forms of financial credit;

(c) The right to participate in recreational activities, sports and all aspects of cultural life.

Article 14

1. States Parties shall take into account the particular problems faced by rural women and the significant roles which rural women play in the economic survival of their families, including their work in the non-monetized sectors of the economy, and shall take all appropriate measures to ensure the application of the provisions of the present Convention to women in rural areas.

2. States Parties shall take all appropriate measures to eliminate discrimination against women in rural areas in order to ensure, on a basis of equality of men and women, that they participate in and benefit from rural development and, in particular, shall ensure to such women the right:

(a) To participate in the elaboration and implementation of development planning at all levels;

(b) To have access to adequate health care facilities, including information, counselling and services in family planning;

(c) To benefit directly from social security programmes;

(d) To obtain all types of training and education, formal and non-formal, including that relating to functional literacy, as well as, inter alia, the benefit of all community and extension services, in order to increase their technical proficiency;

(e) To organize self-help groups and co-operatives in order to obtain equal access to economic opportunities through employment or self employment;

(f) To participate in all community activities;

(g) To have access to agricultural credit and loans, marketing facilities, appropriate technology and equal treatment in land and agrarian reform as well as in land resettlement schemes;

(h) To enjoy adequate living conditions, particularly in relation to housing, sanitation, electricity and water supply, transport and communications.

NOTES AND QUESTIONS

1. CERD and CEDAW are among the treaties most often invoked by critics of disaster relief efforts around the world. Why do you suppose this is so? Is it because of the prominence of discrimination issues in times of disaster, or because of the lack of more forceful treaties dealing with disaster in general?

2. Recall the descriptions of Cyclone Nargis, the Sichuan earthquake, and other disasters recounted in the excerpt by Professor Verchick earlier in this chapter. What possible violations of CERD or CEDAW do you see in those accounts? Myanmar ratified CEDAW in 1997 (with some stated reservations), but has not ratified CERD. China ratified CEDAW in 1980 and CERD in 1981. Keep these treaties in mind when we present a description of the 2004 Asian tsunami later in this chapter.

3. PROTECTING INTERNALLY DISPLACED PERSONS

Days after Hurricane Katrina, when it became clear that the two million residents who had fled their homes would not be returning for a while, Americans wondered what to call them. Some news organizations referred to them as "refugees." But many Louisianans resented that term. They pointed out, correctly, that in legal parlance the word *refugee* refers to a person who has fled to another country, not just crossed a state line. Given the government's insensitive response to their rescue, calling them "refugees" reinforced the view that individuals—many of whom were urban, poor, and Black—were not part of the "real" America. So the press and the public settled instead on "evacuees," or "storm victims," or in casual conversation, "Katrina people."

What many did not know is that the United Nations had already established a phrase to describe people who have been forced to flee their homes, for reasons of armed conflict or disaster, but who remain in their country. It calls them "internally displaced persons," or "IDPs." Although numbers are wildly uncertain, experts believe there are roughly 24 million IDPs in the world at any given time. Most are probably displaced for reasons of war or other violent conflict. But disasters, both natural and manmade, contribute significantly to the problem, as in Ethiopia (drought), Pakistan (earthquake), India (flood), and China (earthquake). As we saw in the example of Myanmar after Cyclone Nargis, the internally displaced are at special risk of being neglected or mistreated for reasons of ethnicity, sex, age, or other characteristics.

International law offers no special protections to IDPs as it does to international refugees. Moreover, the United Nations scatters responsibility for IDP issues across many agencies, making comprehensive solutions more difficult. The United Nations, however, has endorsed a document called the Guiding Principles on Internal Displacement, assembled at the request of then-U.N. Secretary-General Boutros Boutros-Ghali in 1992. U.N. Office of the High Commissioner for Human Rights, Guiding Principles on Internal Displacement, www.unhchr.ch (Dec. 1, 2008). Like the HFA, the Guiding Principles are another attempt to reduce risk by attacking oppression and set a sensible foundation for future legal development. Though not binding, they are said to reflect "international human rights and humanitarian law and analogous refugee law." Francis M. Deng, Introductory Note by the Representative of the Secretary-General on Internally Displaced Persons, U.N. Office for the Coordination of Humanitarian Affairs (undated), www.reliefweb.int (Dec. 28, 2008). Some provisions concerning physical security and the right to travel, for instance, are drawn from the Covenant on Civil and Political Rights, to which the United States is a party. The Guiding Principles detail, in thirty principles, the guarantees that nations owe to IDPs in all three phases of internal displacement: the predisplacement phase, the phase of actual displacement, and the phase of return or resettlement.

GUIDING PRINCIPLES ON INTERNAL DISPLACEMENT
U.N. Doc. E/CN.4/1998/53/Add.2 (1998)

Introduction: Scope and Purpose

1. These Guiding Principles address the specific needs of internally displaced persons worldwide. They identify rights and guarantees relevant to the protection of persons from forced displacement and to their protection and assistance during displacement as well as during return or resettlement and reintegration.

2. For the purposes of these Principles, internally displaced persons are persons or groups of persons who have been forced or obliged to flee or to leave their homes or places of habitual residence, in particular as a result of or in order to avoid the effects of armed conflict, situations of generalized violence, violations of human rights or natural or human-made disasters, and who have not crossed an internationally recognized State border....

Section I—General Principles

Principle 1

1. Internally displaced persons shall enjoy, in full equality, the same rights and freedoms under international and domestic law as do other persons in their country. They shall not be discriminated against in the enjoyment of any rights and freedoms on the ground that they are internally displaced....

Principle 2

1. These Principles shall be observed by all authorities, groups and persons irrespective of their legal status and applied without any adverse distinction....

Principle 3

1. National authorities have the primary duty and responsibility to provide protection and humanitarian assistance to internally displaced persons within their jurisdiction.

2. Internally displaced persons have the right to request and to receive protection and humanitarian assistance from these authorities. They shall not be persecuted or punished for making such a request.

Principle 4

1. These Principles shall be applied without discrimination of any kind, such as race, color, sex, language, religion or belief, political or other opinion, national, ethnic or social origin, legal or social status, age, disability, property, birth, or on any other similar criteria.

2. Certain internally displaced persons, such as children, especially unaccompanied minors, expectant mothers, mothers with young children, female heads of household, persons with disabilities and elderly persons, shall be entitled to protection and assistance required by their condition and to treatment which takes into account their special needs.

Section II—Principles Relating to Protection from Displacement

Principle 5

All authorities and international actors shall respect and ensure respect for their obligations under international law, including human rights and humanitarian law, in all circumstances, so as to prevent and avoid conditions that might lead to displacement of persons.

Principle 6

1. Every human being shall have the right to be protected against being arbitrarily displaced from his or her home or place of habitual residence.

2. The prohibition of arbitrary displacement includes displacement:

(a) When it is based on policies of apartheid, "ethnic cleansing" or similar practices aimed at/or resulting in altering the ethnic, religious or racial composition of the affected population;...

(c) In cases of large-scale development projects, which are not justified by compelling and overriding public interests;

(d) In cases of disasters, unless the safety and health of those affected requires their evacuation;...

3. Displacement shall last no longer than required by the circumstances.

Principle 7

1. Prior to any decision requiring the displacement of persons, the authorities concerned shall ensure that all feasible alternatives are explored in order to avoid displacement altogether. Where no alternatives exist, all measures shall be taken to minimize displacement and its adverse effects.

2. The authorities undertaking such displacement shall ensure, to the greatest practicable extent, that proper accommodation is provided to the displaced persons, that such displacements are effected in satisfactory conditions of safety, nutrition, health and hygiene, and that members of the same family are not separated....

Principle 8

Displacement shall not be carried out in a manner that violates the rights to life, dignity, liberty and security of those affected.

Principle 9

States are under a particular obligation to protect against the displacement of indigenous peoples, minorities, peasants, pastoralists and other groups with a special dependency on and attachment to their lands.

Section III—Principles Relating to Protection During Displacement

Principle 10

1. Every human being has the inherent right to life which shall be protected by law. No one shall be arbitrarily deprived of his or her life....

Principle 11

1. Every human being has the right to dignity and physical, mental and moral integrity.

2. Internally displaced persons, whether or not their liberty has been restricted, shall be protected in particular against:

(a) Rape, mutilation, torture, cruel, inhuman or degrading treatment or punishment, and other outrages upon personal dignity, such as acts of gender-specific violence, forced prostitution and any form of indecent assault;

(b) Slavery or any contemporary form of slavery, such as sale into marriage, sexual exploitation, or forced labour of children; and

(c) Acts of violence intended to spread terror among internally displaced persons. Threats and incitement to commit any of the foregoing acts shall be prohibited.

Principle 12

1. Every human being has the right to liberty and security of person. No one shall be subjected to arbitrary arrest or detention.

2. To give effect to this right for internally displaced persons, they shall not be interned in or confined to a camp. If in exceptional circumstances such internment or confinement is absolutely necessary, it shall not last longer than required by the circumstances.

3. Internally displaced persons shall be protected from discriminatory arrest and detention as a result of their displacement....

Principle 14

1. Every internally displaced person has the right to liberty of movement and freedom to choose his or her residence.

2. In particular, internally displaced persons have the right to move freely in and out of camps or other settlements.

Principle 15

Internally displaced persons have:

(a) The right to seek safety in another part of the country;

(b) The right to leave their country;

(c) The right to seek asylum in another country; and

(d) The right to be protected against forcible return to or resettlement in any place where their life, safety, liberty and/or health would be at risk.

Principle 16

1. All internally displaced persons have the right to know the fate and whereabouts of missing relatives.

2. The authorities concerned shall endeavour to establish the fate and whereabouts of internally displaced persons reported missing....They shall inform the next of kin on the progress of the investigation and notify them of any result.

3. The authorities concerned shall endeavour to collect and identify the mortal remains of those deceased, prevent their despoliation or mutilation, and facilitate the return of those remains to the next of kin or dispose of them respectfully....

Principle 17

1. Every human being has the right to respect of his or her family life.

2. To give effect to this right for internally displaced persons, family members who wish to remain together shall be allowed to do so.

3. Families which are separated by displacement should be reunited as quickly as possible. All appropriate steps shall be taken to expedite the reunion of such families, particularly when children are involved. The responsible authorities shall facilitate inquiries made by family members and encourage and cooperate with the work of humanitarian organizations engaged in the task of family reunification.

4. Members of internally displaced families whose personal liberty has been restricted by internment or confinement in camps shall have the right to remain together.

Principle 18

1. All internally displaced persons have the right to an adequate standard of living.

2. At the minimum, regardless of the circumstances, and without discrimination, competent authorities shall provide internally displaced persons with and ensure safe access to:

    (a) Essential food and potable water;

    (b) Basic shelter and housing;

    (c) Appropriate clothing; and

    (d) Essential medical services and sanitation.

3. Special efforts should be made to ensure the full participation of women in the planning and distribution of these basic supplies.

Principle 19

1. All wounded and sick internally displaced persons as well as those with disabilities shall receive to the fullest extent practicable and with the least possible delay, the medical care and attention they require, without distinction on any grounds other than medical ones....

2. Special attention should be paid to the health needs of women, including access to female health care providers and services, such as reproductive health care, as well as appropriate counselling for victims of sexual and other abuses.

3. Special attention should also be given to the prevention of contagious and infectious diseases, including AIDS, among internally displaced persons.

Principle 20

1. Every human being has the right to recognition everywhere as a person before the law.

2. To give effect to this right for internally displaced persons, the authorities concerned shall issue to them all documents necessary for the

enjoyment and exercise of their legal rights, such as passports, personal identification documents, birth certificates and marriage certificates. In particular, the authorities shall facilitate the issuance of new documents or the replacement of documents lost in the course of displacement, without imposing unreasonable conditions, such as requiring the return to one's area of habitual residence ....

Principle 21

1. No one shall be arbitrarily deprived of property and possessions.

2. The property and possessions of internally displaced persons shall in all circumstances be protected, in particular, against the following acts:

(a) Pillage; [and]

(b) Direct or indiscriminate attacks or other acts of violence;...

3. Property and possessions left behind by internally displaced persons should be protected against destruction and arbitrary and illegal appropriation, occupation or use....

Principle 22

1. Internally displaced persons, whether or not they are living in camps, shall not be discriminated against as a result of their displacement in the enjoyment of the following rights:

(a) The rights to freedom of thought, conscience, religion or belief, opinion and expression;...

(d) The right to vote and to participate in governmental and public affairs, including the right to have access to the means necessary to exercise this right; and

(e) The right to communicate in a language they understand.

Principle 23

1. Every human being has the right to education.

2. To give effect to this right for internally displaced persons, the authorities concerned shall ensure that such persons, in particular displaced children, receive education which shall be free and compulsory at the primary level....

Section IV—Principles Relating to Humanitarian Assistance

Principle 24

1. All humanitarian assistance shall be carried out in accordance with the principles of humanity and impartiality and without discrimination....

Principle 25

1. The primary duty and responsibility for providing humanitarian assistance to internally displaced persons lies with national authorities.

2. International humanitarian organizations and other appropriate actors have the right to offer their services in support of the internally displaced. Such an offer shall not be regarded as an unfriendly act or an interference in a State's internal affairs and shall be considered in good faith....

3. All authorities concerned shall grant and facilitate the free passage of humanitarian assistance and grant persons engaged in the provision of such assistance rapid and unimpeded access to the internally displaced.

Principle 26

Persons engaged in humanitarian assistance, their transport and supplies shall be respected and protected. They shall not be the object of attack or other acts of violence....

Section V—Principles Relating to Return, Resettlement and Reintegration

Principle 28

1. Competent authorities have the primary duty and responsibility to establish conditions, as well as provide the means, which allow internally displaced persons to return voluntarily, in safety and with dignity, to their homes or places of habitual residence, or to resettle voluntarily in another part of the country. Such authorities shall endeavour to facilitate the reintegration of returned or resettled internally displaced persons.

2. Special efforts should be made to ensure the full participation of internally displaced persons in the planning and management of their return or resettlement and reintegration.

Principle 29

1. Internally displaced persons who have returned to their homes or places of habitual residence or who have resettled in another part of the country shall not be discriminated against as a result of their having been displaced. They shall have the right to participate fully and equally in public affairs at all levels and have equal access to public services.

2. Competent authorities have the duty and responsibility to assist returned and/or resettled internally displaced persons to recover, to the extent possible, their property and possessions which they left behind or were dispossessed of upon their displacement. When recovery of such property and possessions is not possible, competent authorities shall provide or assist these persons in obtaining appropriate compensation or another form of just reparation....

NOTES AND QUESTIONS

1. At first glance, the Guiding Principles seem straightforward, but there is mischief in the details. How would you answer the following questions?

a. The Guiding Principles forbid "discrimination of any kind" and say that families have the "right to remain together" when housed in camps. Should a country like Pakistan (to pick just one example) be able to segregate relief camps by sex in order to comport with religious custom or to protect women from abuse or violence? Should India be able to segregate relief camps by religious caste for similar reasons?

b. The Guiding Principles emphasize the needs of women and children. Principle 19, for instance, says "special attention should be paid to the health needs of women, including access to female health care providers and services, such as reproductive health care." What does that access include? Birth control (with or without a partner's consent)? Reversal of a tubal ligation (for women wishing to become pregnant again after losing a child)? Abortion? Principle 4 says children should be provided "assistance... which takes into account their special needs." This includes appropriate schooling (Principle 23). Are children entitled to child counseling? Organized recreational activities? Education in their native language? Special education for those with mental or physical disabilities?

c. Principle 4 says all provisions will be applied without discrimination based on "legal...status." Does this prevent a country from checking the identification papers of IDPs before providing them with transportation or relief services? Suppose a country finds within its relief camps illegal residents seeking services. May these persons be legally deported? If so, what is the chance illegal residents will seek the aid that the Guiding Principles say they are entitled to? After Hurricane Gustav hit the Texas coast in 2008, some legal aid workers reported that U.S. immigration officials were checking the residency documents of evacuees returning to their home cities. Is this a violation of Principle 4? How about Principles 28 and 29?

d. Principle 29 requires state officials to assist IDPs in recovering their property and possessions, or, where recovery is impossible, assist IDPs with "appropriate compensation" or "just reparation." What does that mean? If the government is partly responsible for the failure of a levee or a dam, does that mean the dispossessed are owed compensation? Is that a reversal of sovereign immunity? If not, what practical effect does Principle 29 have?

If your class has trouble reaching consensus, don't worry. At this point none of the questions has been definitively resolved. The debates will continue.

2. Following hurricanes Katrina and Rita in 2005, some human rights experts argued that the U.S. federal government and some state governments had violated several of the Guiding Principles. *See, e.g.,* Lolita Buckner Inniss, *A Domestic Right of Return? Race, Rights, and Residency in New Orleans in the Aftermath of Hurricane* Katrina, 27 B.C. Third World L.J. 325, 368-369 (2007); Frederic L. Kirgis, "Hurricane Katrina and Internally Displaced Persons," American Society of International Law, Sept. 21, 2005, http://www.asil.org/insights050921.cfm (July 1, 2009).

    Some experts claimed that the U.S. response to Hurricane Katrina, by allowing a disproportionate burden to fall upon African Americans, had also violated CERD. In 2008, a UN treaty committee agreed and urged U.S. officials to afford displaced residents a greater say in decisions affecting their ability to return to New Orleans, including decisions about the future of public housing. U.N. Committee on the Elimination of All Forms of Racial Discrimination, Consideration of Reports Submitted by States Parties under Article 9 of the Convention, May 8, 2008, http://www.universalhumanrightsindex.org/documents/824/1310/document/en/text.html (July 1, 2009). American officials immediately downplayed the significance of the committee's report and suggested it was misinformed. (Though standing behind the report's conclusion, committee members would later concede they had not visited New Orleans.) *See* David Hammer, *Critics Admit They Didn't Visit, Research Post-Katrina New Orleans*, Times-Picayune, March 5, 2008, http://blog.nola.com/updates/2008/03/critics_admit_they_didnt_visit.html (July 1, 2009).

    As already pointed out, the United States has not agreed to the Guiding Principles on Internally Displaced Persons, and in any event the agreement is unenforceable. The United States is a party to CERD, but that agreement is not enforceable either. What, then, is the value of calling attention to suspected violations of international agreements such as these? What if the alleged violator is *not* a global power? How does that change the calculus?

3. Critics fault the Guiding Principles for their lack of binding effect. Bahame Tom Nyanduga, a Special Rapporteur for the African Commission on Human and Peoples' Rights, has called the absence of binding protection for IDPs "a grave lacuna in international law." Bahame Tom Nyanduga, *The Challenge of Internal Displacement in Africa*, Forced Migration Review 21, 58 (September 2004).

    Despite that omission, the Guiding Principles are gaining some traction and are presumably making a difference in people's lives. Several U.N. entities—such as the U.N. Development Programme, the High Commissioner for Human Rights, and UNICEF—have incorporated the Guiding Principles into their actions and policies. U.N. treaty bodies, which monitor the implementation of U.N. human rights conventions, have referred to the Guiding Principles in their observations of member states. A few countries—including Burundi, Colombia, the Philippines, Sri Lanka, and Uganda—have integrated some of the principles into their national policies.

Although the U.S government does not recognize the Guiding Principles as law, the U.S. Agency for International Development (USAID) explicitly uses the principles to guide foreign assistance efforts in regions of disaster or war. Take a look at this excerpt from USAID's statement on IPDs.

U.S. AGENCY FOR INTERNATIONAL DEVELOPMENT, USAID ASSISTANCE TO INTERNALLY DISPLACED PERSONS

1-3 (Oct. 2004)

At least 25 million people are uprooted within the borders of their own countries by armed conflict, generalized violence, persecution, and natural and human-caused disasters. The plight of these internally displaced persons (IDPs) in some 52 countries is a pressing humanitarian, human rights, development, and political challenge for the global community....

The U.S. Agency for International Development (USAID) recognizes that the 25 million people displaced within their own countries are a pressing humanitarian, human rights, development, and political challenge for the global community. There are nearly twice as many internally displaced persons (IDPs) as the 13 million civilians classified as refugees who have crossed international frontiers, thereby gaining protection under international laws.

USAID's interest in internal displacement is driven by humanitarian and development concerns as well as political and security considerations. Involuntary displacement can lead to disaffection that could be exploited to threaten regional stability. The National Security Strategy of the United States, issued in 2002, elevated the importance of development, citing it—along with defense and diplomacy—as a fundamental element of U.S. security.

Since IDPs remain within the territorial jurisdiction of their own countries, the primary responsibility for their welfare and protection lies with the respective governing authorities. The international community should provide assistance and support to ensure this responsibility is being fulfilled. USAID advocates that IDPs should be granted the full security and protection provided for under applicable norms of international human rights law, international humanitarian law, and national law. Population displacement can endure for a few days, several years, or even decades, creating a wide range of needs. Basic protection for at-risk populations requires attention during the immediate humanitarian response to population displacement as well as during the longer-term transition toward development and stability.

The inclusion of a comprehensive response to the problem of internal displacement in the broader USAID strategy is a priority. This reflects the growing understanding of how population displacement can negatively affect stability and development prospects. USAID is committed to a long-term perspective that promotes durable solutions and eventual self-reliance for displaced persons, reinforcing the principle that internal displacement is an Agency-wide concern.

With its strong operational presence in the field, USAID will address the broad array of needs confronting all phases of displacement, ranging from emergency relief to transitional aid to long-term development assistance. The transitional phase is critical, requiring the coordinated efforts of all partners to develop a comprehensive strategy that facilitates IDP resettlement and reintegration. The ultimate goal is to enable IDPs to become fully productive contributors to economic and social progress in their local communities.

USAID will serve as the U.S. Government's lead coordinator on internal displacement to ensure a coherent response from the U.S. Government and the international community. The Agency will work closely with the U.S. Department of State and other U.S. Government entities, U.N. agencies, international organizations, nongovernmental organizations (NGOs), host governments, and local institutions in affected countries. As part of its advocacy role, USAID promotes

- lifesaving humanitarian access to needy populations
- information sharing to forge common understanding of the problems and build consensus on policy and strategic approaches
- the protection of IDPs during all phases of displacement
- accountability and evaluation of programs
- wider international recognition of the U.N. Guiding Principles on Internal Displacement as a useful framework for dealing with internal displacement

Internal population displacement and the factors that cause it pose difficult challenges and present complex legal and sovereignty issues. The availability of resources, security, and humanitarian access will affect the scale of assistance and protection that USAID and the international community can provide. USAID will review these challenging issues on a regular basis to develop and update effective strategies.

NOTES AND QUESTIONS

In this statement, USAID says it promotes "wider international recognition" of the Guiding Principles as a policy framework. Why, then, has the U.S. government not recognized the application of those principles on American soil? What specific provisions, if any, do you think the government objects to?

E. PULLING IT TOGETHER

As a way of synthesizing the many issues in this chapter—geographic distribution, ecological exposure, social vulnerability, and international law—we ask you to review this last case study of one of the most devastating and broad-scaled catastrophes of the last half-century: the 2004 Asian tsunami.

ACTION AID INTERNATIONAL, TSUNAMI RESPONSE: A HUMAN RIGHTS ASSESSMENT
3, 17, 20, 25, 28, 35, 43-44, 51-52 (January 2006)

The December 2004 tsunami unleashed loss and destruction of horrific magnitude in 12 countries in Asia and Africa. One year after the tragedy, despite the tremendous efforts of local, national and international agencies, the rehabilitation and reconstruction process is fraught with difficulties.

Even though all the affected countries have ratified international human rights instruments, they are failing to meet these standards in post-tsunami relief and rehabilitation work. Allegations of human rights violations in tsunami-affected areas are rampant. These include discrimination in aid distribution, forced relocation, arbitrary arrests and sexual and gender-based violence. One year on, tsunami reconstruction efforts are plagued with serious delays and have not been given the priority they warrant....

Inadequate response and a lack of consideration for the human rights of victims creates a human-induced tragedy that exacerbates the plight of those already suffering the effects of a disaster brought on by natural causes. Therefore, individual states, international agencies including the UN and its programmes, civil society and the private sector, must redouble efforts towards the realisation of human rights worldwide, including rights to disaster-preparedness and disaster-response. Indeed this is essential if we are to reduce the loss of life, human suffering and homelessness resulting from disasters in the future. It is only through national and international cooperation based on human rights standards that people uprooted and at risk as a result of devastating natural disasters can be effectively protected. This report is a significant contribution. It assesses the status of post-tsunami reconstruction and clearly highlights multiple human rights violations in Indonesia, Thailand, Sri Lanka, India and the Maldives. It makes the demand for human rights standards in resettlement and reconstruction all the more urgent. Non-discriminatory access to relief and rehabilitation, mechanisms to ensure transparency and accountability, and provision for the active participation of survivors are fundamental, while all efforts must take into account the special needs and concerns of women....

Land

The right to land is one of the most contentious issues to have arisen in the wake of the tsunami. Across the region there are cases of conflict between communities who have historically lived along the coastline and government departments, major land-owners and developers. With coastal land at a premium for tourism and sea areas coveted by industrial fishing companies, the governments of India, Sri Lanka, Indonesia and Thailand are discouraging—and even preventing—people from returning to their original land and fishing areas. In some cases governments have made compensation contingent on people relinquishing their rights to coastal land. In other cases, governments have failed to compensate local residents and farmers for land that has become uninhabitable or barren due to sea water. Survivors from Kuala Bubon in West Aceh, Indonesia, are still awaiting compensation for lost land and earnings, despite repeated promises from the chief of Indonesia's National Land Agency.

Buffer Zones

An aspect of government policy that has caused great hardship to tsunami survivors has been the imposition of "buffer zones" preventing people from rebuilding homes along the coast. India, Indonesia, Sri Lanka, Thailand and the Maldives have all created restricted areas or islands, supposedly to mitigate the impact of future storms or tsunamis. With moving inland often a pre-condition for receiving a new house, poorer families are left with little choice but to relocate....

In India, the "coastal regulation zone" (CRZ), in existence since 1991, restricts dwellings and other residential activity within 500 metres of the hightide line. Post-tsunami, the government declared its intention to enforce this regulation rigorously. This generated a huge outcry from fishing communities along the coast of Tamil Nadu as it would have meant relocating several hundreds of villages. Not only would it prevent fishing communities from earning a living but it would deny their customary rights to land by the sea. For a number of those surveyed, renewed enforcement of the CRZ would mean relinquishing legal tenure for coastal land and properties to the state under the guise of safety concerns. After an intense three-month campaign by fisher people's organizations, the government of Tamil Nadu has recently amended legislation, accepting their right to remain close to the sea but withholding benefits from those who choose to do so. People are now allowed to rebuild and repair houses within 200 metres of the hightide line but they must pay for it themselves. On the other hand, if they choose to move more than 200 metres from the hightide line, they are eligible to receive a new house from the government. In the case of Manginpudi Beach village in Andhra Pradesh, residents have been forcibly relocated two kilometres away from their original village, making way for new tourist resorts. The government promised to allocate new land to them and build them new homes, but to date residents have no information as to when these will be ready.

In Sri Lanka, in response to popular pressure in the run-up to presidential elections, the 100-200 metre "buffer zone" established in the aftermath of the tsunami was reduced to 35 metres in the south and west, and 50 metres in the east. In Jaffna in the north it remains at 100 metres. Throughout 2005, the Sri Lankan buffer zone led to confusion and concern among families living in temporary camps who did not know when or whether they would be able to rebuild on the site of their old homes.

In the Maldives, the government is seeking to implement a "safe island" programme which will lead to the displacement of more people. The programme's stated aims are to develop a few islands as economically and socially sustainable. The government argues that this will enable cost-effective delivery of services and will provide protection from natural and other disasters. It will also, according to the government, divert the influx of migrants to its capital, Male. This plan, in existence since 1998, is now being funded by the European Union, World Bank, United Nations Development Programme (UNDP) and others through a trust fund managed by the government in collaboration with the UNDP. At present the entire population of three islands…and part of the population of a further 10 islands, are being relocated to other islands. People are left with no choice but to move as it is a precondition of housing and livelihood rehabilitation. Those affected by this programme have expressed their doubts about the safety rationale of the government and ask why the populations of more than 180 islands in similar circumstances (in terms of elevation, topography, proximity of homes to the sea) are not also being moved.

…

Land for Permanent Housing

One of the main reasons for slow progress on permanent housing is the paucity of land. In several cases, government agencies have been slow to acquire land from private parties or have been reluctant to pay the market price. In two areas of Prakasham in Andhra Pradesh, India, a local NGO had taken on responsibility for the construction of permanent housing but the price quoted to purchase the 2.5 acres of land needed was considered by the government to be extremely high. Progress has now stalled and there is confusion over who will bear the cost. Residents doubt whether the plan will go ahead.

In Iraimandurai, Tamil Nadu, India, residents have had to give up their rights to their coastal land in order to be eligible for government land and a house farther from the sea. Although many were unhappy about relinquishing their land rights, they felt there was no other option if they were to receive help. The relocation will damage their livelihoods and increase other costs, including the cost of transport for children to get to school. Residents also feel it will mean the loss of social networks and their sense of community.

Housing

The human right to adequate housing cannot be interpreted as merely being the right to four walls and a roof. The concept of adequacy in relation to the right to housing is understood as adequacy of privacy, space, security, lighting and ventilation, basic infrastructure and location with regard to work and basic facilities.

Temporary Housing

One of the most appalling facts in post-tsunami rehabilitation is that a year on from the disaster a large number of people are still living in temporary shelters and some even in tents. There are also many living in damaged houses. Living conditions in all these forms of shelter are uniformly poor.

In Indonesia, official sources confirmed in September 2005 that more than 470,000 people were living as internally displaced people in temporary shelters or with relatives. In the Maldives, the number of internally displaced people stands at more than 11,000. Of these some 5,200 are living in temporary shelters. The rest are living with their friends and relatives, either because temporary shelter was not available or because they refused it as they found the living conditions unacceptable....

In India, temporary housing consists of one-room structures, irrespective of family size. At all sites, women and men have complained about the inadequate size of the shelters, which range from 2.4×3.0 metres to 3.6×4.5 metres and house between four and seven people each....

Temporary shelters provided by the government in...the Maldives are 4.9×7.6 meters each....Most shelters house two families (nine to twelve people in total)....Lack of privacy and sleeping space is a particular concern for women and adolescent girls....Children of all ages and both sexes sleep together, making the younger ones, particularly girls, vulnerable to abuse. . . .

Livelihood

The right to earn a living is fundamental. It provides people with the power to control their lives with dignity. Estimations from the [United Nations] and the World Bank suggest the loss of livelihoods in India alone post-tsunami was US$700 million. In Indonesia, unemployment has risen by more than 30 per cent since the tsunami. The loss of earning capacity not only affects household income but contributes to the psychological depression that often follows a disaster.

In Andhra Pradesh, India, fishermen complain that, despite compensation and aid they have received, they are still unable to cope with the loss of income because of a change in sea patterns after the tsunami. Most of their former fishing sites are no longer remunerative. They no longer have a fixed place for fishing and have to hunt out new locations. Generally their catch is lower or different, resulting in lower income....

In Thailand, migrant workers are protected by the 1998 Labour Protection Act, which deals with issues including the minimum wage, overtime wages, working hours and holidays. Since the tsunami, local landlords and factories will only employ migrant workers on the condition that they forgo their rights under this Act. In tsunami-affected areas of Thailand, most migrant workers have been found to be receiving less than the legal minimum wage or are compelled to work more than the stipulated 48-hour week. Many migrant workers are being cheated out of their wages with the money "disappearing" between the employer and the middleman.

Our field research shows that government response to the massive loss of livelihoods is far from satisfactory. Employment initiatives by government have only begun in a third of villages surveyed; none have begun in Indonesia and India. Where employment generation has begun, workers are often brought in from outside the area, rather than using local people who need the work and have a vested interest in the quick reconstruction of their environment....

Women

Women the world over tend to have more responsibility for looking after children, providing food and running a home than men. In a post-disaster situation, when support systems—including physical infrastructure—break down, women bear the additional burden. Indeed, they are often the ones leading the recovery process in their families and communities. In responding to the tsunami, governments have, once again, largely neglected the particular needs of women. Women have not been included in decision-making regarding damage assessment, allocation of plots, land surveys or design of shelters and permanent houses. Orphaned girls, single women, women heading their households and women who are elderly, disabled or part of minority and vulnerable communities remain the most neglected.

Relief Distribution

Immediately after the tsunami, aid was often distributed in places and ways that were more accessible to men. It was a struggle for women to be recognized as heads of households and receive their dues. Only in a very few cases was special attention given to the needs of single women, including widows. In all countries, compensation was almost always handed out to male members of the family who did not necessarily share it with the women.

In Sri Lanka, women who owned land in their own names prior to the tsunami, particularly Muslim women who had received property as part of their dowry, have raised concerns that they are not considered eligible for compensation. Even in cases where the original house or land was in the woman's name, the government deposits compensation payments in the name of the man. Banks in the northeast of Sri Lanka reportedly asked women to sign a letter relinquishing their rights to the house and land to their husbands in order to facilitate compensation payments....

Water and Sanitation

The absence of proper sanitation facilities is a serious cause for concern. Not only are people's rights to adequate housing violated but also their right to health. And there are grave implications for women's mobility and security. One of the most common complaints across all countries was the inadequacy of toilets....

In both Sri Lanka and India [, for instance,] women complain that toilets built close to temporary shelters lack water or that they have to walk long distances to use toilet facilities. The absence of proper street lighting in most resettlement camps makes it unsafe for women walking to the toilets....

Reproductive Rights

The notion of a woman's body as a site of her spouse's and his family's reproductive demands is an old one. In India, in families who lost children in the tsunami, women are under great pressure to replace dead offspring. The fact that many women had previously been convinced to go through sterilization operations makes the situation all the more tragic. Scores of women flocked to health centers in search of the "miracle"—a reversal of tubectomy, known in medical terminology as "recanalization."...

Relief camps all over Asia report an almost complete lack of healthcare services for expectant women and mothers with newborn babies. Government relief measures have also completely ignored the needs of menstruating women and girls. In Tamil Nadu in India most families received only dhotis and saris (outer clothing), but no undergarments or sanitary napkins for women....

Violence

Violence against women was manifest soon after the tsunami struck and included shocking reports of women being pulled out of the water and then raped. Vulnerability to sexual violence increases manifold under camp conditions where toilet facilities and living quarters are forced out into the public domain....

In Thailand, women immigrant labourers have reported the increased risk of being drawn into human trafficking and say that they regularly face sexual violence, including rape by employment agents. Women report that difficult camp conditions, trauma and unemployment are contributing to increased alcoholism among men. This often results in increased violence in the home. In Beureugang in West Aceh, [Indonesia,] women living in government temporary settlements have explained that husbands who are not working are more likely to inflict psychological and physical abuse.

Livelihoods

Women's concerns have once again largely been ignored in schemes to restore livelihoods. In spite of their obvious contribution to both fishing and agriculture, women are rarely recognised as fisherfolk or farmers; and therefore when schemes of livelihood restoration are taken up, they rarely involve women. While fishermen in India carry out the visibly strenuous and dangerous task of deep-sea fishing, once the fish is offloaded, women take over completely. Little has been done to compensate women in the fishing community who perform important tasks such as cleaning, drying and selling the fish catch. Women from fishing communities who were widowed by the tsunami and therefore lost access to the catch that their husbands would have normally brought in, have not been considered in government livelihood programmes.

Discrimination

...

Discrimination is evident in all countries [affected by the tsunami] and has been a major factor in impeding people's access to relief and rehabilitation post-tsunami.

For dalits (members of the "lowest" caste) in India, discrimination that existed before the tsunami increased afterwards when they were even more vulnerable....

In the Andamans [a chain of islands in the Indian Ocean] there is evidence that compensation has been hijacked by local political groups. Residents complain that people have received compensation on the basis of party political affiliation rather than need....

[In Thailand,] discrimination by the state has severely affected the rights of...Mokens or sea gypsies. In a temple in Phang Nga, while everyone else received large relief packages, Moken families were given a box of milk or canned sardines. Mokens were also denied help by the government as many are not Thai citizens....

Some religious foundations in Thailand have made it a precondition of help that Mokens must change their religion and participate in the religious activities of the foundation. In other places, religious foundations will only help those who paste a sticker displaying a religious symbol in front of their tent or house.

E. One More Thing: Climate Change

Consider an excerpt from this guidebook, published by Catholic Relief Services.

MARILISE TURNBULL, CHARLOTTE L. STERRETT, & AMY HILLEBOE, TOWARD RESILIENCE: A
GUIDE TO DISASTER RISK REDUCTION AND CLIMATE CHANGE ADAPTATION

1-5, 7, 11-13 (2013)

Disaster Risk

Development and humanitarian practitioners share a common goal: the empowerment of women, men and children to enjoy their human rights, and the ongoing protection of those rights. Development strategies and humanitarian responses need, therefore, to incorporate measures to reduce the main risks to achieving this goal.

But the impacts of disasters continue to be a major obstacle to this. Recorded disasters alone from 2001 to 2010 affected, on average, 232 million people per year, killed 106 million others, and caused US$108 billion in economic damages. In addition, countless small-scale, unreported disasters put a cumulative strain on health, lives and livelihoods....

Disaster Risk Reduction

...People around the world constantly seek ways to reduce disaster risks. Some combine diverse livelihood strategies, such as fishing, farming and selling manual labor, to reduce their vulnerability to losses in one area; some use social networks to obtain information about good pasture, or impending hazards, such as swollen rivers, and plan their actions accordingly. But in many cases poverty and marginalization restrict their effectiveness and options, and rural-to-urban migration exposes them to unfamiliar situations in which they lack the knowledge and means to manage new risks.

Today, there is increasing awareness that states—within their obligation to respect, fulfill and protect human rights—have primary responsibility for reducing disaster risk, and that the international community has a duty to provide support and create an enabling environment for this obligation to be met....

[Under] the Hyogo Framework for Action (HFA)..., many governments have introduced legislative and policy frameworks for disaster risk reduction, established early warning systems and increased their level of preparedness to respond to disasters. However, the goals of the HFA are still far from being achieved, particularly in terms of addressing the causes of risk and ensuring full participation of at-risk populations in risk assessments, planning processes and programs. A massive effort is needed to bring about change at the heart of each country's 'development system' through the involvement of all sectors and all stakeholders—from local to national—in disaster risk reduction.

Climate Change Risk

As scientific knowledge of global climate change increases and its impacts are experienced around the world, there is a clear need for a broader approach to reducing risks.

...

Projected changes in the climate include temperature increases on land and at sea, sea-level rise, melting of glaciers and ice caps, and changing and irregular rainfall patterns. These changes affect almost every aspect of human life and the ecosystems on which it depends.

Climate change will result in increases in the frequency and intensity of extreme weather events, as well as significant impacts from more gradual changes....

Understanding Disaster Risk Reduction and Climate Change Adaptation

Governments and institutions are coming to realize that security, poverty reduction and prosperity will depend on the integration of climate change adaptation strategies in all sectors, and their implementation at all levels. Development and humanitarian practitioners also have an important role to play in terms of advocating for the rights of the women, men and children at greatest risk to be prioritized, and incorporating climate change adaptation strategies into their own programs.

As an approach, climate change adaptation is a dynamic process and not an end state, given the uncertainty in climate change impacts and the need to support at-risk populations to: address current hazards, increased variability and emerging trends; manage risk and uncertainty; and build their capacity to adapt.

Principles of an Integrated Approach
to Disaster Risk Reduction and Climate Change Adaptation

...Most recently, interest among development and humanitarian actors in improving understanding of how to generate greater resilience to shocks and stresses, including hazards and the effects of climate change, is resulting in constructive debate. There is significant convergence in the lessons, recommendations and challenges emerging from each of these spheres of activity, and a growing consensus on the need for an integrated approach.

The following [abridged list of principles] provide[s] development and humanitarian practitioners with a set of criteria for building disaster and climate resilience that is applicable across the program cycle in multiple sectors and varied contexts.

Increase understanding of the hazard and climate change context: An understanding of past trends, present experiences and future projections of hazard occurrence, climate variability and the range of effects of climate change on the area and population concerned should underpin any decisions or actions to build disaster and climate resilience. It should include mapping at different scales, to allow for regional and local hazards and effects of climate change. The risk analysis process itself should increase understanding among all stakeholders, both as a result of its participatory nature, and through sharing of the results.

Increase understanding of exposure, vulnerability and capacity: An assessment of the vulnerabilities and capacities of the population, systems and resources should be the foundation for decisions on the location, target populations (including understanding differential vulnerability), objectives and approach of measures to build disaster and climate resilience. It should include analysis of the projected effects of climate change as well as of those currently observed. The assessment should also increase understanding among all stakeholders of the causes of exposure, vulnerability and capacity, both as a result of a participatory process, and through sharing of the results.

Recognize rights and responsibilities: Disaster risk reduction and climate change adaptation should be regarded among the responsibilities of states and governments as duty-bearers for the realization and enjoyment of human rights. Governancesystems and the political environment should enable people at risk or affected by disasters and climate change to demand accountability for their decisions, actions and omissions. The role of other stakeholders, including NGOs, should be complementary to, and enabling of, the relationship between duty-bearers and right-holders.

Strengthen participation of, and action by, the population at risk: All people at risk have the right to participate in decisions that affect their lives. Their first-hand knowledge of the issues affecting them is critical to ensuring that analysis and subsequent actions are based on empirical evidence. In addition, the sustainability of resilience-building strategies depends on their ownership and agency. Therefore all decision-making processes and actions should directly involve the population at risk ensuring that women, men and children, as well as high-risk groups, are included.

Address different timescales: Analysis, strategies and programs should address current, identified risks and likely future scenarios. Preparing for the occurrence of known hazards should not be neglected in favor of building capacities to adapt to medium- and long-term effects of climate change, and other, potentially unknown shocks or stresses. Resource allocation and activities should be planned accordingly.

Do no harm: Processes to define strategies and programs to build disaster and climate resilience should always incorporate an assessment of their potential negative impacts, including their contribution to conflict and effects on the environment. In cases where potential harm is identified, measures to substantially reduce or remove them should be built into the strategy and program design. To avoid creating a false sense of security, or promoting mal-adaptation, programs should always be based on a multi-hazard, multi- effect assessment.

NOTES AND QUESTIONS

1.   Readers wanting to know more about climate impacts and climate change adaptation on the global scale should see Climate Change 2014: Impacts, Adaptation and Vulnerability (Intergovernmental Panel on Climate Change Fifth Assessment Report) (2014) (Final Draft), *available at* https://www.ipcc.ch/report/ar5/wg2/and The Law of Adaptation to Climate Change: United States and International Aspects (Michael B. Gerrard & Katrina Fischer Kuh, eds., 2012).

2.   Does it matter whether a nation's vulnerability is classified as related mostly to "natural disaster" or to "climate change"? Some experts think that it does. Vulnerabilities triggered by climate change imply a human cause and, therefore, a set of *responsible* parties—including wealthy, industrialized countries (the "Global North"). Vulnerabilities posed by natural disaster amount to an international concern; but they are harder to blame directly on rich countries. As such, the international responsibility for reducing climate change risk may be viewed as more compelling than the desire to reduce "ordinary" disaster risk. *See* M.J. Mace & Michiel Schaeffer, Loss and Damage under the UNFCC: What Relationship to the Hyogo Framework 3 (Climate Analytics, Oct. 2013), *available at* http://www.lossanddamage.net/download/7248.pdf. Thus, nations of the Global South often oppose efforts from the North to house international climate adaptation strategies in the HFA rather than in the U.N. Framework Convention on Climate Change. As they see it, such a strategy enables the North to downplay its contribution to climate risk and to avoid full financial responsibility. *See* Paul Govind & Robert R.M. Verchick, *Climate Change and Natural Disasters,* in International Environmental Law and the Global South: Comparative Perspectives 491, 491 (Shawkat Alam, Sumudu Atapattu, Carmen G. Gonzalez, & Jona Razzaque, eds., 2015).

F. EXERCISE

In preparation for a future cyclone or another tsunami, imagine that India decides to develop a disaster response strategy using the U.N. Guiding Principles on Internal Displacement as an important policy framework. Since India is also a party to CERD and CEDAW, it wants its disaster response strategy to comply with these agreements too. As a first step, India's national Ministry of Home Affairs agrees to collaborate with the Indian state of Andhra Pradesh to develop practical strategies for protecting the socially and economically vulnerable.

Located on India's southeastern coast, Andhra Pradesh is known for its rich agricultural lands and busy fishing villages. Its 600-mile coastline is the second longest in India. (Gujarat has the longest.) Andhra Pradesh is also one of India's most populous states, with nearly 76 million people, mostly Hindu with a small minority (about 15 percent) of Christians and Muslims.

Since Andhra Pradesh was so heavily damaged during the Asian Tsunami, it is hoped that the region will be a source of lessons for the future. Local citizens' organizations are also being invited to collaborate. Recently, USAID has expressed an interest in helping to plan and modestly fund parts of the project.

A small meeting has been called to lay out the possibilities and address some fundamental concerns.

The participants are

1. a representative from India's Ministry of Home Affairs,
2. a representative from the state government of Andhra Pradesh,
3. a representative from the Kattumaram Fishing Project, a nongovernmental organization that promotes the interests of rural fisherfolk in Andhra Pradesh,
4. a representative of the Many Hands Network, a nongovernmental organization that promotes the interests of rural women in southern India, and
5. a representative from USAID.

The questions to be discussed are the following:

1. What are the most important aspects of the Guiding Principles? That is, what values provide the "framework" on which the state's policy should be based?
2. What reforms or improvements are most needed to promote those values? Try to agree on the top three reforms.
3. How should compliance with the reforms be enforced? What level of government should be responsible for implementation? For enforcement? For evaluation?
4. How should the reforms be funded?

Choose a role and divide into groups to address these questions. Be prepared to report on the results.

TABLE OF CASES

Principal case decisions reproduced or excerpted are noted by italic font.

TABLE OF AUTHORITIES

Books and Treatises

Alexandre, Michèle, Navigating the Topography of Inequality Post-Disaster: A Proposal for Remedying Past Geographic Segregation during Rebuilding, in Law and Recovery from Disaster: Hurricane Katrina (Robin Paul Malloy ed., 2009), 255

Apt, Jay et al., Electricity: Protecting Essential Services, in Seeds of Disaster, Roots of Response: How Private Action Can Reduce Public Vulnerability (Philip E. Auerswald et al. eds., 2006), 19

Auerswald, Philip E., Complexity and Interdependence, in Seeds of Disaster, Roots of Response: How Private Action Can Reduce Public Vulnerability (Philip E. Auerswald et al. eds., 2006), 16

Auerswald, Philip E. et al., Where Private Efficiency Meets Public Vulnerability: The Critical Infrastructure Challenge, in Seeds of Disaster, Roots of Response: How Private Action Can Reduce Public Vulnerability (Philip E. Auerswald et al. eds., 2006), 24, 25

Barry, John M., Rising Tide: The Great Mississippi Flood of 1927 and How It Changed America (1998), 216

Bassett, Debra Lyn, Place, Disasters, and Disabilities, in Law and Recovery from Disaster: Hurricane Katrina (Robin Paul Malloy ed., 2009), 267

Beck, Ulrich, Risk Society: Toward a New Modernity (1986), 228

Blaikie, Piers, Cannon, Terry, Davis, Ian & Wisner, Ben, At Risk: Natural Hazards, People's Vulnerability and Disasters (1994), 243

Blakely, Ed, My Storm: Managing the Recovery of New Orleans in the Wake of Katrina (2011), 430

Branscomb, Lewis M. & Michel-Kerjan, Erwann O., Public-Private Collaboration on a National and International Scale, in Seeds of Disaster, Roots of Response: How Private Action Can Reduce Public Vulnerability (Philip E. Auerswald et al. eds., 2006), 21

Breyer, Stephen, Breaking the Vicious Circle: Toward Effective Risk Regulation (Harvard 1993), 299

Bullard, Robert D., Dumping in Dixie: Race, Class and Environmental Quality (3d ed. 2000), 252

Burby, Raymond J., Cooperating with Nature (1998), 46

Button, Gregory, Disaster Culture: Knowledge and Uncertainty in the Wake of Human and Environmental Catastrophe (2010), 280

Campanella, Richard, Bienville's Dilemma: A Historical Geography of New Orleans (2008), 427

Cawardine, William, The Pullman Strike (1973), 143

Chen, Jim, Law Among the Ruins in Law and Recovery from Disaster: Hurricane Katrina (Robin Paul Malloy ed., 2009), 233

Chomsky, Noam, Language and Mind (enlarged ed. 1972), 162

Kormos, Michael & Bowe, Thomas, Coordinated and Uncoordinated Crisis Responses by the Electric Industry, in Seeds of Disaster, Roots of Response: How Private Action Can Reduce Public Vulnerability (Philip E. Auerswald et al. eds., 2006), 17, 19

Kousky, Carolyn et al., In Harm's Way: Homeowner Behavior and Wildland Fire Policy, in Wildfire Policy: Law and Economics Perspectives (Karen M. Bradshaw & Dean Lueck eds., 2012), 41

Kunreuther, Howard C. & Michel-Kerjan, Erwann O., At War with the Weather: Managing Large-Scale Risks in a New Era of Catastrophes (2009), 37, 232

Lagadec, Patrick & Michel-Kerjan, Erwann O., The Paris Initiative, "Anthrax and Beyond," in Seeds of Disaster, Roots of Response: How Private Action Can Reduce Public Vulnerability 164, 178 (Philip E. Auerswald et al. eds., 2006), 17, 21

La Porte, T.M., Managing for the Unexpected: Reliability and Organizational Resilience, in Seeds of Disaster, Roots of Response: How Private Action Can Reduce Public Vulnerability (Philip E. Auerswald et al. eds., 2006), 16

The Law of Adaptation to Climate Change: United States and International Aspects (Michael B. Gerrard & Katrina Fischer Kuh, eds., 2012), 403, 500

Lawton, Raymond et al., Model State Protocols for Critical Infrastructure Protection Cost Recovery (2004), 15

Lemann, Nicholas, The Promised Land: The Great Black Migration and How It Changed America (1991), 216

Lewis, J., Law of Eminent Domain (1888), 420

Lipsey, Richard G. & Steiner, Peter O., Economics (5th ed. 1978), 275

Locke, John, Second Treatise on Civil Government (1689, 1998), 63

Lord, Janet E., Waterstone, Michael E. & Stein, Michael Ashley, Natural Disasters and Persons with Disabilities, in Law and Recovery from Disaster: Hurricane Katrina (Robin Paul Malloy ed., 2009), 267

Margolis, Howard, Dealing with Risk: Why the Public and the Experts Disagree on Environmental Issues (1996), 288

Mileti, Dennis S., Disasters by Design (1999), 26, 85

Morgan, M. Granger & Henrion, Max, Uncertainty: A Guide to Dealing with Uncertainty in Quantitative Risk and Policy Analysis (1990), 284

Nelson, Arthur C. & Lang, Robert E., Megapolitan America (2011), 27

Ollenburger, Jane C. & Tobin, Graham A., Women and Postdisaster Stress, in The Gendered Terrain of Disaster: Through Women's Eyes (Elaine Enarson & Betty Hearn Morrow eds., 1998), 262

Perrow, Charles, The Next Catastrophe: Reducing Our Vulnerabilities to Natural, Industrial, and Terrorist Disasters (2007), 10, 26, 38

Petroski, Henry, To Engineer Is Human: The Role of Failure in Successful Design (1982), 305

Prieto, Daniel B., III, Information Sharing with the Private Sector, in Seeds of Disaster, Roots of Response: How Private Action Can Reduce Public Vulnerability (Philip E. Auerswald et al. eds., 2006), 23

Rabin, Robert L. & Bratis, Suzanne A., Financial Compensation for Catastrophic Loss in the United States, Financial Compensation for Victims after Catastrophe (M. Faure & T. Honlief eds., 2005), 332, 383

Randle, Timothy J. et al., Geomorphology and River Hydraulics of the Teton River Upstream of Teton Dam, Teton River, Idaho (2000), 80

Revesz, Richard L. & Livermore, Michael A., Retaking Rationality: How Cost-Benefit Analysis Can Better Protect the Environment and Our Health (2008), 306

Rose, Carol M., The Story of Lucas: Environmental Land Use Regulation Between Developers and the Deep Blue Sea, in Richard J. Lazarus & Oliver A. Houck, Environmental Law Stories (2005), 62

Ryan, Erin, Federalism and the Tug of War Within (2012), 105

Salkin, Patricia E., Sustainability at the Edge: The Opportunity and Responsibility of Local Governments to Effectively Plan for Natural Disaster Mitigation, in Losing Ground: A Nation on Edge (John Nolon & Daniel Rodriguez eds., 2007), 413

Schroeder, Manfred, Fractals, Chaos, Power Laws: Minutes from an Infinite Paradise (1991), 284

Schulman, Paul R. & Roe, Emery, Managing for Reliability in an Age of Terrorism, in Seeds of Disaster, Roots of Response: How Private Action Can Reduce Public Vulnerability (Philip E. Auerswald et al. eds., 2006), 19, 20

Schumpeter, Joseph A., Capitalism, Socialism and Democracy (1975, 1st ed. 1942), 255

Schwab, Anna K. & Brower, David J., Increasing Resilience to Natural Hazards: Obstacles and Opportunities for Local Governments under the Disaster Mitigation Act of 2000, in Losing Ground: A Nation on Edge (John Nolon & Daniel Rodriguez eds., 2007), 404

Seed, R.B. et al., Investigation of the Performance of the New Orleans Flood Protection Systems in Hurricane Katrina on August 29, 2005 (Final Report), July 31, 2006, http://works.bepress.com/rmoss/17, 2, 76

Shogren, Jason F. & Toman, Michael A., How Much Climate Change Is Too Much?, in Climate Change Economics and Policy: An RFF Anthology (Michael A. Toman ed., 2001), 317

Slovic, P., Fischhoff, B., & Lichtenstein, S., Facts and Fears: Understanding Perceived Risk, in Societal Risk Assessment: How Safe Is Safe Enough? (R. Schwing & W. Albers, Jr., eds., 1980), 286

Slovic, P., Fischhoff, B., & Lichtenstein, S., Regulation of Risk: A Psychological Perspective, in Regulatory Policy and the Social Sciences (R. Noll ed., 1985), 286

The Sphere Project Handbook: Humanitarian Charter and Minimum Standards in Disaster Response (2004), 238

Squires, Gregory & Hartman, Chester, There's No Such Thing as a Natural Disaster: Race, Class, and Hurricane Katrina (2006), 228

Stern, Nicholas, The Stern Review of the Economics of Climate Change (2007), 317

Sunstein, Cass R., The Cost-benefit State (2002), 318

Sunstein, Cass R., Risk and Reason: Safety, Law, and the Environment (2002), 302

Taylor, J. Edward, Differential Migration, Networks, Information and Risk, in Migration Theory, Human Capital and Development (Oded Stark ed., 1986), 272

Troy, Austin & Romm, Jeff, Living on the Edge: Economic, Institutional and Management Perspectives on Wildfire Hazard in the Urban Interface, in Advances in the Economics of Environmental Resources (Austin Troy & Roger G. Kennedy eds., 2007), 41

Turnbull, Marilise, Sterrett, Charlotte L., & Hilleboe, Amy, Toward Resilience: A Guide to Disaster Risk Reduction and Climate Change Adaptation (2013), 497

Vale, Lawrence J. & Campanella, Thomas J., Introduction: The Cities Rise Again, in The Resilient City: How Modern Cities Recover from Disaster (Lawrence J. Vale & Thomas J. Campanella eds., 2005), 426

Verchick, Robert R.M., Facing Catastrophe: Environmental Action for a Post-Katrina World (2010), 65, 457

White, Gilbert F., Human Adjustment to Floods, in Geography, Resources, and Environment: Selected Writings of Gilbert F. White (Robert W. Kates & Ian Burton eds., 1986), 228

Yonder, Ayse, Akcar, Sengul & Gopalan, Prema, Women's Participation in Disaster Relief and Recovery (2005), 262

Zeichner, Lee M., Private Sector Integration, in American Bar Association, Hurricane Katrina Task Force Subcommittee Report (Feb. 2006), 201

Zocchetti, David, Public Disclosure of Information by Emergency Services Agencies: A Post-September 11 Paradigm Shift, in A Legal Guide to Homeland Security and Emergency Management for State and Local Governments (Ernest B. Abbott & Otto J. Hetzel eds., 2005), 22

Articles

AAA OFFERS New Disaster Recovery Services, 60-JAN Disp. Res. J. 4 (2005), 372

Abbott, Ernest B., Representing Local Governments in Catastrophic Events: DHS/FEMA Response and Recovery Issues, 37 Urb. Law. 467 (2005), 112

Abbott, Ernest B., Hetzel, Otto J., & Cohn, Alan D., State, Local, and First Responder Issues, in American Bar Association, Hurricane Katrina Task Force Subcommittee Report 14 (Feb. 2006), 185, 186

Ackerman, Frank & Heinzerling, Lisa, Pricing the Priceless: Cost-benefit Analysis of Environmental Protection, 150 U. Pa. L. Rev. 1553 (2002), 312

Adler, Jonathan H., More Sorry Than Safe: Assessing the Precautionary Principle and the Proposed International Safety Protocol, 35 Tex. Int'l L.J. 194 (2000), 323

Adler, Matthew D., Policy Analysis for Natural Hazards: Some Cautionary Lessons from Environmental Policy Analysis, 56 Duke L.J. 1 (2006), 303

Aguirre, B.E., Dialectics of Vulnerability and Resilience, 14 Geo. J. on Poverty L. & Pol'y 39 (2007), 243

Alexander, Frank S., Louisiana Land Reform in the Storm's Aftermath, 53 Loy. L. Rev. 727 (2007), 421

Aloisi, Silvia, Italy Quake Exposes Poor Building Standards, Reuters, Apr. 7, 2009, http://www.alertnet.org/thenews/newsdesk/L7932819.htm, 82

Anderson, Charles, Christchurch: After the Earthquake, a City Rebuilt in Whose Image, The Guardian (London) Jan. 27, 2014, http://www.theguardian.com/cities/2014/jan/27/christchurch-after-earthquake-rebuild-image-new-zealand, 434

Annas, George J., Bioterrorism, Public Health, and Civil Liberties, 346 New Eng. J. Med. 1337 (2002), http://www.nejm.org/doi/full/10.1056/NEJM200204253461722, 192

Annas, George J., Blinded by Bioterrorism: Public Health and Liberty in the 21st Century, 13 Health Matrix 33 (2003), 192

Balcius, James & Liang, Bryan A., Public Health Law & Military Medical Assets: Legal Issues in Federalizing National Guard Personnel, 18 Annals Health L. 35 (2009), 136

Barnes, Julian E. & Walsh, Kenneth T., A Uniform Response?, U.S. News & World Rep., Oct. 3, 2005, 146

Baron, Robert A. & Weinkopf, Mary K., Potential Effects of Proposed Price Gouging Legislation on the Cost and Severity of Gas Supply Interruptions, 3 J. Compet. L. & Econ. 357 (2007), 276

Barron, David J. & Lederman, Martin S., The Commander in Chief at the Lowest Ebb– A Constitutional History, 121 Harv. L. Rev. 941 (2008), 99

Bayer, Ronald & Colgrove, James, Public Health vs. Civil Liberties, 297 Science 1811 (2002), 192

Beito, David & Smith, Daniel J., Tornado Recovery, How Joplin Is Beating Tuscaloosa, Wall Street Journal, April 13, 2012, http://online.wsj.com/news/articles /SB10001424052702303404704577309220933715082, 431

Bennett, Dan, Note, The Domestic Role of the Military in America: Why Modifying or Repealing the Posse Comitatus Act Would Be a Mistake, 10 Lewis & Clark L. Rev. 935 (2006), 137, 138

Blevins, Sue, The Model State Emergency Health Powers Act: An Assault on Civil Liberties in the Name of Homeland Security, Heritage Found. Lecture 748 (2002), http://www.heritage.org/research/lecture/the-model-state-emergency-health-powers-act, 192

Boburg, Shawn, Rebuild v. Retreat: Christie and Cuomo Offer Contrasting Plans in Wake of Sandy, The Record (Bergen County), March 15, 2013, http://www.northjersey.com/news/rebuild-vs-retreat-christie-and-cuomo-offer-contrasting-plans-in-wake-of-sandy-1.589124, 442

Bolin, Robert & Stanford, Lois, The Northridge Earthquake: Community-Based Approaches to Unmet Recovery Needs, 22 Disasters 21 (1998), 258

Borden, Kevin A. & Cutter, Susan L., Spatial Patterns of Natural Hazards Mortality in the United States, Int'l J. Health Geographics 7:64 (2008), 27

Braine, Theresa, Was 2005 the Year of Natural Disasters?, 84:1 Bull. World Health Org. 4 (Jan. 2006), 229

Brodsky, Emily E. & Lay, Thorne, Recognizing Foreshocks from the 1 April 2014 Chile Earthquake, 344 Science 700 (May 16, 2014), 190

Bronin, Sara C., Curbing Energy Sprawl with Microgrids, 43 Conn. L. Rev. 547 (2010), 19

Brook, C., Note, Federalizing the First Responders to Acts of Terrorism via the Militia Clauses, 54 Duke L.J. 999 (2005), 97

Bucci, Steven P. et al., After Hurricane Sandy: Time to Learn and Implement the Lessons in Preparedness, Response, and Resilience, The Heritage Foundation, http://www.heritage.org/research/reports/2013/10/after-hurricane-sandy-time-to-learn-and-implement-the-lessons, 114, 209

Burkett, Maxine, Duty and Breach in an Era of Uncertainty, 20 Geo. Mason L. Rev. 775 (2013), 42, 87

Burton, Lloyd, Wildfire Mitigation Law in the Mountain States of the American West: A Comparative Assessment (2012), http://www.ucdenver.edu/academics/colleges/SPA/Research/EAWG/Research/wildfires/Documents/WhtPprIntrstStdy15jul13.pdf, 52

Byrnes, P.D., Lowry, W.J., & Bondurant, E.J., II, Product Shortages, Allocation and the Antitrust Laws, 20 Antitrust Bull. 713 (1975), 275

Calandrillo, Steve P., Responsible Regulation: A Sensible Cost-benefit, Risk Versus Risk Approach to Federal Health and Safety Regulation, 81 B.U. L. Rev. 957 (2001), 308

Caldwell, Alicia A., Zombie Apocalypse: "The Zombies Are Coming," Homeland Security Warns, Huffington Post Sept. 6, 2012, http://www.huffingtonpost.com/2012/09/06 /homeland-security-warns-the-zombies-are-coming_n_1862768.html, 171

Carey, Christopher, Cities Look to Flood Plains for Jobs, Growth, Tax Dollars, St. Louis Post-Dispatch, July 29, 2003, at A1, 39

Carlson, Ann, The President, Climate Change, and California, 125 Harv. L. Rev. F. 156 (2013), 88

Carlson, Ann E. & Pollak, Daniel, Takings on the Ground: How the Supreme Court's Takings Jurisprudence Affects Local Land Use Decisions, 35 U.C. Davis L. Rev. 103 (2001), 64

Charest, Stephen, Bayesian Approaches to the Precautionary Principle, 12 Duke Envtl. L. & Pol'y F. 265 (2002), 324

Chen, Jim, The Nature of the Public Utility: Infrastructure, the Market, and the Law, 98 Nw. U. L. Rev. 1617 (2004), 201

Chen, Jim, Of Agriculture's First Disobedience and Its Fruit, 48 Vand. L. Rev. 1261 (1995), 216

Chong, Jia-Rui & Becerra, Hector, Katrina's Aftermath: California Earthquake Could Be the Next Katrina, L.A. Times, Sept. 8, 2005, at A2, 45, 83

Citizen Corps, FEMA, Citizen Preparedness Review: Community Resilience through Civil Responsibility and Self-Reliance, Issue 5, Update on Citizen Preparedness Research 12 (Fall 2007), 27

Cohen, Tom, Disaster Relief: Obama, Romney Differ on Federal Role, CNN (Oct. 31, 2012), http://www.cnn.com/2012/10/30/politics/disaster-role-government/, 108

Colburn, Jamison, The Fire Next Time: Land Use Planning in the Wildland/Urban Interface, 28 J. Land Resources & Envtl. L. 223 (2008), 52

Corley, Cheryl, States, Lawmakers Want Feds to Use New Math for FEMA Calculations, April 9, 2014, http://www.npr.org/2014/04/09/300519019/states-lawmakers-want-feds-to-use-new-math-for-fema-calculations, 114

Costanza, Robert et al., The Value of the World's Ecosystem Services and Natural Capital, Nature, vol. 387: 253 (May 15, 1997), 65

Cross, Frank B., Paradoxical Perils of the Precautionary Principle, 53 Wash. & Lee L. Rev. 851 (1996), 323

Cunningham, Michael T., The Military's Involvement in Law Enforcement: The Threat Is Not What You Think, 26 Seattle U. L. Rev. 699 (2003), 137

Cutter, Susan L., Boruff, Bryan J. & Shirley, W. Lynn, Social Vulnerability to Environmental Hazards, 84 Soc. Sci. Q. 242 (2003), 242

Dana, David A., A Behavioral Economic Defense of the Precautionary Principle, 97 Nw. U. L. Rev. 1315 (2003), 325

Furman, H.W.C., Restrictions upon Use of the Army Imposed by the Posse Comitatus Act, 27 Mil. L. Rev. 85 (1960), 132

Gardina, Jackie, Toward Military Rule? A Critique of Executive Discretion to Use the Military in Domestic Emergencies, 91 Marq. L. Rev. 1027 (2008), 149

Gerrard, Michael B., Disasters First: Rethinking Environmental Law After September 11, 9 Widener L. Symp. J. 223 (2003), 185

Gigerenzer, Rerd, Dread Risk, September 11, and Fatal Traffic Accidents, 15 Psych. Sci. 286 (2004), 288

Gilette, Clayton P. & Krier, James E., Risk, Court, and Agencies, 138 U. Pa. L. Rev. 1027 (1990), 285

Gill, James, Ed Blakely Can't Get Anything Right, Times-Picayune (New Orleans), Jan. 18, 2012, http://www.nola.com/opinions/index.ssf/2012/01/ed_blakely_cant_get_anything_r.html, 430

Gilles, Myriam, Public-Private Approaches to Mass Tort Victim Compensation: Some Thoughts on the Gulf Coast Claims Facility, 61 DePaul L. Rev. 419 (2012), 340

Gillette, Clayton P. & Krier, James E., Risk, Courts, and Agencies, 138 U. Pa. L. Rev. 1027 (1990), 280

Gollier, Christian, Jullien, Bruno & Treich, Nicolas, Scientific Progress and Irreversibility: An Economic Interpretation of the "Precautionary Principle," 75 J. Pub. Econ. 229 (2000), 324

Goodwin, Liz, A Year After Sandy, Red Cross Still Dogged by Criticism, Yahoo News, Oct. 23, 2013, http://news.yahoo.com/a-year-later-after-sandy--red-cross-still-dogged-by-criticism-145155111.html, 206

Gostin, Lawrence O., The Model State Emergency Health Powers Act: Public Health and Civil Liberties in a Time of Terrorism, 13 Health Matrix 3 (2003), 191

Grace, Stephanie, Defiant Rumsfeld Left City to Suffer, Time-Picayune, May 21, 2009, 144

Greenberger, Michael, Yes, Virginia, the President Can Deploy Federal Troops to Prevent the Loss of a Major American City from a Devastating Natural Catastrophe, 26 Miss. C. L. Rev. 107 (2006), 148

Griffin, Stephen M., Stop Federalism Before It Kills Again: Reflections on Hurricane Katrina, 21 St. John's J. Legal Comment 527 (2007), 100, 106

Guarino, Mark, Fear the Almighty Wrath: Five Natural Disasters "Caused" by Gays, Salon, Oct. 30, 2012, http://www.salon.com/2012/10/30/fear_the_almighty_wrath_five_natural_disasters_caused_by_gays, 263

Gude, Patricia et al., Potential for Future Development on Fire-Prone Lands, J. Forestry, 106(4) 198 (June 2008), 47, 53, 54

Gurian, Scott, NJ Sandy Recovery Fails to Consider Long-Term Climate Predictions, NJ Spotlight, Nov. 12, 2013, http://www .njspotlight.com/stories/13/11/11/nj-sandy-recovery-fails-to-consider-long-term-climate-predictions/?p=all, 445

Gwartney, Kurt, Moore Approves Tornado Resistant Building Codes, Mar. 18, 2014, http://kgou.org/post/moore-approves-tornado-resistant-building-codes, 81

Haacke, Jürgen, Myanmar, the Responsibility to Protect, and the Need for Practical Assistance, 1 Global Responsibility to Protect 156 (2009), 461

Hahn, Robert W., The Economics of Rebuilding Cities: Reflections after Katrina, The Economists' Voice, Vol. 2 (2005), No. 4, Article 1, http://www.bepress.com/ev/vol2/iss4/art1, 426

Hammer, David, Critics Admit They Didn't Visit, Research Post-Katrina New Orleans, Times-Picayune, March 5, 2008, http://blog.nola.com/updates/2008/03/critics_admit_they_didnt_visit.html, 487

Hammond, Matthew Carlton, Note, The Posse Comitatus Act: A Principle in Need of Renewal, 75 Wash. U. L.Q. 953 (1997), 132

Haskell, Bonnie, Sexuality and Natural Disaster: Challenges of LGBT Communities Facing Hurricane Katrina (May 2010), http://papers.ssrn.com/sol3/papers.cfm?abstract_id=2513650, 263

Hausrath, Katherine, Tough Love: Should We Analyze Federal Emergency Management Agency Disaster Planning under the National Environmental Policy Act?, 13 Hastings W.-Nw. J. Envtl. L. & Pol'y 161 (2007), 178-182, 75

Hecht, Sean, Climate Change and the Transformation of Risk: Insurance Matters, 55 UCLA L. Rev. 1559 (2008), 376

Hodge, Jr., James G. & Anderson, Evan D., Principles and Practice of Legal Triage during Public Health Emergencies, 64 N.Y.U. Ann. Surv. Am. L. 249 (2008), 192

Hollander, Jack M., The Real Environmental Crisis: Why Poverty, Not Affluence, Is the Environment's Number One Enemy (2003), 238

Hopper, Lindsey J., Note, Striking a Balance: An Open Courts Analysis of the Uniform Emergency Volunteer Health Practitioners Act, 92 Minn. L. Rev. 1924 (2008), 267

Horne, Jed, Carving a Better City, Times-Picayune (New Orleans), Nov. 13, 2005, at A1, 421

Horwitz, Steven, Making Hurricane Response More Effective: Lessons from the Private Sector and the Coast Guard During Katrina (March 2008), mercatus.org/uploadedFiles/Mercatus/Publications/PDF_20080319_MakingHurricaneReponseEffective.pdf, 204

Houck, Oliver A., Rising Water: The National Flood Insurance Program and Louisiana, 60 Tul. L. Rev. 61-164 (1985), 355

Hudson, Blake, Reconstituting Land Use Federalism to Address Transitory and Perpetual Disasters: The Bimodal Federalism Framework, 2011 B.Y.U. L. Rev. 1991 (2011), 94

Husted, Thomas & Nickerson, David, Political Economy of Presidential Disaster Declarations and Federal Disaster Assistance, 42 Public Finance R. 35 (2014), 114

Inniss, Lolita Buckner, A Domestic Right of Return? Race, Rights, and Residency in New Orleans in the Aftermath of Hurricane Katrina, 27 B.C. Third World L.J. 325 (2007), 487

Jiang Jie, The Death of Beijing's Dust Shield, Global Times (Sept. 23, 2013), http://www.globaltimes.cn/content/813288.shtml#.U0gxDeZdXlQ, 70

Jolls, Christine, Sunstein, Cass R., & Thaler, Richard, A Behavioral Approach to Law and Economics, 50 Stan. L. Rev. 1471 (1998), 279

Jordan, Mary, President Orders Military to Aid Florida, Wash. Post, Aug 28, 1992, at A1, 106

Kahan, Dan M., Two Conceptions of Emotion in Risk Regulation, 156 U. Pa. L. Rev. 741 (2008), 280, 290

Kaswan, Alice, Domestic Climate Change Adaptation and Equity, 42 Envtl. L. Rep. 11125 (2012), 88

Keiter, Robert B., The Law of Fire: Reshaping Public Land Policy in an Era of Ecology and Litigation, 36 Envt'l Law 301 (2006), 52

Keohane, Georgia Levenson, Preparing for Disaster While Betting Against It, N.Y. Times, Feb. 12, 2014, 391

Kimmelman, Michael, Vetoing Business as Usual After the Storm, N.Y. Times, Nov. 19, 2012, 31

Kircher, Charles A. et al., When the Big One Strikes Again: Estimated Losses due to a Repeat of the 1906 San Francisco Earthquake, 22 Earthquake Spectra S297 (April 2006), 45, 84

Kirgis, Frederic L., "Hurricane Katrina and Internally Displaced Persons," American Soc'y of Int'l Law, Sept. 21, 2005, http://www.asil.org/insights050921.cfm, 487

Kirsch, Gregory R., Note, Hurricanes and Windfalls: Takings and Price Controls in Emergencies, 79 Va. L. Rev. 1235 (1993), 279

Klein, Christine A., The New Nuisance: An Antidote to Wetland Loss, Sprawl, and Global Warming, 48 B.C. L. Rev. 1155 (2007), 62

Koch, Wendy, Post Sandy, U.S. Pushes Microgrids for Backup Power, USA Today, Oct. 31, 2013, http://www.usatoday.com/story/news/nation/2013/10/31/microgrids-increase-post-sandy/3305379/, 19

Kousky, Carolyn et al., Strategically Placing Green Infrastructure: Cost-Effective Land Conservation in the Floodplain, 47 Environ. Sci. Technol. 3563 (2013), 38

Krupa, Michelle, "Black, Hispanic Numbers Jump," Times-Picayune (New Orleans), May 14, 2009, at A1, 431

Kuo, Susan S., Disaster Tradeoffs: The Doubtful Case for Public Necessity, 54 B.C. L. Rev. 127 (2013), 187

Kuo, Susan S. & Means, Benjamin, Corporate Social Responsibility After Disaster, 89 Wash. U. L. Rev. 973 (2012), 203, 205, 277

Kuran, Timur & Sunstein, Cass R., Availability Cascades and Risk Regulation, 51 Stan. L. Rev. 683, 685-86 (1999), 280

Kysar, Douglas A., It Might Have Been: Risk, Precaution and Opportunity Costs, 22 J. Land Use & Envtl. L. 1 (2006), 318

Lafferty, Sean P., Consumer Protection, Emergencies–Protection against Price Gouging, 26 Pac. L.J. 215 (1995), 274

Landis, Michele L., Let Me Next Time Be "Tried by Fire": Disaster Relief and the Origins of the American Welfare State 1789-1874, 92 Nw. U. L. Rev. 967 (1998), 96

Lazarus, Richard J., The Measure of a Justice: Justice Scalia and the Faltering of the Property Rights Movement within the Supreme Court, 57 Hastings L.J. 759 (2006), 62

Leaderman, Dan & Ward, John, Inauguration Declared "Emergency," Wash. Times, Jan. 14, 2009, 113

Lefcoe, George, Property Condition Disclosure Forms: How the Real Estate Industry Eased the Transition from Caveat Emptor to "Seller Tell All," 39 Real Prop. Prob. & Tr. J. 193 (2004), 41, 42

Lehman, Gary E., Price Gouging: Application of Florida's Unfair Trade Practices Act in the Aftermath of Hurricane Andrew, 17 Nova L. Rev. 1029 (1993), 274

Lerner, Ken, Governmental Negligence Liability Exposure in Disaster Management, 23 Urb. Law. 333 (1991), 245

Lindlaw, Scott, Homeowners Willing to Gamble, Houston Chron., March 20, 2006, 47

Lipton, Eric et al., Storm and Crisis: Military Response; Political Issues Snarled Plans for Troop Aid, N.Y. Times, Sept. 9, 2005, at A1, 136, 144

Liu, Yongqiang et al., Wildland Fire Emissions, Carbon and Climate: Wildfire Climate Interactions, 317 Forest Ecology & Mgmt. 80 (2014), 54

Lopez, Todd M., A Look at Climate Change and the Evolution of the Kyoto Protocol, 43 Nat. Resources J. 285 (2003), 88

Low, Patrick, Trade and the Environment: What Worries the Developing Countries?, 23 Envtl. L. 705 (1993), 238

Lowenstein, Laura J. & Revesz, Richard L., Anti-Regulation under the Guise of Rational Regulation: The Bush Administration's Approaches to Valuing Human Lives in Environmental Cost-Benefit Analyses, 34 Envtl. L. Rep. 10954 (2004), 307

Margolis, Howard, A New Account of Expert/Lay Conflicts of Risk Intuition, 8 Duke Envtl. L. & Pol'y F. 115 (1997), 288

Massey, Douglas S. & Espinosa, Kristin, What's Driving Mexico-US Migration? A Theoretical, Empirical and Policy Analysis, 102 Am. J. Sociology 939 (1997), 272

Masterman, Vicki O., Worst Case Analysis: The Final Chapter?, 19 Envtl. L. Rep. 10026 (1989), 326, 327

Matthews, William, Two Hats Are Better Than One, National Guard Magazine, http://nationalguardmagazine.com/article/Two+Hats+Are+Better+Than+One/1341937/149143/article.html (May 27, 2014), 140

Mazzetti, Mark & Johnston, David, Bush Weighed Using Military in U.S. Arrests, N.Y. Times, July 25, 2009, at A1, 99

Mazzone, Jason, The Commandeerer in Chief, 83 Notre Dame L. Rev. 265 (2007), 97, 98

Mazzone, Jason, The Security Constitution, 53 UCLA Law Rev. 29 (2005), 96

McClam, Erin, Oklahoma Politics Snarl Push for Tornado Shelters at Schools, NBCNews.com, April 7, 2014, http://www.nbcnews.com/news/us-news/oklahoma-politics-snarl-push-tornado-shelters-schools-n70196, 81

McGarvey, Joe & Wilhelm, John D., National Association of Regulatory Utility Commissioners/National Regulatory Research Institute, 2003 Survey on Critical Infrastructure Security 3-4, nrri.org/pubs/multiutility/04-01pdf, 14

Montgomery, W. David & Smith, Anne E., Global Climate Change and the Precautionary Principle, 6 Hum. & Ecological Risk Assessment 399 (2000), 324

Moss, Mitchell et al., The Stafford Act and Priorities for Reform, 6 J. Homeland Security & Emergency Mgmt. 8 (2009), 184

Nathan, Richard P. & Luncy, Marc, Who's in Charge? Who Should Be? The Role of the Federal Government in Megadisasters: Based on Lessons from Hurricane Katrina (June 2, 2009), http://www.rockinst.org/pdf/disaster_recovery/gulfgov/gulfgov_reports/2009-06-02-Whos_in_Charge.PDF, 217

Nelson, Arthur C. & Lang, Robert E., The Next 100 Million, Planning Magazine 73(1): 4 (2007), 10

Nickelsbur, Stephen M., Note, Mere Volunteers? The Promise and Limits of Community-Based Environmental Protection, 84 Va. L. Rev. 1371 (1998), 232

Noll, Roger G. & Krier, James E., Some Implications of Cognitive Psychology for Risk Regulation, 19 J. Legal Stud. 747 (1990), 288

Nyanduga, Bahame Tom, The Challenge of Internal Displacement in Africa, Forced Migration Review 21 (September 2004), 487

Ollenburger, Jane C. & Tobin, Graham A., Women, Aging, and Post-Disaster Stress: Risk Factors, 17 Intl. J. Mass Emergencies & Disasters 65 (1999), 262

Orfield, Myron, Land Use and Housing Policies to Reduce Concentrated Poverty and Racial Segregation, 33 Fordham Urb. L.J. 877 (2006), 255

Palinkas, Lawrence A. et al., Social, Cultural, and Psychological Impacts of the Exxon Valdez Oil Spill, 52 Human Org. 1 (1993), 262

Palmberg, Elizabeth, "Teach a Woman to Fish...and Everyone Eats." Why Women Are Key to Fighting Global Poverty, Sojourners Mag., June 2005, 263

Pelling, Mark, Urbanization and Disaster Risk, http://www.populationenvironmentresearch.org/papers/Pelling_urbanization_disaster_risk.pdf, 27

Perlman, David, Sure Bet: Big Quake in Next 30 Years, S.F. Chron., April 15, 2008, at A1, 45

Petrolia, Daniel R. et al., Why Don't Coastal Residents Choose to Evacuate for Hurricanes? 38 Coastal Management 97 (2010), 188

Phillips, Almarin & Hall, George R., The Salk Vaccine Case: Parallelism, Conspiracy and Other Hypotheses, 46 Va. L. Rev. 717 (1960), 275

Pidot, Justin, Deconstructing Disaster, 2013 B.Y.U. L. Rev. 213, 37, 280, 302

Rabin, Robert L., The Quest for Fairness in Compensating Victims of September 11, 49 Clev. St. L. Rev. 573 (2001), 332

Rachlinsky, Jeffrey J., Selling Heuristics, 64 Alabama L. Rev. 389 (2012), 302

Raman, Papri Sri, Mangroves "Do Not Protect against Tsunamis," SciDevNet (Jan. 14, 2009), http://www.scidev.net/en/news/mangroves-do-not-protect-against-tsunamis-.html, 68

Rao, Gautham, The Federal Posse Comitatus Doctrine: Slavery, Compulsion, and Statecraft in Mid-Nineteenth Century America, 26 Law & Hist. Rev. 1 (2008), 131

Rapp, Geoffrey C., Gouging: Terrorist Attacks, Hurricanes, and the Legal and Economic Aspects of Post-Disaster Price Regulation, 94 Ky. L.J. 535 (2005-06), 276

Redlener, Irwin, Abramson, David M., & Garfield, Richard, Lessons from Katrina: What Went Wrong, What Was Learned, Who's Most Vulnerable, 13 Cardozo J.L. & Gender 783 (2008), 262

Richards, Edward P. & Rathbun, Katharine C., Legislative Alternatives to the Model State Emergency Health Powers Act (MSEHPA), LSU Program in Law, Science, and Public Health White Paper #2 (April 21, 2003), http://biotech.law.lsu.edu/blaw/bt/MSEHPA_review.htm, 192

Ritter, John, Several Cities Dependent on Vulnerable Levees, U.S.A. Today, Sept. 11, 2005, 79

Robson, Gregory J., Kelo v. City of New London: Its Ironic Impact on Takings Authority, 44 Urb. Law. 865 (2012), 421

Romano, Jay, Protecting Pets in a Disaster, N.Y. Times, Sept. 25, 2005, 122

Verchick, Robert R.M., Culture, Cognition, and Climate, 2016 U. Ill. L. Rev. ___ (forthcoming), 299

Verchick, Robert R.M., Disaster Justice: The Geography of Human Capability, 23 Duke Envt'l L. & Pol'y For. 23 (2012), 63

Verchick, Robert R.M. & Hall, Abby, Adapting to Climate Change while Planning for Disaster: Footholds, Rope Lines, and the Iowa Floods, 2011 B.Y.U. L. Rev. 2201 (2011), 413

Verchick, Robert R.M. & Johnson, Lynsey Rae, When FEMA Heads for the Hills: Climate Retreat and the Flood Insurance Reform Act, 47 J. Marshall L. Rev. 695 (2014)., 392, 400

Villa, Clifford J., Law and Lawyers in the Incident Command System, 36 Seattle U. L. Rev. 1855 (2013), 172

Viscusi, W. Kip & Hamilton, James T., Are Risk Regulators Rational? Evidence from Hazardous Waste Cleanup Decisions, 89 Am. Econ. Rev. 1012 (1999), 302

Vladeck, Stephen I., The Domestic Commander in Chief, 29 Cardozo L. Rev. 1091 (2008), 96, 98, 141

Vladeck, Stephen I., Note, Emergency Power and the Militia Acts, 114 Yale L.J. 149 (2004), 96

Vock, Daniel C., Disaster Declaration Denials Exasperate Governors, Aug. 23, 2013, http://www.pewstates.org/projects/stateline/headlines/disaster-declaration-denials-exasperate-governors-85899499704, 113

Volokh, Alexander, Rationality or Rationalism? The Positive and Normative Flaws of Cost-Benefit Analysis, 48 Houston L. Rev. 1 (2011), 316

Wald, Matthew L., The Blackout: What Went Wrong; Experts Asking Why Problems Spread So Far, N.Y. Times, August 16, 2003, at A1, 18

Webb, Julia C., Responsible Response: Do the Emergency and Major Disaster Exceptions to Federal Environmental Laws Make Sense from a Restoration and Mitigation Perspective?, 31 Wm. & Mary Envtl. L. & Pol'y Rev. 529 (2007), 185

Weiss, Charles, Note, Federal Agency Treatment of Uncertainty in Environmental Impact Statements under the EPA's Amended NEAP Regulation §1502.22: Worst Case Analysis or Risk Threshold?, 86 Mich. L. Rev. 777 (1988), 326

Weiss, Debra Cassens, Will Swine Flu Merit Quarantines? If So, New Laws Give States Authority, ABA Journal, Apr. 27, 2009, http://www.abajournal.com/mobile/article/will_swine_flu_merit_quarantines_if_so_new_laws_give_states_authority/Swine%20Flu%20Fear%20Prompts%20Some%20Changes%20in%20Law%20Firm%20Protocol, 191

Wilson, Molly J. Walker, Cultural Understandings of Risk and the Tyranny of the Experts, 90 Ore. L. Rev. 113 (2011), 299

Wines, Michael, To Protect an Ancient City, China Moves to Raze It, N.Y. Times, May 27, 2009, 84

Winthrop, Jim, The Oklahoma City Bombing: Immediate Response Authority and Other Military Assistance to Civil Authority (MACA), 1997-JUL Army Law 3, 115

Wishnie, Lauren, Student Article, Fire and Federalism: A Forest Fire Is Always an Emergency, 17 N.Y.U. Envtl. L.J. 1006 (2008), 53

Wood, Hugh L., Jr., Comment, The Insurance Fallout Following Hurricane Andrew: Whether Insurance Companies Are Legally Obligated to Pay for Building Code

Upgrades Despite the "Ordinance or Law" Exclusion Contained in Most
Homeowners Policies, 48 U. Miami L. Rev. 949 (1994), 372

Xiao, Fan, Did the Zipingpu Dam Trigger China's 2008 Earthquake? (Dec. 2012),
http://probeinternational.org/library/wp-content/uploads/2012/12/Fan-Xiao12-
12.pdf, 82

Congressional Reports

Bea, Keith, Disaster Evacuation and Displacement Policy: Issues for Congress (CRS
Report for Congress, Order Code RS22235, Sept. 2, 2005), 164

Bea, Keith, Federal Emergency Management Policy Changes after Hurricane Katrina:
A Summary of Statutory Provisions (CRS Report for Congress, Order Code
RL33729, Dec. 15, 2006), 155

Brown, Jared T., Presidential Policy Directive 8 and the National Preparedness
System: Background and Issues for Congress (CRS Report for Congress, Order
Code R42073, Oct. 21, 2011), 171

Brown, Jared T., The Hurricane Sandy Rebuilding Strategy: In Brief, Congressional
Research Service, Feb. 10, 2014, http://www.fas.org/sgp/crs/misc/R43396.pdf,
441

Elsea, Jennifer & Swendiman, Kathleen, Federal and State Quarantine and Isolation
Authority (CRS Report for Congress, Order Code RL33201, Aug. 16, 2006), 145

Hogue, Henry B., Federal Emergency Management and Homeland Security
Organization: Historical Developments and Legislative Options (CRS Report for
Congress, Order Code RL33369, June 1, 2006), 156

H.R. Rep. No. 97-71, Part II, 97th Cong., 1st Sess. 4 (1981), 131

H.R. Rep. No. 106-710 (2000), 7

Hurricane Katrina: Insurance Losses and National Capacities for Financing Disaster
Risk, Congressional Research Service (Sept. 15, 2005), 360

King, Rawle O., Hurricane Katrina: Insurance Losses and National Capacities for
Financing Disaster Risks, Congressional Budget Office (January 31, 2008), 385

King, Rawle O., The National Flood Insurance Program: Status and Remaining Issues
for Congress (Congressional Research Serv. 2013), 363

Lindsay, Bruce R. et al., An Examination of Federal Disaster Relief Under the Budget
Control Act (CRS Report for Congress, Order Code R42352, Nov. 18, 2013), 123

Liu, Edward C., Would an Influenza Pandemic Qualify as a Major Disaster under the
Stafford Act? (CRS Report for Congress, Order Code RL34724, Oct. 20, 2008), 112

U.S. House of Representatives, A Failure of Initiative, Final Report of the Select
Bipartisan Committee to Investigate the Preparation for and Response to
Hurricane Katrina (2006), 160, 183, 188, 198, 206, 239

Legislative Proceedings

152 Cong. Rec. S10808-09 (daily ed. Sept. 29, 2006), 147

Hurricane Katrina: The Role of the Governors in Managing the Catastrophe: Hearing
before the S. Comm. on Homeland Sec. and Governmental Affairs, 109th Cong.
25 (2006), 138

U.S. Constitution

Federal Statutes

Federal Regulations

State Statutes

Web-Based Materials

United Nations

U.N. Committee on the Elimination of All Forms of Racial Discrimination, Consideration of Reports Submitted by States Parties under Article 9 of the Convention, May 8, 2008, http://www.universalhumanrightsindex.org/documents/824/1310 /document/en/text.html, 487

U.N. International Strategy for Disaster Reduction, Global Assessment Report on Disaster Risk Reduction (2009), 456

U.N. International Strategy for Disaster Reduction, Global Assessment Report on Disaster Risk Reduction: Revealing Risk, Redefining Development (2011), http://www .preventionweb.net/english/hyogo/gar/?pid:222&pil:1, 469

U.N. International Strategy for Disaster Reduction, Synthesis Report: Consultations on a Post-2015 Framework on Disaster Risk Reduction (HFA2), April 2012, 472

U.N. International Strategy for Disaster Reduction, Towards a Post-2015 Framework for Disaster Risk Reduction, March 2012, http://www.unisdr.org/files/25129_ towardsapost2015frameworkfordisaste.pdf, 472

United Nations, 2009 Global Assessment Report on Disaster Risk Reduction: Risk and Poverty in a Changing Climate, 9, 71

United Nations, 2013 Global Assessment Report on Disaster Risk Reduction: The Business Case for Disaster Reduction 30, 15

United Nations International Strategy for Disaster Reduction, Global Assessment Report on Disaster Risk Reduction (2009), 452

United States Coast Guard, BP Deepwater Horizon Oil Spill: Incident Specific Preparedness Review (Jan. 2011), 173

Restatements

Restatement (Second) of Torts §402A, 162

Restatement (Second) of Torts §826, 59

Restatement (Second) of Torts §827, 59

Restatement (Second) of Torts §827, Comment g, 59

Restatement (Second) of Torts §827(e), 59

Restatement (Second) of Torts §828(a), 59

Restatement (Second) of Torts §828(b), 59

Restatement (Second) of Torts §828(c), 59

Restatement (Second) of Torts §830, 59

Restatement (Second) of Torts §831, 59

Restatement (Third) of Torts: Products Liability §2(b), 162

Miscellaneous Documents

96 FERC ¶61, 299, Docket PL01-6-000 (September 14, 2001), 14

2005 World Resources Institute Millennium Ecosystem Assessment Report, Ecosystems and Human Well-Being: Wetlands and Water, 69

2013 Report Card, Levees: Condition & Capacity, 78

Action Aid International, Tsunami Response: A Human Rights Assessment, 3 (January 2006), 490

Ainsworth, Jack & Doss, Troy Alan, Cal. Coastal Comm'n, Presentation to the Post-Fire Hazard Assessment Planning and Mitigation Workshop at the University of California, Santa Barbara: Natural History of Fire & Flood (Aug. 18, 1995), 54

American Society of Civil Engineers (ASCE) 2013 Report Card for America's Infrastructure, 78, 80

Army Corps of Engineers, Final Report of the Interagency Performance Evaluation Taskforce (IPET) (June 1, 2006), 154, 260

ASCE 2009 Report Card for America's Infrastructure, 79

Association of State Floodplain Managers, Critical Facilities and Flood Risk (2011), http://www.ncpc.gov/floodseminar/handouts/ASFPM_Critical_Facilities_and_Flood_Risk.pdf, 40

Association of State Floodplain Managers, Floodplain Management 2050, A Report of the 2007 Assembly of the Gilbert F. White National Flood Policy Forum (2007), 10, 31, 37, 38, 40, 43

Association of State Floodplain Managers, Managing Flood Risks and Floodplain Resources (2010), http://www.asfpmfoundation.org/forum/2010_Forum_Report.pdf, 36

Building Codes in the National Flood Insurance Program (Oct. 2013), 81

Bush administration's now-rescinded predecessor (HSPD-8), 171

A California Challenge–Flooding in the Central Valley, A Report from an Independent Review Panel to the Department of Water Resources, State of California (Oct. 15, 2007), 29, 36

California Department of Water Resources, 2007 California Flood Legislation Summary, 42

California Department of Water Resources, Flood Warnings: Responding to California's Flood Crisis (Jan. 2005), 30

California Seismic Safety Commission, 2006 Report to the Legislature, Status of the Unreinforced Masonry Building Law (Nov. 2006), http://www.seismic.ca.gov/pub.html, 82, 83

Center for Law and the Public's Health, The Model State Emergency Health Powers Act (2001), http://www.publichealthlaw.net/ModelLaws/MSEHPA.ph, 190, 191

Center for Law & Military Operations, Domestic Operational Law (DOPLAW) Handbook for Judge Advocates 71 (2013), 139, 140

Center for Progressive Reform, An Unnatural Disaster: The Aftermath of Hurricane Katrina (2005), 228, 251, 252

Centers for Disease Control, Zombie Preparedness, at http://www.cdc.gov/phpr/zombies.htm, 171

CERA: Canterbury Earthquake Recovery Authority, http://cera.govt.nz, 437

Climate Change 2014: Impacts, Adaptation and Vulnerability (Intergovernmental Panel on Climate Change Fifth Assessment Report) (2014) (Final Draft), https://www.ipcc.ch/report/ar5/wg2/, 403, 500

Climate Change Impacts in the United States: The Third National Climate Assessment (U.S. Global Change Research Program) (Jerry M. Melillo et al. eds., 2014), http://nca2014.globalchange.gov/downloads, 403

CNN Live Republican Debate (CNN television broadcast June 13, 2011), http://transcripts.cnn.com/TRANSCRIPTS/1106/13/se.02.html, 108

Coast 2050: Toward a Sustainable Coastal Louisiana, 66

GLOSSARY OF ACRONYMS

ACE	Army Corps of Engineers
ADA	Americans with Disabilities Act
BCEGS	Building Code Effectiveness Grading Schedule
CBA	Cost-Benefit Analysis
CDC	Centers for Disease Control
CEDAW	Convention on the Elimination of All Forms of Discrimination Against Women
CEQ	Council on Environmental Quality
CERD	Convention on the Elimination of All Forms of Racial Discrimination
CERT	Community Emergency Response Team
CFR	Code of Federal Regulations
CIDRAP	Center for Infectious Disease Research and Policy
CI/KR	Critical Infrastructure and Key Resources
CRS	Congressional Research Service
CRZ	Coastal Regulation Zone
CSIRO	Australian Commonwealth Scientific and Industrial Research Organization
CVFPP	Central Valley Flood Protection Plan
CWA	Clean Water Act
DED	Deferred Enforced Departure
DFE	Discretionary-Function Exception
DHS	Department of Homeland Security
DOD	Department of Defense
DRF	Disaster Relief Fund
DWR	Department of Water Resources
EIA	Environmental Impact Assessment
EIS	Environmental Impact Statement
EMAC	Emergency Management Assistance Compact
EPA	Environmental Protection Agency
ESF	Emergency Support Functions
EVD	Extended Voluntary Departure
FCA	Flood Control Act
FCO	Federal Coordinating Officer
FDA	Food and Drug Administration
FEMA	Federal Emergency Management Agency
FERC	Federal Energy Regulatory Commission
FLAME	Federal Land Assistance, Management, and Enhancement
FMV	Fair Market Value
FTCA	Federal Tort Claims Act
GAO	Government Accountability Office
GDP	Gross Domestic Product
GHG	Greenhouse Gas

HCA	Hospital Corporation of America
HFA	Hyogo Framework for Action
HFRA	Healthy Forests Restoration Act
HHS	Health and Human Services
HMGP	Hazard Mitigation Grant Program
HSC	Homeland Security Council
HSOC	Homeland Security Operations Center
HSPD-5	Homeland Security Presidential Directive 5
HSRS	Hurricane Sandy Rebuilding Strategy
HUD	Housing and Urban Development
ICS	Incident Command System
IDP	Internally Displaced Persons
IFRC	International Federation of Red Cross
IHNC	Inner Harbor Navigation Canal
IIMG	Interagency Incident Management Group
IIPLR	Insurance Institute for Property Loss Reduction
ILS	Insurance-Linked Securities
IMAT	Incident Management Assistance Team
INA	Immigration and Nationality Act
INS	Incidents of National Significance
IPCC	Intergovernmental Panel on Climate Change
IPET	Interagency Performance Evaluation Task Force
JFO	Joint Field Office
LGBT	Lesbian, Gay, Bisexual, Transgender
LPV	Lake Pontchartrain and Vicinity Hurricane Protection Plan
LTFI	Long-Term Flood Insurance
MRGO	Mississippi River Gulf Outlet
MSEHPA	Model State Emergency Health Powers Act
MSPHA	Model State Public Health Act
NDRF	National Disaster Recovery Framework
NEPA	National Environmental Policy Act
NERC	North American Electric Reliability Corporation
NFIP	National Flood Insurance Program
NGO	Non-Governmental Organization
NIMS	National Incident Management System
NLSA	National Logistics Staging Area
NRCC	National Response Coordination Center
NRF	National Response Framework
NRF-CIA	National Response Framework's Catastrophic Incident Annex
NRF-CIS	National Response Framework Catastrophic Incident Supplement
NRP	National Response Plan
NRP-CIA	National Response Plan's Catastrophic Incident Annex
NRT	National Response Team
OMB	Office of Management and Budget
PAHO	Pan American Health Organization
PCA	Posse Comitatus Act
PES	Payment for Ecosystem Services

PETS	Pet Evacuation and Transportation Standards Act
PFO	Principal Federal Official
PP	Precautionary Principle
PPD-8	Presidential Policy Directive 8: National Preparedness
PRB	Powder River Basin
PRWOR	Personal Responsibility and Work Opportunity Reconciliation act
RRCC	Regional Response Coordination Center
RSF	Recovery Support Functions
SAD	State Active Duty
SFI	Strategic Foresight Initiative
SNRA	Strategic National Risk Assessment
SNS	Strategic National Stockpile
SPR	Strategic Petroleum Reserve
SREMAC	Southern Regional Emergency Management Assistance Compact
SRFCP	Sacramento River Flood Control Project
SSA	Social Security Act
SSDI	Social Security Disability Insurance
TPS	Temporary Protected Status
TRIA	Terrorism Risk Insurance Act of 2002
UCG	Unified Coordination Group
UNDP	United Nations Development Programme
UNICEF	United Nations Children's Fund
UNISDR	United Nations International Strategy for Disaster Reduction
URM	Unreinforced Masonry Buildings
USAID	U.S. Agency for International Development
WHO	World Health Organization
WMD	Weapon of Mass Destruction
WUI	Wildland-Urban Interface

INDEX